# Readings in Sociology:
# Contemporary Perspectives

Harper & Row's
CONTEMPORARY PERSPECTIVES READER SERIES
Phillip Whitten, Series Editor

# Readings in Sociology:
# Contemporary Perspectives
## second edition

edited by
Phillip Whitten

Harper & Row, Publishers
New York   Hagerstown   Philadelphia   San Francisco   London

Sponsoring Editor: Dale Tharp
Project Editor: Pamela Landau
Production Manager: Stefania J. Taflinska
Printer and Binder: The Murray Printing Company
Art Studio: Danmark & Michaels, Inc.

Cover: Detail from Pablo Picasso, *The Fourteenth of July*, 1901. Courtesy The Solomon R. Guggenheim Museum, New York. Photo Credit: Robert E. Mates.

**Readings in Sociology: Contemporary Perspectives,**
*Second Edition*

Copyright © 1979 by Phillip Whitten

Library of Congress Cataloging in Publication Data

Readings in sociology, contemporary perspectives.

(Harper & Row's contemporary perspectives
reader series)
    1. Sociology—Addresses, essays, lectures.
2. Social problems—Addresses, essays, lectures.
I. Robertson, Ian.   II. Whitten, Phillip.
HM51.R37   1979   301   79-579
ISBN 0-06-045503-9

# ACKNOWLEDGMENTS

I.  INTRODUCTION TO SOCIOLOGY

1. INVITATION TO SOCIOLOGY by Peter Berger from INVITATION TO SOCIOLOGY, copyright © 1963. Reprinted by permission of Doubleday & Co., Inc.

II.  CULTURE, SOCIETY, AND THE INDIVIDUAL

2. SEEING IS BELIEVING by Alan Dundes. Reprinted with permission from NATURAL HISTORY Magazine, May 1972. Copyright © The American Museum of Natural History, 1972.
3. BODY RITUAL AMONG THE NACIREMA by Horace Miner is reproduced by permission of the American Anthropological Association from the AMERICAN ANTHROPOLOGIST, Vol. 58, No. 3, 1956, and the author.
4. THE MOUNTAIN PEOPLE by Colin M. Turnbull is reprinted by permission from Colin M. Turnbull. Copyright © 1972.
5. THE AMERICAN OBSESSION WITH FUN by Ann Nietzke is reprinted by permission from SATURDAY REVIEW, copyright © 1972.
6. SOCIOBIOLOGY: THE AESOP'S FABLES OF SCIENCE by Michael A. Simon is reprinted by permission from The Sciences, February 1978. © 1978 by The New York Academy of Sciences.
7. SEXUAL ADEQUACY IN AMERICA by Philip E. Slater. Copyright © 1972 by Philip E. Slater. Reprinted by permission of the author.
8. TERRITORIES OF THE LOBSTERMEN by James M. Acheson. Reprinted with permission from NATURAL HISTORY Magazine, April 1972. Copyright © The American Museum of Natural History, 1972. Photo by Douglas Faulkner.
9. ERIK ERIKSON'S EIGHT AGES OF MAN by David Elkind. Copyright © 1971 by The New York Times Company. Reprinted by permission. Photo courtesy of Phillip Whitten.
10. COMING OF AGE IN AMERICA by Peter and Jane Davison. Copyright © 1975 by The New York Times Company. Reprinted by permission. Drawing by Carol Howie Eldridge.
11. FACING UP TO DEATH by Elisabeth Kubler Ross. Reprinted by permission from TODAY'S EDUCATION, Journal of the National Education Association and Elisabeth Kübler-Ross.

12. THE HUMAN GAZE: SILENT LANGUAGE OF THE EYES by Michael Argyle is printed by permission from the author.
13. GROUPTHINK by Irving L. Janis. Reprinted with permission from the January 1973 issue of the YALE ALUMNI MAGAZINE; copyright by Yale Alumni Publications, Inc. Artwork by William Hersey, reprinted by permission.
14. TEEN-AGE INTERRACIAL DATING by Frank A. Petroni. Published by permission of Transaction, Inc., from TRANSACTION, Volume 8 #11. Copyright © 1971 by Transaction, Inc. Photo by Jean-Claude LeJeune.
15. PATHOLOGY OF IMPRISONMENT by Philip Zimbardo. Published by permission of Transaction, Inc., from SOCIETY, Volume 9 #6. Copyright © 1972, by Transaction Inc.
16. NEW CLUES TO THE CAUSES OF VIOLENCE by Gene Bylinsky. Reprinted from the January 1973 issue of FORTUNE Magazine by special permission; copyright © 1972 TIME INC.
17. LOCK 'EM UP AND OTHER THOUGHTS ON CRIME by James Q. Wilson. Copyright © 1975 by The New York Times Company. Reprinted by permission. Photo courtesy of Magnum Photos, Inc.
18. ON BEING SANE IN INSANE PLACES by D. L. Rosenhan. Copyright © 1973 by the American Association for the Advancement of Science. Reprinted by permission from D. L. Rosenhan.
19. BEHIND BARS by Tom Miller. Reprinted by permission from The Progressive, 408 West Gorham Street, Madison, Wisconsin 53703. Copyright © 1976, The Progressive, Inc.
20. WHY WOMEN FEAR SUCCESS by Vivian Gornick. Copyright © 1971 by NYM Corp. Reprinted with the permission of NEW YORK Magazine.
21. WOMEN IN THE WORKPLACE by Louise Kapp Howe. This article first appeared in THE HUMANIST, September/October 1973 issue, and is reprinted by permission.
22. THE BISEXUAL DEBATE by Martin Duberman. Copyright © 1974 by Martin Duberman. First appeared in NEW TIMES Magazine.

III.  SOCIAL INEQUALITY

23. THE ROBIN HOOD SYNDROME by Edwin Kuh.

IV. SOCIAL INSTITUTIONS

V. SOCIAL CHANGE

# CONTENTS

Is the human species fundamentally bisexual? Duberman surveys biological, cross-cultural, and historical evidence, and predicts that overt bisexuality will become more common.

The distribution of income in the United States is highly unequal—and will remain so, argues Kuh, until myths about "incentives" are swept aside.

An upper-class gang, the Saints, committed more delinquent acts than a lower-class gang, the Roughnecks. Yet the Saints were never prosecuted, while the Roughnecks were always in trouble. Selective perception and labeling, according to Chambliss, provide the explanation.

Poverty persists in America, suggests Gans, because it provides a number of convenient functions for that part of society which is not poor. But this does not mean that poverty is necessary or inevitable.

The white blue-collar workers in America are becoming increasingly discontented and alienated. Tyler examines some reasons for the white workers' "backlash."

The formal "rights" of the accused have little meaning in the actual judicial process, argues Amsterdam. The safeguards of the accused are available only to those who can buy them.

Opinion surveys show that whites of all social backgrounds are becoming steadily more liberal in their attitudes to blacks. Blacks, on the other hand, are becoming more suspicious of whites.

A graduate student recounts how he was forced to lose his Mexican-American heritage in the process of his education, and how he is now rediscovering his Chicano roots.

Perhaps no group in the United States has been as cruelly and falsely stereotyped as the American Indian. Faherty provides a factual overview of Indian history and culture.

The recent resurgence of group identity and pride among the "white ethnics" took most sociologists by surprise. Michael Novak writes about ethnic consciousness among the "PIGS"—Poles, Italians, Greeks, and Slavs.

How do young children perceive sex roles in America, and how do they visualize their future adult roles? Iglitzin shows that traditional stereotypes set in very early.

American males are taught, explicitly and implicitly, to be inexpressive. One result is the creation of such personality types as the "cowboy" and the "playboy," who are unable to relate to women as people.

The nuclear family is under unprecedented attack in America. Mace suggests that these attacks are misdirected and that the nuclear family is here to stay.

evolutionary wisdom of billions of years by creating new plants, new animals, and even new forms of human beings. How will this incredible power be used? And who will make the crucial decisions?

## Topic 19: Social Movements and Social Change

58. The Rebels of '70: Confessions of a Middle-Class Drifter **316**
By James S. Kunen
*New York Times Magazine*, October 28, 1973.

What happened to the student rebels of the 1960s counterculture? Kunen, one of the leaders of the movement, revisited his former comrades in order to find out, and wryly presents his findings.

59. They Changed Rock, Which Changed the Culture, Which Changed Us **324**
By Jeff Greenfield
*New York Times Magazine*, February 16, 1975.

The Beatles revolutionized rock music, making it the main medium of a movement that has profoundly changed our culture. Greenfield shows how the Beatles changed us all in the process.

# PREFACE

This anthology is intended to be a distinctive one. Its distinctiveness lies in that the selection of articles has been determined primarily by the needs and interests of beginning students in sociology, who are so easily turned off by the relentless jargon and abstruseness of many of the articles in more conventional readers. The aims of this selection have been to reveal the breadth of the discipline, to demonstrate the direct relevance of sociology to everyday life, and to capture and retain the interest of the student. Moreover, the publisher has made every effort to keep down the cost of the book to the student by reproducing articles in facsimile form wherever this procedure does not detract from the overall design of the book; it has thus been possible to include an unusually large number of selections in relatively inexpensive form.

The articles in the anthology were chosen in accordance with several basic criteria. First, they must be sound sociology. Second, they must be highly readable. Third, they must appeal to the student through their intrinsically interesting and challenging content. Fourth, they must relate to the introductory sociology course as it is taught in most American colleges. And fifth, they must have relevance to contemporary social experience. All of the articles in this book, nearly sixty in number, meet these criteria.

In this, the second edition of *Readings in Sociology: Contemporary Perspectives*, we have retained the best of the articles from the first edition, and have added a number of superb new articles on issues of central importance in modern society and its analysis. These articles cut across the discipline of sociology and include sociobiology, the implications of genetic engineering, terrorism, health care in America, the recent rise of the "new right," open admissions, a case of corporate irresponsibility and its devastating human consequences, the "laws of looking," prisons, political socialization in South Africa, secret files, Eastern religious cults, and communal living.

In addition, we have improved the design format of the book and reorganized it so that it can be used more easily in conjunction with a number of the leading texts in the field.

The articles in the book were carefully selected from a broad range of contemporary sources—books, journals, and semipopular magazines. The work of many leading social scientists has been included, among others, Peter Berger, Colin M. Turnbull, David Elkind, Philip G. Zimbardo, William J. Chambliss, Harvey Cox, Richard Borshay Lee, Walter Laqueur, Herbert J. Gans, Christopher Jencks, James Q. Wilson, and Peter F. Drucker. The range of issues covers virtually every topic taught in contemporary introductory courses, and should provide a thorough and readable background introduction to the fascination of the discipline.

This edition of *Readings in Sociology: Contemporary Perspectives* was revised with the assistance of feedback from hundreds of instructors and students who used the first edition. They sent us the Response Card that appears in the back of the book and let us know which articles they thought should be retained, which articles should be deleted, and why. Analysis of these cards provided us with some of the guidelines we used in preparing this second edition.

We will continue to revise this anthology regularly—not only in response to changes in the discipline itself, but also as a result of the suggestions and criticisms of students and instructors who use it. For this reason, we have retained the Response Card, which can be located at the back of the book. Please take a moment to fill out the card and send it to the publisher after you have used the book. Your comments will be much appreciated and gratefully received.

PHILLIP WHITTEN
Series Editor

# Readings in Sociology:
# Contemporary Perspectives

# I. Introduction to Sociology

The excitement of sociology lies in its liberating potential. In effect, the sociological perspective is a special form of human consciousness: a consciousness that enables its possessor to see beyond the taken-for-granted realities of everyday life, to recognize that "common sense" explanations of social behavior are often hopelessly misguided, and to appreciate that what is unthinkingly accepted as "natural" is often merely a social product—created over the generations by countless men and women, and hence capable of being changed by them as well. The great American sociologist C. Wright Mills defined the "sociological imagination" as the ability to perceive the crucial connection between the individual and the society in which he or she lives: between personal concerns and troubles—drug addiction, divorce, poverty—and the broader social context that provides the origin and context of private experience.

The subject matter of sociology provides its fascination. Unlike the natural scientist, the sociologist is part of the subject matter that he or she investigates. Also unlike the natural scientist, the sociologist deals with subjects that have consciousness, feelings, intentions, and rational (or irrational) thoughts. Under these circumstances, most sociologists now agree that full objectivity and precise understanding are not possible.

Topic 1 concerns the nature of sociology and consists of only one selection: Peter L. Berger's now-classic "Invitation to Sociology." In this excerpt from his book of the same name, Berger describes the discipline of sociology, the work of the sociologist, and the fascination inherent in the study of people and society.

1

# Invitation to Sociology

Peter L. Berger

The sociologist (that is, the one we would really like to invite to our game) is a person intensively, endlessly, shamelessly interested in the doings of men. His natural habitat is all the human gathering places of the world, wherever men come together. The sociologist may be interested in many other things. But his consuming interest remains in the world of men, their institutions, their history, their passions. And since he is interested in men, nothing that men do can be altogether tedious for him. He will naturally be interested in the events that engage men's ultimate beliefs, their moments of tragedy and grandeur and ecstasy. But he will also be fascinated by the commonplace, the everyday. He will know reverence, but this reverence will not prevent him from wanting to see and to understand. He may sometimes feel revulsion or contempt. But this also will not deter him from wanting to have his questions answered. The sociologist, in his quest for understanding, moves through the world of men without respect for the usual lines of demarcation. Nobility and degradation, power and obscurity, intelligence and folly — these are equally *interesting* to him, however unequal they may be in his personal values or tastes. Thus his questions may lead him to all possible levels of society, the best and the least known places, the most respected and the most despised. And, if he is a good sociologist, he will find himself in all these places because his own questions have so taken possession of him that he has little choice but to seek for answers.

It would be possible to say the same things in a lower key. We could say that the sociologist, but for the grace of his academic title, is the man who must listen to gossip despite himself, who is tempted to look through keyholes, to read other people's mail, to open closed cabinets. Before some otherwise unoccupied psychologist sets out now to construct an aptitude test for sociologists on the basis of sublimated voyeurism, let us quickly say that we are speaking merely by way of analogy. Perhaps some little boys consumed with curiosity to watch their maiden aunts in the bathroom later become inveterate sociologists. This is quite uninteresting. What interests us is the curiosity that grips any sociologist in front of a closed door behind which there are human voices. If he is a good sociologist, he will want to open that door, to understand these voices. Behind each closed door he will anticipate some new facet of human life not yet perceived and understood.

The sociologist will occupy himself with matters that others regard as too sacred or as too distasteful for dispassionate investigation. He will find rewarding the company of priests or of prostitutes, depending not on his personal preferences but on the questions he happens to be asking at the moment. He will also concern himself with matters that others may find much too boring. He will be interested in the human interaction that goes with warfare or with great intellectual discoveries, but also in the relations between people employed in a restaurant or between a group of little girls playing with their dolls. His main focus of attention is not the ultimate significance of what men do, but the action in itself, as another example of the infinite richness of human conduct. So much for the image of our playmate.

In these journeys through the world of men the sociologist will inevitably encounter other professional Peeping Toms. Sometimes these will resent his presence, feeling that he is poaching on their preserves. In some places the sociologist will meet up with the economist, in others with the political scientist, in yet others with the psychologist or the ethnologist. Yet chances are that the questions that have brought him to these same places are different from the ones that propelled his fellow-trespassers. The sociologist's questions always remain essentially the same: "What are people doing with each other here?" "What are their relationships to each other?" "How are these relationships organized in institutions?" "What are the collective ideas that move men and institutions?" In trying to answer these questions in specific instances, the sociologist will, of course, have to deal with economic or political matters, but he will do so in a way rather different from that of the economist or the political scientist. The scene that he contemplates is the same human scene that these other scientists concern themselves with. But the sociologist's angle of vision is different. When this is understood, it becomes clear that it makes little sense to try to stake out a special enclave within which the sociologist will carry on business in his own right. Like Wesley the sociologist will have to confess that his parish is the world. But unlike some latter-day Wesleyans he will gladly share this parish with others. There is, however, one traveler whose path the sociologist will cross more often than anyone else's on his journeys. This is the historian. Indeed, as soon as the sociologist turns from the present to the past, his preoccupations are very hard indeed to distinguish from those of the historian. However, we shall leave this relationship to a later part of our considerations. Suffice it to say here that the sociological journey will be much impoverished unless it is punctuated frequently by conversation with that other particular traveler.

Any intellectual activity derives excitement from the moment it becomes a trail of discovery. In some fields of learning this is the discovery of worlds previously unthought and unthinkable. This is the excitement of the astronomer or of the nuclear physicist on the antipodal boundaries of the realities that man is capable of conceiving. But it can also be the excitement of bacteriology or geology. In a different way it can be the excitement of the linguist discovering new realms of human expression or of the anthropologist exploring human customs in faraway countries. In such discovery, when undertaken with passion, a widening of awareness, sometimes a veritable transformation of consciousness, occurs. The universe turns out to be much more wonderful than one had ever dreamed. The excitement of sociology is usually of a different sort. Sometimes, it is true, the sociologist penetrates into worlds that had previously been quite unknown to him — for instance, the world of crime, or the world of some bizarre religious sect, or the world fashioned by the exclusive concerns of some group such as medical specialists or military leaders or advertising executives. However, much of the time the sociologist moves in sectors of experience that are familiar to him and to most people in his society. He investigates communities, institutions and activities that one can read about every day in the newspapers. Yet there is another excitement of discovery beckoning in his investigations. It is not the excitement of coming upon the totally unfamiliar, but rather the excitement of finding the familiar becoming transformed in its meaning. The fascination of sociology lies in the fact that its perspective makes us see in a new light the very world in which we have lived all our lives. This also constitutes a transformation of consciousness. Moreover, this transformation is more relevant existentially than that of many other intellectual disciplines, because it is more difficult to segregate in some special compartment of the mind. The astronomer does not live in the remote galaxies, and the nuclear physicist can, outside his laboratory, eat and laugh and marry and vote without thinking about the insides of the atom. The geologist looks at rocks only at appropriate times, and the linguist speaks English with his wife. The sociologist lives in society, on the job and off it. His own life, inevitably, is part of his subject matter. Men being what they are, sociologists too manage to segregate their professional insights from their everyday affairs. But it is a rather difficult feat to perform in good faith.

The sociologist moves in the common world of men, close to what most of them would call real. The categories he employs in his analyses are only refinements of the categories by which other men live — power, class, status, race, ethnicity. As a result, there is a deceptive simplicity and obviousness about some sociological investigations. One reads them, nods at the familiar scene, remarks that one has heard all this before and don't people have better things to do than to waste their time on truisms — until one is suddenly brought up against an insight that radically questions everything one had previously assumed about this familiar scene. This is the point at which one begins to sense the excitement of sociology.

Let us take a specific example. Imagine a sociology class in a Southern college where almost all the students are white Southerners. Imagine a lecture on the subject of the racial system of the South. The lecturer is talking here of matters that have been familiar to his students from the time of their infancy. Indeed, it may be that they are much more familiar with the minutiae of this system than he is. They are quite bored as a result. It seems to them that he is only using more pretentious words to describe what they already know. Thus he may use the term "caste," one commonly used now by American sociologists to describe the Southern racial system. But in explaining the term he shifts to traditional Hindu society, to make it clearer. He then goes on to analyze the magical beliefs inherent in caste tabus, the social dynamics of commensalism and connubium, the economic interests concealed within the system, the way in which religious beliefs relate to the tabus, the effects of the caste system upon the industrial development of the society and vice versa — all in India. But suddenly India is not very far away at all. The lecture then goes back to its Southern theme. The familiar now seems not quite so familiar any more. Questions are raised that are new, perhaps raised angrily, but raised all the same. And at least some of the students have begun to understand that there are functions involved in this business of race that they have not read about in the newspapers (at least not those in their hometowns) and that their parents have not told them — partly, at least, because neither the newspapers nor the parents knew about them.

It can be said that the first wisdom of sociology is this — things are not what they seem. This too is a deceptively simple statement. It ceases to be simple after a while. Social reality turns out to have many layers of meaning. The discovery of each new layer changes the perception of the whole.

Anthropologists use the term "culture shock" to describe the impact of a totally new culture upon a newcomer. In an extreme instance such shock will be experienced by the Western explorer who is told, halfway through dinner, that he is eating the nice old lady he had been chatting with the previous day — a shock with predictable physiological if not moral consequences. Most explorers no longer encounter cannibalism in their travels today. However, the first encounters with polygamy or with puberty rites or even with the way some nations drive their automobiles can be quite a shock to an American visitor. With the shock may go not only disapproval or disgust but a sense of excitement that things can *really* be that different from what they are at home. To some extent, at least, this is the excitement of any first travel abroad. The experience of sociological discovery could be described as "culture shock" minus geographical displacement. In other words, the sociologist travels at home — with shocking results. He is unlikely to find that he is eating a nice old lady for dinner. But the discovery, for instance, that his own church has considerable money invested in the missile industry or that a few blocks from his home there are people who engage in cultic orgies may not be drastically different in emotional impact. Yet we would not want to imply that sociological discoveries are always or even usually outrageous to moral sentiment. Not at all. What they have in common with exploration in distant lands, however, is the sudden illumunation of new and unsuspected facets of human existence in society. This is the excitement and, as we shall try to show later, the humanistic justification of sociology.

People who like to avoid shocking discoveries, who prefer to believe that society is just what they were taught in Sunday School, who like the safety of the rules and the maxims of what Alfred Schutz has called the "world-taken-for-granted," should stay away from sociology. People who feel no temptation before closed doors, who have no curiosity about human beings, who are content to admire scenery without wondering about the people who live in those houses on the other side of that river, should probably also stay away from sociology. They will find it unpleasant or, at any rate, unrewarding. People who are interested in human beings only if they can change, convert or reform them should also be warned, for they will find sociology much less useful than they hoped. And people whose interest is mainly in their own conceptual constructions will do just as well to turn to the study of little white mice. Sociology will be satisfying, in the long run, only to those who can think of nothing more entrancing than to watch men and to understand things human.

It may now be clear that we have, albeit deliberately, understated the case in the title of this chapter. To be sure, sociology is an individual pastime in the sense that it interests some men and bores others. Some like to observe human beings, others to experiment with mice. The world is big enough to hold all kinds and there is no logical priority for one interest as against another. But the word "pastime" is weak in describing what we mean. Sociology is more like a passion. The sociological perspective is more like a demon that possesses one, that drives one compellingly, again and again, to the questions that are its own. An introduction to sociology is, therefore, an invitation to a very special kind of passion.

# II. Culture, Society, and the Individual

The term *culture* refers to all the human products of a society, material and immaterial: language, hair styles, philosophy, music, values, government, religion, art, space technology. A person born into a particular culture normally takes that culture for granted and views all others as somehow "odd," even "wrong," an attitude sociologists term *ethnocentrism*. We are all ethnocentric to some degree. A fundamental tenet of sociology is that our reality is socially constructed: each society creates its own culture, and the individual members become "imprisoned" within it, implicitly assuming that their own values and way of life are superior to and more "normal" than all others. If you were a male traveler in traditional Eskimo society, your host would automatically make his wife available to you for the night, and in order to enhance her attractiveness, she might smear her face with whale blubber and sprinkle urine on her hair. You would doubtless be highly discomforted, for your culture tells you that such behavior is entirely inappropriate. But if you failed to take advantage of the Eskimo's offer, he would be fully within his rights to kill you for what his culture tells him is a gross insult.

Topic 2 concerns culture, which structures our lives and provides us with the opportunity to become fully human; in fact, without culture human society could not exist. Cultural assumptions structure the way we perceive reality. In the first article in Topic 2 Alan Dundes explores how language defines the way we interpret the world around us. Generally, we take our own cultural habits so much for granted that we are often blissfully unaware of them, as Horace Miner implies in his now-classic article about the Nacirema, a North American group. Colin M. Turnbull's study of the Ik, a traditional African people whose culture has been utterly disrupted by the impact of modern society, provides a chilling and deeply disturbing vision of what life without an integrated culture and society can be like. Ann Nietzke's article on the "obsession with fun" in American society looks beneath the surface of our hedonistic way of life and finds a deeply unhappy people so out of touch with themselves that they have forgotten what fun truly is.

Topic 3 explores three very different aspects of society. Since the publication of Edward O. Wilson's *Sociobiology: A New Synthesis*, sociobiology has engendered fierce debate among sociologists about the extent to which our evolutionary heritage defines human social behavior. Unfortunately, the debate involves major political issues, which has tended to obscure the scientific issues. Michael A. Simon's article explores the concept of sociobiology and the controversy surrounding it. Philip E. Slater's article deals with sexuality and American society. He presents a cogent argument for the view that our prevalent stereotypes are crippling the sexuality of American men and women. James M. Acheson writes about the territorial norms of the

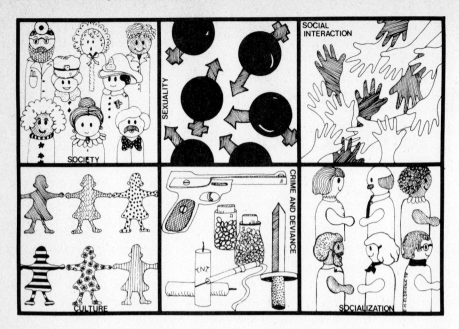

"society" of Maine lobstermen and about how these norms are enforced by an escalating series of negative sanctions.

Socialization, the subject of Topic 4, is the process by which the human animal becomes the human being. The process is a lifelong one in which, day by day, the individual learns the culture in which he or she lives, and internalizes its norms, taking social customs, attitudes, and values into his or her own developing personality. Our capacity for socialization is without parallel in the animal world. Other animal species rely, to a greater or lesser extent, on instinctive patterns of behavior. However, virtually all human behavior is learned behavior, and in this feature lies that unique capacity for flexibility and adaptation which has made our species such an evolutionary success. Various agencies of socialization—family, schools, peer group, media, and other specialized agencies such as the workplace—all operate, deliberately or otherwise, to socialize us into the behavior patterns appropriate for our particular culture and our place within it. Our personalities, behavior, and attitudes therefore depend very much on the precise content of our socialization.

This insight into the relationship between social context and personal development is the underlying theme of the work of Erik Erikson, outlined in the article by David Elkind. Erikson's analysis of the human life cycle systematically relates each stage of the developmental process from infancy to old age to the pressures, demands, and opportunities of the prevailing social environment. The next article, by Peter and Jane Davison, deals with adolescence in America, that "great waiting room" of turmoil and confusion in which young people, unlike their counterparts in simpler societies, have no clearly defined role. The essay by Elisabeth Kubler Ross deals with a topic that is almost taboo in the United States: death. She points out that society has insulated itself from death—people even die in specialized institutions rather than at home—and that our fear of the subject has made death even more harrowing, both for the dying and for their friends and relatives.

Social interaction and social groups are the focus for Topic 5. One form of interaction often overlooked in texts (and until recently in social scientific research) is nonverbal communication. People communicate verbally to a degree without parallel in the animal kingdom. But we also communicate through our "body language." The "laws of looking" are an important aspect of nonverbal communication. The human gaze can convey a wide variety of meaning: from hatred to love and a host of other emotions. Research on the silent language of the eyes is neatly summed up in an original essay by British social psychologist Michael Argyle. Human interaction takes on peculiar forms within the context of groups. Irving L. Janis studies various "fiascoes" of American policy in terms of the process he calls "groupthink," the tendency for individual members in decision-making groups to suppress their private doubts in order to conform to what they believe are group expectations. Frank A. Petroni looks at one of the most sensitive and taboo-laden areas of human interaction in the United States: interracial dating, with its overtones of forbidden sex. The topic closes with Philip G. Zimbardo's account of an experiment he conducted involving the temporary resocialization of students into the roles of prisoners and guards—an experiment the consequences of which were so frightening that Zimbardo had to abandon it before completion.

Crime, deviance, and social control form the subject of Topic 6. Deviance is behavior that departs significantly from social norms. Although the sociologist uses the term in a strictly neutral sense to refer to behavior that does not conform to social expectations, most people are disapproving of deviant behavior, which they regard as an affront to their assumptions and values. However, though deviants tend to be stigmatized, a certain amount of deviance may serve important social functions. First, deviance can be an important source of social change: what is deviant today may well become the conventional behavior of tomorrow. Second, the existence of deviance may contribute to social cohesion and solidarity: by applying sanctions to the deviant, the majority who consider themselves nondeviant are able to assert their own "normality" and to reaffirm the boundaries of permissible behavior.

In the early years of American sociology, deviance tended to be regarded as an intrinsic attribute of the deviants themselves: there was something "wrong" with them. This notion was rather ethnocentric, for it assumed that the middle-class norms of the time were right and all others self-evidently wrong. The obvious difficulty with such an approach is that behavior which seems deviant in one context may be quite acceptable, or even required, at a different time and place. Sociologist are now much more sensitive to the relativity of the concept of deviance, and two newer sociological approaches to the topic have become popular. The first approach regards deviance as the product of *anomie*, a term referring to a state of confusion about norms. In this view, the deviant is a person who desires socially acceptable goals (like wealth) but lacks the socially acceptable means (like high salary) of achieving them. Faced with this tension, the person may resort to disapproved or deviant means (like theft) in order to attain the approved goal. The second approach regards deviance, not as a characteristic of the deviant, but as a *label* that one group attaches to another. Labeling theorists point out that everyone is a deviant from someone else's point of view; which group gets labeled and which group does the labeling depends on which has the greater power and influence in society.

Social norms are the rules, formal and informal, that specify the appropriate expectations and behavior of a society and of the people filling various roles within it. The existence and preservation of these norms is vital for the smooth functioning of society: sudden and radical changes in behavior and expectations, or widespread variances from the established norms, introduces uncertainty and confusion into social relationships. These changes may, of course, often be necessary, but every society has both formal and informal means of social control—means of ensuring that, on the whole, the norms are adhered to. The main mode of social control is the use of sanctions, that is, rewards for adherence to the norms and punishments for violating them. These sanctions may take many forms. Positive sanctions, for example, might range from formal public acclaim to the informal approval of friends; negative sanctions might range from a death sentence to the mildly disapproving reactions of others.

The readings in this topic explore facets of deviant behavior and the methods used by society to control such behavior. The first article, by Gene Bylinsky, deals with one of the most disturbing forms of deviant behavior in contemporary America—violence. In his essay, James Q. Wilson presents a reasoned argument for adopting a hard line against certain categories of criminals, especially habitual offenders. D. L. Rosenhan's study, which excited great attention when it was published, details what happened when a number of quite normal people deliberately tried to gain entrance into mental hospitals. Although their behavior once inside the hospitals did not violate norms of reality, it was interpreted in terms of the norms of the institution, and the most trivial everyday behavior was seen as evidence of schizophrenia. Finally, Tom Miller's remarkable article, written when he was a Yale undergraduate, looks at conditions in a federal penitentiary.

Sexuality and society is the subject for the final topic in Part II. At birth every individual in almost every society is classified on the basis of physical characteristics into one of two categories: male or female. However, in every society, biological differences between the sexes are elaborated into secondary, nonbiological differences—cultural notions of "masculine" and "feminine." Masculinity and femininity refer not to physical differences but to social and psychological ones: differences in clothing, occupational roles, personality, and so on. It is all too easy to assume that these culturally created characteristics of the sexes are inevitably linked to their physical characteristics, that the differences are innate, or somehow "natural."

Social science research shows how mistaken that assumption is. Historical, and cross-cultural studies have clearly demonstrated that human beings can be socialized into a very wide range of different roles, some of them very unlike our own. In her highly influential studies of some New Guinea peoples, for example, Margaret Mead found one tribe in which both males and females were passive, one in which both males and females were aggressive, and in one in which females were domineering while males were gentle and nurturant. Many other studies have shown the great flexibility of sex roles and their frequent dissimilarity from our own. To take another example, it has been found that in most traditional societies the carrying of heavy burdens is a woman's job, not a man's. The rise in the last decade of the Women's Movement, which has challenged our existing sex roles and which may lead to fundamental changes in our family structure, is in a sense the result of the application of the sociological perspective to a new area of society: what was once taken for granted as part of the natural order is now seen as part of the social order and therefore as modifiable.

Vivian Gornick summarizes important research suggesting that women in college are actually motivated to perform below their abilities: both their male and female peers react negatively to the woman who gains academic success. Louise Kapp Howe surveys the progress that women have made in the workplace in recent years. Finally, Martin Duberman offers his views on bisexuality, a form of sexual behavior that has attracted growing attention since the mid-1970s.

# Seeing Is Believing

A brief look at visual terms
used in American speech illustrates just
how much culture affects perception

Alan Dundes

Whether from early memories of playing "peek-a-boo," "showing and telling" in school, or learning the opening phrase of the national anthem—"Oh, say can you see"—the primacy of vision in American culture is affirmed again and again as infants grow to adulthood. Americans are conditioned from childhood to believe that "what you see is what you get."

There is more to such a phenomenon than immediately meets the eye. That Americans rely more on vision than on other senses doesn't mean that they are aware of it. Nor does it mean that it is a peculiarly American trait. People everywhere rely on their senses to perceive their world and order their experiences, but since my data are derived from American folk speech, I cannot speak about others. In any case, because I have been taught to mistrust hearsay, I have decided to take a look at the evidence for a visual bias and to see for myself.

In Western thought, a distinction has commonly been made between sensory perception and reasoning. The power of reason is presumably the superior of the two. According to Aristotle, there are five senses—sight, hearing, smell, taste, and touch—which provide data generally deemed less trustworthy or, at least, frequently illusory, compared to the information that is provided by the faculties of rational thought. Subjective versus objective and body versus mind are other expressions of this distinction between the sensory and the rational. If we assume, however, that reasoning cannot take place without some reference to metaphor, then it is certainly possible that much American logic and reasoning is closely tied to metaphor in general and to visual metaphor in particular.

The allegedly inferior sensory experiences seem to be ranked according to how effective or reliable a given sense is assumed to be. In American culture, the sense of sight is normally the first of the five senses to be listed. However, whether sight is actually more useful or crucial for perception than the other senses is a moot question and, in fact, does not require an answer to show that a cultural bias for the sense of sight really exists. In the present context, it is not the literal meaning of sight that is important, but the metaphorical. I believe that, metaphorically speaking, Americans tend to *see* the world around them, rather than hear, feel, smell, or taste it. It may be no accident that Americans *observe* laws and holidays.

American speech provides persuasive evidence to support the notion that "vision" is used as a metaphor for "understanding." Consider, for example, the classic punning proverb, " 'I see,' said the blind man, as he picked up his hammer and saw." The oppositional structure in this text is produced by the juxtaposition of sight and blindness. Here is a clear distinction between literal and metaphorical seeing. Literally a blind man cannot see, but figuratively he certainly can.

Americans consistently speak of "seeing" the point of an argument when, in fact, an argument is not really seen but comprehended. Intellectual positions, or "perspectives," are frequently referred to as points of *view*. When articulated, they may be introduced by such formulas as, "As I see it" or "It all depends on how you look at it."

American culture is pronouncedly concerned with empiricism, and this empiricism is explicitly visual. "Seeing is believing" and "I'm from Missouri" (which means "you've got to show me") are indications of the emphasis on seeing something for oneself and the tendency to distrust anyone else's report of a given event. "I saw it with my own (two)

eyes" is a common authenticating formula, as is the invitation to "see for yourself."

Without sight, there may be disbelief or lack of faith: "I'll believe it when I see it," "That I've got to see," or "I can't picture that." Even though the reliability of vision may be questioned—"There's more to this than meets the eye"—in general, people tend to believe what they see. Thus, when something is really out of the ordinary, we say, "I couldn't believe my eyes." Something that is incredible or unbelievable is termed "out of sight," a phrase dating from before the end of the nineteenth century.

Imagination is sometimes called "the mind's eye," but why should the mind have an eye? Probably for the same reason that patients want doctors "to see them." Telephone conversations or other purely oral–aural channels are not considered entirely satisfactory. Actually, the patient is probably relieved by *his* seeing the doctor. Seeing the doctor, in turn, is part of the widespread cultural insistence upon interviews. Literally, the word *interview* refers to A seeing B and B seeing A.

Consider the nature of American tourist philosophy—sightseeing. To "see the sights" is a common goal of tourists, a goal also reflected in the mania for snapping pictures as permanent records of what was seen. Typical travel boasting consists of inflicting an evening of slide viewing on unwary friends so that they may see what their hosts saw.

This is surely a strange way of defining tourism. Visiting a foreign locale certainly involves all of the sensory apparatus. There are exotic smells and tastes, and the opportunity to savor new foods and experience the "feel" of a foreign setting is as important in understanding a country and its people as seeing them. One reason Americans frequently fail to enjoy touring as much as they might may be their al-

most compulsive tendency to see as many sights as possible. The seeing of many sights is, of course, consistent with a tendency to quantify living, and, specifically, with the desire to get one's money's worth.

When shopping, whether in foreign countries or at home, Americans are reluctant to buy anything "sight unseen." They prefer "to look something over," "to walk into something with their eyes open." A thorough inspection theoretically allows one to "see through" a pretense or fake. And obviously, a product can only "catch a person's eye" if he sees it.

Public "images," too, are part of the visual pattern. But why, after all, should a person have to be depicted in a term such as image? Even though looks may be deceiving ("Never judge a book by its cover"), it seems clear that packaging that appeals to visual esthetics is equally effective whether one is hawking cigarettes or automobiles or selling political candidates.

The reduction of persons or events to purely visual terms is also evident in the use of the popular slang phrase for a detective: "private eye." By the same token, sleep is commonly referred to as "shuteye," which obviously singles out only one aspect of the dormant state. Furthermore, this suggestion that sleep is shut-eye also implies that the waking state is marked chiefly by having one's eyes open.

As I collected examples of folk speech, I soon found that comparison of vision with the other senses reaffirmed the superiority of sight. That a "seer" can make predictions by gazing into a crystal ball, for example, suggests that vision is more effective than the other senses in fore*seeing* future events.

The same bias in favor of the visual is found in American greeting and leave-taking formulas. Examples include: "See you around," "I'll be seeing you," or "I haven't seen so-and-so in ages." Greetings may also be couched in visual terms. "It's good to see you," Americans say, rather than, "It's good to hear, smell, or feel you."

There seem to be relatively few complimentary references to hearers, smellers, talkers, and touchers. "Look, but don't touch" hints at a delight in gawking (girl-watching), and possibly at a cultural distaste for body contact. Someone who is "touchy" is not pleasant to have around. A "soft touch," which sounds as if it should have a positive connotation, is a slang term for a dupe or easy mark.

One of the most interesting pieces of evidence supporting the notion of visual superiority over the other senses is that the original version of "Seeing's believing" was presumably "Seeing's believing, but feeling's the truth." That most Americans have dropped the second portion of the proverb does not seem to be an accident. Rather, it reflects a definite penchant for the visual in contrast to the tactual. Originally, the proverb denigrated "seeing" in favor of "feeling."

Comparisons between the visual and the aural are the most common, however, with hearing considered second best. Consider "Believe nothing of what you hear and only half of what you see." Although

caution is urged against believing everything one sees, seeing is surely depicted as being more reliable and trustworthy than hearing. Compare the following two statements: "I hear that X has just moved to Miami," and "I see that X has just moved to Miami." The first statement is possibly true, possibly not true: there is an element of doubt. The second, in contrast, seems to be a statement of fact.

Other instances are found in legal parlance. Although judges hear cases, there is no doubt that *hearsay*, that is, aural–oral, evidence is not in the same league as that offered by an eyewitness. Actually, the word *witness* indicates that the person was physically present during an event and saw with his own eyes the activities in question. If so, then the term *eyewitness* is redundant. Strangely enough, at *hearings* there is an insistence that *hearsay* evidence be rejected and that only *eyewitness* testimony be accepted. On the other hand, it is interesting to recall that Justice is depicted as being blind. Justice cannot see and presumably blindness guarantees fairness. But of course, sometimes even an innocent man may be guilty "in the eyes of the law."

The eye is also more powerful than the ear insofar as it is regarded as an active rather than a passive agent. The eye looks, peers, or gazes. There is seductive power in the eye, as in "giving a girl the eye," and the malevolent power of the eye is manifested in "the evil eye." The ear, by contrast, is a passive receptacle. There is little evidence of evil ears. Remember also that "big brother is watching you," not listening to you, although bugging rooms with microphones makes listening more likely than watching. Note also that voyeurs, such as Peeping Toms, are considered to be worse than eavesdroppers. The active versus passive with respect to seeing and hearing may also be implied by the connotative

differences between "spectators" and "audience."

Marshall McLuhan and his followers have suggested that the oral–aural channels of preliterate, or rather, nonliterate man may be enjoying a renaissance. According to this view, as man becomes literate, written language—which must be seen to be read—takes priority over the oral. Recently, however, radio and television have created postliterate man, whose world is once more primarily oral–aural. Many Americans learn the news of the day by hearing it on the radio rather than by reading it in newspapers. Even on television, the argument says, the news is mainly told, not shown. Then, too, telephone conversations are replacing letter writing more and more.

One can contend, however, that television has replaced radio, and thus the visual still supersedes the purely aural. Americans still prefer to get agreements in writing rather than to trust a gentleman's handshake (a tactile sign) or take someone's word or say-so (oral sign) for a contract. Once an agreement is down in black and white, Americans watch out for, and read, the small print, with an "eye" toward avoiding an unfavorable set of conditions.

If Americans do have a deep-seated penchant for the visual sense, as I have tried to suggest by examining American folk speech, the question of what it means remains to be answered. It is not just a matter of being able to see more clearly why Americans tend to look for men of vision to lead them. Much more important is the influence of folk metaphors on scientific thought. American science is not culture-free, no matter how devoutly American scientists wish that it were or think that it is.

As an anthropologist, I am struck by the fact that American anthropologists insist upon being participant observers (not voyeurs!) when they go into the field so as to gain insight into the world-views of other cultures. Why "insight"? Do all examples of problem solving by insight actually involve visual perception? And why world-view?

Anthropologists do not always agree whether man is active or passive with regard to world-view. Bronislaw Malinowski, for example, tended to consider man passive: he depicted man as being molded by the impress of a culturally patterned, cookie cutter kind of world-view, which imposed its structure upon human minds. "What interests me really in the study of the native," Malinowski said, "is his outlook on things, his *Weltanschauung*. Every human culture gives its members a definite vision of the world." In contrast, Robert Redfield, by defining world-view as "the way a people characteristically look outward upon the universe," suggested that man was a more active participant. In any case, whether man passively accepts a culturally determined world-view or actively creates a world-view system, the visual bias in the very search by anthropologists for world-view is evident.

It has been observed that for Americans the universe is essentially something they can draw a picture or diagram of. But surely a person's world is felt, smelled, tasted, and heard as well. This propensity for visual metaphorical categories may produce distortion in attempts to describe facets of American culture. It is unlikely that such distortion would even be noticed, since the distortion, like beauty, is strictly in the subjective eye of the beholder. But what happens when Americans or American scientists seek to describe features of other cultures or the features of the natural world?

It is at least possible that by looking for the world-view of other peoples, we run the risk of imposing our own rank-ordering of the senses upon data that may not be perceived in the same way by the people whose cultures are being described. If we are truly interested in understanding how other peoples perceive reality, we must recognize their cognitive categories and try to escape the confines of our own.

The history of man is full of instances of one group's conscious or unconscious attempts to impose its particular set of cognitive categories upon another group. The imposing group typically claims that its categories represent the true nature of reality (as opposed to the categories of the victimized group, which are deemed odd at best and false at worst). Whether it is nineteenth-century American linguists searching in vain for Latin cases (for example, the dative or accusative) in American Indian languages, or a modern Western physician, imbued with the number three, trying to persuade an American Indian, who believes in the sacredness of the number four, that only three doses or inoculations are sufficient (as in a series of three polio shots), the issue is the same.

This is why it is essential for Americans (and for other peoples as well) to become aware of their dependence upon cognitive categories such as the visual metaphorical mode I have been talking about. Armed with this awareness, it is possible to appreciate more fully the aptness of the visual metaphor Ruth Benedict used to explain why so many social theorists failed to notice custom or culture: "We do not see the lens through which we look." A conscious recognition of our visual bias may help make the lens visible. We must never forget the possible relativity of our own sensory perception categories.

Inventories of the same or similar sense categories found in other cultures may help. Clifford Geertz reports, for example, that the Javanese have five senses (seeing, hearing, *talking*, smelling, and feeling), which do not coincide exactly with our five. The delineation of such differences may teach us just how culture-bound or culture-specific our own observations of nature may be. We tend to delude ourselves into thinking we are studying the nature of nature, foolishly forgetting that we cannot observe raw or pure nature. We can perceive nature only through the mediation of culture, with its panoply of culturally relative cognitive categories.

Much of the study of "natural history" often turns out to be "cultural history" in disguise. Theories and ideas about the natural world are invariably couched in terms of a specific human language and are based upon data obtained from human observation. With human observation expressed in human language, one simply cannot avoid cultural bias. Searching for culture-free descriptions of nature may be a worthwhile goal, and perhaps man will one day succeed in achieving it. In the meantime, we must be wary of mistaking relatives for absolutes, of mistaking culture for nature. Cross-cultural comparisons of sense categories may not only reveal critical differences in the specific senses, but also whether or not the apparent priority of vision over the other senses is a human universal. For the moment, we can do little more than wait and *see*.  ∎

# 3

## Body Ritual among the Nacirema

HORACE MINER

*University of Michigan*

THE anthropologist has become so familiar with the diversity of ways in which different peoples behave in similar situations that he is not apt to be surprised by even the most exotic customs. In fact, if all of the logically possible combinations of behavior have not been found somewhere in the world, he is apt to suspect that they must be present in some yet undescribed tribe. This point has, in fact, been expressed with respect to clan organization by Murdock (1949:71). In this light, the magical beliefs and practices of the Nacirema present such unusual aspects that it seems desirable to describe them as an example of the extremes to which human behavior can go.

Professor Linton first brought the ritual of the Nacirema to the attention of anthropologists twenty years ago (1936:326), but the culture of this people is still very poorly understood. They are a North American group living in the territory between the Canadian Cree, the Yaqui and Tarahumare of Mexico, and the Carib and Arawak of the Antilles. Little is known of their origin, although tradition states that they came from the east. According to Nacirema mythology, their nation was originated by a culture hero, Notgnihsaw, who is otherwise known for two great feats of strength—the throwing of a piece of wampum across the river Pa-To-Mac and the chopping down of a cherry tree in which the Spirit of Truth resided.

Nacirema culture is characterized by a highly developed market economy which has evolved in a rich natural habitat. While much of the people's time is devoted to economic pursuits, a large part of the fruits of these labors and a considerable portion of the day are spent in ritual activity. The focus of this activity is the human body, the appearance and health of which loom as a dominant concern in the ethos of the people. While such a concern is certainly not unusual, its ceremonial aspects and associated philosophy are unique.

The fundamental belief underlying the whole system appears to be that the human body is ugly and that its natural tendency is to debility and disease. Incarcerated in such a body, man's only hope is to avert these characteristics through the use of the powerful influences of ritual and ceremony. Every household has one or more shrines devoted to this purpose. The more powerful individuals in the society have several shrines in their houses and, in fact, the opulence of a house is often referred to in terms of the number of such ritual centers it possesses. Most houses are of wattle and daub construction, but the shrine rooms of the more wealthy are walled with stone. Poorer families imitate the rich by applying pottery plaques to their shrine walls.

While each family has at least one such shrine, the rituals associated with it are not family ceremonies but are private and secret. The rites are normally only discussed with children, and then only during the period when they are being initiated into these mysteries. I was able, however, to establish sufficient rapport with the natives to examine these shrines and to have the rituals described to me.

The focal point of the shrine is a box or chest which is built into the wall. In this chest are kept the many charms and magical potions without which no native believes he could live. These preparations are secured from a variety of specialized practitioners. The most powerful of these are the medicine men, whose assistance must be rewarded with substantial gifts. However, the medicine men do not provide the curative potions for their clients, but decide what the ingredients should be and then write them down in an ancient and secret language. This writing is understood only by the medicine men and by the herbalists who, for another gift, provide the required charm.

The charm is not disposed of after it has served its purpose, but is placed in the charm-box of the household shrine. As these magical materials are specific for certain ills, and the real or imagined maladies of the people are many, the charm-box is usually full to overflowing. The magical packets are so numerous that people forget what their purposes were and fear to use them again. While the natives are very vague on this point, we can only assume that the idea in retaining all the old magical materials is that their presence in the charm-box, before which the body rituals are conducted, will in some way protect the worshipper.

Beneath the charm-box is a small font. Each day every member of the family, in succession, enters the shrine room, bows his head before the charm-box, mingles different sorts of holy water in the font, and proceeds with a brief rite of ablution. The holy waters are secured from the Water Temple of the community, where the priests conduct elaborate ceremonies to make the liquid ritually pure.

In the hierarchy of magical practitioners, and below the medicine men in prestige, are specialists whose designation is best translated "holy-mouth-men." The Nacirema have an almost pathological horror of and fascination with the mouth, the condition of which is believed to have a supernatural influence on all social relationships. Were it not for the rituals of the mouth, they believe that their teeth would fall out, their gums bleed, their jaws shrink, their friends desert them, and their lovers reject them. They also believe that a strong relationship exists between oral and moral characteristics. For example, there is a ritual ablution of the mouth for children which is supposed to improve their moral fiber.

The daily body ritual performed by everyone includes a mouth-rite. Despite the fact that these people are so punctilious about care of the mouth, this rite involves a practice which strikes the uninitiated stranger as revolting. It was reported to me that the ritual consists of inserting a small bundle of hog hairs into the mouth, along with certain magical powders, and then moving the bundle in a highly formalized series of gestures.

In addition to the private mouth-rite, the people seek out a holy-mouth-man once or twice a year. These practitioners have an impressive set of paraphernalia, consisting of a variety of augers, awls, probes, and prods. The use of these objects in the exorcism of the evils of the mouth involves almost unbelievable ritual torture of the client. The holy-mouth-man opens the client's mouth and, using the above mentioned tools, enlarges any holes which decay may have created in the teeth. Magical materials are put into these holes. If there are no naturally occurring holes in the teeth, large sections of one or more teeth are gouged out so that the supernatural substance can be applied. In the client's view, the purpose of these ministrations is to arrest decay and to draw friends. The extremely sacred and traditional character of the rite is evident in the fact that the natives return to the holy-mouth-men year after year, despite the fact that their teeth continue to decay.

It is to be hoped that, when a thorough study of the Nacirema is made, there will be careful inquiry into the personality structure of these people. One has but to watch the gleam in the eye of a holy-mouth-man, as he jabs an awl into an exposed nerve, to suspect that a certain amount of sadism is involved. If this can be established, a very interesting pattern emerges, for most of the population shows definite masochistic tendencies. It was to these that Professor Linton referred in discussing a distinctive part of the daily body ritual which is performed only by men. This part of the rite involves scraping and lacerating the surface of the face with a sharp instrument. Special women's rites are performed only four times during each lunar month, but what they lack in frequency is made up in barbarity. As part of this ceremony, women bake their heads in small ovens for about an hour. The theoretically interesting point is that what seems to be a preponderantly masochistic people have developed sadistic specialists.

The medicine men have an imposing temple, or *latipso*, in every community of any size. The more elaborate ceremonies required to treat very sick patients can only be performed at this temple. These ceremonies involve not only the thaumaturge but a permanent group of vestal maidens who move sedately about the temple chambers in distinctive costume and headdress.

The *latipso* ceremonies are so harsh that it is phenomenal that a fair proportion of the really sick natives who enter the temple ever recover. Small children whose indoctrination is still incomplete have been known to resist attempts to take them to the temple because "that is where you go to die." Despite this fact, sick adults are not only willing but eager to undergo the protracted ritual purification, if they can afford to do so. No matter how ill the supplicant or how grave the emergency, the guardians of many temples will not admit a client if he cannot give a rich gift to the custodian. Even after one has gained admission and survived the ceremonies, the guardians will not permit the neophyte to leave until he makes still another gift.

The supplicant entering the temple is first stripped of all his or her clothes. In every-day life the Nacirema avoids exposure of his body and its natural functions. Bathing and excretory acts are performed only in the secrecy of the household shrine, where they are ritualized as part of the body-rites. Psychological shock results from the fact that body secrecy is suddenly lost upon entry into the *latipso*. A man, whose own wife has never seen him in an excretory act, suddenly finds himself naked and assisted by a vestal maiden while he performs his natural functions into a sacred vessel. This sort of ceremonial treatment is necessitated by the fact that the excreta are used by a diviner to ascertain the course and nature of the client's sickness. Female clients, on the other hand, find their naked bodies are subjected to the scrutiny, manipulation and prodding of the medicine men.

Few supplicants in the temple are well enough to do anything but lie on their hard beds. The daily ceremonies, like the rites of the holy-mouth-men, involve discomfort and torture. With ritual precision, the vestals awaken their miserable charges each dawn and roll them about on their beds of pain while performing ablutions, in the formal movements of which the maidens are highly trained. At other times they insert magic wands in the supplicant's mouth or force him to eat substances which are supposed to be healing. From time to time the medicine men come to their clients and jab magically treated needles into their flesh. The fact that these temple ceremonies may not cure, and may even kill the neophyte. in no way decreases the people's faith in the medicine men.

There remains one other kind of practitioner, known as a "listener." This witch-doctor has the power to exorcise the devils that lodge in the heads of people who have been bewitched. The Nacirema believe that parents bewitch their own children. Mothers are particularly suspected of putting a curse on children while teaching them the secret body rituals. The counter-magic of the witch-doctor is unusual in its lack of ritual. The patient simply tells the "listener" all his troubles and fears, beginning with the earliest difficulties he can remember. The memory displayed by the Nacirema in these exorcism sessions is truly remarkable. It is not uncommon for the patient to bemoan the rejection he felt upon being weaned as a babe, and a few individuals even see their troubles going back to the traumatic effects of their own birth.

In conclusion, mention must be made of certain practices which have their base in native esthetics but which depend upon the pervasive aversion to the natural body and its functions. There are ritual fasts to make fat people thin and ceremonial feasts to make thin people fat. Still other rites are used to make women's breasts larger if they are small, and smaller if they are large. General dissatisfaction with breast shape is symbolized in the fact that the ideal form is virtually outside the range of human variation. A few women afflicted with almost inhuman hypermammary development are so idolized that they make a handsome living by simply going from village to village and permitting the natives to stare at them for a fee.

Reference has already been made to the fact that excretory functions are ritualized, routinized, and relegated to secrecy. Natural reproductive functions are similarly distorted. Intercourse is taboo as a topic and scheduled as an act. Efforts are made to avoid pregnancy by the use of magical materials or by limiting intercourse to certain phases of the moon. Conception is actually very infrequent. When pregnant, women dress so as to hide their condition. Parturition takes place in secret, without friends or relatives to assist, and the majority of women do not nurse their infants.

Our review of the ritual life of the Nacirema has certainly shown them to be a magic-ridden people. It is hard to understand how they have managed to exist so long under the burdens which they have imposed upon themselves. But even such exotic customs as these take on real meaning when they are viewed with the insight provided by Malinowski when he wrote (1948:70):

Looking from far and above, from our high places of safety in the developed civilization, it is easy to see all the crudity and irrelevance of magic. But without its power and guidance early man could not have mastered his practical difficulties as he has done, nor could man have advanced to the higher stages of civilization.

**REFERENCES CITED**

Linton, Ralph
    1936   The Study of Man. New York, D. Appleton-Century Co.
Malinowski, Bronislaw
    1948   Magic, Science, and Religion. Glencoe, The Free Press.
Murdock, George P.
    1949   Social Structure. New York, The Macmillan Co.

# 4

# The Mountain People

By Colin M. Turnbull

**Can human beings survive without love? Is society merely a survival mechanism? The Ik may hold the answers—for us.**

### PREFACE

In what follows, there will be much to shock, and the reader will be tempted to say, "how primitive, how savage, how disgusting," and, above all, "how inhuman." The first judgments are typical of the kind of ethno- and egocentricism from which we can never quite escape. But "how inhuman" is of a different order and supposes that there are certain values inherent in humanity itself, from which the people described here seem to depart in a most drastic manner. In living the experience, however, and perhaps in reading it, one finds that it is oneself one is looking at and questioning; it is a voyage in quest of the basic human and a discovery of his potential for inhumanity, a potential that lies within us all.

Just before World War II the Ik tribe had been encouraged to settle in northern Uganda, in the mountainous northeast corner bordering on Kenya to the east and Sudan to the north. Until then they had roamed in nomadic bands, as hunters and gatherers, through a vast region in all three countries. The Kidepo Valley below Mount Morungole was their major hunting territory. After they were confined to a part of their former area, Kidepo was made a national park and they were forbidden to hunt or gather there.

The concept of family in a nomadic society is a broad one; what really counts most in everyday life is community of residence, and those who live close to each other are likely to see each other as effectively related, whether there is any kinship bond or not. Full brothers, on the other hand, who live in different parts of the camp may have little concern for each other.

It is not possible, then, to think of the family as a simple, basic unit. A child is brought up to regard any adult living in the same camp as a parent, any age-mate as a brother or sister. The Ik had this essentially social attitude toward kinship, and it readily lent itself to the rapid and disastrous changes that took place following the restriction of their movement and hunting activities. The family simply ceased to exist.

It is a mistake to think of small-scale societies as "primitive" or "simple." Hunters and gatherers, most of all, appear simple and straightforward in terms of their social organization, yet tnat is far from true. If we can learn about the nature of society from a study of small-scale societies, we can also learn about human relationships. The smaller the society, the less emphasis there is on the formal system and the more there is on interpersonal and intergroup relations. Security is seen in terms of these relationships, and so is survival. The result, which appears so deceptively simple, is that hunters frequently display those characteristics that we find so admirable in man: kindness, generosity, consideration, affection, honesty, hospitality, compassion, charity. For them, in their tiny, close-knit society, these are necessities for survival. In our society anyone possessing even half these qualities would find it hard to survive, yet we think these virtues are inherent in man. I took it for granted that the Ik would possess these same qualities. But they were as unfriendly, uncharitable, inhospitable and generally mean as any people can be. For those positive qualities we value so highly are no longer functional for them; even more than in our own society they spell ruin and disaster. It seems that, far from being basic human qualities, they are luxuries we can afford in times of plenty or are mere mechanisms for survival and security. Given the situation in which the Ik found themselves, man has no time for such luxuries, and a much more basic man appears, using more basic survival tactics.

*Turnbull had to wait in Kaabong, a remote administration outpost, for permission from the Uganda government to continue to Pirre, the Ik water hole and police post. While there he began to learn the Ik language and became used to their constant demands for food and tobacco. An official in Kaabong gave him, as a "gift," 20 Ik workers to build a house and a road up to it. When they arrived at Pirre, however, wages for the workers were negotiated by wily Atum, "the senior of all the Ik on Morungole."*

The police seemed as glad to see me as I was to see them. They hungrily asked for news of Kaabong, as though it were the hub of the universe. They had a borehole and pump for water, to which they said I was welcome, since the water holes used by the Ik were not fit for drinking or even for washing. The police were not able to tell me much about the Ik, because every time they went to visit an Ik village, there was nobody there. Only in times of real hunger did they see much of the Ik, and then only enough to know that they were hungry.

The next morning I rose early, but even though it was barely daylight, by the time I had washed and dressed, the Ik were already outside. They were sitting silently, staring at the Land Rover. As impassive as they seemed, there was an air of expectancy, and I was reminded that these were, after all, hunters, and the likelihood was that I was their morning's prey. So I left the Land Rover curtains closed and as silently as possible prepared a frugal breakfast.

Atum was waiting for me. He said that he had told all the Ik that Iciebam [friend of the Ik] had arrived to live with them and that I had given the workers a "holiday" so they could greet me. They were waiting in the villages. They were very hungry, he added, and many were dying. That was probably one of the few true statements he ever made, and I never even considered believing it.

There were seven villages in all. Village Number One was built on a steep slope, and even the houses tilted at a crazy angle. Atum rapped on the outer stockade with his cane and shouted a greeting, but there was no response. This was Giriko's village, he said, and he was one of my workers.

"But I thought you told them to go back to their villages," I said.

"Yes, but you gave them a holiday, so they are probably in their fields," answered Atum, looking me straight in the eye.

At Village Number Two there was indisputably someone inside, for I could hear loud singing. The singing stopped, a pair of hands gripped the stockade and a craggy head rose into view, giving me an undeniably welcoming smile. This was Lokeléa.

When I asked him what he had been singing about, he answered, "Because I'm hungry."

Village Number Three, the smallest of all, was empty. Village Number Four had only 8 huts, as against the 12 or so in Lokeléa's village and the 18 in Giriko's. The outer stockade was broken in one section, and we walked right in. We ducked through a low opening and entered a compound in which a woman was making pottery. She kept on at her work but gave us a cheery welcome and laughed her head off when I tried to speak in Icietot. She willingly showed me details of her work and did not seem unduly surprised at my interest. She said that everyone else had left for the fields except old Nangoli, who, on hearing her name mentioned, appeared at a hole in the stockade shutting off the next compound. Nangoli mumbled toothlessly at Losiké, who told Atum to pour her some water.

As we climbed up to his own village, Number Five, Atum said that Losiké never gave anything away. Later I remembered that gift of water to Nangoli. At the time I did not stop to think that in this country a gift of water could be a gift of life.

Atum's village had nearly 50 houses, each within its compound within the stout outer stockade. Atum did not invite me in.

A hundred yards away stood Village Number Six. Kauar, one of the workers, was sitting on a rocky slab just outside the village. He had a smile like Losiké's, open and warm, and he said he had been waiting for me all morning. He offered us water and showed me his own small compound and that of his mother.

Coming up from Village Number Seven, at quite a respectable speed, was a blind man. This was Logwara, emaciated but alive and remarkably active. He had heard us and had come to greet me, he said, but he added the inevitable demand for tobacco in the same breath. We sat down in the open sunlight. For a brief moment I felt at peace.

After a short time Atum said we should start back and called over his shoulder to his village. A muffled sound came from within, and he said, "That's my wife, she is very sick—and hungry." I offered to go and see her, but he shook his head. Back at the Land Rover I gave Atum some food and some aspirin, not knowing what else to give him to help his wife.

I was awakened well before dawn by the lowing of cattle. I made an extra pot of tea and let Atum distribute it, and then we divided the workers into two teams. Kauar

was to head the team building the house, and Lokelatom, Losiké's husband, was to take charge of the road workers.

While the Ik were working, their heads kept turning as though they were expecting something to happen. Every now and again one would stand up and peer into the distance and then take off into the bush for an hour or so. On one such occasion, after the person had been gone two hours, the others started drifting off. By then I knew them better; I looked for a wisp of smoke and followed it to where the road team was cooking a goat. Smoke was a giveaway, though, so they economized on cooking and ate most food nearly raw. It is a curious hangover from what must once have been a moral code that Ik will offer food if surprised in the act of eating, though they now go to enormous pains not to be so surprised.

I was always up before dawn, but by the time I got up to the villages they were always deserted. One morning I followed the little *oror* [gulley] up from *oror a pirre'i* [Ravine of Pirre] while it was still quite dark, and I met Lomeja on his way down. He took me on my first illicit hunt in Kidepo. He told me that if he got anything he would share it with me and with anyone else who managed to join us but that he certainly would not take anything back to his family. "Each one of them is out seeing what he can get for himself, and do you think they will bring any back for me?"

Lomeja was one of the very few Ik who seemed glad to volunteer information. Unlike many of the others, he did not get up and leave as I approached. Apart from him, I spent most of my time, those days, with Losiké, the potter. She told me that Nangoli, the old lady in the adjoining compound, and her husband, Amuarkuar, were rather peculiar. They helped each other get food and water, and they brought it back to their compound to eat together.

I still do not know how much real hunger there was at that time, for most of the younger people seemed fairly well fed, and the few skinny old people seemed healthy and active. But my laboriously extracted genealogies showed that there were quite a number of old people still alive and allegedly in these villages, though they were never to be seen. Then Atum's wife died.

Atum told me nothing about it but kept up his demands for food and medicine. After a while the beady-eyed Lomongin told me that Atum was selling the medicine I was giving him for his wife. I was not unduly surprised and merely remarked that that was too bad for his wife. "Oh no," said Lomongin, "she has been dead for weeks."

It must have been then that I began to notice other things that I suppose I had chosen to ignore before. Only a very few of the Ik helped me with the language. Others would understand when it suited them and would pretend they did not understand when they did not want to listen. I began to be forced into a similar isolationist attitude myself, and although I cannot say I enjoyed it, it did make life much easier. I even began to enjoy, in a peculiar way, the company of the silent Ik. And the more I accepted it, the less often people got up and left as I approached. On one occasion I sat on the *di* [sitting place] by Atum's rain tree for three days with a group of Ik, and for three days not one word was exchanged.

The work teams were more lively, but only while working. Kauar always played and joked with the children when they came back from foraging. He used to volunteer to make the two-day walk into Kaabong and the even more tiring two-day climb back to get mail for me or to buy a few things for others. He always asked if he had made the trip more quickly than the last time.

Then one day Kauar went to Kaabong and did not come back. He was found on the last peak of the trail, cold and dead. Those who found him took the things he had been carrying and pushed his body into the bush. I still see his open, laughing face, see him giving precious tidbits to the children, comforting some child who was crying, and watching me read the letters he carried so lovingly for me. And I still think of him probably running up that viciously steep mountainside so he could break his time record and falling dead in his pathetic prime because he was starving.

Once I settled down into my new home, I was able to work more effectively. Having recovered at least some of my anthropological detachment, when I heard the telltale rustling of someone at my stockade, I merely threw a stone. If when out walking I stumbled during a difficult descent and the Ik shrieked with laughter, I no longer even noticed it.

Anyone falling down was good for a laugh, but I never saw anyone actually trip anyone else. The adults were content to let

things happen and then enjoy them; it was probably conservation of energy. The children, however, sought their pleasures with vigor. The best game of all, at this time, was teasing poor little Adupa. She was not so little—in fact she should have been an adult, for she was nearly 13 years old—but Adupa was a little mad. Or you might say she was the only sane one, depending on your point of view. Adupa did not jump on other people's play houses, and she lavished enormous care on hers and would curl up inside it. That made it all the more jump-on-able. The other children beat her viciously.

Children are not allowed to sleep in the house after they are "put out," which is at about three years old, four at the latest. From then on they sleep in the open courtyard, taking what shelter they can against the stockade. They may ask for permission to sit in the doorway of their parents' house but may not lie down or sleep there. "The same thing applies to old people," said Atum, "if they can't build a house of their own and, of course, *if* their children let them stay in their compounds."

I saw a few old people, most of whom had taken over abandoned huts. For the first time I realized that there really was starvation and saw why I had never known it before: it was confined to the aged. Down in Giriko's village the old ritual priest, Lolim, confidentially told me that he was sheltering an old man who had been refused shelter by his son. But Lolim did not have enough food for himself, let alone his guest; could I . . . I liked old Lolim, so, not believing that Lolim had a visitor at all, I brought him a double ration that evening. There was a rustling in the back of the hut, and Lolim helped ancient Lomeraniang to the entrance. They shook with delight at the sight of the food.

When the two old men had finished eating, I left; I found a hungry-looking and disapproving little crowd clustered outside. They muttered to each other about wasting food. From then on I brought food daily, but in a very short time Lomeraniang was dead, and his son refused to come down from the village above to bury him. Lolim scratched a hole and covered the body with a pile of stones he carried himself, one by one.

Hunger was indeed more severe than I knew, and, after the old people, the children were the next to go. It was all quite impersonal— even to me, in most cases, since I had been immunized by the Ik themselves against sorrow on their behalf. But Adupa

was an exception. Her madness was such that she did not know just how vicious humans could be. Even worse, she thought that parents were for loving, for giving as well as receiving. Her parents were not given to fantasies. When she came for shelter, they drove her out; and when she came because she was hungry, they laughed that Icien laugh, as if she had made them happy.

Adupa's reactions became slower and slower. When she managed to find food— fruit peels, skins, bits of bone, half-eaten berries—she held it in her hand and looked at it with wonder and delight. Her playmates caught on quickly; they put tidbits in her way and watched her simple drawn little face wrinkle in a smile. Then as she raised her hand to her mouth, they set on her with cries of excitement, fun and laughter, beating her savagely over the head. But that is not how she died. I took to feeding her, which is probably the cruelest thing I could have done, a gross selfishness on my part to try to salve my own rapidly disappearing conscience. I had to protect her, physically, as I fed her. But the others would beat her anyway, and Adupa cried, not because of the pain in her body but because of the pain she felt at the great, vast, empty wasteland where love should have been.

It was *that* that killed her. She demanded that her parents love her. Finally they took her in, and Adupa was happy and stopped crying. She stopped crying forever because her parents went away and closed the door tight behind them, so tight that weak little Adupa could never have moved it.

The Ik seem to tell us that the family is not such a fundamental unit as we usually suppose, that it is not essential to social life. In the crisis of survival facing the Ik, the family was one of the first institutions to go, and the Ik as a society have survived.

The other quality of life that we hold to be necessary for survival—love —the Ik dismiss as idiotic and highly dangerous. But we need to see more of the Ik before their absolute lovelessness becomes truly apparent.

In this curious society there is one common value to which all Ik hold tenaciously. It is *ngag*, "food." That is the one standard by which they measure right and wrong, goodness and badness. The very word for "good" is defined in terms of food. "Goodness" is "the possession of food," or the "*individual* possession of food." If you try to discover their concept of a "good man," you get the truly Icien answer: one who has a full stomach.

We should not be surprised, then, when the mother throws her child out at three years old. At that age a series of *rites de passage* begins. In this environment a child has no chance of survival on his own until he is about 13, so children form age bands. The junior band consists of children between three and seven, the senior of eight- to twelve-year-olds. Within the band each child seeks another close to him in age for defense against the older children. These friendships are temporary, however, and inevitably there comes a time when each turns on the one that up to then had been the closest to him; that is the *rite de passage*, the destruction of that fragile bond called friendship. When this has happened three or

four times, the child is ready for the world.

The weakest are soon thinned out, and the strongest survive to achieve leadership of the band. Such a leader is eventually driven out, turned against by his fellow band members. Then the process starts all over again; he joins the senior age band as its most junior member.

The final *rite de passage* is into adulthood, at the age of 12 or 13. By then the candidate has learned the wisdom of acting on his own, for his own good, while acknowledging that on occasion it is profitable to associate temporarily with others.

One year in four the Ik can count on a complete drought. About this time it began to be apparent that there were going to be two consecutive years of drought and fam-

ine. Men as well as women took to gathering what wild fruits and berries they could find, digging up roots, cutting grass that was going to seed, threshing and eating the seed.

Old Nangoli went to the other side of Kidepo, where food and water were more plentiful. But she had to leave her husband, Amuarkuar, behind. One day he appeared at my *odok* and asked for water. I gave him some and was going to get him food when Atum came storming over and argued with me about wasting water. In the midst of the dispute Amuarkuar quietly left. He wandered over to a rocky outcrop and lay down there to rest. Nearby was a small bundle of grass that evidently he had cut and had been dragging painfully to the ruins of his village to make a rough shelter. The grass was his supreme effort to keep a home going until Nangoli returned. When I went over to him, he looked up and smiled and said that my water tasted good. He lay back and went to sleep with a smile on his face. That is how Amuarkuar died, happily.

There are measures that can be taken for survival involving the classical institutions of gift and sacrifice. These are weapons, sharp and aggressive. The object is to build up a series of obligations so that in times of crisis you have a number of debts you can recall; with luck one of them may be repaid. To this end, in the circumstances of Ik life, considerable sacrifice would be justified, so you have the odd phenomenon of these otherwise singularly self-interested people going out of their way to "help" each other. Their help may very well be resented in the extreme, but is done in such a way that it cannot be refused, for it has already been given. Someone may hoe another's field in his absence or rebuild his stockade or join in the building of a house.

The danger in this system was that the debtor might not be around when collection was called for and, by the same token, neither might the creditor. The future was too uncertain for this to be anything but one additional survival measure, though some developed it to a fine technique.

There seemed to be increasingly little among the Ik that could by any stretch of the imagination be called social life, let alone social organization. The family does not hold itself together; economic interest is centered on as many stomachs as there are people; and cooperation is merely a device for furthering an interest that is consciously selfish. We often do the same thing in our so-called "altruistic" practices, but we tell ourselves it is for the good of others. The Ik have dispensed with the myth of altruism. Though they have no centralized leadership or means of physical coercion, they do hold together with remarkable tenacity.

In our world, where the family has also lost much of its value as a social unit and where religious belief no longer binds us into communities, we maintain order only through coercive power that is ready to uphold a rigid law and through an equally rigid penal system. The Ik, however, have learned to do without coercion, either spiritual or physical. It seems that they have come to a recognition of what they accept as man's basic selfishness, of his natural determination to survive as an individual before all else. This they consider to be man's basic right, and they allow others to pursue that right without recrimination.

In large-scale societies such as our own,

where members are individual beings rather than social beings, we rely on law for order. The absence of both a common law and a common belief would surely result in lack of any community of behavior; yet Ik society is not anarchical. One might well expect religion, then, to play a powerful role in Icien life, providing a source of unity.

The Ik, as may be expected, do not run true to form. When I arrived, there were still three ritual priests alive. From them and from the few other old people, I learned something of the Ik's belief and practice as they had been before their world was so terribly changed. There had been a powerful unity of belief in Didigwari—a sky god—and a body of ritual practice reinforcing secular behavior that was truly social.

Didigwari himself is too remote to be of much practical significance to the Ik. He created them and abandoned them and retreated into his domain somewhere in the

sky. He never came down to earth, but the *abang* [ancestors] have all known life on earth; it is only against them that one can sin and only to them that one can turn for help, through the ritual priest.

While Morungole has no legends attached to it by the Ik, it nonetheless figures in their ideology and is in some ways regarded by them as sacred. I had noticed this by the almost reverential way in which they looked at it—none of the shrewd cunning and cold appraisal with which they regard the rest of the world. When they talked about it, there was a different quality to their voices. They seemed incapable of talking about Morungole in any other way, which is probably why they talked about it so very seldom. Even that weasel Lomongin became gentle the only time he talked about it to me. He said, "If Atum and I were there, we would not argue. It is a good place." I asked if he meant that it was full of food. He said

yes. "Then why do Ik never go there?" "They do go there." "But if hunting is good there, why not live there?" "We don't hunt there, we just go there." "Why?" "I told you, it is a good place." If I did not understand him, that was my fault; for once he was doing his best to communicate something to me. With others it was the same. All agreed that it was "a good place." One added, "That is the Place of God."

Lolim, the oldest and greatest of the ritual priests, was also the last. He was not much in demand any longer, but he was still held in awe, which means kept at a distance. Whenever he approached a *di*, people cleared a space for him, as far away from themselves as possible. The Ik rarely called on his services, for they had little to pay him with, and he had equally little to offer them. The main things they did try to get out of him were certain forms of medicine, both herbal and magical.

Lolim said that he had inherited his power from his father. His father had taught him well but could not give him the power to hear the *abang*—that had to come from the *abang* themselves. He had wanted his oldest son to inherit and had taught him everything he could. But his son, Longoli, was bad, and the *abang* refused to talk to him. They talked instead to his oldest daughter, bald Nangoli. But there soon came the time when all the Ik needed was food in their stomachs, and Lolim could not supply that. The time came when Lolim was too weak to go out and collect the medicines he needed. His children all refused to go except Nangoli, and then she was jailed for gathering in Kidepo Park.

Lolim became ill and had to be protected while eating the food I gave him. Then the children began openly ridiculing him and teasing him, dancing in front of him and kneeling down so that he would trip over them. His grandson used to creep up behind him and with a pair of hard sticks drum a lively tattoo on the old man's bald head.

I fed him whenever I could, but often he did not want more than a bite. Once I found him rolled up in his protective ball, crying. He had had nothing to eat for four days and no water for two. He had asked his children, who all told him not to come near them.

The next day I saw him leaving Atum's village, where his son Longoli lived. Longoli swore that he had been giving his father food and was looking after him. Lolim was not shuffling away; it was almost a run, the run of a drunken man, staggering from side to side. I called to him, but he made no reply, just a kind of long, continuous and horrible

moan. He had been to Longoli to beg him to let him into his compound because he knew he was going to die in a few hours, Longoli calmly told me afterward. Obviously Longoli could not do a thing like that: a man of Lolim's importance would have called for an enormous funeral feast. So he refused. Lolim begged Longoli then to open up Nangoli's *asak* for him so that he could die in *her* compound. But Longoli drove him out, and he died alone.

Atum pulled some stones over the body where it had fallen into a kind of hollow. I saw that the body must have lain parallel with the *oror*. Atum answered without waiting for the question: "He was lying looking up at Mount Meraniang."

Insofar as ritual survived at all, it could hardly be said to be religious, for it did little or nothing to bind Icien society together. But the question still remained: Did this lack of social behavior and communal ritual or religious expression mean that there was no community of belief?

Belief may manifest itself, at either the individual or the communal level, in what we call morality, when we behave according to certain principles supported by our belief even when it seems against our personal interest. When we call ourselves moral, however, we tend to ignore that ultimately our morality benefits us even as individuals, insofar as we are social individuals and live in a society. In the absence of belief, law takes over and morality has little role. If there was such a thing as an Icien morality, I had not yet perceived it, though traces of a moral past remained. But it still remained a possibility, as did the existence of an unspoken, unmanifest belief that might yet reveal itself and provide a basis for the reintegration of society. I was somewhat encouraged in this hope by the unexpected flight of old Nangoli, widow of Amuarkuar.

When Nangoli returned and found her husband dead, she did an odd thing: she grieved. She tore down what was left of their home, uprooted the stockade, tore up whatever was growing in her little field. Then she fled with a few belongings.

Some weeks later I heard that she and her children had gone over to the Sudan and built a village there. This migration was so unusual that I decided to see whether this runaway village was different.

Lojieri led the way, and Atum came along. One long day's trek got us there. Lojieri pulled part of the brush fence aside, and we went in and wandered around. He and Atum looked inside all the huts,

and Lojieri helped himself to tobacco from one and water from another. Surprises were coming thick and fast. That households should be left open and untended with such wealth inside . . . That there should have been such wealth, for as well as tobacco and jars of water there were baskets of food, and meat was drying on racks. There were half a dozen or so compounds, but they were separated from each other only by a short line of sticks and brush. It was a village, and these were homes, the first and last I was to see.

The dusk had already fallen, and Nangoli came in with her children and grandchildren. They had heard us and came in with warm welcomes. There was no hunger here, and in a very short time each kitchen hearth had a pot of food cooking. Then we sat around the central fire and talked until late, and it was another universe.

There was no talk of "how much better it is here than there"; talk revolved around what had happened on the hunt that day. Loron was lying on the ground in front of the fire as his mother made gentle fun of him. His wife, Kinimei, whom I had never seen even speak to him at Pirre, put a bowl of fresh-cooked berries and fruit in front of him. It was all like a nightmare rather than a fantasy, for it made the reality of Pirre seem all the more frightening.

The unpleasantness of returning was somewhat alleviated by Atum's suffering on the way up the stony trail. Several times he slipped, which made Lojieri and me laugh. It was a pleasure to move rapidly ahead and leave Atum gasping behind so that we could be sitting up on the *di* when he finally appeared and could laugh at his discomfort.

The days of drought wore on into weeks and months and, like everyone else, I became rather bored with sickness and death. I survived rather as did the young adults, by diligent attention to my own needs while ignoring those of others.

More and more it was only the young who could go far from the village as hunger became starvation. Famine relief had been initiated down at Kasilé, and those fit enough to make the trip set off. When they came back, the contrast between them and the others was that between life and death. Villages were villages of the dead and dying, and there was little difference between the two. People crawled rather than walked. After a few feet some would lie down to rest, but they could not be sure of ever being able to sit up again, so they mostly stayed upright until they reached their destination. They were going nowhere, these semianimate bags of skin and bone; they just wanted to be with others, and they stopped whenever they met. Perhaps it was the most important demonstration of sociality I ever saw among the Ik. Once they met, they neither spoke nor did anything together.

Early one morning, before dawn, the village moved. In the midst of a hive of activity were the aged and crippled, soon to be abandoned, in danger of being trampled but seemingly unaware of it. Lolim's widow, Lo'ono, whom I had never seen before, also had been abandoned and had tried to make her way down the mountainside. But she was totally blind and had tripped and rolled to the bottom of the *oror a pirre'i;* there she lay on her back, her legs and arms thrashing feebly, while a little crowd laughed.

At this time a colleague was with me. He kept the others away while I ran to get medicine and food and water, for Lo'ono was obviously near dead from hunger and thirst as well as from the fall. We treated her and fed her and asked her to come back with us. But she asked us to point her in the direction of her son's new village. I said I did not think she would get much of a welcome there, and she replied that she knew it but wanted to be near him when she died. So we gave her more food, put her stick in her hand and pointed her the right way. She suddenly cried. She was crying, she said, because we had reminded her that there had been a time when people had helped each other, when people had been kind and good. Still crying, she set off.

The Ik up to this point had been tolerant of my activities, but all this was too much. They said that what we were doing was wrong. Food and medicine were for the living, not the dead. I thought of Lo'ono. And I thought of other old people who had joined in the merriment when they had been teased or had a precious morsel of food taken from their mouths. They knew that it was silly of them to expect to go on living, and, having watched others, they knew that the spectacle really was quite funny. So they joined in the laughter. Perhaps if we had left Lo'ono, she would have died laughing. But we prolonged her misery for no more than a few brief days. Even worse, we reminded her of when things had been different, of days when children had cared for parents and parents for children. She was already dead, and we made her unhappy as well. At the time I was sure we were right, doing the only "human" thing. In a way we *were*—we were making life more comfortable for our-

selves. But now I wonder if the Ik way was not right, if I too should not have laughed as Lo'ono flapped about, then left her to die.

Ngorok was a man at 12. Lomer, his older brother, at 15 was showing signs of strain; when he was carrying a load, his face took on a curious expression of pain that was no physical pain. Giriko, at 25 was 40, Atum at 40 was 65, and the very oldest, perhaps a bare 50, were centenarians. And I, at 40, was younger than any of them, for I still enjoyed life, which they had learned was not "adult" when they were 3. But they retained their will to survive and so offered grudging respect to those who had survived for long.

Even in the teasing of the old there was a glimmer of hope. It denoted a certain intimacy that did not exist between adjacent generations. This is quite common in small-scale societies. The very old and the very young look at each other as representing the future and the past. To the child, the aged represent a world that existed before their own birth and the unknown world to come.

And now that all the old are dead, what is left? Every Ik who is old today was thrown out at three and has survived, and in consequence has thrown his own children out and knows that they will not help him in his old age any more than he helped his parents. The system has turned one full cycle and is now self-perpetuating; it has eradicated what we know as "humanity" and has turned the world into a chilly void where man does not seem to care even for himself, but survives. Yet into this hideous world Nangoli and her family quietly returned because they could not bear to be alone.

For the moment abandoning the very old and the very young, the Ik as a whole must be searched for one last lingering trace of humanity. They appear to have disposed of virtually all the qualities that we normally think of as differentiating us from other primates, yet they survive without seeming to be greatly different from ourselves in terms of behavior. Their behavior is more extreme, for we do not start throwing our children out until kindergarten. We have shifted responsibility from family to state, the Ik have shifted it to the individual.

It has been claimed that human beings are capable of love and, indeed, are dependent upon it for survival and sanity. The Ik offer us an opportunity for testing this cherished notion that love is essential to survival. If it is, the Ik should have it.

Love in human relationships implies mutuality, a willingness to sacrifice the self that springs from a consciousness of iden-

tity. This seems to bring us back to the Ik, for it implies that love is self-oriented, that even the supreme sacrifice of one's life is no more than selfishness, for the victim feels amply rewarded by the pleasure he feels in making the sacrifice. The Ik, however, do not value emotion above survival, and they are without love.

But I kept looking, for it was the one thing that could fill the void their survival tactics had created; and if love was not there in some form, it meant that for humanity love is not a necessity at all, but a luxury or an illusion. And if it was not among the Ik, it meant that mankind can lose it.

The only possibility for any discovery of love lay in the realm of interpersonal relationships. But they were, each one, simply alone, and seemingly content to be alone. It was this acceptance of individual isolation that made love almost impossible. Contact, when made, was usually for a specific practical purpose having to do with food and the filling of a stomach, a single stomach. Such contacts did not have anything like the permanence or duration required to develop a situation in which love was possible.

The isolation that made love impossible, however, was not completely proof against loneliness. I no longer noticed normal behavior, such as the way people ate, running as they gobbled, so as to have it all for themselves. But I did notice that when someone was making twine or straightening a spear shaft, the focus of attention for the spectators was not the person but the action. If they were caught watching by the one being watched and their eyes met, the reaction was a sharp retreat on both sides.

When the rains failed for the second year running, I knew that the Ik as a society were almost certainly finished and that the monster they had created in its place, that passionless, feelingless association of individuals, would spread like a fungus, contaminating all it touched. When I left, I too had been contaminated. I was not upset when I said good-bye to old Loiangorok. I told him I had left a sack of *posho* [ground corn meal] with the police for him, and I said I would send money for more when that ran out. He dragged himself slowly toward the *di* every day, and he always clutched a knife. When he got there, or as far as he could, he squatted down and whittled at some wood, thus proving that he was still alive and able to do things. The *posho* was enough to last him for months, but I felt no emotion when I estimated that he would last one month, even with the *posho* in the hands of the police. I underestimated his son, who within two days had persuaded the police that it would save a lot of bother if he looked after the *posho.* I heard later that Loiangorok died of starvation within two weeks.

So, I departed with a kind of forced gaiety, feeling that I should be glad to be gone but having forgotten how to be glad. I certainly was not thinking of returning within a year, but I did. The following spring I heard that rain had come at last and that the fields of the Ik had never looked so prosperous, nor the country so green and fertile. A few months away had refreshed me, and I wondered if my conclusions had not been excessively pessimistic. So, early that summer, I set off to be present for the first harvests in three years.

I was not surprised too much when two days after my arrival and installation at the police post I found Logwara, the blind man, lying on the roadside bleeding, while a hundred yards up other Ik were squabbling over the body of a hyena. Logwara had tried to get there ahead of the others to grab the meat and had been trampled on.

First I looked at the villages. The lush outer covering concealed an inner decay. All the villages were like this to some extent, except for Lokeléa's. There the tomatoes and pumpkins were carefully pruned and cleaned, so that the fruits were larger and healthier. In what had been my own compound the shade trees had been cut down for firewood, and the lovely hanging nests of the weaver birds were gone.

The fields were even more desolate. Every field without exception had yielded in abundance, and it was a new sensation to have vision cut off by thick crops. But every crop was rotting from sheer neglect.

The Ik said that they had no need to bother guarding the fields. There was so much food they could never eat it all, so why not let the birds and baboons take some? The Ik had full bellies; they were good. The *di* at Atum's village was much the same as usual, people sitting or lying about. People were still stealing from each other's fields, and nobody thought of saving for the future.

It was obvious that nothing had really changed due to the sudden glut of food except that interpersonal relationships had deteriorated still further and that Icien individualism had heightened beyond what I thought even Ik to be capable of.

The Ik had faced a conscious choice between being humans and being parasites and had chosen the latter. When they saw their fields come alive, they were confronted with a problem. If they reaped the harvest, they would have to store grain for eating and planting, and every Ik knew that trying to store anything was a waste of time. Further, if they made their fields look too promising, the government would stop famine relief. So the Ik let their fields rot and continued to draw famine relief.

The Ik were not starving any longer; the old and infirm had all died the previous year, and the younger survivors were doing quite well. But the famine relief was administered in a way that was little short of criminal. As before, only the young and well were able to get down from Pirre to collect the relief; they were given relief for those who could not come and told to take it back. But they never did—they ate it themselves.

The facts are there, though those that can be read here form but a fraction of what one person was able to gather in under two years. There can be no mistaking the direction in which those facts point, and that is the most important thing of all, for it may affect the rest of mankind as it has affected the Ik. The Ik have "progressed," one might say, since the change that has come to them came with the advent of civilization to Africa. They have made of a world that was alive a world that is dead—a cold, dispassionate world that is without ugliness because it is without beauty, without hate because it is without love, and without any realization of truth even, because it simply is. And the symptoms of change in our own society indicate that we are heading in the same direction.

Those values we cherish so highly may indeed be basic to human society but not to humanity, and that means that the Ik show that society itself is not indispensable for man's survival and that man is capable of associating for purposes of survival without being social. The Ik have replaced human society with a mere survival system that does not take human emotion into account. As yet the system is imperfect, for although survival is assured, it is at a minimal level and there is still competition between individuals. With our intellectual sophistication and advanced technology we should be able to perfect the system and eliminate competition, guaranteeing survival for a given number of years for all, reducing the demands made upon us by a social system, abolishing desire and consequently that ever-present and vital gap between desire and achievement, treating us, in a word, as individuals with one basic individual right— the right to survive.

Such interaction as there is within this system is one of mutual exploitation. That is how it already is with the Ik. In our own world the mainstays of a society based on a truly social sense of mutuality are breaking down, indicating that perhaps society as we know it has outworn its usefulness and that by clinging to an outworn system we are bringing about our own destruction.

Family, economy, government and religion, the basic categories of social activity and behavior, no longer create any sense of social unity involving a shared and mutual responsibility among all members of our society. At best they enable the individual to survive as an individual. It is the world of the individual, as is the world of the Ik.

The sorry state of society in the civilized world today is in large measure due to the fact that social change has not kept up with technological change. This mad, senseless, unthinking commitment to technological change that we call progress may be sufficient to exterminate the human race in a very short time even without the assistance of nuclear warfare. But since we have already become individualized and desocialized, we say that extermination will not come in our time, which shows about as much sense of family devotion as one might expect from the Ik.

Even supposing that we can avert nuclear holocaust or the almost universal famine that may be expected if population keeps expanding and pollution remains unchecked, what will be the cost if not the same already paid by the Ik? They too were driven by the need to survive, and they succeeded at the cost of their humanity. We are already beginning to pay the same price, but we not only still have the choice (though we may not have the will or courage to make it), we also have the intellectual and technological ability to avert an Icien end. Any change as radical as will be necessary is not likely to bring material benefits to the present generation, but only then will there be a future.

The Ik teach us that our much vaunted human values are not inherent in humanity at all but are associated only with a particular form of survival called society and that all, even society itself, are luxuries that can be dispensed with. That does not make them any less wonderful, and if man has any greatness, it is surely in his ability to maintain these values, even shortening an already pitifully short life rather than sacrifice his humanity. But that too involves choice, and the Ik teach us that man can lose the will to make it. That is the point at which there is an end to truth, to goodness and to beauty, an end to the struggle for their achievement, which gives life to the individual and strength and meaning to society. The Ik have relinquished all luxury in the name of individual survival, and they live on as a people without life, without passion, beyond humanity. We pursue those trivial, idiotic technological encumbrances, and all the time we are losing our potential for social rather than individual survival, for hating as well as loving, losing perhaps our last chance to enjoy life with all the passion that is our nature. ◼

# The American Obsession with FUN

# 5

The way we stress the importance of being "alive," says the author, betrays "a diminution in the sense of the self." Too often we discover our identity in the products we buy.

BY ANN NIETZKE

In John Barth's *The End of the Road*, Jacob Horner describes a dream he once had in which, after several futile attempts to find out the weather forecast, he learns from the chief meteorologist that there simply will not be any weather the next day. He tells us about the dream in order to explain a particular state of mind that he often experiences, a state he has come to call "weatherless." Though analogies between moods and weather are commonplace, Horner questions their appropriateness in his case because a day without weather is almost impossible to imagine, and yet he frequently has days without any mood at all. At such times Horner is without a personality, is nonexistent in his own mind, except in the purely physical sense. He compares himself to those microscopic specimens that must be dyed before they can be seen: Horner needs to be colored by some mood or other in order to recognize himself. On his weatherless days he sits blankly in his rocking chair, rocking sometimes for hours until some external event colors him back into being.

Throughout the book Horner suffers from varying degrees of weatherlessness, the most extreme being a trancelike state of complete immobility. His standard device for warding off emptiness of mind is to repeat over and over an advertising jingle from the 1950s: "Pepsi-Cola hits the spot./Twelve full ounces—that's a lot." This jingle serves as the test pattern of his consciousness: As long as he can say it, he knows he still exists. Once, when the jingle failed him, he sat frozen on a bench in Penn Station all night long. By the end of the book the jingle has lost its effectiveness because Horner cannot even remember to say it at the right times. In the final scene he sits in his rocking chair, totally weatherless. When he gets in a cab and says, "Terminal," we know he will take the bus to the nameless "Doctor," recognizing himself to be a spiritual terminal case.

Ann Nietzke, who lives in Normal, Illinois, is a housewife and freelance writer with a special interest in psychology.

I have a friend, a teacher at a junior college in a large midwestern city, who sometimes suffers similar periods of weatherlessness. Her attacks are less severe and less pervasive than Jacob Horner's; I think they are, in part, just a defense against being overwhelmed by modern urban living. When things become a bit too much, she simply tunes out temporarily while her strength, the strength necessary for living a feeling life, gets replenished. Nevertheless, finding yourself in the company of someone who is in no mood at all, whatever the reasons behind it, is an unsettling experience. You just plain don't know how to act, since nothing you say or do seems to matter. There is nothing to interact with, no mood, emotion, or viewpoint to oppose or complement. You can't cheer your friend up, because she's not sad; you can't convince her of anything, because she's all too agreeable; and you can't make her feel better, because she doesn't feel bad. A few years ago, when I was visiting my friend during one of her weatherless bouts, I became exasperated and then saddened by my own helplessness in the situation. But as the weekend wore on, my sadness, interestingly enough, dissolved itself into moodlessness, too, so that finally the two of us sat there staring vacantly into space and feeling quite at home with each other. The only thing to do on such a weatherless Saturday night,

of course, was to look at television.

At that time Pepsi had just begun a new series of commercials, which must have proved very successful since it is still being used almost three years later. The main theme, familiar to everyone by now, is in the refrain: "You've got a lot to live,/And Pepsi's got a lot to give." That night, after hearing those words, my friend turned to me with the first spark of life I had seen in her eyes all weekend. "Don't you just *love* that?" she said. And I had to admit that I did. The tune and the words together conveyed a spirit of vivacity and affirmation that was somehow irresistibly appealing. The rest of the evening and all the next day we couldn't get the song out of our minds. We sang it aloud, together or solo, and, like Jacob Horner, we found ourselves intoning it under our breath, tapping a foot or waving a hand breezily through the air to mark the time. The thing had gotten through to us and in some mysterious way filled the emotional vacuum we were in.

Well, the coincidental relationship among my friends and me and Jacob Horner and weatherlessness and Pepsi-Cola ads all came together in an intriguing way when I recently reread Barth's *The End of the Road*. I began to listen carefully to Pepsi ads and then to Coke ads, and, as is usually the case when advertising is analyzed, I learned much less about the products than about the public for which the ads are designed. As almost any American can tell you, "Pepsi helps you come alive" and "Coke is the real thing." These slogans seem simple enough, but a close look at what they imply leads us into some sociopsychological considerations that are not simple.

When I was trying to help my friend that weekend, I didn't yet understand that moodlessness is a kind of death, that "aliveness" of some sort might be just the thing required to dispel it. Of course, even if I had realized this, I don't know specifically what I might have done for her, but I think it helps explain our response to the Pepsi commercial. In its various ads on radio and TV, Pepsi uses two main stanzas, always followed by the refrain, "You've got a lot to live,/And Pepsi's got a lot to give."

It's the Pepsi generation
Comin' at ya, goin' strong.
Put yourself behind a Pepsi—
If you're livin', you belong.

There's a whole new way of livin'—
Pepsi helps supply the drive.
It's got a lot to give for those who like to live,
'Cause it helps 'em come alive.

On television the music accompanies scenes of people having good times. Not all the people look young, but we're made to realize that they all are "young in heart," that they are "living" and so are members of the Pepsi generation. On radio rock-'n'-roll stations various well-known recording stars sing the lyrics. I was particularly struck by the idea of deadness that underlies "coming alive" when I heard Johnny Cash sing about it in his most spiritless style.

The relationship depicted in the ads between being "alive" and having fun is psychologically a sound one, and it is in the sexual experience, of course, that the two are most closely related. Alexander Lowen, a medical doctor who has written a book on the subject of pleasure, believes that "the foundation for a joyful life is the pleasure we feel in our bodies, and that, without this bodily pleasure of aliveness, living becomes the grim necessity of survival." Every imaginable kind of product is advertised as holding the key to fun, good times, and sexual fulfillment. But, as Dr. Lowen points out, the American obsession with fun probably betrays a lack of true pleasure in our lives. Similarly, one reason the advertising business relies so heavily on sexual appeals is, not that America has become sexually liberated, but rather that many people are so out of touch with their own bodies that they derive little pleaure from them and will therefore seek the missing pleasure through the use of products which, in one way or another, promise to replace it.

Lowen suggests that the common element in all neurotic-behavior patterns is a diminution in the sense of self, which includes "a loss of the feeling of identity, a reduced awareness of one's individuality, a decrease in self-expression, and a diminshed capacity for pleasure." Certainly Jake Horner and my friend exhibited all of these symptoms in their states of weatherlessness, though they were chronic for him and temporary for her. What is frightening to contemplate is that anyone who spends as much time watching television as the average American does must, almost by definition, exhibit these symptoms to some degree.

*know you're the best you can b*

*feelin' free!*

*The REAL Thing!*

*COKE IS.*

*Join the Pepsi generation*

*under your own two arms*

*because I'm worth it.*

*"OF THE FOUR LOTIONS I USE EVERY DAY*

*easure, double your FUN*

"The price we pay for avoiding the pain of being fully alive is that we are excluded from the pleasure as well."

For, if he were fully aware of himself as an individual, he would not constantly want to be treated as part of an audience. If he felt the need for self-expression, he would want to put himself in a situation that would give him a chance to fulfill it. And if he had a real capacity for pleasure, he would engage in pleasurable activities himself, not watch others so engaged on television. This is not to say, of course, that TV causes neuroses, but only that the neurotic as described by Lowen would naturally be drawn to watching it. And advertisers, to be sure, take full advantage of this fact.

My friend and I knew instinctively to

turn on the television that weatherless Saturday night, although neither of us is an avid viewer. I would venture to guess that the difference between us and many full-time TV addicts is that we were quite conscious of our moodlessness because, for us, it is a sometime thing. Those who lack the strength to live lives of feeling, and in whom the sense of self is always ill-defined, are no doubt much less conscious of that state, although they may vaguely sense that something is missing from their lives. The price they pay for avoiding the pain of being fully alive is that they are excluded from the pleasure of it as well. They are, therefore, always tempted by any promise of pleasure, hoping that perhaps this time it will not elude them.

I understood the most sinister aspect of the phenomenon Vance Packard termed "hidden persuasion" when I began to consider what it might mean to be weatherless most of the time and not even realize it. There is nothing obviously "hidden" about what the Pepsi ad is saying; in fact, upon close examination it is hard to believe how straightforward the words are. But the psychological success of the commercial depends upon a lack of self-awareness in the viewer. For while it gives the impression of appealing to the "living" and those with a "zest for life," the ad is actually aimed at the "dead" who experience so little pleasure that they need something to help them "come alive." Thus, on the conscious level the ad provides support for the viewer's illusion that he is "alive" and capable of enjoying things and himself, while at the same time, on a deeper level, it is touching that vague sense of deadness that so many people experience. Even if the "dead" viewer were to take part in all the fun-filled activities shown in the ads, he still would not be capable of having any real fun. That is too terrible a thing for him to face consciously; it is easier to accept the notion, however irrational, that Pepsi might make a difference ("Put yourself behind a Pepsi-/If you're livin', you belong"). The point is that the persuasion depends, not on something hidden in the commercial, but on something the viewer has hidden from himself.

The neurotic, with his diminished sense of self-identity, has no way of really knowing when he is fooling himself. Because he feels that at the center of his being there is only emptiness rather than an integrated personality, he lives with a permanent sense of unreality. It is this realization that brings many neurotics to the analyst's couch, and, of course, the realization itself is a step in the right direction. For most, however, the realization probably never crystallizes; they go on existing with their weatherlessness and a vague awareness that their lives are unfulfilled.

At its deepest level the Coca-Cola pitch for "the real thing" appeals to this neurotic sense of unreality:

It's the real thing, Coke is.
That's the way it should be.
What the world wants to see
Is the real thing.

It's the real thing, Coke is.
In the back of your mind
What you're hoping to find
Is the real thing.

On one level of interpretation, Coke is held up as something genuine in a world of automation and imitation. (Interestingly enough, Coke became "the real thing" only after 7-Up billed itself as the "Uncola"—apparently in an attempt to imply that 7-Up is not a genuine soft drink.) It becomes associated in our minds with a nostalgia for the superior products of the past —"real" bread, "real" ice cream, "real" cars, "real" wood, etc. And, of course, people who are living imitation lives will be doubly attracted by the idea of "authentic" products.

The other meaning of "the real thing" is *love*, and this association is conveyed partly through the pleasant, soft-rock style of the song in the commercials. In the back of our minds we are all looking for the real thing—genuine affection—and would be ready and willing to buy any products that might help us find it.

A more complex and subtle use of the concept of love lies behind the familiar Coca-Cola commercial in which young people from all over the world are brought together on a hilltop in Italy, where they sing (in perfect harmony):

I'd like to teach the world to sing
In perfect harmony.
I'd like to buy the world a Coke
And keep it company.

I find the appeal of this ad, the music combined with the idea of buying the world a Coke, almost irresistible, a fact that disturbs me when I consider its implications. For one thing, the ad embodies the all too American theory and practice of *buying* good will, friendship, or even love. This notion is so pervasive at every level of our society that it is pretty much taken for granted—and for some reason has always been neatly associated with Coca-Cola. I remember that when I was in junior high school, if a guy bought me a Coke it was the first sign he was "interested" in me; later, if the relationship turned out to be "the real thing," he might ask you to go steady with him. The ad illustrates perfectly, if unintentionally, how this economic aspect of courtship is projected onto the global plane in American foreign relations. We are always happy to buy the world a Coke if we believe that this will keep it in our "company" rather than the Soviet Union's or China's. (I am incidentally reminded of that outrageous scene in *Dr. Strangelove* in which Peter Sellers is begging Keenan Wynn to shoot open the coin box of a Coke machine so he can get a dime to call the President and explain why the world may be about to end. Keenan Wynn reluctantly complies with the request, saying, "Okay, but you're gonna have to answer to the Coca-Cola Company for this.")

Of course, this kind of sociological analysis is somewhat remote from the ad's ability to touch people emotionally. On a more personal level, I think it appeals to that sense of community that many of us long for but so rarely experience in contemporary urban life —in fact, may have lost the knack to experience. The irony about an idea like buying the world a Coke and keeping it company, though, is that it is so abstract it can be employed only in the mind, which means everyone has to experience it alone.

Still, the ad always puts me in a mood of buoyancy and good will, although then I don't quite know what to *do* with these feelings. The words and music inevitably make me smile and think any day now I will begin to show the world all the love I have in my heart, but, needless to say, I never do. Unfortunately, the "world" is made up of individual people, any one of whom is much more difficult to love than is mankind in general. I can sit alone and respond to that ad with a sense of joy; but later that same day, if I see an acquaintance who doesn't see me in the supermarket, I may still duck down some aisle and linger behind the shelves until he or she is out of sight. It is not that I dislike the person but that I wish to avoid the degree of involvement required for even the most casual conversation. What makes the jingle in the Coke ad so appealing is that it allows you to participate momentarily in a kind of love that is not dangerous or painful to you, a kind that makes no demands. Actually, loving another individual (the *real* "real thing") always involves the terrible risk of being hurt, which simply does not enter into the notion of buying the world a Coke and keeping it company.

The other day I noticed in a magazine advertisement that the Pepsi-Cola Company has come up with a new slogan: "Pepsi people—the smilin' majority." My first reaction was to connect the slogan with those signs and buttons and bumper stickers cropping up all over that remind people to smile, as if it were something to be done on cue. That in itself is a little scary. Then I remembered a couple of people I've known who smiled almost constantly, even when they didn't mean to or perhaps even when a smile was most inappropriate. The thought of them led me to recall a theory about the development of the human smile that some cultural anthropologists have expounded—that a smile actually represents a passive defense against the threat of aggression, a symbolic baring of the teeth to demonstrate that they will not be used in hostility. Like the smile, a lot more than meets the eyes lies behind those seemingly innocent soft-drink ads. □

# Sociobiology:

*Charles H. Bennett's (1903) illustration of the Aesop's fable in which the lion is elected king of the beasts.*

# 6

# The Aesop's Fables of Science

by Michael A. Simon

How relevant is biology
to understanding human behavior?

Is there such a thing as "human nature"? If biological research can help to discover what it is, biology would prove itself extremely valuable as a means to understanding how human societies work. If we could discover what is natural for the human species, what people are really like—independent of cultural influences—we would then know what is fixed by biology and what needs to be explained as a result of our environment.

If we knew what sorts of human social patterns could be expected to remain stable, regardless of major cultural changes, and if we knew what sorts might be modifiable, we would have a powerful social tool. If we knew how deeply (or shallowly) rooted human aggressive or territorial behavior is, for instance, we might have a better idea as to whether certain social institutions could maintain peace.

Given the apparent desirability of obtaining an adequate biological conception of human nature, what have the ethologists and sociobiologists achieved thus far? Their results have been extremely meager or, at best, highly controversial. Apart from those aspects of human behavior that are trivial or uninteresting from the point of view of social science, such as eating, sleeping and excreting, there seems to be no human behavior sufficiently invariable to count as instinctive or which can be established as fully heritable. The problem is not that animal behavior has not been adequately investigated but rather that what has been discovered has not shed much light on humans. Nobel laureate Konrad Lorenz' studies of geese, wolves and rats, for example, have definitely not succeeded in demonstrating the presence of an instinctive aggressive drive in humans, nor have the studies by George Schaller on gorillas and Jane Goodall on chimpanzees, indicating a lack of aggression in the higher primates, proven that humans are *not* innately aggressive. Sociobiologists have speculated that behavior such as

*Michael Simon, associate professor of philosophy at the University of Connecticut, is currently visiting associate professor at the State University of New York at Stony Brook. He is the author of* The Matter of Life: Philosophical Problems of Biology *(Yale, 1971) and is nearing completion of a book on the philosophy of the social sciences. This article is based on a chapter from that book.*

human altruism, social conformity, and even creativity and entrepreneurship is controlled by genetic factors, but there appears to be no direct scientific evidence for these claims.

What would we have to do to establish that a human behavioral trait is based on genetic inheritance? First, we would have to become convinced that the trait is universal. A way of discovering whether a trait is universal is to make cross-cultural comparisons. But would this show that the trait is genetically based, rather than a result of common environmental influences? E.O. Wilson, in his book, *Sociobiology* (Harvard, 1976), suggests we can make the assumption of universality, especially when the trait is found in all, or nearly all, other primates. Although he allows for the possibility that some traits that are present throughout the rest of the primates "might nevertheless have changed [i.e. mutated] during the origin of man," he does not seem to consider seriously the possibility that they may be environmentally induced in humans. The fact that Wilson says of qualities that are "distinctively ineluctably human," that "they can be safely classified as genetically based," indicates that he simply *assumes* that whatever is universal in humans must be fixed in their common genotype.

Another possibility—not ruled out by the evidence—is that what is most distinctive in humans, beyond their "distinctively ineluctably human" traits, is their adaptability, their capacity to learn what in other animals is already programmed into the genes. Humans have no instinct to eat only edible food or to drink only safe water, but must acquire these tendencies on an individual basis in order to survive. It is very likely true that whatever is universal in humans is biologically significant, in the sense of contributing to the perpetuation of the species, but it does not follow that any of these qualities must be determined genetically.

One of the features of social behavior in humans, and at least certain other animals, is its susceptibility to modification. Almost any kind of social behavior can be inhibited or provoked by means of sufficiently drastic manipulation of the creature's environment. Dogs can be domesticated, ordinarily peaceful monkeys can be trained in aggressiveness, and birds can be made to ignore their young.

We cannot justly characterize as instinctive or as rooted in human nature any kind of social behavior for which exceptions are known, unless we are prepared to explain away the exceptions as results of abnormal or unnatural conditions. We are able to justify calling eating instinctive, but only because we recognize as extraordinary the conditions under which a person will voluntarily starve to death. We could not, on the other hand, maintain that human aggression is innate, in the face of evidence indicating the existence of nonaggressive tribes.

## Universal Traits

A number of cross-cultural universals have been suggested by sociobiologists. Male-male competition, for example, is something that has not been specified as absent in any culture that has been studied. Another universal seems to be the avoidance of incest by taboo. Others that have been mentioned include sexual inhibition and shyness, play, male dominance, and territoriality. There is no evidence that any of these characteristics is genetically based, but neither is there any evidence that they are not.

Let us assume, nevertheless—perhaps on the grounds that no alternative assumption is any better supported—that these patterns are genetically based and reveal certain characteristics of human nature.

Consider human *territoriality*: such behavior is not simply a matter of turning away unwanted visitors by means of a pattern of signals and responses common to the whole species. Rules regarding property are culturally determined and vary widely among different societies, and it is these variations that are ordinarily of primary interest to us. If one group is blatantly territorial and has elaborate legal institutions concerning private property, and another group is nomadic, it is hardly enlightening to insist, as Wilson seems to, that even the latter group is territorial as well, but merely in a subtle and extended sense.

And what about *altruism?* When Wilson defines an act of altruism as what occurs "when a person or animal increases the fitness of another at the expense of his own fitness," he ignores the distinction between acts that are performed with the intention and for the purpose of benefiting others and acts that *turn out* to have this effect. It is this definition that allows Wilson to label as cases of altruism, not only the behavior of dolphins in cooperating to rescue their wounded, but also the labors of sexually neuter workers among the social insects, the warning calls of small birds, the defense of a colony by the soldier caste of termites, and even the case of bees that lose both their stings and their lives when attacking a predator, thereby leaving a chemical deposit to summon additional defenders.

Wilson, in a popular presentation of this example, refers to these as "Kamikaze attacks." One would, I think, be unlikely to call an *actual* Kamikaze attack a case of altruism unless the mission were a *voluntary* one. By disregarding what makes the creature do the beneficial acts it performs—its reasons, if you will—the biologist is likely to miss the entire point of designating a piece of behavior as altruistic. We would hardly be willing to accredit a putative study of suicide that failed to distinguish it from accidental death.

One way—perhaps the only way—that human biology could influence voluntary behavior, other than by setting the limits that fix capacities, would be through the determination of certain feelings and inclinations. The idea is that what people do in any given situation depends on their natural urges, their inborn desires, and the tastes and preferences that are part of their biological makeup. All of these features are supposed to be fixed by the genotypes; the genotypes are the result of natural selection; and natural selection is based on the adaptive advantages that the genotypes confer, or did confer at an earlier time, either on the individuals who perform the actions to which these genotypes lead or on populations in which these actions occur.

What the theory—if that is what it may be called—implies is that social practices that persist do so not because they are adaptive or because of the weight of cultural tradition but because of propensities that reside in the genes. The theory also seems to require that when people opt for what their tradition and their cultural inputs encourage them to do, it is because of their innate tendencies. Not only is such a proposition unsupported by evidence, but it is entirely gratuitious, especially when other explanations, notably cultural ones, are readily available.

We do not need to invoke innate tendencies to account for racism, for example, especially when we already have available to us equally well-supported explanations in terms of social and economic factors. The problem with explanations of social practices in terms of innate preferences and propensities is that, whenever one is confronted with a counterinstance, either one must suppose that the tendency can be overridden, in which case the factor in question is too weak to have explanatory force, or else one must make an *ad hoc* postulation of a genetic difference in order to account for the exception.

## Incest Taboo

These considerations apply to the attempt to provide a biological explanation of the apparently ubiquitous *incest* taboo. There is evidence, albeit indirect, that the avoidance of the dangers of excess homozygosity—physical and mental defects—might very well be the basis of the taboo, but this, the giving of a biological reason, would not show that incest avoidance has a genetic basis. At the very least, what would be needed is knowledge of a biological mechanism, one that works through natural preferences, to make individuals not *want* to mate with kin. As the wags have pointed out, if incest avoidance were instinctive, incest would not have to be illegal.

Wilson has suggested that the way a cultural tradition may become established is by means of social reinforcement of natural tendencies that have been selected for the adaptive advantages they confer. With regard to the incest taboo, a mechanism that has been supposed to operate involves what has been called "the precluding of bonds": kinship relationships such as between fathers and daughters, mothers and son, and brothers and sisters seem to exclude the possible formation of other types of bonds.

Evidence cited for this hypothesis include studies in Israeli kibbutzim, where it was found that, among unrelated members of the same kibbutz peer group who had been together since birth, there were no recorded instances of heterosexual activity, despite the absence of formal or informal pressure, and that all of the marriages that occurred were with persons outside the kibbutz. The inference drawn is that social prohibitions on incest may have arisen as a result of evolved natural inhibitions, inhibitions that have persisted because those who have them tend to leave a larger number of fertile offspring than do those who lack them.

The problem with this model—apart from the fact that it lacks direct empirical support—is that these preferences, since they are known to be overridable, are too weak to provide any significant explanatory power. As many anthropological studies have shown, human beings are capable of internalizing a number of quite different norms. Innate preferences of the sort invoked are clearly not strong enough to prevent some tribes from drawing the incest line between cross-cousin and parallel-cousin marriages, for example. It is very tempting to try to derive norms from natural tendencies; but it is impossible to say which norms *must* be so derived. A norm is something that governs *voluntary* behavior, and there is no norm that is not capable of being replaced by a substitute.

Or consider the matter of the *sexual division of labor*. As Wilson puts it, "women and children remain in the residential area while the men forage for game or its symbolic equivalent in the form of barter of money." Wilson has suggested that the basis for this division of labor, which he takes as revealing a genetic bias, may lie in the fact that males are, on the average, demonstrably more aggressive than females from the beginnings of social play in infancy, and that they tend to show less verbal and great-

er mathematical ability.

These facts, if true, may help to explain why some people dominate others, and also why certain professions have a disproportionate number of men in them. They do not explain the extent to which the social patterns that are actually observed reveal polarizations that are much more pronounced than the essentially statistical findings would dictate. A basketball team may dominate another team whose members are on the average shorter than those of the first team, but only because each team is organized as a unity for the sake of demonstrating its collective dominance. You cannot derive a culture of male/female dominance, or deduce a strict or nearly strict sexual division of labor, from a set of statistical differences between classes of males and females.

*Reliance on Analogy*
What the biologist who seeks a basis for understanding human social behavior in the study of nonhuman animals is trying to show is that some of what we know about animals is also true of human beings. Since human behavioral traits, unlike anatomical features, cannot, for the most part, be established as homologous—based on common phylogenetic descent—the ethologist is forced to rely on analogy. But analogies which concern patterns of human social behavior and similar displays among animals are unconvincing. The behavior typically is either disanalogous or not known to be analogous just at the point where analogy is the most crucial: the way the behavior is mediated. If behavior that is rigidly determined by a specific releaser that triggers off an internal mechanism has, as its counterpart in human beings, behavior that is subject to nothing like such rigid causal determination, we are not licensed to infer anything whatever concerning the biological basis of the behavior in question.

If what is true of animal societies is also true of human societies, this can be established only by studying human beings on their own. We cannot *assume* that animals in different species will behave in similar ways under similar circumstances, nor can we assume that behavior that is common to two or more species and has a genetic basis in one is equally heritable in the others. We simply do not know what to make of our observations of animals, nor are we able to show these data to be relevant to a scientific understanding of the human species. There is not enough force in any conclusion that could be reached regarding nonhuman animals to give its extension to human beings a significantly higher likelihood of being true than could be given to the proposition that people are exceptions.

Because discoveries about the way animals behave are often so *interesting*, it is tempting to believe that there must be something that we can learn about humans as a result of these studies. One can readily be impressed by seeing the way monkeys or wolves avoid destructive intraspecies fighting by means of dominance hierarchies, or by observing the effects of crowding on social harmony among rats and hippopotamuses. By telling us a lot about animals that we did not know, it seems that animal behaviorists can help us to discover that we are more like animals than we thought we were.

## Aesop's Fables

Nothing that is a possible source of ideas deserves to be summarily dismissed, of course, and animal behavior studies may be a particularly rich source. They may be a no better source of ideas about human behavior than might be afforded by travel to foreign lands or by reading imaginative fiction. I suspect that what makes animal societies a particularly attractive source is not so much the wealth of illustrations they afford as is the unsupported notion that what is true of animals and can be applied to humans is likely to be true of them.

Citing ethological discoveries in the context of considering human social behavior has an effect that is largely rhetorical. Like Aesop's fables, facts about the ways animals behave are often thought to provide us with "lessons" as to how we ourselves might behave, quite apart from whether or not they reveal the way we actually do behave. Specific findings with regard to animals, like stories or myths, neither establish nor refute assertions concerning what human behavior is or ought to be; the most they can do is serve to counter other claims that have been made based on other examples. Finding that higher primates seem to lack intraspecies aggression does not lead to any reliable conclusion concerning humans, but it may serve as an antidote to the claim, based on analogies between humans and certain animals that do fight, that human beings are innately given to fighting. The popularity of books by Konrad Lorenz, Desmond Morris, and Robert Ardrey is mainly due to these rhetorical effects.

There is in these accounts a definite undercurrent that suggests that people do what they do, not for reasons or as a result of conditions that are brought about by other people or by cultural influences, but because of internal forces that we have all inherited from our remote animal ancestors and which cannot easily be resisted. Thus Lorenz suggests that the reason "why reasonable beings . . . . behave so unreasonably," is that human social behavior "is still subject to all the laws prevailing in all phylogenetically adapted instinctive behavior." The lesson being taught is that we ought to resign ourselves to accepting a non-rational basis to our social behavior.

Scientific inference need not be regarded as the sole vehicle of truth. Myths and fables, as well as true stories about other people and other animals, often are repositories of truths of a very important sort. What I deny is that what can be learned about people from observing animals has any more credibility, is any more proven by evidence, than are the insights of Aesop's fables.

Consider an example from the work of Lorenz. One of the things that he found in studying pair-formation in ravens is that it is the sex of a newly introduced prospective sexual partner that determines whether an individual that has been raised in isolation will act like a male or a female: regardless of its own biological sex, the isolated bird will adopt the courting behavior appropriate to the sex opposite to that of the introduced bird. Lorenz' finding offers no basis for inference concerning a potentially analogous human situation—any suggestiveness is merely implicit, that being part of the rhetorical effect of the example—though it could very well express something that is true of human beings. The suggestion is not altogether dissimilar to one that is found in D. H. Lawrence's story, "The Fox," in which the role that a young woman has assumed in a homosexual relationship is seen abruptly to change from that of a male to that of a female when a young man enters the scene. The writer and the ethologist are both in the position of being able to point out, but not to prove, something significant about the way the human creature behaves.    □

# SEXUAL ADEQUACY IN AMERICA

7

*Our obsession with achievement pervades our sexual lives. We strive to perfect the "product," orgasm, and ignore the pleasures of leisurely love.*

## By Philip E. Slater

The use of an engineering term like "adequacy" in relation to an act of pleasure exemplifies the American gift for turning everything into a task. Even more curious is that the criteria of adequacy are not the same for men and women. For men, adequacy is usually focused on erection; for women, on orgasm. A man tends to be defined as "adequate" to the degree that he is able to bring a women to orgasm, preferably through the use of his penis ("Look, Ma, no hands!"). A woman, however, tends to be defined as adequate to the degree to which she is able to "achieve" orgasm rapidly through the same method. A woman gets defined as sexually adequate only insofar as she can make the man feel that *he* is sexually adequate. Note that by these definitions a man is considered adequate when he can delay climax, while a woman is considered adequate when she can accelerate it. Why isn't the same standard of adequacy applied to both sexes?

Some might argue that women have a different timing pattern than men and that the goal of these definitions is to bring men and women into synchrony. We live, after all, in a highly scheduled, clock-oriented society, and it is important that people arrive at the same place at the same time. But who can say whether these much-discussed timing differences are biological or cultural. The implicit attitude behind most discussions of female orgasm is that the longer time period preceding it is an unfortunate defect of feminine physiology. But why wouldn't it be just as appropriate to say that the shorter time period before the typical male orgasm is due to a defect in men? Don't men say that brevity equals "inadequacy" among men? Then why not say that brevity equals inadequacy for men *in relation to women*? That, in other words, men as a sex are less adequate than women.

Suppose we were to say not that "it takes a woman longer to reach orgasm than a man" but rather that a woman can delay orgasm longer than a man. If we are going to use terms as absurd as "adequacy" in relation to pleasure at all, this seems to me the more reasonable statement. We are talking about the "ability" to tolerate and sustain pleasurable stimulation without release: the simple fact is that women can absorb and tolerate more pleasure than men can and hence are more adequate to the "business" of enjoyment.

I have always been fascinated that women seem to be far more capable of being attracted to a homely male than vice versa. Why is it that a homely woman, or an older one, is so much more likely to be disqualified as a sexual partner? Many men in our society are attracted only to women who are young, thin, long legged, large breasted, madeup, depilated and deodorized. Does the fact that men are so easily turned off — by age, weight and sundry other departures from some narrow *Playboy* ideal — mean that they really don't like women much? Is their heterosexual desire so weak that only some weirdly specialized feminine image can flog it into being? Why is it that women can be turned on by men who are old or ugly? Are they sexier than men? Less squeamish and fastidious? Or do they really like men more than men like women?

Psychiatrists tend to respond to such observations by talking vaguely about latent homosexuality. Yet a large proportion of male homosexuals can be aroused only by *men* who are young or exceptionally good-looking. Reaching the age of 40 can be as great a disaster for a gay male as for a heterosexual woman. In fact, men, whether homosexual or heterosexual, seem far more exacting in their standards of attractiveness than are females of either persuasion. This is another way of saying that women are more easily turned on than men — that they can take their sex with fewer condiments.

This statement flies in the face of the old-fashioned idea that men were "more sexual" than women, but this idea has had a relatively brief history and has been largely limited to the Western world. Historically and cross-culturally it has more often been women who are portrayed as the sexual, earthy beings, with men viewed as more restrained, controlled, spiritual and less susceptible to demands of the flesh. Women, usually seen as the source of evil, have appeared frequently in folklore and literature as sexually insatiable creatures, undermining the efforts of men to pursue chaste and lofty enterprises.

> The longer time period preceding female orgasm is considered a defect of feminine physiology. Why not say that the shorter time period before the typical male orgasm is due to a defect in men?

Men throughout history have devoted a surprising amount of energy to the construction of a Feminine Ideal. These ideals have varied from culture to culture, but they share a large area of agreement. Women should be sexually accessible but not sexually demanding, docile and servile but yet not totally uninteresting. The contradictions are worked out in different ways, usually by emphasizing the passivity of the feminine role (always willing but never asking). The Ideal Woman is sometimes encouraged to develop pleasing little skills that will make her interesting to the male without threatening his vanity. In other instances, it is stated flatly that the Ideal Woman should be an ignorant booby. On one point all writers are in complete agreement: the Ideal Woman exists only for men.

It is difficult to read this literature — whether English, Greek, Chinese, Moslem or American — without sensing the profound pathology that lies beneath them: the obsessional detail, the writer's exhausting struggle to resolve his ambivalence by controlling and constricting another person's behavior; the zealous effort to pretend that the problem lies outside the author's perverse brain; the inability to recognize that a completely accommodating individual can be only a nonperson, a robot. One suspects that these lectures are really misdirected. Intended perhaps for the frantic, seductive, demanding and overpowering mothers of their authors, they are delivered instead to their wives, who, thereby constricted and constrained, transfer all their frantic, seductive and overpowering needs onto their sons, thus continuing the cycle.

Women rarely write such documents, perhaps because fathers, as a rule, are less omnipresent in the life of a small child than are mothers. In any case, women seem to have been able to take men pretty much as they found them.

They may have tried to make improvements on a given man, and they may have longed for some perfect Prince Charming, but by and large they have not wasted paper writing treatises on how the Ideal Male should behave in the daily fulfillment of his role.

All this suggests that men feel at a severe sexual disadvantage with women. They want them passive, docile, exciting yet undemanding. They continually argue that if only women could walk this or that psychological tightrope, *then* men would feel safe and be attracted to them. A man, it seems, has difficulty feeling like a man if a woman approaches him as a free, independent, fully sexual being. It is as if he feels handicapped in sexual encounters and needs to create a comparable handicap for the woman.

Perhaps men *have* become sexually handicapped relative to women — not just in the physiological sense of having a more finite capacity for repetition, but culturally, in the sense of having evolved a social role that limits their capacity for physical pleasure. In all civilized societies men have sacrificed a part of their eroticism to the pursuit of wealth, status, power and political dominance over women. They have then harassed their womenfolk in a variety of ways to compensate for the feelings of sexual inferiority that this sacrifice engendered.

Work and sex are natural enemies, and the more personal commitment the work generates, the more inroads it makes into erotic life. For the ambitious careerist, as John Cuber and Peggy Harroff found in their study of successful executives, government officials and professionals (*Sex and the Significant Americans*), eroticism tends to become perfunctory — a release rather than a pastime. Clearly if pleasure is something to be caught on the fly in the interstices of effortful striving, then the quicker it is done with, the better. Men tend to define themselves by their professions — a man is a banker or a lawyer first, a person second, and it is difficult for one who thinks this way to invest himself totally in a love relationship or spend days in leisurely lovemaking.

It is often said that love is only a part of a man's life, the whole of a woman's. Although the intent of this sentiment is to keep women in their place, it expresses a historical reality. Men have invested in professions a part of the energy and interest that women devote to relationships. Eroticism thereby became women's domain, into which men enter as dilettantes in some sense.

The history of sexual mores in civilized societies is a chronicle of the efforts of men to use their political advantage to rectify this sexual disadvantage. The most common form of harassment has been through sexual restrictions, such as premarital virginity and marital fidelity. These restrictions have usually been applied exclusively to women and have succeeded to some extent in warping, crippling and blocking their sexual spontaneity. Nineteenth-century Europe produced a more subtle and insidious form of sexual control. Men began to impose upon women a feminine ideal stripped of sexual impulse. Reversing the usual idea of the spiritual male opposed to the carnal female, they made allowances for the "animal nature" of men and denied that any respectable woman had such a thing. This was a more powerful device since it crippled feminine sexuality at the core. Its transparent absurdity, however, made it vulnerable to social reform.

Ironically, the efforts of psychoanalysts to achieve such reform produced what was by far the most powerful technique yet devised for giving women a sexual handicap comparable to that borne by men. This was the dictum that mature female sexuality should center in the vagina and should de-emphasize the clitoris — a brilliant gambit inasmuch as the clitoris is the center of erotic sensation. Before the researches of Masters and Johnson undermined this dogma, two generations of women had felt guilty and inadequate because of a man's fantasy about how their bodies should function. Thus the psychiatric profession was for some years able to achieve psychically the same goal sought by certain primitive tribes, who limit the sexuality of their women by cutting away the clitoris at puberty.

> Before Masters and Johnson undermined the dogma of vaginal orgasm "two generations of women had felt guilty and inadequate because of a man's fantasy about how their bodies should function."

Whoever makes the labels holds the power, and all these devices have been invented by men. Each has served in one way or another to cause women to doubt their natural sexual impulses, and this limitation on feminine sexuality has in turn served to make men feel more competent in the sexual sphere.

Discussions of sexuality in America have always centered on the orgasm rather than on pleasure in general. This seems to be another example of our tendency to focus on the *product* of any activity at the expense of the *process*. It may seem odd to refer to an orgasm as a product, but this is the tone taken in such discussions. Most sex manuals give the impression that the partners in love-making are performing some sort of task; by dint of a great cooperative effort and technical skill (primarily the man's), an orgasm (primarily the woman's, which masculine mystification has made problematic) is ultimately produced. The bigger the orgasm, the more "successful" the task performance.

This thought pattern owes much to the masculine preoccupation with technical mastery. Women in popular sexual literature become manipulable mechanical objects — like pianos ("It's amazing what sounds he can get out of that instrument"). Even more pronounced is the competitive note in writers such as D. H. Lawrence and Norman Mailer, who often make it seem as if lovemaking were a game in which the first person to reach a climax loses.

The emphasis on orgasm also reveals, paradoxically, a vestigial puritanism. The term "climax" expresses not only the idea of a peak or zenith but also the idea of termination or completion. Discussions of the sexual act in our society are thus primarily concerned with how it *ends*. Leisurely pleasure-seeking is brushed aside, as all acts and all thoughts are directed toward the creation of a successful finale. The better the orgasm, the more enjoyable the whole encounter is retrospectively defined as having been. This insures against too much pleasure obtained in the here and now, since one is always concentrating on the future goal. In such a system you can find out how much you're enjoying yourself only after it's all over, just as many Americans traveling abroad don't know what they've experienced until they've had their films developed.

Eastern love manuals, although rather mechanical and obsessional in their own ways, direct far more attention to the sensations of the moment. The preoccupation in Western sexual literature with orgasm seems to be a natural extension of the Protestant work ethic in which nothing is to be enjoyed for its own sake except striving.

The antithetical attitude would be to view orgasm as a delightful interruption in an otherwise continuous process of generating pleasurable sensations. This would transform our ways of thinking about sex — we would no longer use the orgasm as a kind of unit of lovemaking, as in "we made love three times that day" (. . . "I have two cars," "I played nine holes of golf," "he's worth five million dollars"). The impulse to quantify sex would be sharply diminished, and along with it the tendency to infuse pleasure-seeking with ideas of achievement and competition. Affectionate caresses exchanged in passing would not be so rigidly differentiated from those interludes culminating in orgasm.

Women already espouse this view to a greater degree than men; witness the complaint of many women that their husbands never caress them except in bed. The reason they assign to this behavior, however — "he's only interested in sex, in my body, not in me" — misses the point. A man who behaves this way is not interested in sex, either — he is interested only in releasing tension. Far from enjoying pleasurable stimulation, he cannot tolerate it beyond a minimum level and wants it to end as rapidly as possible within the limits of sexual etiquette and competent "performance."

This desire for release from tension, for escape from stimulation, lies at the root of our cultural preoccupation with orgasm. In a society like ours, which perpetually bombards its participants with bizarre and dissonant stimuli — both sexual and nonsexual — tension release is a a premium. It is this confused and jangling stimulation, together with the absence of simple and meaningful rhythms in our daily lives, that makes Americans long for orgasmic release and shun any casual pleasure-seeking that does not culminate in rapid tension discharge.

It is men who suffer most from this need for tension release, since it is men who have specialized most acutely in sacrificing feelings in the service of ambition — in postponing gratification, in maintaining a stiff upper lip, in avoiding body contact, in emotional coldness. Women often express the feeling in the midst of intense lovemaking that they want it never to end. I wonder how many men are capable of sustaining such a sentiment — are able to imagine themselves enjoying endless inputs of acute pleasurable stimulation?

The emphasis in popular sexual literature on the ecstatic agony thus caters primarily to men. A favorite theme, for example, is that of the inhibited or resistant woman forced by overwhelming sexual arousal into unexpected and explosive orgasm. This sadomasochistic fantasy has two roots. First, it expresses the common masculine wish for some kind of superpotency — one glance and she falls writhing to the ground; one stroke and she explodes in ecstacy. Second, it involves an identification with the woman herself. For it is *men* who have bottled up feelings and long to burst their controls. But since this yearning endangers the whole edifice of our culture, it cannot be allowed direct expression and is projected onto women. Women are the emotional specialists in our society — they are supposed to do the crying, screaming, clinging and so on, not only for themselves, but for the men as well ("It would break your mother's heart if you went away").

The fantasy of the woman propelled into orgasm against her will is just another expression of the general tendency of men to give women the job of releasing masculine tensions vicariously. Indeed, part of the sexual hang-ups suffered by women spring from having to play out this fantasy for men. Many women feel inadequate when they are not consumed with passion at the first approach of their lover and guilty that they have thereby injured his vanity.

It seems to me that when sexual gratification is plentiful, orgasm is not the goal of every erotic encounter from the start but is a possible outcome arising naturally as the lovemaking proceeds. In a comfortable sexual setting, in other words, some lovemaking is nonorgasmic.

This observation should not be considered some sort of ideal. The last thing I want to do is to add another "should" to our already overburdened sexual mores. The notion of sexual "adequacy" seems to have had as poisonous an effect on the American psyche as did simple Puritan prohibitions or Victorian restraints, and the contributions of psychiatry, however well intended and often insightful, have merely added to the confusion. Psychoanalysts have demanded "vaginal" orgasms, have ranked orgasms by degree of total bodily involvement, have demanded fantasy-free sex (which has the amusing effect of consigning all sexual intercourse performed with procreation in mind to the realm of perversion). All these efforts to establish medical grading systems for sexual behavior seem to have had the unfortunate effect of increasing the sexual pathology against which they were directed.

From a cold, detached physiological viewpoint, the "goal" of the human orgasm is to maintain some kind of balance in the sphere of pleasurable stimulation. A degree of tension and excitement is prerequisite to life, and a degree of release is necessary for internal order and serenity. The fantasy of complete discharge — of the perfect, ultimate orgasm — is fundamentally a death fantasy. People we view as particularly alive are those capable of sustaining a lot of pleasurable stimulation without discharging it or blunting their senses; but a person *unable* to discharge often seems nervous and jumpy. These styles are sometimes difficult to distinguish in practice, and, by the same token, a person with a low level of tolerance for stimulation may appear either serene or dead. It is most important to recognize that this balance differs for each person, and no one else can decide for that person the appropriate balance to be maintained or the best way of obtaining it.

But this is, as I said, a cold physiological view of the matter. From a merely human viewpoint an orgasm is simply something that happens involuntarily when pleasure peaks, and probably the less cognitive messing about with it we do, the better.

# 8     Territories of the Lobstermen

by James M. Acheson

According to the law of the State of Maine, anyone with the proper license can fish for lobsters in any waters of the state. Yet every year, fledging lobster fishermen set out strings of traps or summer residents put out a few traps "for fun" only to find their traps opened, damaged, or gone when they return. They soon realize that the local lobstermen consider them interlopers in private fishing territories.

The local legal system, which rules lobstering off the rocky coast, sometimes runs counter to the laws of the state and nation. It may be enforced with surreptitious vio-

lence, which can escalate into "lobster wars" and even homicide.

But the lobstermen are not outlaws, obeying their own code and ignoring state laws. For example, they almost universally obey the conservation laws concerning licensing and the taking of either undersized "short lobsters" or breeding females. But these formal laws are relatively few in comparison with the numerous traditional norms by which lobstermen govern themselves.

The rules for lobster fishing territories are especially critical because they control access to the

lobsters and because they have important ecological implications at a time when some parts of the marine resource are being overexploited.

Growing up in an inland area of Maine, I was for a long time vaguely aware that territoriality existed among lobstermen. Only recently, however, did I find evidence of these territorial rules and investigate them systematically.

About five years ago, I helped a friend, a recently retired New Yorker, who was attempting "to break into the lobster game," as he phrased it. This was going to be a part-time activity for him, a way of supplementing his Navy pension. He only laughed at warnings about any problems, stubbornly insisting that the Atlantic Ocean was part of the public domain and that all one needed was a state license to go lobster fishing.

Accordingly, he bought an old boat and 190 new traps and proceeded to go lobstering. I was with him the first day he pulled his traps. In the first row of traps we pulled, one was missing, possibly destroyed by accident, we decided. But at the second string, the trend became clear: ten traps out of seventeen—at least $150 worth of gear—were missing. The destruction was deliberate, as we found the cut-off buoys floating over a two-mile area. For the rest of the morning it took little to goad my friend to the heights of eloquence concerning the ancestry of lobstermen, their inborn criminal tendencies, and their sneaky and arrogant ways. He was incredulous that lobstermen would "survey off the Atlantic Ocean," as he put it, and have the gall to enforce those boundaries.

Maine lobstering takes place in a spectacular natural setting. Eons ago, the coast of Maine sank. What were once valleys and river basins are now long, indented bays that create a highly irregular coastline. It is only 250 air miles from Eastport, Maine, on the Canadian border to Kittery, across from Portsmouth, New Hampshire, but stretched out, the coastline is some 2,500 miles long. There are a great number of deep, well-protected harbors. The rocky headlands—covered with dark, stunted spruce—are continually pounded and showered with foam by long, rolling waves coming in off the open ocean. Up the bays and rivers are mile after mile of small islands and coves.

The little coastal communities nestle in small, sheltered harbors filled with boats. The shores are covered with a jumble of weatherbeaten docks piled with fishing and lobstering equipment. Clustered behind the waterfront, the people live in plain clapboard or shingled houses from which they can easily watch boats, equipment, and the weather. Behind the houses are evergreen forests.

The cold water off Maine's coast provides an ideal habitat for halibut, shrimp, cod, haddock, sardine, and lobster, but a poor place for swimming. The statement that "only tourists go in the water" is more than a joke. Many lobstermen cannot swim, feeling with some justification that swimming offers them little insurance in such waters. The thick fog, present as much as 180 days a year, adds to the danger. Even with modern safety devices, lobstering is not a safe occupation. Every coastal community has its list of men lost at sea.

At any time of year, lobstering is difficult work. In the summer, men usually haul pots, or traps, every day, starting before daybreak so that they can complete as much of the task as possible in the calm morning hours. In winter, bad weather makes it impossible to go out more than one or two days a week. On a sunny, calm day, winter lobstering can be almost pleasant. But when the temperature hovers around zero and one is wet with spray, eight or ten hours on a bouncing lobster boat can be miserable. At this time of year, one does not have even the compensation of a large catch. Many men prefer to pull all their traps onshore in midwinter and to spend their time working on equipment.

Lobsters are caught in wooden traps about three feet long, made of spruce slats, or lars, over oak frames. The style of trap has remained essentially the same for at least 100 years. The lars are spaced about an inch and a half apart, allowing the undersized lobsters to escape while trapping the legal-sized ones. One end of the trap is left open and rigged with a funnel-shaped nylon net, or head, so that a lobster can easily climb in, but not out of, the narrow opening. Traps are baited with fish remnants, obtained now from fish-processing plants in nearby cities. A "warp" line attaches each trap to a floating buoy, made either of wood or, more commonly, of styrofoam. Buoys are painted a distinctive combination of colors to allow each man to identify his traps at a distance, and the individual designs are registered with the state.

In shallow water, normally one trap is attached to a buoy, while in deep water it is common to attach two to one warp line; this is called "fishing doubles." In the Casco Bay region, the standard procedure, known as "trawl fishing," is to attach several traps to a single line. In all cases, traps are set in rows, or strings, 100 to 300 feet from each other, close enough so that a lobsterman can see from one buoy to the next, even on a foggy day.

The amount of equipment used by individual lobstermen varies greatly. A high school boy, just starting out, might have as few as 20 traps, which he tends with an outboard-powered skiff. An experienced lobsterman, especially in the area where trawl fishing is common, might have more than 1,000 traps, a 40-foot boat costing more than $20,000, and a two-man crew. The average lobster fisherman tends 400 to 600 traps by himself, using a 30-foot boat costing about $15,000.

Lobsters are marketed in the lobsterman's home harbor through a dealer with whom he has close economic ties. The lobsterman will sell his entire catch to his dealer, and purchase gas and supplies from him. In return, the dealer will allow the lobsterman to use his dock, provide him with bait at close to cost, and extend credit for rope and other gear.

To go lobstering, one must be accepted by the men already fishing out of a harbor. These groups of men have no special name, but are referred to by the name of their harbor: the "Friendship gang" or the "Monhegan boys" or the "men from Boothbay." Once a man gains admission to one of these harbor gangs, he usually can fish only in its traditional area.

In cases where townships have two or sometimes three harbors within their boundaries, each harbor has its own gang with its own traditional territory. The men from the village of New Harbor, for example, go lobstering out of Pemaquid Harbor and New Harbor. While they live side by side in one community, they fish in separate traditional areas.

Anyone just starting out as a lobsterman will experience some hostility. Many resign themselves to a long period of harassment before they are accepted; many never make it. However, a man will have the best chance of establishing himself if his family are long-time residents of the town, if his father's family are lobstermen, and if he is well liked in the community. Such a man almost inherits a place in his father's harbor gang. It also helps if he enters lobstering gradually, putting out a few traps while still a teen-ager, then expanding after high school to become a full-time fisherman. Such a boy learns the culture of the community and the norms of the lobster industry as a part of growing up.

A man will have most difficulty entering lobstering if he is an adult, if he comes from a distant area, and if his family has no connection with fishing. However, the most important single factor in gaining admission to a harbor gang is willingness to abide by local traditions. Any man who acquires a reputation for molesting others' gear, a prime taboo, will not last long regardless of local genealogy or ties.

A number of "outsiders" are presently lobstering in Maine waters. For example, mainlanders and even out-of-staters have been allowed to fish in Monhegan Island territory—ostensibly one of the most difficult places to gain entry into—as long as they presently live on Monhegan, prove willing to abide by the local "closed season," and do not go fishing before "trap day," the day when the islanders begin fishing each year. In fact, in every harbor, a surprisingly high proportion of the lobstermen were not born in the community where they are now lobster fishing.

A part-time lobsterman receives a good deal more hostility than a new, full-time fisherman, even though full-time fishermen catch more lobsters. In part this prejudice stems from a strong feeling that part-time men are taking unfair advantage by having two jobs. As one man complained, "They have one job, then after they have collected one pay check, they come on out here and take the food out of our mouths." Another common complaint is that part-time fishermen are not familiar with the norms of the industry.

Lobsters are caught in different places at different seasons. In the winter, when the water near shore is very cold, they are best trapped in water over 30 fathoms deep, which is warmed by an inversion effect from the Gulf Stream. As the water becomes warmer with the approach of summer, they can be caught closer and closer to shore so that by mid-June the buoys are often placed within feet of the surf. During late June and July, when lobsters go among the rocks to molt, or shed, lobstering is so bad that some men pull up all their traps; many others leave only a few in the water. As the water cools off, traps are again moved farther offshore.

Traditional lobstering territories are usually no more than 100 square miles, which means that a lobsterman spends most of his life in one small, intimately known area. Even in winter, most men rarely go more than ten miles from their home harbor.

Close to shore, traditional territorial boundaries are clearly demarcated and defended. Farther out, the boundaries become vaguer, so that six or eight miles offshore there are no effective boundaries to speak of. A man from the southern part of the state put it well when he said, "The whole ocean is free if you go out far enough."

While lobstermen will discuss boundaries in terms of major geographical features, such as the Damariscotta River or Pemaquid Point, actual boundaries are usually drawn with reference to minor features—a reef, a small cove, a sand bar, sea buoys—features that have significance only for men intimately acquainted with the area.

Violation of a territorial boundary meets with no set response. An older man, well known in the area, might get away with a territorial intrusion for a long period of time; a younger man, a new fisherman, or an unpopular man might quickly be sanctioned for the violation.

Ordinarily, repeated violation of territorial boundaries will lead to destruction of the offender's gear. It is usual for one man operating completely on his own to first warn an interloper. In some places this is done by tying two half hitches around the spindle of the offending buoys; in other places by damaging the traps slightly. At this point, most intruders will move their traps. If they are not moved, they will be "cut off." This means cutting off the buoy and warp line from the trap, which then sinks to the bottom where the owner has no chance of finding it.

A man who violates a boundary is ordinarily never verbally confronted with the fact of his intrusion, and the man who destroys his gear will traditionally never admit to it. Admitting the destruction of a man's gear could bring retaliation not only from the lobsterman but from the Sea and Shore Fisheries warden as well. Moreover, destroying another man's gear—even the traps of a known interloper—is considered shameful.

In rare instances, boundaries are defended by group action. It is well known that anyone invading the traditional territories of islands such as Monhegan, Matinicus, and Green Island will meet with coordinated resistance from men fishing in those territories.

Men touch each other's lobster gear only with great reluctance. A would-be aggressor knows that he can easily precipitate an incident in which he would be the ultimate victim. As one man said, "The trick to driving a man [driving him out of the area] is to just cut off one or two traps at a time." This makes it unprofitable for him to continue operating in the area, but does not challenge him to open warfare, especially since, in most cases, he can only guess at who cut his traps.

Periodically, a man whose traps have been cut off will retaliate against the wrong man or men, who do the same thing in return. The result is often a comic opera in which the innocent, along with the guilty, retaliate blindly against each other. Some men cut off traps knowing someone else will be blamed. The potentialities for trouble in such situations are enormous.

Small incidents occur continually, but lobster wars—in which hundreds of traps are cut off—are rare, occurring perhaps once a decade. In fact, when one considers that the entire coast of Maine is patrolled by only a handful of Sea and Shore Fisheries wardens, it is amazing that there is so little trouble. The traditional territorial concepts go a long way in maintaining relative peace.

There are times, however, when a group of men, goaded beyond endurance, will launch a large scale "cut war." These lobster wars may lead to court action, violence, and long-standing bitterness. In Maine's midcoast area such incidents are infrequent, although stories about them are repeated so widely that they give the entire coastal region an unsavory reputation. I recall listening to a group of men gleefully recount how men on one of the offshore islands cut off all of each other's gear in a series of forays; then went around burning each other's docks. Such stories have obvious entertainment value. They also remind people of what can happen when traditional norms are violated.

When trouble does occur, those who can muster the most support usually win. This is true whether the fight concerns territorial viola-

tions, attempts to break into a harbor gang, or a personal feud between two men fishing out of the same harbor. Several times I heard it said that "two men who get to fighting just put each other out of business." The older, well-established men from large families are thought to be particularly "bad to play with." This explains why men like my New York friend have less of a chance of breaking into the business. It also explains why such men must be careful about violating territorial boundaries if they are ever accepted by a harbor gang.

An individual can affect boundaries if he doesn't mind a little trouble and is willing to take the economic losses. As one man put it, "One man who doesn't give a damn can cut off more traps in a night than a dozen men can make and set out in a week." The willingness of an individual to engage in trouble is notably increased if he has some other source of income. One man

on one of the offshore islands, for example, maintains a private lobstering area. If anyone invades his area, he merely pulls his traps, cuts off all those of the invader, and works at boat building until the trouble dies down. He said, "That's my area, and if I can't fish there, no one else is going to."

The waters around many of the small, unoccupied islands are the private lobstering grounds of families who have had legal ownership of the islands themselves for generations. These territories are most vigorously defended. In some cases, lobstering is done exclusively by members of the owning family, but in cases where there are not enough family members to utilize the area, other men are allowed to rent lobstering rights. Even these rental rights are inherited, so that men who rent ocean space from a particular owning family are usually descended from previous renters.

Although people are hesitant to

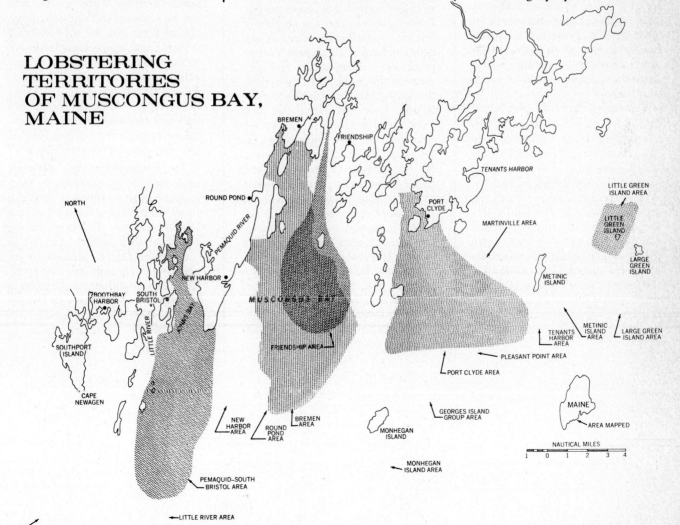

LOBSTERING TERRITORIES OF MUSCONGUS BAY, MAINE

talk about catches and incomes, especially those men fishing private island territories, there is some evidence that holding and defending a private island territory is economically rewarding. For example, early in July, 1971, when mainland fishermen were happy to average a half pound of lobster per trap, a man from one of the strongly defended island areas indicated that he was getting much more: "Some of us out here think that half a pound a trap isn't so good. If all I could get was half a pound a trap, I'd go ashore."

On a recent morning I was talking to some friends on a dock as they brought in their catches. One man—who fishes in an ordinary mainland harbor territory, along with about 40 other men—got eleven pounds of lobsters. Another—fishing five miles away in his family's private island area—caught 172 pounds the same day. The ecology of the two areas is slightly different, and both men do not pull the exact same number of traps. Although the differences in catch are not always this dramatic, men lobstering in exclusive island areas consistently obtain higher yields than men fishing out of mainland harbors.

Before the advent of sophisticated fishing equipment, lobstering territories were small compared with those of today, and boundaries were strongly defended. This pattern was connected to the fishing technology. When fishermen could only gain the intimate knowledge needed for lobstering with a lead sounding line, and could only travel by rowboat or sail, the area that could be effectively fished was limited. Thus, before 1920 the entire coastal waters of Maine were divided into a large number of small territories vigorously defended by their "owners"—often groups of kinsmen.

With the advent of gasoline motors, and more recently with the installation of electronic depth-sounding gear, traditional areas have been growing larger and larger, and the ocean area where mixed fishing is allowed has increased as well. In part, this new technology has allowed men to fish for lobster farther offshore, in areas not claimed exclusively by one harbor. In addition, the new technology also broke down many of the older boundaries. As the capacity to fish a larger area increased, men became much less defensive about maintaining their smaller territories. Moreover, many men seem happy to see some territorial boundaries disappear. As one old man put it, "You might not be too sad to see men invading your area when the fishing was good if you could do the same to him some other time. Both of you might well catch more lobsters that way."

Changes in territoriality relate in very important ways to the major problem now facing the Maine lobstering industry—that of overfishing. In the past few years the number of lobsters caught has decreased drastically, at least a 25 percent decline since 1967. Lobstermen are fully aware of the problem. In their view, the decrease in supply is due to overfishing. One lobsterman said that "the whole problem is due to too many men, fishing too many traps, for too long." This is a simplistic view, for Robert Dow of Maine Sea and Shore Fisheries has evidence that a change in water temperature is one of the factors responsible for the decrease in lobster supply. However, part of the problem is man-made. The number of traps set has increased tremendously. Fifteen years ago, only a few men had as many as 400 traps; the average was well below 200. Now, the average fisherman has perhaps 400, and men with 700 and 800 traps are not uncommon. These in-

creases were made possible by the hydraulic pot hauler.

For the last ten years, the number of lobstermen in Maine has hovered at about 6,000. However, only half of the men who had lobster licenses in 1970 had them ten years previously. This means that a large number of men do not stay in the business for long. But those who leave are immediately replaced by others. It is still difficult to break into a harbor gang and in most places a summer resident cannot go lobstering at all. Nevertheless, the industry is much easier to enter now. When the entire coast consisted of small, strongly defended territories, any stranger moving into an area could expect to be rebuffed by the traditional owners whose income he threatened.

The older territorial system effectively restricted the number of lobstermen. While the system was hard on men attempting to enter the business, it was easier on the lobster as a resource. Even now, those coastal areas that are most difficult to enter, and whose boundaries are strongly defended, continue to provide a sustained yield of lobsters. As one dealer expressed it, "Those islanders are doing all right, and they will continue to earn the highest incomes on the coast as long as the place doesn't get overcrowded."

In comparison, the relatively open areas of the coast where territorial boundaries are weak have suffered from overexploitation of the lobster resource. If lobster fishing and fishermen are to survive in these areas, Maine will have to impose more controls on lobstering. The state would do well, when it prepares new legislation on lobstering, to take into consideration the lobstermen's unwritten rules of territoriality.

# Erik Erikson's Eight Ages Of Man

## *One man in his time plays many psychosocial parts*

**DAVID ELKIND**

AT a recent faculty reception I happened to join a small group in which a young mother was talking about her "identity crisis." She and her husband, she said, had decided not to have any more children and she was depressed at the thought of being past the child-bearing stage. It was as if, she continued, she had been robbed of some part of herself and now needed to find a new function to replace the old one.

When I remarked that her story sounded like a case history from a book by Erik Erikson, she replied, "Who's Erikson?" It is a reflection on the intellectual modesty and literary decorum of Erik H. Erikson, psychoanalyst and professor of developmental psychology at Harvard, that so few of the many people who today talk about the "identity crisis" know anything of the man who pointed out its pervasiveness as a problem in contemporary society two decades ago.

Erikson has, however, contributed more to social science than his delineation of identity problems in modern man. His descriptions of the stages of the life cycle, for example, have advanced psychoanalytic theory to the point where it can now describe the development of the healthy personality on its own terms and not merely as the opposite of a sick one. Likewise, Erikson's emphasis upon the problems unique to adolescents and adults living in today's society has helped to rectify the one-sided emphasis on childhood as the beginning and end of personality development.

Finally, in his biographical studies, such as "Young Man Luther" and "Gandhi's Truth" (which has just won a National Book Award in philosophy and religion), Erikson emphasizes the inherent strengths of the human personality by showing how individuals can use their neurotic symptoms and conflicts for creative and constructive social purposes while healing themselves in the process.

It is important to emphasize that Erikson's contributions are genuine advances in psychoanalysis in the sense that Erikson accepts and builds upon many of the basic tenets of Freudian theory. In this regard, Erikson differs from Freud's early co-workers such as Jung and Adler who, when they broke with Freud, rejected his theories and substituted their own.

Likewise, Erikson also differs from the so-called neo-Freudians such as Horney, Kardiner and Sullivan who (mistakenly, as it turned out) assumed that Freudian theory had nothing to say about man's relation to reality and to his culture. While it is true that Freud emphasized, even mythologized, sexuality, he did so to counteract the rigid sexual taboos of his time, which at that point in history, were frequently the cause of neuroses. In his later writings, however, Freud began to concern himself with the executive agency of the personality, namely, the ego, which is also the repository of the individual's attitudes and concepts about himself and his world.

It is with the psychosocial development of the ego that Erikson's observations and theoretical constructions are primarily concerned. Erikson has thus been able to introduce innovations into psychoanalytic theory without either rejecting or ignoring Freud's monumental contribution.

The man who has accomplished this notable feat is a handsome Dane, whose white hair, mustache, resonant accent and gentle manner are reminiscent of actors like Jean Hersholt and Paul Muni. Although he is warm and outgoing with friends, Erikson is a rather shy man who is uncomfortable in the spotlight of public recognition. This trait, together with his ethical reservations about making public even disguised case material, may help to account for Erikson's reluctance to publish his observations and conceptions (his first book appeared in 1950, when he was 48).

In recent years this reluctance to publish has diminished and he has been appearing in print at an increasing pace. Since 1960 he has published three books, "Insight and Responsibility," "Identity: Youth and Crisis" and "Gandhi's Truth," as well as editing a fourth, "Youth: Change and Challenge." Despite the accolades and recognition these books have won for him, both in America and abroad, Erikson is still surprised at the popular interest they have generated and is a little troubled about the possibility of being misunderstood and misinterpreted. While he would prefer that his books spoke for themselves and that he was left out of the picture, he has had to accede to popular demand for more information about himself and his work.

The course of Erikson's professional career has been as diverse as it has been unconventional. He was born in Frankfurt, Germany, in 1902 of Danish parents. Not long after his birth his father died, and his mother later married the pediatrician who had cured her son of a childhood illness. Erikson's stepfather urged him to become a physician, but the boy declined and became an artist instead—an artist who did portraits of children. Erikson says of his post-adolescent years, "I was an artist then, which in Europe is a euphemism for a young man with some talent and nowhere to go." During this period he settled in Vienna and worked as a tutor in a family friendly with Freud's. He met Freud on informal occasions when the families went on outings together.

These encounters may have been the impetus to accept a teaching appointment at an American school in Vienna founded by Dorothy Burlingham and directed by Peter Blos (both now well known on the American psychiatric scene). During these years (the late nineteen-twenties) he also undertook and completed psychoanalytic training with Anna Freud and August Aichhorn. Even at the outset of his career, Erikson gave evidence of the breadth of his interests and activities by being trained and certified as a Montessori teacher. Not surprisingly, in view of that training. Eriksin's first articles dealth with psychoanalysis and education.

It was while in Vienna that Erikson met and married Joan Mowat Serson, an American artist of Canadian descent. They came to America in 1933, when Erikson was invited to practice and teach in Boston. Erikson was, in fact, one of the first if not the first child-analyst in the Boston area. During the next two decades he held clinical and academic appointments at Harvard, Yale and Berkeley. In 1951 he joined a group of psychiatrists and psychologists who moved to Stockbridge, Mass., to start a new program at the Austen Riggs Center, a private residential treatment center for disturbed young people. Erikson re-

mained at Riggs until 1961, when he was appointed professor of human development and lecturer on psychiatry at Harvard. Throughout his career he has always held two or three appointments simultaneously and has traveled extensively.

PERHAPS because he had been an artist first, Erikson has never been a conventional psychoanalyst. When he was treating children, for example, he always insisted on visiting his young patients' homes and on having dinner with the families. Likewise, in the nineteen-thirties, when anthropological investigation was described to him by his friends Scudder McKeel, Alfred Kroeber and Margaret Mead, he decided to do field work on an Indian reservation. "When I realized that Sioux is the name which we [in Europe] pronounced "See ux" and which for us was *the* American Indian, I could not resist." Erikson thus antedated the anthropologists who swept over the Indian reservations in the post-Depression years. (So numerous were the field workers at that time that the stock joke was that an Indian family could be defined as a mother, a father, children and an anthropologist.)

Erikson did field work not only with the Oglala Sioux of Pine Ridge, S. D. (the tribe that slew Custer and was in turn slaughtered at the Battle of Wounded Knee), but also with the salmon-fishing Yurok of Northern California. His reports on these experiences revealed his special gift for sensing and entering into the world views and modes of thinking of cultures other than his own.

It was while he was working with the Indians that Erikson began to note syndromes which he could not explain within the confines of traditional psychoanalytic theory. Central to many an adult Indian's emotional problems seemed to be his sense of uprootedness and lack of continuity between his present life-style and that portrayed in tribal history. Not only did the Indian sense a break with the past, but he could not identify with a future requiring assimilation of the white culture's values. The problems faced by such men, Erikson recognized, had to do with the ego and with culture and only incidentally with sexual drives.

The impressions Erikson gained on the reservations were reinforced during World War II when he worked at a veterans' rehabilitation center at Mount Zion Hospital in San Francisco. Many of the soldiers he and his colleagues saw seemed not to fit the traditional "shell shock" or "malingerer" cases of World War I. Rather, it seemed to Erikson that many of these men had lost the sense of who and what they were. They were having trouble reconciling their activities, attitudes and feelings as soldiers with the activities, attitudes and feelings they had known before the war. Accordingly, while these men may well have had difficulties with repressed or conflicted drives, their main problem seemed to be, as Erikson came to speak of it all the time, "identity confusion."

It was almost a decade before Erikson set forth the implications of his clinical observations in "Childhood and Society." In that book, the summation and integration of 15 years of research, he made three major contributions to the study of the human ego. He posited (1) that, side by side with the stages of psychosexual development described by Freud (the oral, anal, phallic, genital, Oedipal and pubertal), were psychosocial stages of ego development, in which the individual had to establish new basic orientations to himself and his social world; (2) that personality development continued throughout the whole life cycle; and (3) that each stage had a positive *as well as* a negative component.

Much about these contributions—and about Erikson's way of thinking—can be understood by looking at his scheme of life stages. Erikson identifies eight stages in the human life cycle, in each of which a new dimension of "social interaction" becomes possible—that is, a new dimension in a person's interaction with himself, and with his social environment.

## Trust vs. Mistrust

THE first stage corresponds to the oral stage in classical psychoanalytic theory and usually extends through the first year of life. In Erikson's view, the new dimension of social interaction that emerges during this period involves basic *trust* at the one extreme, and *mistrust* at the other. The degree to which the child comes to trust the world, other people and himself depends to a considerable extent upon the quality of the care that he receives. The infant whose needs are met when they arise, whose discomforts are quickly removed, who is cuddled, fondled, played with and talked to, develops a sense of the world as a safe place to be and of people as helpful and dependable. When, however, the care is inconsistent, inadequate and rejecting, it fosters a basic mistrust, an attitude of fear and suspicion on the part of the infant toward the world in general and people in particular that will carry through to later stages of development.

It should be said at this point that the problem of basic trust-versus-mistrust (as is true for all the later dimensions) is not resolved once and for all during the first year of life; it arises again at each successive stage of development. There is both hope and danger in this. The child who enters school with a sense of mistrust may come to trust a particular teacher who has taken the trouble to make herself trustworthy; with this second chance, he overcomes his early mistrust. On the other hand, the child who comes through infancy with a vital sense of trust can still have his sense of mistrust activated at a later stage if, say, his parents are divorced and separated under acrimonious circumstances.

This point was brought home to me in a very direct way by a 4-year-old patient I saw in a court clinic. He was being seen at the court clinic because his adoptive parents, who had had him for six months, now wanted to give him back to the agency. They claimed that he was cold and unloving, took things and could not be trusted. He was indeed a cold and apathetic boy, but with good reason. About a year after his illegitimate birth, he was taken away from his mother, who had a drinking problem, and was shunted back and forth among several foster homes. Initially he had tried to relate to the persons in the foster homes, but the relationships never had a chance to develop because he was moved at just the wrong times. In the end he gave up trying to reach out to others, because the inevitable separations hurt too much.

Like the burned child who dreads the flame, this emotionally burned child shunned the pain of emotional involvement. He had trusted his mother, but now he trusted no one. Only years of devoted care and patience could now undo the damage that had been done to this child's sense of trust.

## Autonomy vs. Doubt

STAGE Two spans the second and third years of life, the period which Freudian theory calls the anal stage. Erikson sees here the emergence of *autonomy*. This autonomy dimension builds upon the child's new motor and mental abilities. At this stage the child can not only walk but also climb, open and close, drop, push and pull, hold and let go. The child takes pride in these new accomplishments and wants to do everything himself, whether it be pulling the wrapper off a piece of candy, selecting the vitamin out of the bottle or flushing the toilet. If parents recognize the young child's need to do what he is capable of doing at his own pace and in his own time, then he develops a sense that he is able to control his muscles, his impulses, himself and, not insignificantly, his environment—the sense of autonomy.

When, however, his caretakers are impatient and do for him what he is capable of doing himself, they reinforce a sense of shame and doubt. To be sure, every parent has rushed a child at times and children are hardy enough to endure such lapses. It is only when caretaking is consistently overprotective and criticism of "accidents" (whether these be wetting, soiling, spilling or breaking things) is harsh and unthinking that the child develops an excessive sense of shame with respect to other people and an excessive sense of doubt about own abilities to control his world and himself.

If the child leaves this stage with less autonomy than shame or doubt, he will be handicapped in his attempts to achieve autonomy in adolescence and adulthood. Contrariwise, the child who moves through this stage with his sense of autonomy buoyantly outbalancing his feelings of shame and doubt is well prepared to be autonomous at later phases in the life cycle. Again, however, the balance of autonomy to shame and doubt set up during this period can be changed in either positive or negative directions by later events.

It might be well to note, in addition, that too much autonomy can be as harmful as too little. I have in mind a patient of 7 who had a heart condition. He had learned very quickly how terrified his parents were of any signs in him of cardiac difficulty. With the psychological acuity given to children, he soon ruled the household. The family could not go shopping, or for a drive, or on a holiday if he did not approve. On those rare occasions when the parents had had enough and defied him, he would get angry and his purple hue and gagging would frighten them into submission.

Actually, this boy was frightened of this power (as all children would be) and was really eager to give it up. When the parents and the boy came to realize this, and to recognize that a little shame and doubt were a healthy counterpoise to an inflated sense of autonomy, the three of them could once again assume their normal roles.

## Initiative vs. Guilt

IN this stage (the genital stage of classical psychoanaysis) the child, age 4 to 5, is pretty much master of his body and can ride a tricycle, run, cut and hit. He can thus initiate motor acivities of various sorts on his own and no longer merely responds to or imitates the actions of other children. The same holds true for his language and fantasy activities. Accordingly, Erikson argues that the social dimension that appears at this stage has *initiative* at one of its poles and *guilt* at the other.

Whether the child will leave this stage with his sense of initiative far outbalancing his sense of guilt depends to a considerable extent upon how parents respond to his self-initiated activities. Children who are given much freedom and opportunity to initiate motor play such as running, bike riding, sliding, skating, tussling and wrestling have their sense of initiative reinforced. Initiative is also reinforced when parents answer their children's questions (intellectual initiative) and do not deride or inhibit fantasy or play activity. On the other hand, if the child is made to feel that his motor activity is bad, that his questions are a nuisance and that his play is silly and stupid, then he may develop a sense of guilt over self-initiated activities in general that will persist through later life stages.

## Industry vs. Inferiority

STAGE Four is the age period from 6 to 11, the elementary school years (described by classical psychoanalysis as the *latency phase*). It is a time during which the child's love for the parent of the opposite sex and rivalry with the same sexed parent (elements in the so-called family romance) are quiescent. It is also a period during which the child becomes capable of deductive reasoning, and of playing and learning by rules. It is not until this period, for example, that children can really play marbles, checkers and other "take turn" games that require obedience to rules. Erikson argues that the psychosocial dimension that emerges during this period has a sense of *industry* at one extreme and a sense of *inferiority* at the other.

The term industry nicely captures a dominant theme of this period during which the concern with how things are made, how they work and what they do predominates. It is the Robinson Crusoe age in the sense that the enthusiasm and minute detail with which Crusoe describes his activities appeals to the child's own budding sense of industry. When children are encouraged in their efforts to make, do, or build practical things (whether it be to construct creepy crawlers, tree houses, or airplane models—or to cook, bake or sew), are allowed to finish their prod-

*This nine-year-old youngster is at Stage Four of Erikson's psychosocial stages, Industry vs. Inferiority. In this case, it is clear that industry predominates.*

ucts, and are praised and rewarded for the results, then the sense of industry is enhanced. But parents who see their children's efforts at making and doing as "mischief," and as simply "making a mess," help to encourage in children a sense of inferiority.

During these elementary-school years, however, the child's world includes more than the home. Now social institutions other than the family come to play a central role in the developmental crisis of the individual. (Here Erikson introduced still another advance in psychoanalytic theory, which heretofore concerned itself only with the effects of the parents' behavior upon the child's development.)

A child's school experiences affect his industry-inferiority balance. The child, for example, with an IQ of 80 to 90 has a particularly traumatic school experience, even when his sense of industry is rewarded and encouraged at home. He is "too bright" to be in special classes, but "too slow" to compete with children of average ability. Consequently he experiences constant failures in his academic efforts that reinforce a sense of inferiority.

On the other hand, the child who had his sense of industry derogated at home can have it revitalized at school through the offices of a sensitive and committed teacher. Whether the child develops a sense of industry or inferiority, therefore, no longer depends solely on the caretaking efforts of the parents but on the actions and offices of other adults as well.

## Identity vs. Role confusion

WHEN the child moves into adolescence (Stage Five—roughly the ages 12-18), he encounters, according to traditional psychoanalytic theory, a reawakening of the family-romance problem of early childhood. His means of resolving the problem is to seek and find a romantic partner of his own generation. While Erikson does not deny this aspect of adolescence, he points out that there are other problems as well. The adolescent matures mentally as well as physiologically and, in addition to the new feelings, sensations and desires he experiences as a result of changes in his body, he develops a multitude of new ways of looking at and thinking about the world. Among other things, those in adolescence can now think about other people's thinking and wonder about what other people think of them. They can also conceive of ideal families, religions and societies which they can then compare with the imperfect families, religions and societies of their own experience. Finally, adolescents become capable of constructing theories and philosophies designed to bring all the varied and conflicting aspects of society into a working, harmonious and peaceful whole. The adolescent, in a word, is an impatient idealist who believes that it is as easy to realize an ideal as it is to imagine it.

Erikson believes that the new interpersonal dimension which emerges during this period has to do with a sense of *ego identity* at the positive end and a sense of *role confusion* at the negative end. That is to say, given the adolescent's newfound integrative abilities, his task is to bring together all of the things he has learned about himself as a son, student, athlete, friend, Scout, newspaper boy, and so on, and integrate these different images of himself into a whole that makes sense and that shows continuity with the past while preparing for the future. To the extent that the young person succeeds in this endeavor, he arrives at a sense of psychological identity, a sense of who he is, where he has been and where he is going.

## Freud's "Ages of Man"

Erik Erikson's definition of the "eight ages of man" is a work of synthesis and insight by a psychoanalytically trained and worldly mind. Sigmund Freud's description of human phases stems from his epic psychological discoveries and centers almost exclusively on the early years of life. A brief summary of the phases posited by Freud:

*Oral stage*—roughly the first year of life, the period during which the mouth region provides the greatest sensual satisfaction. Some derivative behavioral traits which may be seen at this time are *incorporativeness* (first six months of life) and *aggressiveness* (second six months of life).

*Anal stage*—roughly the second and third years of life. During this period the site of greatest sensual pleasure shifts to the anal and urethral areas. Derivative behavioral traits are *retentiveness* and *expulsiveness*.

*Phallic stage*—roughly the third and fourth years of life. The site of greatest sensual pleasure during this stage is the genital region. Behavior traits derived from this period include *intrusiveness* (male) and *receptiveness* (female).

*Oedipal stage*—roughly the fourth and fifth years of life. At this stage the young person takes the parent of the opposite sex as the object or provider of sensual satisfaction and regards the same-sexed parent as a rival. (The "family romance.") Behavior traits originating in this period are *seductiveness* and *competitiveness*.

*Latency stage*—roughly the years from age 6 to 11. The child resolves the Oedipus conflict by identifying with the parent of the opposite sex and by so doing satisfies sensual needs vicariously. Behavior traits developed during this period include *conscience* (or the internalization of parental moral and ethical demands).

*Puberty stage*—roughly 11 to 14. During this period there is an integration and subordination of oral, anal and phallic sensuality to an overriding and unitary genital *sexuality*. The genital sexuality of puberty has another young person of the opposite sex as its object, and discharge (at least for boys) as its aim. Derivative behavior traits (associated with the control and regulation of genital sexuality) are *intellectualization* and *estheticism*.

—D.E.

In contrast to the earlier stages, where parents play a more or less direct role in the determination of the result of the developmental crises, the influence of parents during this stage is much more indirect. If the young person reaches adolescence with, thanks to his parents, a vital sense of trust, autonomy, initiative and industry, then his chances of arriving at a meaningful sense of ego identity are much enhanced. The reverse, of course, holds true for the young person who enters adolescence with considerable mistrust, shame, doubt, guilt and inferiority. Preparation for a successful adolescence, and the attainment of an integrated psychosocial identity must, therefore, begin in the cradle.

OVER and above what the individual brings with him from his childhood, the attainment of a sense of personal identity dpends upon the social milieu in which he or she grows up. For example, in a society where women are to some extent second-class citizens, it may be harder for females to arrive at a sense of psychosocial identity. Likewise at times, such as the present, when rapid social and technological change breaks down many traditional values, it may be more difficult for young people to find continuity between what they learned and experienced as children and what they learn and experience as adolescents. At such times young people often seek causes that give their lives meaning and direction. The activism of the current generation of young people may well stem, in part at least, from this search.

When the young person cannot attain a sense of personal identity, either because of an unfortunate childhood or difficult social circumstances, he shows a certain amount of *role confusion*—a sense of not knowing what he is, where he belongs or whom he belongs to. Such confusion is a frequent symptom in delinquent young people. Promiscuous adolescent girls, for example, often seem to have a fragmented sense of ego identity. Some young people seek a "negative identity," an identity opposite to the one prescribed for them by their family and friends. Having an identity as a "delinquent," or as a "hippie," or even as an "acid head," may sometimes be preferable to having no identity at all.

In some cases young people do not seek a negative identity so much as they have it thrust upon them. I remember another court case in which the defendant was an attractive 16-year-old girl who had been found "tricking it" in a trailer located just outside the grounds of an Air Force base. From about the age of 12, her mother had encouraged her to dress seductively and to go out with boys. When she returned from dates, her sexually frustrated mother demanded a kiss-by-kiss, caress-by-caress description of the evening's activities. After the mother had vicariously satisfied her sexual needs, she proceeded to call her daughter a "whore" and a "dirty tramp." As the girl told me, "Hell, I have the name, so I might as well play the role."

Failure to establish a clear sense of personal identity at adolescence does not guarantee perpetual failure. And the person who attains a working sense of ego identity in adolescence will of necessity encounter challenges and threats to that identity as he moves through life. Erikson, perhaps more than any other personality theorist, has emphasized that life is constant change and that confronting problems at one stage in life is not a guarantee against the reappearance of these problems at later stages, or against the finding of new solutions to them.

## Intimacy vs. Isolation

STAGE Six in the life cycle is young adulthood; roughly the period of courtship and early family life that extends from late adolescence till early middle age. For this stage, and the stages described hereafter, classical psychoanalysis has nothing new or major to say. For Erikson, however, the previous attainment of a sense of personal identity and the engagement in productive work that marks this period gives rise to a new interpersonal dimension of *intimacy* at the one extreme and *isolation* at the other.

When Erikson speaks of intimacy he means much more than love-making alone; he means the ability to share with and care about another person without fear of losing oneself in the process. In the case of intimacy, as in the case of identity, success or failure no longer depends directly upon the parents but only indirectly as they have contributed to the individual's success or failure at the earlier stages. Here, too, as in the case of identity, social conditions may help or hinder the establishment of a sense of intimacy. Likewise, intimacy need not involve sexuality; it includes the relationship between friends. Soldiers who have served together under the most dangerous circumstances often develop a sense of commitment to one another that exemplifies intimacy in its broadest sense. If a sense of intimacy is not established with friends or a marriage partner, the result, in Erikson's view, is a sense of isolation—of being alone without anyone to share with or care for.

## Generativity vs. Self-absorption

THIS stage—middle age—brings with it what Erikson speaks of as either *generativity* or *self-absorption*, and stagnation. What Erikson means by generativity is that the person begins to be concerned with others beyond his immediate family, with future generations and the nature of the society and world in which those generations will live. Generativity does not reside only in parents; it can be found in any individual who actively concerns himself with the welfare of young people and with making the world a better place for them to live and to work.

Those who fail to establish a sense of generativity fall into a state of self-absorption in which their personal needs and comforts are of predominant concern. A fictional case of self-absorption is Dickens's Scrooge in "A Christmas Carol." In his one-sided concern with money and in his disregard for the interests and welfare of his young employe, Bob Cratchit, Scrooge exemplifies the self-absorbed, embittered (the two often go together) old man. Dickens also illustrated, however, what Erikson points out: namely, that unhappy solutions to life's crises are not irreversible. Scrooge, at the end of the tale, manifested both a sense of generativity and of intimacy which he had not experienced before.

## Integrity vs. Despair

STAGE Eight in the Eriksonian scheme corresponds roughly to the period when the individual's major efforts are nearing completion and when there is time for reflection—and for the enjoyment of grandchildren, if any. The psychosocial dimension that comes into prominence now has *integrity* on one hand and *despair* on the other.

The sense of integrity arises from the individual's ability to look back on his life with satisfaction. At the other extreme is the individual who looks back upon his life as a series of missed opportunities and missed directions; now in the twilight years he realizes that it is too late to start again. For such a person the inevitable result is a sense of despair at what might have been.

THESE, then, are the major stages in the life cycle as described by Erikson. Their presentation, for one thing, frees the clinician to treat adult emotional problems as failures (in part at least) to solve genuinely adult personality crises and not, as heretofore, as mere residuals of infantile frustrations and conflicts. This view of personality growth, moreover, takes some of the onus off parents and takes account of the role which society and the person himself play in the formation of an individual personality. Finally, Erikson has offered hope for us all by demonstrating that each phase of growth has its strengths as well as its weaknesses and that failures at one stage of development can be rectified by successes at later stages.

The reason that these ideas, which sound so agreeable to "common sense," are in fact so revolutionary has a lot to do with the state of psychoanalysis in America. As formulated by Freud, psychoanalysis encompassed a theory of personality development, a method of studying the human mind and, finally, procedures for treating troubled and unhappy people. Freud viewed this system as a scientific one, open to revision as new facts and observations accumulated.

The system was, however, so vehemently attacked that Freud's followers were constantly in the position of having to defend Freud's views. Perhaps because of this situation, Freud's system became, in the hands of some of his followers and defenders, a dogma upon which all theoretical innovation, clinical observation and therapeutic practice had to be grounded. That this attitude persists is evidenced in the recent remark by a psychoanalyst that he believed psychotic patients could not be treated by psychoanalysis because "Freud said so." Such attitudes, in which Freud's authority rather than observation and data is the basis of deciding what is true and what is false, has contributed to the disrepute in which psychoanalysis is widely held today.

Erik Erikson has broken out of this scholasticism and has had the courage to say that Freud's discoveries and practices were the start and not the end of the study and treatment of the human personality. In addition to advocating the modifications of psychoanalytic theory outlined above, Erikson has also suggested modifications in therapeutic practice, particularly in the treatment of young patients. "Young people in severe trouble are not fit for the couch," he writes. "They want to face you, and they want you to face them, not as a facsimile of a parent, or wearing the mask of a professional helper, but as a kind of over-all individual a young person can live with or despair of."

Erikson has had the boldness to remark on some of the negative effects that distorted notions of psychoanaly-

sis have had on society at large. Psychoanalysis, he says, has contributed to a widespread fatalism—"even as we were trying to devise, with scientific determinism, a therapy for the few, we were led to promote an ethical disease among the many."

PERHAPS Erikson's innovations in psychoanalytic theory are best exemplified in his psycho-historical writings, in which he combines psychoanalytic insight with a true historical imagination. After the publication of "Childhood and Society," Erikson undertook the application of his scheme of the human life cycle to the study of historical persons. He wrote a series of brilliant essays on men as varied as Maxim Gorky, George Bernard Shaw and Freud himself. These studies were not narrow case histories but rather reflected Erikson's remarkable grasp of Europe's social and political history, as well as of its literature. (His mastery of American folklore, history and literature is equally remarkable.)

While Erikson's major biographical studies were yet to come, these early essays already revealed his unique psycho-history method. For one thing, Erikson always chose men whose lives fascinated him in one way or another, perhaps because of some conscious or unconscious affinity with them. Erikson thus had a sense of community with his subjects which he adroitly used (he calls it *disciplined subjectivity*) to take his subject's point of view and to experience the world as that person might.

Secondly, Erikson chose to elaborate a particular crisis or episode in the individual's life which seemed to crystallize a life-theme that united the activities of his past and gave direction to his activities for the future. Then, much as an artist might, Erikson proceeded to fill in the background of the episode and add social and historical perspective. In a very real sense Erikson's biographical sketches are like paintings which direct the viewer's gaze from a focal point of attention to background and back again, so that one's appreciation of the focal area is enriched by having pursued the picture in its entirety.

THIS method was given its first major test in Erikson's study of "Young Man Luther." Originally, Erikson planned only a brief study of Luther, but "Luther proved too bulky a man to be merely a chapter in a book." Erikson's involvement with Luther dated from his youth, when, as a wandering artist, he happened to hear the Lord's Prayer in Luther's German. "Never knowingly having heard it, I had the experience, as seldom before or after, of a wholeness captured in a few simple words, of poetry fusing the esthetic and the moral; those who have suddenly 'heard' the Gettysburg Address will know what I mean."

Erikson's interest in Luther may have had other roots as well. In some ways, Luther's unhappiness with the papal intermediaries of Christianity resembled on a grand scale Erikson's own dissatisfaction with the intermediaries of Freud's system. In both cases some of the intermediaries had so distorted the original teachings that what was being preached in the name of the master came close to being the opposite of what he had himself proclaimed. While it is not possible to describe Erikson's treatment of Luther here, one can get some feeling for Erikson's brand of historical analysis from his sketch of Luther:

"Luther was a very troubled and a very gifted young man who had to create his own cause on which to focus his fidelity in the Roman Catholic world as it was then. . . . He first became a monk and tried to solve his scruples by being an exceptionally good monk. But even his superiors thought that he tried much too hard. He felt himself to be such a sinner that he began to lose faith in the charity of God and his superiors told him, 'Look, God doesn't hate you, you hate God or else you would trust Him to accept your prayers.' But I would like to make it clear that someone like Luther becomes a historical person only because he also has an acute understanding of historical actuality and knows how to 'speak to the condition' of his times. Only then do inner struggles become representative of those of a large number of vigorous and sincere young people—and begin to interest some troublemakers and hangers-on."

After Erikson's study of "Young Man Luther" (1958), he turned his attention to "middle-aged" Gandhi. As did Luther, Gandhi evoked for Erikson childhood memories. Gandhi led his first nonviolent protest in India in 1918 on behalf of some mill workers, and Erikson, then a young man of 16, had read glowing accounts of the event. Almost a half a century later Erikson was invited to Ahmedabad, an industrial city in western India, to give a seminar on the human life cycle. Erikson discovered that Ahmedabad was the city in which Gandhi had led the demonstration about which Erikson had read as a youth. Indeed, Erikson's host was none other than Ambalal Sarabahai, the benevolent industrialist who had been Gandhi's host—as well as antagonist—in the 1918 wage dispute. Throughout his stay in Ahmedabad, Erikson continued to encounter people and places that were related to Gandhi's initial experiments with nonviolent techniques.

The more Erikson learned about the event at Ahmedabad, the more intrigued he became with its pivotal importance in Gandhi's career. It seemed to be the historical moment upon which all the earlier events of Gandhi's life converged and from which diverged all of his later endeavors. So captured was Erikson by the event at Ahmedabad, that he returned the following year to research a book on Gandhi in which the event would serve as a fulcrum.

AT least part of Erikson's interest in Gandhi may have stemmed from certain parallels in their lives. The 1918 event marked Gandhi's emergence as a national political leader. He was 48 at the time, and had become involved reluctantly, not so much out of a need for power or fame as out of a genuine conviction that something had to be done about the disintegration of Indian culture. Coincidentally, Erikson's book, "Childhood and Society," appeared in 1950 when Erikson was 48, and it is that book which brought him national prominence in the mental health field. Like Gandhi, too, Erikson reluctantly did what he felt he had to do (namely, publish his observations and conclusions) for the benefit of his ailing profession and for the patients treated by its practitioners. So while Erikson's affinity with Luther seemed to derive from comparable professional identity crises, his affinity for Gandhi appears to derive from a parallel crisis of generativity. A

passage from "Gandhi's Truth" (from a chapter wherein Erikson addresses himself directly to his subject) helps to convey Erikson's feeling for his subject.

"So far, I have followed you through the loneliness of your childhood and through the experiments and the scruples of your youth. I have affirmed my belief in your ceaseless endeavor to perfect yourself as a man who came to feel that he was the only one available to reverse India's fate. You experimented with what to you were debilitating temptations and you did gain vigor and agility from your victories over yourself. Your identity could be no less than that of universal man, although you had to become an Indian—and one close to the masses—first."

The following passage speaks to Erikson's belief in the general significance of Gandhi's efforts:

"We have seen in Gandhi's development the strong attraction of one of those more inclusive identities: that of an enlightened citizen of the British Empire. In proving himself willing neither to abandon vital ties to his native tradition nor to sacrifice lightly a Western education which eventually contributed to his ability to help defeat British hegemony—in all of these seeming contradictions Gandhi showed himself on intimate terms with the actualities of his era. For in all parts of the world, the struggle now is for the *anticipatory development of more inclusive identities* . . . I submit then, that Gandhi, in his immense intuition for historical actuality and his capacity to assume leadership in 'truth in action,' may have created a ritualization through which men, equipped with both realism and strength, can face each other with mutual confidence."

THERE is now more and more teaching of Erikson's concepts in psychiatry, psychology, education and social work in America and in other parts of the world. His description of the stages of the life cycle are summarized in major textbooks in all of these fields and clinicians are increasingly looking at their cases in Eriksonian terms.

Research investigators have, however, found Erikson's formulations somewhat difficult to test. This is not surprising, inasmuch as Erikson's conceptions, like Freud's, take into account the infinite complexity of the human personality. Current research methodologies are, by and large, still not able to deal with these complexities at their own level, and distortions are inevitable when such concepts as "identity" come to be defined in terms of responses to a questionnaire.

Likewise, although Erikson's life-stages have an intuitive "rightness" about them, not everyone agrees with his formulations. Douvan and Adelson in their book, "The Adolescent Experience," argue that while his identity theory may hold true for boys, it doesn't for girls. This argument is based on findings which suggest that girls postpone identity consolidation until after marriage (and intimacy) have been established. Such postponement occurs, says Douvan and Adelson, because a woman's identity is partially defined by the identity of the man whom she marries. This view does not really contradict Erikson's, since he recognizes that later events, such as marriage, can help to resolve both current and past developmental crises. For the woman, but not for the man, the problems of identity and intimacy may be solved concurrently.

Objections to Erikson's formulations have come from

other directions as well. Robert W. White, Erikson's good friend and colleague at Harvard, has a long-standing (and warm-hearted) debate with Erikson over his life-stages. White believes that his own theory of "competence motivation," a theory which has received wide recognition, can account for the phenomena of ego development much more economically than can Erikson's stages. Erikson has, however, little interest in debating the validity of the stages he has described. As an artist he recognizes that there are many different ways to view one and the same phenomenon and that a perspective that is congenial to one person will be repugnant to another. He offers his stage-wise description of the life cycle for those who find such perspectives congenial and not as a world view that everyone should adopt.

It is this lack of dogmatism and sensitivity to the diversity and complexity of the human personality which help to account for the growing recognition of Erikson's contribution within as well as without the helping professions. Indeed, his psycho-historical investigations have originated a whole new field of study which has caught the interest of historians and political scientists alike. (It has also intrigued his wife, Joan, who has published pieces on Eleanor Roosevelt and who has a book on Saint Francis in press.) A recent issue of Daedalus, the journal for the American Academy of Arts and Sciences, was entirely devoted to psycho-historical and psycho-political investigations of creative leaders by authors from diverse disciplines who have been stimulated by Erikson's work.

NOW in his 68th year, Erikson maintains the pattern of multiple activities and appointments which has characterized his entire career. He spends the fall in Cambridge, Mass., where he teaches a large course on "the human life cycle" for Harvard seniors. The spring semester is spent at his home in Stockbridge, Mass., where he participates in case conferences and staff seminars at the Austen Riggs Center. His summers are spent on Cape Cod. Although Erikson's major commitment these days is to his psycho-historical investigation, he is embarking on a study of pre-school children's play constructions in different settings and countries, a follow-up of some research he conducted with preadolescents more than a quarter-century ago. He is also planning to review other early observations in the light of contemporary change. In his approach to his work, Erikson appears neither drawn nor driven, but rather to be following an inner schedule as natural as the life cycle itself.

Although Erikson, during his decade of college teaching, has not seen any patients or taught at psychoanalytic institutions, he maintains his dedication to psychoanalysis and views his psycho-historical investigations as an applied branch of that discipline. While some older analysts continue to ignore Erikson's work, there is increasing evidence (including a recent poll of psychiatrists and psychoanalysts) that he is having a rejuvenating influence upon a discipline which many regard as dead or dying. Young analysts are today proclaiming a "new freedom" to see Freud in historical perspective—which reflects the Eriksonian view that one can recognize Freud's greatness without bowing to conceptual precedent.

Accordingly, the reports of the demise of psychoanalysis may have been somewhat premature. In the work of Erik Erikson, at any rate, psychoanalysis lives and continues to beget life.

# 10

C.H. ELDRIDGE '76

Learning to love, learning to work

# Coming of age in America

By Peter and Jane Davison

Our sons and daughters emerge from childhood into what? Into that big waiting room that is adolescence in America.

"He's a mere child, you're a typical teen-ager, we're sort of middle-aged, she's really getting on, and he's practically dead." How ironic that technological America can accept so vaguely calibrated a continuum to tick off the ages of man. The way we dress now expresses the way we gloss over society's compartmentalization by age and generation. Lately, the young, in rebellion against tailormade conformity, broke out into a revolution of dress, if not ultimately one in fact, and now, like most revolutions, it has become a model for antirevolutionary imitation. A grandmother in St. Petersburg strolls under the palms in a size 16½ duplicate of the double-knit pants suit her daughter-in-law wears while car-pooling her jersey-clad children to school in Mamaroneck — yet their life expectations are as different as chalk and cheese. Now, less than five

*Peter and Jane Davison are regarded by their two children as uncanny but not necessarily inimical. He is a poet and editor, whose most recent book is "Walking the Boundaries: Poems 1957-1974."*

years after Kent State, college students (boys or girls) dip into their mother's bureau for her Yves Saint Laurent shirt, silk scarf or bulky cardigan. Even at the height of what may be described as the Mannerist Sixties, when inspired originality was the universal cry, the with-it people from Harvard Square to Haight-Ashbury ended up looking like so many interchangeable characters in an all-American ethno-historico-theatrical motley. The laws of costume have a certain leveling inevitability.

The homogenization of the way we look has begun to shatter the merchandising category known as Children's Clothes — yet children's clothes of any kind are a surprisingly recent development in Western civilization. In his fascinating book, "Dress and Society: 1560-1970," Geoffrey Squire states that not until the last decades of the 18th century, under the influence of Rousseau, did it occur to parents to abandon the age-old practice of dressing children like miniature adults. The well-dressed child, with sighs of relief, cast aside knee breeches and corselets to slip into loose trousers and smocks.

This innovation coincided, moreover, with a movement in both adult dress and manners to separate the sexes and intensify the differences between them. This reached its most elaborate and dramatic phase in the 19th century, the age of vapors and the double standard, when the fabrics as well as the silhouettes of men's and women's clothes reached their extremes of polarization. Who could mistake Scarlett O'Hara for Rhett Butler? Ultimately, all the adult and juvenile categories of dress became part of the Byzantine inventories of the 20th-century department store. In Children's Clothes alone, we had to learn to make our way through 3-6x, Young Subdebs, Older Preps, Junior Chubbettes and other exotic subdivisions. Now in the seventies we seem to be leaving those distinctions of age and sex behind us.

The way we dress, Squire contends, reflects the way we are. Costume is "only a unit in the complete production, which is illuminated by the spirit of the age in which we live." We have moved into an era of democratization, of attempting to dispense with social and economic distinctions, of welcoming cradle-to-grave blue denim "work clothes." We have mass production and mass media and, if you like, a mass mess. Our clothes have followed our customs. As we have blurred or eliminated social differences in the name of equality, ritual distinctions among us have faded. Many changes have been morally and socially beneficial — the abolition of slavery and the relative liberation of women, for example — but enlightened progress has its casualties. We sense uneasily that something has been lost.

Less complicated, confused cultures have been able to preserve a variety of social ceremonies marking the major, irreversible biological/social stages of an individual's life. Although age-old and universal in one form or another, these rituals had no generic name until 1909 when the anthropologist A. L. Van Gennep coined the term "rites of passage."

As Carleton Coon points out in "The Hunting Peoples," a rite of passage is therapeutic both for the "patient" and for those close to him, such as his immediate family. It eases difficult adjustments to change for all concerned. We agree that it provides a boy or girl, man or woman with a navigational fix on his position in the society that surrounds him like a sea. Moreover, it helps reduce the individual's fear of the future; it reassures him with its public announcement that he has changed and must henceforth be regarded differently by society; it keeps the society informed of who has got to what stage of life, and how, accordingly, he should be treated. If rituals are erased or suppressed, an emotional geography haltingly tamed through the millennia is delivered over to wilderness.

To what extent has this happened to us? As a nation we expend ourselves on two rites of passage which we regard as major events in human life: marriages, with their picturesque folkways — like white veils, champagne receptions, engraved announcements and competitive gift-giving — and funerals, with their euphemistic language and cosmetic disguising of the facts of death. (Note that what others do is ritual; what we do is The Way It's Done.) Coming of age is a happening we seem to neglect, certainly in comparison to such cultures as that the Mbuti pygmies of the Ituri Forest, in northwest Zaire.

For several months after their first menstruation, Mbuti girls are segregated in what is called an *elima* house to undergo an experience something like a summer camp crossed with a slumber party. They sing special *elima* songs, make a lot of noise and are told the facts of life. If any boys approach, the girls beat them with sticks. Eventually, they begin to let certain suitors in, and the wooing is on. At this point the mothers step in and harass the suitors with all sorts of deterrents, from a little more run-of-the-mill stick-beating to throwing particularly unattractive prospects into a stream. The battle of the sexes and generations intensifies, and the boys retaliate by such horseplay as slapping their prospective mothers-in-law with banana skins. Somehow in the melee betrothals are negotiated, whereupon a girl busies herself with prenuptial activities, like painting white clay stars on her buttocks or rings on her breasts. Meanwhile, the boy hunts for a nice large antelope to give to her parents to seal the deal.

To us these carryings-on seem amusing enough, but no more so perhaps than a visiting Mbuti pygmy would find the mummery of a first-class interment at Forest Lawn. It might be instructive to imagine a modern American adaptation of the perky coed rite of passage described above, but the mind boggles at the possibilities for such a living theater hoedown. Think of the by-products. "Celebrate your lovely daughter's coming of age with the all-new Pandora's Box, her very own simulated-gold coffer containing a six months' supply of The Pill! Available in better stores across the country." No, such revels cannot be invented; they have to grow out of the inner needs of a society.

If they do, they work. After weeks of being the center of the Mbuti hullabaloo, you must certainly know (1) that you are no longer the same as before, and (2) that certain new expectations now rest upon you, whether they be signalized by stars on your rear, king-size antelopes or more private and personal engagements, like sex and children.

Our sons and daughters emerge from childhood into what? Into that big waiting room that is adolescence in America. Here the boy or girl puts away childish things and takes up adult concerns and entertainments, but not adult duties. In middle-class America Daddy pays the tuition and the piper, and the principal emotions rise over the rights, not the rites, of passage. It is a terrifying and terrible time, in that no one, neither the parent nor the child, has any way to measure when it will ever end, and what few yardsticks are available keep changing.

Erik H. Erikson wrote in "Childhood and Society," "The adolescent mind is essentially a mind of the moratorium, a psychosocial stage between childhood and adulthood, and between the morality learned by the child, and the ethics developed by the adult. It is an ideological mind — and indeed it is the ideological outlook of a society that speaks most clearly to the adolescent who is eager to be confirmed by his peers, and is ready to be confirmed by the rituals, creeds, and programs which at the same time define what is evil, uncanny, and inimical." Because we as a society have shucked off, one by one, and mostly in the name of ideology, the "rituals, creeds, and programs" that help define the adult, a vacuum remains, and it is filled by the adolescent's peers. Yet how unsatisfactory. How can one pass a test in a course where there is no teacher?

Only a few specific acknowledgments of entrance into an adult community still exist — the bar mitzvahs and first communions of formal but receding religions. The ideologies, however, are all too ready at hand, and new ones keep arriving — old ideas in new disguises — offering panaceas that can be dropped as quickly as they were adopted. "Historically," as C. G. Jung wrote in "The Undiscovered Self," it is chiefly in times of physical, political, economic, and spiritual distress that men's eyes turn with anxious hope to the future, and when anticipations, utopias, and apocalyptic visions multiply." If our adolescents a decade ago gave themselves to the cause of civil rights, how soon they neglected that cause when they became more nearly threatened by the Vietnam war. Once we were out of the war, they turned to the ecological threats posed by technology, and their next cause well may be world famine.

Who would call these causes unworthy? No one. But the adolescent, who is given nothing by society to assure him of first-class membership, has fewer defenses against fads and panics than anyone else. As Jung went on to write, "Resistance to the organized mass can be effected only by the man who is as well organized in his individuality as the mass itself. I realize that this proposition must sound well-nigh unintelligible to the man of today."

Perhaps it sounds less unintelligible now than when it was first written in 1957. No longer militant, the young seem to be turning inward, or at least away from social struggle. Perhaps they have come to suspect that one element in their protests was retribution against their parents for not having provided them with the satisfying "rituals, creeds, and programs" that define the "evil, uncanny, and inimical."

Parents themselves went through a lot in those bitter years of the nineteen-sixties, and they still do. On certain dark winter mornings they recognize themselves as "uncanny"; they can see themselves mirrored in their children's eyes as "inimical." Some of them run away from their lives into divorce, second professions, new homes and surroundings; others take no action but drift into a worrisome limbo — the *Weltschmerz* of a second adolescence, the acknowledged but totally unritualized mid-life crisis, an increasingly familiar neurosis that arises, as much as anything, from the absence of any rite of passage into age. Undeniably, becoming a respected elder reassures one more than simply growing older.

There is nothing new about the feelings of a father in his forties, aware of the waning of his seemingly illimitable sexual powers, watching with rueful amusement the stretching and preening of his 13-year-old son, who is wearing a sleeveless Italian shirt so that no one can avoid noticing the new tufts of hair under his arms. Nor is there anything new about the emotions of a mother, who looks up from the latest magazine article on breast cancer and sees her blossoming braless daughter jounce by, seemingly unaware of the aura she casts. Parents have no doubt always held such feelings about their children, but there were once the compensations of eldership. Those few who survived past middle age gained a certain status in the society; their experience seemed a source of wisdom; the young looked to them for answers to famine, inflation and war, though it may be we still believe in the elders of the Supreme Court as wise and just.

With so few specific rites of passage to mark our adolescent coming of age, clothes have assumed a symbolic importance — or they did so 30 years ago. We girls were children as long as we dressed up in tweed reefers from Best & Co. (just like Princess Margaret Rose's),

and patent leather Mary Janes with fine white cotton socks, and a velveteen party dress with heavy white lace at the neck. Only with the first pimple and the first box of sanitary supplies (a euphemism that ranks for quaintness with *sal volatile* and the vapors) did we cast aside the trappings of childhood and harness up in bra, garter belt, "hose" and "heels." Or, as boys, we seemed to change when we traded our curly hair and shorts (after a long battle with our mothers) for crew cuts and long corduroys from J. C. Penney.

When we won these minor battles for status, we knew something significant had happened in our lives, but it hardly constituted adult recognition. We had a feeling that whatever else was wanted had more to do with sex than anyone was letting on. "I see you're growing up," one of those little blue-haired ladies who knew your mother would say, peering through her specs, and we wondered uneasily exactly what she could see. When in the nineteen-sixties one generation dramatized its differences with the preceding one far more overtly than we ever had, there was no question that sex as an issue underlay adult hysteria about long hair and dirty jeans.

Not knowing what the world had a right to expect, we had no idea what to expect from ourselves as semi-adults, except to *keep going*. For a white middle-class child, particularly a boy, this meant an endless slogging upward on the academic and business slopes. No graduation, whether from high school or from college or from graduate school, could replace the rites of passage invented by our "primitive" ancestors. We were herded along through the decades in the increasingly frightening knowledge that next year or next week or even perhaps tomorrow we would be expected to comport ourselves like adults, to be as ruthless and tough as adults, without, of course, making any of the mistakes the older generation had made. The worst of it was that we had no way of judging our own performance, until our children came along to mark us, and we began to fear we had flunked out. We had no ceremony to give us the sense of where we were now in the procession. The occasion never arose when we might taste the pride of public recognition of our achievement, when we might, so to speak, introduce the succession to a cheering populace, "My son, the Prince of Wales, and my daughter, the future Queen of France."

The traditional acknowledgments of coming of age have been very directly, if symbolically, linked with sex and reproduction: the girl is now of an age to bear children; the boy is equipped to father them. In an age of population explosion, years of suspended animation are required of young people, and reproduction is to be prevented, not encouraged. The major difference between adolescence today and 30 years ago is more than that between anxious backseat groping and sexual freedom or coed dorms, far more than that between velveteen dresses and Levi's. Thirty years ago how many of our contemporaries discussed, seriously and as a matter of choice, not having children? Girls never even talked about not marrying, except as one would speak of the possibility of some cataclysm.

Today, even as fashion begins to move away from the unisex effect of the blue denim uniform, educators confer and speculate on the advantages of adrogyny, or at least of the androgynous mind. A recent study at Stanford University seemed to prove that a young mind that balances attributes traditionally viewed as male or female is likely to be more adept at problem solving than one more sexually polarized. The trend in education may be to discourage sexual stereotyping, at least for a time, and probably it is desirable, but we are moving still father away from conceiving of adulthood as a confirmation of our sexual identities, and the biological fact of puberty will continue to lose its traditional social significance.

In the absence of sexually defined rites of passage, some people have groped for substitutes to replace our vanished rituals. Artificial and exclusive subgroups have sprung into being, small communes as well as those societies ordered and financed on a larger scale — the Jesus Freaks and Maharishis and Esalens and Hare Krishnas and Reverend Moons. If an industrial civilization cannot provide us with a purified social order containing those rites of passage and progress which our soul loveth, some of us will feel obliged to turn again, in the American way, and run up a society out of whole cloth to satisfy the heart's desire.

Alas, the record is not encouraging for this do-it-yourself kind of social enterprise. Our New Harmonys, Shakers, Amanas, Amish and Doukhobors don't seem to be much more fertile than the mules they drive, and have a sad way of fading into extinction after a generation or two. For ritual to perform its functions of refreshment, vitalization and renewal, it must truly reflect the human needs and realities of the society that decrees it. What rites would a technological society decree that all members could consent to?

When Freud was asked what a mature adult should be able to do well, his answer was short and awesomely simple: *"Lieben und arbeiten."* To love and to work. The standard is so profound that it can apply to Mbuti pygmies or anyone in America. Whether we are young adolescents seeking reassurance of growth or recidivists in our forties, we would have received little help toward either goal from sex-oriented rites of passage. The discouraging thing about so exalted and rational a goal as Freud's is that it will not admit of the thrill of initiation, the graduate's self-satisfaction, the parents' gratification, the recognition and intensification of a social pattern in which all generations have a set role. Loving and working are somehow left to the individual to learn for himself or herself.

The only rites of passage left are those which each of us must set up for ourselves. There is cause for celebration the first time we say, "No, I won't go to bed with you just because you want me." "Yes, I will go to bed with you because I want you." "No, I won't smoke dope just because everyone else does," "No, I won't follow my parents' pattern of competitive expertise." "No, I won't challenge my parents just because all my peers say it's the thing to do." Simplistic? Perhaps. But such considered assents and refusals, weighed against the demands and bounties of a society that so far has seemed to offer us everything and refuse us nothing, are the only acts by which we can define ourselves, while telling our world that we have at last — at whatever age, 13 or 39 — become adults.

# 11

# FACING UP TO DEATH

**ELISABETH KUBLER ROSS, M.D.,** *medical director, South Cook County Mental Health and Family Services, Chicago Heights, Illinois.*

☐ **People used to be born at home and die at home.** In the old days, children were familiar with birth and death as part of life. This is perhaps the first generation of American youngsters who have never been close by during the birth of a baby and have never experienced the death of a beloved family member.

Nowadays when people grow old, we often send them to nursing homes. When they get sick, we transfer them to a hospital, where children are usually unwelcome and are forbidden to visit terminally ill patients—even when those patients are their parents. This deprives the dying patient of significant family members during the last few days of his life and it deprives the children of an experience of death, which is an important learning experience.

**At the University of Chicago's Billings Hospital,** some of my colleagues and I interviewed and followed approximately 500 terminally ill patients in order to find out what they could teach us and how we could be of more benefit, not just to them but to the members of their families as well. We were most impressed by the fact that even those patients who were not told of their serious illness were quite aware of its potential outcome. They were not only able to say that they were close to dying, but many were able to predict the approximate time of their death.

It is important for next of kin and members of the helping professions to understand these patients' communications in order to truly understand their needs, fears, and fantasies. Most of our patients welcomed another human being with whom they could talk openly, honestly, and frankly about their predicament. Many of them shared with us their tremendous need to be informed, to be kept up-to-date on their medical condition, and to be told when the end was near. We found out that patients who had been dealt with openly and frankly were better able to cope with the imminence of death and finally to reach a true stage of acceptance prior to death.

Two things seem to determine the ultimate adjustment to a terminal illness. When patients were allowed hope at the beginning of a fatal illness and when they were informed that they would not be deserted "no matter what," they were able to drop their initial shock and denial rather quickly and could arrive at a peaceful acceptance of their finiteness.

Most patients respond to the awareness that they have a terminal illness with the statement, "Oh no, this can't happen to me." After the first shock, numbness, and need to deny the reality of the situation, the patient begins to send out cues that he is ready to "talk about it." If *we*, at that point, need to deny the reality of the situation, the patient will often feel deserted, isolated, and lonely and unable to communicate with another human being what he needs so desperately to share.

When, on the other hand, the patient has one person with whom he can talk freely, he will be able to talk (often for only a few minutes at a time) about his illness and about the consequences of his deteriorating health, and he will be able to ask for help. Sometimes, he'll need to talk about financial matters; and, toward the end of the life, he will frequently ask for some spiritual help.

Most patients who have passed the stage of denial will become angry as they ask the question, "Why me?" Many look at others in their environment and express envy, jealousy, anger, and rage toward those who are young, healthy, and full of life. These are the patients who make life difficult for nurses, physicians, social workers, clergymen, and members of their families. Without justification they criticize everyone.

What we have to learn is that the stage of anger in terminal illness is a blessing, not a curse. These patients are not angry at their families or at the members of the helping professions. Rather, they are angry at what these people represent: health, pep, energy.

Without being judgmental, we must allow these patients to express their anger and dismay. We must try to understand that the patients have to ask, "Why me?" and that there is no need on our part to answer this question concretely. Once a patient has ventilated his rage and his envy, then he can arrive at the bargaining stage. During this time, he's usually able to say, "Yes, it is happening to me—*but*." The *but* usually includes a prayer to God: "If you give me one more year to live, I will be a good Christian (or I'll go to the synagogue every day)."

Most patients promise something in exchange for prolongation of life. Many a patient wants to live just long enough for the children to get out of school. The moment they have completed high school, he may ask to live until the son gets married. And the moment the wedding is over, he hopes to live until the grandchild arrives. These kinds of bargains are compromises, the patient's beginning acknowledgement that his time is limited, and an expression of finiteness, all necessary in reaching a stage of acceptance. When a patient drops the *but*, then he is able to say, "Yes, me." At this point, he usually becomes very depressed. And here again we have to allow him to express his grief and his mourning.

**If we stop and think how much we would grieve if** we lost a beloved spouse, it will make us realize what courage it takes for a man to face his own impending death, which involves the loss of everyone and everything he has ever loved. This is a thousand times more crushing than to become a widow or a widower.

To such patients, we should never say, "Come on now, cheer up." We should allow them to grieve, to cry. And we should even convey to them that "it takes a brave person to cry," meaning that it takes courage to face death. If the patient expresses his grief, he will feel more comfortable, and he will usually go through the stage of depression much more rapidly than he will if he has to suppress it or hide his tears.

Only through this kind of behavior on our part are our patients able to reach the stage of acceptance. Here, they begin to separate themselves from the interpersonal relationships in their environment. Here, they begin to ask for fewer and fewer visitors. Finally, they will require only one beloved person who can sit quietly and comfortably near.

This is the time when a touch becomes more important than words, the time when a patient may simply say one day, "My time is very close now, and it's all right." It is not necessarily a happy stage, but the patient now shows no more fear, bitterness, anguish, or concern over unfinished business. People who have been able to sit through this stage with patients and who have experienced the beautiful feeling of inner and outer peace that they show will soon appreciate that working with terminally ill patients is not a morbid, depressing job but can be an inspiring experience.

The tragedy is that in our death-denying society, people grow up uncomfortable in the presence of a dying patient, unable to talk to the terminally ill and lost for words when they face a grieving person.

**We tried to use dying patients as teachers. We talked** with these patients so they could teach our young medical students, social work students, nurses, and members of the clergy about one part of life that all of us eventually have to face. When we interviewed them, we had a screened window setup in which we were able to talk with them in privacy while our students observed and listened. Needless to say this observation was done with the knowledge and agreement of our patients.

This teaching by dying patients who volunteered this service to us enabled them to share some of their turmoil and some of their needs with us. But perhaps more important than that, they were able to help our own young students to face the reality of death, to identify at times with our dying patients, and to become aware of their own finiteness.

Many of our young students who originally were petrified at the thought of facing dying patients were eventually able to express to us their own concerns, their own fears, and their own fantasies about dying. Most of our students who have been able to attend one quarter or perhaps a semester of these weekly death-and-dying seminars have learned to come to grips with their own fears of death and have ultimately become good counselors to terminally ill patients.

One thing this teaches us is that it would be helpful if we could rear our children with the awareness of death and of their own finiteness. Even in a death-denying society, this can be and has been done.

In our hospital we saw a small child with acute leukemia. She made the rounds and asked the adults, "What is it going to be like when I die?" The grown-ups responded in a variety of ways, most of them unhelpful or even harmful for this little girl who was searching for an answer. The only message she really received through the grown-ups' response was that they had a lot of fear when it came to talking about dying.

When the child confronted the hospital chaplain with the same question, he turned to her and asked, "What do you think it's going to be like?" She looked at him and said, "One of these days I'm going to fall asleep and when I wake up I'm going to be with Jesus and my little sister." He then said something like "That should be very beautiful." The child nodded and happily returned to play. Perhaps this is an exaggerated example, but I think it conveys how children face the reality even of their own death if the adults in their environment don't make it a frightening, horrible experience to be avoided at all costs.

**The most forgotten people in the environment of** the dying patient are the brothers and sisters of dying children. We have seen rather tragic examples of siblings who were terribly neglected during the terminal illness of a brother or a sister. Very often those children are left alone with many unanswered questions while the mother attends the dying child in the hospital and the father doesn't come home from work because he wants to visit the hospital in the evening.

The tragedy is that these children at home not only are anxious, lonely, and frightened at the thought of their sibling's death, but they also feel that somehow their wish for a sibling to "drop dead" (which all children have at times) is being fulfilled. When such a sibling actually dies, they feel responsible for the death, just as they do when they lose a parent during the preschool years. If these children receive no help prior to, and especially immediately after, the death of a parent or a sibling, they are likely to grow up with abnormal fears of death and a lot of unresolved conflicts that often result in emotional illness later on in life.

We hope that teachers are aware of the needs of these children and can make themselves available to them in order to elicit expression of their fears, their fantasies, their needs. If they're allowed to express their anger for being neglected and their shame for having "committed a crime," then these children can be helped before they develop permanent emotional conflict.

**A beautiful example of death education in an indirect way** is expressed in a letter I received from a man who became aware of my work and felt the need to convey some of his life experiences to me. I will quote his letter verbatim because it shows what an early childhood memory can do for a man when he's faced with the imminent death of his own father.

Dear Dr. Ross: May I commend you and your colleagues who took part in the Conference on "death. . . ."

I am a production-line brewery worker here in Milwaukee who feels strongly on this subject. Because of your efforts, maybe one day we can all look death in the eye. . . . In reading and rereading the enclosed account of your meeting, I found myself with the urge to relate to you a personal experience of my own.

About six years ago, my dad was a victim of terminal cancer. He was a tough, life-loving 73-year-old father of 10 with 10 grandchildren who kept him aglow and always on the go. It just couldn't be that his time had come. The last time I saw him alive was the result of an urgent phone call from my sister. "You'd better come home as soon as possible; it's Pa."

The 500-mile drive to northern Minnesota wasn't the enjoyable trip that so many others had been. I learned after I arrived that he wasn't in the hospital, but at home. I also learned that "he didn't know." The doctor told the family that it was up to us to tell him or not tell him. My brother and sisters who live in the area thought it best "not to" and so advised me.

When I walked in on him, we embraced as we always did when we'd visit about twice or so each year. But this time it was different—sort of restrained and lacking the spirit of earlier get-togethers; and each of us, I know, sensed this difference.

Then, some hours later, after the usual kinds of questions and answers and talk, it was plain to me that he appeared so alone and withdrawn, almost moody or sulk-

ing. It was scary to see him just sitting there, head in hand, covering his eyes. I didn't know what to say or do. I asked if he'd care for a drink—no response. Something had to give. It all seemed so cruel. So I stepped into the kitchen and poured me a good one—and another. This was it, and if he didn't "know," he would now.

I went over and sat down beside and sort of facing him, and I was scared. I was always scared of my father, but it was a good kind of fear, the respectful kind. I put one hand on his shoulder and the other on his knee. I said, "Pa, you know why I came home, don't you? This is the last time we will be together." The dam burst. He threw his arms around me, and just hung on.

And here's the part I'll never forget and yet always cherish. I remember when our tears met, I recalled, in a sort of vivid flashback, a time 30 years before when I was five or six and he took me out into the woods to pick hazelnuts. My very first big adventure! I remembered being afraid of the woods. Afraid of bears or monsters or something that would eat me up. But even though I was afraid, I at the same time was brave, because my big strong daddy was with me.

Needless to say, thanks to that hazelnut hunt, I knew how my dad was feeling at that moment. And I could only hope that I gave him some small measure of courage; the kind he had given me. I do know he was grateful and appreciated my understanding. As I remember, he regained his composure and authority enough to scold *me* for crying. It was at the kitchen table, after a couple or three fingers of brandy, that we talked and reminisced and planned. I would even guess he was eager to start a long search for his wife, who also had known how to die. . . .

**What I am trying to convey is that everything depends** on the way we rear our children. If we help them to face fear and show them that through strength and sharing we can overcome even the fear of dying, then they will be better prepared to face any kind of crisis that might confront them, including the ultimate reality of death. □

# The Human Gaze: Silent Language of the Eyes

## Michael Argyle

Former heavyweight champion Sonny Liston used to transfix his opponents with his famous "hate stare"—at least until young Cassius Clay appeared on the scene. It was a modern version of the "evil eye," and it communicated an unmistakable message of menace. However, just as gaze can be used to attack, it can also be used to attract.

The Roman poet Ovid knew the seductive powers of the eyes when he counseled, "Let your eyes gaze into hers; let the gazing be a confession." A modern songwriter sounded the same theme when he wrote, "A fleeting glance can say so many lovely things; suddenly you know why my heart sings." Whether it is a look of hate or a look of love, we all understand implicitly the silent language of the eyes. Looking at other people, being looked at, and having eye contact (or mutual gaze) are familiar experiences often mentioned by poets and novelists. They were, however, neglected by social scientists until the early 1960s.

It can be argued that looking at others is of central importance in social behavior. Psychologists have long recognized the importance of the perception of others—reactions to others depend on how others are perceived and how their behavior is interpreted. But how are people and their behavior perceived? Mainly by looking at them. It follows that how much people look, and when and where they look are crucial for their social performance. Gaze acts here as a channel for the reception of signals, mainly nonverbal signals, from others.

There is only one established approach to social psychology which recognizes gaze at all—the non-verbal communication tradition. However, most research in this tradition treats gaze only as a signal, along with facial expression, bodily posture, and so on. One of the main points I want to make in this article is that gaze operates in two quite different ways simultaneously—as a channel and as a signal. Gaze is also part of verbal communication, in that gaze is closely coordinated with

speaking and listening, serves to provide feedback, and is one of the signals used for coordinating the stopping and starting of speech by different speakers. Here again the same glance can act as a channel to one person and a signal for another.

## METHODS OF RECORDING GAZE

The earliest studies of gaze used a human observer looking through a one-way screen and operating a cumulative stopwatch, which added up, for example, the amount of gaze at a second person in a three minute period of interaction. Human observers are still used sometimes, but it is more common to make a more permanent record by using two video cameras, whose images are combined side-by-side on one video tape by using a video mixer.

## GAZE AS A SIGNAL FOR INTERPERSONAL ATTITUDES AND EMOTIONS

If person A likes person B more than C, then A will look at B more than at C. This has been shown in a variety of experiments. In one of the best of these, Exline and Winters manipulated the attitudes of subjects to two experimental confederates, so that subjects liked one more than the other. It was found that subjects looked much more at the one they liked. Rubin found that couples who were more in love, according to his questionnaire scale, engaged in more mutual gaze than couples less deeply in love.

Janet Dean and I put forward a theory to the effect that pairs of people form an equilibrium level of intimacy, based on conflicting approach and avoidance forces. This degree of intimacy is expressed by a combination of affiliative signals, such as gaze, proximity, or smiling. If the equilibrium is disturbed, for example by an increase of distance, compensating signals would be expected, such as more smiling, more gaze, and so on. We first tested this in an experiment in which gaze was measured at different distances. The experiment has been replicated a number of times under different conditions, and the results of three experiments are shown in Figure 1.

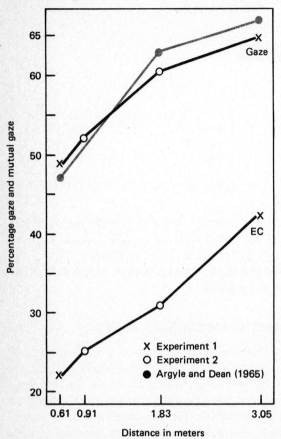

*Figure 1. The effects of distance on gaze and mutual gaze.*

It can be seen that both gaze and mutual gaze increase continuously with distance, as predicted. Various other findings confirm the hypothesis; for example, Exline and others have found less gaze and mutual gaze where intimate topics are being discussed.

Gaze can signal other attitudes besides liking and loving. Hostility can be signaled by a special kind of stare, such as the familiar blank or hostile facial expression of boxers. It can also be signaled by aversion of gaze, as when visibly ignoring another person. Dominance is rather complex. Two people who have not yet established a relationship may try to stare each other down; but in an established hierarchy, the subordinate individual looks more, especially while listening.

When people are embarrassed, they look away. When they are not telling the truth most people look less: Exline and colleagues implicated subjects in cheating by another supposed subject; when interviewed about the other's behavior, subjects looked less—unless they were "Machiavellian personalities." Other emotions produce characteristic gaze patterns; for example, depression is shown by gazing downward.

The main finding here is that positive attitudes and emotions, such as liking and happiness, are shown by more gaze, while negative ones, such as dislike and depression, are shown by less gaze. People look at those with whom they are interpersonally involved. They may also look at those they like because the sheer appearance and the friendly behavior of the other are rewarding. There is aversion of gaze if the other is not expected to send friendly signals back, and it may be dissonant to look too much if there are feelings of guilt, about deception for example. The total level of gaze reflects the balance between such approach and avoidance forces. In addition, the kind of gaze (e.g., staring or looking downward) conveys further information about the attitudes and emotions of the sender.

## THE PERCEPTION OF GAZE

How is gaze perceived and decoded by others? In the first place, several studies have shown that there is a rather low degree of awareness of gaze. When people are aware of being gazed at, the first impression is that of being the object of the other's attention. The feeling of "being observed" is heightened if the other can see better, for example, if he is wearing dark glasses or is behind a one-way screen. There is another gaze experience which has a special quality—mutual gaze, in which two people realize that each is open to signals from the other.

Human beings are able to use the additional cues of context and body language to interpret a gaze. Most people find a steady gaze to be pleasant if they like the gazer and want to be liked by him. The same gaze will be irritating if they think the gazer has undue sexual interests or is seething with anger. If the gazer's stare seems meaningless and vacant, and no other cues allow one to interpret his intentions, the gaze will be even more disturbing.

Usually, though, people within a culture show an excellent ability to decode the message sent in a look. They can readily distinguish affectionate gazes, worried gazes that request help, or threatening gazes. Although the specific meaning of a look may shift across cultures, people everywhere recognize that a gaze means that the other person is attending, and therefore requires a reaction.

It was stated earlier that if A likes B, A will look more at B. It is also the case that if B is looked at a lot by A, B will recognize that A likes him or her and will in turn like A. According to the Argyle and Dean theory, however, *two much gaze* will be felt to be too intimate a signal and cause anxiety and withdrawal.

Among animals, gaze is often used as a threat signal. Exline and Yellin found that if an experimenter stared at a monkey (in a cage), the monkey attacked or gave a threat display on 76 percent of the trials. If the experimenter looked away again, there was an aggressive response in only 40 percent of the trials. Phoebe Ellsworth and her coworkers found that continuous staring caused motorists to move off more rapidly from stoplights. Peter Marsh has found that a glance by a member of a rival group of football fans may be enough to start a fight, with cries of "He looked at me!" However, gaze is only seen as a threat under certain social conditions. Ellsworth has recently reported that a stare by someone who has collapsed on the subway leads to help rather than flight or attack.

Gaze is used to some extent as a clue for emotions and personality. If the same person is judged by one group of subjects who each see him looking at them 15 percent of the time and by another group who see him looking at them 85 percent of the time, in the low level of gaze he is seen as nervous and lacking in confidence, evasive, cautious and defensive while with the high level of gaze he is seen as self-confident. The way the eyes are opened is also made use of. Nummenmaa in Finland found that emotions could be decoded with above-chance accuracy from photos of the eyes alone, while for certain mixed emotional states, like pleasure and anger, this was the most informative area of the face.

There is quite a good correspondence between the encoding and decoding of gaze. For example, if A likes B, A looks more at B, and under many conditions this is correctly decoded by B. It is likely that when there is such a match, the decoded message has been learned or has developed during evolution. Gaze can also be a signal for submission and appeasement. A threatened animal submits by looking away—to avoid the terrifying sight of the other. This act becomes ritualized as an appeasement signal and eventually becomes an unlearned signal for it.

However, the meaning of gaze varies, as we have seen, with the situation: a glance from a stranger can be decoded as threat or an appeal for help. The universal meaning given to gaze is that the other is attending; this produces a heightened arousal, a preparedness to deal with an interpersonal event. But different events can be expected, the arousal labeled accordingly, and the gaze interpreted differently.

It should be added that being looked at is reinforcing under many conditions, for example, when a mother is looked at by her child and vice versa. On the other hand, being stared at by strangers or being the object of attention of a lot of people can be very disturbing.

## GAZE AND SEQUENCES OF SOCIAL BEHAVIOR

Social interaction consists of a rapid and closely coordinated exchange of verbal and nonverbal signals. Gaze plays several central roles in this process, operating simultaneously as channel and signal. Let us look first at some of the basic situations. For two people, sitting about 6 feet apart, talking on fairly easy subjects such as favorite television programs, the levels of gaze are typically as shown in Table 1. These figures refer to gaze at the other person's eyes or face.

TABLE 1.  **Typical levels of gaze**

| | Level of gaze (%) | Length of glance (sec) |
|---|---|---|
| Individual gaze | 61 | 2.95 |
| while listening | 75 | |
| while looking | 41 | |
| Mutual gaze | 31 | 1.18 |

However these levels of gaze vary greatly between different social encounters. Here are some of the main variables.

1. *Liking for the other person.* The level of gaze is greater to a person who is liked rather than disliked.
2. *Distance.* Gaze is greater at greater distances.
3. *Presence of relevant objects.* The results given above were obtained in a rather bare laboratory, with no objects present which were relevant to the topic of interaction. In a later experiment, we studied the amount of gaze at another person when various objects were introduced. In some conditions a map of central Europe was placed between two interactors; sometimes this was relevant to their conversation, for example, discussing a possible vacation in the area; sometimes it was possible to look out of the window. It was found that gaze at the other person drops from 76.6 percent to 6.4 perecnt when a relevant map is present, and that gaze is mainly directed to the map (81.9 percent). People look either at each other, at objects relevant to the encounter, or vaguely into space and out of the window.

We now turn to the more detailed linkages between gaze and other aspects of social interaction. The conceptual model which led us to the study of gaze in the first place was the social skill model (Fig. 2), which uses the analogies between social behavior and the performance of a motor skill.

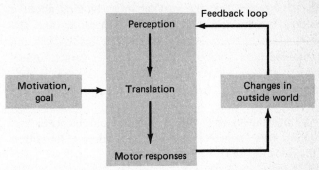

*Figure 2. Social skill model.*

People in social situations and performers of motor skills (e.g., car drivers) are pursuing goals that can be defined in terms of the desired responses of other people or physical objects. They make skilled moves designed to bring about these consequences, and they modify their behavior as the result of feedback. This feedback is partly obtained by looking in the right direction at the right time and interpreting what is seen. It is found that gaze is timed to provide feedback at those points where it is most needed—at the ends of long utterances and at grammatical breaks in these utterances. Adam Kendon studied the timing of gaze in relation to speech for ten subjects, with the results shown in Figure 3.

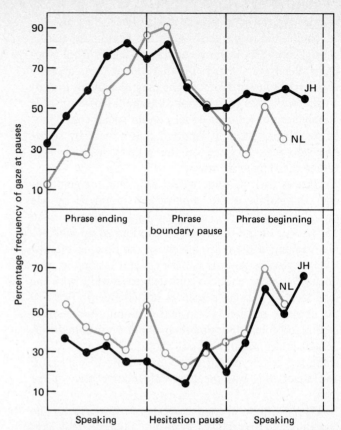

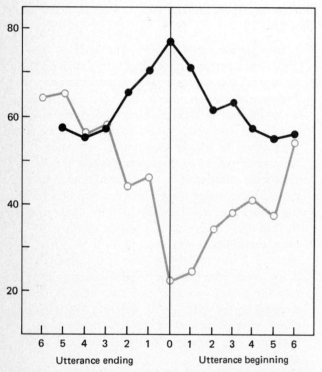

*Figure 3. Patterns of gaze at the beginning and end of long utterances (from Kendon, 1967). Frequency of looks at other person, before and after the beginning (broken line) and ending (continuous line) of long utterances.*

It can be seen that the speaker starts looking about a second before the end of a long utterance, and the other person starts looking away. The feedback being obtained here is about whether the other person understood, agreed, and so on with the utterance that is ending. Kendon also found gazes at grammatical breaks during utterances—perhaps to obtain feedback on whether the listener was willing to continue listening. There was, however, *reduced* gaze during hesitation pauses (Fig. 4).

*Figure 4. Patterns of gaze at phrase boundaries and hesitation pauses (from Kendon, 1967). Data from two individuals summarizing 48 phrase boundaries and 43 hesitation pauses.*

So while a person is speaking—sending verbal signals to another—the other person is sending back nonverbal signals. The verbal and nonverbal signals go in opposite directions simultaneously. An utterance may be altered when it is halfway through if feedback from the other indicates lack of understanding or dislike. And this feedback is mainly obtained by gaze at crucial points during the utterance. It is useless to say something unless someone else is listening. The same applies to nonverbal messages. As the social skill model suggests, there has to be monitoring of the other's responses, to make sure that the message has been received and to find out what effect it had. So an accompanying gaze is an important part of both verbal and nonverbal social acts.

As was shown in Table 1, there is much more gaze while listening than when speaking—nearly twice as much. The probable reason for this is that while people are speaking most attention is directed toward planning what is to be said, particularly at the beginning of utterances. People nearly always look away when they are asked a question. There has been a lot of research into the direction of looking away. There is some evidence that questions about words produce a shift to the right (and downward), while questions about spatial matters lead to a shift of gaze to the left (and upward). Other studies shown that electrical stimulation of one side of the brain produces a gaze shift in the opposite direction. So verbal questions, which primarily activate the left hemisphere tend to produce a right shift, while spatial questions, which activate the right hemisphere more, do the opposite.

During conversation, two or more individuals have to take turns speaking and usually succeed in doing so without much overlap or interruption. This process of turn taking is mainly managed by a number of non-verbal cues, of which gaze is one. Figure 3 shows the long gaze used at the ends of utterances by the speaker to collect feedback on how the utterance was received. The same gaze functions as a full-stop signal; in the same study it was found that if there was no terminal gaze, it was some time before the other person replied. So the same glance serves to collect feedback for the speaker and as a full-stop signal for the listener. However, closer inspections of Figure 3 raises an interesting question. If the listener is not looking when the terminal gaze takes place, how does he know about it? We do not know, but it could be either by peripheral vision or by seeing the beginning of the terminal gaze and the larger bodily movements that go with it. There are a number of other signals for negotiating turn taking: A speaker who wants to hold the floor, for example, does not pause at the end of a sentence, and gives no terminal gaze, but keeps a hand in midgesture. If he is interrupted, he increases the volume of his voice, and if necessary speaks louder than the interrupter. Other signals are used by those who want to take or decline the floor.

We have shown that gaze acts as a channel (for the speaker) and as a synchronizing signal (for the listener). Gaze acts as a signal in several other ways during conversation. A speaker may use gaze as an emphasizer, to underline part of what he says. Sometimes this is done by an "eye flash," a sudden widening of the eye. A speaker can look in particular directions, instead of pointing at objects or persons, to suggest, for example, who should speak next. A listener indicates his general level of attention by looking, nodding and smiling, and also his interest or approval of particular points in utterances. These glances act as reinforcers, increasing the speaker's tendency to talk about particular topics. While glances act as reinforcers, gaze can itself be reinforced: If A smiles when looked at by B, B's level of gaze increases. In addition, increased gaze by one person leads to increased gaze by another, either through reinforcement or imitation.

We tried to separate some of the different functions of gaze in an experiment in which two subjects conversed across a one-way screen, so that A could see B, but B could not see A (Fig. 5).

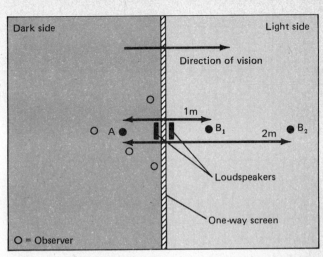

*Figure 5. Laboratory arrangements for experiment on the different functions of gaze.*

The amount of time each person looked in the direction of the other's face was recorded. It was found that A (who could see) looked 67 percent of the time while B (who could not) looked only 23 percent of the time. Person A looked to receive information; however, B still looked 23 percent of the time, accompanied by nods, smiles, eyebrow raises, and so on, apparently to *send* information. Also, the level of gaze was higher when interactors had real conversations (67 percent) than when they exchanged monologues (46 percent), probably reflecting the need for gaze as a synchronizing signal in the real conversation.

We have seen that the sequence of glances is of central importance in conversation. This is probably true of social behavior in general: Two individuals need to know that the other is attending, and gaze can be used to send a variety of messages. Gaze also plays a part in rather more complex social sequences like greetings and partings. The different phases of a greeting have been described by Kendon and others. There is a mutual gaze in the first stage, the "distant salutation"; aversion during the approach phase, and a second mutual gaze in the third, or close, phase, when a bodily contact also occurs. A similar set of phases in reverse occur in partings, again with two mutual glances.

## INDIVIDUAL DIFFERENCES IN GAZE

Individuals vary a lot in how much they look and in other measures of gaze. They are fairly consistent across situations, so that if person A looks more and with longer glances than B, this is the case when interacting with C, D, and E. However, the social situation also affects gaze: As we have seen, people look more at people they like, when at greater distances, and so on. Both person and situation affect how much a person will look.

## Autistic Children

Autistic children show so much gaze aversion that this is one of the main criteria for diagnosis. They look in very short glances (½ sec.) or through their fingers, and often turn their backs or pull hats over their heads. Richer and Coss found that autistic children look more at an experimenter when he covered his eyes. While they avoid eyes and faces, they do not avoid all social contact, and can be led by the hand or will sit on a knee with gaze averted.

## Schizophrenics

Schizophrenics have been found to have approximately 65 percent less gaze than have normal controls, as well as shorter glances. However, these results were obtained when the patients were talking to psychologists about their personal problems. Rutter has recently found that schizophrenic patients look just as much as nonpsychiatric hospital patient controls if talking about an impersonal topic. It has sometimes been reported that schizophrenics who have spent a long time in an institution avert gaze more, but Rutter found only a small difference in this direction. Williams, however, did find that schizophrenics averted gaze and preferred to look at television when a stranger approached them and tried to start a conversation. It seems that schizophrenics use gaze aversion as a method of avoiding unwanted encounters.

## Depression

It has been found that depressives have a reduced level of gaze and look downward, again when talking to psychologists about their problems. As with schizophrenics, their level of gaze is much the same as normals when they are talking about impersonal topics.

## Neurotics

There is no general gaze pattern for neurotics, but we have found that quite a number have some aversion of gaze (18 percent), while others stare inappropriately (34 percent), at least during clinic conversations with strangers.

## Extraverts

A lot of British studies have compared the gaze of people high and low on questionnaire measures of extraversion. It is always found that extraverts look more than introverts, but there are conflicting results on the details. The best-confirmed finding is that extraverts glance more frequently, especially while talking, and that they look for a greater percentage of the time.

## Sex

Females look more than males, on all indexes of gaze. The difference is greatest for mutual gaze and for looking while talking. Why do females look more? It has been found that girls attend to faces more than boys do at the age of six months, so there may be an innate difference. On the other hand, this early difference increases during childhood, and is greater for adults. It seems likely that gaze is used more for affiliative purposes by females, in addition to which affiliative needs are stronger in females. Furthermore, being looked at for a female is interpreted in terms of affiliation or sexual choice, rather than threat. Argyle and Williams found that young women in mixed sex encounters felt "observed," reflecting the relation between the sexes at the time.

## THE BIOLOGICAL AND SOCIAL ORIGINS OF GAZE

Gaze appears, both as signal and channel, quite early in the evolutionary scale. Its earliest use is as a threat signal, to provide a defense against predators. Some butterflies, for example, have developed eye patterns on their wings. Blest found that if these are removed, birds attack the butterflies more readily. However, work by Scaife suggests that the function of eyespots is to deflect attacks from the real eyes. Some fish have eyespots that expand during fights; it seems as if these spots provoke attack when small and encourage avoidance when large. Similar considerations may apply to primate facial-threat displays, involving circular designs of eyebrows and other features that produce an enlarged eye-pattern display (Fig. 6).

Coss has found that two pairs of concentric circles horizontally arranged produced aversive behavior in animals, while pupil dilation produced the same effect in humans. However, this does not prove that there is an innate human reaction to eyes, for it might have been acquired in infancy.

Michael Chance has observed that in groups of primates there is an "attention structure," in which attention is directed upward to more dominant animals —from infants to mothers, from mothers to mates, and from subordinate males to dominant males. This serves to maintain both social cohesion and the dominance hierarchy and makes rapid response to the initiative of leaders possible. This gaze pattern also reflects the social bonds in the group. Izard and Walker found that severing the facial muscles of rhesus monkey mothers and infants led to less affiliative and more aggressive behavior. This suggests that bonding requires visual awareness of facial responsiveness, rather than mutual gaze alone. Gaze in humans operates rather differently from gaze in animals; it is closely linked with speech in most kinds of interaction, and it is used more for affiliation than for threat.

Pygmy marmoset
*(Cebuella pygmaea)*

White-throated capuchin
*(Cebus capuchin)*

White-collared mangabey
*(Cerocebus torquatus)*

Dusky leaf-monkey
*(Presbytus obscurus)*

Bornean orangutan
*(Pongo p. pygmaeus)*

Man
*(Homo sapiens)*

*Figure 6. Examples of eye rings (from Coss, 1972; reprinted Argyle and Cook, 1976).*

Gaze operates as a social signal early in the life of human infants. By the third week of life infants smile at a nodding head, and by the end of the fourth week there is mutual gaze between mother and infant. Experiments by Fantz and others show that this response is partly innate in the sense that infants have an unlearned response to stimuli with certain properties, and their eyes are focused at a range of from 20 to 30 centimeters; the mother's eyes while the baby is feeding fit this specification, and the pattern of the mother's eyes and face is learned. Infants respond positively to eyes and eyelike patterns: they smile, and their pupils dilate. In addition, gaze plays an important part in the development of attachment to the mother. Martin Richards at Cambridge has found that at eight weeks mother-infant interaction consists of a number of repeated cycles in which, for example, the mother smiles, looks, vocalizes and moves rhythmically toward and away from the baby. The latter responds by periods of rapt attention and widening of the eyes. Bruner and colleagues at Oxford have found similar repeated routines at 7 to 17 months, with games like peek-a-boo, which consist basically of making and breaking mutual gaze. Schaffer and Emerson found that while all infants seek the company of their mothers, some of them are content with visual contact. There are presumably differences of early learning in connection with gaze that generate this reaction as well as the opposite one of autism. The coordination of gaze with speech is not found in young

children, but develops later. The level of gaze declines up to adolescence and then increases again.

The gaze phenomena that we have described have been found in all cultures studied so far. However, there are differences, particularly in the average level of gaze. A number of cultures, known as "contact cultures," where people stand closer and touch each other a lot, gaze more than Americans or western Europeans. It has been found by Watson and others that gaze levels are high for Arabs, South Americans Greeks and Italians. On the other hand, there are rather low levels of gaze in certain South American Indian tribes. The finding that gaze is higher for contact cultures goes against the affiliative balance hypothesis: we do not know whether social relations are more intimate (in terms of subjective feelings) in these cultures, or whether the same signals simply have different meanings there.

Cultural differences in gaze can be regarded as rules governing the use of gaze. Children are often instructed not to stare at strangers, or to look at the person they are talking to. In some cultures there are taboos: It is common not to be allowed to look at mothers-in-law, and in some South American Indian tribes a storyteller faces the back of the hut. In Japan people do not look others in the eye much. It would be unacceptable in the United States or Europe to look at certain parts of another's anatomy or to look just past their heads. In every culture people notice if gaze is done incorrectly, indicating the presence of cultural rules. Too much gaze is regarded as intrusive or disrespectful, especially by Africans, Asians, and Indians, while too little gaze is regarded as insincere and cold, especially by Arabs and South Americans.

Gaze can also vary in meaning between different cultures. The most striking example is belief in the evil eye, which is still common in some Mediterranean countries. It is believed that certain women or priests, who have squints or deep-set eyes, cast a curse on people they look at, particularly brides on their wedding day. It is interesting to note that in a study at Stanford University by Gifford, 72 percent of men and 84 percent of women thought they could tell when someone behind their backs was looking at them. These ideas perhaps arise out of the discomfort of being stared at by strangers, combined with fallacious ideas about the physics of vision and a belief in witchcraft.

## SUMMARY

We can now put together the main points of a biological-cultural explanation of the phenomenon of gaze. Animals and people look at each other when they are interested in the other and their reactions, particularly when social behavior is directed or is about to be directed toward the other. This leads to gaze acquiring meaning as a social signal. There may be evolutionary development of gaze as a ritualized signal whose meaning is innate, as in the case of eyespots and other threat signals. There may be individual learning of the significance of certain kinds of gaze, for example, learning the meaning of the evil eye. Especially for humans, the meaning of gaze varies with contextual cues, such as facial expression and the general social setting. Gaze comes to play a central part in the process of communication, and is closely coordinated with the timing of speech, to provide feedback, to manage synchronizing, and to add to the meaning of utterances. These skills appear to be acquired during childhood and are learned along with the use of language. The use of gaze can go wrong in a variety of way; aversion of gaze and staring are common in mental patients.

# GROUPTHINK

by Irving L. Janis

**A Yale psychologist isolates the disease that caused our worst foreign policy fiascoes: a compulsion by the decision-makers to have each other's approval, even at the cost of critical thinking.**

The idea of "groupthink" occurred to me while reading Arthur M. Schlesinger's chapters on the Bay of Pigs in *A Thousand Days*. At first I was puzzled: How could bright men like John F. Kennedy and his advisers be taken in by such a stupid, patchwork plan as the one presented to them by the C.I.A. representatives? I began wondering if some psychological contagion of complacency might have interfered with their mental alertness.

I kept thinking about this notion until one day I found myself talking about it in a seminar I was conducting at Yale on the psychology of small groups. I suggested that the poor decision-making performance of those high officials might be akin to the lapses in judgment of ordinary citizens who become more concerned with retaining the approval of the fellow members of their work group than with coming up with good solutions to the tasks at hand.

When I re-read Schlesinger's account I was struck by many further observations that fit into exactly the pattern of concurrence-seeking that has impressed me in my research on other face-to-face groups when a "we" feeling of solidarity is running high. I concluded that a group process was subtly at work in Kennedy's team which prevented the members from debating the real issues posed by the C.I.A.'s plan and from carefully appraising its serious risks.

By now I was sufficiently fascinated by what I called the "groupthink" hypothesis to start looking into similar historic

*Irving L. Janis, professor of psychology at Yale, teaches courses in attitude change, decision-making, leadership and small-group behavior. This material is adapted from his "Victims of Groupthink: A Psychological Study of Foreign Policy Decisions and Fiascoes," just published by Houghton Mifflin.*

fiascoes. I selected for intensive analysis three that were made during the administrations of three other American presidents: Franklin D. Roosevelt (failure to be prepared for Pearl Harbor), Harry S. Truman (the invasion of North Korea) and Lyndon B. Johnson (escalation of the Vietnam war). Each decision was a group product, issuing from a series of meetings held by a small and cohesive group of government officials and advisers. In each case I found the same kind of detrimental group process that was at work in the Bay of Pigs decision.

In my earlier research with ordinary citizens I had been impressed by the effects—both unfavorable and favorable—of the social pressures that develop in cohesive groups: in infantry platoons, air crews, therapy groups, seminars and self-study or encounter groups. Members tend to evolve informal objectives to preserve friendly intra-group relations, and this becomes part of the hidden agenda at their meetings. When conducting research on groups of heavy smokers, for example, at a clinic established to help people stop smoking, I noticed a seemingly irrational tendency for the members to exert pressure on each other to increase their smoking as the time for the final meeting approached. This appeared to be a collusive effort to display mutual dependence and resistance to the termination of the sessions.

Sometimes, even long before the final separation, pressures toward uniformity subverted the fundamental purpose. At the second meeting of one group of smokers, consisting of 12 middle-class American men and women, two of the most dominant members took the position that heavy smoking was an almost incurable addiction. Most of the others soon agreed that nobody could be expected to cut down drastically. One man took issue with this consensus, arguing that he had stopped smoking since joining the group and that everyone else could do the same. His declaration was followed by an angry discussion. Most of the others ganged up against the man who was deviating from the consensus.

At the next meeting the deviant an-

nounced that he had made an important decision. "When I joined," he said, "I agreed to follow the two main rules required by the clinic—to make a conscientious effort to stop smoking, and to attend every meeting. But I have learned that you can only follow one of the rules, not both. I will continue to attend every meeting but I have gone back to smoking two packs a day and I won't make any effort to stop again until after the last meeting." Whereupon the other members applauded, welcoming him back to the fold.

No one mentioned that the whole point of the meetings was to help each person to cut down as rapidly as possible. As a psychological consultant to the group, I tried to call this to the members' attention and so did my collaborator, Dr. Michael Kahn. But the members ignored our comments and reiterated their consensus that heavy smoking was an addiction from which no one would be cured except by cutting down gradually over a long period of time.

This episode—an extreme form of groupthink—was only one manifestation of a general pattern that the group displayed. At every meeting the members were amiable, reasserted their warm feelings of solidarity and sought concurrence on every important topic, with no reappearance of the unpleasant bickering that would spoil the cozy atmosphere. This tendency could be maintained, however, only at the expense of ignoring realistic challenges—like those posed by the psychologists.

The term "groupthink" is of the same order as the words in the "newspeak" vocabulary that George Orwell uses in *1984*—a vocabulary with terms such as "doublethink" and "crimethink." By putting "groupthink" with those Orwellian words, I realize that it takes on an invidious connotation. This is intentional: groupthink refers to a deterioration of mental efficiency, reality testing and moral judgment that results from in-group pressures.

When I investigated the Bay of Pigs invasion and other fiascoes, I found that there were at least six major defects in

with a rival nation, policy-makers constituting an amiable group find it relatively easy to authorize dehumanizing solutions such as large-scale bombings. An affable group of government officials is unlikely to pursue the difficult issues that arise when alternatives to a harsh military solution come up for discussion. Nor are they inclined to raise ethical issues that imply that this "fine group of ours, with its humanitarianism and its high-minded principles, could adopt a course that is inhumane and immoral."

The greater the threat to the self-esteem of the members of a cohesive group, the greater will be their inclination to resort to concurrence-seeking at the expense of critical thinking. Symptoms of groupthink will therefore be found most often when a decision poses a moral dilemma, especially if the most advantageous course requires the policy-makers to violate their own standards of humanitarian behavior. Each member is likely to become more dependent than ever on the in-group for maintaining his self-image as a decent human being and will therefore be more strongly motivated to maintain group unity by striving for concurrence.

decision-making which contributed to failures to solve problems adequately.

First, the group's discussions were limited to a few alternatives (often only two) without a survey of the full range of alternatives. Second, the members failed to re-examine their initial decision from the standpoint of non-obvious drawbacks that had not been originally considered. Third, they neglected courses of action initially evaluated as unsatisfactory; they almost never discussed whether they had overlooked any non-obvious gains.

Fourth, members made little or no attempt to obtain information from experts who could supply sound estimates of losses and gains to be expected from alternative courses. Fifth, selective bias was shown in the way the members reacted to information and judgments from experts, the media and outside critics; they were only interested in facts and opinions that supported their preferred

policy. Finally, they spent little time deliberating how the policy might be hindered by bureaucratic inertia, sabotaged by political opponents or derailed by the accidents that happen to the best of well-laid plans. Consequently, they failed to work out contingency plans to cope with foreseeable setbacks that could endanger their success.

I was surprised by the extent to which the groups involved in these fiascoes adhered to group norms and pressures toward uniformity, even when their policy was working badly and had unintended consequences that disturbed the conscience of the members. Members consider loyalty to the group the highest form of morality. That loyalty requires each member to avoid raising controversial issues, questioning weak arguments or calling a halt to soft-headed thinking.

Paradoxically, soft-headed groups are likely to be extremely hard-hearted toward out-groups and enemies. In dealing

Although it is risky to make huge inferential leaps from theory to practice, we should not be inhibited from drawing tentative inferences from these fiascoes. Perhaps the worst mistakes can be prevented if we take steps to avoid the circumstances in which groupthink is most likely to flourish. But all the prescriptive hypotheses that follow must be validated by systematic research before they can be applied with any confidence.

The leader of a policy-forming group should, for example, assign the role of critical evaluator to each member, encouraging the group to give high priority to airing objections and doubts. He should also be impartial at the outset, instead of stating his own preferences and expectations. He should limit his briefings to unbiased statements about the scope of the problem and the limitations of available resources.

The organization should routinely

## Pearl Harbor: Geniality and Security

establish several independent planning and evaluation groups to work on the same policy question, each carrying out its deliberations under a different leader.

One or more qualified colleagues within the organization who are not core members of the policy-making group should be invited to each meeting and encouraged to challenge the views of the core members.

At every meeting, at least one member should be assigned the role of devil's advocate, to function like a good lawyer in challenging the testimony of those who advocate the majority position.

Whenever the policy issue involves relations with a rival nation, a sizable block of time should be spent surveying all warning signals from the rivals and constructing alternative scenarios.

After reaching a preliminary consensus the policy-making group should hold a "second chance" meeting at which all the members are expected to express their residual doubts and to rethink the entire issue They might take as their model a statement made by Alfred P. Sloan, a former chairman of General Motors, at a meeting of policymakers:

"Gentlemen, I take it we are all in complete agreement on the decision here. Then I propose we postpone further discussion until our next meeting to give ourselves time to develop disagreement and perhaps gain some understanding of what the decision is all about."

It might not be a bad idea for the second-chance meeting to take place in a relaxed atmosphere far from the executive suite, perhaps over drinks. According to a report by Herodotus dating from about 450 B.C., whenever the ancient Persians made a decision following sober deliberations, they would always reconsider the matter under the influence of wine. Tacitus claimed that during Roman times the Germans also had a custom of arriving at each decision twice—once sober, once drunk.

Some institutionalized form of allowing second thoughts to be freely expressed might be remarkably effective for breaking down a false sense of unanimity and related illusions, without endangering anyone's reputation or liver.

On the night of Dec. 6, 1941—just 12 hours before the Japanese struck—Admiral Husband E. Kimmel (Commander in Chief of the Pacific Fleet) attended a dinner party given by his old crony, Rear Admiral H. Fairfax Leary, and his wife. Other members of the in-group of naval commanders and their wives were also present. Seated next to Admiral Kimmel was Fanny Halsey, wife of Admiral Halsey, who had left Hawaii to take his task force to the Far East. Mrs. Halsey said that she was certain the Japanese were going to attack. "She was a brilliant woman," according to Captain Joel Bunkley, who described the party, "but everybody thought she was crazy."

Admiral Leary, at a naval inquiry in 1944, summarized the complacency at that dinner party and at the daily conferences held by Admiral Kimmel during the preceding weeks. When asked whether any thought had been given to the possibility of a surprise attack by the Japanese, he said, "We all felt that the contingency was remote . . . and the feeling strongly existed that the Fleet would have adequate warning of any chance of an air attack." The same attitude was epitomized in testimony given by Captain J. B. Earle, chief of staff, Fourteenth Naval District. "Somehow or other," he said, "we always felt that 'it couldn't happen here.'"

From the consistent testimony given by Admiral Kimmel's advisers, they all acted on the basis of an "unwarranted feeling of immunity from attack," though they had been given a series of impressive warnings that they should be prepared for war with Japan.

Most illuminating of the norm-setting behavior that contributed to the complacency of Kimmel's in-group is a brief exchange between Admiral Kimmel and Lieutenant Commander Layton. Perturbed by the loss of radio contact with the Japanese aircraft carriers, Admiral Kimmel asked Layton on Dec. 1, 1941, to check with the Far East Command for additional information. The next day, discussing the lost carriers again with Layton, he remarked jokingly: "What, you don't know where the carriers are?

Do you mean to say that they could be rounding Diamond Head [at Honolulu] and you wouldn't know it?" Layton said he hoped they would be sighted well before that.

This exchange implies an "atmosphere of geniality and security." Having relegated the Japanese threat to the category of laughing matters, the admiral was making it clear that he would be inclined to laugh derisively at anyone who thought otherwise. "I did not at any time suggest," Layton later acknowledged at a Congressional hearing, "that the Japanese carriers were under radio silence approaching Oahu. I wish I had."

But the admiral's foolish little joke may have induced Layton to remain silent about any vague, lingering doubts he may have had. Either man would risk the scornful laughter of the other—whether expressed to his face or behind his back—if he were to express second thoughts such as, "Seriously, though, shouldn't we do something about the slight possibility that those carriers might *really* be headed this way?" Because this ominous inference was never drawn, not a single reconnaissance plane was sent out to the north of the Hawaiian Islands, allowing the Japanese to win the incredible gamble they were taking in trying to send their aircraft carriers within bombing distance of Pearl Harbor without being detected.

That joking exchange was merely the visible part of a huge iceberg of solid faith in Pearl Harbor's invulnerability. If a few warm advocates of preparedness had been within the Navy group, steamed up by the accumulating warning signals, they might have been able to melt it. But they would certainly have had a cold reception. To urge a full alert would have required presenting unwelcome arguments that countered the myth of Pearl Harbor's impregnability. Anyone who was tempted to do so knew that he would be deviating from the group norm: the others were likely to consider him "crazy," just as the in-group regarded Mrs. Halsey at the dinner party on the eve of the disaster when she announced her deviant opinion that the Japanese would attack.

## A Perfect Fiasco: The Bay of Pigs

Why did President Kennedy's main advisers, whom he had selected as core members of his team, fail to pursue the issues sufficiently to discover the shaky ground on which the faulty assumptions of the Cuban invasion plan rested? Why didn't they pose a barrage of penetrating and embarrassing questions to the representatives of the C.I.A. and the Joint Chiefs of Staff? Why were they taken in by the incomplete and inconsistent answers they were given in response to the relatively few critical questions they raised?

Schlesinger says that "for all the utter irrationality with which retrospect endowed the project, it had a certain queer logic at the time as it emerged from the bowels of government." Why? What was the source of the queer logic" with which the plan was endowed? If the available accounts describe the deliberations accurately, many typical symptoms of groupthink can be discerned among the members of the Kennedy team: an illusion of invulnerability, a collective effort to rationalize their decision, an unquestioned belief in the group's inherent morality, a stereotyped view of enemy leaders as too evil to warrant genuine attempts to negotiate, and the emergence of self-appointed mind-guards.

Robert Kennedy, for example, who had been constantly informed about the Cuban invasion plan, asked Schlesinger privately why he was opposed. The President's brother listened coldly and then said: "You may be right or you may be wrong, but the President has made his mind up. Don't push it any further. Now is the time for everyone to help him all they can."

Here is a symptom of groupthink, displayed by a highly intelligent man whose ethical code committed him to freedom of dissent.

Robert Kennedy was functioning in a self-appointed role that I call being a "mind-guard." Just as a bodyguard protects the President and other high officials from physical harm, a mind-guard protects them from thoughts that might damage their confidence in the soundness of the policies which they are about to launch.

## Escalation in Vietnam: How Could It Happen?

A highly revealing episode occurred soon after Robert McNamara told a Senate committee some impressive facts about the ineffectiveness of the bombings. President Johnson made a number of bitter comments about McNamara's statement. "That military genius, McNamara, has gone dovish on me," he complained to one Senator. To someone on his White House staff he spoke even more heatedly, accusing McNamara of playing into the hands of the enemy. He drew the analogy of "a man trying to sell his house while one of his sons went to the prospective buyer to point out that

there were leaks in the basement."

This strongly suggests that Johnson regarded his in-group of policy advisers as a family and its leading dissident member as an irresponsible son who was sabotaging the family's interest. Underlying this revealing imagery are two implicit assumptions that epitomize groupthink: We are a good group, so any deceitful acts that we perpetrate are fully justified. Anyone who is unwilling to distort the truth to help us is disloyal.

This is only one of the many examples of how groupthink was manifested in Johnson's inner circle.

# Teen-age Interracial Dating

## Frank A. Petroni

# 14

Early in the still unfolding story of school desegregation, many observers were saying that what white opponents of integration were most afraid of was interracial sex. People who had been comforting themselves with such abstractions as "Negroes are OK, but I wouldn't want my daughter to marry one," now, with desegregation, had suddenly to cope (they thought) with a real possibility, not a farfetched hypothesis.

Be this as it may, I doubt there are many Americans who have not, at one time or another had to cope with the question of interracial sex, either in imagination—"what would happen if . . ."—or in fact. Interracial dating and interracial marriage are social realities, however much white racists and black nationalists may deplore it.

A few years ago, while I was with the Menninger Foundation in Topeka, Kansas, my wife and I had an opportunity to study the extent of, and students' feelings about, interracial dating at a desegregated high school. Our procedure was rather unorthodox. Instead of trying to gather a 5 percent random sample of the 3,000-member student body, we began slowly by letting our initial student contacts tell us what they considered to be the principal "types" of student in the school. They distinguished 12 such types: middle-class whites, hippies, peaceniks, white trash, "sedits" (upper-class blacks), elites, conservatives, racists, niggers, militants, athletes and hoods. Then, and again through our initial contacts, we brought in other students and roughly classified them according to "type." In this way, I believe we got a representative cross section of the social world of this high school. We interviewed the boys and girls in groups of three or four, and in time 25 groups came to our house for these conversations. We had two refusals: a black girl canceled her appointment after Martin Luther King was killed, and a boy told us he wouldn't talk to white people.

Few topics demonstrate the multiple pressures students are subject to better than interracial dating. These pressures come from parents, teachers, counselors, school administrators and peers. However, mixed dating is emphatically not a barometer of the amount of "integration" in a desegrated school; that is not the reason we chose to study it.

Needless to say, the students did not all share the same point of view on interracial dating. Yet, most of them—independent of race—did feel that it was none of the school's business: if students wanted to date interracially, the school had no right to stop them.

### White Boys and Black Girls

Not one student knew of a case of interracial dating involving a white boy and a black girl. There was considerable speculation about why. A conservative white girl said that white boys are too proud to date blacks. The two white boys with her disagreed: both said that it's because black girls aren't as pretty as white girls. One of the two also suggested that blacks and whites have little in common and so he would not consider dating a black. Note the popular stereotypes in this answer:

Well, there are cultural differences, and their attitudes are different. I think that's what makes the difference. They're easygoing. They like to have a lot of fun. They don't think about the future, about things that are important like getting a job, or supporting a family. They don't try for grades. They're just out to have a good time.

Even when black girls met an individual's standard of physical attractiveness, however, white boys spoke of other obstacles: where to go, how to ignore community disapproval and what to do about family and friends who disapprove. These conflicts are cogently summarized in the response of a white boy who considered dating a black:

I think if you dated a Negro, you would lose a lot of so-called friends. But you would probably gain some Negro friends. I contemplated asking this Negro girl for a date, but I chickened out. I thought, where would I take her? The only place where people wouldn't stare at me would be a drive-in movie, and I don't have a car. If you went to a restaurant, you would get dirty looks from people. I couldn't take her home and introduce her to my mom; she'd probably kill me.

Social obstacles apart, there is some doubt in my mind whether a black girl, in the school we studied, would go out with a white boy even if asked. Each black girl we interviewed was asked, "Suppose a white boy asked you out, how easy would it be for you to accept?" One girl answered: "Any white boy who asked me out, I would know what he wants. For a Negro boy to have a white girl is some sort of status symbol, but if a white boy asked me out, it would be a step down for him. I would think he wants something I'm not about to give him."

Other black girls spoke of the double standard between boys and girls, and how girls were less free to date interracially because their reputations would be ruined. Fear for one's reputation was also a factor among white girls. The students associated interracial dating with sex;

and girls, be they black or white, stood to lose the most. Yet sex was not always associated with dating. There was no reference to sex when respondents talked about dating within one's race. Sometimes the reference to sex in interracial dating was subtle, but nonetheless it was present. A white girl's comment demonstrates this: "When you think of mixed dating, you always think of a colored boy with a white girl. And you always think it is the white girl who is low. If it was a white boy with a colored girl, then it would be the white boy who was low."

When asked for the meaning of low, another white girl said: "Well, generally the public thinks that the girl has low standards and low morals, if she's willing to go out with a Negro."

Particularly among "elite" blacks, parental disapproval of interracial dating also stood between black young women and dates with white boys. Most of the black students in this strata stated that their parents would not tolerate interracial dating. The parents expected their children to compete with white students academically, for school offices, and in extracurricular activities; socially, however, they expected them to stay with blacks.

Still other respondents saw the white boys' reluctance to date blacks as essentially a matter of status considerations. If the belief that *all* whites are better than *all* blacks is general in this society (and it showed up among some of the blacks in our sample as well), then the response of an 18-year-old black girl, who was given the highest academic award the school has to offer, makes sense:

White boys would be scared to ask us out anyway. The Negro boys will ask white girls out, but white boys will never ask Negro girls out. For a Negro boy, going out with a white girl is an accomplishment; it raises his status, even if the white girl is lower-class. All white kids are supposed to be better than Negro kids. If a white boy dated a Negro, even if the white boy was one of the "trashy" kind, and the girl was, say me, his status would drop. They would ask him if he was hard-up or something. White boys would be stepping down if they asked Negro girls for dates.

Aside from the black girl's fear of parental disapproval and loss of her reputation, we were told that few blacks would accept a date from a white boy because of pressures from black young men, who would object if black girls dated whites. However, this pressure doesn't appear to count for much with the elite, college-bound black girl; it was the athletic girl who gave us this answer. Unlike her elite counterpart, the athletic black girl was not preoccupied with achieving what the white man prized for whites: academic achievement, social popularity and a svelte figure. The reference group for these girls was the black community. A star on the girl's track team said:

No Negro girls that I know of have ever been dated by a white guy. There are some that wish they could. In fact, I know some white guys, myself, I wouldn't mind going out with, but the Negro girls are mostly afraid. Even if a white guy asked them out, they wouldn't go out with them. Negro boys don't like for Negro girls to date white guys. Sometimes I see white guys who look nice, and I stop and talk to them. The Negro boys get upset. They are real screwy. They can date white girls, but we can't date white guys.

**The Reaction of Black Males**

The black young men in our sample at times disagreed on how they would react to dating between white boys and black girls, but in general their answers fell into one of the categories predicted by the black girls. A boy, who has dated white girls, admitted to the double standard alleged by the girl athlete. He told us:

You know, I think that Negro boys would detest having a Negro girl go out with a white boy. They don't want Negro girls to date white boys. They don't like it. I feel like that, and I think I'm a hypocrite. I've been out with white girls, but I don't like it if a Negro girl goes out with a white boy. If I see a colored girl with a white boy, I think, why didn't she date me, or another Negro? What's he got that I ain't got?

Not all blacks who date whites felt this way. The young man whom we just quoted identified positively with the black community. But another young man, with a steady white girl friend, and who prized white over black, had this to say: "I don't think most of the white boys would ask Negro girls out. Maybe I shouldn't say this, but I think any Negro girl would consider it a privilege to have a white boy ask her out. I feel if a colored girl is good enough to get a white boy, they should go out together."

It was easier for most of the students, white or black, to talk about interracial dating in which the girl is white. This is the kind of dating most of them have seen. Some students, however, had seen black girls with white boys at the state university and in larger communities. One black spoke frankly of his reactions when he first saw a white man with a black woman:

You see this at the colleges [white boys with Negro girls]. You know, it's a funny thing now that you mention it, you never see Negro girls with white boys here. I was in New York once. It was kind of funny; I saw this Negro girl with a white guy. I was shocked. You know, I looked, and it seemed kind of funny to me. I mean you see white girls with Negro boys, but you never see a Negro girl with a white guy; it kind of shocks you at first.

**Black Males and White Girls**

The pressures from parents, teachers, counselors, peers and the community are also brought to bear on the black boy and white girl who cross the barrier against interracial dating. As one student poignantly put it, "For those who violate this convention, the tuition is high." Just how high is exemplified by the white girl in the most talked about relationship involving an interracial couple.

Around Christmas time, I got to know this colored guy real well and wanted to date him. There was a big mix-up; my parents didn't like it. My parents put a lot of pressure on me not to go out with him. They are the type people, like Dad, who says he's not prejudiced. He even has *them* working in his office, but he wants them to stay in their place. At school there was a lot of talking behind my back and snickering when I walked down the hallway. I tried to tell myself it didn't matter what people thought, but it still hurt. It hurt an awful lot. My parents made me feel so guilty. They made me feel so cheap. They were worried about what people would say. They made me feel like two pieces of dirt. You know, I never thought interracial dating was a good idea, but when I met this colored guy, it changed me. I never went with anyone I really liked before. I think this changes your outlook. It gives you hope, when you find someone you really like.

## Sex and Dating

That sexual intercourse is associated with interracial dating is indicated by the fact that one reaction to such dating is to question the girl's moral standards. We heard this frequently from both white girls and boys, but particularly the latter. Prior to dating a black, however, the girl's personal conduct is rarely mentioned. It seems as if the disbelief among the white community that a white girl would date a black is softened by the rationalization that she "'must be immoral." One white girl found it hard to accept this student reaction: "I got kind of sick of the kids throwing her to the dogs. There were times when you had to take a stand. You either turned the other cheek, or you fought back for her. They thought she was cheap, and they said nasty things about her. Even the guy I'm dating, he's that way, too."

However, a white girl doesn't have to date a black to have others question her morality. Just talking to a black student can result in the same labeling process. A liberal white girl, identified as a hippie, told us: "One day we were talking to some black power students in front of school. Some adults going by in cars made some filthy remarks. You can imagine what they think of white women, hanging around talking to Negroes. They shot it right out as they drove by. These are the good, white middle-class people."

A very articulate black youth described a similar incident in which he was talking to a white girl: "One time I was walking down the stairs outside school. I was standing with this white girl, and we were talking. About six white kids drove by and yelled, 'White trash, you're nothing but white trash.' I guess because she was white and I'm black, and we were talking, she was white trash."

Other blacks, aware of the white community's reaction to white girls who date or talk in public with blacks, were prevented from asking white girls out because they did not want to ruin the girls' reputations. The son of a prominent black professional, who was a football letterman, in the student government and extremely popular, refused to date a white girl for this reason.

> In general, I would say that just the fact that I was taking out a white girl, the imaginations would go wild. They think the moral standards are lower in interracial dating. There's this one white girl I goofed around with a lot. It's gone beyond the friendship stage, but we never dated. If I did go out with a white girl, it would be hard to take her anyplace. I would have to think about it for a while before I took out a white girl, because I feel she would be downgraded. I wouldn't want to ruin her reputation.

White girls who date across the color line find themselves unacceptable to white boys. Most of the students agreed that to date interracially limited a girl's field of potential dates. For many white girls, knowledge of this reaction on the part of white boys served as a deterrent to interracial dating. Nevertheless, a number of white girls told us they were attracted to certain black young men. One of the girls who did defy her society reported this also. She said, "When I was dating him, I was surprised at how many girls wanted to date colored guys. They would come up to me and ask me things. They really wanted to date colored guys, but they were afraid."

## White "Boycott"

We found, too, that the white boycott (as it were) persisted after the interracial couple no longer dated, albeit only among white boys still in school. Girls who broke off their relationship with blacks were dated by older whites in the community. But to regain admission as an acceptable date among the high school boys, a girl would have to move to a new community to lose the pejorative label, which is part of the price for dating interracially.

The black male who dates a white girl does not escape criticism from his own race, particularly the black girls. Part of their disapproval is motivated, again, by the lack of reciprocity: black girls were not dated by whites. When a high status black, generally an athlete, dated a white girl, he was replaced by neither a high status nor low status white. The black girls' resentment is summarized in the answer of one of our respondents, identified as a "militant."

> Well, in junior high, the Negro girls resented the fact that I went out with a white girl, and they really got onto me. They feel inferior. The white girls get all the guys. Some hostility between the Negro girls and white girls comes from this. The Negro girls kind of feel left out. She doesn't have white guys to date, and she doesn't have Negro guys to date. She says, "Hey, gal, you dating that Negro, and I can't get a date with him." This kind of builds up a resentment in her.

Pressure on the black male comes in two forms. First, his racial identification may be questioned. Often he is accused of thinking he is white. Second, retaliation by black girls can be more direct and swift. There were reports of boys physically beaten for dating a white girl. However, this response was the exception; it was more common for girls to spread the rumor that a boy is an "Uncle Tom."

## Parental Pressures

The double threat of losing one's reputation and losing favor among the white boys prevented many white girls from dating blacks. Yet the pressures do not end there. Interracial dating is a test of the white liberal's commitment to civil rights—a test that few have passed. A number of white students spoke of their disappointment in their parents who gave lipservice to "liberalism" but in the final analysis were prejudiced. White girls reported this more often than white boys. However, white girls *tested* their parents more often. A white girl who sensed this in one of her parents said:

> This Negro friend of mine gets along beautifully with my mother, but not my father. He senses this, too. After meeting my father, he said my father didn't like him. This is something new for me because my father and mother have always been liberal. Now that he has been over to my house a couple of times, my father is acting strange. I guess I'm learning something about him I didn't know before.

Sometimes the parental reaction isn't as subtle as the feeling that one's father doesn't approve of interracial dating. A rather tough black girl, who admitted that at one time she was a hood, told us what happened to a white girl, who used to date her ex-boy friend:

> For many Negro boys, dating white girls is their way of showing their superiority, their way of trying to hurt the white man. This boy I used to date went with a white girl once. She went through hell with her parents and everyone else to go out with him. But he didn't really care. He was just showing off. Her father even spit in her face. Her parents attacked her; they beat her and called her a slut.

Parental disapproval of interracial dating is not restricted to whites. The blacks reported a generation gap between themselves, their parents and their grandparents on this issue. In general, they reported that the intensity of the disapproval varied directly with age. Thus, grandparents showed more disapproval than parents. By and large, however, the black students agreed that the mixed couple that chooses to go out together should have that choice without interference from members of the adult community, be they parents, teachers, counselors, school administrators or anonymous members of the community.

The sample included few Mexican-Americans; those interviewed, however, reported the same phenomenon: Mexican parents, like white and black parents, objected to interracial dating. An outspoken Mexican-American girl related the Mexican parents' position. Her answer reveals the confusion parental inconsistencies can create for a young person.

Mom always said have your fun as long as you're young, and as long as you marry a Mexican. I don't feel that way. If I fall in love with a Negro, I'll marry him. If I fall in love with a white, I'll marry a white. My parents would frown on us dating a Negro, even if he has higher standards than the Mexicans we date now: even if the Negro's father was a lawyer or a doctor, and he was a better person than many of the lower-class Mexicans we date now. I don't understand it. They would rather see us go out with white people, who aren't as good, just because of skin color. They say they want the best for us; if the best meant going out with a Negro, they would say no!

## The School

As if the pressures of peers, parents and community were not enough, those who try to break down the barrier against interracial dating, or who ignore it, must also cope with teachers, counselors and school administrators, who, by and large, are united on this issue. In a word, boy-girl relationships should be white-white, or black-black, but not black-white.

It became apparent to us that when we discussed the school's position on interracial dating, the students' objections to interference became more emotionally charged. This suggested to us that the students perceived the school and its functionaries as having less legitimacy than either parents or peers in attempting to control and dictate norms for their social life.

The hostility was increased by the fact that both black and white students perceived a selective interference by the school. The teachers, counselors and school administrators did not interfere with interracial dating per se. Their interference increased in direct proportion to the white girl's social status. A black girl described this selective process to us.

I think it's their business, not the school's. She was crazy about him, and he was crazy about her. They went to school to get an education, and that's what the school should be concerned with: giving them an education. Instead, they threatened him, they said he wouldn't get an athletic scholarship. I felt this was entirely wrong for the school to interfere. It's not the school's affair to concern itself with whether or not the students have companionship. It's their business to teach. These kids aren't the only couple at school. But she was somebody. With some of the other couples, the girls aren't

important. In fact, one of the other girls is just white "trash." They don't say too much to these others; it's the important ones they want to save.

Another girl left little doubt of the painful slur implicit in this attitude of the school functionaries: "If you're a low white person, the administration could care less, but if you're a higher white person, they're worried that you might be dragged down by a Negro."

Although we cannot be certain, there is a possibility that the school's policy in these matters is dictated by the reality of the situation. There was little that the school could do to low status students who dated across the color line; the school did not have an effective lever to stop them from continuing except to inform the parents, and most parents already knew. The only other course open to them was to expel the students for the slightest infraction of the rules. Among high status students, however, the school could threaten removal from the very positions the students worked to achieve. Black athletes were called in and ordered to desist or forfeit their chances for an athletic scholarship; others were threatened with removal from the team. And white girls were told they could not run for a school office, they were not eligible to become cheerleaders and they would receive no assistance in obtaining a scholarship.

## Summary and Conclusions

Interracial dating was one of the most emotionally charged subjects in our discussions with these young people. Although we have not cited all our respondents in this brief presentation, all of them had opinions on the issue. There was complete agreement on the type of interracial dating that occurred. In no case was the male white and the female black. Generally the black male, who dated a white girl, was a high status athlete; however, by high status we are not referring to his father's socioeconomic position in the community. This may, or may not, have been high; in most cases it was not.

The fact that black students with prestige took up with white girls was a source of tension between black and white girls. More than her male counterpart, the black girl preached black separatism. Some students felt that this was because the girls did not share a sports experience such as that shared by black and white boys. On the surface, that may appear to be right. However, since there was little camaraderie between black and white athletes off the field or court, direct competition for high status blacks in the dating-mating complex seems to be a more plausible explanation for the friction between white and black girls.

While interracial dating was not commonplace, it did exist, and those who did it paid a heavy price. Payment was exacted from peers, parents, the community, teachers, counselors and other school administrators. In short, the entire social world of these teen-agers was united against them. There was no citadel to protect them. When school and peers were allied against them, there was no comfort from their parents. The couple had each other, and a small enclave of "friends," but even among the latter, the attrition rate was high.

Join this to the implication that their moral standards were lower if they dated interracially, and it is small wonder that few felt strong enough to weather all these assaults.

# 15

# Pathology of Imprisonment
## Philip G. Zimbardo

*I was recently released from solitary confinement after being held therein for 37 months [months!]. A silent system was imposed upon me and to even whisper to the man in the next cell resulted in being beaten by guards, sprayed with chemical mace, blackjacked, stomped and thrown into a strip-cell naked to sleep on a concrete floor without bedding, covering, wash basin or even a toilet. The floor served as toilet and bed, and even there the silent system was enforced. To let a moan escape your lips because of the pain and discomfort . . . resulted in another beating. I spent not days, but months there during my 37 months in solitary. . . . I have filed every writ possible against the administrative acts of brutality. The state courts have all denied the petitions. Because of my refusal to let the things die down and forget all that happened during my 37 months in solitary . . . I am the most hated prisoner in [this] penitentiary, and called a "hard-core incorrigible."*

*Maybe I am an incorrigible, but if true, it's because I would rather die than to accept being treated as less than a human being. I have never complained of my prison sentence as being unjustified except through legal means of appeals. I have never put a knife on a guard's throat and demanded my release. I know that thieves must be punished and I don't justify stealing, even though I am a thief myself. But now I don't think I will be a thief when I am released. No, I'm not rehabilitated. It's just that I no longer think of becoming wealthy by stealing. I now only think of killing—killing those who have beaten me and treated me as if I were a dog. I hope and pray for the sake of my own soul and future life of freedom that I am able to overcome the bitterness and hatred which eats daily at my soul, but I know to overcome it will not be easy.*

This eloquent plea for prison reform—for humane treatment of human beings, for the basic dignity that is the right of every American—came to me secretly in a letter from a prisoner who cannot be identified because he is still in a state correctional institution. He sent it to me because he read of an experiment I recently conducted at Stanford University. In an attempt to understand just what it means psychologically to be a prisoner or a prison guard, Craig Haney, Curt Banks, Dave Jaffe and I created our own prison. We carefully screened over 70 volunteers who answered an ad in a Palo Alto city newspaper and ended up with about two dozen young men who were selected to be part of this study. They were mature, emotionally stable, normal, intelligent college students from middle-class homes throughout the United States and Canada. They ap-

peared to represent the cream of the crop of this generation. None had any criminal record and all were relatively homogeneous on many dimensions initially.

Half were arbitrarily designated as prisoners by a flip of a coin, the others as guards. These were the roles they were to play in our simulated prison. The guards were made aware of the potential seriousness and danger of the situation and their own vulnerability. They made up their own formal rules for maintaining law, order and respect, and were generally free to improvise new ones during their eight-hour, three-man shifts. The prisoners were unexpectedly picked up at their homes by a city policeman in a squad car, searched, handcuffed, fingerprinted, booked at the Palo Alto station house and taken blindfolded to our jail. There they were stripped, deloused,

put into a uniform, given a number and put into a cell with two other prisoners where they expected to live for the next two weeks. The pay was good ($15 a day) and their motivation was to make money.

We observed and recorded on videotape the events that occurred in the prison, and we interviewed and tested the prisoners and guards at various points throughout the study. Some of the videotapes of the actual encounters between the prisoners and guards were seen on the NBC News feature "Chronolog" on November 26, 1971.

At the end of only six days we had to close down our mock prison because what we saw was frightening. It was no longer apparent to most of the subjects (or to us) where reality ended and their roles began. The majority had indeed become prisoners or guards, no longer able to clearly differentiate between role playing and self. There were dramatic changes in virtually every aspect of their behavior, thinking and feeling. In less than a week the experience of imprisonment undid (temporarily) a lifetime of learning; human values were suspended, self-concepts were challenged and the ugliest, most base, pathological side of human nature surfaced. We were horrified because we saw some boys (guards) treat others as if they were despicable animals, taking pleasure in cruelty, while other boys (prisoners) became servile, dehumanized robots who thought only of escape, of their own individual survival and of their mounting hatred for the guards.

We had to release three prisoners in the first four days because they had such acute situational traumatic reactions as hysterical crying, confusion in thinking and severe depression. Others begged to be paroled, and all but three were willing to forfeit all the money they had earned if they could be paroled. By then (the fifth day) they had been so programmed to think of themselves as prisoners that when their request for parole was denied, they returned docilely to their cells. Now, had they been thinking as college students acting in an oppressive experiment, they would have quit once they no longer wanted the $15 a day we used as our only incentive. However, the reality was not quitting an experiment but "being paroled by the parole board from the Stanford County Jail." By the last days, the earlier solidarity among the prisoners (systematically broken by the guards) dissolved into "each man for himself." Finally, when one of their fellows was put in solitary confinement (a small closet) for refusing to eat, the prisoners were given a choice by one of the guards: give up their blankets and the incorrigible prisoner would be let out, or keep their blankets and he would be kept in all night. They voted to keep their blankets and to abandon their brother.

About a third of the guards became tyrannical in their arbitrary use of power, in enjoying their control over other people. They were corrupted by the power of their roles and became quite inventive in their techniques of breaking the spirit of the prisoners and making them feel they were worthless. Some of the guards merely did their jobs as tough but fair correctional officers, and several were good guards from the prisoners' point of view since they did them small favors and were friendly. However, no good guard ever interfered with a command by any of the bad guards; they never intervened on the side of the prisoners, they never told the others to ease off because it was only an experiment, and they never even came to me as prison superintendent or experimenter in charge to complain. In part, they were good because the others were bad; they needed the others to help establish their own egos in a positive light. In a sense, the good guards perpetuated the prison more than the other guards because their own needs to be liked prevented them from disobeying or violating the implicit guards' code. At the same time, the act of befriending the prisoners created a social reality which made the prisoners less likely to rebel.

By the end of the week the experiment had become a reality, as if it were a Pirandello play directed by Kafka that just keeps going after the audience has left. The consultant for our prison, Carlo Prescott, an ex-convict with 16 years of imprisonment in California's jails, would get so depressed and furious each time he visited our prison, because of its psychological similarity to his experiences, that he would have to leave. A Catholic priest who was a former prison chaplain in Washington, D. C. talked to our prisoners after four days and said they were just like the other first-timers he had seen.

But in the end, I called off the experiment not because of the horror I saw out there in the prison yard, but because of the horror of realizing that *I* could have easily traded places with the most brutal guard or become the weakest prisoner full of hatred at being so powerless that I could not eat, sleep or go to the toilet without permission of the authorities. *I* could have become Calley at My Lai, George Jackson at San Quentin, one of the men at Attica or the prisoner quoted at the beginning of this article.

Individual behavior is largely under the control of social forces and environmental contingencies rather than personality traits, character, will power or other empirically unvalidated constructs. Thus we create an illusion of freedom by attributing more internal control to ourselves, to the individual, than actually exists. We thus underestimate the power and pervasiveness of situational controls over behavior because: a) they are often non-obvious and subtle, b) we can often avoid entering situations where we might be so controlled, c) we label as "weak" or "deviant" people in those situations who do behave differently from how we believe we would.

Each of us carries around in our heads a favorable self-image in which we are essentially just, fair, humane and understanding. For example, we could not imagine inflicting pain on others without much provocation or hurting people who had done nothing to us, who in fact were even liked by us. However, there is a growing body of social psychological research which underscores the conclusion derived from this prison study. Many people, perhaps the majority, can be made to do almost anything when put into psychologically compelling situations— regardless of their morals, ethics, values, attitudes, beliefs or personal convictions. My colleague, Stanley Milgram, has shown that more than 60 percent of the population will deliver what they think is a series of painful electric shocks to another person even after the victim cries for mercy, begs them to stop and then apparently passes out. The subjects complained that they did not want to inflict more pain but blindly obeyed the command of the authority figure (the experimenter) who said that they must go on. In my own research on violence, I have seen mild-mannered co-eds repeatedly give shocks (which they thought were causing pain) to another girl, a stranger whom they had rated very favorably, simply by being made to feel anonymous and put in a situation where they were expected to engage in this activity.

Observers of these and similar experimental situations never predict their outcomes and estimate that it is unlikely that they themselves would behave similarly. They can be so confident only when they were outside the situation. However, since the majority of people in these studies do act in non-rational, non-obvious ways, it follows that the majority of observers would also succumb to the social psychological forces in the situation.

With regard to prisons, we can state that the mere act of assigning labels to people and putting them into a situation where those labels acquire validity and meaning is sufficient to elicit pathological behavior. This pathology is not predictable from any available diagnostic indicators we have in the social sciences, and is extreme enough to modify in very significant ways fundamental attitudes and behavior. The prison situation, as presently arranged, is guaranteed to generate severe enough pathological reactions in both guards and prisoners as to debase their humanity, lower their feelings of self-worth and make it difficult for them to be part of a society outside of their prison.

For years our national leaders have been pointing to the enemies of freedom, to the fascist or communist threat to the American way of life. In so doing they have overlooked the threat of social anarchy that is building within our own country without any outside agitation. As soon as a person comes to the realization that he is being imprisoned by his society or individuals in it, then, in the best American tradition, he demands liberty and rebels, accepting death as an alternative. The third alternative, however, is to allow oneself to become a good prisoner—docile, cooperative, uncomplaining, conforming in thought and complying in deed.

Our prison authorities now point to the militant agitators who are still vaguely referred to as part of some communist plot, as the irresponsible, incorrigible troublemakers. They imply that there would be no trouble, riots, hostages or deaths if it weren't for this small band of bad prisoners. In other words, then, everything would return to "normal" again in the life of our nation's prisons if they could break these men.

The riots in prison are coming from within—from within every man and woman who refuses to let the system turn them into an object, a number, a thing or a no-thing. It is not communist inspired, but inspired by the spirit of American freedom. No man wants to be enslaved. To be powerless, to be subject to the arbitrary exercise of power, to not be recognized as a human being is to be a slave.

To be a militant prisoner is to become aware that the physical jails are but more blatant extensions of the forms of social and psychological oppression experienced daily in the nation's ghettos. They are trying to awaken the conscience of the nation to the ways in which the American ideals are being perverted, apparently in the name of justice but actually under the banner of apathy, fear and hatred. If we do not listen to the pleas of the prisoners at Attica to be treated like human beings, then we have all become brutalized by our priorities for property rights over human rights. The consequence will not only be more prison riots but a loss of all those ideals on which this country was founded.

The public should be aware that they own the prisons and that their business is failing. The 70 percent recidivism rate and the escalation in severity of crimes committed by graduates of our prisons are evidence that current prisons fail to rehabilitate the inmates in any positive way. Rather, they are breeding grounds for hatred of the establishment, a hatred that makes every citizen a target of violent assault. Prisons are a bad investment for us taxpayers. Until now we have not cared, we have turned over to wardens and prison authorities the unpleasant job of keeping people who threaten us out of our sight. Now we are shocked to learn that their management practices have failed to improve the product and instead turn petty thieves into murderers. We must insist upon new management or improved operating procedures.

The cloak of secrecy should be removed from the prisons. Prisoners claim they are brutalized by the guards, guards say it is a lie. Where is the impartial test of the truth in such a situation? Prison officials have forgotten that they work for us, that they are only public servants whose salaries are paid by our taxes. They act as if it is their prison, like a child with a toy he won't share. Neither lawyers, judges, the legislature nor the public is allowed into prisons to ascertain the truth unless the visit is sanctioned by authorities and until all is prepared for their visit. I was shocked to learn that my request to join a congressional investigating committee's tour of San Quentin and Soledad was refused, as was that of the news media.

There should be an ombudsman in every prison, not under the pay or control of the prison authority, and responsible only to the courts, state legislature and the public. Such a person could report on violations of constitutional and human rights.

Guards must be given better training than they now receive for the difficult job society imposes upon them. To be a prison guard as now constituted is to be put in a situation of constant threat from within the prison, with no social recognition from the society at large. As was shown graphically at Attica, prison guards are also prisoners of the system who can be sacrificed to the demands of the public to be punitive and the needs of politicians to preserve an image. Social scientists and business administrators should be called upon to design and help carry out this training.

The relationship between the individual (who is sentenced by the courts to a prison term) and his community must be maintained. How can a prisoner return to a dynamically changing society that most of us cannot cope with after being out of it for a number of years? There should be more community involvement in these rehabilitation centers, more ties encouraged and promoted between the trainees and family and friends, more educational opportunities to prepare them for returning to their communities as more valuable members of it than they were before they left.

Finally, the main ingredient necessary to effect any change at all in prison reform, in the rehabilitation of a single prisoner or even in the optimal development of a child is caring. Reform must start with people—especially people with power—caring about the well-being of others. Underneath the toughest, society-hating convict, rebel or anarchist is a human being who wants his existence to be recognized by his fellows and who wants someone else to care about whether he lives or dies and to grieve if he lives imprisoned rather than lives free. □

*Philip G. Zimbardo is professor of social psychology at Stanford University.*

# 16

# NEW CLUES TO THE CAUSES OF
# VIOLENCE

**Scientists studying
over-aggressive behavior
are now implicating
brain damage from
hitherto hidden sources.**

*by Gene Bylinsky*

Assassinations, vicious muggings, and the high and rising U.S. murder rate have pushed the subject of violence to the forefront among American concerns. At times, the nation appears to be oddly fascinated by the phenomenon. Consider, for example, the recent proliferation of grisly movies, some of which seem to glorify violence as a cult. We have been hearing an abundance of theories about the causes of violence, which variously attribute it to the war in Vietnam, to permissiveness, to drug addiction, to racial frustrations, and even to the legacy of the wild frontier.

Now science is venturing into this area of speculation and dispute. A broad interdisciplinary effort is getting under way to explore the biological nature and origins of violence. Biologists, biochemists, neurophysiologists, geneticists, and other natural scientists are probing with increasingly precise tools and techniques in a field where supposition and speculation have long prevailed. Their work is beginning to provide new clues to the complex ways in which the brain shapes violent behavior. It is also shedding new light on how environmental influences, by affecting the brain, can trigger violence. In time, these insights and discoveries could lead to practical action that may inhibit violent acts—perhaps, for example, a change in the way children are brought up, or treatment with "anti-violence" drugs. Such preventive steps might in the long run be more effective in controlling violent crime than either "law and order" or social reform.

By tradition, students of aggression and violence have been divided into two separate camps that hardly ever communicated with each other. On one side stood the ethologists, students of animal behavior in the wild, many of whom held that man is biologically fated to violence. At the other extreme were social scientists, who knew, or cared, little about biology. They argued that violent crime is strictly a social phenomenon, best dealt with by eliminating slums, urban crowding, and racial discrimination, and by alleviating poverty and improving the prison system.

### An imprint on the brain

The most recent research suggests that the biological and environmental causes of violence are so closely intertwined as to require a less fragmented search for remedies. The research is showing, among other things, that the environment itself can leave a physical imprint on a developing brain. The

wrong kind of upbringing can make a young animal, and probably a child too, more inclined to violent behavior as an adolescent or an adult. The hopeful augury of this research is that such behavior can be prevented if steps are taken to assure that young brains develop properly.

Until a few years ago, scientists knew comparatively little about the intricate inner mechanisms of the brain that initiate and control violence. These mechanisms lie deep in an inaccessible area called the limbic system, wrapped around the brain stem, as shown in the drawing on page 136. In the limbic system, the hypothalamus stands out as the single most important control center. Regulating many of man's primitive drives, its networks of nerve cells, or neurons, direct not only aggressive and violent behavior but also the states of sleep and wakefulness, as well as sexual and feeding behavior. The front part of the hypothalamus contains networks of nerve cells that promote calmness and tranquillity. The back part regulates aggression and rage.

### Restraining the hypothalamus

Nearby lies the almond-shaped amygdala, which restrains the impulses from the hypothalamus. Another close-by structure, the septum, seems to inhibit messages from both the hypothalamus and the amygdala. The cerebellum, the large structure at the back of the brain, filters sensory impulses. The hippocampus, a short-term memory bank in front of the cerebellum, is importantly involved in ways that brain researchers do not yet adequately understand.

All these structures are functionally as well as anatomically interrelated. Electrical signals, arising in response to sensory or internal cues (e.g., sight or thought), speed along nerve pathways to activate or block the function of other nerve cells. Chemicals such as noradrenaline and dopamine, which are normally present in the brain and are known as neurotransmitters, apparently ferry these electrical signals across the tiny gaps between nerve cells, called synapses, to such control centers as the hypothalamus. At the same time, the neurons are constantly bathed in waves of background electrical activity. In still unknown ways, this background "music" apparently conveys information, too.

So complex are the organization and function of the human brain that some of its estimated 10 billion nerve cells may have

*Research associate: Bro Uttal*

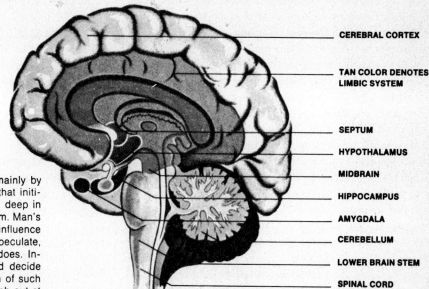

CEREBRAL CORTEX

TAN COLOR DENOTES
LIMBIC SYSTEM

SEPTUM

HYPOTHALAMUS

MIDBRAIN

HIPPOCAMPUS

AMYGDALA

CEREBELLUM

LOWER BRAIN STEM

SPINAL CORD

**The brain's decisions about violence** are made mainly by some of the structures depicted here. The centers that initiate aggressive acts, such as the hypothalamus, lie deep in the primitive part of the brain called the limbic system. Man's more intellectual cortex exercises a restraining influence over the lower brain regions. The brain, scientists speculate, reaches decisions much as a democratic society does. Individual neurons sort out conflicting impulses and decide whether to fire an electrical pulse or not. The sum of such decisions tells a person, for instance, whether to lash out at an enemy or to remain calm.

as many as 100,000 connections to adjoining cells. When an aggressive act escalates into a violent one, apparently more and more of these neurons are recruited to create bigger pathways for the flow of pulses. Thus violence, as some scientists define it, is aggression gone awry.

**The case of the enraged cat**

Fortunately for the advance of knowledge about human aggression, the limbic systems of animals have recently been found to bear an amazing functional resemblance to that of man. So laboratory experiments with animals (notably monkeys, cats, and mice) underpin the still limited investigations of aggression systems in the human brain.

Using fine electrodes inserted into animal brains, researchers have induced a fascinating range of aggressive behavior. Cats that normally do not attack rats, for instance, will stalk and kill a rat when stimulated in a certain area of the hypothalamus. On the other hand, a cat stimulated in another nearby region of the hypothalamus may ignore an available rat and attack the experimenter instead. Destruction of the nucleus of the amygdala will turn a friendly cat into a raging beast that claws and bites without provocation, because the signals from the hypothalamus are no longer dampened by the amygdala.

Similarly, a tumor in the hypothalamus or the amygdala can turn a peaceful person into a violent one. Such tumors occur infrequently. Corrective brain surgery remains highly controversial, however, mainly because surgeons lack precise knowledge of the aggression systems and know little about the risk of unwanted side effects from such operations. A surgical lesion—a scar-producing cut, freeze, or burn intended to destroy tissue—can increase or decrease hostile behavior, depending on its location.

Similar gaps in medical information inhibit manipulation of aggressive behavior with drugs that structurally mimic the

neurotransmitter chemicals. Recent experiments by Peter Bradley, a British neuropharmacologist, show that a brain cell can be affected in different ways by the same neurotransmitter, depending on the state of the cell, the amount of neurotransmitter, and how often the chemical is administered. It also appears that during an aggressive act a general arousal of the physiological system occurs—the same type of arousal that can be produced by such peaceful activities as jogging or even a concentrated mental effort.

**Dynamite in the genes?**

The complex anatomical and biochemical systems of the brain get their "orders" from the genes that determine behavior. Recent studies suggest that males have more brain cells that specialize in aggression than do females. This means that boys are more likely than girls to inherit aggressive tendencies. Very little is yet known, though, about the relationship between specific genetic defects and violence, how many such defects exist, and how frequently they might be inherited. Among the handful of anomalies discovered so far that some scientists have connected with violent behavior is the famous extra Y chromosome, which luckily appears to be inherited by fewer than two men in a thousand. (X and Y are sex chromosomes, with a normal male having an X and a Y, and a normal woman two X's.)

The Y chromosome leaped from the quiet of the laboratory four years ago and landed with a splash in newspaper headlines and courtrooms. The XYY males, usually tall, were said to have a natural propensity for violent crime. Some lawyers tried to gain reduced sentences or acquittal for their clients on the basis of their real or imagined extra Y chromosome. In France, at least, one attorney succeeded.

Some imaginative work now in progress at the University of Connecticut suggests that the Y chromosome story isn't all that simple. Researchers in the department of biobehavioral sciences, led by Benson E. Ginsburg, a noted geneticist, have designed animal breeding techniques that allow them to "tease out," as Ginsburg puts it, the contributions of individual genes and chromosomes to behavior. Their findings strongly hint that an XYY male's tendency to aggressiveness depends on whether he inherited his extra Y chromosome from a peaceful or aggressive father. The Y chromosome may act on the brain through the male sex hormones. Ginsburg and other scientists are trying to find out how this process works.

Elevating genetic probing to a new level of precision, Ginsburg and his colleagues have also shown that a Y chromosome from an aggressive father can combine with another genetic anomaly to make an animal twice as aggressive as it would be with just one genetic defect. They worked with an inbred strain of mice known as DBA 1. These mice are genetically susceptible to epileptic-type seizures that can be initiated by a high-frequency sound from a buzzer, or a bell, or even a jangling set of keys. The sound activates an enzyme system, controlled by a gene as all enzymes are, and located in the hippocampus. In a mouse, the network of neurons involved makes up an area the size of a pinpoint. The enzyme activated by sound, nucleoside triphosphatase, generates epileptic-like brain waves that can be recorded.

### Stormy weather in the hippocampus

The DBA mice, particularly males, are abnormally aggressive, apparently because of the defect in their hippocampus. In such mice, complex chemical reactions are superimposed on abnormal electrical activity in their hippocampal neurons. "You whip up an electrical storm in that region of the brain," says Ginsburg, describing his work with a touch of poetic license. Chemicals in the brain intensify the storm, he says, "as if you poured gasoline on a fire—and it went whoosh!"

The same type of storm, and in the same spot, rages in the brains of certain humans. They are either pathologically aggressive or have been made aggressive by hippocampal stimulation. This suggests, of course, that Ginsburg and his colleagues have found a genetic anomaly underlying aggression in both mice and men. In recent years, surgeons in some hospitals have been stimulating different parts of the brains of cancer patients in an effort to find an area that might block unbearable pain. In a number of instances, where doctors have stimulated the hippocampus by administering a very mild electrical shock through an electrode, patients showed the type of rage that Ginsburg and his associates found in those DBA mice. One mild-mannered patient in his fifties suddenly brandished his bedpan as a weapon against the nurses and whoever else happened to be around. He later felt quite embarrassed and contrite.

The discovery of the consequences of these anomalies and of other types of brain damage shatters the assumption made by criminologists and sociologists that the vast majority of cases of violent behavior involve people with completely normal brains. Studies of criminals who have repeatedly committed violent offenses show that they have a higher incidence of brain damage than the general population. Moreover, recent research is uncovering subtle forms of brain damage, unrecognized until now. No one knows for sure how many people in the U.S. suffer from brain damage, but some doctors place the number at 10 million to 20 million. Not all of them are violent, of course, but in addition there are many thousands who suffer from delusions or other forms of mental disturbance that make them dangerous. David Hamburg, head of the psychiatry department at Stanford University Medical School, estimates that the nation harbors some 200,000 potential presidential assassins. "Many manage their delusions on the fantasy level," says Hamburg. "Others engage in other forms of violent behavior."

What many people with brain abnormalities may have in common are pathways in the brain that failed to develop properly in infancy because of faulty upbringing, just as visual nerve pathways fail to develop properly in animals deprived of light. The fault, especially during the first two years of life when the brain is growing the fastest, lies in lack of physical affection, which an infant needs as much as nourishment. Earlier researchers had usually blamed emotional, social, or learning deficiencies for behavioral disturbances in infants raised in a foundling home. But James Prescott, a young neuropsychologist at the U.S. National Institute of Child Health and Human Development, suggests that there is a more fundamental biological reason. He maintains that normal pathways in the brain do not fully develop in children deprived of such expressions of affection as touching, cuddling, and being carried about. Instead, he says, this "somatosensory deprivation" leaves them with damaged central nervous systems.

### A chicken-wire mother

In a dramatic series of experiments, Harry F. Harlow, a University of Wisconsin psychologist, has demonstrated what happens when baby rhesus monkeys are deprived of their mothers. Harlow placed an infant monkey in a cage with two inanimate mother substitutes. One, covered with terry cloth and equipped with bicycle-reflector eyes, was designed to feel and look somewhat like a real rhesus mother but had no apparatus for feeding the infant. The other "mother," made of unadorned chicken wire, was unattractive to touch but contained a baby's bottle from which the infant could drink milk. Harlow found that the infant rhesus clearly preferred to spend all of its time with the nonfeeding surrogate. Even when feeding from the chicken-wire "mother," the infant would cling to his terry-cloth favorite. Harlow concluded that in infant-mother love, holding and cuddling are even more important than feeding. He also found that female monkeys who grew up with mother surrogates failed to develop maternal affection: they all seemed indifferent to their own children. Like parents who abuse their children, these monkey mothers frequently attacked, and sometimes even killed, their infants. Other researchers have recently traced three generations of human parents who batter and abuse their children. The only common characteristic of such parents, regardless of social or economic class, was that they themselves had suffered from lack of mothering and affection. Harlow wryly concluded a recent paper:

*Hell hath no fury like a woman spurned.*
*With love not given, love is not returned.*
*The loveless female, human or macaque,*
*In place of love will substitute attack.*

Can such deprived, aggressive monkeys be restored to normalcy? Experiments in Harlow's laboratory indicate that rehabilitation is possible if it is done early enough. Young monkey mothers reared in isolation sometimes regain most of their normal maternal behavior when locked in a cage with their own babies. The infant clings to the mother so persistently, despite her efforts to push it away, that eventually the baby monkey begins to serve as a therapist. Similarly, some young male monkeys reared in isolation become less aggressive when forced to play with monkeys their own age or younger.

Research into the brains of monkeys raised in isolation is just beginning, but indirect evidence already hints that such treatment induces brain damage. In humans, brain waves with abnormal, jagged "spikes" are often a telltale sign of damage. Robert G. Heath and Bernard Saltzberg, researchers at Tulane University, have recorded such spikes in the brain waves of monkeys reared by Harlow. The spikes reflect abnormal electrical activity, particularly in the cerebellum.

## Why Ding feared Dong

Further evidence of the cerebellum's role in violence comes from the work of A. J. Berman, a neurosurgeon at Mount Sinai Medical School and the Jewish Hospital in Brooklyn. He has successfuly modified autistic and aggressive behavior in isolation-reared monkeys by removing presumably abnormal sections of cerebellum that deal with the reception of sensory signals. In one experiment, Berman performed similar surgery on two monkeys called Ding and Dong, who had fought viciously and continuously. The operation turned Ding into a submissive animal, while Dong remained as aggressive as ever. Berman attributes the difference to the location of the surgery. Some tissue was removed from the midline section of Ding's cerebellum while the excision on Dong was microscopically closer to the side of that brain structure.

Berman suggests that his findings may one day be relevant to treating humans. "Walk into the back wards of any mental institution," he says, "and you'll find children whose behavior is identical with that of Harlow's monkeys."

All these and many other experiments have led a number of scientists to conclude that people who behave overaggressively may have an abnormality in the mechanism by which they perceive pleasure. In animals reared in isolation, as in pathologically violent people, the impulses resulting from the stimulation of movement and skin sensations may not be reaching their normal destinations in the brain. The feeling of pleasure may thus be experienced only partially or not at all.

This may explain, among other things, why both institutionalized children and monkeys brought up in isolation generally rock back and forth for hours on end and respond violently if touched. Adults with damaged pleasure systems similarly may be trying to derive pleasure from the rough physical contact involved in violent acts; they may, in effect be seeking an additional stimulus. Researchers have also found that electrical stimulation of pleasure centers in the brain eliminates feelings of rage, because the brain seems to contain rival nerve systems that suppress opposing emotions chemically and electrically.

## The scientist plays victim

Aggressive behavior doesn't necessarily have to arise as a result of damaged networks of nerve cells; it can be easily learned, too. Albert Bandura, a pioneering psychologist at Stanford University, demonstrated almost a decade ago how effectively aggression can be taught through the power of example. He used as "victims" large, inflated plastic figures known as Bobo dolls. Small children watched both real-life and filmed attacks on the dolls, then were given an opportunity to act aggressively themselves.

In study after study, researchers discovered that boys, especially, easily learn and retain aggressive behavior. They readily act out what they have learned not only on Bobo dolls but on other children and even adults. In one typical and recent experiment, conducted by psychologist Robert M. Liebert and his associates at New York State University at Stony Brook, kindergarten children watched a short film. Later they spontaneously attacked a scientist who had appeared in the film dressed up as a hard-luck clown and had been beaten up by another researcher. Many studies show that televised violence affects children in similar ways.

Violent behavior can be set off by many other environmental conditions. For instance, Leonard Berkowitz, a University of Wisconsin psychologist, showed that the mere presence of firearms can stimulate aggressive action. He tested groups of students who were provoked and insulted by one of his colleagues. Later, the groups had a chance to administer electric shocks to their tormentor. Students in a room where a gun was casually displayed gave the investigator about 25 percent more shocks than those in a room containing no weapons. The findings suggest to Berkowitz and others that easy access to lethal weapons—about 65 percent of homicides in the U.S. are committed with guns—not only facilitates the commission of crimes but creates an atmosphere in which violence is more likely to occur.

As in the laboratory, violence in real life often begets more violence. Marvin E. Wolfgang, a noted criminologist at the University of Pennsylvania, has coined the term "subculture of violence" to describe the cluster of values, attitudes, and life styles prominent among the poor living in the slums. Violence in that setting is so common as a problem-solving mechanism, says Wolfgang, that there is no shortage of real-life models for the young to imitate.

Many other factors—frequent absence of fathers, low income, unstable employment, poor living conditions—also bend the behavior of underprivileged youths toward violence, according to Wolfgang. Under all these pressures, plus in some cases a lack of physical affection at home, adolescent blacks have the highest homicide rate of any group in the U.S.

To complicate matters, they, like other adolescents, undergo a hormonal upheaval. Boys in particular become more aggressive as the amount of sex hormones in their bodies increases. Electron microscopy at Oxford University has recently begun to reveal structural differences between males and females in such control centers of aggression as the hypothalamus, for which sex hormones have a particular affinity.

## Are men stronger than mice?

The still mysterious workings of hormones on the brain constitute only a small part of the enormous gap between what scientists have discovered and what remains to be learned about the physiology and biochemistry of violence. For example, says Benson Ginsburg, the University of Connecticut geneticist, scientists should find out whether men, through conscious control and training, can override the physiological changes involved in aggression much more effectively than, say, mice can. Another unknown is whether genetic instructions are so strong in some people as to completely mold their behavior. Answers to such questions could open the way to far more specific therapies. More effective antiviolence drugs, for instance, could be developed if we could delineate the particular enzymatic mechanisms in the brain that affect aggression.

Treatment with existing drugs, many scientists feel, is something like using a shotgun where a rifle is needed. Even so, some investigators propose that methadone-type clinics be set up to dispense drugs available now to persons prone to violence. Lithium might be useful because it appears to speed up the release of serotonin, a brain chemical that seems to inhibit aggression. Michael H. Sheard, a Yale neuropharmacologist, has had some success in modifying the behavior of violent prisoners with lithium.

Other novel approaches may emerge from studies that are under way. For example, development of a vastly improved brain-wave recording machine, now in progress at Tulane, would enable doctors to detect signals of trouble from deep in the brain without surgically implanting recording electrodes there. It may also become possible to treat damaged deep-nerve networks ultrasonically, thereby avoiding surgery.

It is clear that much more specific therapies than those in use today are needed for people who have brain damage. Vernon H. Mark and Frank R. Ervin observe in their recent book, *Violence and the Brain:* "Hoping to rehabilitate such a violent individual through psychotherapy or education, or to improve his character by sending him to jail or by giving him love and understanding—all these methods are irrelevant and will not work. It is the malfunction itself that must be dealt with, and only if this fact is recognized is there any chance of changing his behavior."

## No trouble in Tahiti

To prevent brain damage that may lead to violence, some

new tactics could be tried now. "Changing child-rearing practices is probably the most important single thing we can do as a society," says Prescott. "We have to make sure that the children we have are wanted children." Prescott and others also suggest that it might be a good idea to evaluate and treat children as early as age five if they show a tendency to brutalize other children or animals or have episodes of uncontrolled rage. Such youngsters, scientists say, are good candidates for violent behavior later.

Anthropologists have gained some intriguing clues about child rearing by studying peaceful societies. Prescott surveyed data from forty-nine primitive cultures and found in thirty-six of them an amazingly strong correlation between physical affection toward infants and lack of violence. In societies where infants were treated cruelly, violence prevailed. Robert Levy, an anthropologist at the University of California at San Diego who has studied tranquil Tahiti, found that parents on the island seldom punish children by hitting them. Thus the children have no aggressive models to emulate.

Another deterrent to violence may be the habit of arguing it out. Societies that have developed highly elaborate ways of verbalizing violence are quite peaceful. In Tahiti and other Polynesian islands, people engage in "talking out acute anger, rather than taking physical action," says Levy. Similarly, Italians sometimes sound violent, but according to scientists who have studied Italy, there is far less incidence of violent offenses there than in the U.S.

This nation leads the advanced industrialized countries of the world in homicide and other violent crimes. Assaults in the U.S. occur nearly twice as often per capita as in England and Wales, and robberies are ten times as common. In 1971, the latest full year for which figures are available, 17,630 people in the U.S. were murdered. In England and Wales, West Germany, France, and Italy, which have a combined population about 3 percent larger than ours, there were only 1,948 murders—a rate almost ten times lower than that in the U.S.

By contrast with the U.S., these other industrial countries have more homogeneous populations, exert greater control over firearms, and operate with somewhat more rigid social structures. These differences may explain some, though not necessarily all, of the disparities in the rates of violence. In any case, it is clear that our methods of dealing with the problem have not proved particularly effective. Scientific investigation at last is beginning to provide surprising insights into why this is so. In time, the new research may lead to a much broader understanding of violent behavior, and, eventually, to effective means of discouraging it.   END

# 17

Intellectuals do not wish to be caught saying uncomplimentary
things about mankind. But wicked people exist.

# LOCK 'EM UP
## AND OTHER THOUGHTS ON CRIME

## By James Q. Wilson

As much as anything, our futile efforts to curb
or even understand the dramatic and continuing
rise in crime have been frustrated by our optimistic
and unrealistic assumptions about human nature.
Considering that our society is in the grip of a
decade-old crime wave despite a decade-long period of prosperity, it is strange that we should persist in the view that we can find and alleviate the
"causes" of crime, that serious criminals can be
rehabilitated, that the police can somehow be
made to catch more criminals faster, and that
prosecutors and judges have the wisdom to tailor
sentences to fit the "needs" of the individual offender.

I argue for a sober view of man and his institutions that would permit reasonable things to be
accomplished, foolish things abandoned, and utopian things forgotten. A sober view of man requires
a modest definition of progress. A 20-per cent reduction in robbery would still leave us with the

highest robbery rate of almost any Western nation
but would prevent about 60,000 robberies a year.
A small gain for society, a large one for the would-
be victims. Yet a 20 per cent reduction is unlikely
if we concentrate our efforts on dealing with the
causes of crime or even if we concentrate on improving police efficiency. But were we to devote
those resources to a strategy that is well within
our abilities — to incapacitating a larger fraction of the convicted serious robbers—then not only
is a 20 per cent reduction possible, even larger
ones are conceivable.

Most serious crime is committed by repeaters.
What we do with first offenders is probably far
less important than what we do with habitual offenders. A genuine first offender (and not merely
a habitual offender caught for the first time) is in
all likelihood a young person who, in the majority
of cases, will stop stealing when he gets older. This
is not to say we should forgive first offenses, for
that would be to license the offense and erode the
moral judgments that must underlie any society's
attitude toward crime. The gravity of the offense
must be appropriately impressed on the first offender, but the effort to devise ways of re-educat-
ing or uplifting him in order

*James Q. Wilson is Henry Lee Shattuck Professor
of Government at Harvard.*

to insure that he does not steal again is likely to be wasted—both because we do not know how to re-educate or uplift and because most young delinquents seem to re-educate themselves no matter what society does.

After tracing the history of nearly 10,000 Philadelphia boys born in 1945, Marvin Wolfgang and his colleagues at the University of Pennsylvania found that more than one-third were picked up by the police for something more serious than a traffic offense but that 46 per cent of these delinquents had no further police contact after their first offense. Though one-third started on crime, nearly half seemed to stop spontaneously —a good thing, because otherwise the criminal justice system in that city, already sorely taxed, would in all likelihood have collapsed. Out of the 10,000 boys, however, there were 627—only 6 per cent—who committed five or more offenses before they were 18. Yet these few chronic offenders accounted for *more than half* of all the recorded delinquencies and about *two-thirds* of all the violent crimes committed by the entire cohort.

Only a tiny fraction of all serious crimes leads immediately to an arrest, and only a slightly larger fraction is ultimately "cleared" by an arrest, but this does not mean that the police function is meaningless. Because most serious crime is committed by repeaters, most criminals eventually get arrested. The Wolfgang findings and other studies suggest that the chances of a persistent burglar or robber living out his life, or even going a year, with no arrest are quite small. Yet a large proportion of repeat offenders suffers little or no loss of freedom. Whether or not one believes that such a penalty, if inflicted, would act as a deterrent, it is obvious that it could serve to incapacitate these offenders, and thus, for the period of the incapacitation, prevent them from committing additional crimes.

We have a limited (and declining) supply of detention facilities, and many of those that exist are decrepit, unsafe, and overcrowded. But as important as expanding the supply and improving the decency of the facilities is the need to think seriously about how we wish to allocate those spaces that exist. At present, that allocation is hit or miss. A 1966 survey of more than 15 juvenile correctional institutions disclosed that about 30 per cent of the inmates were young persons who had been committed for conduct that would not have been judged criminal were it committed by adults. They were runaways, "stubborn children," or chronic truants—problem children, to be sure, but scarcely major threats to society. Using scarce detention space for them when in Los Angeles more than 90 per cent of burglars with a major prior record receive no state prison sentence seems, to put it mildly, anomalous.

In a joint study, Prof. Reuel Shinnar of City College of New York and his son Shlomo have estimated the effect on crime rates in New York State of a judicial policy other than than that followed during the last decade or so. Given the present level of police efficiency and making some assumptions about how many crimes each offender commits per year, they conclude that the rate of serious crime would be only *one-third* what it is today if every person convicted of a serious offense were imprisoned for three years. This reduction would be less if it turned out (as seems unlikely) that most serious crime is committed by first-time offenders, and it would be much greater if the proportion of crimes resulting in an arrest and conviction were increased (as also seems unlikely). The reduction, it should be noted, would be solely the result of incapacitation, making no allowance for such additional reductions as might result from enhanced deterrence or rehabilitation.

The Shinnar estimates are based on uncertain data and involve assumptions that can be challenged. But even assuming they are overly optim-

istic by a factor of two, a sizable reduction in crime would still ensue. In other countries such a policy of greater incapacitation is in fact followed. A robber arrested in England, for example, is more than three times as likely as one arrested in New York to go to prison. That difference in sentencing does not account for all the difference between English and American crime rates, but it may well account for a substantial fraction of it.

That these gains are possible does not mean that society should adopt such a policy. One would first want to know the costs, in additional prison space and judicial resources, of greater use of incapacitation. One would want to debate the propriety and humanity of a mandatory three-year term; perhaps, in order to accommodate differences in the character of criminals and their crimes, one would want to have a range of sentences from, say, one to five years. One would want to know what is likely to happen to the process of charging and pleading if every person arrested for a serious crime faced a mandatory minimum sentence, however mild. These and other difficult and important questions must first be confronted. But the central fact is that *these are reasonable questions* around which facts can be gathered and intelligent arguments mustered. To discuss them requires us to make few optimistic assumptions about the malleability of human nature, the skills of officials who operate complex institutions, or the capacity of society to improve the fundamental aspects of familial and communal life.

Persons who criticize an emphasis on changing the police and courts to cope with crime are fond of saying that such measures cannot work so long as unemployment and poverty exist. We must acknowledge that we have not done very well at inducting young persons, especially but not only blacks, into the work force. Teen-age unemployment rates continue to exceed 20 per cent and show little sign of abating. Nor should we assume that declining birth rates will soon reduce either the youthful demand for jobs or the supply of young criminals. The birth rates are now very low; it will not be until the mid- or late-nineteen-eighties that these low rates will affect the proportion of the population that is entering the job-seeking and crime-prone ages of 16 through 26.

In the meantime, while anti-crime policies may be hampered by the failure of employment policies, it would be equally correct to say that so long as the criminal-justice system does not impede crime, efforts to reduce unemployment will not work. If legitimate opportunities for work are unavailable, many young persons will turn to crime; but if criminal opportunities are profitable, many young persons will not take those legitimate jobs that exist. The benefits of work and the costs of crime must be increased simultaneously; to increase one but not the other makes sense only if one assumes that young people are irrational.

One rejoinder to this view is the argument that if legitimate jobs are made absolutely more attractive than stealing, stealing will decline even without any increase in penalties for it. That may be true provided there is no practical limit on the amount that can be paid in wages. Since the average "take" from a burglary or mugging is quite small, it would seem easy to make the income from a job exceed the income from crime.

But this neglects the advantages of a criminal income: One works at crime at one's convenience, enjoys the esteem of colleagues who think a "straight" job is stupid and skill at stealing is commendable, looks forward to the occasional "big score" that may make further work unnecessary for weeks, and relishes the risk and adventure associated with theft. The money value of all these benefits—that is, what one who is not shocked by crime would want in cash to forgo crime—is hard to estimate

but is almost certainly far larger than what either public or private employers could offer to unskilled or semiskilled young workers. The only alternative for society is so to increase the risks of theft that its value is depreciated below what society can afford to pay in legal wages, and then take whatever steps are necessary to insure that those legal wages are available.

Another rejoinder to the "attack poverty" approach to crime is this: The desire to reduce crime is the worst possible reason for reducing poverty. Most poor persons are not criminals; many are either retired or have regular jobs and lead conventional family lives. The elderly, the working poor, and the willing-to-work poor could benefit greatly from economic conditions and government programs that enhance their incomes without there being the slightest reduction in crime—indeed, if the experience of the nineteen-sixties is any guide, there might well be, through no fault of most such beneficiaries, an increase in crime. Reducing poverty and breaking up the ghettos are desirable policies in their own right, whatever their effects on crime. It is the duty of government to devise other measures to cope with crime: not only to permit anti-poverty programs to succeed without unfair competition from criminal opportunities, but also to insure that such programs do not inadvertently shift the costs of progress, in terms of higher crime rates, onto innocent parties, not the least of whom are the poor themselves.

One cannot press this economic reasoning too far. Some persons will commit crimes whatever the risks; indeed, for some, the greater the risk, the greater the thrill, while others—the alcoholic wife beater, for example—are only dimly aware that there are any risks. But more important than the insensitivity of certain criminal offenders to changes in risks and benefits is the impropriety of casting the crime problem wholly in terms of a util-

itarian calculus. The most serious offenses are crimes not simply because society finds them inconvenient, but because it regards them with moral horror. To steal, to rape, to rob, to assault—these acts are destructive of the very possibility of society and affronts to the humanity of their victims. It is my experience that parents do not instruct their children to be law-abiding merely by pointing to the risks of being caught, but by explaining that these acts are wrong whether or not one is caught. I conjecture that those parents who simply warn their offspring about the risks of crime produce a disproportionate number of young persons willing to take those risks.

Even the deterrent capacity of the criminal-justice system depends in no small part on its ability to evoke sentiments of shame in the accused. If all it evoked were a sense of being unlucky, crime rates would be even higher. James Fitzjames Stephens, the 19th-century British jurist, makes the point by analogy. To what extent, he asks, would a man be deterred from theft by the knowledge that by committing it he was exposing himself to 1 chance in 50 of catching a serious but not fatal illness—say, a bad fever? Rather little, we would imagine—indeed, all of us regularly take risks as great as or greater than that: when we drive after drinking, when we smoke cigarettes, when we go hunting in the woods. The criminal sanction, Stephens concludes, "operates not only on the fears of criminals, but upon the habitual sentiments of those who are not criminals. [A] great part of the general detestation of crime . . . arises from the fact that the commission of offenses is associated . . . with the solemn and deliberate infliction of punishment wherever crime is proved."

Much is made today of the fact that the criminal-justice system "stigmatizes" those caught up in it, and thus unfairly marks such persons and perhaps even furthers their criminal careers by having "labeled" them as criminals. Whether the labeling process operates in this way is as yet unproved, but it would indeed be unfortunate if society treated a convicted offender in such a way that he had no reasonable alternative but to make crime a career. To prevent this, society ought to insure that one can "pay one's debt" without suffering permanent loss of civil rights, the continuing and pointless indignity of parole supervision, and frustration in being unable to find a job. But doing these things is very different from eliminating the "stigma" from crime. To destigmatize crime would be to lift from it the weight of moral judgment and to make crime simply a particular occupation or avocation which society has chosen to reward less (or perhaps more!) than other pursuits. If there is no stigma attached to an activity, then society has no business making it a crime. Indeed, before the invention of the prison in the late 18th and early 19th centuries, the stigma attached to criminals was the major deterrent to and principal form of protection from criminal activity. The purpose of the criminal-justice system is not to expose would-be criminals to a lottery in which they either win or lose, but to expose them in addition and more importantly to the solemn condemnation of the community should they yield to temptation.

Anyone familiar with the police stations, jails and courts of some of our larger cities is keenly aware that accused persons caught up in the system are exposed to very little that involves either judgment or solemnity. They are instead processed through a bureaucratic maze in which a bargain is offered and a haggle ensues at every turn—over the amount of bail, the degree of the charged offense and the nature of the plea. Much of what observers find objectionable about this process could be alleviated by devoting many more resources to it, so that an ample supply of prosecutors, defense attorneys and judges was available.

That we do not devote those additional resources in a country obsessed with the crime problem is one of the more interesting illustrations of the maxim, familiar to all political scientists, that one cannot predict public policy simply from knowing popular attitudes. Whatever the cause, it remains the case that in New York County (Manhattan) there were, in 1973, 31,098 felony arrests to be handled by only 125 prosecutors, 119 public defenders and 59 Criminal-Court judges. The result was predictable: Of those arrested, only 4,130 pleaded guilty to or were convicted on a felony charge; 81 per cent of the felony arrests were disposed of by pleading guilty to a misdemeanor or by discharging the case.

One wonders whether the stigma properly associated with crime retains much deterrent or educative value. My strong inclination is to resist explanations for rising crime that are based on the alleged moral breakdown of society, the community or the family. I resist in part because most of the families and communities I know have not broken down, and in part because, had they broken down, I cannot imagine any collective action we could take consistent with our civil liberties that would restore a moral consensus, and yet the facts are hard to ignore. Take the family: More than one-third of all black children and 1 in 14 of all white children live in single-parent families. More than two million children live in single-parent households (usually the father absent), almost *double* the number of 10 years ago. In 1950, 18 per cent of black families were headed by females; in 1969 the proportion had risen to 27 per cent; by 1973 it exceeded 35 per cent. The average income for a single-parent family with children under 6 years of age was, in 1970, only $3,100, well below the official "poverty line."

Studies done in the late nineteen-fifties and the early nineteen-sixties showed that children from broken homes were more likely than others to become delinquent. In New York State, 58 per cent of the variation in pupil achievement in 300 schools could be predicted by but three variables —broken homes, overcrowded housing and parental educational level. Family disorganization, writes Prof. Urie Bronfenbrenner of Cornell University, has been shown in thousands of studies to be an "omnipresent overriding factor" in behavior disorders and social pathology. And that disorganization is increasing.

These facts may explain some elements of the rising crime rate that cannot be attributed to the increased number of young persons, high teen-age unemployment or changed judicial policies. The age of persons arrested has been declining for more than 15 years and the median age of convicted defendants (in jurisdictions for which data are available) has been declining for the last six years. Apparently, the age at which persons begin to commit serious crime has been falling. For some young people, thus, whatever forces weaken their resistance to criminal activity have been increasing in magnitude, and these forces may well include the continued disorganization of the family and the continued deterioration of the social structure of inner-city communities.

One wants to be objective, if not optimistic. Perhaps single-parent families today are less disorganized—or have a different significance—than such families in the past. Perhaps the relationship between family structure and social pathology will change. After all, for at least a brief while, the heroin epidemic on the East Coast showed signs of abating as law enforcement reduced the supply of narcotics, treatment programs took many addicts off the streets and popular revulsion against addiction mounted. Perhaps other aspects of the relationship among family, personality and crime will change. Perhaps. But even as this is being written, and after the book from which it is taken went to press, there have appeared ominous signs that the East Coast heroin shortage may be ending and the use of heroin once again increasing.

No one can say how much of crime results from its increased profitability and how much from its decreased shamefulness. But one or both factors must be at work, for population changes alone simply cannot account for the increases. Crime in our cities has increased far faster than the number of young people, or poor people, or black people, or just plain people who live in those cities. In short, objective conditions alone, whether demographic or economic, cannot account for the crime increases; ideas, attitudes, values have played a great part, though in ways hard to define and impossible to measure. An assessment of the effect of these changes on crime would provide a partial understanding of changes in the moral structure of our society.

But to understand is not to change. If few of the demographic factors contributing to crime are subject to planned change, virtually none of the subjective ones are. Though intellectually rewarding, from a practical point of view it is a mistake to think about crime in terms of its "causes" and then to search for ways to alleviate those causes. We must think instead of what it is feasible for a government or a community to do, and then try to discover, by experimentation and observation, which of those things will produce, at acceptable costs, desirable changes in the level of criminal victimization.

There are, we now know, certain things we can change in accordance with our intentions, and certain ones we cannot. We cannot alter the number of juveniles who first experiment with minor crimes. We cannot lower the recidivism rate, though within reason we should keep trying. We are not yet certain whe-

ther we can increase significantly the police apprehension rate. We may be able to change the teen-age unemployment rate, though we have learned by painful trial and error that doing this is much more difficult than once supposed. We can probably reduce the time it takes to bring an arrested person to trial, even though we have as yet made few serious efforts to do so. We can certainly reduce the arbitrary and socially irrational exercise of prosecutorial discretion over whom to charge and whom to release, and we can most definitely stop pretending that judges know, any better than the rest of us, how to provide "individualized justice." We can confine a larger proportion of the serious offenders and repeaters and fewer of the common drunks and truant children. We know that confining criminals prevents them from harming society, and we have grounds for suspecting that some would-be criminals can be deterred by the confinement of others.

Above all, we can try to learn more about what works, and in the process abandon our ideological preconceptions about what *ought* to work. Nearly 10 years ago I wrote that the billions of dollars the Federal Government was then preparing to spend on crime control would be wasted and indeed might even make matters worse if they were merely pumped into the existing criminal-justice system. They were, and they have. In the next 10 years I hope we can learn to experiment rather than simply spend, to test our theories rather than fund our fears. This is advice, not simply or even primarily to government — for governments are run by men and women who are under irresistible pressures to pretend they know more than they do— but to my colleagues: academics, theoreticians, writers, advisers. We may feel ourselves under pressure to pretend we know things, but we are also under a positive obligation to admit what we do not know and to avoid cant and sloganizing. The Govern-

ment agency, the Law Enforcement Assistance Administration, that has futilely spent those billions was created in consequence of an act passed by Congress on the advice of a Presidential commission staffed by academics, myself included.

It is easy and popular to criticize yesterday's empty hopes and mistaken beliefs, especially if they seemed supportive of law enforcement. It is harder, and certainly most unpopular, to criticize today's pieties and pretensions, especially if they are uttered in the name of progress and humanity. But if we were wrong in thinking that more money spent on the police would bring down crime rates, we are equally wrong in supposing that closing our prisons, emptying our jails and supporting "community-based" programs will do any better. Indeed, there is some evidence that these steps will make matters worse, and we ignore it at our peril.

Since the days of the crime commission we have learned a great deal, more than we are prepared to admit. Perhaps we fear to admit it because of a new-found modesty about the foundations of our knowledge, but perhaps also because the implications of that knowledge suggest an unflattering view of man. Intellectuals, although they often dislike the common person as an individual, do not wish to be caught saying uncomplimentary things about humankind. Nevertheless, some persons will shun crime even if we do nothing to deter them, while others will seek it out even if we do everything to reform them. Wicked people exist. Nothing avails except to set them apart from innocent people. And many people, neither wicked nor innocent, but watchful, dissembling and calculating of their opportunities, ponder our reaction to wickedness as a cue to what they might profitably do. We have trifled with the wicked, made sport of the innocent and encouraged the calculators. Justice suffers, and so do we all. ■

# 18 On Being Sane in Insane Places

D. L. Rosenhan

If sanity and insanity exist, how shall we know them?

The question is neither capricious nor itself insane. However much we may be personally convinced that we can tell the normal from the abnormal, the evidence is simply not compelling. It is commonplace, for example, to read about murder trials wherein eminent psychiatrists for the defense are contradicted by equally eminent psychiatrists for the prosecution on the matter of the defendant's sanity. More generally, there are a great deal of conflicting data on the reliability, utility, and meaning of such terms as "sanity," "insanity," "mental illness," and "schizophrenia" (1). Finally, as early as 1934, Benedict suggested that normality and abnormality are not universal (2): What is viewed as normal in one culture may be seen as quite aberrant in another. Thus, notions of normality and abnormality may not be quite as accurate as people believe they are.

To raise questions regarding normality and abnormality is in no way to question the fact that some behaviors are deviant or odd. Murder is deviant. So, too, are hallucinations. Nor does raising such questions deny the existence of the personal anguish that is often associated with "mental illness." Anxiety and depression exist. Psychological suffering exists. But normality and abnormality, sanity and insanity, and the diagnoses that flow from them may be less substantive than many believe them to be.

At its heart, the question of whether the sane can be distinguished from the insane (and whether degrees of insanity can be distinguished from each other) is a simple matter: do the salient characteristics that lead to diagnoses reside in the patients themselves or in the environments and contexts in which observers find them? From Bleuler, through Kretchmer, through the formulators of the recently revised *Diagnostic and Statistical Manual* of the American Psychiatric Association, the belief has been strong that patients present symptoms, that those symptoms can be categorized, and, implicitly, that the sane are distinguishable from the insane. More recently, however, this belief has been questioned. Based in part on theoretical and anthropological considerations, but also on philosophical, legal, and therapeutic ones, the view has grown that psychological categorization of mental illness is useless at best and downright harmful, misleading, and pejorative at worst. Psychiatric diagnoses, in this view, are in the minds of the observers and are not valid summaries of characteristics displayed by the observed (3–5).

Gains can be made in deciding which of these is more nearly accurate by getting normal people (that is, people who do not have, and have never suffered, symptoms of serious psychiatric disorders) admitted to psychiatric hospitals and then determining whether they were discovered to be sane and, if so, how. If the sanity of such pseudopatients were always detected, there would be prima facie evidence that a sane individual can be distinguished from the insane context in which he is found. Normality (and presumably abnormality) is distinct enough that it can be recognized wherever it occurs, for it is carried within the person. If, on the other hand, the sanity of the pseudopatients were never discovered, serious difficulties would arise for those who support traditional modes of psychiatric diagnosis. Given that the hospital staff was not incompetent, that the pseudopatient had been behaving as sanely as he had been outside of the hospital, and that it had never been previously suggested that he belonged in a psychiatric hospital, such an unlikely outcome would support the view that psychiatric diagnosis betrays little about the patient but much about the environment in which an observer finds him.

This article describes such an experiment. Eight sane people gained secret admission to 12 different hospitals (6). Their diagnostic experiences constitute the data of the first part of this article; the remainder is devoted to a description of their experiences in psychiatric institutions. Too few psychiatrists and psychologists, even those who have worked in such hospitals, know what the experience is like. They rarely talk about it with former patients, perhaps because they distrust information coming from the previously insane. Those who have worked in psychiatric hospitals are likely to have adapted so thoroughly to the settings that they are insensitive to the impact of that experience. And while there have been occasional reports of researchers who submitted themselves to psychiatric hospitalization (7), these researchers have commonly remained in the hospitals for short periods of time, often with the knowledge of the hospital staff. It is difficult to know the extent to which they were treated like patients or like research colleagues. Nevertheless, their reports about the inside of the psychiatric hospital have been valuable. This article extends those efforts.

## Pseudopatients and Their Settings

The eight pseudopatients were a varied group. One was a psychology graduate student in his 20's. The remaining seven were older and "established." Among them were three psychologists, a pediatrician, a psychiatrist, a painter, and a housewife. Three pseudopatients were women, five were men. All of them employed pseudonyms, lest their alleged diagnoses embarrass them later. Those who were in mental health professions alleged another occupation in order to avoid the special attentions that might be accorded by staff, as a matter of courtesy or caution, to ailing colleagues (8) With the exception of myself (I was the first pseudopatient and my presence was known to the hospital administrator and chief psychologist and, so far as I can tell, to them alone), the presence of pseudopatients and the nature of the research program was not known to the hospital staffs (9).

The settings were similarly varied. In order to generalize the findings, admission into a variety of hospitals was sought. The 12 hospitals in the sample were located in five different states on the East and West coasts. Some were old and shabby, some were quite new. Some were research-oriented, others not. Some had good staff-patient ratios, others were quite understaffed. Only one was a strictly private hospital. All of the others were supported by state or federal funds or, in one instance, by university funds.

The author is professor of psychology and law at Stanford University, Stanford, California 94305. Portions of these data were presented to colloquiums of the psychology departments at the University of California at Berkeley and at Santa Barbara; University of Arizona, Tucson; and Harvard University, Cambridge, Massachusetts.

After calling the hospital for an appointment, the pseudopatient arrived at the admissions office complaining that he had been hearing voices. Asked what the voices said, he replied that they were often unclear, but as far as he could tell they said "empty," "hollow," and "thud." The voices were unfamiliar and were of the same sex as the pseudopatient. The choice of these symptoms was occasioned by their apparent similarity to existential symptoms. Such symptoms are alleged to arise from painful concerns about the perceived meaninglessness of one's life. It is as if the hallucinating person were saying, "My life is empty and hollow." The choice of these symptoms was also determined by the *absence* of a single report of existential psychoses in the literature.

Beyond alleging the symptoms and falsifying name, vocation, and employment, no further alterations of person, history, or circumstances were made. The significant events of the pseudopatient's life history were presented as they had actually occurred. Relationships with parents and siblings, with spouse and children, with people at work and in school, consistent with the aforementioned exceptions, were described as they were or had been. Frustrations and upsets were described along with joys and satisfactions. These facts are important to remember. If anything, they strongly biased the subsequent results in favor of detecting sanity, since none of their histories or current behaviors were seriously pathological in any way.

Immediately upon admission to the psychiatric ward, the pseudopatient ceased simulating *any* symptoms of abnormality. In some cases, there was a brief period of mild nervousness and anxiety, since none of the pseudopatients really believed that they would be admitted so easily. Indeed, their shared fear was that they would be immediately exposed as frauds and greatly embarrassed. Moreover, many of them had never visited a psychiatric ward; even those who had, nevertheless had some genuine fears about what might happen to them. Their nervousness, then, was quite appropriate to the novelty of the hospital setting, and it abated rapidly.

Apart from that short-lived nervousness, the pseudopatient behaved on the ward as he "normally" behaved. The pseudopatient spoke to patients and staff as he might ordinarily. Because there is uncommonly little to do on a psychiatric ward, he attempted to engage others in conversation. When asked by staff how he was feeling, he indicated that he was fine, that he no longer experienced symptoms. He responded to instructions from attendants, to calls for medication (which was not swallowed), and to dining-hall instructions. Beyond such activities as were available to him on the admissions ward, he spent his time writing down his observations about the ward, its patients, and the staff. Initially these notes were written "secretly," but as it soon became clear that no one much cared, they were subsequently written on standard tablets of paper in such public places as the dayroom. No secret was made of these activities.

The pseudopatient, very much as a true psychiatric patient, entered a hospital with no foreknowledge of when he would be discharged. Each was told that he would have to get out by his own devices, essentially by convincing the staff that he was sane. The psychological stresses associated with hospitalization were considerable, and all but one of the pseudopatients desired to be discharged almost immediately after being admitted. They were, therefore, motivated not only to behave sanely, but to be paragons of cooperation. That their behavior was in no way disruptive is confirmed by nursing reports, which have been obtained on most of the patients. These reports uniformly indicate that the patients were "friendly," "cooperative," and "exhibited no abnormal indications."

## The Normal Are Not Detectably Sane

Despite their public "show" of sanity, the pseudopatients were never detected. Admitted, except in one case, with a diagnosis of schizophrenia (*10*), each was discharged with a diagnosis of schizophrenia "in remission." The label "in remission" should in no way be dismissed as a formality, for at no time during any hospitalization had any question been raised about any pseudopatient's simulation. Nor are there any indications in the hospital records that the pseudopatient's status was suspect. Rather, the evidence is strong that, once labeled schizophrenic, the pseudopatient was stuck with that label. If the pseudopatient was to be discharged, he must

naturally be "in remission"; but he was not sane, nor, in the institution's view, had he ever been sane.

The uniform failure to recognize sanity cannot be attributed to the quality of the hospitals, for, although there were considerable variations among them, several are considered excellent. Nor can it be alleged that there was simply not enough time to observe the pseudopatients. Length of hospitalization ranged from 7 to 52 days, with an average of 19 days. The pseudopatients were not, in fact, carefully observed, but this failure clearly speaks more to traditions within psychiatric hospitals than to lack of opportunity.

Finally, it cannot be said that the failure to recognize the pseudopatients' sanity was due to the fact that they were not behaving sanely. While there was clearly some tension present in all of them, their daily visitors could detect no serious behavioral consequences— nor, indeed, could other patients. It was quite common for the patients to "detect" the pseudopatients' sanity. During the first three hospitalizations, when accurate counts were kept, 35 of a total of 118 patients on the admissions ward voiced their suspicions, some vigorously. "You're not crazy. You're a journalist, or a professor [referring to the continual note-taking]. You're checking up on the hospital." While most of the patients were reassured by the pseudopatient's insistence that he had been sick before he came in but was fine now, some continued to believe that the pseudopatient was sane throughout his hospitalization (*11*). The fact that the patients often recognized normality when staff did not raises important questions.

Failure to detect sanity during the course of hospitalization may be due to the fact that physicians operate with a strong bias toward what statisticians call the type 2 error (*5*). This is to say that physicians are more inclined to call a healthy person sick (a false positive, type 2) than a sick person healthy (a false negative, type 1). The reasons for this are not hard to find: it is clearly more dangerous to misdiagnose illness than health. Better to err on the side of caution, to suspect illness even among the healthy.

But what holds for medicine does not hold equally well for psychiatry. Medical illnesses, while unfortunate, are not commonly pejorative. Psychiatric diagnoses, on the contrary, carry with them personal, legal, and social stigmas (*12*). It was therefore important to see whether the tendency toward diagnosing the sane insane could be reversed. The following experiment was arranged at a research and teaching hospital whose staff had heard these findings but doubted that such an error could occur in their hospital. The staff was informed that at some time during the following 3 months, one or more pseudopatients would attempt to be admitted into the psychiatric hospital. Each staff member was asked to rate each patient who presented himself at admissions or on the ward according to the likelihood that the patient was a pseudopatient. A 10-point scale was used, with a 1 and 2 reflecting high confidence that the patient was a pseudopatient.

Judgments were obtained on 193 patients who were admitted for psychiatric treatment. All staff who had had sustained contact with or primary responsibility for the patient—attendants, nurses, psychiatrists, physicians, and psychologists—were asked to make judgments. Forty-one patients were alleged, with high confidence, to be pseudopatients by at least one member of the staff. Twenty-three were considered suspect by at least one psychiatrist. Nineteen were suspected by one psychiatrist *and* one other staff member. Actually, no genuine pseudopatient (at least from my group) presented himself during this period.

The experiment is instructive. It indicates that the tendency to designate sane people as insane can be reversed when the stakes (in this case, prestige and diagnostic acumen) are high. But what can be said of the 19 people who were suspected of being "sane" by one psychiatrist and another staff member? Were these people truly "sane," or was it rather the case that in the course of avoiding the type 2 error the staff tended to make more errors of the first sort—calling the crazy "sane"? There is no way of knowing. But one thing is certain: any diagnostic process that lends itself so readily to massive errors of this sort cannot be a very reliable one.

## The Stickiness of Psychodiagnostic Labels

Beyond the tendency to call the healthy sick—a tendency that accounts better for diagnostic behavior on admission than it does for such behavior after a lengthy period of exposure—the data speak to the massive role of labeling in psychiatric assessment. Having once been labeled schizophrenic, there is nothing the pseudopatient can do to overcome the tag. The tag profoundly colors others' perceptions of him and his behavior.

From one viewpoint, these data are hardly surprising, for it has long been known that elements are given meaning by the context in which they occur. Gestalt psychology made this point vigorously, and Asch (*13*) demonstrated that there are "central" personality traits (such as "warm" versus "cold") which are so powerful that they markedly color the meaning of other information in forming an impression of a given personality (*14*). "Insane," "schizophrenic," "manic-depressive," and "crazy" are probably among the most powerful of such central traits. Once a person is designated abnormal, all of his other behaviors and characteristics are colored by that label. Indeed, that label is so powerful that many of the pseudopatients' normal behaviors were overlooked entirely or profoundly misinterpreted. Some examples may clarify this issue.

Earlier I indicated that there were no changes in the pseudopatient's personal history and current status beyond those of name, employment, and, where necessary, vocation. Otherwise, a veridical description of personal history and circumstances was offered. Those circumstances were not psychotic. How were they made consonant with the diagnosis of psychosis? Or were those diagnoses modified in such a way as to bring them into accord with the circumstances of the pseudopatient's life, as described by him?

As far as I can determine, diagnoses were in no way affected by the relative health of the circumstances of a pseudopatient's life. Rather, the reverse occurred: the perception of his circumstances was shaped entirely by the diagnosis. A clear example of such translation is found in the case of a pseudopatient who had had a close relationship with his mother but was rather remote from his father during his early childhood. During adolescence and beyond, however, his father became a close friend, while his relationship with his mother cooled. His present relationship with his wife was characteristically close and warm. Apart from occasional angry exchanges, friction was minimal. The children had rarely been spanked. Surely there is nothing especially pathological about such a history. Indeed, many readers may see a similar pattern in their own experiences, with no markedly deleterious consequences. Observe, however, how such a history was translated in the psychopathological context, this from the case summary prepared after the patient was discharged.

> This white 39-year-old male . . . manifests a long history of considerable ambivalence in close relationships, which begins in early childhood. A warm relationship with his mother cools during his adolescence. A distant relationship to his father is described as becoming very intense. Affective stability is absent. His attempts to control emotionality with his wife and children are punctuated by angry outbursts and, in the case of the children, spankings. And while he says that he has several good friends, one senses considerable ambivalence embedded in those relationships also. . . .

The facts of the case were unintentionally distorted by the staff to achieve consistency with a popular theory of the dynamics of a schizophrenic reaction (*15*). Nothing of an ambivalent nature had been described in relations with parents, spouse, or friends. To the extent that ambivalence could be inferred, it was probably not greater than is found in all human relationships. It is true the pseudopatient's relationships with his parents changed over time, but in the ordinary context that would hardly be remarkable—indeed, it might very well be expected. Clearly, the meaning ascribed to his verbalizations (that is, ambivalence, affective instability) was determined by the diagnosis: schizophrenia. An entirely different meaning would have been ascribed if it were known that the man was "normal."

All pseudopatients took extensive notes publicly. Under ordinary circumstances, such behavior would have raised questions in the minds of observers, as, in fact, it did among patients. Indeed, it seemed so certain that the notes would elicit suspicion that elaborate precautions were taken to remove them from the ward each day. But the precautions proved needless. The closest any staff member came to questioning these notes occurred when one pseudopatient asked his physician what kind of medication he was receiving and began to write down the response. "You needn't write it," he was told gently. "If you have trouble remembering, just ask me again."

If no questions were asked of the pseudopatients, how was their writing interpreted? Nursing records for three patients indicate that the writing was seen as an aspect of their pathological behavior. "Patient engages in writing behavior" was the daily nursing comment on one of the pseudopatients who was never questioned about his writing. Given that the patient is in the hospital, he must be psychologically disturbed. And given that he is disturbed, continuous writing must be a behavioral manifestation of that disturbance, perhaps a subset of the compulsive behaviors that are sometimes correlated with schizophrenia.

One tacit characteristic of psychiatric diagnosis is that it locates the sources of aberration within the individual and only rarely within the complex of stimuli that surrounds him. Consequently, behaviors that are stimulated by the environment are commonly misattributed to the patient's disorder. For example, one kindly nurse found a pseudopatient pacing the long hospital corridors. "Nervous, Mr. X?" she asked. "No, bored," he said.

The notes kept by pseudopatients are full of patient behaviors that were misinterpreted by well-intentioned staff. Often enough, a patient would go "berserk" because he had, wittingly or unwittingly, been mistreated by, say, an attendant. A nurse coming upon the scene would rarely inquire even cursorily into the environmental stimuli of the patient's behavior. Rather, she assumed that his upset derived from his pathology, not from his present interactions with other staff members. Occasionally, the staff might assume that the patient's family (especially when they had recently visited) or other patients had stimulated the outburst. But never were the staff found to assume that one of themselves or the structure of the hospital had anything to do with a patient's behavior. One psychiatrist pointed to a group of patients who were sitting outside the cafeteria entrance half an hour before lunchtime. To a group of young residents he indicated that such behavior was characteristic of the oral-acquisitive nature of the syndrome. It seemed not to occur to him that there were very few things to anticipate in a psychiatric hospital besides eating.

A psychiatric label has a life and an influence of its own. Once the impression has been formed that the patient is schizophrenic, the expectation is that he will continue to be schizophrenic. When a sufficient amount of time has passed, during which the patient has done nothing bizarre, he is considered to be in remission and available for discharge. But the label endures beyond discharge, with the unconfirmed expectation that he will behave as a schizophrenic again. Such labels, conferred by mental health professionals, are as influential on the patient as they are on his relatives and friends, and it should not surprise anyone that the diagnosis acts on all of them as a self-fulfilling prophecy. Eventually, the patient himself accepts the diagnosis, with all of its surplus meanings and expectations, and behaves accordingly (5).

The inferences to be made from these matters are quite simple. Much as Zigler and Phillips have demonstrated that there is enormous overlap in the symptoms presented by patients who have been variously diagnosed (16), so there is enormous overlap in the behaviors of the sane and the insane. The sane are not "sane" all of the time. We lose our tempers "for no good reason." We are occasionally depressed or anxious, again for no good reason. And we may find it difficult to get along with one or another person—again for no reason that we can specify. Similarly, the insane are not always insane. Indeed, it was the impression of the pseudopatients while living with them that they were sane for long periods of time—that the bizarre behaviors upon which their diagnoses were allegedly predicated constituted only a small fraction of their total behavior. If it makes no sense to label ourselves permanently depressed on the basis of an occasional depression, then it takes better evidence than is presently available to label all patients insane or schizophrenic on the basis of bizarre behaviors or cognitions. It seems more useful, as Mischel (17) has pointed out, to limit our discussions to *behaviors*, the stimuli that provoke them, and their correlates.

It is not known why powerful impressions of personality traits, such as "crazy" or "insane," arise. Conceivably, when the origins of and stimuli that give rise to a behavior are remote or unknown, or when the behavior strikes us as immutable, trait labels regarding the *behaver* arise. When, on the other hand, the origins and stimuli are known and available, discourse is limited to the behavior itself. Thus, I may hallucinate because I am sleeping, or I may hallucinate because I have ingested a peculiar drug. These are termed sleep-induced hallucinations, or dreams, and drug-induced hallucinations, respectively. But when the stimuli to my hallucinations are unknown, that is called craziness, or schizophrenia—as if that inference were somehow as illuminating as the others.

## The Experience of Psychiatric Hospitalization

The term "mental illness" is of recent origin. It was coined by people who were humane in their inclinations and who wanted very much to raise the station of (and the public's sympathies toward) the psychologically disturbed from that of witches and "crazies" to one that was akin to the physically ill. And they were at least partially successful, for the treatment of the mentally ill *has* improved considerably over the years. But while treatment has improved, it is doubtful that people really regard the mentally ill in the same way that they view the physically ill. A broken leg is something one recovers from, but mental illness allegedly endures forever (18). A broken leg does not threaten the observer, but a crazy schizophrenic? There is by now a host of evidence that attitudes toward the mentally ill are characterized by fear, hostility, aloofness, suspicion, and dread (19). The mentally ill are society's lepers.

That such attitudes infect the general population is perhaps not surprising, only upsetting. But that they affect the professionals—attendants, nurses, physicians, psychologists, and social workers—who treat and deal with the mentally ill is more disconcerting, both because such attitudes are self-evidently pernicious and because they are unwitting. Most mental health professionals would insist that they are sympathetic toward the mentally ill, that they are neither avoidant nor hostile. But it is more likely that an exquisite ambivalence characterizes their relations with psychiatric patients, such that their avowed impulses are only part of their entire attitude. Negative attitudes are there too and can easily be detected. Such attitudes should not surprise us.

They are the natural offspring of the labels patients wear and the places in which they are found.

Consider the structure of the typical psychiatric hospital. Staff and patients are strictly segregated. Staff have their own living space, including their dining facilities, bathrooms, and assembly places. The glassed quarters that contain the professional staff, which the pseudopatients came to call "the cage," sit out on every dayroom. The staff emerge primarily for caretaking purposes—to give medication, to conduct a therapy or group meeting, to instruct or reprimand a patient. Otherwise, staff keep to themselves, almost as if the disorder that afflicts their charges is somehow catching.

So much is patient-staff segregation the rule that, for four public hospitals in which an attempt was made to measure the degree to which staff and patients mingle, it was necessary to use "time out of the staff cage" as the operational measure. While it was not the case that all time spent out of the cage was spent mingling with patients (attendants, for example, would occasionally emerge to watch television in the dayroom), it was the only way in which one could gather reliable data on time for measuring.

The average amount of time spent by attendants outside of the cage was 11.3 percent (range, 3 to 52 percent). This figure does not represent only time spent mingling with patients, but also includes time spent on such chores as folding laundry, supervising patients while they shave, directing ward cleanup, and sending patients to off-ward activities. It was the relatively rare attendant who spent time talking with patients or playing games with them. It proved impossible to obtain a "percent

mingling time" for nurses, since the amount of time they spent out of the cage was too brief. Rather, we counted instances of emergence from the cage. On the average, daytime nurses emerged from the cage 11.5 times per shift, including instances when they left the ward entirely (range, 4 to 39 times). Late afternoon and night nurses were even less available, emerging on the average 9.4 times per shift (range, 4 to 41 times). Data on early morning nurses, who arrived usually after midnight and departed at 8 a.m., are not available because patients were asleep during most of this period.

Physicians, especially psychiatrists, were even less available. They were rarely seen on the wards. Quite commonly, they would be seen only when they arrived and departed, with the remaining time being spent in their offices or in the cage. On the average, physicians emerged on the ward 6.7 times per day (range, 1 to 17 times). It proved difficult to make an accurate estimate in this regard, since physicians often maintained hours that allowed them to come and go at different times.

The hierarchical organization of the psychiatric hospital has been commented on before (20), but the latent meaning of that kind of organization is worth noting again. Those with the most power have least to do with patients, and those with the least power are most involved with them. Recall, however, that the acquisition of role-appropriate behaviors occurs mainly through the observation of others, with the most powerful having the most influence. Consequently, it is understandable that attendants not only spend more time with patients than do any other members of the staff—that is required by their station in the hierarchy

—but also, insofar as they learn from their superiors' behavior, spend as little time with patients as they can. Attendants are seen mainly in the cage, which is where the models, the action, and the power are.

I turn now to a different set of studies, these dealing with staff response to patient-initiated contact. It has long been known that the amount of time a person spends with you can be an index of your significance to him. If he initiates and maintains eye contact, there is reason to believe that he is considering your requests and needs. If he pauses to chat or actually stops and talks, there is added reason to infer that he is individuating you. In four hospitals, the pseudopatient approached the staff member with a request which took the following form: "Pardon me, Mr. [or Dr. or Mrs.] X, could you tell me when I will be eligible for grounds privileges?" (or " . . . when I will be presented at the staff meeting?" or ". . . when I am likely to be discharged?"). While the content of the question varied according to the appropriateness of the target and the pseudopatient's (apparent) current needs the form was always a courteous and relevant request for information. Care was taken never to approach a particular member of the staff more than once a day, lest the staff member become suspicious or irritated. In examining these data, remember that the behavior of the pseudopatients was neither bizarre nor disruptive. One could indeed engage in good conversation with them.

The data for these experiments are shown in Table 1, separately for physicians (column 1) and for nurses and attendants (column 2). Minor differences between these four institutions were overwhelmed by the degree to

Table 1. Self-initiated contact by pseudopatients with psychiatrists and nurses and attendants, compared to contact with other groups.

| Contact | Psychiatric hospitals | | University campus (nonmedical) | University medical center | | |
|---|---|---|---|---|---|---|
| | | | | Physicians | | |
| | (1) Psychiatrists | (2) Nurses and attendants | (3) Faculty | (4) "Looking for a psychiatrist" | (5) "Looking for an internist" | (6) No additional comment |
| **Responses** | | | | | | |
| Moves on, head averted (%) | 71 | 88 | 0 | 0 | 0 | 0 |
| Makes eye contact (%) | 23 | 10 | 0 | 11 | 0 | 0 |
| Pauses and chats (%) | 2 | 2 | 0 | 11 | 0 | 10 |
| Stops and talks (%) | 4 | 0.5 | 100 | 78 | 100 | 90 |
| Mean number of questions answered (out of 6) | * | * | 6 | 3.8 | 4.8 | 4.5 |
| Respondents (No.) | 13 | 47 | 14 | 18 | 15 | 10 |
| Attempts (No.) | 185 | 1283 | 14 | 18 | 15 | 10 |

* Not applicable.

which staff avoided continuing contacts that patients had initiated. By far, their most common response consisted of either a brief response to the question, offered while they were "on the move" and with head averted, or no response at all.

The encounter frequently took the following bizarre form: (pseudopatient) "Pardon me, Dr. X. Could you tell me when I am eligible for grounds privileges?" (physician) "Good morning, Dave. How are you today?" (Moves off without waiting for a response.)

It is instructive to compare these data with data recently obtained at Stanford University. It has been alleged that large and eminent universities are characterized by faculty who are so busy that they have no time for students. For this comparison, a young lady approached individual faculty members who seemed to be walking purposefully to some meeting or teaching engagement and asked them the following six questions.

1) "Pardon me, could you direct me to Encina Hall?" (at the medical school: ". . . to the Clinical Research Center?").

2) "Do you know where Fish Annex is?" (there is no Fish Annex at Stanford).

3) "Do you teach here?"

4) "How does one apply for admission to the college?" (at the medical school: ". . . to the medical school?").

5) "Is it difficult to get in?"

6) "Is there financial aid?"

Without exception, as can be seen in Table 1 (column 3), all of the questions were answered. No matter how rushed they were, all respondents not only maintained eye contact, but stopped to talk. Indeed, many of the respondents went out of their way to direct or take the questioner to the office she was seeking, to try to locate "Fish Annex," or to discuss with her the possibilities of being admitted to the university.

Similar data, also shown in Table 1 (columns 4, 5, and 6), were obtained in the hospital. Here too, the young lady came prepared with six questions. After the first question, however, she remarked to 18 of her respondents (column 4), "I'm looking for a psychiatrist," and to 15 others (column 5), "I'm looking for an internist." Ten other respondents received no inserted comment (column 6). The general degree of cooperative responses is considerably higher for these university

groups than it was for pseudopatients in psychiatric hospitals. Even so, differences are apparent within the medical school setting. Once having indicated that she was looking for a psychiatrist, the degree of cooperation elicited was less than when she sought an internist.

## Powerlessness and Depersonalization

Eye contact and verbal contact reflect concern and individuation; their absence, avoidance and depersonalization. The data I have presented do not do justice to the rich daily encounters that grew up around matters of depersonalization and avoidance. I have records of patients who were beaten by staff for the sin of having initiated verbal contact. During my own experience, for example, one patient was beaten in the presence of other patients for having approached an attendant and told him, "I like you." Occasionally, punishment meted out to patients for misdemeanors seemed so excessive that it could not be justified by the most radical interpretations of psychiatric canon. Nevertheless, they appeared to go unquestioned. Tempers were often short. A patient who had not heard a call for medication would be roundly excoriated, and the morning attendants would often wake patients with, "Come on, you m-----f-----s, out of bed!"

Neither anecdotal nor "hard" data can convey the overwhelming sense of powerlessness which invades the individual as he is continually exposed to the depersonalization of the psychiatric hospital. It hardly matters which psychiatric hospital—the excellent public ones and the very plush private hospital were better than the rural and shabby ones in this regard, but, again, the features that psychiatric hospitals had in common overwhelmed by far their apparent differences.

Powerlessness was evident everywhere. The patient is deprived of many of his legal rights by dint of his psychiatric commitment (21). He is shorn of credibility by virtue of his psychiatric label. His freedom of movement is restricted. He cannot initiate contact with the staff, but may only respond to such overtures as they make. Personal privacy is minimal. Patient quarters and possessions can be entered and examined by any staff member, for whatever reason. His personal history and anguish is available to any staff member

(often including the "grey lady" and "candy striper" volunteer) who chooses to read his folder, regardless of their therapeutic relationship to him. His personal hygiene and waste evacuation are often monitored. The water closets may have no doors.

At times, depersonalization reached such proportions that pseudopatients had the sense that they were invisible, or at least unworthy of account. Upon being admitted, I and other pseudopatients took the initial physical examinations in a semipublic room, where staff members went about their own business as if we were not there.

On the ward, attendants delivered verbal and occasionally serious physical abuse to patients in the presence of other observing patients, some of whom (the pseudopatients) were writing it all down. Abusive behavior, on the other hand, terminated quite abruptly when other staff members were known to be coming. Staff are credible witnesses. Patients are not.

A nurse unbuttoned her uniform to adjust her brassiere in the presence of an entire ward of viewing men. One did not have the sense that she was being seductive. Rather, she didn't notice us. A group of staff persons might point to a patient in the dayroom and discuss him animatedly, as if he were not there.

One illuminating instance of depersonalization and invisibility occurred with regard to medications. All told, the pseudopatients were administered nearly 2100 pills, including Elavil, Stelazine, Compazine, and Thorazine, to name but a few. (That such a variety of medications should have been administered to patients presenting identical symptoms is itself worthy of note.) Only two were swallowed. The rest were either pocketed or deposited in the toilet. The pseudopatients were not alone in this. Although I have no precise records on how many patients rejected their medications, the pseudopatients frequently found the medications of other patients in the toilet before they deposited their own. As long as they were cooperative, their behavior and the pseudopatients' own in this matter, as in other important matters, went unnoticed throughout.

Reactions to such depersonalization among pseudopatients were intense. Although they had come to the hospital as participant observers and were fully aware that they did not "belong," they nevertheless found themselves caught up in and fighting the process of depersonalization. Some examples: a graduate student in psychology asked his wife to bring his textbooks to the hospital so he could "catch up on his homework"—this despite the elaborate precautions taken to conceal his professional association. The same student, who had trained for quite some time to get into the hospital, and who had looked forward to the experience, "remembered" some drag races that he had wanted to see on the weekend and insisted that he be discharged by that time. Another pseudopatient attempted a romance with a nurse. Subsequently, he informed the staff that he was applying for admission to graduate school in psychology and was very likely to be admitted, since a graduate professor was one of his regular hospital visitors. The same person began to engage in psychotherapy with other patients—all of this as a way of becoming a person in an impersonal environment.

**The Sources of Depersonalization**

What are the origins of depersonalization? I have already mentioned two. First are attitudes held by all of us toward the mentally ill—including those who treat them—attitudes characterized by fear, distrust, and horrible expectations on the one hand, and benevolent intentions on the other. Our ambivalence leads, in this instance as in others, to avoidance.

Second, and not entirely separate, the hierarchical structure of the psychiatric hospital facilitates depersonalization. Those who are at the top have least to do with patients, and their behavior inspires the rest of the staff. Average daily contact with psychiatrists, psychologists, residents, and physicians combined ranged from 3.9 to 25.1 minutes, with an overall mean of 6.8 (six pseudopatients over a total of 129 days of hospitalization). Included in this average are time spent in the admissions interview, ward meetings in the presence of a senior staff member, group and individual psychotherapy contacts, case presentation conferences, and discharge meetings. Clearly, patients do not spend much time in interpersonal contact with doctoral staff. And doctoral staff serve as models for nurses and attendants.

There are probably other sources. Psychiatric installations are presently in serious financial straits. Staff shortages are pervasive, staff time at a premium. Something has to give, and that something is patient contact. Yet, while financial stresses are realities, too much can be made of them. I have the impression that the psychological forces that result in depersonalization are much stronger than the fiscal ones and that the addition of more staff would not correspondingly improve patient care in this regard. The incidence of staff meetings and the enormous amount of record-keeping on patients, for example, have not been as substantially reduced as has patient contact. Priorities exist, even during hard times. Patient contact is not a significant priority in the traditional psychiatric hospital, and fiscal pressures do not account for this. Avoidance and depersonalization may.

Heavy reliance upon psychotropic medication tacitly contributes to depersonalization by convincing staff that treatment is indeed being conducted and that further patient contact may not be necessary. Even here, however, caution needs to be exercised in understanding the role of psychotropic drugs. If patients were powerful rather than powerless, if they were viewed as interesting individuals rather than diagnostic entities, if they were socially significant rather than social lepers, if their anguish truly and wholly compelled our sympathies and concerns, would we not *seek* contact with them, despite the availability of medications? Perhaps for the pleasure of it all?

**The Consequences of Labeling and Depersonalization**

Whenever the ratio of what is known to what needs to be known approaches zero, we tend to invent "knowledge" and assume that we understand more than we actually do. We seem unable to acknowledge that we simply don't know. The needs for diagnosis and remediation of behavioral and emotional problems are enormous. But rather than acknowledge that we are just embarking on understanding, we continue to label patients "schizophrenic," "manic-depressive," and "insane," as if in those words we had captured the essence of understanding. The facts of the matter are that we have known for a long time that diagnoses are often not useful or reliable, but we have nevertheless continued to use them. We now know that we cannot distinguish insanity from sanity. It is depressing to consider how that information will be used.

Not merely depressing, but frightening. How many people, one wonders, are sane but not recognized as such in our psychiatric institutions? How many have been needlessly stripped of their privileges of citizenship, from the right to vote and drive to that of handling their own accounts? How many have feigned insanity in order to avoid the criminal consequences of their behavior, and, conversely, how many would rather stand trial than live interminably in a psychiatric hospital—but are wrongly thought to be mentally ill? How many have been stigmatized by well-intentioned, but nevertheless erroneous, diagnoses? On the last point, recall again that a "type 2 error" in psychiatric dia nosis does not have the same consequences it does in medical diagnosis. A diagnosis of cancer that has been found to be in error is cause for celebration. But psychiatric diagnoses are rarely found to be in error. The label sticks, a mark of inadequacy forever.

Finally, how many patients might be "sane" outside the psychiatric hospital but seem insane in it—not because craziness resides in them, as it were, but because they are responding to a bizarre setting, one that may be unique to institutions which harbor nether people? Goffman (4) calls the process of socialization to such institutions "mortification"—an apt metaphor that includes the processes of depersonalization that have been described here. And while it is impossible to know whether the pseudopatients' responses to these processes are characteristic of all inmates—they were, after all, not real patients—it is difficult to believe that these processes of socialization to a psychiatric hospital provide useful attitudes or habits of response for living in the "real world."

**Summary and Conclusions**

It is clear that we cannot distinguish the sane from the insane in psychiatric hospitals. The hospital itself imposes a special environment in which the meanings of behavior can easily be misunderstood. The consequences to patients hospitalized in such an environment—

the powerlessness, depersonalization, segregation, mortification, and self-labeling—seem undoubtedly counter-therapeutic.

I do not, even now, understand this problem well enough to perceive solutions. But two matters seem to have some promise. The first concerns the proliferation of community mental health facilities, of crisis intervention centers, of the human potential movement, and of behavior therapies that, for all of their own problems, tend to avoid psychiatric labels, to focus on specific problems and behaviors, and to retain the individual in a relatively non-pejorative environment. Clearly, to the extent that we refrain from sending the distressed to insane places, our impressions of them are less likely to be distorted. (The risk of distorted perceptions, it seems to me, is always present, since we are much more sensitive to an individual's behaviors and verbalizations than we are to the subtle contextual stimuli that often promote them. At issue here is a matter of magnitude. And, as I have shown, the magnitude of distortion is exceedingly high in the extreme context that is a psychiatric hospital.)

The second matter that might prove promising speaks to the need to increase the sensitivity of mental health workers and researchers to the *Catch 22* position of psychiatric patients. Simply reading materials in this area will be of help to some such workers and researchers. For others, directly experiencing the impact of psychiatric hospitalization will be of enormous use. Clearly, further research into the social psychology of such total institutions will both facilitate treatment and deepen understanding.

I and the other pseudopatients in the psychiatric setting had distinctly negative reactions. We do not pretend to describe the subjective experiences of true patients. Theirs may be different from ours, particularly with the passage of time and the necessary process of adaptation to one's environment. But we can and do speak to the relatively more objective indices of treatment within the hospital. It could be a mistake, and a very unfortunate one, to consider that what happened to us derived from malice or stupidity on the part of the staff. Quite the contrary, our overwhelming impression of them was of people who really cared, who were committed and who were uncom-

monly intelligent. Where they failed, as they sometimes did painfully, it would be more accurate to attribute those failures to the environment in which they, too, found themselves than to personal callousness. Their perceptions and behavior were controlled by the situation, rather than being motivated by a malicious disposition. In a more benign environment, one that was less attached to global diagnosis, their behaviors and judgments might have been more benign and effective.

### References and Notes

1. P. Ash, *J. Abnorm. Soc. Psychol.* **44**, 272 (1949); A. T. Beck, *Amer. J. Psychiat.* **119**, 210 (1962); A. T. Boisen, *Psychiatry* **2**, 233 (1938); N. Kreitman, *J. Ment. Sci.* **107**, 876 (1961); N. Kreitman, P. Sainsbury, J. Morrisey, J. Towers, J. Scrivener, *ibid.*, p. 887; H. O. Schmitt and C. P. Fonda, *J. Abnorm. Soc. Psychol.* **52**, 262 (1956); W. Seeman, *J. Nerv. Ment. Dis.* **118**, 541 (1953). For an analysis of these artifacts and summaries of the disputes, see J. Zubin, *Annu. Rev. Psychol.* **18**, 373 (1967); L. Phillips and J. G. Draguns, *ibid.* **22**, 447 (1971).
2. R. Benedict, *J. Gen. Psychol.* **10**, 59 (1934).
3. See in this regard H. Becker, *Outsiders: Studies in the Sociology of Deviance* (Free Press, New York, 1963); B. M. Braginsky, D. D. Braginsky, K. Ring, *Methods of Madness: The Mental Hospital as a Last Resort* (Holt, Rinehart & Winston, New York, 1969); G. M. Crocetti and P. V. Lemkau, *Amer. Sociol. Rev.* **30**, 577 (1965); E. Goffman, *Behavior in Public Places* (Free Press, New York, 1964); R. D. Laing, *The Divided Self: A Study of Sanity and Madness* (Quadrangle, Chicago, 1960); D. L. Phillips, *Amer. Sociol. Rev.* **28**, 963 (1963); T. R. Sarbin, *Psychol. Today* **6**, 18 (1972); E. Schur, *Amer. J. Sociol.* **75**, 309 (1969); T. Szasz, *Law, Liberty and Psychiatry* (Macmillan, New York, 1963); *The Myth of Mental Illness: Foundations of a Theory of Mental Illness* (Hoeber-Harper, New York, 1963). For a critique of some of these views, see W. R. Gove, *Amer. Sociol. Rev.* **35**, 873 (1970).
4. E. Goffman, *Asylums* (Doubleday, Garden City, N.Y., 1961).
5. T. J. Scheff, *Being Mentally Ill: A Sociological Theory* (Aldine, Chicago, 1966).
6. Data from a ninth pseudopatient are not incorporated in this report because, although his sanity went undetected, he falsified aspects of his personal history, including his marital status and parental relationships. His experimental behaviors therefore were not identical to those of the other pseudopatients.
7. A. Barry, *Bellevue Is a State of Mind* (Harcourt Brace Jovanovich, New York, 1971); I. Belknap, *Human Problems of a State Mental Hospital* (McGraw-Hill, New York, 1956); W. Caudill, F. C. Redlich, H. R. Gilmore, E. B. Brody, *Amer. J. Orthopsychiat.* **22**, 314 (1952); A. R. Goldman, R. H. Bohr, T. A. Steinberg, *Prof. Psychol.* **1**, 427 (1970); unauthored, *Roche Report* **1** (No. 13), 8 (1971).
8. Beyond the personal difficulties that the pseudopatient is likely to experience in the hospital, there are legal and social ones that,

combined, require considerable attention before entry. For example, once admitted to a psychiatric institution, it is difficult, if not impossible, to be discharged on short notice, state law to the contrary notwithstanding. I was not sensitive to these difficulties at the outset of the project, nor to the personal and situational emergencies that can arise, but later a writ of habeas corpus was prepared for each of the entering pseudopatients and an attorney was kept "on call" during every hospitalization. I am grateful to John Kaplan and Robert Bartels for legal advice and assistance in these matters.
9. However distasteful such concealment is, it was a necessary first step to examining these questions. Without concealment, there would have been no way to know how valid these experiences were; nor was there any way of knowing whether whatever detections occurred were a tribute to the diagnostic acumen of the staff or to the hospital's rumor network. Obviously, since my concerns are general ones that cut across individual hospitals and staffs, I have respected their anonymity and have eliminated clues that might lead to their identification.
10. Interestingly, of the 12 admissions, 11 were diagnosed as schizophrenic and one, with the identical symptomatology, as manic-depressive psychosis. This diagnosis has a more favorable prognosis, and it was given by the only private hospital in our sample. On the relations between social class and psychiatric diagnosis, see A. deB. Hollingshead and F. C. Redlich, *Social Class and Mental Illness: A Community Study* (Wiley, New York, 1958).
11. It is possible, of course, that patients have quite broad latitudes in diagnosis and therefore are inclined to call many people sane, even those whose behavior is patently aberrant. However, although we have no hard data on this matter, it was our distinct impression that this was not the case. In many instances, patients not only singled us out for attention, but came to imitate our behaviors and styles.
12. J. Cumming and E. Cumming, *Community Ment. Health* **1**, 135 (1965); A. Farina and K. Ring, *J. Abnorm. Psychol.* **70**, 47 (1965); H. E. Freeman and O. G. Simmons, *The Mental Patient Comes Home* (Wiley, New York, 1963); W. J. Johannsen, *Ment. Hygiene* **53**, 218 (1969); A. S. Linsky, *Soc. Psychiat.* **5**, 166 (1970).
13. S. E. Asch, *J. Abnorm. Soc. Psychol.* **41**, 258 (1946); *Social Psychology* (Prentice-Hall, New York, 1952).
14. See also I. N. Mensh and J. Wishner, *J. Personality* **16**, 188 (1947); J. Wishner, *Psychol. Rev.* **67**, 96 (1960); J. S. Bruner and R. Tagiuri, in *Handbook of Social Psychology*, G. Lindzey, Ed. (Addison-Wesley, Cambridge, Mass., 1954), vol. 2, pp. 634–654; J. S. Bruner, D. Shapiro, R. Tagiuri, in *Person Perception and Interpersonal Behavior*, R. Tagiuri and L. Petrullo, Eds. (Stanford Univ. Press, Stanford, Calif., 1958), pp. 277–288.
15. For an example of a similar self-fulfilling prophecy, in this instance dealing with the "central" trait of intelligence, see R. Rosenthal and L. Jacobson, *Pygmalion in the Classroom* (Holt, Rinehart & Winston, New York, 1968).
16. E. Zigler and L. Phillips, *J. Abnorm. Soc. Psychol.* **63**, 69 (1961). See also R. K. Freudenberg and J. P. Robertson, *A.M.A. Arch. Neurol. Psychiatr.* **76**, 14 (1956).
17. W. Mischel, *Personality and Assessment* (Wiley, New York, 1968).
18. The most recent and unfortunate instance of this tenet is that of Senator Thomas Eagleton.
19. T. R. Sarbin and J. C. Mancuso, *J. Clin. Consult. Psychol.* **35**, 159 (1970); T. R. Sarbin, *ibid.* **31**, 447 (1967); J. C. Nunnally, Jr., *Popular Conceptions of Mental Health* (Holt, Rinehart & Winston, New York, 1961).
20. A. H. Stanton and M. S. Schwartz, *The Mental Hospital: A Study of Institutional Participation in Psychiatric Illness and Treatment* (Basic, New York, 1954).
21. D. B. Wexler and S. E. Scoville, *Ariz. Law Rev.* **13**, 1 (1971).
22. I thank W. Mischel, E. Orne, and M. S. Rosenhan for comments on an earlier draft of this manuscript.

# 19

# Behind Bars

## TOM MILLER

"The degree of civilization in a society can be judged by entering its prisons."

— *Feodor Dostoevsky, author*

"Living in the control unit is impossible for a free person to understand. The only way you could understand it is to go into your bathroom, lock the door, lie down in the bathtub, and remain there for three to four years. Cut off contact from your family and your friends, and you will start to glimpse the feeling we go through."

— *Earl X. Gaither, inmate*

The United States Penitentiary at Marion is set back in the rolling hills of rural southern Illinois. The prison is about ten miles from Marion, a town of 12,000, and is accessible only by driving on the small back roads off the main two-lane highway. The route is marked by two unassuming green signs. At the entrance to the prison grounds, another sign warns "all unauthorized personnel" to turn around and a gravel circle on the left side of the road is conveniently provided for this purpose. The entrance road winds gently through well-tended fields of grass and beautiful stands of trees — an unusually scenic (and inappropriate) landscape. To the right of the road is a cluster of suburban-style houses, where some prison employes and their families live. On the sweltering mid-August afternoon when I first arrived at Marion, shirtless children were frolicking in the front yards of these houses. The penitentiary loomed large in the background.

From a distance, the prison complex seems to consist of several concrete and steel boxes; no windows are readily discernible from the road. The structure is low-lying — about two stories tall at most — and massive, sprawling over several acres. Guard towers protrude into the skyline; two tall wire mesh fences, with barbed wire at the top of each and coiled between them, enclose the penitentiary. All visitors approaching the prison must stop at an intercom alongside the road and report their business to a guard in a nearby tower, who then issues clearance to proceed to the prison itself.

You enter the prison through the administration building. Inside the main glass doors is a large lobby, furnished sparsely with a few sofas and chairs. Above one sofa hangs a group of photographs depicting, in chronological order, the past and present wardens of Marion. Tributes to John F. Kennedy — under whose Administration Marion was completed in 1963 — and to former Attorneys General and directors of the Federal Bureau of Prisons adorn the other walls. At the far end of the lobby, a solidly built guard sits at the registration desk. Behind him, an iron-barred, plexiglass gate separates visitors from Marion's 525 inmates.

The size and solemnity of the place are intimidating. Walking from the front doors to the registration desk, I felt conspicuous as my footsteps echoed through the lobby As I neared the desk to sign in, the iron gate behind it suddenly began to whir and slide open, and two officials emerged from the passageway that connects to the prisoners' quarters. The gate decisively clanged shut behind them — a final, authoritative sound that reverberated in the expanse of the lobby. All of the gates in Marion — those partitioning the prison into sections and those sealing off each individual cell — are electronically controlled. It can no longer be said, in a strict sense, that prisoners are kept under lock and key.

It is not difficult to see why Marion is called the New Alcatraz. In fact, Marion was specifically designed to replace Alcatraz, which was closed in 1962, as the most closely guarded of all Federal prisons. The prisoners confined in Marion, Warden Charles Fenton told me, are serving an average sentence of twenty years, a grim statistic which places the penitentiary first in terms of serious offenders; the Federal penitentiary at Leavenworth, whose inmates have been sentenced to an average of ten years, is a distant second.

Security at Marion has lived up to the expectations of its designers: Since 1971, when the barbed wire was placed between the fences on the perimeter of the prison, there has been only one successful escape from Marion. On October 10, 1975, five prisoners manufactured a device that somehow opened the electronic gates, allowing them to walk out of the penitentiary. Although all the escapees were subsequently recaptured, prison officials are still trying to figure out how the device worked and how the prisoners could surreptitiously have built it.

Last July, the Bureau of Prisons announced a temporary change in its policy governing press access to Federal prisons. For the first time, representatives of "legitimate" news media were allowed to interview prisoners in maximum security institutions whom they could designate by name. Because of this new policy, which was to remain in effect only until December, I was able to visit the Marion Federal Penitentiary and talk to eight prisoners. I was particularly interested in Marion's "control unit," a prison-within-a-prison that is perhaps the most severe sanction in modern American penology, short of capital punishment.

The control unit, or Controlled Unit Treatment Program (CTP), is the up-to-date version of solitary confinement. It consists of seventy-two long-term segregation cells. The Bureau of Prisons regards the men who are incarcerated in these cells as the most dangerous and aggressive convicts among the 27,000 inmates currently serving time in Federal penal institutions. Control unit prisoners are not allowed out of their six-foot by eight-foot cells for more than one half hour a day. Whenever they are transported from one area of the prison to another, they are placed in handcuffs. According to Dr. Robert Levinson, the Inmate Program Services Administrator at the Bureau of Prisons who helped design the CTP, the control unit is "the end of the line of the end of the line."

Established in 1972 by the prison officials at Marion in the wake of a work stoppage by inmates, the control unit program was not regulated by Bureau of Prisons guidelines until almost a year later. The Bureau policy statement on the CTP, which was released in June 1973, stated that the purpose of the control unit is "to separate those offenders whose behavior seriously disrupts the orderly operation of an institution from the vast majority of offenders who wish to participate in regular institution programs."

Prisoners with "proven and demonstrated behavior problems" can be assigned to the control unit for committing repeated assaults or serious threats, participating in group disturbances, or attempting to escape. Although the first occupants of the control unit came from the Marion penitentiary's own population, inmates from all thirty-seven Federal prisons can now be transferred to the Marion control unit, and state prisons can send disruptive prisoners to the CTP by paying a "boarding fee" to the Federal Prisons System.

As defined by the Bureau of Prisons policy statement, the control unit is a behavior modification program, "designed to assist the individual in changing his attitude and behavior so he may be returned to a regular institution program." A central concept of the CTP is a progression system, consisting of at least three levels of privileges, responsibilities, and rewards, through which offenders are to be motivated to improve their conduct: "Each level should offer some advantages to the participant and assist in creating an incentive to advance."

This progression system, according to the policy statement, is "essential" and must be "specifically spelled out in a program plan." The policy statement also guarantees each prisoner in the control unit "humane living conditions and an opportunity to engage in self-improvement activities." Examples of individual activities that should be made available to the prisoners include a work program, an educational program "for all levels of academic needs," and a cultural program.

Since its inception, however, the control unit has been enveloped in controversy. Prisoners have constantly complained of conditions in the unit, alleging frequent beatings by guards, administration of drugs on unconsenting inmates, inadequate diet, the routine denial of physical exercise, and other abuses. They cite the "boxcar cells" — a group of cells sealed off by an outer steel door — in which inmates often are fed only cold bag lunches. They claim that censorship of reading material, deliberate delays in the delivery of mail, and confiscation of egal papers are regular occurrences in the control unit They contend that a progression system which would enable them to work their way out of the unit does not exist, that the work program is exploitative, that the educational opportunities are pitifully inadequate, and that the cultural program is an insult to their intelligence.

The inmates in Marion's CTP have twice taken their grievances to court. In *Adams* v. *Carlson*, a suit decided in December 1973, the prisoners persuaded a Federal judge to order the release from the control unit of thirty-six men who, he said, were being excessively punished, not "treated." These men had been confined to the control unit for sixteen months because they had taken part in the work strike of July 1972 in protest against prison conditions.

A more recent class-action suit, *Bono* v. *Saxbe*, which was initiated in April 1974 and is still in litigation, seeks to close down the control unit entirely. It not only challenges the "severely punitive conditions" in the CTP, but raises serious questions about its functions. The suit alleges that prisoners are arbitrarily placed in the CTP because of their political and religious beliefs and activities. The complaining prisoners, their lawyers, and the National Prison Project of the American Civil Liberties Union contend that the control unit is merely a convenient "hole" in which prison administrators can isolate prison activists.

The control unit was designed to achieve total security, and its physical arrangements are quite different from those provided for other prisoners at Marion. In H-unit, the cellblock devoted to the CTP, each cell has an outer vestibule enclosed by a door, in addition to the usual iron-barred gate enclosing the cell. When the outer doors are closed, the prisoner is effectively isolated from the inmates in neighboring cells. There are four rows, or "ranges," of eighteen cells each in the control unit and, unlike the ranges in other cellblocks, these are caged in by steel gratings that extend from floor to ceiling.

Recreational facilities for control unit prisoners are far more limited than those available to other prisoners. There is one television set in the control unit, which can be seen from about twelve of the seventy-two cells. A small courtyard, with one basketball hoop, is the only outdoor facility which control unit prisoners can use. In contrast, inmates who are not in segregation have access to several baseball and football fields, bowling alleys, weight-lifting machines, pool tables, television sets, an indoor gymnasium, handball courts, and a miniature golf course that was built by prisoners.

Prisoners in the general population — those who are not segregated — are often outside eight to ten hours a day when the weather permits; the men in the control unit usually do not get out of their cells for more than two hours a week, and their exercise generally consists of walking or jogging along the range in front of their cells. Meals are served to control unit prisoners in their cells, not in the regular dining hall.

This extreme degree of isolation, prison officials contend, is justified by the criminal histories of the prisoners in the control unit. A compilation of the offenses committed by those prisoners, which was given to me by the warden while I was at Marion, lists a total of 190 crimes committed by the sixty-eight men then in H-unit, including twenty-one murders, eighteen assaults, seven kidnappings, forty-nine bank robberies, seventeen robberies, and twenty-three escapes or attempted escapes. About a fourth of the offenses listed had been committed by the inmates while they were in prison. According to Warden Fenton, the inmates who were in the control unit at the time of my visit were serving an average sentence of thirty-eight years.

Of the eight prisoners I interviewed at Marion, four were confined in the control unit. Two others were in disciplinary segregation, or I-unit, in which the living conditions are identical to H-unit; the difference is in the time served in each form of segregation. Prisoners are not sentenced to the control unit for a specific period; they are told that their stay in the "hole" is indeterminate. Unless an inmate takes his case to court, the duration of his stay in the CTP rests solely with the prison administration. The

R. Nass, Ampersand Design

average stay in the control unit is nine months to a year, though many remain for twice as long, while in I-unit the average duration of disciplinary segregation is three to six months.

I chose the prisoners I interviewed from lists provided by the National Prison Project; by attorney Arpiar Saunders, who is representing the prisoners in the *Bono* v. *Saxbe* suit, and by the National Committee to Support the Marion Brothers, a St. Louis-based organization that is trying to have the control unit closed down permanently.

I had originally asked to meet with nine prisoners, but one refused to see me. A letter from the National Prison Project introducing me to the prisoners, which was mailed two weeks before my arrival at Marion, was not delivered to this man until after he had been given an interview release form by prison officials. Not knowing who I was, this control unit prisoner indicated on the form that he would not consent to be interviewed. Several days afterwards, he received the letter of introduction, reconsidered, and asked the warden to be allowed to meet with me. While at Marion, I twice asked the warden to give this prisoner a second interview release form. The requests were denied. In a later letter to the National Prison Project, this prisoner referred to the "hold-the-letter-back ploy": "It worked," he wrote.

All but one of my interviews were conducted in a small, isolated room beyond the regular visiting area. After having my briefcase inspected and being asked if I was carrying contraband, I was admitted to the main prison corridor, where I passed through a metal detector. About eighty feet along the central corridor, I reached another gate, which was buzzed open for me. A guard directed me to the improvised "press room," formerly a visiting area for segregated prisoners, where four metal and plexiglass booths were lined up side by side; the two booths farthest from the door had the pane of unbreakable plexiglass between them removed, leaving a four-foot by six-foot enclosure separated by a two-foot-high metal divider. Two telephones, which prisoners in segregation must use to communicate with their visitors, sat, disconnected, on a narrow ledge in the booth. There was barely room enough for a chair in each of the closet-like compartments. I was led to the last booth, and locked in.

Opposite me sat a black man with shoulder-length hair, clad in a frayed khaki shirt and work pants. Victor M. Daniel, thirty-four years old, told me he was born in Detroit "of a working-class background," his father an independent plasterer and his mother employed by a Michigan social services agency. For nineteen of the past twenty-one years, Daniel has been confined in one form or another — in a boys' camp, a mental hospital, and, twice, in prison. He is currently serving time for robbery and was, when I spoke with him, in disciplinary segregation.

Articulate and obviously intelligent — Daniel received nationwide press attention when he graduated from Southern Illinois University while imprisoned at Marion — he was outspoken on the function and nature of the segregation units. He was originally placed in segregation, Daniel told me, for his participation in a prisoner-organized seminar on "The Black Soldier: From the Civil War to Modern Ones." The notes he took as secretary of the group were considered "illegal" by prison officials, and his supposed "clandestine" activities were perceived as a threat to the "orderly functioning of the institution." As a result of being put in the "hole," Daniel lost his job in the prison factory and his chance for parole.

This is how Vic Daniel described to me what he believes to be the rationale used in selecting prisoners for the control unit and for disciplinary segregation: "The prison [administrators] focus in on people that they consider to be leaders. They are hung up on this idea of leaders. But the men that they lock up are, if anything, the crystallization of a consciousness that is current in the population itself. These are guys who simply pursue that line of consciousness.... They get off into their books and read." A major aim in segregating prisoners for long periods, he continued, is to "modify" beliefs that "contradict the so-called American values — the Protestant work ethic, and things of that sort." The principle that officials want prisoners to accept, he stressed, is that "however the system was made to run, that is the right thing."

This attempted modification of beliefs, Daniel said, "also fits in with the concept that you're a prisoner, you're ignorant, you're not supposed to think, and you're not supposed to do research." His own education has been pursued despite formidable obstacles. After being accepted into graduate school at Southern Illinois, he was transferred to Leavenworth — "a most effective means of stopping my education." Previously, some people from the university who were helping him in his studies were removed from his visiting list. And he has found it difficult to obtain political reading matter: "I just got the *Anti-Duhring* by Engels, but," he laughed, "I don't think they know who Fred Engels is."

There is "little food for thought" in the control unit or the disciplinary segregation unit, Daniel said. Any book or magazine that a prisoner requests must come from the prison library, through a loan from a local library, or directly from the publisher; family and friends are not allowed to send reading material into the prison. Furthermore, as the personnel officer at Marion told me, literature that is "inflammatory" or "likely to create a disturbance" is returned to the sender. Publications from the National Lawyers' Guild or prisoners' support groups which advocate prisoner involvement in penal reform movements — such as *The Midnight Special, The Conspiracy,* and *The Outlaw* — are generally banned.

The education supervisor at Marion told me that thirty to forty of the men in the control unit were involved in education programs ranging from high school equivalency courses to college correspondence courses. But prisoners in the control unit must bear the total cost of a correspondence course, unless they can procure veterans' benefits or a scholarship. According to a prisoner in the general population who has taken several of these courses by means of a scholarship and loans, the average cost runs from about $50 to $70. Since only a minority of the prisoners are gainfully employed, and even their wages provide no more than a paltry income, college-level study is virtually out of bounds. There is little formal instruction given to students in the control unit; the very nature of the segregation units means that most of the material must be self-taught through independent study.

There was agreement among all the prisoners with whom I spoke that the "individual activities" outlined in the Bureau of Prisons policy statement on the control unit were more fiction than reality. For example, the Bureau's guidelines detail the need for an industry or work program within the control unit. Yet profits, not the welfare of prisoners, are the primary consideration here: The industry, according to Bureau policy, "will be of such a nature that the number of men participating can vary without significantly affecting productivity."

At the time of my visit, fifteen of the sixty-eight men in the control unit were employed. For assembling computer patchcords, these "privileged" prisoners receive a starting wage of twenty-eight cents an hour; if they prove themselves good workers, they may be able to earn as much as forty-two cents per hour. Vocational training is not a goal in the industries at Marion, the warden told me during my tour of Marion's print shop and furniture plant; the industries, he said, are first and foremost "profit-making enterprises."

Though this is their only opportunity to earn money, many of the prisoners in the control unit feel that the work program not only is exploitative but also is used as a manipulative device by the prison administration. As Stephen Kessler, a control unit prisoner, told me: "They really use it to play people off from each other. They use it like the carrot-in-front-of-the-donkey trick. Myself, I would refuse to participate."

Kessler was another inmate I interviewed in my little cubicle. A white man of medium build, he looked gaunt and told me that he had a kidney ailment. Though he had been temporarily taken out of the control unit to a prison hospital, he said he had lost thirty pounds because of inadequate medical attention at the hospital and poor food.

When I asked Kessler about leisure activity, which the Bureau of Prisons policy statement says should "assist [the inmate]in keeping mentally alert" and is "limited only to the imagination" of prison officials, he told me about the arts and crafts program in Marion's control unit. "I've been here ten months," he said, "and two times they brought us 'doodle art' — it's for a little kid. It's like a coloring book, only you do it with felt-tip pens instead of crayons." The public information officer at Marion later verified the "doodle-art" story, but hastened to add that prisoners could buy art supplies from the commissary, if they could afford them. Nevertheless, a prisoner's participation in "doodle-art" is one of the few positive indicators used to measure his "adjustment."

I was impressed with Steve Kessler's concern for some of the men who, in his words, do not have "a larger analysis" or an "ideological basis" to help them cope with the solitary life of the control unit. Kessler says his philosophy, "based on Marxism and Leninism," puts the prison experience in perspective: "The prison system," he said, "only perpetrates what the Government creates in the first place, because [the Government] cannot economically take care of the working class. In times of unemployment, the [prison] population rises. The purpose of the prison is to make people conform to the system — in the capitalist system, it is the idea of profits to the few. Another purpose of the prison is to break the will of people who resist."

Kessler admitted to me that he had committed the crime of which he was originally convicted — armed robbery. He said he now sees his offense as a reaction to "material conditions in a blind, instinctive way" and as "rebelliousness toward something I really couldn't define at the time."

While serving time at the Atlanta Federal Penitentiary in 1968, Kessler participated in the creation of the Church of the New Song, a controversial religious movement organized by prisoners. The Church, according to its members, is a multi-racial, nonviolent organization that encourages solidarity and activism among prisoners. Federal prison officials, on the other hand, maintain that the only

# Crime and Class

The common opinion that economic crime is uniquely the province of the poor is dead wrong. It's just prison, not crime, that is reserved for non-whites, for the unemployed, and for the working class. Many of the poorer people behind bars have never been convicted. A U.S. Census study showed that 52 per cent of the people confined in local jails are there because they are awaiting trial and can't afford to post bail. Even more significant is the number of white-collar criminals who will never be arrested, never be indicted, never be convicted.

Take the most extreme example: mass murder. On March 3, 1974, a Turkish Airlines DC-10 jetliner crashed nine minutes after taking off from the Paris airport. At least 246 people were killed. The causes of the crash were a faulty baggage door and a weak cabin floor. The manufacturers of the plane — McDonnell Douglas Aircraft — knew about these weaknesses, which had caused a similar (but non-fatal) accident in Canada two years before. No one was ever indicted, much less imprisoned, for this crime. The only question was how much of the loot which McDonnell Douglas picked up by cutting corners in design and production would have to be paid out in civil damages.

Manufacturing an airplane that kills 246 people is not officially a crime. But many forms of white-collar profiteering are crimes in law as well as fact. In 1965 nationwide losses to robbery of the stick-'em-up variety were $27 million; losses to embezzlement were $200 million. Overall, the cost of white-collar crime totaled $1.7 billion, while the working class crimes of robbery, burglary, and theft cost only $608 million.

White-collar criminals do not only win in money terms. They win in the sentencing game, as well. In 1969, Federal courts convicted 502 individuals of tax frauds averaging $190,000 each. Only ninety-five got jail terms, which averaged 9.5 months. The same courts convicted 254 people for burglaries (of Federal property, post offices, and banks) and almost 4,000 people for interstate car thefts. Though these crimes involved no more violence than tax evasion does, and though they netted the criminals far less of the public's money, the courts sentenced more than 60 per cent of the burglars and car thieves to prison, for terms averaging more than twenty months.

— "Staying Out of Prison Takes a Lot of Class,"
*Dollars and Sense,* November 1976

purpose of the Church is to extort champagne and steak dinners for its religious services. A suit filed several years ago to determine the legitimacy of the Church of the New Song is still awaiting a decision.

While at the Oregon State Prison, Kessler was active in the Oregon Prisoners' Coalition, working for racial unity and calling for investigations into prison conditions. Officials there charged him with being a member of a mysterious group called "The Family" that was plotting to assassinate the warden; an administrative hearing determined his "guilt," and he was sent to Marion's control unit.

I conducted two other interviews in the cubicle on my first day at Marion. Fred Bustillo, a Chicano, was a prisoner in the disciplinary segregation unit. He had been an editor of *Aztlan*, a Chicano publication, at Leavenworth, and after his transfer to Marion he had joined a Chicano cultural group which was eventually disbanded by prison authorities on grounds that it "had abandoned all cultural aspects and was in reality a political revolutionary group."

Bustillo spoke in intense, emotional terms about the hostility between prisoners and guards. Most of the prison guards at Marion come from nearby communities in southern Illinois, an area noted for its political conservatism and durable racism. Many of the prisoners come from urban, minority backgrounds. "There is always an atmosphere of hostility, of tension," Bustillo said, and often it erupts into violence. He claimed to have witnessed several beatings of inmates by guards — in fact, all of the prisoners I interviewed said they had seen, heard, or learned about beatings in the segregation units, and one inmate alleged he had been beaten by six officers on New Year's Day, 1976.

Jazz Jasper, a slender black man from the control unit, mentioned several instances in which black prisoners had been beaten by white guards. He agreed with Stephen Kessler's assessment that prisoners who attempt to promote racial unity are often those who are isolated from the general prison population: "Most of them — white, black, and Chicano — have been going out of their way to try to get the races together. The stabbings, the fighting, the killing, the racial enmity — most of the convicts that I see in the holes are constantly speaking out against this." Jasper also echoed a sentiment I had heard from Vic Daniel: "It's no longer a racial question, it's a class question."

After being locked in the close quarters off the interview room for more than five hours, I was relieved when a corrections officer told me my final interview that day would be conducted in the regular visiting area. Having spent most of the day under circumstances I considered extremely confining, I was jolted to realize that the prisoners with whom I had spoken were going back to a life I could not even begin to comprehend. Most of them had not had an extended, face-to-face conversation in months. As I sat in the visiting room, filled with prisoners and their wives, children, and friends, I thought of another remark Vic

Daniel had made: "That human contact — a guy becomes starved for it."

I was approached by a black man, neatly dressed in a sport shirt and dark brown slacks, who introduced himself as Keith Farries. He looked younger than his twenty-eight years. Originally sentenced to fifteen years for bank robbery, Farries is an active Muslim minister inside Marion. Although he was in the general population at the time of my visit, he had recently spent time in segregation and offered some observations on the problems encountered by Black Muslims in the control unit.

"We don't see the control unit as trying to control uncontrollable prisoners," he told me. "We see the control unit being used to demoralize and emasculate the political consciousness, the religious consciousness, and the legal consciousness that the inmates have developed and are trying to develop." Black Muslims, he added, have traditionally been repressed by prison officials. He said Muslims in the control unit are denied proper religious services and find it difficult to obtain *The Bilalian News*, the official newspaper of the Black Muslim faith.

In May 1976, Farries was placed in disciplinary segregation because he was campaigning for a liberalized telephone call policy at Marion. At the time, prisoners were allowed to make one ten-minute call to family or friends every ninety days. Keith was encouraging prisoners to protest the policy and was helping prisoners file administrative remedies — the official forms which inmates can use to complain about conditions. Marion officials claimed Farries was harassing other inmates and might provoke a violent confrontation. For this reason, they said, he was segregated in I-unit for forty-five days. But Farries maintained he was put in segregation one day before he was due for parole reclassification, and therefore forfeited 180 days of "good time." Since parole cannot be granted to a prisoner who has lost "good time," Farries had his possibility of parole postponed.

The denial of parole, Farries said, is another method prison officials can use to discourage prison activism. Although the Parole Board is supposedly an autonomous body not under the influence of prison administrators, Farries said, Warden Fenton had intervened in a previous instance involving him, and had obtained a reversal of the Parole Board's decision.

In August 1975, Farries was recommended for parole effective January 22, 1976, by a U.S. Parole Board hearing. The parole date was later set back to March 5, 1976. When Warden Fenton received notice of the parole grant, he did not inform Farries of it. Instead, he sent a telegram to Norman Carlson, director of the Federal Bureau of Prisons, requesting that Carlson "inquire" into Farries's parole. The telegram said Farries should not be paroled because he was convicted — along with six other Muslims — on mutiny and riot charges at the Lewisburg Penitentiary in 1970, an uprising which resulted in the severe injury of a guard. In addition, Fenton said, Farries "continues as a negative leader of the Muslim group and still reflects racial hatred."

Although the original parole hearing had acknowledged Farries's complicity in the Lewisburg riot, it had determined that his action there was erased by his "clear conduct record for a period of several years." The report of the original parole hearing for Farries went on to say: "Certainly the subject has done everything possible... has a sound release plan and has both the ability and the desire to receive his bachelor's degree. Since the subject has been fully involved in institutional programs, it is felt that the institution has nothing further to offer him from a treatment point of view." Yet the Parole Board, after being advised of Fenton's position, decided it had made a mistake and denied parole to Farries.

As my conversation with Keith Farries drew to a close, a guard approached and informed me that the warden wanted to see me before I left for the day. I walked out of the visiting room, back through the central corridor, and to the lobby, from which a smaller corridor led to the warden's office. I was hungry and tired by then, after more than six hours of interviews, and was expecting only some sort of official acknowledgment of my presence. But my first encounter with Warden Charles Fenton turned out to be more than a pleasant exchange of greetings. The warden was an angry man.

"Mr. Miller," he said, "I imagine that you have been told lies and are being told lies. It's all lies, and they are all liars." A large man in his mid-forties, about six feet tall and muscular, with graying hair cut in a flat-top crewcut, Fenton appeared to me to be the quintessential "prison man" — a term he later used several times to describe himself. He peered at me through wire-rimmed glasses, his face taut, and made it abundantly clear that if he could have had his way, he would not have let me into the prison; he was only conforming to the new Federal policy, he said.

In the strongest terms, Fenton expressed his intense dislike of "liberal lawyers" and "outside political groups" — he did not refer directly to me — who go into prisons ostensibly to help inmates: "The prisoner becomes a pawn. He is used and discarded as cannon fodder. I despise these people who use prisoners in this way," he told me. Outside interest in prisoners and prison conditions — especially on the part of lawyers like those conducting the suit against the control unit — falsely inflates the prisoners' hopes that "some act of God," as Fenton put it, will have them released; this interest, he told me, encourages prisoners to rebel and lie.

Charles Fenton has been a "prison man" almost all his life. He was raised in Pennsylvania near the Lewisburg Federal Penitentiary, and recently said in an interview with a Pennsylvania newspaper, "When I was five, I aspired to be warden at this [Lewisburg] penitentiary." His father was a correctional officer for thirty-five years. Fenton studied criminology at the University of Maryland and has taught that subject at Indiana State and Southern Illinois University.

After serving in the Army and the Air Force, Fenton joined the Bureau of Prisons and has been with that agency for twenty-two years. He has served as an administrator at Federal prisons in Lewisburg; the District of Columbia; El Reno, Oklahoma, and Terre Haute, Indiana. He was associate warden at Marion, then warden at Oxford, Wisconsin, and warden at Marion. About ten days after I left Marion, Fenton was transferred back to Lewisburg where, fulfilling his childhood dream, he assumed the post of warden.

I hardly knew where to begin, given the nature of the warden's opening remarks. Because Keith Farries's story was still fresh in my mind, I asked Fenton about the decision to put Farries in disciplinary segregation for his actions regarding the prison's telephone call policy. "If Farries was dissatisfied with our phone call policy," Fenton replied, "then he should have communicated his feelings directly to me."

But, I asked, weren't Farries's attempts to enlist support for his views and to help other prisoners in filing administrative remedies an essential form of democratic activity? Prison, Fenton responded, is not a democratic society: "I am in complete control here," he said. "The final authority, and responsibility, resides with me."

Besides, he added, the Marion telephone policy was "adequately liberal." A serious problem was posed, he said, by inmates using the telephone to extort money from family and friends. Fenton said he had received letters from welfare families who could not afford to accept collect calls from their imprisoned relatives. But prisoners with whom I spoke later denied that extortion was the general practice, and Farries had pointed out that as a man with eight members in his immediate family, he would have to spend two years to speak with each of them individually.

Next, I brought up the fact that each inmate I had inter-

R. Nass, Ampersand Design

## Comparative Criminology

"I asked a man in prison once how he happened to be there, and he said he had stolen a pair of shoes. I told him if he had stolen a railroad, he would be a United States Senator."

— *Mary Harris "Mother Jones," labor organizer, about 1900*

viewed had mentioned beatings in the segregation units. On this point, Fenton's denial was unequivocal: "There have been absolutely no beatings here since I have been warden." (Fenton assumed his post as warden on June 8, 1975.) He said he would take immediate and severe disciplinary action against any officer found to be mistreating a prisoner. The warden did not deny that "disturbances" had occurred; in every instance, he asserted, the incident was provoked by prisoners.

Perhaps the most serious allegation of brutality I had heard involved an incident on April 27, 1976, when four Black Muslims were purportedly beaten by white guards. Fenton's version, as he related it to me, was that two of the Muslims threw pails of urine on a corrections officer, one had a contraband spoon clenched in his fist and was loudly threatening the guards, and the fourth was brandishing a contraband cup and was encouraging someone to "come and get him." For these reasons, according to Fenton, a group of guards armed with riot shields, batons, and blackjacks — what prisoners call the "goon squad" — entered each cell and subdued the resisting prisoners. After the violence subsided, Fenton said, a medical technician visited the Muslims and was either refused permission to examine them or found no evidence of injury.

In testimony given to the National Prison Project which is now part of the record in the *Bono* suit, Earl Gaither, one of the four Muslims involved in the incident, told a different story. He said guards, not prisoners, were responsible for throwing the urine, and subsequently handcuffed and beat the prisoners.

"After the assault in April 1976," Gaither said in his testimony, "all four of us were placed on bag lunches... which consisted of, in the morning time, one baloney sandwich; afternoon time, two baloney sandwiches; and in the evening time, one baloney sandwich. None of us eat pork. We complained to the officials concerning this — they all know that our faith is Islam, we are Muslims, and that we, as well as Jews and other people of similar faith, do not eat any pork, especially the flesh of pork. We were laughed at and told that we could eat that or eat nothing at all. Also, we were put on deadlock status; we were allowed no showers at all."

The week after I visited Marion, an investigation was conducted into a series of allegations concerning beatings in the control unit. At the request of Representatives Robert Kastenmeier, Wisconsin Democrat, and Herman Badillo, New York Democrat, the Bureau of Prisons undertook to ascertain the "truth" in all the alleged in-

stances of beatings since January 1, 1976. The investigation was carried out by two members of the Bureau's Kansas City regional office, who interviewed thirty staff members and examined the unit logs for H and I units, disciplinary reports, inmate central files, administrative remedies, and medical records. No prisoners were interviewed.

The National Prison Project and prisoners with whom I have maintained correspondence claim that this "investigation" was a sham — only the guards' side of the story was told. Nevertheless, some interesting admissions have emerged from the report issued by the investigating team. It found that guards as well as prisoners had engaged in throwing urine and quoted guards as admitting "that a container or containers of urine were...kept in a cabinet for such purposes."

As a result of the investigation, the officers who admitted to throwing the urine were cited for "unprofessional judgment" and suspended — but this disciplinary action came nearly five months after the incidents took place. Prison officials consistently maintain that "in the event force is necessary to control an individual, only that force which is necessary is utilized by the correctional officers to gain control of the inmate." Yet James Potts, a former control unit prisoner who is now on the staff of the National Prison Project, poses this question: "If it has been admitted that guards participated in throwing urine, how can they always stress that they use precisely the correct amount of force against prisoners?"

Scott Myers, a co-director of the National Committee to Support the Marion Brothers, summarized the difficulties involved in substantiating allegations made by prisoners: "There is no way, within a prison setting," he told me, "of finding out the truth about a particular crime that has been committed, whether it is the beating of a prisoner or an assault on a guard."

I noticed during my first meeting with Warden Fenton that he had a particular way of dealing with the allegations I brought up. He always asked me which prisoner had made the complaint before he gave me his perception of the incident in question. Then he would tell me "a little something" about that prisoner — his criminal history, the duration of his sentence, and, sometimes, his parole eligibility date. Later, when I was examining correspondence from prison officials to members of Congress, I discovered this same pattern: The officials would first describe the record of the prisoner who had voiced a complaint, and then deal with the allegation at hand.

At the end of our first meeting, Warden Fenton invited me to accompany him on a tour of the penitentiary the next day. He said I could see for myself how the institution was run, and I accepted. An official of the Delaware prison system joined us for the tour.

The warden first took us to the dining hall, which was clean and spacious, resembling — except for the barred windows — a large high school cafeteria. The kitchen was spotless and equipped with modern stainless steel cooking facilities. Some of the prisoners who are not in segregation help prepare the meals, and prisoners in the general population are allowed all the food they want to eat.

I told Warden Fenton that several prisoners had complained to me about the food in the segregation units, claiming that they were not permitted to have second helpings and that the meals served to them were "watered-down" versions of what the other prisoners received. In fact, a petition signed by eleven control unit prisoners in August asserted that they were fed an unbalanced diet, with large quantities of bread and potatoes and few protein foods or nutrients with vitamin C. Fenton admitted that segregated prisoners could not have seconds, but charged that there was extensive food waste in the control unit. Those prisoners had small appetites, he said, because of the lack of physical exercise.

We went from the dining hall to the outside recreation area. Two groups of prisoners were playing cards on a veranda in the shade of the prison. In the hot August sun, several inmates were bare-chested, playing handball, jogging, bowling, doing calisthenics. The warden pointed out a muscular prisoner, his head shaven, who was exercising on the parallel bars; the man, Fenton told me, was a "graduate" of the control unit. "Working on your own Olympic routine?" Fenton called to him. The prisoner smiled.

Along our tour of Marion, Warden Fenton stopped several times to chat with prisoners. He knew many by name. Once in the furniture shop, Fenton borrowed my pen to make some notes about a complaint that a prisoner had made to him. The warden was much more relaxed and responsive than he had been the previous afternoon. He then led us to a regular cellblock. All of the cell doors were open and the cells vacant. Two inmates sat playing cards on the range, while a guard lounged in the corner. A television set, its sound turned down, sat at the far end of the range. Fenton explained that ice machines had been installed in each cellblock so that prisoners could have cold drinks whenever they wanted. He also told us that prisoners habitually wanted the small, slatted windows in each cellblock open, though this made the cells much hotter in the summer.

From the living quarters of non-segregated inmates Warden Fenton guided us to the control unit. The entrance door was locked, unlike the doors to other cellblocks, and had to be opened from the inside by a guard. To get onto the range directly in front of the control unit cells, we passed through two more locked gates. All of the prisoners were locked in their cells. Although it was mid-afternoon, many were asleep, some sprawled on mattresses on the floor. Most of the cells were barren, with nothing on the walls and only a few personal items in each. I noticed how pale these men were compared with the prisoners I had seen outside.

As we stood in the control unit, I asked Fenton about the behavior progression system that the Bureau of Prisons policy statement on the control unit had called essential to the successful operation of the unit. I told him the prisoners had claimed such a program did not exist; they said they did not know what was expected of them or

how they could work their way out of the control unit. I also mentioned a report by the U.S. General Accounting Office (GAO), released in August 1975, that had been extremely critical of the Marion CTP. That investigation found: "No progression system and few, if any, progress goals were set. Essentially, the inmates were expected to behave themselves for several months."

Fenton's reply was that the type of plan that the policy called for was not "an effective organization." "The levels here are not restricted to a handful," he told me, "but are infinite. Essentially, there is a different plan for every individual in the control unit." Each prisoner's "improvement" is judged by his counselor, the staff psychologist, the manager of the control unit, and administration officials, with input from the corrections officers. Formal notification of any change in an inmate's status is announced by a review committee that meets with each inmate every thirty days.

The prisoners, however, maintained that the review committee was more like a kangaroo court. Since they are kept in their cells almost all the time and there are no concrete programs in which they can participate, they said, there are no standards to evaluate a change in a prisoner's behavior. The prisoners regard the decisions of the review committee as completely arbitrary. Vic Daniel had summarized the prisoners' feeling of helplessness: "It's, like, whatever the gods say."

I also asked Fenton about the contention made by prisoners that several mentally unstable men were incarcerated in the control unit. The Bureau of Prisons policy statement, I noted, specified that prisoners in the CTP, "should show little or no evidence of mental disorder." Fenton admitted this was not the case at Marion. He estimated that ten of the men in H-unit at the time were "psychotic," but he said he saw little alternative for them. "It's handy to put them here, but they really don't belong here," he told me. "The hospital doesn't want them and can't handle them because they are serious behavior problems."

By the end of the tour, I had a sense of the difficulties involved in running a prison. Warden Fenton appeared to be on good terms with many of the prisoners, but many others directed hostile stares at him. My impression that the control unit was being mismanaged, to say the least, was strengthened.

---

I interviewed three more prisoners during my final day at Marion. One of them, John Croom, was on my list because I had been told by the National Prison Project that he was being forcibly drugged. When the guards brought Croom to my interviewing cubicle and locked him in with me, it was immediately obvious that Croom was heavily under the influence of drugs. He kept looking wildly around the room, and every few minutes would pause with his head cocked, as if he heard something strange.

His responses to my questions were almost totally incoherent. He spoke rapidly and slurred his words. He often forgot what he was saying. Croom was distressed at his condition and promised that he would "write everything down" for me. Repeatedly he stopped in the middle of a sentence to tell me: "You don't understand me, do you?" Although I tried to assure him that I understood what he was saying — which I did not — Croom became visibly upset, insisting that I didn't understand him. I was frightened; he is a large, muscular man, and there was nothing to stop him from reaching for me over the metal partition. In fact, he reached for my tape recorder several times, mumbling something about his radio, only to draw back at the last minute.

When I finally realized that Croom had no control over himself, I anxiously awaited an opportunity to signal a guard that our interview was over. Throughout my fifteen-minute talk with Croom, I asked him six or seven times whether he consented to taking drugs. Each time he told me that he was pressured, and often forced, into taking thorazine. According to the *Physician's Desk Reference* (1975), thorazine is a tranquilizer that often has wide-ranging side effects. Warden Fenton, however, told me that Croom asked to be put under medication.

Several weeks after I left Marion, I wrote to John Croom and asked him a few follow-up questions. This is an excerpt from his reply to me: "In your note you mentioned you talked to me during your visit here. However, sir, I don't recall being called out to see you, as I was eagerly anticipating.... In response to your query: Yes, the officials here forced and continue to coerce me to ingest drugs (100 to 200 milligrams of thorazine in four daily dosages, plus a 'cogenten' per dosage which supposedly is to offset the side effects of thorazine — an obvious admission of the hazards of thorazine). ... Modern penology has replaced antiquated prison physical brutality with new 'correctional programs' by using euphemistical and/or psychological nomenclatures and mistreatment of the *mind*. The Prisoncrats' new philosophy is: Destroy the mind and you've got the body!" (The *Physician's Desk Reference* says that a daily dosage of 800 milligrams of thorazine "is not uncommon in discharged mental patients." A "cogenten," as Croom wrote, is a drug administered to offset the side effects of another drug.)

I also spoke with Larry Stead, a "jailhouse lawyer" in the general population at Marion, who assists other prisoners in filing suits and writs of habeas corpus. He was director of the JayCees' Legal Rights and Assistance Committee for prisoners at Marion until that committee was terminated by the warden in 1972. Now, after educating himself through correspondence courses from the University of Minnesota, Stead is a member of the National Lawyers' Guild and a para-legal assistant to a Chicago lawyer.

Although he often does preparatory work on cases for this lawyer, he is not allowed to interview prisoners in the control unit. "I had approximately eight cases going for people in H and I units," Stead told me. "The administration blocked our communication. I couldn't get letters to them and I couldn't get pleadings back." Marion policy states that prisoners in the general population can communicate only by open correspondence with inmates of the control unit. Stead's request to gather testimony

through sealed correspondence, which would provide some degree of confidentiality, was turned down.

Stead escaped from prison in 1974, but turned himself in a month later. Because of his escape, his sentence was increased by three years and he forfeited 673 days of "good time." In the two years since the escape, he has not received a disciplinary "shot," or reprimand. Generally, an inmate's "good time" is restored if he maintains a clear conduct record for one year after the incident. This is important because, as in Keith Farries's case, a prisoner is not eligible for parole if he has lost a single day of "good time." Though the Parole Board has recommended that Stead's "good time" be reinstated, the Marion administration has refused to comply. According to Stead, Warden Fenton told him the refusal was not due to his escape, but to the "problems" he was causing by giving legal assistance to inmates.

Fenton had told me that he regarded most jailhouse lawyers as hustlers who extended "false hopes" to prisoners in return for cigarettes or other forms of reimbursement. In a letter to me, Larry Stead declared, "I have *never* charged anyone for my assistance. If there is something I cannot stand to see, it is a prisoner charging another prisoner for anything. Things are hard enough without such petty exploitation. But the Fentons of the prison systems only want to talk about our 'quacks' and make the public believe that we are all a bunch of idiots sucking off of others' misfortunes. Nothing could be more untrue."

The last prisoner I interviewed at Marion was Richard Montgomery, a white inmate who has been in the control unit for almost a year. Like the other prisoners I had met, Montgomery believed that the primary purpose of the control unit is to control dissidents: "They want you to bow and scrape, tap-dance, and everything else," he told me. "They want you to think the way they think, and if you don't, you'll just have to suffer the consequences." Montgomery called himself a socialist and said he believes capitalism is conducive to crime. "A socialist system wouldn't breed crime," he said. "It wouldn't have all this poverty. It wouldn't have these conditions where a person has to go out and steal if they didn't have all these benefits themselves."

My last meeting with Warden Fenton took place in his office. He refused my request to tape-record the session, saying that he did not want to get himself into trouble. I had used a tape recorder in all of my interviews with prisoners.

Almost without exception, the prisoners had insisted to me that the Marion control unit was being used as a type of political prison. These inmates were activists in one form or another — religious, political, or legal activists. Moreover, most of them were radical in their political views. Could there be, I asked the warden, some correlation between their activism, their radicalism, and their confinement in the segregation units?

"Their leadership qualities or radical beliefs," Fenton

replied, "are not what make them dangerous. It is their repeated aggressive behavior." (In my encounters with these men, I perceived them as basically humane, and often intelligent, articulate people.) Rarely, Fenton said, do such prisoners have "an ideological background before they commit their crimes." This was, in fact, a point that several prisoners had made themselves — it was only after they were removed from abject material concerns, they had told me, and had time to read and think, that they developed a radical perspective. Such thinking, Warden Fenton charged as he now paced the room, was "the rationalization of a criminalistic subculture, characteristic of repeated prisoners and slum-dwellers who make their living by illicit means.

"As a prison man," the warden continued, "socialist theories make me very impatient." If the causes of crime are primarily social and beyond an individual's control, then the prisoner might as well lie down "and cut his own throat," Fenton said. "Socialists, Marxists, radicals, Symbionese-whatchamacallits are all destroying these men." These groups encourage prisoners to rebel against a system they have no power to change, he said, and frustrate a prisoner's efforts at self-improvement. Radical theories, he added, encourage prisoners to think, "I'm not the crook — they're the crooks." Every society must have rules to insure social cohesion, the warden concluded, and "the purpose of imprisonment is that it's a better way of punishment" for those who transgress the laws of society.

In the Washington offices of the Federal Bureau of Prisons, I spoke with several officials about the control unit at Marion. Dr. Robert Levinson, who helped draw up the Bureau's policy statement on the control unit, conceded there are difficulties in characterizing the CTP as a behavior modification program. Every penal program, he said, is broadly designed to modify a prisoner's behavior so that he can be reintegrated into society. In a narrower sense, however, behavior modification involves the application of learning theory — by reinforcing positive behavior — to a prisoner's activities. The Bureau of Prisons, he continued, emphasizes rewards for good behavior, not "negative reinforcement" or punishment. The control unit, Levinson told me, "is not as structured, not as precise — not really behavior modification."

Levinson insisted that the control unit was not designed in any way to be a repository for politicized prisoners. "Why should there be some sort of conspiracy in the Government to segregate, to silence political dissidents in the prisons?" he asked. "That was certainly not what we had in mind when we set [the control unit] up."

Why, then, were so many political activists in the control unit? "I think that the guys who get themselves into Marion are that [politically active] and then something else," Levinson said. That "something else," of course, is the pattern of aggressive behavior on the part of control unit prisoners. Levinson firmly believes that the inmates in the CTP at Marion would be extremely dangerous if

they were released to the general population; as he put it, these are "people who cannot live in the free world." And, he concluded, "it's a sad commentary that we don't know what to do with them."

Other officials at the Bureau of Prisons echoed these sentiments. Michael Quinlan, the executive assistant to the director, said the sole purpose of the control unit is to control prisoners with serious behavior problems: "Probably 98 per cent, if not more, of those men are dangerous," he told me. Though Quinlan admitted that some of the prisoners in the control unit may be "malcontent about prison conditions," their criticism of the system was not the reason they were placed in the CTP. Similarly, Mike Aun, the public information officer, dismissed the notion of political repression. "Our purpose is to protect society while preserving the basic constitutional rights of the prisoners," he said. "Of course, their constitutional rights are not the same as those that you enjoy."

Certainly there is some basis for the official assumption that prisoners in Marion's segregation units are "aggressive;" many are in those units because they perpetrated acts of violence. The danger these men may pose to other prisoners who want to serve out their sentences peacefully, or to prison staff members, must be dealt with in one form or another by prison administrators. At the same time, "aggressiveness" on the part of prisoners can be construed by prison officials in an institutional context. Prisoners who criticize prison conditions as unjust, who perceive crime as a social — rather than individual — disease, and who "disrupt" prisons by encouraging protests, strikes, and nonconformity are deemed "aggressive" by

R. Nass, Ampersand Design

the authorities whose job it is to ensure the peaceful and orderly functioning of prisons.

As Warden Fenton told me, a prison society is authoritarian; complete power resides with the administrators. It follows that prisoners who question or challenge such total control must be handled in a different manner than "peaceful" prisoners. It seems that the only "treatment" prison administrators can envision for such "disruptive" prisoners is increased control over their actions, which generally means segregation, deprivation, and isolation.

The General Accounting Office investigation of August 1975, in assessing the reasons for placing prisoners in the Marion control unit, reported to Congress: "We could not, in some instances, determine if the inmates had repeatedly engaged in acts which seriously endangered others." The report also stated that the GAO could "not evaluate the institution's compliance with inmate selection criteria primarily because of the criteria's vagueness and the limited data available."

The investigation listed several reasons given by prison officials for assigning 134 inmates to the control unit over an eighteen-month period. Most prominent among these causes were: work stoppage; past record; disruptive, verbal abuse; noncompliance with prison rules, and escape risk. Only seven prisoners were cited for assaults on staff or other prisoners, only five for participating in a group disturbance, only eleven for being dangerous.

The basic function of the control unit seems to have been defined in testimony given in the *Bono* v. *Saxbe* case one year ago. The suit contends that the control unit violates several constitutional rights — freedom from cruel and unusual punishment, freedom of speech, freedom of religion, freedom of association, and the right to due process of law. In the proceedings, Ralph Aron, the warden who preceded Charles Fenton at Marion, testified, "It [the control unit] is necessary because of the revolutionary attitudes acting throughout our country. It has become necessary just in the last few years." Later in the transcript, Aron was asked by one of the lawyers for the prisoners, "Is the control unit used to control prisoners with revolutionary attitudes and tactics?" Aron replied, "That is correct."

In September 1975, Representative Ralph Metcalfe, the Illinois Democrat who asked the GAO to undertake its investigation into behavior modification programs in Federal prisons, condemned the Bureau of Prisons for its failure to analyze the effects of behavior modification: "These programs can only serve to instill further bitterness, at the very least, upon those inmates it purports to help. All of us, in the end, must pay the price for their bitterness and anger," he said.

Bitterness and anger persist at Marion. Since my visit, there have been some minor changes. Charles Fenton is now warden at the Lewisburg Federal Penitentiary. The telephone call policy, which led Keith Farries into segregation, was liberalized after Fenton's departure to allow inmates a call every thirty, instead of ninety, days. Jazz Jasper and Steve Kessler have been released into the general prison population. But stories of beatings and druggings continue to come from the prisoners in Marion's control unit. The living conditions remain unchanged. And the role of the control unit in repressing prison activism and dissent, although constantly and vehemently denied by prison officials, remains in force.

In a society increasingly preoccupied with preserving "law and order," the Marion control unit — and all of our prison system — poses deeply troubling questions. If we impose a regimen of isolation, deprivation, and brutality in our prisons, is there not a parallel to the current situation and future of our cities? If we condone experimentation with behavior modification techniques on involuntary subjects, could the rest of us not fall victims to such experimentation? If we allow prisoners to be punished for political dissent, will we not be prepared to suppress an alternative social vision?

The word "control" has an insidious meaning for all of us — not just for the men in Marion. And Dostoevsky observed that the degree of civilization in a society can be judged by entering its prisons. □

R. Nass, Ampersand Design

# 20 Why Women Fear Success

## Vivian Gornick

"Psychologists
found
women's data
indicated
a hopeless
will to fail"

Girls get dumber and dumber as they get older and older. We all know that. We have all *always* known that. The girl child matures early, levels off fast, and then slowly retrogresses. Thousands of females who are positively brilliant in grade school become merely bright in high school, simply very good in college, and finally, almost mediocre in graduate school. It is a curious pattern of human development familiar to all of us, one that has come under formal observation very often in the past 75 years.

The explanation for this peculiar reversal has consisted of obscure references to something in the female that turns inward, something that is repelled by competition, some natural lack of aggression. Freud said it, Erikson says it, and the entirety of Western culture repeats it. All of our observations and predilections have traditionally supported the idea that women, in the long haul, simply do not have the constitution for normal competition; that, in women, the inner necessity to succeed which nourishes and sharpens the intelligence seems to be missing. In all of the highly perceptive work done on the relation between motivation and achievement, none of the information contributed by women adds to our understanding of this powerful dynamic in human lives, because women seem unresponsive to the stimulus to achieve. In fact, they seem dominated by a profound wish to fail.

Seven years ago, Matina Horner, an experimental psychologist working on the relation between motivation and achievement at the University of Michigan, was as puzzled as the men in her department by the irregular and disturbing results that came exclusively from female subjects. All sorts of data based on information given by the men were successfully fed into the carefully worked-out test model, but when it came to the women, the model went crazy. Nothing meshed; no two sets of women came up with the same kinds of results —ever. In addition, the women tested out abnormally high on anxiety. Bewildered and dissatisfied, the psychologists reluctantly dismissed the women's data as indicating a hopeless "will to fail," impossible to cope with

*Vivian Gornick is a staff writer for "The Village Voice" and co-editor of the anthology "Women in Sexist Society."*

in achievement-motivation work. Dr. Horner, however, sensed that this was not an adequate explanation for what she felt was going on with the women; she stumbled, ultimately, on the idea that the women involved were not exhibiting a will to fail, but rather an active, anxious desire to *avoid success*.

Matina Horner, a dark-haired, dark-eyed woman in her early thirties, is now assistant professor of clinical psychology at Harvard. She teaches three courses in personality, one of them a graduate seminar in the personality development of women. Her office, in a new Harvard building, is a large, bright room overlooking the city of Cambridge. Recently, I spent a morning in that room with Dr. Horner. We discussed her work, and inevitably—as we were not only a psychologist and a journalist, but two women as well—we discussed our own lives. (After all, were they not proper subjects for a study of the fear of success in women?)

Dr. Horner spoke slowly, in a soft voice; as she warmed to both her subject and her visitor she became more animated.

I asked Dr. Horner what had made her tumble to the idea that it was not the will to fail that was operating in the girl students she had tested, but rather the desire to avoid success.

"Well," she said, smiling, "the desire to fail comes from some deep psychological conviction that the consequences of failure will be *satisfying*. These girls at Michigan were motivated by the opposite; they were positively anxiety-ridden over the prospect of success. They were not simply eager to fail and have done with it; they seemed to be in a state of anxious conflict over what would happen if they succeeded. It was almost as though this conflict was inhibiting their capacity for achievement."

Intrigued by the intellectual problem that these male-female sexual differences seemed to present, Dr. Horner had decided to work up another model for testing, one that would concentrate on discovering women's actual expectancies in relation to achievement. This approach made use of what is known in scientific jargon as an "expectancy-value theory of motivation." Here the experimenter aims to discover what a subject's expectations are regarding the consequences of an action he or she proposes to take. According to the theory, anxiety is aroused when one expects the consequences to be negative. Thus, anxiety acts as an inhibiting force and produces what scientists call an "avoidance motive." This motive doesn't tell us what someone *will* do, but it indicates clearly what he or she will *not* do.

Out of this approach came a theory Dr. Horner called "the Motive to Avoid Success." The compelling evidence for her theory came

from a series of Thematic Apperception Tests she administered to 90 girls and 88 boys, all undergraduates at the University of Michigan. Known to psychologists as T.A.T.s, these tests require the interpretation of a picture or the completion of a story line. The results of those T.A.T.s were startling. As Dr. Horner explains in her first study:

"We asked Phil, a bright young college sophomore . . . to tell us a story based on one clue: *After first-term finals, John finds himself at the top of his medical school class*. Phil writes:

*John is a conscientious young man who worked hard. He is pleased with himself. John has always wanted to go into medicine and is very dedicated. . . .John continues working hard and eventually graduates at the top of his class.*

"Now consider Monica, another honor student. She too has always done well and she too has visions of a flourishing career. We give her the same clue, but with 'Anne' as the successful student. . . . Instead of identifying with Anne's triumph, Monica tells a bizarre tale:

*Anne starts proclaiming her surprise and joy. Her fellow classmates are so disgusted with her behavior that they jump on her in a body and beat her. She is maimed for life.*

"Next we ask Monica and Phil to work on a series of achievement tests by themselves. Monica scores higher than Phil. Then we get them together, competing against each other on the same kinds of tests. Phil performs magnificently; Monica dissolves into a bundle of nerves.

"The glaring contrast between the two stories and the dramatic changes in competitive situations illustrates important differences between men and women in reacting to achievement . . .

"In response to the successful-male cue(*After first-term finals, John finds himself . . .*) more than 90 per cent of the men in the study showed strong positive feelings, indicated increased striving, confidence in the future and a belief that this success would be instrumental to fulfilling other goals such as providing a secure and happy home for some girl. . . . Fewer than 10 per cent of the men responded at all negatively. . . .

"On the other hand, in response to the successful-female cue,65 per cent of the girls were disconcerted, troubled or confused by the cue. Unusual excellence in women was clearly associated for them with the loss of femininity, social rejection, personal or societal destruction or some combination of the above. Their responses were filled with negative consequences and affect, righteous indignation, withdrawal rather than enhanced striving, concern,or even an inability to accept the information presented in the cue. For example:

*Anne will deliberately lower her academic standing the next term, while she does all subtly can to help Carl. . . . His grades come up and Anne soon drops out of med school. They marry and he goes on in school while she raises their family.*

*Anne is a code name for a nonexistent person created by a group of med students. They take turns taking exams and writing papers for Anne. . . .*

*Aggressive, unmarried, wearing Oxford shoes and hair pulled back in a bun, she wears glasses and is terribly bright.*

"In other words, women showed significantly more evidence of the motive to avoid success than did men, with 59 of the 90 women scoring high and 8 of the 88 men doing so."

"What was even more apparent," said Dr. Horner, swiveling her chair around to face me more directly, "was that the fear of success manifested itself mainly in women of demonstrably high intelligence, coming from homes where high achievement was much valued. Which makes great sense, when you think about it. After all, a girl who's not too bright and doesn't have much chance for success to begin with is hardly likely to be frightened by the prospect of success. Whereas, a bright girl from a middle-class home, knowing she actually has it within her possible grasp . . . ."

What happens to most women of this type, continued Dr. Horner, is simple. In this age of lip-service to equality and self-realization for all, parents encourage their daughters to fulfill their entire potential and allow them some of the advantages given to men. The encouragement, however, is essentially hollow. Somewhere around a girl's junior year in college, if not before, the parents' strong desire surfaces: that the girl be securely married, rather than take the unconventional and risky course of becoming a serious working person. The contradictory message that the girl gets, from society as well as from her parents, is that if she is too smart, too independent, and above all, too serious about her work, she is unfeminine and will therefore never get married. (Speculation that the full brunt of anxiety over femininity and academic achievement begins to fall upon a woman student about halfway through college is supported by special studies. For instance, one study revealed that the fear of success in women ranged from a low 47 per cent in a seventh grade junior high school sample to a high 88 per cent in a sample of

high-ability undergraduate students at a prominent Eastern school.)

The woman student in her third year understands then—or primarily then—that she actually has been sent to college to find a husband and to fit herself out as an attractive and educated wife. The important aspect of this reversal of goals is the immediate capitulation in the girl's psyche, a capitulation that parallels the rapidity with which the fear of success then grows in the brightest women students. The implication, clearly, is that the girl is predisposed to accept this notion that femininity and academic achievement are incompatible; that some deep receptivity toward this idea has been developing in her personality almost from birth; some influence beyond the inauthentic encouragement of her parents to become an autonomously developed human being has caused her to internalize the traditional sexual stereotype of passive femininity. Once the thin crust of encouragement is broken, a deep well of social conditioning is discovered underneath. She goes into a tailspin of anxiety as she struggles to reverse her appetite for human fulfillment, an appetite she now learns is in direct contradiction to her *feminine* fulfillment.

As Dr. Horner succinctly puts it in her study: "Our data indicate that the emphasis on the new freedom for women has thus far not been any more effective in doing away with this tendency [to avoid success] than were the vote, trousers, cigarettes, and even changing standards of sexual behavior. If anything, our most recent data indicate something of a backlash phenomenon since the mid-sixties. The negative attitudes we find expressed toward successful women have increased to a disproportionately greater extent than have the positive ones, and this is true of both male and female subjects."

Needless to say, such a contradictory state of being is unthinkable for a man, who is taught *from birth* that his human fulfillment and his masculine fulfillment are one and the same. While it is true that achievement-motivation work has raised the fear of success in men, that fear is always coupled with philosophical issues in the man's mind, i.e., an apprehension regarding the values of succeeding in a materialistic or socially amoral culture. It is never coupled with a deep conflict over the crucial and fundamental issue of his masculinity.

What happens inside the mind of a woman struggling with such a conflict? Since it has never been properly acknowledged until now, the question has remained unaddressed.

One day Dr. Horner separated out into two piles the results of one of her T.A.T.s. She separated them according to the data collected through other T.A.T.s which had identified some of these same subjects as low in fear of success, and others as high in fear of success. The T.A.T. cue was *Anne is sitting in a chair with a smile on her face.* Those low in fear of success had responded to the cue with rather pleasant, neutral tales such as:

*Anne is happy—she's happy with the world because it is so beautiful. It's snowing, and nice outside—she's happy to be alive and this gives her a warm feeling. . . .*

*Anne is alone in her room. It's a beautiful day. . . . Her two closest friends have just met marvelous people and believe they are in love.*

*. . . The beautiful day and her nice friends' happiness create an aura of happiness about her. . . .*

The stories written by the girls high in fear of success were startlingly different:

*Anne is recollecting her conquest of the day. She has just stolen her ex-boyfriend away, right before the High School Senior Prom. . . . She wanted to hurt her friend, and succeeded by taking the boyfriend away underhandedly. . . .*

*Anne is at her father's funeral. There are over 200 people there. . . . Her mother, two brothers and several relations are there. Anne's father committed suicide . . . She knows it is unseemly to smile but cannot help it. . . . Her brother Ralph pokes her in fury but she is uncontrollable. . . . Anne rises dramatically and leaves the room, stopping first to pluck a carnation fom the blanket of flowers on the coffin.*

*(Anne), a woman in her twenties, is sitting, smiling smugly, in a chair in a small restaurant in New York City. She has just successfully (so far) completed her first robbery (a jewelry store). . . . Gun in hand, she is waiting for her stepmother to return home. A short time earlier, her father was murdered and she believes her stepmother did it. . . .*

To think seriously on the meaning of these fantasies in the minds of women who long for and are morbidly afraid of autonomous fulfillment is to come away filled with fear and sadness. Our culture has made a deep split in the souls of its women, and the result is insupportable anxiety which can bear up only by transforming itself into the malevolence of what is known as passive-aggressive behavior. Behind the "passive" exterior of many women there lies a growing anger over lost energies and confused lives, an anger so sharp in its fury but so diffuse in its focus that one can only describe it as the price society must pay for creating a patriarchal system in the first place, and for now refusing to let it go.

And make no mistake, it is not letting go.

Last summer at Harvard University, Dr. Horner tested a group of undergraduate men in order to discover their genuine feelings about successful women. She gave them the T.A.T. cue that she had previously given to women at the University of Michigan, i.e., *After first-term finals, Anne finds herself at the top of her medical school class.* The answers, overwhelmingly, were along the following lines:

*Anne is not a woman. She is really a computer, the best in a new line of machines. . . . Anne rushes out of her smelly formaldehyde laboratory, and runs to the university bar where she knows she will find Bruno! The perfect man!*

*Anne is paralyzed from the waist down. She sits in a wheelchair and studies for medical school. . . .*

This in the summer of 1970. This from Harvard University. This from the men who will marry the girls at Michigan.

"How has this happened to women?" I asked Dr. Horner. " And how can it *un*-happen?"

"Those are both extremely difficult issues even to *speculate* about," Dr. Horner smiled. "How does it all happen? When does it begin to happen? So fast, so early, that it is frightening. My daughter is five years old. One day she came into my room and said to me: 'Mommy, Daddy must love you very much.' 'Why do you say that?' I asked her, pleased that she had made such an assumption. 'Because he doesn't want you to be tired,' she said. 'He does the dishes so that you won't be tired.' . . . Now, it was very nice that the conclusion she came to was that my husband cared for me because he washed the dishes, but the point is, it was a *problem* in her mind, one she had to find a solution for. At five—without any help from us, I can assure you—she knows something is funny if her daddy is doing the dishes!

"The sexual stereotypes are fixed in the minds of girls and of boys almost from birth, and God, do they ever *stay* fixed. I've observed it repeatedly in *myself*. Look, when I was up for my prelims, I went into a state of anxiety like nothing I'd ever known before. I carried on so I frightened my husband and finally, in desperation, he yelled at me: 'For God's sake, maybe women *shouldn't* be in graduate school!' Now, what was I afraid of? I had designed my own prelim, I knew everything I was responsible for. There wasn't the *remotest* possibility of failure; and yet, I was shaking, throwing up, screaming I was stupid and now they'd all know I was stupid.

"Interestingly enough, there was only one time that I remember facing an audience calmly. I rose to speak and was amazed at how quiet and good I felt inside. Then I looked down at myself, and I understood. There I was,

**"There was only one time that I remember facing an audience calmly. I was seven months pregnant—that was my insurance. I was in there being a woman"**

seven months pregnant. Nothing I was about to say could contradict *that*. It was my insurance—I was loved, I was about to have a baby, I was in there being a woman—nothing to be afraid of.

"To alter all this is the most complex problem we face now. And it's what we do here. We sit around and we think about these things. My students here at Harvard are marvelous: very bright, very quick, very much taken with these problems. We sit together in our seminars and we ask hard questions. It's exciting to see these ideas taking hold in their minds.

"What we have to do is to get to the bottom of what is genuinely natural in women. What we now call natural is only normative. It is what our culture has defined as normal for women and normal for men, but it sheds no light on what is *natural*. For instance the assertion that women have no natural aggression in them is absurd. Women can be very aggressive even while using 'passive' methods. Silence can be used aggressively. Two little

girls getting together in a schoolyard and saying to each other: 'You be my friend and I'll be yours, and we won't be *her* friend'—that's aggressive! Aggression is a desire to exercise will. Passivity is not. Well, God knows, enough women are interested in exercising their wills. . . . So which is it? Is woman aggressive or not? What *is* her nature? This we know next to nothing about. It is this vast area of ignorance that we must explore.

"I think, as far as the future is concerned, that everything depends on where society goes. The counter-culture offers some interesting possibilities, but even those, if you look closely enough, don't get to the heart of the matter as far as women are concerned. For instance, one of the ideas of the counter-culture is that competitiveness is bad. You are a bad *person* if you compete. If this idea should begin to dominate the norm, and women seeking to develop themselves for the first time should then rise to high positions, well they're still in bad shape! Because men define the good. It is what *men* do that determines the values of the society, and this no less so in the counter-culture than in the one they left behind.

"But perhaps all these issues—the counter-culture, ecology, liberation from sexual stereotypes—can eventually feed into a new normative world in which women may finally be able to define themselves. I have great hopes."

I walked out into the Cambridge afternoon sun, feeling benign toward every unknown person whose path crossed mine. After all, this campus had given Matina Horner a place to work, a place to continue her search for new answers, and, perhaps more important, a place to examine and discard all those old questions. Here, her gift as a scientist has led her to ask *new* questions about women. And new questions are what Women's Liberation is all about.  ●

# 21

# Women in the Workplace

by Louise Kapp Howe

## I

On the wall (reports the *Wall Street Journal*) is a picture of Israeli Premier Golda Meir captioned "But Can She Type?" There are other feminist posters, too. Seated around the room are forty women—all employees of Westinghouse, all invited to this "motivational" workshop because the company says it is interested in helping them to advance to higher positions within the corporation.

Actually Westinghouse is under the gun to help them do so. Like all major corporations with a history of sex discrimination—in short, *all* major corporations—it could be declared ineligible for federal contracts if it doesn't comply with new regulations to show "affirmative action" (which now means specific goals and time-tables) to recruit and promote women to all levels of its job structure.

That is, of course, why every other week or so we hear of new company plans and programs and occasionally statistical progress such as IBM's announcement of a 35 per cent increase in its female managerial staff over the previous year. Though sounding impressive it was never made clear exactly what *numbers* were involved. More impressive are the recent strides in opening higher-level jobs and awarding back pay to thousands of women working for Ma Bell.

In any case, the Westinghouse workshop takes place in a motel conference room in Pittsburgh. For two days the invited employees debate whether it has been sex discrimination or women's own inadequacies that have kept us from the nation's top ranks of management. Because of the attention given to the Feminist Movement in the past few years, the women respond instantly that it has been the fault of our lousy male chauvinist occupational system—or do they?

Not here, not yet. Doubts and self-doubts instead. The women worry openly about their abilities, or rather their lack of them. They also express concern about losing their femininity or damaging their relationships with men by concentrating on careers. Although less than a quarter of the women present are married and living with their husbands, most still foresee and fear a future conflict between home and career. "Remember," one woman says, "it's more socially acceptable for a man to sacrifice his home for a career than it is for a woman."

Finally, according to *Wall Street Journal* reporter Ellen Graham, they decide to put the question of sex discrimination to a vote. At this point a woman named Janet pulls out a book of statistics showing that women college graduates earn on the average more than $5,000 a year less than their male counterparts. "Now won't you agree women have been discriminated against?" she asks. "Men are making more money because they're more qualified," Irene retorts. "If you're held back, it isn't because you're a woman, it's because of your own inadequacies." The vote is taken. Doubts and self-doubts. Irene wins.

---

*Louise Kapp Howe is now working on a book concerning working women. She was formerly the editor of the journal* **New Generation** *and recently edited a book for Simon & Schuster entitled* **The Future of the Family.**

---

Nevertheless, by the time it's over, the workshop seems to have made a difference in the way the participants feel about themselves. There was only one avowed feminist when they began and now their consciousness has been raised for the future. Bring on the promotions! The workshop is praised.

## II

Doubts and self-doubts still chip away at the potential abilities of how many women? *What should I be, what can I do, what will I have to give up to get there?* Spurred by the Feminist Movement, many thousands of women are refusing to give yesterday's ritual reply: wife-and-mother, period. Many who wouldn't have done so 10 years ago are now seeking careers instead, or careers *as well*, if they can manage it all.

But, as the Westinghouse workshop showed, for other women, for no doubt the vast majority of other women, the old conditioning about sex roles—that a man is your basic security, that his work always comes before your own—has not lost its power in a few short years. How could it? For most women the objective conditions that would breach the doubts have yet to arrive.

On the same day in April, 1973, that the *Wall Street Journal* reported the steps Westinghouse and other corporations were taking to help women advance in work, another item tabulated the latest rate of unemployment among married men (2.5 per cent). Washington experts will tell you that this is the one rate that matters the most. Although the rate is far lower than the overall jobless figure that encompasses us all, officials look at it first when unemployment starts to climb. The overall figure isn't really that critical, John B. Connally announced definitively a couple of years ago. At that time it was 6 per cent and he was Secretary of the Treasury; after all, "it includes so many women and teenagers."

Our employment policies have always been based on the male bread-winner's needs first. During depressions, recessions, recurring periods of high unemployment, his prior right to available work, the *best* available work, has never been seriously questioned. It was he about whom the government worried to the extent it bothered to worry about its job-reduction policies to stem inflation at the beginning of this decade. And of course that was far from a frivolous concern. Nothing could have been more memorable than some of the shocked and saddened faces we saw on television at that time, white, middle-aged breadwinners who had thought they and their families were secure for life; after all, unemployment was something reserved for "lazy kids and blacks." The irony of their past bigotry, in some few instances an awakening to the inequities facing others for so long, came through on the tube as we watched them. But what the television cameras failed to show, what government officials failed to consider, in addition to the then deepening problems among the poor and the black, were the faces of the women who were also being laid off, women who needed work just as badly.

We keep hearing the statistics, but that doesn't mean they are taken seriously. Forty per cent of all women who work are dependent on neither a husband nor a father for their support. Of the 33 million women now in the labor force, more than 20 per cent are single; another 20 per cent are widowed, divorced, or separated; and about 15 per cent more have husbands who are earning less than $5,000 a year. Thirteen million American women who maintain their own households are responsible for the welfare of about 10 million children. The rate of unemployment is consistently higher for women looking for work than it is for men—more than two times higher for female heads of households than male—and the gap has widened in the past decade. Despite the Equal Pay Act of 1964, the disparity in pay has widened. Far from working for pin money, there is evidence, as the *Washington Post* put it, that the "working woman is to some extent doing in this country what the US Government seems incapable of doing. Increasingly, she provides the essentials of life for the poorest of families and is pulling a very substantial number up the ladder into middle class life."

Yet, when we hear about the plight of the unemployed, when we read about the problems of workers in general, for that matter, when the subject of "the worker" comes up in almost any context, what picture is being drawn for us? Yes, most always it is the picture of a man—although 40 per cent of the labor force is now female. Pick up a book about "sex roles" and you will spend most of your time reading about women. Pick up a book about work (the meaning of work, the alienation from work, the value of work) and you will mainly be reading about men. Workers are men. Women are, well, *sometimes*, women workers.

These attitudes obviously did not start with, nor are they confined to, the current administration we have all come to know and love so well. Paradoxically, Nixon and Company appear to have done more to advance and to retard the cause of working women than any administration in recent history. On the one hand he giveth (through enforcement of equal-employment opportunity codes) while on the other he taketh away (by vetoing major child care legislation that would have made it possible or less difficult for working mothers to take advantage of the new opportunities).

Surely, politicians or men of any stripe can compete with Mr. Nixon's ability to make his position on an issue so perfectly confused. But one thing about the President, he may aid and abet you, he may benignly or malignly neglect you, he may even do worse, but he is far too politically astute to ever forget that you exist. Senator Edward Kennedy, on the other hand, last year conducted two full days of hearings on "Worker Alienation." Research has shown that women are nearly twice as likely as men to express discontent with their jobs. Yet neither the Senator nor his staff remembered to call one single woman to testify at those hearings. And in a putatively more radical vein, three scholars from Cambridge and Canada recently edited a 500-page Random House reader on *Worker's Control*, consisting of more than 40 articles on current work life and how to improve it, again without a single article *by* or about a woman.

Of course these gentlemen could argue that, after all, the issue under discussion is not gender but work. The reasons people become dissatisfied with their jobs—the routine, the lack of autonomy, the low status and pay—have nothing to do with their sex. But if these men say this, then they haven't considered why it is that women just happen to be concentrated in the lowest level jobs. And they haven't stopped saying it or tried to perceive what the women at the Westinghouse workshop knew, what all women know, that try as you will it is impossible to separate life into neat, discrete pieces that don't affect each other, that the areas of family and employment are inseparably related, and that for millions of women they are in conflict.

## III

To work or not to work, that is not the question. "The most important fact" to remember, in the words of the HEW reports on *Work in America*, is "that almost all women are working unless they are disabled. Some work in the market for pay; others work in the home; and many do both."

More and more do both. In 1900 about 20 per cent of women were in the paid workforce; today the figure is 50 per cent. In 1900 most job-holding women were young and single (while older, married women then generally confined their labor to the home—working in the fields, doing piecework or other kinds of in-house jobs in addition to child care and housework). The large increase in women workers since World War II resulted mainly from the influx of older, married women to the labor force. The *new* change is due to the sharp rise in the number of working mothers with young children, including currently a third of the mothers with children under six.

There is now every sign that these percentages will grow. The main reason, it would be nice to say, is the impact of the Women's Movement in sparking our sisters to embark on promising careers. Envision all of us going off in the morning to fight disease in the hospitals, defend justice in the courts, wheel and deal with Henry Ford II on the executive floor, in other words, doing all the things that men in the most prestigious, high paying, and "satisfying" occupations have largely kept as their own preserve.

And it is true that in the upper middle class more women are doing just that—invading the so-called male professions. Unhappily it is equally true that, for all the publicity when it happens, the invasion force is abysmally small. In 1970 women received 8.5 per cent of all M.D.'s awarded, 5.6 per cent of the law degrees, and 3.9 per cent of the Master's degrees in business. Hardly a take-over. Still, low as these percentages were, in each case they represented a large increase over the previous year, hopefully indicating a trend that will continue and accelerate.

Meantime in the so-called female professions a very different situation took place. In 1971 women received 74 per cent of the B.A.'s in education, 83 per cent of the library science degrees and 98 per cent of the nursing degrees. If you want to guess the future career of a woman college graduate, your best bet is still teaching—42 per cent of all professional women are teachers; more than one-third of all female students major in education. The reason for the overwhelming popularity of this choice is very important to understand. As Juanita Kreps notes in her book *Sex in the Marketplace* (Johns Hopkins, 1971):

Are there monetary rewards in certain careers that more than offset the low pay? Is elementary school teaching appealing to women because they like the work itself, or because it is viewed as an extension of their feminine roles, or because it can be timed to enable women to perform their regular household duties? . . . It is not merely that their nonmarket work influences their decision as to whether to enter the labor force; the demands of home and family also influence *which* market jobs women are willing to take. Moreover the period of heaviest domestic responsibility occurs fairly early in a woman's work life, when she is likely to be forced to make some quite long-range decisions: whether to acquire further job training or additional formal education; how many children she will have; whether to continue working, at least part-time, during the child-bearing period. *In the face of demands on her time the young wife is likely to find that the scheduling of her job is the most important single consideration* [my italics].

The scheduling of her job! Thus, although a man is able to enjoy the emotional benefits of a rich family life while at the same time pursuing a demanding career to its fullest, a woman who wants a family *and* a career must somehow find a way to juggle the two or else become a kind of superwoman, generally with the help of a stand-in surrogate worker in the home. The originally strong anti-marriage, anti-family position of the Women's Movement was largely based on the realization of this bind: the sacrifice was too great.

The current debate is tempered by a further realization among some feminists that the abandonment of family life may also be too great a sacrifice for many women—in any case, why should it always have to be the woman who must sacrifice? The growing pressures for truly egalitarian marriages or cohabitational arrangements—sharing equally in both the home and work roles—grows out of this feeling. What is still obviously far away, however, is an occupational and economic structure—with shorter and more flexible hours—that would make the model of shared roles possible for more than a relative handful of upper middle class professionals.

The rapid surge in the number of working mothers has *not* been primarily due to the Women's Movement. Inflation, taxes, and the rising cost of living have been far greater factors. The noble view of a job as a road to self-fulfillment and self-expression may indeed seem laughable to many working-class women forced out of their homes to take menial jobs to help ends meet. If she has a high-school education, she most likely will be involved in clerical or secretarial work. If she has less than a high school education, clerical, factory, or service work is most probable. Only farm workers and domestic workers average less income than clerical workers.

Among these persons, work dissatisfaction is profound. It is in these kinds of jobs that the vast majority of women workers are still found. Compounding all the possible problems of boredom and routine that may face anyone involved in such work is the difficulty of coordinating family responsibilities that the upper middle class professional woman also faces. But while the professional woman often has surrogate child care and household help, plus a husband to some extent committed to the notion of equality in marriage, the working-class woman generally has neither. While the professional woman's husband is often pleased at his wife's status, male workers with low income and education register higher dissatisfaction with their own jobs when their wives work. This was the conclusion of Harold Sheppard and Neal Herrick in their book *Where Have All the Robots Gone?* (The Free Press, 1972):

> The phenomenon of two or more earners in the working class family is not the unmixed blessing it is assumed to be. To put the above facts in a different form, only one-fourth of the single-earner Pennsylvania workers have the "blues" but among workers with additional earners in the family, discontent goes up to nearly two-fifths, 38 per cent...Perhaps the belief that satisfaction among male workers should increase as family income is improved through the wife's employment is a projection on the part of the people who

write about such problems. These people are primarily professional, upper middle class individuals. Perhaps these professional males feel no threat to themselves if their wives work. Indeed they may even feel proud and gain satisfaction if their wives are so engaged. And the wives themselves may work, not so much for the purpose of adding needed income to the family budget, but more for 'self-fulfillment ...

The working class context may be sharply different from the professional class situation, and the professional class individuals who write about worker discontent may...be making some wrong assumptions...It may be that these working class men don't feel that they've really succeeded if *all by themselves* they can't provide their families with the necessary income to pay for the level of living to which they aspire.

Here, of course, the emphasis is on the job discontent of the man, not the woman. But the attitudes of a husband are far from unimportant. Among married, professional women, study after study has shown that the supportiveness and encouragement of their husbands has been a crucial factor in their ability to succeed. Among working-class women, the impact of the husband's position toward their working is hardly less crucial. With less commitment generally found in working-class families to the idea of women's liberation, his influence is bound to be even more pronounced. His dissatisfaction with her working adds to her dissatisfaction—his tension to hers. Even if she finds she enjoys her job, even if it turns out to be a relief to have a break from the kitchen and kids, the very hassle of all that surrounds the job—rising early to get the house clean, the kids off to the sitter or school, then rushing home after work to pick them up and start dinner—may outweigh the satisfaction she derives. What to do?

## IV

The acute work discontent of so many women needs to be seen in all these terms—personal, social, economic. The meaning of a job to a woman changes as we go from class to class, primarily because of the differences in opportunities available (with motherhood being far more satisfying than many jobs), but also because of the differences in all the factors surrounding work from class to class—the availability of child care and household help, the attitude of the husband and other family members toward her working—all combine to make a woman glad or sorry to be gainfully employed.

One obvious answer to the discontent that appears to be growing is to make it possible for mothers *forced* to take jobs, including welfare mothers, to return to the home. If a woman—or a man—freely chooses to confine her labor to home and child care—and many do—it should be economically possible. In the 1950's we glorified domesticity for women; in the '70's it is equally senseless to glorify the labor market. Whether 'tis nobler for a woman to dish out the ham-and-eggs-over-easy to her family at home or to a stranger at Schraffts—that is hardly the issue women are struggling over. In either instance the content of the work is the same. In one instance the pay is low; in the other, non-existent. To make home and child care possible for those women who want to devote themselves to it full-time, many people are now suggesting we find a way to pay for that work, through government subsidies, tax deductions, or other imaginative measures.

Overall, however, the trend of two-earner families and working women does appear certain to continue and grow. So it is imperative to make sure that current efforts to open better job opportunities and to equalize pay for women do not fade away with the next economic slump, as many are predicting. The notion of eminent domain for the male breadwinner must finally be put to rest.

To make sure it happens, there is also a need to organize women in the low-paying occupations into unions responsive to their needs. Although only 12 per cent of women workers are currently unionized, there has recently been a flood of organizing among women working in the large banks and insurance offices as well as throughout government employment. And it is the unions with large female memberships (teachers, service employees, and state, county, and municipal employees) that are now growing the fastest.

Indeed, slowly and unsurely something may be happening to the conservative labor movement—as well as the rest of the nation—regarding its attitudes toward women. Externally, unions as well as corporations may now be sued under Title VII of the Civil Rights Act for discriminating against women, and several already have been. Internally, many women union members appear to be going through their consciousness-raising period at conferences and discussion groups where women talk about the discrimination they face on the job and the double burdens they must carry as workers and as women. They are raising issues like child care and maternity (also paternity) with increased force.

Many unions now have women's caucuses. State federations of labor and county labor councils are for the first time starting to adopt resolutions that concern the rights of women. In the San Francisco Bay area a growing group of women from over 70 unions have formed the first voluntary group of trade union women specifically organized to "fight discrimination of women on the job, in unions, and in society." The organization is called Union WAGE (Women's Alliance to Gain Equality), and several groups modeled on it have begun to sprout in other areas of the country.

It was the women of Union WAGE who almost singlehandedly made possible the first statewide women's conference of the California AFL-CIO. Indeed, it took a bitter floor fight at last year's state convention before the women were allowed to conduct it; the male trade union leaders, while willing to make a few concessions to women, obviously didn't want to see women seeking their rightful share of power within the male-dominated unions.

The conference, held in May, 1973, was attended by nearly 400 women from unions all over the state—an historic event. They discussed such topics as working women and the law, how to negotiate women's issues, how to organize the unemployed, how to move into leadership positions within the labor movement. Repeatedly, however, the subject of child care came to the fore. At one point a woman from the Newspaper Guild, a clerk, I believe, rose to voice her irritation about this.

"But what we've said is something else," answered a young woman with a long black braid flowing down her back. "We want women to become more active, to fight for more power. But right now women don't come to union meetings and there are concrete reasons why they don't. Most of the women I work with have to rush home and do all the work on their second jobs as housewives. If we want women to fight for the larger issues, we have to make it possible."

"Yes," said an older woman, a teacher, a mother, a wife, a trade unionist, a person, a veteran juggler of roles. "Yes to child-care centers. The time must come when we can say, 'Listen buddy, tonight it's your turn to start the dinner and take care of the house and the baby. The first battle begins at home."

There are union battles, government battles, business battles, education battles to win if women are ever to gain job equality, but for millions the first battle still begins at home. If the matter of workload is now an issue for negotiation on the job, then it should be no less an issue at home where every working mother moonlights. If job rotation and restructuring are seen as answers to the endlessness and banality of so many work tasks, then the analysis applies with equal force in the nursery and kitchen. If classifying jobs by sex is no longer deemed lawful in business and government, then how can it be fitting at home if both persons also work in the labor market? If wages are still the *sine qua non* of participation in the labor market (and people with the lowest incomes have the lowest satisfaction), then the effect of not assigning an economic value to housework and child care must also be clear. If humanizing the workplace is really a vital issue on the social agenda today, then it is time to recognize that the home is also a place of work.   ●

# The bisexual debate

## By Martin Duberman

*Martin Duberman, historian and playwright (In White America), is currently writing a book on sex and society.*

# 22

About a year ago I made this entry in a sporadic journal I keep:

*"Bisexuals seem to be popping up all over. Until recently, I knew very few, and none well. I could relegate them to some distant category of indecision. Now I know many — and tend to romanticize them as the embodiment of the brave new world struggling into being. They're already acting, one part of me says, on the rhetoric most of us are spouting — that warmth between two individuals should eventuate in physical expression, regardless of the genders involved. But is 'physical expression' the same as 'genital contact?' . . .*

*"When I hear in detail about the lives of [Phil] or [Wally] their bisexuality seems less a function of their free 'polymorphous perversity' than of their delayed recognition that they prefer sex with men. They continue to maintain a bisexual life because they're trapped in marriage obligations, or continue to need the security and support of a 'home life,' or remain unwilling to take on the still onerous image of being homosexual.*

*"I remember [Carol] telling me she'd 'passed through' her bisexual 'phase,' that she thought the current pressures to be bisexual were to be resisted as a cop-out, as a failure of nerve.*

*"I don't know. I think it may be the central — and largely ignored — issue in 'gay liberation.' If, as Freud thought, we all have (or originally had) bisexual capacities, the injunction should be to discover and utilize them. If, as Carol feels, we are either homo- or heterosexual, then those who mix the two become cowards and poseurs . . . but that kind of patronization may be our way of refusing to come to grips with our bisexuality."*

Now, a year after writing that diary entry, the bisexual idea has come increasingly to be touted as the standard against which all who aspire to be *bona fide* members of the Sexual Revolution must measure themselves. The psychiatrist Robert E. Gould, speaking as a heterosexual, has recently declared his new-found conviction that "if there were no social restrictions on sexual object choice, most humans would be functioning bisexuals." Phil Mullen, speaking as a homosexual in a recent issue of *The Gay Alternative,* has expressed a view heard increasingly within homosexual circles: ". . . we gay people . . . have often been heard to argue that the lives of straights would be richer if they could only respond sexually and emotionally to others of their own gender. *Our* gay lives, by the same token, would be richer if we could open up to . . . heterosexual love. . . . Now that we're finally learning that gay is good, we'll have to start learning that gay isn't good enough. . . ."

Probably. But I'm less sure than they of everyone's "innate" bisexual nature, and I'm worried that that assumption — though seemingly on the side of liberation — could prove tyrannical, could become the latest in a long series of "scientific" party lines used to whip deviants — in this case exclusive homosexuals *or* heterosexuals — into line. The recent reading I've done in the scanty literature on bisexuality, along with my proliferating personal contact with practicing bisexuals, has deepened rather than resolved the doubts and questions I expressed in my journal a year ago.

But before exploring the theory and practice of bisexuality, I should make one thing perfectly clear: I am not now and have never been a bisexual. To anyone alive in the Nixon Era, it's obvious that the preceding statement is probably untrue. My sexual activities (not to be equated with desires or fantasies) have always been — give or take a few clouded teenage experiences — exclusively homosexual. For most of my 40 years, I was made to feel guilty about my homosexuality; now, under the sting of new cultural imperatives, I'm learning to feel guilty about my exclusivity. Since guilt is the common denominator (and since I'm Jewish), one might conclude that no shift in social attitudes will appease my unquenchable instinct for self-castigation.

Among my many exclusively homosexual friends, some resent my espousal of the bisexual theme. At first they though I'd found a new tactic for asserting superiority. After I explained that bisexuality was an aspiration and not an actuality for me, they settled for the view that I'm a latter-day Horatio Alger, fixated on some version of insatiable Self-Improvement. To which I respond — the nerve having been hit — that they're fixated on self-congratulation (all the while calling it self-affirmation). So the argument stands. And will stand for a long time to come. For we seem a space age away from accumulating the data — theoretical and personal — that might resolve it.

The "objective" data to date derives from three main sources: biology, anthropology and history. The evidence from all three areas is remarkably thin and often contradictory, either very new (biology) and therefore unreplicated or very old (history) and therefore incapable of replication. First, biology — the argument, as it were, from "nature," from the genetic, chromosomal and hormonal "givens."

### Biology

The genetic sex of the individual embryo is established at the time of fertilization, but sexual differentiation in the fetus doesn't manifest itself until the fifth to sixth week of pregnancy. Freud (and until recently almost everyone else) referred to the undifferentiated genital system of the embryo during these early weeks as a "bisexual" one. Recent research — and especially that of Mary Jane Sherfey — suggests that it would be more accurate to say that mammalian embryos (unlike those of fish and amphibia) are *female* during the first few weeks of life; the strong intervention of the male hormone, androgen, is necessary to "overcome" what would otherwise be a straight-line development of ovarian reproductive organs.*

Freud believed bisexuality was a biological universal — a potential inherent in all cells, tissues, organs, creatures. Since Freud also believed that psychology reflects biology, he assumed that bisexuality is present in the thought/feeling processes of all human beings — even if not in their overt behavior. Some 35 years ago, the distinguished analyst Sandor Rado issued what has become the classic attack on Freud's concept of bisexuality. Rado concentrated his fire on the sloppiness of Freud's conceptualization. "Bipotentiality of differentiation" in the early embryonic stages, Rado argued, had been confused with hermaphroditism, the possession of two complete reproductive systems in the mature organism; and only true hermaphroditism, he insisted, could properly be called "bisexuality."

*For much of this discussion I'm indebted to John Money and Anke A. Ehrhart, *Man & Woman, Boy & Girl,* and to Robert J. Stoller, "Facts and Fancies: An Examination of Freud's Concept of Bisexuality," soon to appear in a fine new book of essays, *Women & Analysis* (Jean Strouse, ed.).

But the absence of a dual reproductive system in human beings has not kept them from seeking pleasure (or relatedness) wherever their psyches cue them to find it. Strict linguistic definitions of bisexuality have as little do with the *fact* of bisexual behavior as they do with the everyday vocabulary used to describe the phenomenon. In common usage, a bisexual is simply a person sexually attracted to people of both genders. Less often, the term is used to describe someone who identifies with *behavioral* traits of the opposite sex — someone who apes presumed "masculine" or "feminine" mannerisms or dress.

Thus the narrow semantic point can be conceded to Rado without any other conclusions about bisexuality necessarily following. Rado is correct that "true hermaphroditism" — a bisexual breeding capacity — is never found in human beings. (Well, almost never: a few rare conditions are known that are marked by genital ambiguity — a mixture of ovarian and testicular structures — or, in the male, by degeneration of the testes.) It is also true that this is in decided contrast with other creatures. A garden worm, for example, produces both eggs and sperm — a condition Money and Ehrhardt call "simultaneous bisexuality." In certain species of fish, bisexuality is sequential rather than simultaneous: the Mexican swordfish, for example, "spends part of its life as a male making sperms, and part of its life as a female making eggs." The only process even remotely comparable in human beings may be that fleeting moment during the gradual buildup in the production of androgen in the male fetus at which, in Mary Jane Sherfey's words, "female and male hormonal influences are equal."

Higher in the phyletic scale, among birds and mammals, we do not find the capacity for hermaphroditic reproduction, but in subhuman mammals we do decidedly find bisexual behavior. The zoologist and physiologist R. H. Denniston has written categorically that "frequent homosexual activity has been described for all species of mammals of which careful observations have been made . . . it has little relation to hormonal or structural abnormality." Whether it relates, however, to "dominance behavior" or to what (if apes were humans) we might call "indiscriminate responsiveness to genital stimulation" has long been a point of argument. And in that argument, the "dominance" theoreticians have long been in the ascendance — with some of them denying that anal intromission (let alone orgasm) actually takes place.

But the balance in the arguments is rapidly shifting. A convenient summary of that shift can be found in the work of Suzanne Chevalier-Skolnikoff. (The arrival of women scientists on the scene, less frightened — like women everywhere — of homosexuality than their male counterparts, will, I believe, produce a wide variety of reevaluations of supposed scientific truths.) In her study of the stumptail monkey, Chevalier-Skolnikoff has come up with some very unambiguous findings: "Homosexual encounters with numerous . . . the term 'homosexual' . . . refers to interactions between individuals of the same sex that involve prolonged (15 sec. or more) intensive genital stimulation of at least one of the animals. This definition excludes most mountings that function mainly as dominance behavior, since these mountings rarely involve prolonged genital stimulation . . . four of the five females in the group were involved in homosexual behavior. . . . Male homosexual interactions were more varied in form. . . . Eight different methods of stimulation were observed. They include extensive manual genital stimulation (which was often mutual), oral genital stimulation or fellatio (also often mutual), as well as dorsal mountings with pelvic thrusts and anal intromission"; orgasms were observed during female, but not male, encounters;

homosexual intercourse took place in essentially the same position assumed in the common heterosexual pattern, and even though heterosexual options for sex were available.*

As we've learned from the works of Lorenz, Ardrey and Desmond Morris, there's great danger in using animal studies to draw simplistic analogies about human behavior. We can tell plainly enough when two male stumptail monkeys are pleasuring each other (in eight observable positions, no less), but we can't be sure whether the incidence or quality is affected by the artificial environment of the laboratory;

*Archives of Sexual Behavior, Vol. 3, No. 2, March 1974.

whether and how the *feelings* of the monkeys relate to their behavior (and thus to our own); whether and how the feelings of scientists watching those prodigies of fellatio affect their "objective" reporting of the material; whether — most basically — the behavior of stumptail monkeys, in or out of the lab, has much of anything to do with that of, say, macaque baboons — let alone the inhabitants of Manhattan Island.

## 49 of 76 societies surveyed regarded homosexuality as a normal variable

Though the evidence from biology and from animal studies suggests the possibility that genes and hormones play a role in programming patterns of sexual behavior, it suggests far more emphatically that such behavior results from the *interaction* between genetic "predispositions" and the models, cues and injunctions provided by the social environment—with social learning playing much the more significant role. The latter point has been made incontrovertibly by John Money in his work on transsexuals; though the anatomical and chromosomal equipment of a given transsexual is entirely intact—it checks out as "correct" against every scientific measurement of gender—the psychological conviction of the individual that he or she has in fact been misassigned overwhelms all the supposed mandates of biology. "I am a woman trapped in a man's body" takes precedence in male transsexuals over all the seeming logic of XY chromosomes, testicles and penis, prostate gland and gonads, androgen levels and hairy chest. Neither psychotherapy nor electric shock, neither the insistence of healers nor the pleas of friends, has ever made the slightest dent in the determination of a transsexual to convert his or her anatomy to conform to the inner conviction that they *were meant to be the* opposite of what their internal biology and external anatomy suggests they are.

### Anthropology
The anthropologists have given us additional evidence that our sexual behavior results largely from cultural, not biological, imperatives. Even a cursory glance at the psychosexual patterns of other cultures confirms how much our own are dependent on parochial social dictates.

More than 20 years ago, Clellan S. Ford and Frank A. Beach, in their classic work *Patterns of Sexual Behavior*, revealed that 49 of the 76 societies (64 percent) they surveyed regarded homosexuality as a normal variable. (They mean male homosexuality; 17 of the societies did sanction female homosexuality, but in anthropological research—as in everything else—female behavior is less visible, less studied.) The 49 cultures vary considerably in the kind of homosexual behavior sanctioned, the degree to which it is formally institutionalized and the extent to which it is merely encouraged, casually accepted or actually prescribed.

Among the fierce Kukukuku people of the New Guinea highlands, the ingesting of semen is magically endowed, considered essential to virile growth—and accordingly prescribed for all preadolescent and adolescent males. Among the Keraki of New Guinea, the prescription for health and character in the growing boy is regularized anal intercourse with an older man. Among the Crow Indians, sodomy is entirely absent—but there is frequent oral-genital contact. Among the Batak people of northern Sumatra, adolescent boys are expected to have anal intercourse with one another —but fellatio is taboo.

Among the Koniag of Alaska and the Tanala of Madagascar, transvestite males ("berdaches") are usually regarded as shamans, persons in possession of supernatural power; and sexual contact with a berdache is thought to confer a variety of blessings. They become wives of other men—though the husband may have another, heterosexual wife, and the berdache sometimes has a female mistress. In Davenport's study of a Melanesian people of the Southwest Pacific, transvestitism is unkown; but acceptable sexual practices include homosexual partnerships between adolescent friends and even brothers, and between adolescents and older men — including their fathers' friends.

It's important to remember that in all these examples— and they could be multiplied many times — we're discussing bisexual behavior. The expected, approved, even prescribed homosexuality in these cultures is never found to the exclusion of heterosexuality. It is always expected (the berdache or shaman may be a partial exception) that if there is same gender sex there will also be opposite gender sex — sometimes simultaneously, sometimes alternately, sometimes progressively (that is, gender choice shifting completely from adolescence to adulthood).

The anthropological data allows for many *near*-generalizations in regard to same gender sex. We can say, for example, that it is *usually* connected with puberty rites and/or religious significance; that it *usually* involves anal intercourse rather than oral-genital contact; that it *usually* occurs prior to marriage and breeding; that a considerable age differential is *usually* present between the partners. But the only complete generalization we can make, the one universal we can point to, is that homosexuality is never found *in opposition to* heterosexuality. The same universal is true in all nonhuman animal studies.

There is but one exception; the Judeo-Christian culture of the West. If exclusive homosexuality is to be found only among human beings, the only human beings among whom it is found are those in our own culture. Even within our own culture, moreover, exclusivity is a relatively recent phenomenon; though known at least as far back as ancient Greece, it was considered a rarity and a subject for mockery (for example, in the plays of Aristophanes and Menander). It's important to keep in mind that the converse is also true; probably more people are exclusively *heterosexual* in our culture than at any previous time in recorded history—and within our culture, the exclusivity (especially for males) is more pronounced now than in earlier epochs.

If this conclusion is correct—and the evidence is sketchy enough (we may, for example, associate exclusive homosexuality with the West simply because the phenomenon has been little studied in Eastern cultures)—it requires explanation, and that in turn requires a closer look at our past.

## History

The history of sexual mores in the West is, for the most part, poorly documented — and therefore susceptible to a wide difference in interpretation. (I've often thought "philosophy" is contingent on limited data.) As the anthropologist Steve Weinstock has remarked. "Incidences are easily demonstrated, but attitudes can only be surmised."

There are but two books in English that survey the subject with any competence: G. Rattray Taylor's pioneering *Sex in History* (first published in the mid-'50s), and Arno Karlen's far more comprehensive *Sexuality and Homosexuality* (published in 1971). Taylor's book, gracefully written and often witty, is burdened with a theoretical superstructure derived from the rigid categories of psychoanalysis (the Oedipal Complex, et al.) and to that degree now seems overinterpreted and outdated. Taylor's inquiry, moreover, is pretty much limited to England (an island not as narrow in its range of sexual expression as generations of exposure to the royal hand-wave might suggest).

Karlen's book, though a little prudish, and more than a little homophobic, is remarkable for its scrupulous detailing and its sophisticated analysis, its blend of a scholar's precision with a journalist's concern with communication. Among Karlen's most firmly held views is that "we must scrap the biologically rooted concepts of bisexuality and latency." Taylor, on the same theme, waffles strangely; not once, but twice in his book, he states that "homosexual elements are present in everyone." Yet he constantly equates homosexuality with "abnormality." How a quality present in everyone can be considered abnormal is never clarified — though the whimsical implications of the converse are certainly tempting: "Normality is that quality which can be recognized by its absence in everyone."

It's possible, obviously, for a behavioral pattern to be commonplace and yet not biologically determined: driving a car is one example. Such behavior, we say, is "learned." Very well. But why through time have human beings been so available for "learning" bisexual behavior? If biology has not been the cause, it has not been a deterrent, either; apparently no biological mechanism has ever existed sufficient to inhibit the capacity to take physical pleasure with people of either gender. "Nature" would seem to be neutral on the subject; we are or we aren't bisexual depending on whether our culture does or does not encourage the activity.

Karlen provides ample evidence for arguing that bisexuality has been so integral an element in human history that statistically speaking we would have to rank it among the few constants of "human nature" — on a par with waging war or using intoxicants. Though Karlen is the first to warn us how scanty the evidence is about the sexuality of early people, he does insist that on one matter "with confidence we can say this: for centuries or even millennia before the Greeks, many peoples from the eastern Mediterranean to Sumeria worshiped a goddess whose rites included both heterosexual and homosexual intercourse." He then names the goddess in her various incarnations — Artemis in Ephesus, Aphrodite in Corinth, Astarte in Phoenicia, Ishtar in Babylon, Isis in Egypt . . . Anitis in Persia . . . Cybele in Phrygia . . . Bendis in Thrace.

Even Sandor Rado — like Karlen, unsympathetic to Freud's notion of a biologically rooted bisexuality — agrees with Karlen that as far back as we have records of human behavior, evidence of bisexuality exists. (We only have records, of course, for about 1 percent of our history — the last 10,000 years; before that, human beings lived in nonliterate hunting and gathering societies.) Rado finds traces of bisexuality in the Upanishads and the Old Testament, and he refers to certain Egyptian gods as being "notoriously bisexual." Curiously — in light of his vigorous argument against biological bisexuality — Rado locates the source of persistent bisexual behavior through history in "primeval, emotional needs of animalistic man." Confusing, to say the least. If "primeval emotions" bear no relation to biology, perhaps biology should no longer be looked to as the source of our "instincts."

Our scattered sources suggest that before 500 B.C. sexual

activity was more uninhibited and homosexuality more acceptable than thereafter. In her fine new book, *Woman Plus Woman: Attitudes Toward Lesbianism*, Dolores Klaich argues persuasively that in Sappho's day (c. 612-558 B.C.) her poems were celebrated throughout the Greek world, coins were minted with her image, statues erected in her honor; in other words, no opprobrium of any kind was attached to her lesbianism (or perhaps, bisexuality — the existence of a husband and — more probable — a daughter, are disputed). It was not until Emperor Theodosius the Great (the Christian hero who massacred 7,000 people at Thessalonica) and the Council of Constantinople that edicts were issued declaring homosexuality a crime punishable by death, and that Sappho's poems were consigned to the flames (390 A.D.).

## In Sparta a boy who had no lover was punished — and a boy who picked a poor lover over a rich one was fined

Any attempt to generalize about "Greek" or "Roman" sexuality involves an absurd compression of a variety of lifestyles spread over some thousand years of human history. Even at any given moment in time, the extent and shape of bisexual behavior is disputed among scholars. Though Rattray Taylor, for example, agrees with other scholars that among the aristocratic class in classical Greece "every man was expected to take to himself a boy" and a boy not chosen by anyone was a boy disgraced, he disagrees with them in confining the relationship to the kind of quaint Victorian roles of Inspirer and Listener that I very much doubt Socrates and Alcibiades would have recognized.

To avoid excessive absurdity in the compression of complex historical data, it's perhaps best to content ourselves with scattered glimpses of the assorted styles of bisexual identification in antiquity:

In the 4th century B.C. a picked band of male lovers fought against Philip of Macedon at Chaeronea and died to a man. In Sparta a boy who had no lover was punished — and a boy who picked a poor lover over a rich one was fined. Julius Caesar's diversity of sexual tastes earned him the reputation as "the husband of every woman and the wife of every man"; but even Caesar was scandalized by the harem of both sexes Mark Antony kept in Rome — perhaps because Caesar did not believe pleasure should be institutionalized.

Though female homosexuality was practiced in Greece, no one knows how widely; among the few bits of extant evidence are the fragments of Sappho's poetry, Plato's comment in the *Symposium* that the existence of lesbians, like that of male homosexuals, was to be explained naturally, as part of bisexual creation, and Plutarch's remark that "at Sparta love was held in such honor that even the most respectable women became infatuated with girls."

If the definition of bisexuality is broadened beyond "sexual desire for the same sex" to include nonsexual identification with the opposite sex, the phenomenon of cross-dressing also becomes a matter of historical interest. Philip Slater (in *The Glory of Hera*) describes "the prevalence, in puberty initiations and other *rites de passage*, of exchange of clothes between the sexes." Among such *rites* was the nuptial ceremony. In both Greek myths and practice we find cross-dressing associated with the wedding night, with a desire, perhaps, to ensure potency. At Argos brides donned false beards on the wedding night; in Sparta the

bride's head was shaved and she put on men's clothing; at Cos the procedure was reversed: the husband put on women's clothing to receive his bride.

The Greeks, as Rattray Taylor puts it, "were deeply preoccupied with understanding the experiences of the other sex." The story of Teresias — the male seer who spent seven years as a woman — is merely the best-known of many legends depicting men and women who changed sex during the course of their lives. The Greek deities also numbered several bisexual or androgynous figures, the most famous being Hermaphroditos.

In Rome, too, cross-dressing was a familiar practice. Will Durant (in *Caesar and Christ*) describes the sons of the rich in the 1st century B.C. who "dressed and walked like courtesans, wore frilled robes and women's sandals, decked themselves with jewelry, sprinkled themselves with perfume, deferred marriage or avoided parentage, and emulated the bisexual impartiality of the Greeks." (Alas for the pansexual swingers of Le Jardin and Max's, for David Bowie and Alice Cooper, for all those pioneers of the new who, in thinking that they are inventing a world, may be merely representing another shift in an age-old cycle — a shift so long delayed, this last time around, that those applying weight to the edge are perhaps entitled to their claims of originality.)

Otto Kiefer, in his book *Sexual Life in Ancient Rome*, comments that "everything relating to sex was regarded as completely natural, and was approached far more simply and innocently than it is now." The comment is suspiciously sweeping and bland, but Kiefer does draw the needed contrast between the acceptance of diverse sexuality in the ancient world and the repression of it — even of the inner wish for it in the Christian era that followed, and continues to linger.

By the time of Leviticus, homosexuality had come to be associated with heresy and was made (for males) a capital offense. (It was disapproved for females too, but penalties were affixed only later.) As Rattray Taylor summarizes the evidence: "a remarkable psychological change" emerged as early as 500 B.C., marked by an increased repression of sexuality and a heightened sense of guilt. The growing homophobia of the Hebraic view eventually overpowered the bisexual ambience of the Greek and Roman period. This is not to say that the Christianized West came merely to exemplify sexual repression: the baudiness of Chaucer's poetry is alone enough to remind us that official disapproval failed to persuade humanity against the pleasures of the sensual life. But the disapproval was fierce, obsessional — as exemplified in the "penitential books" and in the ferocious punishments ordained during the Inquisition. (Its official handbook, the *Malleus Maleficarum* explicitly stated that "all witchcraft comes from carnal lust.") And the triumph of Christianity did mark, in Karlen's phrase, "the West's full transformation from a shame culture to a guilt culture, in which prohibitions are fully internalized and man is ruled by conscience rather than by others' disapproval."

## Faced with crosscurrents of adulation and contempt, it is not surprising that bisexuals sometimes exhibit an incipient chauvinism of their own

It hardly needs demonstrating that the guilt, the internalization of sexual prohibitions, remains very much a part of our culture despite the hopeful signs of a countermovement. Both the continuing repression and the dawning liberation from it are exemplified in a recent controversy in one of our specialized papers, *The Chronicle of Higher Education.* Back in February of this year, the *Chronicle* printed an article by English Professor Louis Crew in which he described his sense of heightened freedom and joy since de-closeting himself as a gay person. Two months later the *Chronicle* printed the outraged response of Albert J. Maier, Comptroller of Marquette University in Milwaukee. Maier, in the thunderous tones of the *Malleus* denounced the publication of Crew's article as "a blunder of unforgivable magnitude and a sign of the general moral decadence." Maier went on to characterize homosexuality as "one of the most vile blasphemies against God, and then with the understatement of a papal bull, warned Louis Crew that "some day he will be called upon to give an accounting of the stewardship entrusted to him by our creator." Maier left no doubt as to the Lord's verdict: "a one-way ticket to hell."

The ravings of an isolated nut? Not when a recent poll reveals that 85 percent (I can't put my hand on the clipping; the figure was perhaps a little higher) of the country disapproves of homosexuals teaching at any level of our school system, and a still higher percentage disapproves of sex between adult members of the same gender even when in private and even within the context of a love relationship. I have no poll to back my hunch that at this particular moment in time there is still less acceptance of bisexuality than of homosexuality. But I do have a personal anecdote.

In the summer of 1972, an evening of my one act plays was being performed at the John Drew Theater in East Hampton. During rehearsals, I stayed in the home of a couple well known in New York for their philanthropic activities and their liberal attitudes. Though we'd known each other a long time. I'd never discussed my sex or love life with "Joan" and "Don"; it was clear they knew I was gay and equally clear they didn't want to talk about it. I was in love at the time with a bisexual man whom I'd been seeing about a year. He wanted to come out to East Hampton for opening night, and I very much wanted him to. I asked Joan if it was all right if "Bob" stayed overnight. (I should add that they lived in a 30-room mansion, lest the false issue of overcrowding arise in anyone's mind.) Initially Joan said "yes," but on the morning of opening night, with Bob on his way out to East Hampton, she told me that Don had called from Manhattan to say "it might be better" if Bob went to a hotel.

I told Joan I couldn't let it go at that, and wanted to talk things out. She made some reference to their teenage sons, a vague hint of possible seduction, an explicit avowal that she and Don believed the "wrong" influence at a critical juncture could turn youngsters down the "wrong" path. Stupefied more than angry, and still affiliated with "old gay" apologetics, I volunteered the information then that Bob had never before been involved with a man, that his earlier love affairs had been with women that he was well, bisexual. "Oh my God!" Joan blurted out, "that's much worse. Don has trouble enough accepting someone who's homosexual, but someone who crosses back and forth . . . ! !"

Those dangling exclamation points say a lot about "liberal" sexual attitudes in this country. "Not to withhold the punchline. Bob came to East Hampton, we stayed in a hotel (the friendship with Joan and Don is ruptured). It's easier I believe, for exclusive heterosexuals to tolerate (and that's the word) exclusive homosexuals than those who rejecting exclusivity, sleep with people not genders. It's easier because in the Cartesian West we've long been taught to think in either/or categories, to believe that one is male *or* female, boss *or* worker, teacher *or* student, child *or* adult,

gay *or* straight. To suggest, as practising bisexuals do, that each of us may contain within ourselves all those supposed diametric opposites we've been taught to divide humanity into is to suggest that we might not know ourselves as well as we like to pretend. It's to suggest, too, that the roles through which most of us define ourselves — "Me, Tarzan", "Me, Jane" — represent transient and even foolish social values.

Such suggestions are discomforting. Few people welcome discomfort. And that includes most gay people. In the 18 months or so that I've been active in "movement" politics I've heard considerable disparagement among exclusively homosexual people of the "confusion" and "cowardice" of their bisexual brothers and sisters. Gay people, struggling to accept their self-worth, do not like hearing that once one mountain's been scaled, another may lie directly ahead.

Bisexuals, in short, seem at the moment very much between the devil and the deep blue sea. And in their struggle for the right to their own lifestyle, there isn't much legitimizing comfort to be drawn from the blurred data of the social sciences. Biology, as I've tried to argue, is neutral on the subject. History and anthropology do provide considerable evidence of the widespread incidence of bisexuality through time and across cultures; but it also provides evidence that most people have been predominantly heterosexual.

The safest conclusion to be drawn from these assorted arguments seems to be that human beings will behave sexually as their culture tells them they should behave — and both the social cues and the behavior have varied wildly through time. *Why* societies have differed so radically in their programming is almost as mysterious as why people have almost always accepted that parochial programming as the equivalent of universal truth. I don't mean that answers to these conundrums are impossible to come by. Freudians, Marxist. Feminists and others have all had their say; but only that the answers to date seem partial and polemical. At any rate, as any good utopian knows, evidence from the past, what has been, is no necessary guide to the future, what might be. Even if it can be conclusively demonstrated that sexual dimorphism has been the dominant pattern in history, that does not mean it will or should remain so. Not, that is, unless the argument from biology clarifies and consolidates. Even then, there would be many who would oppose biological determinism — in the name of the continuing evolution of the species, and conscious that in the evolutionary process deliberate human intervention — building cities, inventing a flying machine — has always been salient. Besides, as psychologist Pamela Oline has put it, "What if more *were* known about connections between body chemistry and certain predispositions? Would that knowledge tell us automatically how to behave?"

As regards our own country, it seems beyond dispute that bisexuality is currently more visible and assertive than at any previous time. And in tight little circles within tight little islands like Manhattan, bisexuals are even being hailed as the exemplars of a brave new world. Faced with crosscurrents of adulation and contempt, it's not surprising that bisexuals can sometimes exhibit an incipient chauvinism of their own. I think here of an ex-student of mine (male) who went to live in a small commune after graduating from college. Its members were paired heterosexually, but the women in the commune were also sleeping with each other. They began increasingly to bait the men as "hung-up Puritans" for their reluctance to do likewise — finally driving the man I knew, desperate to get his credentials in the counterculture, to a homosexual experience that was entirely unsatisfying and has kept him, to date, from further experimentation. "Well," someone might say, "that's the way it has to be for a while, as we try out, often disastrously, possibilities that in the long run will prove enriching." Okay, but the long run is a difficult hike to get started on, and pointing a gun in someone's face may not be the optimal way to get him to put on his track suit. It's possible to argue, moreover, that sexual orientation becomes fixed at so early an age — the homo- or heterosexual pattern so thoroughly imprinted — that most adults, even if they had the will, would be unable to activate their bisexual potential. Why *some* adults can and do is one of the many mysteries.

Besides, the long run, if we're lucky, will allow for more not less diversity; we don't want to exchange one set of harness for another — not, that is, if we believe the rhetoric many of us are currently spouting about the mysterious specialness of every human creature. I myself feel that the future will see many more people relating bisexually — at least in the minimal sense that some day, and perhaps within another generation, most people will more or less regularly enjoy the pleasures of having sex with someone of their own (or opposite) gender, even though they may still prefer

their "core" relationship to be heterosexual (or homosexual).

But the words D. H. Lawrence wrote 50 years ago probably have more value than any prediction — and they are certainly more humane than some of the current ones we're hearing:

"That I am I.
That my soul is a dark forest.
That my known self will never be more
   than a little clearing in the forest.
That gods, strange gods, come forth from
   the forest into the clearing of my known
   self, and then go back.
That I must have the courage to let them
   come and go.
That I will never let mankind put anything
   over me, but that I will try always to recognize
   and submit to the gods in me and the gods
   in other men and women."

# III. Social Inequality

Inequality is a universal feature of human societies. In a few small-scale, simple societies, this inequality is often simply a matter of differences in the status of specific individuals—between, say, the strong and the weak or the wise and the foolish. In nearly all societies, however, social inequality takes the form of social stratification, or the ranking of entire groups of people into a hierarchy of strata with unequal access to the basic economic resources. There are many types of stratification systems. Some are based on slavery; some, like the medieval feudal system, are based on different rights to land; and some, like the Indian caste system or the South African *apartheid* system, are based on arbitrary criteria of religion or color. Most modern societies, however, have a class system in which people are ranked primarily according to their economic status.

Despite the rhetoric of human equality found in our "official" ideology and enshrined in our Declaration of Independence and our Constitution, the United States is actually a very inegalitarian society. There are over 200,000 millionaires in the United States, and over 1000 families enjoy annual incomes of over a million dollars. Yet some 34 million of our citizens live below the poverty line, on incomes acknowledged by the federal government to be

inadequate to meet basic requirements of food, clothing, and shelter. Inequality in American society is usually justified by the ideology (but not the fact) of equal opportunity: everyone is supposed to have much the same chance to get rich, and those who work harder are supposed to gain the greater rewards. In consequence, those who do not get rich (which is most of us) have only themselves to blame, not the rich and not the system as a whole. But despite our belief in the United States as a land of exceptional opportunity, the rate of mobility between the classes is actually rather low and differs very little from that found in other industrialized societies. Social stratification ensures, in fact, that most people remain in their class of origin.

Topic 8 explores two aspects of social stratification. Edwin Kuh's article forcefully presents the case that the "incentive" argument has been greatly overemphasized in the United States, especially in cases where people are wealthy not through their own efforts, but through those of their ancestors. In his study, William J. Chambliss examines the reactions of a community to two delinquent teenage gangs and how this response was determined not by the gangs' actual behavior, but by the community's selective perceptions of how each gang behaved.

Topic 9 contains three articles concerning social class. In his essay, Herbert J. Gans offers the novel view that the poor in America perform so many useful functions to society that it would be highly inconvenient to everyone else to abolish poverty though it would be quite possible to do so. Gus Tyler focuses on the white working class in America and analyzes some of the reasons for their current "backlash." Finally, Anthony G. Amsterdam examines our judicial institutions, whose differential treatment of offenders has become a matter of major concern since the pardon of former President Richard Nixon, the Watergate trials, and the wrist slaps meted out to "white collar" offenders like former Vice-President Spiro Agnew and former CIA Director Richard Helms.

Topic 10 consists of four articles exploring different aspects of race and ethnic relations. The more than 4 billion people in the world today form a bewildering continuum of physical types. In their attempts to impose rough classifications on this continuum, physical anthropologists formerly tended to use three main broad categories: "Caucasoid," covering peoples as different in appearance as the blond, blue-eyed inhabitants of Northern Europe and the dark-skinned peoples of India; "Negroid," ranging from the tall inhabitants of Northern Africa to the diminutive pygmies of tropical jungles of that continent; and "Mongoloid," including peoples as diverse as the Japanese and the South American Indians. Many other peoples, however, are impossible to classify in these terms, such as the tawny-skinned San (Bushmen) of the Kalahari desert, the dark-skinned but often fair-haired Australian aborigines, and the countless millions of other people, such as those in Indonesia, who are between the major groups. In fact, most anthropologists have now abandoned the attempt to classify the human species into races and deny that the word *race* has any scientific meaning at all.

In themselves, the physical differences between human groups are simply a biological fact, nothing more. But because people attach meanings to these differences, and act on these meanings, racial distinctions are of great social significance. To the sociologist, therefore, a racial group is not so much a biological entity as a group of people who, in their interactions with other groups, regard themselves or are regarded as a separate race.

The concept of ethnicity, on the other hand, refers to cultural rather than physical distinctions between people (although the two may overlap). Ethnic differences, therefore, are based on such characteristics as religion, language, or national origin. An Italian-American may be physically indistinguishable from an Irish-American, but each may participate to some extent in a distinctive ethnic subculture, and may have an ethnic as well as a broader American identity. Partly because the ethnic differences in America are not as immediately apparent as the racial differences, antagonism between ethnic groups in our society has rarely been as severe as that between racial groups.

In his article, Howard Schuman details new evidence of changes in the racial attitudes of blacks and whites in America: it appears that whites are becoming more liberal toward blacks, but blacks are becoming more suspicious of whites. Richard Rodriguez writes of his experiences as a Mexican-American: of how his education separated him from his roots and of how he is painfully rediscovering them. Robert L. Faherty's article deals with the American Indians, perhaps the most unjustly treated and stereotyped of all Americans: they were first decimated by diseases brought to these shores by whites and blacks; subjected to the theft of their lands, the destruction of their way of life, and the virtual genocide of entire tribes; and then portrayed in literature and movies as wildly aggressive savages. In fact, Mesoamerican Indians had developed highly complex civilizations while Europeans were still savages; hundreds of years before Columbus landed in the New World, Teotihuacán was the most populated city in the world! Finally, in his article, Michael Novak deals with the newly resurgent white ethnic consciousness in America of the people acronymically known as PIGS—Poles, Italians, Greeks, and Slavs—who are rejecting the "melting pot" ideal and reasserting their group identities.

Topic 11 contains two articles discussing sex roles, other aspects of which were considered in Topic 7. Lynne B. Iglitzin's article reveals that children are socialized into the prevalent sex-role stereotypes at a very young age. In recent years, the traditional stereotype of the American woman has received the most attention, and its disadvantages to women have been widely exposed. In the final article in this section, however, Jack O. Balswick and Charles W. Peek turn the coin over and take a closer look at the disadvantages of traditional male roles.

# The Robin Hood Syndrome

Edwin Kuh

What is the present distribution of income and wealth in the U.S.A.? Wealth is distributed much more unevenly than income; thus, the richest 10 per cent of the population receive 29 per cent of personal income but own 56 per cent of the national wealth, while the poorest 10 per cent receive 1 per cent of the income and are in debt, to boot. At the top of the wealth distribution, 1 per cent of the wealth-holders own 25 per cent of physical and financial wealth. Among those with incomes in excess of $100,000, inherited wealth amounts to 57 per cent of total assets.

Despite the extreme inequality that now prevails, two principles embedded in the American tax structure are that taxes should be levied according to ability to pay and that at least some income should be redistributed to the poor. Taxes paid by the prosperous are used, in a variety of ways, to help the poor. But apart from the need to help the poor, there are other cogent reasons to tax the rich at higher rates and to work for genuine tax reform. First, massive concentrations of wealth or income make a mockery of political democracy. Second, real equality of opportunity is impossible in the presence of extreme wealth or extreme poverty. Reducing inequality at the top would thus yield benefits to the middle class as well.

"One person, one vote" is a sham — for the middle class and poor alike — when the rich can buy political influence. When the President of the United States told an assembly of wealthy Texans that the petroleum percentage depletion allowance should if anything be increased, the outpouring of warmth and financial support was predictably generous. The Federal Election Campaign Act of 1972 was a small step in the right direction, but any law intended to curb the undue political influence of the affluent will be readily evaded as long as large concentrations of wealth exist. It would, moreover, be naive to focus attention on rich individuals to the exclusion of giant corporations. While a saving grace of the present system is that business interests often conflict, it is also true that they coalesce on such basic issues as stiffer capital gains taxes, inheritance taxes and tax reform in general.

The second reason for supporting stiffer inheritance and income taxes has to do with equality of opportunity. Equal opportunity is more of a reality in America than in most countries. Yet it is, and will remain, in part a mirage until large concentrations of wealth are broken up. Large inheritances are the antithesis of equal opportunity. The more unequal the distribution of income and wealth, the more closely we approach Anatole France's characterization of equality before the law — the prohibition of rich and poor alike from sleeping under bridges. While the notion of equality of opportunity does not imply that income and wealth should be equally distributed, extreme concentrations represent an insurmountable barrier to those below and a permanent crutch for those above.

Rational arguments for income and wealth inequality boil down to the need "to preserve incentives." This proposition is usually warped into arguments for the status quo:

that American capitalism will come to an end should these privileges be curtailed, or that economic growth will grind to a halt if incentives are tampered with. In the United States, however, the growth of economic productivity has been substantially greater since World War II than it was before, yet the tax burden has been much greater. Abroad, economic growth rates vary greatly, from 10.8 per cent in Japan to 1.8 per cent in Great Britain (annual compound growth rates in real G.N.P. for the most recent available five year period), yet income distributions are strikingly similar among the advanced industrial countries. Clearly the processes of growth are much more complex than the incentive argument would suggest. While care is required in order not to kill the goose that lays the golden egg, the incentive argument in current discussions about income distribution merely cloaks self-interest in the guise of general welfare.

There is widespread agreement in principle in the United States on the need to redistribute some income from the rich to the poor, since the less fortunate should be provided for as a matter of right in a just society. The advocates of redistribution cover the political spectrum from conservatives such as Milton Friedman and Republicans such as President Nixon (early in his first term) to Democratic liberals such as Senators Kennedy, McGovern and Ribicoff. The recommended programs are as varied as the proponents: negative income taxes for those with children or for everyone; or more emphasis on jobs rather than income maintenance; or support in certain categories through such means as subsidized housing, compensatory education or health insurance.

The attainment of meaningful redistribution of income and wealth through sensible tax reform seems remote at this time, because agreement in principle conflicts with willingness to pay. Congressional rejection of President Nixon's Family Assistance Plan proposal, together with its abandonment by the President, reflect the country's mood accurately enough. Part of the reason, as I have argued, is the ability of the wealthy to buy into the political process, but there is more. One component of American ideology is a belief in rugged individualism. However admirable in its own right, this article of faith has been distorted by the apologists of privilege, who falsely identify the interests of ordinary individuals with those of the wealthy and virtually immortal corporations as well.

Another factor, racism, is also powerfully at work. While a majority of the poor are white, blacks are often seen as the main beneficiaries of income redistribution. Hence, an alliance between wealthy and middle-income whites (many of whom are not racist) has grown stronger. In the process, popular attention has shifted to divisive social issues at the lower end of the income distribution and away from the pernicious effects of extreme disparities at the upper end of the distribution. Yet until the incomes of the wealthy and the middle classes are made more nearly equal, true democracy and equal economic opportunity will suffer.

# 24

Black and white, male and female, rich and poor, American teenagers have the herding instinct. On streetcorners, in shopping centers, in the ghetto and in the suburbs, the boys and the girls hang out. Sometimes the kids get together for fun, sometimes for trouble, sometimes for political purposes. Mostly, they crave recognition, companionship and excitement. Gangs are a way of life for many adolescents—part of the ritual of growing up.

---

# The Saints and the Roughnecks

## William J. Chambliss

Eight promising young men—children of good, stable, white upper-middle-class families, active in school affairs, good pre-college students—were some of the most delinquent boys at Hanibal High School. While community residents and parents knew that these boys occasionally sowed a few wild oats, they were totally unaware that sowing wild oats completely occupied the daily routine of these young men. The Saints were constantly occupied with truancy, drinking, wild driving, petty theft and vandalism. Yet not one was officially arrested for any misdeed during the two years I observed them.

This record was particularly surprising in light of my observations during the same two years of another gang of Hanibal High School students, six lower-class white boys known as the Roughnecks. The Roughnecks were constantly in trouble with police and community even though their rate of delinquency was about equal with that of the Saints. What was the cause of this disparity? the result? The following consideration of the activities, social class and community perceptions of both gangs may provide some answers.

### The Saints from Monday to Friday

The Saints' principal daily concern was with getting out of school as early as possible. The boys managed to get out of school with minimum danger that they would be accused of playing hookey through an elaborate procedure for obtaining "legitimate" release from class. The most common procedure was for one boy to obtain the release of another by fabricating a meeting of some committee, program or recognized club. Charles might raise his hand in his 9:00 chemistry class and asked to be excused—a euphemism for going to the bathroom. Charles would go to Ed's math class and inform the teacher that Ed was needed for a 9:30 rehearsal of the drama club play. The math teacher would recognize Ed and Charles as "good students" involved in numerous school activities and would permit Ed to leave at 9:30. Charles would return to his class, and Ed would go to Tom's English class to obtain his release. Tom would engineer Charles' escape. The strategy would continue until as many of the Saints as possible were freed. After a stealthy trip to the car (which had been parked in a strategic spot), the boys were off for a day of fun.

Over the two years I observed the Saints, this pattern was repeated nearly every day. There were variations on the theme, but in one form or another, the boys used this procedure for getting out of class and then off the school grounds. Rarely did all eight of the Saints manage to leave school at the same time. The average number avoiding school on the days I observed them was five.

Having escaped from the concrete corridors the boys usually went either to a pool hall on the other (lower-class) side of town or to a cafe in the suburbs. Both places were out of the way of people the boys were likely to know (family or school officials), and both provided a source of entertainment. The pool hall entertainment was the generally rough atmosphere, the occasional hustler, the sometimes drunk proprietor and, of course, the game of pool. The cafe's entertainment was provided by the owner. The boys would "accidentally" knock a glass on the floor or spill cola on the counter—not all the time, but enough to be sporting. They would also bend spoons, put salt in sugar bowls and generally tease whoever was working in the cafe. The owner had opened the cafe recently and was dependent on the boys' business which was, in fact, substantial since between the horsing around and the teasing they bought food and drinks.

**The Saints on Weekends**

On weekends the automobile was even more critical than during the week, for on weekends the Saints went to Big Town—a large city with a population of over a million 25 miles from Hanibal. Every Friday and Saturday night most of the Saints would meet between 8:00 and 8:30 and would go into Big Town. Big Town activities included drinking heavily in taverns or nightclubs, driving drunkenly through the streets, and committing acts of vandalism and playing pranks.

By midnight on Fridays and Saturdays the Saints were usually thoroughly high, and one or two of them were often so drunk they had to be carried to the cars. Then the boys drove around town, calling obscenities to women and girls; occasionally trying (unsuccessfully so far as I could tell) to pick girls up; and driving recklessly through red lights and at high speeds with their lights out. Occasionally they played "chicken." One boy would climb out the back window of the car and across the roof to the driver's side of the car while the car was moving at high speed (between 40 and 50 miles an hour); then the driver would move over and the boy who had just crawled across the car roof would take the driver's seat.

Searching for "fair game" for a prank was the boys' principal activity after they left the tavern. The boys would drive alongside a foot patrolman and ask directions to some street. If the policeman leaned on the car in the course of answering the question, the driver would speed away, causing him to lose his balance. The Saints were careful to play this prank only in an area where they were not going to spend much time and where they could quickly disappear around a corner to avoid having their license plate number taken.

Construction sites and road repair areas were the special province of the Saints' mischief. A soon-to-be-repaired hole in the road inevitably invited the Saints to remove lanterns and wooden barricades and put them in the car, leaving the hole unprotected. The boys would find a safe vantage point and wait for an unsuspecting motorist to drive into the hole. Often, though not always, the boys would go up to the motorist and commiserate with him about the dreadful way the city protected its citizenry.

Leaving the scene of the open hole and the motorist, the boys would then go searching for an appropriate place to erect the stolen barricade. An "appropriate place" was often a spot on a highway near a curve in the road where the barricade would not be seen by an on-coming motorist. The boys would wait to watch an unsuspecting motorist attempt to stop and (usually) crash into the wooden barricade. With saintly bearing the boys might offer help and understanding.

A stolen lantern might well find its way onto the back of a police car or hang from a street lamp. Once a lantern served as a prop for a reenactment of the "midnight ride of Paul Revere" until the "play," which was taking place at 2:00 AM in the center of a main street of Big Town, was interrupted by a police car several blocks away. The boys ran, leaving the lanterns on the street, and managed to avoid being apprehended.

Abandoned houses, especially if they were located in out-of-the-way places, were fair game for destruction and spontaneous vandalism. The boys would break windows, remove furniture to the yard and tear it apart, urinate on the walls and scrawl obscenities inside.

Through all the pranks, drinking and reckless driving the boys managed miraculously to avoid being stopped by police. Only twice in two years was I aware that they had been stopped by a Big City policeman. Once was for speeding (which they did every time they drove whether they were drunk or sober), and the driver managed to convince the policeman that it was simply an error. The second time they were stopped they had just left a nightclub and were walking through an alley. Aaron stopped to urinate and the boys began making obscene remarks. A foot patrolman came into the alley, lectured the boys and sent them home. Before the boys got to the car one began talking in a loud voice again. The policeman, who had followed them down the alley, arrested this boy for disturbing the peace and took him to the police station where the other Saints gathered. After paying a $5.00 fine, and with the assurance that there would be no permanent record of the arrest, the boy was released.

The boys had a spirit of frivolity and fun about their escapades. They did not view what they were engaged in as "delinquency," though it surely was by any reasonable definition of that word. They simply viewed themselves as having a little fun and who, they would ask, was really hurt by it? The answer had to be no one, although this fact remains one of the most difficult things to explain about the gang's behavior. Unlikely though it seems, in two years of drinking, driving, carousing and vandalism no one was seriously injured as a result of the Saints' activities.

**The Saints in School**

The Saints were highly successful in school. The average grade for the group was "B," with two of the boys having close to a straight "A" average. Almost all of the boys were popular and many of them held offices in the school. One of the boys was vice-president of the student body one year. Six of the boys played on athletic teams.

At the end of their senior year, the student body selected ten seniors for special recognition as the "school wheels"; four of the ten were Saints. Teachers and school officials saw no problem with any of these boys and anticipated that they would all "make something of themselves."

How the boys managed to maintain this impression is surprising in view of their actual behavior while in school. Their technique for covering truancy was so successful that teachers did not even realize that the boys were absent from school much of the time. Occasionally, of course, the system would backfire and then the boy was on his own. A boy who was caught would be most contrite, would plead guilty and ask for mercy. He inevitably got the mercy he sought.

Cheating on examinations was rampant, even to the point of orally communicating answers to exams as well as looking at one another's papers. Since none of the group studied, and since they were primarily dependent on one another for help, it is surprising that grades were so high. Teachers contributed to the deception in their admitted inclination to give these boys (and presumably others like them) the benefit of the doubt. When asked how the boys did in school, and when pressed on specific examinations, teachers might admit that they were disappointed in John's performance, but would quickly add that they "knew that he was capable of doing better," so John was given a higher grade than he had actually earned. How often this happened is impossible to know. During the time that I observed the group, I never saw any of the boys take homework home. Teachers may have been "understanding" very regularly.

One exception to the gang's generally good performance was Jerry, who had a "C" average in his junior year, experienced disaster the next year and failed to graduate. Jerry had always been a little more nonchalant than the others about the liberties he took in school. Rather than wait for someone to come get him from class, he would offer his own excuse and leave. Although he probably did not miss any more classes than most of the others in the group, he did not take the requisite pains to cover his absences. Jerry was the only Saint whom I ever heard talk back to a teacher. Although teachers often called him a "cut up" or a "smart kid," they never referred to him as a troublemaker or as a kid headed for trouble. It seems likely, then, that Jerry's failure his senior year and his mediocre performance his junior year were consequences of his not playing the game the proper way (possibly because he was disturbed by his parents' divorce). His teachers regarded him as "immature" and not quite ready to get out of high school.

## The Police and the Saints

The local police saw the Saints as good boys who were among the leaders of the youth in the community. Rarely, the boys might be stopped in town for speeding or for running a stop sign. When this happened the boys were always polite, contrite and pled for mercy. As in school, they received the mercy they asked for. None ever received a ticket or was taken into the precinct by the local police.

The situation in Big City, where the boys engaged in most of their delinquency, was only slightly different. The police there did not know the boys at all, although occasionally the boys were stopped by a patrolman. Once they were caught taking a lantern from a construction site. Another time they were stopped for running a stop sign, and on several occasions they were stopped for speeding. Their behavior was as before: contrite, polite and penitent. The urban police, like the local police, accepted their demeanor as sincere. More important, the urban police were convinced that these were good boys just out for a lark.

## The Roughnecks

Hanibal townspeople never perceived the Saints' high level of delinquency. The Saints were good boys who just went in for an occasional prank. After all, they were well dressed, well mannered and had nice cars. The Roughnecks were a different story. Although the two gangs of boys were the same age, and both groups engaged in an equal amount of wild-oat sowing, everyone agreed that the not-so-well-dressed, not-so-well-mannered, not-so-rich boys were heading for trouble. Townspeople would say, "You can see the gang members at the drugstore, night after night, leaning against the storefront (sometimes drunk) or slouching around inside buying cokes, reading magazines, and probably stealing old Mr. Wall blind. When they are outside and girls walk by, even respectable girls, these boys make suggestive remarks. Sometimes their remarks are downright lewd."

From the community's viewpoint, the real indication that these kids were in for trouble was that they were constantly involved with the police. Some of them had been picked up for stealing, mostly small stuff, of course, "but still it's stealing small stuff that leads to big time crimes." "Too bad," people said. "Too bad that these boys couldn't behave like the other kids in town; stay out of trouble, be polite to adults, and look to their future."

The community's impression of the degree to which this group of six boys (ranging in age from 16 to 19) engaged in delinquency was somewhat distorted. In some ways the gang was more delinquent than the community thought; in other ways they were less.

Through all the pranks, drinking and reckless driving the Saints managed miraculously to avoid being stopped by the police. No one was ever seriously injured despite all the carousing and vandalism.

The fighting activities of the group were fairly readily and accurately perceived by almost everyone. At least once a month, the boys would get into some sort of fight, although most fights were scraps between members of the group or involved only one member of the group and some peripheral hanger-on. Only three times in the period of observation did the group fight together: once against a gang from across town, once against two blacks and once against a group of boys from another school. For the first two fights the group went out "looking for trouble"—and they found it both times. The third fight followed a football game and began spontaneously with an argument on the football field between one of the Roughnecks and a member of the opposition's football team.

Jack had a particular propensity for fighting and was involved in most of the brawls. He was a prime mover of the escalation of arguments into fights.

More serious than fighting, had the community been aware of it, was theft. Although almost everyone was aware that the boys occasionally stole things, they did not realize the extent of the activity. Petty stealing was a frequent event for the Roughnecks. Sometimes they stole as a group and coordinated their efforts; other times they stole in pairs. Rarely did they steal alone.

The thefts ranged from very small things like paperback books, comics and ballpoint pens to expensive items like watches. The nature of the thefts varied from time to time. The gang would go through a period of systematically shoplifting items from automobiles or school lockers. Types of thievery varied with the whim of the gang. Some forms of thievery were more profitable than others, but all thefts were for profit, not just thrills.

Roughnecks siphoned gasoline from cars as often as they had access to an automobile, which was not very often. Unlike the Saints, who owned their own cars, the Roughnecks would have to borrow their parents' cars, an event which occured only eight or nine times a year. The boys claimed to have stolen cars for joy rides from time to time.

Ron committed the most serious of the group's offenses. With an unidentified associate the boy attempted to burglarize a gasoline station. Although this station had been robbed twice previously in the same month, Ron denied any involvement in either of the other thefts. When Ron and his accomplice approached the station, the owner was hiding in the bushes beside the station. He fired both barrels of a double-barreled shotgun at the boys. Ron was severely injured; the other boy ran away and was never caught. Though he remained in critical condition for several months, Ron finally recovered and served six months of the following year in reform school. Upon release from reform school, Ron was put back a grade in school, and began running around with a different gang of boys. The Roughnecks considered the new gang less delinquent than themselves, and during the following year Ron had no more trouble with the police.

The Roughnecks, then, engaged mainly in three types of delinquency: theft, drinking and fighting. Although community members perceived that this gang of kids was delinquent, they mistakenly believed that their illegal activities were primarily drinking, fighting and being a nuisance to passersby. Drinking was limited among the gang members, although it did occur, and theft was much more prevalent than anyone realized.

Drinking would doubtless have been more prevalent had the boys had ready access to liquor. Since they rarely had automobiles at their disposal, they could not travel very far, and the bars in town would not serve them. Most of the boys had little money, and this, too, inhibited their purchase of alcohol. Their major source of liquor was a local drunk who would buy them a fifth if they would give him enough extra to buy himself a pint of whiskey or a bottle of wine.

The community's perception of drinking as prevalent stemmed from the fact that it was the most obvious delinquency the boys engaged in. When one of the boys had been drinking, even a casual observer seeing him on the corner would suspect that he was high.

There was a high level of mutual distrust and dislike between the Roughnecks and the police. The boys felt very strongly that the police were unfair and corrupt. Some evidence existed that the boys were correct in their perception.

The main source of the boys' dislike for the police undoubtedly stemmed from the fact that the police would sporadically harass the group. From the standpoint of the boys, these acts of occasional enforcement of the law were whimsical and uncalled for. It made no sense to them, for example, that the police would come to the corner occasionally and threaten them with arrest for loitering when the night before the boys had been out siphoning gasoline from cars and the police had been nowhere in sight. To the boys, the police were stupid on the one hand, for not being where they should have been and catching the boys in a serious offense, and unfair on the other hand, for trumping up "loitering" charges against them.

From the viewpoint of the police, the situation was quite different. They knew, with all the confidence necessary to be a policeman, that these boys were engaged in criminal activities. They knew this partly from occasionally catching them, mostly from circumstantial evidence ("the boys were around when those tires were slashed"), and partly because the police shared the view of the community in general that this was a bad bunch of boys. The best the police could hope to do was to be sensitive to the fact that these boys were engaged in illegal acts and arrest them whenever there was some evidence that they had been involved. Whether or not the boys had in fact committed a particular act in a particular way was not especially important. The police had a broader view: their job was to stamp out these kids' crimes; the tactics were not as important as the end result.

Over the period that the group was under observation, each member was arrested at least once. Several of the boys were arrested a number of times and spent at least one night in jail. While most were never taken to court, two of the boys were sentenced to six months' incarceration in boys' schools.

## The Roughnecks in School

The Roughnecks' behavior in school was not particularly disruptive. During school hours they did not all hang around together, but tended instead to spend most of their time with one or two other members of the gang who were their special buddies. Although every member of the gang attempted to avoid school as much as possible, they were not particularly successful and most of them attended school with surprising regularity. They considered school a burden—something to be gotten through with a minimum of conflict. If they were "bugged" by a particular teacher, it could lead to trouble. One of the boys, Al, once threatened to beat up a teacher and, according to the other boys, the teacher hid under a desk to escape him.

Teachers saw the boys the way the general community did, as heading for trouble, as being uninterested in making something of themselves. Some were also seen as being incapable of meeting the academic standards of the school. Most of the teachers expressed concern for this group of boys and were willing to pass them despite poor performance, in the belief that failing them would only aggravate the problem.

The group of boys had a grade point average just slightly above "C." No one in the group failed either grade, and no one had better than a "C" average. They were very consistent in their achievement or, at least, the teachers were consistent in their perception of the boys' achievement.

Two of the boys were good football players. Herb was acknowledged to be the best player in the school and Jack was almost as good. Both boys were criticized for their failure to abide by training rules, for refusing to come to practice as often as they should, and for not playing their best during practice. What they lacked in sportsmanship they made up for in skill, apparently, and played every game no matter how poorly they had performed in practice or how many practice sessions they had missed.

## Two Questions

Why did the community, the school and the police react to the Saints as though they were good, upstanding, nondelinquent youths with bright futures but to the Roughnecks as though they were tough, young criminals who were headed for trouble? Why did the Roughnecks and the Saints in fact have quite different careers after high school—careers which, by and large, lived up to the expectations of the community?

The most obvious explanation for the differences in the community's and law enforcement agencies' reactions to the two gangs is that one group of boys was "more delinquent" than the other. Which group *was* more delinquent? The answer to this question will determine in part how we explain the differential responses to these groups by the members of the community and, particularly, by law enforcement and school officials.

In sheer number of illegal acts, the Saints were the more delinquent. They were truant from school for at least part of the day almost every day of the week. In addition, their drinking and vandalism occurred with surprising regularity. The Roughnecks, in contrast, engaged sporadically in delinquent episodes. While these episodes were frequent, they certainly did not occur on a daily or even a weekly basis.

The difference in frequency of offenses was probably caused by the Roughnecks' inability to obtain liquor and to manipulate legitimate excuses from school. Since the Roughnecks had less money than the Saints, and teachers carefully supervised their school activities, the Roughnecks' hearts may have been as black as the Saints', but their misdeeds were not nearly as frequent.

There are really no clear-cut criteria by which to measure qualitative differences in antisocial behavior. The most important dimension of the difference is generally referred to as the "seriousness" of the offenses.

If seriousness encompasses the relative economic costs of delinquent acts, then some assessment can be made. The Roughnecks probably stole an average of about $5.00 worth of goods a week. Some weeks the figure was considerably higher, but these times must be balanced against long periods when almost nothing was stolen.

The Saints were more continuously engaged in delinquency but their acts were not for the most part costly to property. Only their vandalism and occasional theft of gasoline would so qualify. Perhaps once or twice a month they would siphon a tankful of gas. The other costly items were street signs, construction lanterns and the like. All of these acts combined probably did not quite average $5.00 a week, partly because much of the stolen equipment was abandoned and presumably could be recovered. The difference in cost of stolen property between the two groups was trivial, but the Roughnecks probably had a slightly more expensive set of activities than did the Saints.

Another meaning of seriousness is the potential threat of physical harm to members of the community and to the boys themselves. The Roughnecks were more prone to physical violence; they not only welcomed an opportunity to fight; they went seeking it. In addition, they fought among themselves frequently. Although the fighting never included deadly weapons, it was still a menace, however minor, to the physical safety of those involved.

The Saints never fought. They avoided physical conflict both inside and outside the group. At the same time, though, the Saints frequently endangered their own and other people's lives. They did so almost every time they drove a car, especially if they had been drinking. Sober, their driving was risky; under the influence of alcohol it was horrendous. In addition, the Saints endangered the lives of others with their pranks. Street excavations left unmarked were a very serious hazard.

Evaluating the relative seriousness of the two gangs' activities is difficult. The community reacted as though the behavior of the Roughnecks was a problem, and they reacted as though the behavior of the Saints was not. But the members of the community were ignorant of the array of delinquent acts that characterized the Saints' behavior. Although concerned citizens were unaware of much of the Roughnecks' behavior as well, they were much better informed about the Roughnecks' involvement in delinquency than they were about the Saints'.

## Visibility

Differential treatment of the two gangs resulted in part because one gang was infinitely more visible than the other. This differential visibility was a direct function of the economic standing of the families. The Saints had access to automobiles and were able to remove themselves from the sight of the community. In as routine a decision as to where to go to have a milkshake after school, the Saints stayed away from the mainstream of community life. Lacking transportation, the Roughnecks could not make it to the edge of town. The center of town was the only practical place for them to meet since their homes were scattered throughout the town and any noncentral meeting place put an undue hardship on some members. Through necessity the Roughnecks congregated in a crowded area where everyone in the community passed frequently, including teachers and law enforcement officers. They could easily see the Roughnecks hanging around the drugstore.

The Roughnecks, of course, made themselves even more visible by making remarks to passersby and by occasionally getting into fights on the corner. Meanwhile, just as regularly, the Saints were either at the cafe on one edge of town or in the pool hall at the other edge of town. Without any particular realization that they were making themselves inconspicuous, the Saints were able to hide their time-wasting. Not only were they removed from the mainstream of traffic, but they were almost always inside a building.

On their escapades the Saints were also relatively invisible, since they left Hanibal and travelled to Big City. Here, too, they were mobile, roaming the city, rarely going to the same area twice.

## Demeanor

To the notion of visibility must be added the difference in the responses of group members to outside intervention with their activities. If one of the Saints was confronted with an accusing policeman, even if he felt he was truly innocent of a wrongdoing, his demeanor was apologetic and penitent. A Roughneck's attitude was almost the polar opposite. When confronted with a threatening adult authority, even one who tried to be pleasant, the Roughneck's hostility and disdain were clearly observable. Sometimes he might attempt to put up a veneer of respect, but it was thin and was not accepted as sincere by the authority.

School was no different from the community at large. The Saints could manipulate the system by feigning compliance with the school norms. The availability of cars at school meant that once free from the immediate sight of the teacher, the boys could disappear rapidly. And this escape was well enough planned that no administrator or teacher was nearby when the boys left. A Roughneck who wished to escape for a few hours was in a bind. If it were possible to get free from class, downtown was still a mile away, and even if he arrived there, he was still very visible. Truancy for the Roughnecks meant almost certain detection, while the Saints enjoyed almost complete immunity from sanctions.

## Bias

Community members were not aware of the transgressions of the Saints. Even if the Saints had been less discreet, their favorite delinquencies would have been perceived as less serious than those of the Roughnecks.

In the eyes of the police and school officials, a boy who drinks in an alley and stands intoxicated on the street corner is committing a more serious offense than is a boy who drinks to inebriation in a nightclub or a tavern and drives around afterwards in a car. Similarly, a boy who steals a wallet from a store will be viewed as having committed a more serious offense than a boy who steals a lantern from a construction site.

Perceptual bias also operates with respect to the demeanor of the boys in the two groups when they are confronted by adults. It is not simply that adults dislike the posture affected by boys of the Roughneck ilk; more important is the conviction that the posture adopted by the Roughnecks is an indication of their devotion and commitment to deviance as a way of life. The posture becomes a cue, just as the type of the offense is a cue, to the degree to which the known transgressions are indicators of the youths' potential for other problems.

Visibility, demeanor and bias are surface variables which explain the day-to-day operations of the police. Why do these surface variables operate as they do? Why did the police choose to disregard the Saints' delinquencies while breathing down the backs of the Roughnecks?

The answer lies in the class structure of American society and the control of legal institutions by those at the top of the class structure. Obviously, no representative of the upper class drew up the operational chart for the police which led them to look in the ghettoes and on streetcorners—which led them to see the demeanor of lower-class youth as troublesome and that of upper-middle-class youth as tolerable. Rather, the procedures simply developed from experience—experience with irate and influential upper-middle-class parents insisting that their son's vandalism was simply a prank and his drunkenness only a momentary "sowing of wild oats" —experience with cooperative or indifferent, powerless, lower-class parents who acquiesced to the laws' definition of their son's behavior.

## Adult Careers of the Saints and the Roughnecks

The community's confidence in the potential of the Saints and the Roughnecks apparently was justified. If anything, the community members underestimated the degree to which these youngsters would turn out "good" or "bad."

Seven of the eight members of the Saints went on to college immediately after high school. Five of the boys graduated from college in four years. The sixth one finished college after two years in the army, and the seventh spent four years in the air force before returning to college and receiving a B.A. degree. Of these seven college graduates, three went on for advanced degrees. One finished law school and is now active in state politics, one finished medical school and is practicing near Hanibal, and one boy is now working for a Ph.D. The other four college graduates entered submanagerial, managerial or executive training positions with larger firms.

The only Saint who did not complete college was Jerry. Jerry had failed to graduate from high school with the other Saints. During his second senior year, after the other Saints had gone on to college, Jerry began to hang around with what several teachers described as a "rough crowd"—the gang that was heir apparent to the Roughnecks. At the end of his second senior year, when he did graduate from high school, Jerry took a job as a used-car salesman, got married and quickly had a child. Although he made several abortive attempts to go to college by attending night school, when I last saw him (ten years after high school) Jerry was unemployed and had been living on unemployment for almost a year. His wife worked as a waitress.

Some of the Roughnecks have lived up to community expectations. A number of them were headed for trouble. A few were not.

Jack and Herb were the athletes among the Roughnecks and their athletic prowess paid off handsomely. Both boys received unsolicited athletic scholarships to college. After Herb received his scholarship (near the end of his senior year), he apparently did an about-face. His demeanor became very similar to that of the Saints. Although he remained a member in good standing of the Roughnecks, he stopped participating in most activities and did not hang on the corner as often.

Jack did not change. If anything, he became more prone to fighting. He even made excuses for accepting the scholarship. He told the other gang members that the school had guaranteed him a "C" average if he would come to play football—an idea that seems far-fetched, even in this day of highly competitive recruiting.

During the summer after graduation from high school, Jack attempted suicide by jumping from a tall building. The jump would certainly have killed most people trying it, but Jack survived. He entered college in the fall and played four years of football. He and Herb graduated in four years, and both are teaching and coaching in high schools. They are married and have sta-

ble families. If anything, Jack appears to have a more prestigious position in the community than does Herb, though both are well respected and secure in their positions.

Two of the boys never finished high school. Tommy left at the end of his junior year and went to another state. That summer he was arrested and placed on probation on a manslaughter charge. Three years later he was arrested for murder; he pleaded guilty to second degree murder and is serving a 30-year sentence in the state penitentiary.

Al, the other boy who did not finish high school, also left the state in his senior year. He is serving a life sentence in a state penitentiary for first degree murder.

Wes is a small-time gambler. He finished high school and "bummed around." After several years he made contact with a bookmaker who employed him as a runner. Later he acquired his own area and has been working it ever since. His position among the bookmakers is almost identical to the position he had in the gang; he is always around but no one is really aware of him. He makes no trouble and he does not get into any. Steady, reliable, capable of keeping his mouth closed, he plays the game by the rules, even though the game is an illegal one.

That leaves only Ron. Some of his former friends reported that they had heard he was "driving a truck up north," but no one could provide any concrete information.

## Reinforcement

The community responded to the Roughnecks as boys in trouble, and the boys agreed with that perception. Their pattern of deviancy was reinforced, and breaking away from it became increasingly unlikely. Once the boys acquired an image of themselves as deviants, they selected new friends who affirmed that self-image. As that self-conception became more firmly entrenched, they also became willing to try new and more extreme deviances. With their growing alienation came freer expression of disrespect and hostility for representatives of the legitimate society. This disrespect increased the community's negativism, perpetuating the entire process of commitment to deviance. Lack of a commitment to deviance works the same way. In either case, the process will perpetuate itself unless some event (like a scholarship to college or a sudden failure) external to the established relationship intervenes. For two of the Roughnecks (Herb and Jack), receiving college athletic scholarships created new relations and culminated in a break with the established pattern of deviance. In the case of one of the Saints (Jerry), his parents' divorce and his failing to graduate from high school changed some of his other relations. Being held back in school for a year and losing his place among the Saints had sufficient impact on Jerry to alter his self-image and virtually to assure that he would not go on to college as his peers did.

Although the experiments of life can rarely be reversed, it seems likely in view of the behavior of the other boys who did not enjoy this special treatment by the school that Jerry, too, would have "become something" had he graduated as anticipated. For Herb and Jack outside intervention worked to their advantage; for Jerry it was his undoing.

---

**Truancy for the Roughnecks meant almost certain detection. The Saints' technique for covering truancy was so successful that teachers did not even realize that the boys were absent from school much of the time.**

---

Selective perception and labelling—finding, processing and punishing some kinds of criminality and not others—means that visible, poor, nonmobile, outspoken, undiplomatic "tough" kids will be noticed, whether their actions are seriously delinquent or not. Other kids, who have established a reputation for being bright (even though underachieving), disciplined and involved in respectable activities, who are mobile and monied, will be invisible when they deviate from sanctioned activities. They'll sow their wild oats—perhaps even wider and thicker than their lower-class cohorts—but they won't be noticed. When it's time to leave adolescence most will follow the expected path, settling into the ways of the middle class, remembering fondly the delinquent but unnoticed fling of their youth. The Roughnecks and others like them may turn around, too. It is more likely that their noticeable deviance will have been so reinforced by police and community that their lives will be effectively channelled into careers consistent with their adolescent background. □

# 25

# The Uses of Poverty: The Poor Pay All

Herbert J. Gans

*The reason poverty resists all our apparent efforts to modify or eliminate it might just be that we are all so dependent on it for our own security and well-being.*

Some twenty years ago Robert K. Merton applied the notion of functional analysis* to explain the continuing though maligned existence of the urban political machine: if it continued to exist, perhaps it fulfilled latent — unintended or unrecognized — positive functions. Clearly it did. Merton pointed out how the political machine provided central authority to get things done when a decentralized local government could not act, humanized the services of the impersonal bureaucracy for fearful citizens, offered concrete help (rather than abstract law or justice) to the poor, and otherwise performed services needed or demanded by many people but considered unconventional or even illegal by formal public agencies.

Today, poverty is more maligned than the political machine ever was; yet it, too, is a persistent social phenomenon. Consequently, there may be some merit in applying functional analysis to poverty, in asking whether it also has positive functions that explain its persistence.

Merton defined functions as "those observed consequences [of a phenomenon] which make for the adaptation or adjustment of a given [social] system." I shall use a slightly different definition; instead of identifying functions for an entire social system, I shall identify them for the interest groups, socioeconomic classes, and other population aggregates with shared values that "inhabit" a social system. I suspect that in a modern heterogeneous society, few phenomena are functional or dysfunctional for the society as a whole, and that most result in benefits to some groups and costs to others. Nor are any phenomena indispensable; in most instances, one can suggest what Merton calls "functional alternatives" or equivalents for them, i.e., other social patterns or policies that achieve the same positive functions but avoid the dysfunctions.†

Associating poverty with positive functions seems at first glance to be unimaginable. Of course, the slumlord and the loan shark are commonly known to profit from the existence of poverty, but they are viewed as evil men, so their activities are classified among the dysfunctions of poverty. However, what is less often recognized, at least by the conventional wisdom, is that poverty also makes possible the existence or expansion of respectable professions and occupations, for example, penology, criminology, social work, and public health. More recently, the poor have provided jobs for professional and paraprofessional "poverty warriors," and for journalists and social scientists, this author included, who have supplied the information demanded by the revival of public interest in poverty.

Clearly, then, poverty and the poor may well satisfy a number of positive functions for many nonpoor groups in American society. I shall describe thirteen such functions — economic, social, and political — that seem to me most significant.

## The Functions of Poverty

*First,* the existence of poverty ensures that society's "dirty work" will be done. Every society has such work: physically dirty or dangerous, temporary, dead-end and underpaid, undignified and menial jobs. Society can fill these jobs by paying higher wages than for "clean" work, or it can force people who have no other choice to do the dirty work — and at low wages. In America, poverty functions to provide a low-wage labor pool that is willing — or, rather, unable to be *un*willing — to perform dirty work at low cost. Indeed, this function of the poor is so important that in some Southern states, welfare payments have been cut off during the summer months when the poor are needed to work in the fields. Moreover, much of the debate about the Negative Income Tax and the Family Assistance Plan has concerned their impact on the work incentive, by which is actually meant the incentive of the poor to do the needed dirty work if the wages therefrom are no larger than the income grant. Many economic activities that involve dirty work depend on the poor for their existence: restaurants, hospitals, parts of the garment industry, and "truck farming," among others, could not persist in their present form without the poor.

*Second,* because the poor are required to work at low wages, they subsidize a variety of economic activities that benefit the affluent. For example, domestics subsidize the upper middle and upper classes, making life easier for

---

*"Manifest and Latent Functions," in *Social Theory and Social Structure* (Glencoe, Ill.: The Free Press, 1949), p. 71.

HERBERT J. GANS *is professor of sociology and planning, Department of Urban Studies and Planning, Massachusetts Institute of Technology, and a faculty associate at the Joint Center for Urban Studies, MIT/Harvard University.*

†I shall henceforth abbreviate positive functions as functions and negative functions as dysfunctions. I shall also describe functions and dysfunctions in the planner's terminology, as benefits and costs.

*". . . poverty creates jobs for a number of occupations and professions that serve or 'service' the poor, or protect the rest of society from them."*

their employers and freeing affluent women for a variety of professional, cultural, civic, and partying activities. Similarly, because the poor pay a higher proportion of their income in property and sales taxes, among others, they subsidize many state and local governmental services that benefit more affluent groups. In addition, the poor support innovation in medical practice as patients in teaching and research hospitals and as guinea pigs in medical experiments.

*Third,* poverty creates jobs for a number of occupations and professions that serve or "service" the poor, or protect the rest of society from them. As already noted, penology would be minuscule without the poor, as would the police. Other activities and groups that flourish because of the existence of poverty are the numbers game, the sale of heroin and cheap wines and liquors, pentecostal ministers, faith healers, prostitutes, pawn shops, and the peacetime army, which recruits its enlisted men mainly from among the poor.

*Fourth,* the poor buy goods others do not want and thus prolong the economic usefulness of such goods — day-old bread, fruit and vegetables that would otherwise have to be thrown out, secondhand clothes, and deteriorating automobiles and buildings. They also provide incomes for doctors, lawyers, teachers, and others who are too old, poorly trained, or incompetent to attract more affluent clients.

In addition to economic functions, the poor perform a number of social functions.

*Fifth,* the poor can be identified and punished as alleged or real deviants in order to uphold the legitimacy of conventional norms. To justify the desirability of hard work, thrift, honesty, and monogamy, for example, the defenders of these norms must be able to find people who can be accused of being lazy, spendthrift, dishonest, and promiscuous. Although there is some evidence that the poor are about as moral and law-abiding as anyone else, they are more likely than middle-class transgressors to be caught and punished when they participate in deviant acts. Moreover, they lack the political and cultural power to correct the stereotypes that other people hold of them and thus continue to be thought of as lazy, spendthrift, etc., by those who need living proof that moral deviance does not pay.

*Sixth,* and conversely, the poor offer vicarious participation to the rest of the population in the uninhibited sexual, alcoholic, and narcotic behavior in which they are alleged to participate and which, being freed from the constraints of affluence, they are often thought to enjoy more than the middle classes. Thus many people, some social scientists included, believe that the poor not only are more given to uninhibited behavior (which may be true, although it is often motivated by despair more than by lack of inhibition) but derive more pleasure from it than affluent people (which research by Lee Rainwater, Walter Miller, and others shows to be patently untrue). However, whether the poor actually have more sex and enjoy it more is irrelevant; so long as middle-class people believe

this to be true, they can participate in it vicariously when instances are reported in factual or fictional form.

*Seventh,* the poor also serve a direct cultural function when culture created by or for them is adopted by the more affluent. The rich often collect artifacts from extinct folk cultures of poor people; and almost all Americans listen to the blues, Negro spirituals, and country music, which originated among the Southern poor. Recently they have enjoyed the rock styles that were born, like the Beatles, in the slums; and in the last year, poetry written by ghetto children has become popular in literary circles. The poor also serve as culture heroes, particularly, of course, to the left; but the hobo, the cowboy, the hipster, and the mythical prostitute with a heart of gold have performed this function for a variety of groups.

*Eighth,* poverty helps to guarantee the status of those who are not poor. In every hierarchical society someone has to be at the bottom; but in American society, in which social mobility is an important goal for many and people need to know where they stand, the poor function as a reliable and relatively permanent measuring rod for status comparisons. This is particularly true for the working class, whose politics is influenced by the need to maintain status distinctions between themselves and the poor, much as the aristocracy must find ways of distinguishing itself from the *nouveaux riches.*

*Ninth,* the poor also aid the upward mobility of groups just above them in the class hierarchy. Thus a goodly number of Americans have entered the middle class through the profits earned from the provision of goods and services in the slums, including illegal or non-respectable ones that upper-class and upper-middle-class businessmen shun because of their low prestige. As a result, members of almost every immigrant group have financed their upward mobility by providing slum housing, entertainment, gambling, narcotics, etc., to later arrivals — most recently to Blacks and Puerto Ricans.

*Tenth,* the poor help to keep the aristocracy busy, thus justifying its continued existence. "Society" uses the poor as clients of settlement houses and beneficiaries of charity affairs; indeed, the aristocracy must have the poor to demonstrate its superiority over other elites who devote themselves to earning money.

*Eleventh,* the poor, being powerless, can be made to absorb the costs of change and growth in American society. During the nineteenth century, they did the backbreaking work that built the cities; today, they are pushed out of their neighborhoods to make room for "progress." Urban renewal projects to hold middle-class taxpayers in the city and expressways to enable suburbanites to commute downtown have typically been located in poor neighborhoods, since no other group will allow itself to be displaced. For the same reason, universities, hospitals, and civic centers also expand into land occupied by the poor. The major costs of the industrialization of agriculture have been borne by the poor, who are pushed off the land without recompense; and they have paid a large share of the human cost of the growth of American power

> ". . . the poor facilitate and stabilize the American political process."

overseas, for they have provided many of the foot soldiers for Vietnam and other wars.

*Twelfth*, the poor facilitate and stabilize the American political process. Because they vote and participate in politics less than other groups, the political system is often free to ignore them. Moreover, since they can rarely support Republicans, they often provide the Democrats with a captive constituency that has no other place to go. As a result, the Democrats can count on their votes, and be more responsive to voters — for example, the white working class — who might otherwise switch to the Republicans.

*Thirteen*, the role of the poor in upholding conventional norms (see the *fifth* point, above) also has a significant political function. An economy based on the ideology of laissez-faire requires a deprived population that is allegedly unwilling to work or that can be considered inferior because it must accept charity or welfare in order to survive. Not only does the alleged moral deviancy of the poor reduce the moral pressure on the present political economy to eliminate poverty but socialist alternatives can be made to look quite unattractive if those who will benefit most from them can be described as lazy spendthrift, dishonest, and promiscuous.

## The Alternatives

I have described thirteen of the more important functions poverty and the poor satisfy in American society, enough to support the functionalist thesis that poverty, like any other social phenomenon, survives in part because it is useful to society or some of its parts. This analysis is not intended to suggest that because it is often functional, poverty *should* exist, or that it *must* exist. For one thing, poverty has many more dysfunctions than functions; for another, it is possible to suggest functional alternatives.

For example, society's dirty work could be done without poverty, either by automation or by paying "dirty workers" decent wages. Nor is it necessary for the poor to subsidize the many activities they support through their low-wage jobs. This would, however, drive up the costs of these activities, which would result in higher prices to their customers and clients. Similarly, many of the professionals who flourish because of the poor could be given other roles. Social workers could provide counseling to the affluent, as they prefer to do anyway; and the police could devote themselves to traffic and organized crime. Other roles would have to be found for badly trained or incompetent professionals now relegated to serving the poor, and someone else would have to pay their salaries. Fewer penologists would be employable, however. And pentecostal religion could probably not survive without the poor — nor would parts of the second- and third-hand-goods market. And in many cities, "used" housing that no one else wants would then have to be torn down at public expense.

Alternatives for the cultural functions of the poor could be found more easily and cheaply. Indeed, entertainers, hippies, and adolescents are already serving as the deviants needed to uphold traditional morality and

as devotees of orgies to "staff" the fantasies of vicarious participation.

The status functions of the poor are another matter. In a hierarchical society, some people must be defined as inferior to everyone else with respect to a variety of attributes, but they need not be poor in the absolute sense. One could conceive of a society in which the "lower class," though last in the pecking order, received 75 percent of the median income, rather than 15-40 percent, as is now the case. Needless to say, this would require considerable income redistribution.

The contribution the poor make to the upward mobility of the groups that provide them with goods and services could also be maintained without the poor's having such low incomes. However, it is true that if the poor were more affluent, they would have access to enough capital to take over the provider role, thus competing with, and perhaps rejecting, the "outsiders." (Indeed, owing in part to antipoverty programs, this is already happening in a number of ghettos, where white storeowners are being replaced by Blacks.) Similarly, if the poor were more affluent, they would make less willing clients for upper-class philanthropy, although some would still use settlement houses to achieve upward mobility, as they do now. Thus "Society" could continue to run its philanthropic activities.

The political functions of the poor would be more difficult to replace. With increased affluence the poor would probably obtain more political power and be more active politically. With higher incomes and more political power, the poor would be likely to resist paying the costs of growth and change. Of course, it is possible to imagine urban renewal and highway projects that properly reimbursed the displaced people, but such projects would then become considerably more expensive, and many might never be built. This, in turn, would reduce the comfort and convenience of those who now benefit from urban renewal and expressways. Finally, hippies could serve also as more deviants to justify the existing political economy — as they already do. Presumably, however, if poverty were eliminated, there would be fewer attacks on that economy.

In sum, then, many of the functions served by the poor could be replaced if poverty were eliminated, but almost always at higher costs to others, particularly more affluent others. Consequently, a functional analysis must conclude that poverty persists not only because it fulfills a number of positive functions but also because many of the functional alternatives to poverty would be quite dysfunctional for the affluent members of society. A functional analysis thus ultimately arrives at much the same conclusion as radical sociology, except that radical thinkers treat as manifest what I describe as latent: that social phenomena that are functional for affluent or powerful groups and dysfunctional for poor or powerless ones persist; that when the elimination of such phenomena through functional alternatives would generate dysfunctions for the affluent or powerful, they will continue to persist; and that phenomena like poverty can be eliminated only when they become dysfunctional for the affluent or powerful, or when the powerless can obtain enough power to change society. ∎

# 26

Gus Tyler

# White Worker / Blue Mood

"It's us they is always chokin' so that the rich folks can stay fat."
—A 28-year-old Kentucky miner on the "freeze."
*New York Times*, September 24, 1971

What are the facts about the American workers—especially white workers? Of the 77.902 million gainfully employed in 1969, 28.237 million wore blue collars; that is, 36 percent. But others might as well have worn that collar. Of the 36.844 million "white-collar" workers, about 18 million were in clerical and sales—an added 22 percent of the employed. In addition, there were another 9.528 million engaged in service trades—a category that earned less than the blue-collar, clerical, or sales people. The total in all these blue and bluish jobs comes to 69 percent of the employed.

Who, beside farm workers, is not included? There is the class listed as professional, technical, managerial, as officials and proprietors, who make up about a quarter of the employed. Despite their lofty titles millions of these are just plain, worried workers. Consider that Italian "professional" who teaches in Franklin K. Lane High School or that Jewish "proprietor" who owns a candy store in Harlem.

The white worker is currently called "middle American," a description that evokes the image of a man and his family at the center of American affluence. But what is the reality?

The white worker is not affluent—not even near-affluent. The median *family* income in 1968 (pre-Nixon) was $8,632, about $1,000 short of what the Bureau of Labor Statistics calls a "modest but adequate" income. That this median family cannot meet the American standard of living refutes the mischievous myth that poor means black, and white means affluent. The myth is mischievous because it turns an ethnic difference into a class struggle and implies—and sometimes states —that the way to end poverty is simply to end racism. This myth, as that of "the vanishing American worker," is based upon a truth that when exaggerated becomes an untruth.

While it is true that a much higher percentage of nonwhites than whites is officially poor, it is equally true that in 1968 two-thirds of the poor were white. Nor is this white poverty limited to Appalachia.

Our latest report on who is poor (March 1970) reveals that of the 5.047 million U.S. families listed as living in poverty, 1.363 million or 25 percent are black: only one out of four poor families is black. In the metropolitan areas of America, in 1968, there were 2.477 million poor families of which 777,000 were black: less than one-third. In the central cities of these metropoles, there were 748,000 poor families, of which 358,000 were black: less than half.

The poor are not mainly the unemployed. One-third of the family heads listed as officially poor work full weeks at least 50 weeks a year. Others work part years. Most of the poor have jobs—and are white.

While families with incomes under $3,000 are officially poor, those with incomes above $3,000 are not all rich. Twelve percent of the families in America have an income between $3,000 and $5,000. (A recent Labor Department study found that an urban family of four needed at least $5,895 a year to meet its basic needs. If $6,000 a year were used as a cut-off poverty line, then 29.3 percent of the families in America are living in poverty.) A high 52 percent of the families had an income of less than $9,000 a year— a figure still below the official "modest but adequate" income. Seventy-two percent of the families have an income below $12,000 a year—a sum just above what the BLS considers adequate for a family of four in New York City. In round figures, about three out of four families struggle along.

If so many Americans are nonaffluent, who gets the money in this affluent society? Here are some facts on income distribution.

In 1968, the bottom fifth of the nation's families received 5.7 percent of the country's income; the top fifth received 40.6 percent. The middle three-fifths were bunched between 12 and 23 percent. These figures, from the U.S. Department of Commerce publication *Consumer Income* (December 1969), actually understate the great gap be-tween top and bottom. In calculating income, the Department of Commerce excludes "money received from the sale of property, such as stocks, bonds, a house, or a car . . . gifts . . . and lump sum inheritances or insurance payments." If these items were included, the income of the top fifth would be appreciably increased—and, by the inclusion of these receipts in the total calculation of income, the percentage of income of the other fifths would be automatically decreased.

Between 1947 and 1967, income shares did not change. The bottom moved from 5 percent to 5.4 percent; the top from 43

---

**TABLE 1**

BREAKDOWN OF EMPLOYED PERSONS AGE 16 AND OVER BY OCCUPATION AND COLOR:

| (in thousands) | White | Nonwhite |
|---|---|---|
| Blue Collar | 24,647 | 3,591 |
| Service | 7,289 | 2,239 |
| Clerical | 12,314 | 1,083 |
| Sales | 4,527 | 166 |
| Professional-Technical | 10,074 | 695 |
| Manager, Officials | 7,733 | 254 |
| Proprietors, Farmers | 2,935 | 356 |
| Total | 69,519 | 8,384 |

---

**TABLE 2**

PERCENTAGE OF THE TOTAL EMPLOYED IN VARIOUS CATEGORIES OF WHITE LABOR

| (percent) | White Percentage of Total Employed of All Races |
|---|---|
| Blue Collar | 32 |
| Service | 9.3 |
| Clerical | 16 |
| Sales | 6 |
| Professional-Technical | 13 |
| Managers, Officials | 10 |
| Proprietors, Farmers | 1.7 |
| Total | 88 |

Whites, then, make up 88 percent of the employed; nonwhites 12 percent. Of the whites, the categories that compose the blue-mooded (exclude farmers and include about half of those in the professional, proprietor, etc., category) make up about 75 percent of the employed.

percent to 41.2 percent. The change is negligible—and, after allowance for other receipts not counted as income, we find that there has been no meaningful redistribution of income in the quarter-century since the end of World War II.

This iron law of maldistribution applies not only to the nation as a whole but also to the nonwhite families of America, which darkly mirror the class structure of the mother culture. Among nonwhite families, in 1968 the lowest fifth got 4.8 percent of the income and the top fifth 43.6 percent; in 1947, the lowest fifth got 4.3 percent and the highest 45.7 percent. In sum, whether we look at white or dark America, in 1947 or 1968, the maldistribution remains almost constant—an economic fact regardless of race, creed, etc.

Recently, a young man at Harvard undertook a study of income distribution reaching all the way back to 1910. Although his findings may be subject to some refinement, his rough conclusions—reached after more than casual digging—tell us a bit more about the rigidities of our class structure. In 1910, he finds, the lowest tenth received 3.5 percent of the income; in 1961, it received a mere 1 percent. The bottom tenth got a smaller share of the GNP in 1961 than it did in 1910. In 1910, the top tenth received 33.9 percent of the income; in 1961, it received 30 percent. The table below records the economic truism that the more times change the more they remain the same.

In a recent study by Herman P. Miller and Roger A. Herriott, in which they recalculated income to include some of the factors excluded from the Commerce Department reports, they found that in 1968 the top 1.4 percent of families and individuals drew 11 percent of the nation's income, while bottom 16 percent drew only 2 percent and the next-from-the-bottom 18 percent drew only 7 percent of the national income. In sum, a top 1.4 percent drew more than the bottom 34 percent.

This maldistribution of income is repeated in a maldistribution of wealth (ownership) which is the major cause of our economic inequities. A study by Robert Lampman points out that although there was less concentration of wealth in the period after World War II than after World War I, a creeping concentration began to set in after 1949. That year, the top 1 percent held 21 percent of the wealth. In 1956, this rose to 26 percent —by 1962, to 33.3 percent (Data are drawn from statistics provided by the Internal Revenue Service, based on estate tax returns that offer loopholes for the most affluent. It is therefore not unreasonable to conclude that all of these figures understate the true concentration of wealth in America.) By 1970, if this trend has continued, we were back to 1929, when the top 1 percent held 36.3 percent of the nation's wealth.

If, however, the maldistribution of income is an inequity of ancient origin, whose persistence we have noted for this whole century, why is the white worker turning restless at this particular moment? The reasons: (1) a quantitative erosion of income; (2) a qualitative erosion of living; (3) a frightening erosion of social order.

Although not living in affluence, the white worker was better off in the '60s than at any other time of this century. In the recovery years following the Great Depression of the early 1930s, he and his family were enjoying an ever-rising standard of living. In 1947, the median family income (in constant 1968 dollars) was $4,716; by 1967, it rose to $8,318, an increase of about $4,000—after allowing for inflation.

During the same period, the percentage of families making under $7,000 a year decreased and the percentage making more increased sharply—again in constant dollars. In 1947, 75 percent of the families had an income of less than $7,000, and 25 percent had an income above that figure. In 1967, on the contrary, 63 percent of the families had an income above $7,000 and only 36 percent had an income below that figure.

$A$ll this was happening, however, without any basic redistribution of income in America. Per capita income was growing because the total national income was growing at a rate faster than that of the population. There was more available for everybody.

The rise in income was reflected in a lifestyle based on rising expectations. You mortgaged your life for a home, because you expected to earn more in the days to come. You bought on the installment plan, everything from baby carriage to auto. You planned a future for your kids: a nice neighborhood, a good school, a savings plan to put the kids through one of the better colleges—maybe even Harvard or Vassar. You were out to "make it," no matter how hard you worked, how much you scrimped, how often you borrowed, how late you moonlighted. You had hope!

You didn't even mind paying ever-higher taxes, so long as your take-home pay was bigger. The tax was an investment in the future—a town or a country where things would be better. You would enjoy it tomorrow, and the kids would enjoy it for generations. You were future-minded.

As a result, this numerous class became the mass base of social stability in America. It was not status quo-ish in the sense that it would be happy to have its present frozen forever; it was constantly pushing for change. But it sought change within a system that it felt was yielding more and could continue to yield more. And to keep moving, this class joined unions for economic advance and voted Democratic for socioeconomic legislation.

Sometime in the mid-60s, however, this social structure began to fall apart. Almost unnoticed by the media was the decline in the real income of the nonsupervisory employee. Between 1965 and 1969, the buying power of the worker was in steady decline—despite wage increases. Pay envelopes were chewed up by inflation and taxation.

The year 1965 was the first of the escalated involvement in Vietnam, and this imposed a triple burden on the American worker. First, he had to pay a greater tax to help finance the war. Second, he had to pay more for consumer goods because this war, like any other, automatically increases demand without increasing supply. Third, he supplied his sons for the military; the affluent found ways to escape in schools and special occupations, the poor were often too ill or illiterate.

The year 1965 is also the mid-point of a decade in which America began to respond to poverty and discrimination. The Johnson years produced a spate of national legislation to provide income and opportunities for the poor, especially the blacks. Local govern-

---

TABLE 3

PERCENTAGE OF NATIONAL PERSONAL INCOME, BEFORE TAXES, RECEIVED BY EACH INCOME-TENTH *

|  | Highest Tenth | 2nd | 3rd | 4th | 5th | 6th | 7th | 8th | 9th | Lowest Tenth |
|---|---|---|---|---|---|---|---|---|---|---|
| 1910 | 33.9 | 12.3 | 10.2 | 8.8 | 8.0 | 7.0 | 6.0 | 5.5 | 4.9 | 3.4 |
| 1960 | 28.0 | 16.0 | 13.0 | 11.0 | 9.0 | 8.0 | 6.0 | 5.0 | 3.0 | 1.0 |

* In terms of "recipients" for 1910–37 and "spending units" for 1941–59. Data for 1960–61 were available in rounded form only. Figures for 1910 were taken from National Industrial Conference Board *Studies in Enterprise and Social Progress,* (New York: National Industrial Conference Board, 1939), p. 125; data for 1960–61 were calculated by the Survey Research Center.

ments were trying to cope with their crises. At all levels, America began to spend public money to resolve pressing problems.

The American worker supported these social measures, through the unions and the Democratic party. He saw these bits and pieces of socioeconomic legislation as a spur and parallel to his upward effort.

It was not apparent to this same worker that the upside-down system of taxation in the United States placed the cost of these measures on the shoulders of the huge "middle" sector—the sector neither poor nor rich enough to escape taxes. Although the federal income tax supposedly is graduated so as to make the wealthy pay at a higher rate, this expressed intent is annulled by the many loopholes for those who derive income from sources other than wages or salaries. At the local level, it is the small homeowner who pays the tariff through *ad valorem* property taxes and the small consumer who pays through the nose for city, county, and state sales taxes.

The worker feels that he is paying triple: he pays for his own way; he pays for the poor; he pays for the rich. He is ready to do the first; he resists the others.

Finally, this same worker has been squeezed by a system of private taxation, operated through monopoly pricing. Everything from electricity to eggs is manipulated in closed and increasingly enclosed markets. As buying power goes up (current dollars in income), the response of dominant sectors of the economy is not to *increase* supply but to *limit* production (or distribution) to keep the consumer on the same level while increasing profits for the seller.

To add insult to injury, the worker is advised by the media and, more recently, by the Administration, that if prices are going up, it is his own fault: high wages make high prices. If he wants to buy for less, he must work for less. This logic boggles the worker who cannot understand how he can live better by earning less. Once more, he is the victim of a myth. The truth was stated in an editorial by the sober *Wall Street Journal* on August 5, 1968:

> In the past 20 years, there have been three distinct periods in which factory prices climbed substantially over a prolonged interval. In each instance, labor costs per unit of factory output were *declining* when the price climb began—and these costs continued to decline for a considerable period after the price rise was underway. In each case, corporate profits began to increase sharply well before the price climb started.

To keep up with rising prices, workers demand higher wages and salaries—through unions and as individuals. But they never catch up, for in a monopoly-oligopoly conglomerate economy, the man who can fix the prices must always end up winning the game.

The result is that millions of workers feel they are paying more and more for less and less. They are paying for a war—with their sons, their taxes, and their overcharged purchases—only to feel they are losing the war. They are paying more for what they buy—and get more cars doomed for early obsolescence, phones that ring wrong numbers, homes that are jerry-built, doctors who make no home visits. They pay more and more in local taxes—and feel they are subsidizing crime and riot.

Hard work seems to have brought nothing but hard times. After federal taxes are taken out of the pay, after local taxes are paid, and then the rest is used to buy debased goods and services at inflated prices, the worker knows—and his wife knows still better—that he is no longer moving up.

The worker in urban America, however, is the victim not only of income maldistribution—but also of population maldistribution, which is a catastrophe whose impact he cannot stand and whose origin he does not understand. Few city dwellers even suspect that much of their urban crisis started down on the farm.

Since World War II, about a million Americans a year have moved from a rural to an urban culture. This massive shift of about 20 million people in one generation has been described as the most gigantic migration in the history of man. Such a collision of cultures has always meant crowding, crime, and conflict. In the 1960s, history repeated itself—except that the immigrant was invisible because he was an in-migrant.

What set this wave in motion? Two contradictory national policies: to increase agricultural productivity and to restrict its production. Subsidized science found ways to make four stalks grow where one grew before. Subsidies to farmers, then, reversed the process by rewarding growers for nonproduction. The result was less and less need for labor on the soil. Farm workers went jobless; small farm owners went bankrupt or were bought out. Rural Americans were driven from their familiar farms into the unfamiliar cities, from warm earth to cold concrete.

This rural-push–urban-pull has been in motion ever since the turn of the century. But what was once a drift became a flood in the 1960s. The discomfort and disorder that followed set another dynamic in motion: the urban-push-suburban-pull.

If the worker can afford it, he generally flees—to outskirts and suburbs. He does so whether he is black or white. (Between 1964 and 1969, 600,000 blacks fled the central cities for other parts of the metropolitan areas.) Those who cannot flee, stay and get ready for the fight.

A current notion holds that the central cities are black and the suburbs white, dividing metros into separate but unequal societies in geographic separation. Again this is a half-truth which, if it were totally true, might well lessen social conflict. But the truth is that many whites cannot move, because they cannot afford to. Typically, they are white workers of more recent stock: economically unmonied and geographically immobile. Often, their neighborhoods abut black ghettos where—after the flight of the more affluent blacks—there are left, according to James Q. Wilson, "only the most deprived, the least mobile, and the most pathological."

Through the '60s, the crush became a crunch—not simply because there were more bodies in the central cities but also because there were fewer places to put them. By public action, we have torn down about twice as many housing units as we have put up. Private builders have bulldozed slums to erect luxury highrisers. Hundreds of thousands of units are abandoned annually by their landlords, because the rotting property is all pain and no profit. As decay sets in at the ghetto core, rats and rain and fleas and fire take over to deprive the most deprived of their turf. So these newly dispossessed become the latest in-migrants, driven from their holes into the surrounding neighborhoods, spreading panic in their path.

Under these pressures, the ethnics—white and black—move from economic frustration and personal fear to political fury. The physical stage on which this tragedy is unfolding is a tiny piece of turf. Now 70 percent of the people—our urban population—live on 1.6 percent of the total land area. The American worker—white or black—is the victim of maldistribution—of people as well as income and wealth.

In the 1970s fury comes easily to the white worker. It's stylish. He sees it everywhere. In the form of common crime—in the subway, on the street, at his doorstop; in the form of riots in the ghettos or the campus or the prison. The present generation of workers has grown up in an age of war: World War II, Korea, Vietnam. For three decades, they have lived with mass violence, directly and vicariously.

Retribalization reawakens ancient feelings.

The white worker has always had the sense of belonging to some special group. There were constant reminders of ethnicity in neighborhood names, groceries, bars, funeral parlors, holidays, papers, ward politics, gang leaders, subtle prides and prejudices. But in an America that was devoted to the mythos of the melting pot and in a period dedicated to the ethos of one world, the white worker tucked his ethnicity up his sleeve. Now, in a retribalized world, he displays his ethnicity —as a pennant to carry into battle.

The young among the white workers, like the young everywhere, add their special stridency to the clamor. They are high on expectations and low on boiling point. To a civilizational distemper, they add their hot tempers, turning ethnic salvation into a moral justification for violence.

Our white worker is ready for battle. But he does not quite know against whom to declare war.

As a child of toilers he holds the traditional view of those who labor about those who don't. He feels that those inflated prices, those high taxes, those inadequate wages are all part of a schema for fattening up the fat. While he rarely, if ever, uses the words "establishment" or "system," he instinctively assumes there's an establishment that exploits him through a devilishly devised system.

Part of the system, his experience teaches, is for the rich to use the poorest to keep the once-poor and the possibly-poor as poor as possible. For generations, employers who demanded protection against foreign imports were importing foreigners to depress wages and break strikes. Out of this arose the Know-Nothing party that threatened, within a couple of years, to become a major national movement. In the mid-19th century, Irish workers (themselves recent immigrants) feared that the Emancipation Proclamation,

ending chattel slavery for the blacks, would intensify wage slavery for the whites. Out of this fear rose the sadistic Draft Riot of 1863 with its lynching and burning of blacks. In the 1920s, the white worker opted for immigration legislation to stem the flow of cheap hands.

As we move into the '70s, many workers fear that the Brass is using Underclass to undermine the Working Class. They seldom use this language, but often feel these sentiments. As they hear it, this is what the rich are saying: "We must fight poverty and discrimination to the last drop of *your* blood. Share *your* job; share *your* neighborhood; pay *your* taxes." These moral exhortations come from the high and mighty, economically ensconced in tax havens far from the madding crowd.

In protest against this establishment, the worker turns to strikes for higher wages and revolt against taxes. But neither remedy works. Wage gains are offset by higher prices. Lower taxes mean lower services—schools, streets, travel, sanitation, police, medical care. What looked like a direct way out turns out to be a maze.

Since our worker does not know how to deal with the system, he tries to do the next best thing: to act within the system to protect his own skin. And in our torn and turbulent cities, it is too often his "skin" that determines his mood.

This mood is generally called "backlash," a reawakening of ancient prejudice directed against blacks because they have dared to raise their heads and voices. But to explain the growing tension simply as "backlash" is once more to create a mischievous myth out of partial truth. To deny that prejudice exists is naive; to ascribe rising racial clash to a simple proliferation of prejudice, equally naive. The white worker feels economically

threatened, personally imperiled, politically suckered. His anxieties make him meaner than he means to be. Racial suspicion turns into tribal war when people—no matter their color—are oppressed by their circumstances. Maldistribution of income and people must multiply strife. This strife, ironically, tends not to change but to continue the system that produced the conflict. So long as black battles white and poor battle not-so-poor, the establishment can continue to "divide and rule."

The further irony is the innocence of those on top who are, in a depersonalized way, responsible for the turmoil on the shrinking turf. The upper 1 percent rarely suspects that its incredible wealth is the prime reason the lesser people, without urging, are at one another's throats. As the wealthiest see their role, they are the great creators: investing, employing, making. They are the great givers, turning tax exempt funds to do God's work.

In short, there is no devil: those at the top merely move their money around in a depersonalized way through impersonal channels (corporations) to multiply their money so they may do man's and God's work better; those in the middle merely try to lift their real income so they and their family can live —better; those at the bottom merely want what man needs to stay alive and kicking. Yet somehow they all end up in a fight, with the top acting genteelly through finances, and the lesser people resorting intemperately to fists.

If there is a devil, he is—as he always is— invisible, ubiquitous, and working his evil will through the way of all flesh. In our case, he is the inherent imperative in a culture that has badly distributed its wealth and people: the devil still is the system.

# 27

# WE HAVE TWO KINDS OF JUSTICE: ONE FOR THE POOR AND ONE FOR US

## Anthony G. Amsterdam

Anthony Amsterdam, who has been on the Stanford University law faculty since 1969, served as a clerk to Justice Felix Frank-furter and as an assistant U.S. attorney. He and Jack Greenberg, as attorneys for the NAACP Legal Defense Fund, argued two of three cases in which the Supreme Court declared the death penalty uncon-stitutional on June 29, 1972.

In its aspirations for justice, America ranks among the most ambitious countries in history. We profess to a respect for the individual that elevates the concept of individual rights to a new high. These aspirations are so noble that they blind us to reality. Our pride in our fine profes-sions makes us refuse to admit or to see that they are largely honored in the breach. Breaches that cannot be wholly ignored are excused with the observation that they are, after all, breaches only of the very highest standards.

An article by one of President Nixon's Supreme Court appointees, Justice Lewis F. Powell, Jr., is typical of the common mystique. Powell paints a picture of Ameri-can criminal justice in which the defend-ant has every safeguard. He has the rights to pretrial bail and to counsel. He has a privilege against self-incrimination. He must not be convicted except after a jury trial and a unanimous guilty verdict. This verdict must be supported by proof beyond a reasonable doubt. Then there are appeals and proceedings in which he may repeat-edly challenge his conviction.

But these are paper rights. The ordinary criminal defendant remains caged in atro-cious jails before trial because he lacks the money to make bail. His court-appointed lawyer convinces him to plead guilty be-cause the vaunted right to jury trial can be bought only at the price of protracted pretrial incarceration and a heavier sen-tence. The lawyer has inadequate time and resources to prepare the case properly for trial; and even with good preparation, the lawyer knows that proof "beyond a reason-able doubt" is a mockery, easily found in doubtful cases by crime-frightened middle-class juries. There are no appeals from guilty pleas or from wrong-headed jury verdicts. And postconviction proceedings — the last hope for correction of this abysmal set of preconviction failures of justice — usually end in postcard denials of writs scribbled illegibly by unlettered and unrepresented prisoners.

We don't talk much about these re-alities. We focus our attention upon cer-tain supposedly very liberal rulings by the Supreme Court giving defendants criminal trial rights. Liberals praise, and law-and-order people decry, these decisions. But these decisions are virtually inconsequen-tial in the actual function of the crim-inal process.

What *is* important in the criminal pro-cess is the money-bail system, under which indigent defendants are incarcerated in default of bail. Under this system, liberty is for sale. So, also, are trials. The fact that the indigent defendant is incarcerated puts tremendous pressure on him to make a quick disposition of his case instead of going to trial and raising the legal claims available. But the Supreme Court has never agreed to review the constitutional-ity of the money-bail system, although it is a plain and invidious discrimination against the poor.

Another thing that is important in the actual criminal process is the adequacy of defense counsel. The lawyers made avail-able to the poor are often overburdened public defenders or conscripted private lawyers who do not have the time and energy to give to indigent cases. The Su-preme Court has never undertaken to set decent standards for the performance of defense lawyers or for the resources that must be given to them.

As a result of pretrial incarceration and inadequate counsel, the defendant is ordi-narily forced to negotiate a guilty-plea dis-position from a position of weakness. The plea-bargaining process is the third impor-tant aspect of criminal justice. Again, the Supreme Court has failed to erect adequate safeguards to protect defendants against the unfairness and coercion inherent in this process.

Next, the defendant is sentenced by a procedure that is utterly lawless. Ameri-can courts have discretion to mete out incredibly harsh sentences. There is no sentencing "law"; and sentencing proce-dure lacks the most basic rudiments of a fair hearing. The Supreme Court has scru-pulously avoided reviewing this process.

Finally, the sentenced defendant is sub-mitted to a regime of penal administration that is both lawless and barbaric. He is denied any rights, his human integrity it-self is denied, his personality is brutalized, and he is subjected to the tyranny and caprice of correctional officials while he is imprisoned and of parole boards after he gets out. The Supreme Court has also avoided any scrutiny of prison administra-tion or of the parole process.

Why does the gap between our profes-sions and our practice exist? There are several reasons.

First, we invariably think about justice as a set of "rights" that the individual "has" rather than as the treatment he actually gets. Some rights are high and holy; some are controversial. We adulate the first and debate the second, while both distract our attention from the real insti-tutions that deliver or withhold justice in our system. We maintain this unworldly outlook because most Americans who hold political power or can influence popular opinion have never been subjected to those institutions; and most people who are lack power and influence.

Second, the mass of Americans does not care much about safeguards designed to protect individuals against the unjust or oppressive functioning of institutions like the criminal law system. These systems operate on the other guy, never on *me* or on *my* family or on *my* friends. *We* may be the victims of crime; but we never expect to be the victims of the criminal courts. So we do not think or care about protections for those who are.

This attitude characterizes the public, as well as those who run the criminal law institutions: policemen, prosecutors, judges, correctional and parole officials. It characterizes journalists, who reinforce it. We read daily about atrocious crimes; but when do we read about an atrocious criminal sentence?

Politicians exploit the same attitude, partly because they share it and partly because it is good politics. Real answers to our deepest social problems, such as crime, are costly; in these days of the taxpayers' revolt, it is cheaper and easier to find scapegoats than solutions. So we hear a rhetoric in which the "criminal forces" are set off against the "peace forces" in society; and when the President engages in that sort of rhetoric, it is difficult to get anyone to inspect the realities of the criminal law system.

In the last analysis, the problem is that we are unwilling to pay the costs of realizing our professions. Government that is properly attentive to individual concerns costs more money than we are willing to invest in it. Paper rights are cheap, so we have them. Decent treatment of people is expensive, so we do not have it.

But strong pressures for productive change are reflected in the political structure from time to time. However gross his error in Vietnam, some of Lyndon Johnson's domestic policies were very fine. But for the reversal of those policies under the Nixon Administration, significant progress might well have been made.

The approach of the Johnson Administration to the crime problem was essentially a realization that crime has to be attacked at its roots: poverty, ignorance, disease, disadvantage. The Johnson Administration put its primary thrust on social programs that would have attacked those root causes. It refused to be alarmist about crime.

The Nixon Administration has turned the crime problem around, largely neglecting the causes and concerning itself simply with assuaging public hysteria about crime. Or, rather, with capitalizing upon public hysteria about crime.

The most significant thing about the Nixon Administration's approach to crime is that it has not inaugurated a single program that could conceivably reduce the incidence of crime fifteen years, or five years, or even two years from now. Criminals will be shot at with bigger guns, but there will be no fewer of them. And some of those guns will hit innocent citizens.

One visible example of the change is the Johnson Administration's refusal to use wiretapping and the Nixon Administration's use of wiretapping, both judicially sanctioned and not judicially sanctioned. That reflects a major shift in values.

The Johnson Administration acted as it did out of constitutional concerns and out of a pragmatic sense that wiretapping was not worth the cost. Its law-enforcement yield was relatively slight compared with the violence that it did to the basic security of a society where people could breathe more freely knowing that Big Brother was not watching.

The Nixon Administration does not seem to feel that there are any costs involved in Big Brother practices, because it does not put a very high value on respect for the individual. And the Nixon Administration has a notably two-faced approach to the constitutional question.

On the one hand, Nixon has lambasted the Supreme Court for a lack of judicial conservatism—that is, for putting its views forward in opposition to those of the Executive and Congress. On the other hand, the Nixon Administration castigates Ramsey Clark for not using the powers given him by Congress to wiretap, on the ground that it was the *Court's* job, not his, to decide the constitutionality of wiretapping.

Nixon's attitude toward the Court resembles Roosevelt's. The blatantly political methods of his appointment process seem designed—as was Roosevelt's Court-packing plan—to cheapen, belittle, discredit and ultimately cow the Court. Like Roosevelt, Nixon has demonstrated a shocking lack of respect for the Court: he has systematically set out to force the Court into his mold both by choosing nominees who will decide cases according to his views and by denigrating its stature so that it will not be strong enough to stand against the President.

Such an attitude by a President toward the Supreme Court spreads popular disrespect for the Court and fans the fires of lawlessness. The acceptability of the

> he Warren Court's 'criminal law revolution' was not the activist enterprise it is sometimes portrayed to be."

Court's decisions depends upon popular belief in the Court's independence and integrity. When they are impugned, there is no reason to obey the law.

This is a very important point, often forgotten by those who urge "civility," as Chief Justice Burger does. The call for civility is explicitly addressed to people who feel themselves oppressed by society, and it tells them: "Cool it. See if you can't get recognition of your just claims through the orderly processes of the law." But the processes of government, which are majoritarian and include both the legislative and the executive, are not likely to give much ear to the just claims of minorities, so it largely remains for the courts to do so. And when the Supreme Court is seen as a reflection of the President, itself shaped by the transient majority that brings him into office, then minorities lose their faith in the enduring power of the Court to bring them justice.

Further, Court-packing seriously weakens the internal strength and integrity of the Court, not only because of the Justices who get on but also because of its impact on all the Justices. The Nixon experience is teaching the Justices that if the Court stands too firm in defense of unpopular individual liberties, it will be subject to savage recrimination by the popular organs of government—which have more raw power than the Court has—so that the Court must either follow the elections or fear the man who does.

The impact of that fear on the entire structure of the law is likely to be devastating. If the Supreme Court becomes timid, the result will be to destroy the outstanding feature of American legal institutions: that is, the interposition of independent courts between the individual's basic and inalienable rights and the will of the majority.

The Supreme Court is the only court with sufficient stature consistently to protect individual rights against the constant pressure of the majority to trample them. Therefore it is the major function of the

Supreme Court not only to respond to claims of individual rights but also to assure that all the lower courts do the same. It is the Court's job to embolden the lower courts to stand firm in defense of individual rights, to take the heat off the lower courts when they do so, and to keep them honest by the threat of reversal.

When the Supreme Court becomes afraid to play this critical role, the lower courts are likely to cave in quickly. So the courts lose their independence, and the individual loses his foremost protection against repression.

Some critics say that the Supreme Court tries to "make law," which is the prerogative of the legislature. But when no legislative or executive judgment of any sort has been expressed, the Supreme Court may have to pass upon a question on which no other branch of government has expressed a policy.

In this situation, the Court is obviously forced to make law. If it decides, for example, that a policeman may not take a confession without warning a suspect, it is making law. If it decides that a policeman *may* take a confession without warning a suspect, it is making law. Either way it makes law because no one else did before the Court got the case.

This situation has been too much ignored by the critics of the Court. The fact is that the Warren Court's so-called criminal law revolution was not the activist enterprise that it is sometimes portrayed to be. The Court did not, for the large part, upset the judgments of any other branch of government. Rather, the Court became "activist" because no other branch had assumed any responsibility for regulating the behavior of policemen.

There is a second situation, though, where complaints about the Court making law have more substance. When the Court reviews a judgment made by a legislature or by the executive, the complaint is that it is overstepping its judicial role and assuming a decision-making responsibility that the legislature or the executive branch should exercise.

Again, however, it is inevitable in our system of law that the Supreme Court must review at least *some* judgments of Congress and of the President and of the state legislatures and executives. The Bill of Rights says that there are things that the executive and Congress cannot do to a citizen, and the Supreme Court sits to enforce those restrictions.

That people should be upset when a policy determined by the elected representatives of the people is set aside by nine appointed justices — or a slim majority of five or six of them — is understandable. But just as the legislative and executive branches derive their legitimacy from their majoritarian character, so the Court derives its legitimacy from its antimajoritarian character. That character is no accident but the careful design of a constitution built upon the principle of separation of powers. Separation of powers does not mean three similar kinds of decision makers either second-guessing *or* deferring to each other. It implies that three branches of government having different roles, responsibilities and functions will check each other.

And the specific and unique role, responsibility and function of a court is to respond to the one-man lobby. Nobody else in our scheme of government does.

This point is as important as the point that nine old men should not substitute their views for those of the elected representatives of the people. The two points must be reconciled; and their proper reconciliation depends upon the nature of the legal issue being presented for the Court's consideration.

If it is an issue of contention between large power blocs or forces in society, and the contending forces are all reasonably capable of holding their own in the halls of the legislature or the back rooms of the executive, then the legislative and executive resolutions of the issue should generally prevail.

But in cases of minority rights, equal protection of the laws, freedom of speech and the Bill of Rights guarantees, the legislatures and the executives have no mandate to defend these interests and often every motivation to destroy them.

These interests are, and institutionally must be, in the special keeping of the Court. Where they are threatened, the Court has a special responsibility; and it must, independently, sometimes unhappily but always firmly, follow its own lights against those of the states, the President and Congress.

# 28

### Racial Attitude Change

# Are Whites Really More Liberal?
# Blacks Aren't Impressed

**by Howard Schuman**

Whites believe their
acceptance of blacks is on
the rise; simultaneously,
black trust in white intentions
is clearly on the way down.
What sounds at first like a
new form of black bigotry is
more likely the voice of rising
expectations shouting down
the racism whites still feel.

AMERICANS ARE CONFRONTED with a paradox: as whites are becoming less hostile to blacks, blacks are becoming more suspicious of whites.

The steady liberalization of white attitudes on all racial issues has been documented by many attitude surveys since World War II, including an early series by the National Opinion Research Center at the University of Chicago and a more recent series by the Institute for Social Research (ISR) at the University of Michigan. The white edifice of antiblack attitudes has been eroding for at least three decades.

Although information on trends in black racial attitudes is much less extensive than that on whites, recent surveys indicate that black beliefs are shifting too, but in the opposite direction from white attitudes.

For a closer look at these shifts, we can examine data collected in Detroit since 1956 by Michigan's Detroit Area Study (DAS). Although there are geographical differences in racial attitudes in America, Detroit residents' beliefs are fairly typical of those in most Northern cities. This was shown by a 1968 ISR study of 15 Northern and border cities in which we found that Detroit white residents scored about average in racial liberalism. Black attitudes in Detroit were somewhat less militant than in other cities, despite the occurrence of a major riot there the previous year.

Four questions in DAS surveys measured white racial attitudes at different points in time; two questions were about residential desegregation, and two concerned interpersonal relations.

**The First Black on the Block.** In 1958 and again in 1971, DAS asked a cross-section of white Detroit residents, "Would you be at all disturbed or unhappy if a Negro with the same income and education as you moved into your block?" The majority (54 percent) of our respondents in 1958 said yes. By 1971 that percentage was cut almost in half (28 percent). The interim period included the major urban riots of the late '60s, the rise of black-power sym-

bolism and rhetoric, and many other events that may have frightened white moderates. Despite this obvious opportunity for white backlash, we found a very substantial change toward a more liberal view on the issue. I might note here that a number of nonracial issues measured over this same period showed no shift at all.

We found a similar change when we asked, "Personally do you think white students and Negro students should go to the same schools or to separate schools?" In 1958 one third of our respondents said "separate schools." Thirteen years later only 17 percent agreed with the segregationist viewpoint. This shift was really remarkable when we consider that in 1958 most Detroit residents thought school integration was only a Southern problem; by 1971 the proposed busing of students in Detroit brought the issue home.

The changes described above dealt with public issues that are the focus of institutional pressure. We wondered if attitudes toward racial issues that did not receive national attention were also changing. They were.

**Intermarriage: Still a Barrier.** In 1969 and in 1971 we asked whites: "If a very close relative married a Negro, would you mind it a lot, a little, or not at all?" As Gunnar Myrdal noted some years ago, intermarriage is an issue of great symbolic importance to whites. It appeared to us that a liberal answer to this question would be an unusually good verbal index of acceptance by whites of equal status for blacks, an acceptance not required by law or custom.

A majority of whites objected strongly to intermarriage in both 1969 (68 percent) and in 1971 (51 percent). But the downward shift of 17 percent in just two years is striking and particularly significant on an issue that lacks institutional support and is still highly controversial.

The second question about interpersonal relations provided further evidence of increasing white liberalism. In 1956 only 40 percent of the white public in Detroit thought children of mixed races should play together freely; by 1971 this figure had nearly doubled to 79 percent. In 1971, we also asked our subjects how they *thought* most whites would answer this question. While four out of five respondents said they would encourage interracial play, less than a third of these same people believed most other whites agreed with them. Thus, public opinion on this issue is well ahead of what the public believes it is. The white population is more liberal than it realizes.

Significantly, these liberalizing trends are not confined to one segment of the white population. Men and women, young and old, more-educated and less-educated white persons are all becoming more tolerant on racial issues.

At any one point in time, however, educated youth are noticeably more liberal than less-educated older people. This suggests that, barring some new force in the opposite direction, we can expect further liberalization of white attitudes as the total educational level of the population continues to rise. But education alone does not account for the liberalizing trends. We are witnessing a process of cultural change larger and more sweeping than any single element that contributes to it.

**Black Suspicions.** Something very different is happening among blacks. We have information only on short-term change between early 1968 and 1971, but this was a crucial three-year period for black racial attitudes. "Black power" captured national attention, and the move toward black community control assumed considerable strength during these three years. And our survey data suggest that important changes in black racial attitudes indeed took place at that time.

One of the largest changes concerned how blacks viewed white intentions toward them. In 1968, 42 percent of the Detroit blacks believed that whites wanted "to see Negroes get a better break"; this figure dropped to 28 percent in 1971. At the same time, the percentage of blacks who believed that whites wanted "to keep Negroes down" rose from 23 percent in 1968 to 41 percent in 1971. Thus, blacks were becoming more distrusting of white intentions toward them.

When we asked blacks whether they would prefer to live in a largely black neighborhood or a mixed neighborhood, we found a small, but significant increase in preference for black neighborhoods between 1968 (12 percent) and 1971 (19 percent), though it must be noted that the percentage is not very high in either year. There was also a small but reliable increase in the percentage of people who felt violence might be a necessary means in their struggle for equal rights.

Finally, we found that slightly more blacks in 1971 (63 percent) than in 1968

---

## Blacks, especially the young, are obviously more concerned with current frustrations than with historical trends pointed out by social scientists.

---

(57 percent) thought that many places in Detroit would hire a white over an equally qualified black. But this change was not significant; it was probably due to sampling error, as were several other minor shifts in these data.

Thus, not all black attitudes and perceptions have changed dramatically. Change seems to be going on primarily in the area of black perceptions of general white attitudes, and to a lesser degree in black reactions to these changed perceptions.

**The Racist American System.** Other surveys at ISR lend support to these findings. Patricia Gurin and Edgar Epps studied students in 10 black colleges in 1965 and 1970. They found a substantial increase in what they called "system blame" by blacks. This is the belief that the major obstacle to personal success is the racist structure of American society.

In a study of the 1972 election, Arthur H. Miller, Thad A. Brown and Alden S. Raine found a very marked increase since 1968 in political cynicism among blacks. Whites showed a similar trend, but it was not nearly as striking. The available data suggest that the slide in blacks' trust of whites and white society dated particularly from the 1967-1968 period of urban riots.

There are good explanations for the disparity between trends in white attitudes and black suspicions. Whatever liberalization has occurred, from the black perspective white racism is far from gone. Half the white population in 1971 still reported "minding a lot" if a close relative married across the color line—as against only seven percent of the black population's feeling this way. And the amount of black opposition to mixed neighborhoods is tiny compared to white resistance to true residential integration. There is still enough white hostility to equal treatment to justify the black perceptions we have noted.

Moreover, the average black citizen reacts to what he sees and hears every day. Blacks, especially the young, are obviously more concerned with current frustrations than with historical trends pointed out by social scientists. And age is a critical factor in conditioning black beliefs; young blacks are noticeably more alienated than older blacks. They want change and they want it now, not a lecture on improvements in the past. It is also important to note that level of education is not a main source of variation in black attitudes, as it is for whites. Distrust of whites has been growing among both educated and uneducated blacks.

**Black Criticism, White Liberalism.** It is also true that blacks, on the average, have simply become more open in their criticism of whites. This openness, like the liberalization of white racial attitudes, seems to be a cultural trend that has its own momentum. The two trends are not necessarily in conflict; indeed, black criticism of whites may be a factor promoting further white liberalization, and such liberalization may allow greater black expression of criticism.

The practical implications of shifts in racial attitudes are not easy to interpret. First, we must examine very carefully what our questions really measure. While two thirds of the white population in Detroit claim they would not be disturbed or unhappy at having a black neighbor, this does not mean these same whites would favor open-housing laws. There is no logical contradiction between sincere willingness to accept one educated black neighbor and unwillingness to vote for laws which prohibit all discrimination in rental or sale of housing. As a matter of fact, other data show that fewer than one third of the general white population favors such laws. And less than a third of the white population would accept living in a heavily black neighborhood. So, though our earlier questions indicate genuine attitude shifts, they may not get at the willingness to accept fundamental structural change.

**Bradley, Black Mayor in a White City.** In fact the same question can take on different meanings in different situations. In 1968 we found that about 60 percent of the whites in 15 cities said they would be willing to vote for a capable black mayoral candidate of their own party. Yet in a number of later elections, even successful black candidates like Maynard Jackson (Atlanta) and Coleman Young (Detroit) received far less than half the white vote. Los Angeles is the only major city where

**Black criticism of whites may be a factor promoting further white liberalization, and such liberalization may allow greater black criticism.**

close to a majority of whites voted for a black candidate, Thomas Bradley, in preference to the white incumbent, Sam Yorty.

Why did Los Angeles confirm our earlier survey results, while most cities with black-white mayoral contests did not? No doubt the answer lies partly in the specific candidates, and partly in a more liberal than average outlook in Los Angeles. But I suspect the most important explanation has roots in the relatively small black population in Los Angeles (18 percent).

In Los Angeles, white voters apparently separated the question of the candidate's own race from the quite different issue of which race would "control" the city. But in Atlanta and Detroit whites were becoming the minority population, and the elections became full-scale battles over which race would run the city. In such situations, we could not expect our question about voting for a black mayor to predict the actual vote very well. In Los Angeles it could.

A related factor to keep in mind is that attitudes vary greatly in strength and intensity, especially when they conflict with other values and pressures. Recently we asked whites whether they thought

employers should hire men for top-management positions without paying attention to their race. More than four out of five (87 percent) favored equal treatment for black and white job applicants. But when we asked the same persons what a personnel director should do if he knew that hiring a black executive would cause friction in the organization, only 59 percent of the respondents supported equal treatment.

**Token Liberals.** This does not necessarily mean that the whites who shifted are all hypocrites, but it does mean that they think racial equality is considerably less important than some of their other values. Such value conflicts are common in all areas of life, so it is no surprise that they occur on racial issues. Thus, while an increasing proportion of white Americans hold liberal views on racial issues, many of them are not prepared to undergo a great deal of discomfort to see those opinions become reality.

This last point has positive as well as negative implications. Prejudiced individuals are also rarely willing to suffer much for their views. Indeed it is this basic weakness of most values that makes it possible for the Government to intervene in racial issues even against majority wishes. Of course, in a democracy it is neither possible nor necessarily desirable to push people too far for too long. Coercive measures to achieve equality that conflict with pervasive attitudes of the general public may well go aground in an election. The real meaning of "backlash" is seldom a

**Coercive measures to achieve equality that conflict with pervasive attitudes of the general public may well go aground in an election.**

genuine change backwards, but rather a resistance to new and stronger steps forward.

**Backlash to Busing.** My own guess is that *large-scale* busing may be just such an issue, although I have no data to support this feeling. Undoubtedly the success of such busing would have a decisive effect on its impact. We know that most citizens tend to accept a successful *fait accompli.*

A strong Government support of a program can have an important influence on the public. In normal times the attitudes of 10 to 20 percent of the population on many issues shift when we preface a question with the phrase: "Do you agree with the President that . . ." On broad issues of public life, people take guidance from authority figures—respected Presidents, the Supreme Court, and other leaders. There is considerable room for moral leadership to change white attitudes. Such leadership could move whites even faster toward positions supporting full racial equality. But because whites still have a long distance to travel, and black skepticism is increasing, it is unrealistic to believe the racial schism will disappear in America in the foreseeable future.

# 29

# On Becoming a Chicano

**An American graduate student recalls how he sloughed off his Spanish-Mexican heritage and then painfully rediscovered his Chicano roots.**

by Richard Rodriguez

Today I am only technically the person I once felt myself to be—a Mexican-American, a Chicano. Partly because I had no way of comprehending my racial identity except in this technical sense, I gave up long ago the cultural consequences of being a Chicano.

The change came gradually but early. When I was beginning grade school, I noted to myself the fact that the classroom environment was so different in its styles and assumptions from my own family environment that survival would essentially entail a choice between both worlds. When I became a student, I was literally "remade"; neither I nor my teachers considered anything I had known before as relevant. I had to forget most of what my culture had provided, because to remember it was a disadvantage. The past and its cultural values became detachable, like a piece of clothing grown heavy on a warm day and finally put away.

Strangely, the discovery that I have been inattentive to my cultural past has arisen because others—student colleagues and faculty members—have started to assume that I am a Chicano. The ease with which the assumption is made forces me to suspect that the label is not meant to suggest cultural, but racial, identity. Nonetheless, as a graduate student and a prospective university faculty member, I am routinely expected to assume intellectual leadership *as a member of a racial minority.* Recently, for example, I heard the moderator of a panel discussion introduce me as "Richard Rodriguez, a Chicano intellectual." I wanted to cor-

*Richard Rodriguez is currently teaching English at the University of California, Berkeley.*

rect the speaker—because I felt guilty representing a non-academic cultural tradition that I had willingly abandoned. So I can only guess what it would have meant to have retained my culture as I entered the classroom, what it would mean for me to be today a *Chicano intellectual.* (The two words juxtaposed excite me; for years I thought a Chicano had to decide between being one or the other.)

Does the fact that I barely spoke any English until I was nine, or that as a child I felt a surge of *self*-hatred whenever a passing teenager would yell a racial slur, or that I saw my skin darken each summer—do any of these facts shape the ideas which I have or am capable of having? Today, I suspect they do—in ways I doubt the moderator who referred to me as a "Chicano intellectual" intended. The peculiar status of being a "Chicano intellectual" makes me grow restless at the thought that I have lost at least as much as I have gained through education.

I remember when, 20 years ago, two grammar-school nuns visited my childhood home. They had come to suggest—with more tact than was necessary, because my parents accepted without question the church's authority—that we make a greater effort to speak as much English around the house as possible. The nuns realized that my brothers and I led solitary lives largely because we were barely able to comprehend English in a school where we were the only Spanish-speaking students. My mother and father complied as best they could. Heroically, they gave up speaking to us in Spanish—the language that formed so much of the family's sense of intimacy in an alien world—and began to speak a broken English. Instead of Spanish sounds, I began hearing sounds that were new, harder, less friendly. More important, I was encouraged to respond in English.

The change in language was the most dramatic and obvious indication that I would become very much like the "gringo"—a term which was used descriptively rather than pejoratively in my home—and unlike the Spanish-speaking relatives who largely constituted my preschool world. Gradually, Spanish became a sound freighted with only a kind of sentimental significance, like the sound of the bedroom clock I listened to in my aunt's house when I spent the night. Just as gradually, English became the language I came not to *hear* because it was the language I used every day, as I gained access to a new, larger society. But the memory of Spanish persisted as a reminder of the society I had left. I can remember occasions when I entered a room and my parents were speaking to one another in Spanish; seeing me, they shifted into their more formalized English. Hearing them speak to me in English troubled me. The bonds their voices once secured were loosened by the new tongue.

This is not to suggest that I was being *forced* to give up my Chicano past. After the initial awkwardness of transition, I committed myself, fully and freely, to the culture of the classroom. Soon what I was learning in school was so antithetical to what my parents knew and did that I was careful about the way I talked about myself at the evening dinner table. Occasionally, there were moments of childish cruelty: a son's condescending to instruct either one of his parents about a "simple" point of English pronunciation or grammar.

Social scientists often remark, about situations such as mine, that children feel a sense of loss as they move away from their working-class identifications and models. Certainly, what I experienced, others have also—whatever their race. Like other generations of, say, Polish-American or Irish-American children coming home from college, I was to know the silence that ensues so quickly after the quick exchange of news and the dwindling of common interests.

In addition, however, education seemed to mean not only a gradual dissolving of familial and class ties but also a change of racial identity. The new language I spoke was only the most obvious reason for my associating the classroom with "gringo" society. The society I knew as Chicano was barely literate—in English *or* Spanish—and so impatient with either prolonged reflection or abstraction that I found the academic environment a sharp contrast. Sharpening the contrast was the stereotype of the Mexican as a mental inferior. (The fear of this stereotype has been so deep that only recently have I been willing to listen to those, like D. H. Lawrence, who celebrate the "noncerebral" Mexican as an alternative to the rational and scientific European man.) Because I did not know how to distinguish the healthy non-rationality of Chicano culture from the mental incompetency of which Chicanos were unjustly accused, I was willing to abandon my non-mental skills in order to disprove the racist's stereotype.

I was wise enough not to feel proud of the person education had helped me to become. I knew that education had led me to repudiate my race. I was frequently labeled a *pocho*, a Mexican with gringo pretensions, not only because I could not speak Spanish but also because I would respond in English with precise and careful sentences. Uncles would laugh good-naturedly, but I detected scorn in their voices. For my grandmother, the least assimilated of my relations, the changes in her grandson since entering school were especially troubling. She remains today a dark and silently critical figure in my memory, a reminder of the Mexican-Indian ancestry that somehow my educational success has violated.

Nonetheless, I became more comfortable reading or writing careful prose than talking to a kitchen filled with listeners, withdrawing from situations to reflect on their significance rather than grasping for meaning at the scene. I remember, one August evening, slipping away from a gathering of aunts and uncles in the backyard, going into a bedroom tenderly lighted by a late sun, and opening a novel about life in nineteenth-century England. There, by an open window, reading, I was barely conscious of the sounds of laughter outside.

With so few fellow Chicanos in the university, I had no chance to develop

"I frankly do not know how my academic autobiography will end. Sometimes I think I will have to leave the campus, in order to reconcile my past and present."

an alternative consciousness. When I spent occasional weekends tutoring lower-class Chicano teenagers or when I talked with Mexican-American janitors and maids around the campus, there was a kind of sympathy—a sense, however privately held—that we knew something about one another. But I regarded them all primarily as people from my past. The maids reminded me of my aunts (similarly employed); the students I tutored reminded me of my cousins (who also spoke English with barrio accents).

WHEN I WAS YOUNG, I was taught to refer to my ancestry as Mexican-American. *Chicano* was a word used among friends or relatives. It implied a familiarity based on shared experience. Spoken casually, the term easily became an insult. In 1968 the word *Chicano* was about to become a political term. I heard it shouted into microphones as Third World groups agitated for increased student and faculty representation in higher education. It was not long before I *became* a Chicano in the eyes of students and faculty members. My racial identity was assumed for only the simplest reasons: my skin color and last name.

On occasion I was asked to account for my interests in Renaissance English literature. When I explained them, declaring a need for cultural assimilation on the campus, my listener would disagree. I sensed suspicion on the part of a number of my fellow minority students. When I could not imitate Spanish pronunciations or the dialect of the barrio, when I was plainly uninterested in wearing ethnic costumes and could not master a special handshake that minority students often used with one another, they knew I was different. And I was. I was assimilated into the culture of a graduate department of English. As a result, I watched how in less than five years nearly every minority graduate student I knew dropped out of school, largely for cultural reasons. Often they didn't understand the value of analyzing literature in professional jargon, which others around them readily adopted. Nor did they move as readily to lofty heights of abstraction. They became easily depressed by the seeming uselessness of the

talk they heard around them. "It's not for real," I still hear a minority student murmur to herself and perhaps to me, shaking her head slowly, as we sat together in a class listening to a discussion on punctuation in a Renaissance epic.

I survived—thanks to the accommodation I had made long before. In fact, I prospered, partly as a result of the political movement designed to increase the enrollment of minority students less assimilated than I in higher education. Suddenly grants, fellowships, and teaching offers became abundant.

In 1972 I went to England on a Fulbright scholarship. I hoped the months of brooding about racial identity were behind me. I wanted to concentrate on my dissertation, which the distractions of an American campus had not permitted. But the freedom I anticipated did not last for long. Barely a month after I had begun working regularly in the reading room of the British Museum, I was surprised, and even frightened, to have to acknowledge that I was not at ease living the rarefied life of the academic. With my pile of research file cards growing taller, the mass of secondary materials and opinions was making it harder for me to say anything original about my subject. Every sentence I wrote, every thought I had, became so loaded with qualifications and footnotes that it said very little. My scholarship became little more than an exercise in caution. I had an accompanying suspicion that whatever I did manage to write and call my dissertation would be of little use. Opening books so dusty that they must not have been used in decades, I began to doubt the value of writing what only a few people would read.

Obviously, I was going through the fairly typical crisis of the American graduate student. But with one difference: After four years of involvement with questions of racial identity, I now saw my problems as a scholar in the context of the cultural issues that had been raised by my racial situation. So much of what my work in the British Museum lacked, my parents' culture possessed. They were people not afraid to generalize or to find insights in their generalities. More important, they had the capacity to make passionate statements, something I was beginning to doubt my dissertation would ever allow me to do. I needed to learn how to trust the use of "I" in my writing the way they trusted its use in their speech. Thus developed a persistent yearning for the very Chicano culture that I had abandoned as useless.

Feelings of depression came occasionally but forcefully. Some days I found my work so oppressive that I had to leave the reading room and stroll through the museum. One afternoon, appropriately enough, I found myself in an upstairs gallery containing Mayan and Aztec sculptures. Even there the sudden yearning for a Chicano past seemed available to me only as nostalgia. One morning, as I was reading a book about Puritan autobiography, I overheard two Spaniards whispering to one another. I did not hear what they said, but I did hear the sound of their Spanish—and it embraced me, filling my mind with swirling images of a past long abandoned.

I RETURNED FROM ENGLAND, disheartened, a few months later. My dissertation was coming along well, but I did not know whether I wanted to submit it. Worse, I did not know whether I wanted a career in higher education. I detested the prospect of spending the rest of my life in libraries and classrooms, in touch with my past only through the binoculars nostalgia makes available. I knew that I could not simply re-create a version of what I would have been like had I not become an academic. There was no possibility of going back. But if the culture of my birth was to survive, it would have to animate my academic work. That was the lesson of the British Museum.

I frankly do not know how my academic autobiography will end. Sometimes I think I will have to leave the campus, in order to reconcile my past and present. Other times, more optimistically, I think that a kind of negative reconciliation is already in progress, that I can make creative use of my sense of loss. For instance, with my sense of the cleavage between past and present, I can, as a literary critic, identify issues in Renaissance pastoral—a literature which records the feelings of the courtly when confronted by the alternatives of rural and rustic life. And perhaps I can speak with unusual feeling about the price we must pay, or have paid, as a rational society for confessing seventeenth-century Cartesian faiths. Likewise, because of my sense of cultural loss, I may be able to identify more readily than another the ways in which language has meaning simply as sound and what the printed word can and cannot give us. At the very least, I can point up the academy's tendency to ignore the cultures beyond its own horizons.

*February 1974*
On my job interview the department chairman has been listening to an oral version of what I have just written. I tell him he should be very clear about the fact that I am not, at the moment, confident enough to call myself a Chicano. Perhaps I never will be. But as I say all this, I look at the interviewer. He smiles softly. Has he heard what I have been trying to say? I wonder. I repeat: I have lost the ability to bring my past into my present; I do not know how to be a Chicano reader of Spenser or Shakespeare. All that remains is a desire for the past. He sighs, preoccupied, looking at my records. Would I be interested in teaching a course on the Mexican novel in translation? Do I understand that part of my duties would require that I become a counselor of minority students? What was the subject of that dissertation I did in England? Have I read the book on the same subject that was just published this month?

Behind the questioner, a figure forms in my imagination: my grandmother, her face solemn and still. ☐

# 30

# The American Indian:
# An Overview

By ROBERT L. FAHERTY

*Eddie Big Beaver. Blackfeet. Browning, Montana, 1937.*

FOR ALMOST FIVE centuries, the original inhabitants of what is now the United States and
those people who have come to call themselves
Americans have remained largely strangers. This
situation is beginning to change, but years of mis-
understanding, suspicion, and mistreatment are not
easily brushed aside. Misconceptions that have become deeply enrooted are difficult to eradicate.

Perhaps most devastating is the image of the Indian
as savage, an image that has influenced the view of
white society toward the Indian since the earliest days
of contact. Either a nomadic, hostile brute impeding
the civilizing process of advancing settlers or a noble,
unspoiled child of nature symbolizing freedom for
Rousseau and others, the Indian was stereotyped as
uncivilized, and mentally, culturally, and religiously
inferior to the white. Denied equal status as a person,
he could be converted, removed, exploited.

Sometimes early writers stated bluntly that Indians
were warlike, crude, lazy, simple, unreliable, or the
like; at other times they used words that implied the
same moral judgments. When Indians killed whites,
it was a "massacre," but whites only "fought" or
"battled" Indians. The whites farmed the land,
while Indians were depicted essentially as hunters and
gatherers. White people are pictured protecting their
homes and families from the savage "menace" or
"peril." But it is rare to find a description of the
Indian defending his life or his homeland against the

ever encroaching white. According to the whites, the
westward-moving frontier was the manifest destiny of
the white culture, and the Indians gave ground inevitably and deservedly to that superior culture.

This conception has colored the official relationship
between the United States government and the Indian
societies. During his Second Annual Message in
December, 1830, President Andrew Jackson justified
his signing of the Indian Removal Act some months
previously in the following words:

> What good man would prefer a country covered with
> forests and ranged by a few thousand savages to our
> extensive Republic, studded with cities, towns, and pros-
> perous farms, embellished with more than twelve million
> happy people, and filled with all the blessings of liberty,
> civilization, and religion?[1]

In 1871, Congress terminated the making of treaties
with Indian tribes on the theory that it was degrading
for Congress to give equal status to nations of primitive
people. Government policy—whether it be the allot-
ment policy legislated in 1887, whereby reservation
Indians would be granted private property, or the
reservation-termination policy of the 1950's, whereby
Indians would be relocated to urban centers—has
returned time and time again to the idea of civilizing
the Indian by assimilating him into white society.

The image of the savage Indian has been subtly
reinforced in other ways. Anthropological literature
has concentrated almost totally on aspects of Indian
life that could be thought of as "aboriginal" or "native." Anthropologists and ethnologists have tended
to present not the dynamic, living, changing complex

---

[1] Quoted in Roy Harvey Pearce, *The Savages of America*
(Baltimore: Johns Hopkins Press, 1953), p. 57.

150

that is the Indian community under study, but only the more traditional elements in that culture. For example, one of the most often described ethnographic events among Indians in the southwestern United States is the Hopi snake dance. From a survey of available literature, it would be natural for the casual reader to infer that the snake dance is the most significant event in the lives of the Hopi people. Instead, the focus on the snake dance only reflects the fascination that the handling of live rattlesnakes holds for members of the non-Indian culture.[2]

Popular literature, movies, and television have contributed to the stereotype. Even television documentaries that attempt to present the story of Indian people have inevitably shown little more than the poverty on a few reservations. Although these conditions certainly exist, their exclusive showing tends to label the Indian as someone who is not quite able to survive on his own.

In a recent article, Vine Deloria expressed great concern that at Wounded Knee, South Dakota, in 1972, the Indian activists had resorted to racing around on horseback before the television cameras like warriors of old. Thus the relevant social issues of the protest were lost and the worst suspicions of whites were reinforced at a time when the ancient image of the savage could have been buried once and for all.[3]

A second lingering misconception is that Indians are a vanishing race. This image, which gained prominence at the beginning of the twentieth century, was captured in James E. Fraser's statue of a bent and battered Indian sitting on an equally forlorn horse, both with heads bowed. According to the title of the statue, this was "The End of the Trail." At about the same time, in 1909, Joseph K. Dixon, working with the Bureau of Indian Affairs, arranged "The Last Great Indian Council." It included 21 representative Indian chiefs, scouts, and warriors, and was intended to be a farewell to a people on the verge of extinction.[4]

On the contrary, however, Indians are increasing in greater numbers than any other group in the United States, although the Indian population decreased dramatically by the end of the last century as a result of warfare, removal, disease, and the destruction of the buffalo. During the last decade, the rate of population growth in Indian communities on or near federal trust land averaged about 2.5 percent, although this figure seems to be tapering off.

Furthermore, the cultures of the native Americans have not withered and died through the process of assimilation. Indian cultures are changing, yet traditional values and institutions live on.

A third mistaken notion is that Indians are all alike. They were not alike in the past, and they are not alike today. There is no such creature as *the* American Indian. As Harold E. Fey and D'Arcy McNickle pointed out in their study, *Indians and Other Americans,* "There is no 'Indian language,' no 'Indian religion,' no 'Indian character'—even the racial strain was a mixture of several physical types."[5]

At the time of the first contact between Indians and whites, there was far greater linguistic and cultural diversity in the New World than in Europe. The number of distinct languages depends upon the recognition of what constitutes a separate language. Some 200 languages have been claimed for aboriginal California alone. Anthropologists' estimates range from a conservative 200 to between 600 and 800 as the number of languages in use in the area that was to become the United States.

Besides speaking different languages, tribes varied widely in their philosophies, in their social, political, and religious institutions, and in their practices. Indian governments, for example, ranged from a loose grouping of family groups and village communities among California Indians to the complex Iroquois Confederation of highly organized tribes. The mode of obtaining food or of building homes, of raising children or of burying the dead varied notably from tribe to tribe. What is more, there was considerable diversity within most of the tribes.

Though it may take different forms, Indian cultural pluralism continues. Overlaid on the legacy of distinct tribal traditions is, of course, the reservation-urban dichotomy. Many Indians have moved off the reservations to urban areas. Yet even this distinction is not sufficient to explain the highly complex social-cultural character of the Indian people. Reservations are not all the same. On some reservations, per capita income is no more than a few dollars per year; on others, like the vast Navajo reservation, tribal organization, tourism, industry, government aid, utilization of resources, and so on have provided a fair source of income for much of the Indian population. Indians in the cities, though normally poor, show the same variation.

As a further complication, urbanism is moving onto some reservations. Peter MacDonald, the tribal chairman, has announced the inauguration of a new Navajo nation, with a capital city that will be centered in a reservation as large as the states of Massachusetts,

[2] See Bernard L. Fontana, "Savage Anthropologists and Unvanishing Indians in the American Southwest." Paper read at the 67th meeting of the American Anthropological Association (unpublished manuscript).

[3] Vine Deloria, Jr., "The American Indian Image," *Encyclopedia of Indians of the Americas,* vol. 1, 1974, p. 41.

[4] See Joseph K. Dixon, *The Vanishing Race: The Last Great Indian Council* (New York: Popular Library, 1972). This book was originally published in 1913.

[5] Harold E. Fey and D'Arcy McNickle, *Indians and Other Americans* (New York: Harper & Row, 1970), p. 14.

Vermont, and New Hampshire combined. MacDonald has indicated that the new state will reflect in all its aspects the character of Navajo culture. Other examples could be cited for what might be termed emerging new states and on-reservation urbanism.

The range and character of Indian organizations is another indication of the intricacy of the Indian community. National organizations include the National Congress of American Indians and the National Tribal Chairmen's Association. Such groups as the American Indian Movement, the National Indian Youth Movement, and numerous university student organizations represent the younger and often more activist elements among native Americans. Particular groups are represented by such organizations as the National Indian Physician's Association, the National Indian Education Association, the National Indian Women's Association, and others. Among the urban Indians, there are some 50 different organizations in the Los Angeles area alone.

A fourth stereotype is the belief that the Indian does not change; he is as unbending in the face of time as he is pictured to be in the face of torture. Indian cultures and societies are examined and understood as they once were, before contact with the white man. Subsequent changes, when they are noted, are attributed not to any internal, creative, adaptive dynamism on the part of the Indian communities but only to a passive acceptance of external relationships with, and influences from, the white culture. The post-contact history of a tribe thus becomes solely the story of Indian response to white stimulus, and there is virtually no account of the recent history of the tribe.[6]

## WHO AND HOW MANY?

Who, then, is the Indian? The answer to the question is both simple and complex. It is simple enough to say that an Indian is an individual who can trace his or her origins to the indigenous peoples of America. But to go beyond this involves consideration of a number of different factors.

Ethnologically, must an individual be a full-blooded Indian, or three-quarters, or half? Culturally, how much of the traditional life style or religion must he maintain? Sociologically, must he live on a reservation or, at the least, be enrolled in an Indian community.

In the legal sense, the question of who is an Indian is most important, because of the distinct rights and obligations of Indian citizens as opposed to non-Indian citizens. For example, an Indian may share in his tribe's land holdings, which may be quite extensive. Yet there is no clear-cut general legal definition of "Indian" in the United States. In each legal case, the question of whether or not an individual is an Indian must be sought in the applicable statutes, administrative decisions, and opinions. As a rule of thumb, however, there are two basic qualifications: (1) that some of the individual's ancestors lived in America before its discovery by the Europeans, and (2) that the individual is accepted as an Indian by the legally constituted Indian community in which he lives.[7]

The legal question actually becomes more social and political than biological. A full-blooded Indian can withdraw from a tribe and thereby, for all legal purposes, cease to be an Indian. On the contrary, an individual with only the most tenuous Indian ancestry can be accepted by the tribe and thus can be legally an Indian. It is interesting to note that a Wyandot tribal roll that was proposed to Congress in the 1930's listed a person with only 1/256 degree of Wyandot blood.[8]

This indicates the importance of two factors operating on a deeply internal, personal level. Does the tribe or community consider the individual to be one of them? Does the individual consider himself to be part of the tribe or community? If an individual has left the reservation or village, how long can he stay away from the ceremonies, festivals, and major moments in the life of his people—that is, how long can he miss his "Indianness"—before either the tribe or the individual decides he no longer belongs? There are some traditionalists who believe that once an individual has left the community—even to take a professional or academic position—he has abandoned his Indianness. This is an extreme attitude, but most groups demand at least periodic contact.

All of this renders perplexing the question of how many Indians there are in the United States. Population estimates vary in accordance with the definition of Indian. Furthermore, accurate demographic figures are extremely difficult to obtain. Some Indians still live in remote areas that are difficult to reach, and many a census taker obtains his information about the numbers, names, and ages of families from a convenient trading post. The fact that an individual Indian may be known under a variety of names is a further hazard.

Bearing these observations in mind, we can note that according to the 1970 census the total number of Indians in the United States was 827,091; they constituted slightly more than 0.4 percent of the country's total population. Unofficial estimates place the Indian population as high as 15 million. It is safe to say that there are several million people in the coun-

---

[6] See Robert F. Berkhofer, Jr., "Indian Americans and United States History," *National Council for Social Studies Yearbook,* 1973.

[7] See *Federal Indian Law* (Washington, D.C.: U.S. Government Printing Office, 1958), pp. 4–12. *Federal Indian Law* is a revision and updating through 1956 of the *Handbook of Federal Indian Law* prepared by Felix S. Cohen and first printed in 1940.

[8] *Federal Indian Law,* p. 986n2.

try who, according to one or another valid definition, are Indians.

Despite the conservative nature of its population figures, the 1970 census provided interesting data. The state with the largest Indian population was Oklahoma, with 97,731 Indians; this was followed by Arizona (95,812), California (91,018), New Mexico (72,788), and Alaska (51,528). These five states account for almost one-half of the Indian population. The state with the highest percentage of Indian population was Alaska—where Indians constitute more than 17 percent of the total population—followed by New Mexico, Arizona, and South Dakota. A total of ten states have an Indian population that is one percent or more of their total population. These statistics show that, though Indians constitute a small minority of the total national population, they are highly concentrated in the Southwest, Oklahoma, the Dakotas, and Alaska. In these regions, the Indians can be a powerful social and political force.

Of the Indians reported in the census, 37 percent live in "Standard Metropolitan Statistical Areas." This metropolitan Indian group, however, is less than one-fourth of one percent (.22) of the total metropolitan population in the United States. The Los Angeles-Long Beach metropolitan area has by far the largest Indian population—numbering almost 25,000 —followed in order by Tulsa, Oklahoma City, New York, San Francisco-Oakland, Phoenix, Minneapolis-St. Paul, Seattle-Everett, Chicago, and Tucson. According to these figures, Indians have moved in large numbers to metropolitan areas. The reasons for this shift are largely economic. The Indian is attracted by the idea of finding a job and making more money then he can on the reservation.

There are, however, some indications that a "return to the reservation" movement is also taking place. One Gros Ventre Indian, a recent graduate of the University of California at Berkeley who spent some time with the Indian community on Alcatraz, recently reported that perhaps as many as 80 percent of the Indians that he knew in the San Francisco Bay area were returning to their tribal communities. He himself was returning to work toward the establishment of a tribal museum and culture center on his reservation. According to this young man, many Indians who had moved to the urban area had made a fair living, but they were deciding that the violence, the cost of living, the hassle—in short, the quality of life —in the urban environment were not worth it. Even for those who periodically go to the city for a while, the reservation remains a sanctuary to which they can return, a sacred place where they can be at home with their families. According to him, this is something that neither the white, the black, the Puerto Rican, the chicano, nor any other group in the United States has.

If, indeed, non-Indians have been generally misinformed about the Indian peoples, what are some of the steps that might be taken to correct this situation? The following observations may provide some broad guidelines.

The non-Indian has to recognize that there are fundamental differences between the majority white culture and the cultures of the Indian peoples. Many differences could be cited, but the point should be sufficiently made by briefly examining how the two cultures differ in their conception of time, decision making, and being.

To the white culture, time is a regularized object whose symbol is the clock. Our schools, offices, means of transportation, television, and all our institutions are ordered according to arbitrarily established units. We speak of "saving" time, of "wasting" time, or of "spending" time. We pay people for their time rather than for what they do or how well they do it. Punctuality geared to the clock is a virtue and, in fact, a necessity in our highly industrialized society.

Set off against this is natural time, a fluid continuum that is geared to the rising and setting of the sun and to the changes in seasons. It is this sense of time that most Indians—many of whom have been reared in the essentially rural, non-industrialized environment of the reservation—have internalized. Indians joke among themselves about operating "on Indian time." This means, for example, that a community meeting will start this evening sharp. Whether the meeting starts at seven o'clock, eight o'clock, or nine o'clock, it will be held, and it will continue until everyone who wishes has had his or her say.

This leads into the next area of cultural difference. Within the white culture, decision making is based on a concept of authority that is exercised on a vertical plane. Power is exerted by those above on those below. We recognize that some people are more legit-

*Almost a century of wisdom and service is reflected in the dignity of the face of Blackfeet Chief Wades-In-Water, who served as chief of Indian police on his reservation for 25 years, oftentimes the uneasy liaison between white law and Indian custom. He was the son of another famous chief—Running Crane.*

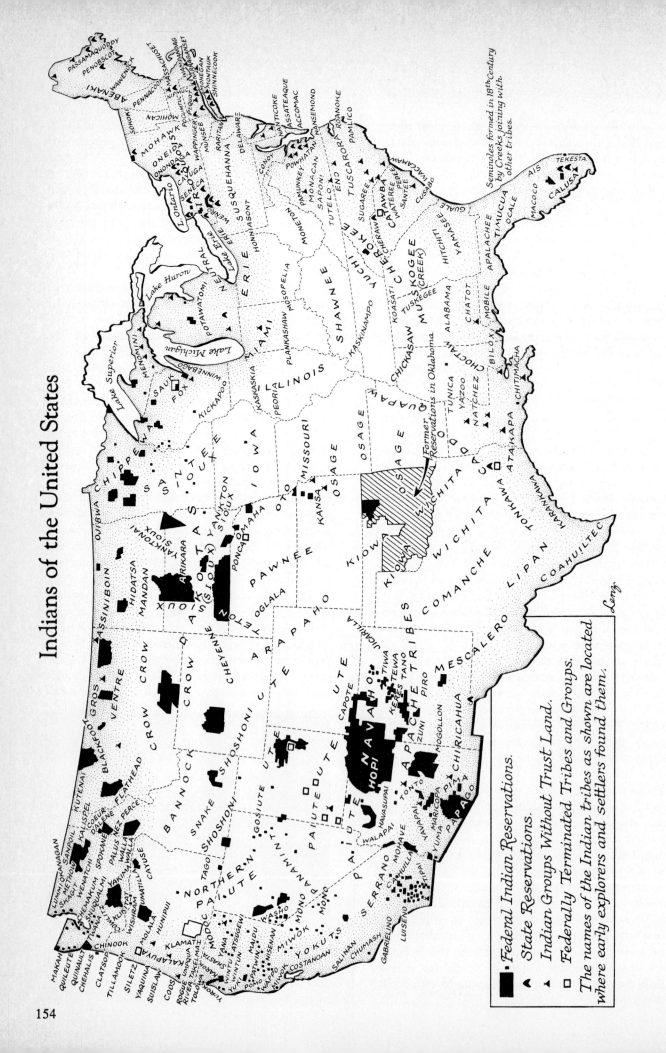

Indians of the United States

imately in power than others; someone makes decisions—usually after a certain amount of discussion or debate—and issues orders that others then act upon.

Authority in the Indian cultures is of a more horizontal type. The councils of many Indian tribes last for days because of the necessity of reaching unanimity on a decision. Orders are not issued; consensus agreements are reached.

Another cultural difference regards the identification of self and of how one regards self in relation to the world outside. Individuals who have been raised in the white culture have learned to think of themselves in a perpetual state of becoming. They are taught as children to live for the future—to be discontent with what they are and forever to plan to improve. A white American looks forward to being smarter, to having more money, to owning a larger house, to being the first or the most or the best.

In contrast, it makes little sense to ask an Indian child what he wants to be when he grows up. Indian children already are. They are children. They do not have to wait to be. And so it is through life. One is what one is; one is continually in a state of being rather than of becoming. One will become other things, of course, but the important thing is improving oneself as he is now.

Once the non-Indian accepts the fact that there are cultural differences, then he must appreciate the value of cultural pluralism in the United States. We must abandon the older national ideal of assimilation, the "melting pot" into which diverse peoples would be blended to lose their distinctive character. We must accept the idea that the United States is strong precisely because of its diversity; the contributions of each group should be honored, preserved, and enhanced in the enrichment of the whole.

The non-Indian must turn to the Indians themselves for more information about and appreciation of their history and their culture as it was and as it is. For far too long the dispensers of knowledge about the Indian have been the non-Indian explorer, soldier, missionary, government official, or scholar. The Indian has been described in various ways, sometimes not accurately, always from the non-Indian point of view. In most instances the Indian and his community have emerged as static and passive elements in society. The Indian's role in history and the reality of his continuity from the past to the present have been vague at best and often completely lost.

In recent years, several tribes (*e. g.*, Zuni, Southern Ute, Nez Perce, Cheyenne-Arapaho, and Navajo) have begun systematically to gather and publish their own materials about their history, language, literature,

music, and other elements of their culture. They have especially asked their old people to record on tape their memories of past years, ancient legends, and important leaders and events.[9]

For professionals in history, anthropology, and other appropriate disciplines, these projects can provide important insights into the past, present, and future of the Indian peoples. There is, however, discussion among these professionals about the merit of the projects because, for the most part, they are being conducted by non-academics. Questions have been raised about the validity of the use of oral history or whether these are "authorized" histories. Regarding oral history, it might be mentioned that Western civilization's grandest records began with oral history: the Iliad, the Odyssey, and the Old Testament attest to this fact. Regarding authorized history, it might be said that previous history written by outside parties about Indian people was unauthorized. This is not to say that every work that is written by an Indian will be a good work or even an accurate work; nonetheless, these projects should be welcomed with an open mind by the academic community.

## DIALOGUES BEGINNING

Several recent items give evidence of what is hopefully the beginning of a dialogue between the white scholarly community and the Indian peoples. Indians from the United States took part in two presentations at the International Congress of Americanists held in September, 1974, at Mexico City. The congress is a biennial gathering of scholars, almost exclusively white, from Europe and the Americas to exchange ideas and research about questions relating to the native populations of the Americas. One of the seminars during the recent congress involved a group of Indian academics who discussed their attempts to establish Native American Studies programs at various universities. Another even more remarkable seminar included presentations by non-academic Indians who explained the work they are doing in their tribal history and culture projects. In December, 1974, a group of tribal historians will be on the program at the American Historical Association meeting. Furthermore, organizations like the National Anthropological Archives at the Smithsonian Institution and the Center for the History of the American Indian at the Newberry Library are beginning to work closely with a diversified and growing group of tribal historians and archivists.

If this type of dialogue blossoms and finds its way into print and the other popular means of communication, it could open the door to a deeper and more accurate understanding of the Indian peoples and to a better and more truly pluralistic society in which every individual can respect another's right to express his culture. ∎

[9] See Dave Warren, "Concepts and Significance of Tribal History/Literature Projects." Paper prepared for the Research and Cultural Studies Development Section, Institute of American Indian Arts (Santa Fe, 1973).

# 31

Michael Novak

# WHITE ETHNIC

The anger of a man disinherited by the authorized American fantasy

GROWING UP IN AMERICA has been an assault upon my sense of worthiness. It has also been a kind of liberation and delight.

There must be countless women in America who have known for years that something is peculiarly unfair, yet who have found it only recently possible, because of Women's Liberation, to give tongue to their pain. In recent months, I have experienced a similar inner thaw, a gradual relaxation, a willingness to think about feelings heretofore shepherded out of sight.

I am born of PIGS—those Poles, Italians, Greeks, and Slavs, non-English-speaking immigrants, numbered so heavily among the workingmen of this nation. Not particularly liberal, nor radical, born into a history not white Anglo-Saxon and not Jewish—born outside what in America is considered the intellectual mainstream. And thus privy to neither power nor status nor intellectual voice.

Those Poles of Buffalo and Milwaukee—so notoriously taciturn, sullen, nearly speechless. Who has ever understood them? It is not that Poles do not feel emotion: what is their history if not dark passion, romanticism, betrayal, courage, blood? But where in America is there anywhere a language for voicing what a Christian Pole in this nation feels? He has no Polish culture left him, no Polish tongue. Yet Polish feelings do not go easily into the idiom of happy America, the America of the Anglo-Saxons and, yes, in the arts, the Jews. (The Jews have long been a culture of the word, accustomed to exile, skilled in scholarship and in reflection. The Christian Poles are largely of peasant origin, free men for hardly more than a hundred years.) Of what shall the man of Buffalo think, on his way to work in the mills, departing from his relatively dreary home and street? What roots does he have? What language of the heart is available to him?

The PIGS are not silent willingly. The silence burns like hidden coals in the chest.

All four of my grandparents, unknown to one another, arrived in America from the same county in Slovakia. My grandfather had a small farm in Pennsylvania; his wife died in a wagon accident. Meanwhile, a girl of fifteen arrived on Ellis Island, dizzy, a little ill from witnessing births and deaths and illnesses aboard the crowded ship, with a sign around her neck lettered "PASSAIC." There an aunt told her of the man who had lost his wife in Pennsylvania. She went. They were married. Inheriting his three children, each year for five years she had one of her own; she was among the lucky, only one died. When she was twenty-two, mother of seven, her husband died. And she resumed the work she had begun in Slovakia at the town home of a man known to us now only as "the Professor": she housecleaned and she laundered.

I heard this story only weeks ago. Strange that I had not asked insistently before. Odd that I should have such shallow knowledge of my roots. Amazing to me that I do not know what my family suffered, endured, learned, hoped these past six or seven generations. It is as if there were no project on which we all have been involved. As if history, in some way, began with my father and with me.

Let me hasten to add that the estrangement I have come to feel derives not only from a lack of family history. All my life, I have been made to feel a slight uneasiness when I must say my name. Under challenge in grammar school concerning my nationality, I had been instructed by my father to announce proudly: "American." When my family moved from the Slovak ghetto of Johnstown to the WASP suburb on the hill, my mother impressed upon us how well we must be dressed, and show good manners, and behave —people think of us as "different" and we mustn't give them any cause. "Whatever you do, marry a Slovak girl," was other advice to a similar end: "They cook. They clean. They take good care of you. For your own good."

When it was revealed to me that most movie stars and many other professionals had abandoned European names in order to feed American fantasies, I felt only a little sadness. One of my uncles, for business reasons and rather late in life, changed his name too, to a simple German variant. Not long, either, after World War II.

Nowhere in my schooling do I recall an attempt to put me in touch with my own history. The strategy was clearly to make an American of me. English literature, American literature; and even the history books, as I recall them, were peopled mainly by Anglo-Saxons from Boston (where most historians seemed to live). Not even my native Pennsylvania, let alone my Slovak forebears, counted for very many paragraphs. I don't remember feeling envy or regret: a feeling, perhaps, of unimportance, of remoteness, of not having heft enough to count.

The fact that I was born a Catholic also complicated life. What is a Catholic but what everybody else is in reaction against? Protestants reformed "the Whore of Babylon," others were "enlightened" from it, and Jews had reason to help Catholicism and the social structures it was rooted in to fall apart. My history books and the whole of education hummed in upon that point (during crucial years I attended a public, not a parochial, school): to be modern is decidedly not to be medieval; to be reasonable is not to be dogmatic; to be free is clearly not to live under ecclesiastical authority; to be scientific is not to attend ancient rituals, cherish irrational symbols, indulge in mythic practices. It is hard to grow up

Catholic in America without becoming defensive, perhaps a little paranoid, feeling forced to divide the world between "us" and "them."

We had a special language all our own, our own pronunciation for words we shared in common with others (Augustine, contemplative), sights and sounds and smells in which few others participated (incense at Benediction of the Most Blessed Sacrament, Forty Hours, wakes, and altar bells at the silent consecration of the Host); and we had our own politics and slant on world affairs. Since earliest childhood, I have known about a "power elite" that runs America: the boys from the Ivy League in the State Department, as opposed to the Catholic boys from Hoover's FBI who, as Daniel Moynihan once put it, keep watch on them. And on a whole host of issues, my people have been, though largely Democratic, conservative: on censorship, on Communism, on abortion, on religious schools . . . Harvard and Yale long meant "them" to us.

The language of Spiro Agnew, the language of George Wallace, excepting its idiom, awakens childhood memories in me of men arguing in the barbershop, of my uncle drinking so much beer he threatened to lay his dick upon the porch rail and wash the whole damn street with steaming piss---while cursing the niggers in the mill, below, and the Yankees in the mill, above: mill-

"Nowhere in my schooling do I recall an attempt to put me in touch with my own history. The strategy was clearly to make an American of me."

CHARLES GATEWOOD

stones he felt pressing him. Other relatives were duly shocked, but everybody loved Uncle George: he said what he thought.

We did not feel this country belonged to us. We felt fierce pride in it, more loyalty than anyone could know. But we felt blocked at every turn. There were not many intellectuals among us, not even very many professional men. Laborers mostly. Small businessmen, agents for corporations perhaps. Content with a little, yes, modest in expectation. But somehow feeling cheated. For a thousand years the Slovaks survived Hungarian hegemony, and our strategy here remained the same: endurance and steady work. Slowly, one day, we would overcome.

A special word is required about a complicated symbol: sex. To this day my mother finds it hard to spell the word intact, preferring to write "s--." Not that much was made of sex in our environment. And that's the point: silence. Demonstrative affection, emotive dances, exuberance Anglo-Saxons seldom seem to share; but on the realities of sex, discretion. Reverence, perhaps; seriousness, surely. On intimacies, it is as though our tongues had been stolen. As though in peasant life for a thousand years the context had been otherwise. Passion, yes; romance, yes; family and children, certainly; but sex, rather a minor part of life.

Imagine, then, the conflict in the generation of my brothers, sister, and myself. (The book critic for the *New York Times* reviews on the same day two new novels of fantasy: one a pornographic fantasy to end all such fantasies [he writes], the other about a mad family representing in some comic way the redemption wrought by Jesus Christ. In language and verve, the books are rated even. In theme, the reviewer notes his embarrassment in reporting a religious fantasy, but no embarrassment at all about the preposterous pornography.) Suddenly, what for a thousand years was minor becomes an all-absorbing investigation. It is, perhaps, one drama when the ruling classes (I mean subscribers to *The New Yorker*, I suppose) move progressively, generation by generation since Sigmund Freud, toward consciousness-raising sessions in Clit. Lib., but wholly another when we stumble suddenly upon mores staggering any expectation our grandparents ever cherished.

YET MORE SIGNIFICANT in the ethnic experience in America is the intellectual world one meets: the definition of values, ideas, and purposes emanating from universities, books, magazines, radio, and television. One hears one's own voice echoed back neither by spokesmen of "Middle America" (so complacent, smug, nativist, and Protestant), nor by "the intellectuals." Almost unavoidably, perhaps, education in America leads the student who entrusts his soul to it in a direction that, lacking a better word, we might call liberal: respect for individual conscience, a sense of social responsibility, trust in the free exchange of ideas and procedures of dissent, a certain confidence in the ability of men to "reason together" and to adjudicate their differences, a frank recognition of the vitality of the unconscious, a willingness to protect workers and the poor against the vast economic power of industrial corporations, and the like.

On the other hand, the liberal imagination has appeared to be astonishingly universalist, and relentlessly missionary. Perhaps the metaphor "enlightenment" offers a key. One is initiated into light. Liberal education tends to separate children from their parents, from their roots, from their history, in the cause of a universal and superior religion. One is taught, regarding the unenlightened (even if they be one's Uncles George and Peter, one's parents, one's brothers perhaps), what can only be called a modern equivalent of *odium theologicum*. Richard Hofstadter described anti-intellectualism in America, more acurately in nativist America than in ethnic America, but I have yet to encounter a comparable treatment of anti-unenlightenment among our educated classes.

In particular, I have regretted and keenly felt the absence of that sympathy for PIGS that simple human feeling might have prodded intelligence to muster: that same sympathy that the educated find so easy to conjure up for black culture, Chicano culture, Indian culture, and other cultures of the poor. In such cases, one finds, the universalist pretensions of liberal culture are suspended: some groups, at least, are entitled to be both different and respected. Why do the educated classes find it so difficult to want to understand the man who drives a beer truck, or the fellow with a helmet working on a site across the street with plumbers and electricians, while their sensitivities race easily to Mississippi or even Bedford-Stuyvesant?

There are deep secrets here, no doubt, unvoiced fantasies and scarcely admitted historical resentments. Few persons, in describing "Middle Americans," "the Silent Majority," or Scammon and Wattenberg's "typical American voter," distinguish clearly enough between the nativist American and the ethnic American. The first is likely to be Protestant, the second Catholic. Both may be, in various ways, conservative, loyalist, and unenlightened. Each has his own agonies, fears, betrayed expectations. Neither is ready, quite, to become an ally of the other. Neither has the same history behind him here. Neither has the same hopes. Neither is living out the same psychic voyage. Neither shares the same symbols or has the same sense of reality. The rhetoric and metaphors differ.

There is overlap, of course. But country music is not a polka; a successful politician in a Chicago ward needs a very different "common touch" from the one used by the county clerk in Normal; the urban experience of immigration lacks that mellifluous, optimistic, biblical vision of the good America that springs naturally to the lips of politicians from the Bible Belt. The nativist tends to believe with Richard Nixon that he "knows America and the American heart is good." The ethnic tends to believe that every American who preceded him has an angle, and that he, by God, will one day find one too. (Often, ethnics complain that by working hard, obeying the law, trusting their political leaders, and relying upon the American Dream they now have only their own naïveté to blame for rising no higher than they have.)

It goes without saying that the intellectuals do not love Middle America, and that for all the good warm discovery of America that preoccupied them during the 1950s, no strong tide of respect accumulated in their hearts for the Yahoos, Babbitts, Agnews, and Nixons of the land. Willie Morris, in *North Toward Home*, writes poignantly of the chill, parochial outreach of the liberal sensibility, its failure to engage the humanity of the modest, ordinary little man west of the Hudson. The intellectual's map of the United States is succinct: "Two coasts connected by United Airlines."

Unfortunately, it seems, the ethnics erred in attempting to Americanize themselves, before clearing the project with the educated classes. They learned to wave the flag and to send their sons to war. (The Poles in World War I were 4 per cent of the population but took 12 per cent of the casualties.) They learned to support their President—an easy task, after all, for those accustomed abroad to obeying authority. And where would they have been if Franklin Roosevelt had not sided with them against established interests? They knew a little about Communism, the radicals among them in one way, and by far the larger number of conservatives in another. Not a few exchange letters to this day with cousins and uncles who did not leave for America when they might have, whose lot is demonstrably harder and less than free.

Finally, the ethnics do not like, or trust, or even understand the intellectuals. It is not easy to feel uncomplicated affection for those who call you "pig," "fascist," "racist." One had not yet grown accustomed not to hearing "Hunkie," "Polack," "Spic," "Mick," "Dago," and the rest. At no little sacrifice, one had apologized for foods that smelled too strong for Anglo-Saxon noses, moderated the wide swings of Slavic and Italian emotion, learned decorum, given oneself to education American style, tried to learn tolerance and assimilation. Each generation criticized the earlier for its authoritarian and European and old-fashioned ways. "Up-to-date" was a moral lever. And now when the process nears completion, when a generation appears that speaks without accent and goes to college, still you are considered pigs, fascists, and racists.

Racists? Our ancestors owned no slaves. Most of us ceased being serfs only in the last 200 years —the Russians in 1861. What have we got against blacks or blacks against us? Competition, yes, for jobs and homes and communities; competition, even, for political power. Italians, Lithuanians, Slovaks, Poles are not, in principle, against "community control," or even against ghettos of our own. Whereas the Anglo-Saxon model appears to be a system of atomic individuals and high mobility, our model has tended to stress communities of our own, attachment to family and relatives, stability, and roots. We tend to have a fierce sense of attachment to our homes, having been homeowners less than three generations: a home is almost fulfillment enough for one man's life. We have most ambivalent feelings about suburban assimilation and mobility. The melting pot is a kind of homogenized soup, and its mores only partly appeal to us: to some, yes, and to others, no.

It must be said that we think we are better people than the blacks. Smarter, tougher, harder working, stronger in our families. But maybe many of us are not so sure. Maybe we are uneasy. Emotions here are delicate. One can understand the immensely more difficult circumstances under which the blacks have suffered, and one is not unaware of peculiar forms of fear, envy, and suspicion across color lines. How much of all this we learned in America, by being made conscious of our olive skin, brawny backs, accents, names, and cultural quirks, is not plain to us. Racism is not our invention; we did not bring it with us; we found it here. And should we pay the price for America's guilt? Must all the gains of the blacks, long overdue, be chiefly at our expense? Have we, once again, no defenders but ourselves?

TELEVISION ANNOUNCERS and college professors seem so often to us to be speaking in a code. When they say "white racism," it does not seem to be their own traditions they are impugning. Perhaps it is paranoia, but it seems that the affect accompanying such words is directed at steelworkers, auto workers, truck drivers, and police—at us. When they say "humanism" or "progress," it seems to us like moral pressure to abandon our own traditions, our faith, our associations, in order to reap higher rewards in the culture of the national corporations—that culture of quantity, homogeneity, replaceability, and mobility. They want to grind off all the angles, hold us to the lathes, shape us to be objective, meritocratic, orderly, and fully American.

In recent years, of course, a new cleavage has sprung open among the intellectuals. Some seem to speak for technocracy—for that alliance of science, industry, and humanism whose heaven is "progress." Others seem to be taking the view once ascribed to ecclesiastical conservatives and traditionalists: that commitment to enlightenment is narrow, ideological, and hostile to the best interests of mankind. In the past, the great alliance for progress sprang from the conviction that "knowledge is power." Both humanists and scientists could agree on that, and labored in their separate ways to make the institutions of knowledge dominant in society: break the shackles of the Church, extend suffrage to the middle classes and finally to all, win untrammeled liberty for the marketplace of ideas. Today it is no longer plain that the power brought by knowledge is humanistic. Thus the parting of the ways.

Science has ever carried with it the stories and symbols of a major religion. It is ruthlessly universalist. If its participants are not "saved," they are nonetheless "enlightened," which isn't bad. And every single action of the practicing scientist, no matter how humble, could once be understood as a contribution to the welfare of the human race; each smallest gesture was invested with meaning, given a place in a scheme, and weighted with redemptive power. Moreover, the scientist was in possession of "the truth," indeed of the very meaning of and validating procedures for the word. His role was therefore sacred.

Imagine, then, a young strapping Slovak entering an introductory course in the Sociology of Religion at the nearby state university or community college. Is he sent back to his Slovak roots, led to recover paths of experience latent in all his instincts and reflexes, given an image of the life of his grandfather that suddenly, in recog-

"The ethnic tends to believe that every American who preceded him has an angle, and that he, by God, will one day find one too."

GEORGE GARDNER

nition, brings tears to his eyes? Is he brought to a deeper appreciation of his Lutheran or Catholic heritage and its resonances with other bodies of religious experience? On the contrary, he is secretly taught disdain for what his grandfather *thought* he was doing when he acted or felt or imagined through religious forms. In the boy's psyche, a new religion is implanted: power over others, enlightenment, an atomic (rather than a communitarian) sensibility, a contempt for mystery, ritual, transcendence, soul, absurdity, and tragedy; and deep confidence in the possibilities of building a better world through scientific understanding. He is led to feel ashamed for the statistical portrait of Slovak immigrants which shows them to be conservative, authoritarian, not given to dissent, etc. His teachers instruct him with the purest of intentions, in a way that is value free.

To be sure, certain radical writers in America have begun to bewail "the laying on of culture" and to unmask the cultural religion implicit in the American way of science. Yet radicals, one learns, often have an agenda of their own. What fascinates *them* among working-class ethnics are the traces, now almost lost, of *radical* activities among the working class two or three generations ago. Scratch the resentful boredom of a classroom of working-class youths, we are told, and you will find hidden in their past some formerly imprisoned organizer for the CIO, some Sacco/Vanzetti, some bold pamphleteer for the IWW. All this is true. But supposing that a study of the ethnic past reveals that most ethnics have been, are, and wish to remain, culturally conservative? Suppose, for example, they wish to deepen their religious roots and defend their ethnic enclaves? Must a radical culture be "laid on" them?

America has never confronted squarely the problem of preserving diversity. I can remember hearing in my youth bitter arguments that parochial schools were "divisive." Now the public schools are attacked for their commitment to homogenization. Well, how *does* a nation of no one culture, no one language, no one race, no one history, no one ethnic stock continue to exist as one, while encouraging diversity? How can the rights of all, and particularly of the weak, be defended if power is decentralized and left to local interests? The weak have ever found strength in this country through local chapters of national organizations. But what happens when the national organizations themselves—the schools, the unions, the federal government—become vehicles of a new, universalistic, thoroughly rationalized, technological culture?

Still, it is not that larger question that concerns me here. I am content today to voice the difficulties in the way of saying what I wish to say, when I wish to say it. The tradition of liberalism is a tradition I have had to acquire, despite an innate skepticism about many of its structural metaphors (free marketplace, individual autonomy, reason naked and undisguised, enlightenment). Radicalism, with its bold and simple optimism about human potential and its anarchic tendencies, has been, despite its appeal to me as a vehicle for criticizing liberalism, freighted with emotions, sentiments, and convictions about men that I cannot bring myself to share.

In my guts, I do not feel that institutions are "repressive" in any meaning of the word that leaves it meaningful; the "state of nature" seems to me, emotionally, far less liberating, far more undifferentiated and confining. I have not dwelt for so long in the profession of the intellectual life that I find it easy to be critical and harsh. In almost everything I see or hear or read, I am struck first, rather undiscriminatingly, by all the things I like in it. Only with second effort can I bring myself to discern the flaws. My emotions and values seem to run in affirmative patterns.

My interest is not, in fact, in defining myself over against the American people and the American way of life. I do not expect as much of it as all that. What I should like to do is come to a better and more profound knowledge of who I am, whence my community came, and whither my son and daughter, and their children's children, might wish to head in the future: I want to have a history.

More and more, I think in family terms, less ambitiously, on a less than national scale. The differences implicit in being Slovak, and Catholic, and lower-middle class seem more and more important to me. Perhaps it is too much to try to speak to all peoples in this very various nation of ours. Yet it does not seem evident that by becoming more concrete, accepting one's finite and limited identity, one necessarily becomes parochial. Quite the opposite. It seems more likely that by each of us becoming more profoundly what we are, we shall find greater unity, in those depths in which unity irradiates diversity, than by attempting through the artifices of the American "melting pot" and the cultural religion of science to become what we are not.

There is, I take it, a form of liberalism not wedded to universal Reason, whose ambition is not to homogenize all peoples on this planet, and whose base lies rather in the imagination and in the diversity of human stories: a liberalism I should be happy to have others help me to find. □

# 32

# A Child's-Eye View of Sex Roles

THE SCHOOLS AND SEX-ROLE STEREOTYPING

**LYNNE B. IGLITZIN,** *lecturer, Department of Political Science, University of Washington.*

In 1971 and 1972, two studies dealing with sex stereotyping were conducted on schoolchildren in three suburbs of Seattle. In the first study, 290 fifth graders (141 boys, 149 girls) took part; in the second study, 147 fifth graders (80 boys, 67 girls).

The first study (in which I collaborated with sociologist Judith Fiedler) involved a series of questions designed to show sex stereotyping based on views of career and employment patterns, social roles in home and family, and the child's view of his/her future life as an adult. Both boys and girls demonstrated sex stereotyping (as measured by the response "men" or "women" rather than "either" or "both" to the questions). However, significantly higher proportions of girls had nonstereotyped responses in all categories.

*Career and employment patterns.* We gave the children a list of jobs and asked them to indicate whether "men," "women," or "both men and women" should perform these tasks. A majority of both sexes thought that bosses, taxi drivers, mayors, factory workers, and lawyers should be men and that nurses and house cleaners should be women.

Stereotyping was common for both boys and girls. In fact, in some cases, girls were even less inclined than boys to see traditionally masculine jobs become feminine jobs. For example, 3.6 percent of the boys said mayors should be women, but only 2 percent of the girls said this. Although girls were as little inclined as boys to reverse sex roles in traditionally sex-tied jobs, girls were much more willing to see jobs open to either sex.

*Home and family.* The results for this part of the study showed that fifth graders have been thoroughly inculcated with a sex-typed view of home and household: Women wash dishes, cook, dust, scrub floors, and get up at night with a sick child. Men pay bills, fix things, and weed the yard. The men's list was shorter than the women's—even taking out the garbage was bestowed by our children on women! Girls' views were as traditional as boys', though the girls showed a slightly greater tendency to see both parents performing household tasks.

*Personality traits.* At least 60 percent of the girls saw themselves as kinder, better behaved, more serious, and better in math than boys; by a smaller

majority the girls thought they "figured things out" better, too. The majority of girls saw boys as fighting more and as better in science. Children of both sexes tended to see most traits as distinctly masculine or feminine, though they did not always agree on which sex should be linked to a particular trait. The aggressive-gentleness continuum offered a striking example of agreement by both sexes: Close to 90 percent of boys and girls saw boys as fighting more, and about 75 percent of boys and 85 percent of girls saw girls as kinder.

Although the girls in the sample were traditional in their sex-typed view of some personality traits, more of them saw both sexes exhibiting these traits.

*Sex typing in girls' view of their future.* The pattern of traditional sex typing which emerged in girls' views of social roles and personality traits carried over into their career aspirations and descriptions of their lives as adults. While the boys wanted to be craftsmen, engineers or scientists, professionals (doctors, lawyers, dentists), sportsmen, and pilots, the girls wanted to be teachers, artists, stewardesses, nurses, and veterinarians.

Overall, the girls had varied job and career aspirations, albeit heavily weighted toward traditional female occupations. They seemed in little doubt that

Dr. Iglitzin spoke at greater length on this topic at the 1972 meeting of the American Political Science Association in Washington, DC.

they would have careers. Only 6 percent said they would be simply a mother or a housewife.

Yet when we correlated the career-choice question with an open-ended essay, "Imagine you are grown up. Describe how you would spend a typical day," a different picture emerged. The girls showed a marked discrepancy between their stated career goals and their descriptions of an actual day.

Girls in the sample emphasized marriage and family much more than boys in the sample. Despite the small number (6 percent) who said they would be housewives and mothers, well over 25 percent of the girls (compared to 10 percent of the boys) made marriage and family the predominant focus of their projected day, and an even larger group (38 percent of the girls, compared to 14 percent of the boys) emphasized details of family life in their descriptions. In contrast, boys overwhelmingly ignored domestic life—well over 83 percent (compared to 63 percent of the girls) gave no details of family activities and fewer than one-fourth even mentioned marriage or family.

Typically, many of the girls commented extensively and in detail on housewifely routine. Even girls who had chosen a variety of careers in the earlier question saw themselves doing traditional "women's work" around the house. In fact, for many, the description of the household chores seemed far more salient than the job. A girl who had said she wanted to be "an artist, maybe a beautician" described her typical day as follows:

I would start the morning after getting out of bed by eating breakfast. Then I would clean house. If I was done before lunch I would probably visit a friend. Then eat lunch. After lunch I would go shopping. Then I would come home and rest for a while. When my husband came home (if I was married) he would probably tell me how his day went and I would tell him how mine went. If he was in a real good mood he would take me out to dinner. When we were done with dinner we would go to a movie. Then we would go home and go to bed.

Boys tended much more to focus exclusively on details of job and career. The following statement by a boy who wants to be a lawyer and who never discusses marriage, family, or home was quite typical:

I would talk to my clients on what their problems were. If I thought his thoughts were right I would explain the right procedures to take depending on his problems, and I would fight for his thoughts.

The comments of girls who said they wanted to be housewives could be described as typical of persons leading what has been called the "contingent life"— seeing one's actions as derived from and dependent on the wishes of others. Thus such statements as "I would try to please my husband" or "If my children wanted to" were common in their essays.

**This study indicated that the degree of traditional sex stereotyping of the major social roles in society is very strong by the fifth grade level.**

Of particular interest is the fact that so many of the girls clearly opted for career choices that they appear to be unwilling or unable to translate into consequences in their own lives.

What is the explanation for this dichotomy between career choice and visualization of future life that our data showed applied unequally to the boys and girls in our sample? It appears that social stereotypes restrict girls in expressing a free choice of future roles. If this is true, it may be that the first question, "What would you like to be when you grow up?" by suggesting that such decisions are possible, permitted the girls freedom to state their wildest wishes. The later question, however, brought them down to earth by asking them to imagine a typical day. The realities of societal pressure took over, they saw themselves doing things women always do, and thus fell back into the traditional activities society sanctions for women.

In our view, the most significant finding of all was that the girls were consistently less stereotyped in their views than the boys. This was a puzzling finding that we were at a loss to explain, particularly in view of the literature that attests to women as traditional bearers and upholders of conservative values.

One variable that seemed to be relevant in determining which children had less traditional sex-stereotyped attitudes was whether or not their mothers worked. As other studies have shown, our data indicated that children with working mothers—especially girls—had more liberal views on roles of men and women in society.

**A year later, I decided to try a follow-up study** in the same schools and with the same age children to determine what effect, if any, the strongly stereotyped views children hold have on their political attitudes and beliefs. More particularly, my interest was with girls, who had always emerged as less politically interested and aware than boys in previous socialization studies. I wondered whether a relationship exists between strong adherence to traditional feminine values and weak political interest among girls.

As in the 1971 study, the new questionnaire dealt with children's own view of their future roles in job and family; the degree of openness/stereotyping in their view of social roles for men and women; and, new in this study, a series of questions designed to explore their political information and awareness.

*Sex differences and political responses.* A number of questions attempted to deal with the degree of stereotyping in children's views of both public and private roles. I was curious to see if the sexual division of labor that we had seen extended into family and social roles also held true for the civil and political areas.

The democratic norm of equal opportunity implies that anyone can be President, a goal theoretically open to both sexes. Which was more salient for the girls, the rhetoric of equal access or the reality of male dominance in virtually all positions of political power? For boys, the log-cabin-to-Presidency myth or an impenetrable "power elite"? Do 11-year-olds find the prospect of becoming powerful political leaders someday attractive? What degree of realism do they have about their actual chances of attaining such posts?

To get answers to some of these queries, I asked a number of questions dealing with national and local politics. First, I asked the children to assume that they were adults and could choose any political job, such as President, governor, judge, head of the school board, and mayor. Strikingly, well over half of the children picked none of these posts. Strong sex differences were apparent in the answers of those who picked political jobs, however. Although about the same small proportion of boys and girls chose President, a sizable number of boys wanted to be mayor, yet not a single girl chose this. For girls, the popular choices were head of the school board and judge.

Then, I asked the children to assess which of the positions they thought they had a realistic chance of attaining. Here I wanted to find out if the girls, more than the boys, would sense the great difficulty of achieving these high prestige roles in our society. This pattern did not occur. Percentages were almost identical to the previous question.

Several interpretations are possible. Probably many of the children did not understand the concept of "realistic" and simply copied the answer they had given in the previous question. Or else, their political concepts are still so naïve that they truly think they can become anything they want to be. Or maybe their initial choices are already calibrated to what is possible: They sense the impossibility of the "you-too-can-be-President-someday" myth and refuse to play that game.

Other sex differences emerged that were in line with previous socialization studies. When asked to decide why they might vote for a candidate, girls were more likely to choose candidates who were peace-oriented and honest and sincere. Over twice as many boys as girls chose the candidate whose ideas would contribute to the country's economic wealth.

I drew up a composite index to include the determinants of political information and awareness. The information score consisted of correct answers to the various political identification questions; the awareness score was composed of any response other than "don't know" to the various questions dealing with voting and elections. On each of these scores, the girls did more poorly than the boys.

In areas beside the political, sex stereotyping was as strong in the attitudes of these children as it had been in their counterparts the year before. Girls saw themselves eventually marrying and having children; boys saw themselves as adults in terms of jobs. Over half the children thought only men should do certain jobs and only women, certain others. A very low 10.6 percent of the girls and 14.7 percent of the boys said a woman should work "anytime she wants to."

*Stereotyping and politicalization.* Once the existence of sex differences had been established, I attempted to see if a common variable, stereotyping, could be isolated as a determinant of low politicalization. The measurement of stereotyping was the degree to which the children saw social roles (housework, medical care, and so on) in the traditional terms of sexual dichotomy. For all the children, I matched the stereotyping index against the separate political information and awareness indices and, in addition, for girls, I matched the femininity index (measured by their adherence to traditional female careers and values) against the political scores.

Results were inconclusive. Stereotyping clearly exists, but the data did not show any strong relationship with level of political information and awareness except in a few cases at the extremes.

The main concern was to see the effect of stereotyping and feminizing influences upon the girls. Here girls did seem more strongly affected than did boys. There were some indications that girls who had the least narrowly feminine aspirations scored higher on political information and awareness, but the relationship was weak. Similarly, the occupation of the mother (housewife vs. job holder) clearly affected the girls' aspirations and degree of stereotyping but was less apparent in influencing their politicalization scores. In contrast to the earlier study, such a small percent of the mothers of these girls were job holders that it would be misleading to draw any conclusions based on the daughters of working mothers.

*Summary.* The expected strong sex differences on political, social, and economic roles in society emerged. Moreover, the existence of very strong sex typing in children's views of jobs and functions in the world, as well as their own personal role within it had been again confirmed. But the hoped for correlation between stereotyping and feminization in the girls as an explanation for their low politicalization scores proved inconclusive.

Why? Two explanations are possible. First, very few of the girls identified themselves in terms other than marriage and family; the sample failed to turn up more than a tiny handful of girls who had not been feminized. Therefore, comparisons weren't possible.

Second, perhaps the questionnaire reflects an unconscious ideology of sexism because of the sexist subject matter with which the questions concern themselves. (Before undertaking the study, I had attempted to control for sexist language. For example, I used "he/she" instead of the ubiquitous "he" and included women as examples of political leaders.) The subject matter of the questionnaire, as well as that of others dealing with this same subject, is male-oriented because political posts have historically always been occupied by men.

When politics is conceptualized in terms of power, aggression, and conflict, it is not surprising that women, trained in submissiveness, dependence, and passivity, should find little in it to interest them.

For too long, political scientists have focused only on the macro level of politics, dealing with formal power as exercised in institutions and by government officials. It is no wonder that children, and indeed many adults, feel alienated and removed from its concerns. Political scientists need to emphasize the micro level of politics—power hierarchies in family, peer groups, and classrooms. Undoubtedly, children can tell political scientists a great deal about this dimension of politics. □

# The Inexpressive Male: A Tragedy of American Society*

# 33

Jack O. Balswick and Charles W. Peek**

*The position is taken in this paper that inexpressiveness is a culturally produced temperament trait which is characteristic of many American males. It is suggested that in growing up, boys are taught that expressiveness is inconsistent with masculinity. Inexpressive males come in two varieties: the cowboy who, although he does have feelings toward women, does not or cannot express them; and the playboy who is a non-feeling man void of even unexpressed emotional feelings toward women. In light of the increase in importance of the companionship and affection function in marriage, across-the-board inexpressiveness of married males (that is, inexpressiveness toward all women, wife included) can be highly dysfunctional to their marital relationships, while selective inexpressiveness (that is, inexpressiveness toward women other than their wives) may be just as functional to maintaining these relationships.*

The problem of what it means to be "male" and "female" is a problem which is faced and dealt with in its own way in every society. Through cross-cultural research one now surmises that culture rather than "nature" is the major influence in determining the temperamental differences between the sexes. It may be no accident that a woman, Margaret Mead, did the classic study demonstrating that temperamental differences between the sexes are explained very little in terms of innateness, but rather in terms of culture. In her book, *Sex and Temperament*, Mead reported on the differences in sex roles for three New Guinea societies. Using ethnocentric western standards in defining sex roles, she found that the ideal sex role for both the male and female was essentially "feminine" among the Arapesh, "masculine" among the Mundugumor, and "feminine" for the male and "masculine" for the female among the Tchambuli. The Tchambuli represents a society that defines sex roles in a complete reversal of the traditional distinctions made between masculine and feminine roles in the United States.

It is the purpose of this paper to consider a particular temperament trait that often characterizes the male in American society. As sex role distinctions have developed in America, the male sex role, as compared to the female sex role, carries with it prescriptions which encourage inexpressiveness. In some of its extreme contemporary forms, the inexpressive male has even come to be glorified as the epitome of a real man. This will be discussed later in the paper when two types of inexpressive male are examined.

## The Creation of the Inexpressive Male

Children, from the time they are born both explicitly and implicitly are taught how to be a man or how to be a woman. While the girl is taught to act "feminine" and to desire "feminine" objects, the boy is taught how to be a man. In learning to be a man, the boy in American society comes to value expressions of masculinity and devalue expressions of femininity. Masculinity is expressed largely through physical courage, toughness, competitiveness, and aggressiveness, whereas femininity is, in contrast, expressed largely through gentleness, expressiveness, and responsiveness. When a young boy begins to express his emotions through crying, his parents are quick to assert, "You're a big boy and big boys don't cry." Parents often use the term, "he's all boy," in reference to their son, and by this term usually refer to behavior which is an expression of aggressiveness, getting into mischief, getting dirty, etc., but never use the term to denote behavior which is an expression of affection, tenderness, or emotion. What parents are really telling their son is that a real man does not show his emotions and if he is a real man he will not allow his emotions to be expressed. These outward expressions of emotion are viewed as a sign of femininity, and undesirable for a male.

Is it any wonder, then, that during the most emotional peak of a play or movie, when many in the audience have lumps in their throats and tears in their eyes, that the adolescent boy guffaws loudly or quickly suppresses any tears which may be threatening to emerge, thus demonstrating to the world that he is above such emotional feeling?

## The Inexpressive Male as a Single Man

At least two basic types of inexpressive male seem to result from this socialization process: the cowboy and the playboy. Manville (1969) has referred to the *cowboy type* in terms of a "John Wayne Neurosis" which stresses the strong, silent, and two-fisted male as the 100 percent American he-man. For present purposes, it is especially in his relationship with women that the John Wayne neurosis is particularly significant in representing many American males. As portrayed by Wayne in any one of his many type-cast roles, the mark of a real man is that he does not show any tenderness or affection toward girls because his culturally-acquired male image dictates that such a show of emotions would be distinctly unmanly. If he does have anything to do with girls, it is on a "man to man" basis: the girl is treated roughly (but not sadistically), with little hint of gentleness or affection. As Manville puts it:

"The on-screen John Wayne doesn't feel comfortable around women. He does like them sometimes—God knows he's not *queer*. But at the right time, and in the right place — which he chooses. And always with his car/horse parked directly outside, in/on which he will ride away to his more important business back in Marlboro country." (1969, 111)

Alfred Auerback, a psychiatrist, has commented more directly (1970) on the cowboy type. He describes the American male's inexpressiveness with women as part of the "cowboy syndrome." He quite rightly states that "the cowboy in moving pictures has conveyed the image of the rugged 'he-man,' strong, resilient, resourceful, capable of coping with over-

* A revised version of a paper read at the meetings of the American Sociological Association, Washington, D.C., September, 1970.
** Jack O. Balswick, Ph.D., is Associate Professor of Sociology, Department of Sociology, University of Georgia, Athens, Georgia 30601, and Charles W. Peek, Ph.D., is Assistant Professor of Sociology, Department of Sociology and Anthropology, University of Georgia, Athens, Georgia 30601.

whelming odds. His attitude toward women is courteous but reserved." As the cowboy equally loved his girlfriend and his horse, so the present day American male loves his car or motorcycle and his girlfriend. Basic to both these descriptions is the notion that the cowboy does have feelings toward women but does not express them, since ironically such expression would conflict with his image of what a male is.

The *playboy type* has recently been epitomized in *Playboy* magazine and by James Bond. As with the cowboy type, he is resourceful and shrewd, and interacts with his girlfriend with a certain detachment which is expressed as "playing it cool." While Bond's relationship with women is more in terms of a Don Juan, he still treats women with an air of emotional detachment and independence similar to that of the cowboy. The playboy departs from the cowboy, however, in that he is also "non-feeling." Bond and the playboy he caricatures are in a sense "dead" inside. They have no emotional feelings toward women, while Wayne, although unwilling and perhaps unable to express them does have such feelings. Bond rejects women as women, treating them as consumer commodities; Wayne puts women on a pedestal. The playboy's relationship with women represents the culmination of Fromm's description of a marketing-oriented personality in which a person comes to see both himself and others as persons to be manipulated and exploited. Sexuality is reduced to a packageable consumption item which the playboy can handle because it demands no responsibility. The woman in the process, becomes reduced to a playboy accessory. A successful "love affair" is one in which the bed was shared, but the playboy emerges having avoided personal involvement or a shared relationship with the woman.

The playboy, then, in part is the old cowboy in modern dress. Instead of the crude mannerisms of John Wayne, the playboy is a skilled manipulator of women, knowing when to turn the lights down, what music to play on the stereo, which drinks to serve, and what topics of conversation to pursue. The playboy, however, is not a perfect likeness; for unlike the cowboy, he does not seem to care for the women from whom he withholds his emotions. Thus, the inexpressive male as a single man comes in two types: the inexpressive feeling man (the cowboy) and the inexpressive non-feeling man (the playboy).

## The Inexpressive Male as a Married Man

When the inexpressive male marries, his inexpressiveness can become highly dysfunctional to his marital relationship *if* he continues to apply it across-the-board to all women, his wife included. The modern American family places a greater demand upon the marriage relationship than did the family of the past. In the typical marriage of 100 or even 50 years ago, the roles of both the husband and the wife were clearly defined as demanding, task-oriented functions. If the husband successfully performed the role of provider and protector of his wife and family and if the wife performed the role of homemaker and mother to her children, chances were the marriage was defined as successful, both from a personal and a societal point of view. The traditional task functions which in the past were performed by the husband and wife are today often taken care of by individuals and organizations outside the home. Concomitant with the decline of the task functions in marriage has been the increase in the importance of the companionship and affectionate function in marriage. As Blood and Wolfe (1960, 172) concluded in their study of the modern American marriage, "companionship has emerged as the most valued aspect of marriage today."

As American society has become increasingly mechanized and depersonalized, the family remains as one of the few social groups where what sociologists call the primary relationship has still managed to survive. As such, a greater and greater demand has been placed upon the modern family and especially the modern marriage to provide for affection and companionship. Indeed, it is highly plausible to explain the increased rate of divorce during the last 70 years, not in terms of a breakdown in marriage relationships, but instead, as resulting from the increased load which marriage has been asked to carry. When the husband and wife no longer find affection and companionship from their marriage relationship, they most likely question the wisdom of attempting to continue in their conjugal relationship. When affection is gone, the main reason for the marriage relationship disappears.

Thus, within the newly defined affectively-oriented marriage relationship male inexpressiveness toward *all* women, wife included, would be dysfunctional. But what may happen for many males is that through progressively more serious involvements with women (such as going steady, being pinned, engagement, and the honeymoon period of marriage), they begin to make some exceptions. That is, they may learn to be *situationally rather than totally inexpressive*, inexpressive toward women in most situations but not in all. As the child who learns a rule and then, through further experience, begins to understand the exceptions to it, many American males may pick up the principle of inexpressiveness toward women, discovering its exceptions as they become more and more experienced in the full range of man-woman relationships. Consequently, they may become more expressive toward their wives while remaining essentially inexpressive toward other women; they learn that the conjugal relationship is one situation that is an exception to the cultural requirement of male inexpressiveness. Thus, what was once a double *sexual* standard, where men had one standard of sexual conduct toward their fiancee or wife and another toward other women, may now be primarily a double *emotional* standard, where men learn to be expressive toward their fiancee or wife but remain inexpressive toward women in general.

To the extent that such situational inexpressiveness exists among males, it should be functional to the maintenance of the marriage relationship. Continued inexpressiveness by married males toward women other than their wives would seem to prohibit their forming meaningful relationships with these women. Such a situation would seem to be advantageous to preserving their marital relationships, since "promiscuous" expressiveness toward other women could easily threaten the stability of these companionship-oriented marital relationships.

In short, the authors' suggestion is that situational inexpressiveness, in which male expressiveness is essentially limited to the marital relationship, may be one of the basic timbers shoring up many American marriages, especially if indications of increasing extramarital sexual relations are correct. In a sense, then, the consequences of situational inexpressiveness for marital relationships do not seem very different from those of prostitution down through the centuries, where prostitution provided for extramarital sex under circumstances which discouraged personal affection toward the female partner strong enough to undermine the marital relationship. In the case of the situationally inexpressive husband, his inexpressiveness in relations with women other than his wife may serve as a line of defense against the possible negative consequences of such involvement toward marital stability. By acting as the cowboy or playboy, therefore, the married male may effectively rob extramarital relationships of their expressiveness and thus preserve his marital relationship.

The inexpressiveness which the American male early acquires may be bothersome in that he has to partially unlearn it in order to effectively relate to his wife. However, if he is successful in partially unlearning it (or learning a few exceptions to it), then it can be highly functional to maintaining the conjugal relationship.

But what if the husband does not partially unlearn his inexpressiveness? Within the newly defined expressive function of the marriage relationship, he is likely to be found inadequate. The possibility of an affectionate and companionship conjugal relationship carries with it the assumption that both the husband and wife are bringing into marriage the expressive capabilities to make such a relationship work. This being the case, American society is ironically short changing males in terms of their ability to fulfill this role expectation. Thus, society inconsistently teaches the male that to be masculine is to be inexpressive, while at the same time, expectations in the marital role are defined in terms of sharing affection and companionship which involves the ability to communicate and express feelings. What exists apparently, is another example of a discontinuity in cultural conditioning of which Benedict (1938) spoke more than 30 years ago.

## Conclusion and Summary

It has been suggested that many American males are incapable of expressing themselves emotionally to a woman, and that this inexpressiveness is a result of the way society socialized males into their sex role. However, there is an alternative explanation which should be explored, namely, that the learning by the male of his sex role may not actually result in his inability to be expressive, but rather only in his thinking that he is not supposed to be expressive. Granted, according to the first explanation, the male cannot express himself precisely because he was taught that he was not supposed to be expressive, but in this second explanation inexpressiveness is a result of present perceived expectations and not a psychological condition which resulted from past socialization. The male perceives cultural expectations as saying, "don't express yourself to women," and although the male may be capable of such expressiveness, he "fits" into cultural expectations. In the case of the married male, where familial norms do call for expressiveness to one's wife, it may be that the expectations for the ex-

pression of emotions to his wife are not communicated to him.

There has been a trickle of evidence which would lend support to the first explanation, which stresses the male's incapacity to be expressive. Several studies (Balswick, 1970; Hurvitz, 1964; Komarovsky, 1962; Rainwater, 1965) have suggested that especially among the lowly educated, it is the wife playing the feminine role who is often disappointed in the lack of emotional concern shown by her husband. The husband, on the other hand, cannot understand the relatively greater concern and emotional expressiveness which his wife desires, since he does not usually feel this need himself. As a result of her research, Komarovsky (1962, 156) has suggested that "the ideal of masculinity into which ....(men are) ... socialized inhibits expressiveness both directly, with its emphasis on reserve, and indirectly, by identifying personal interchange with the feminine role." Balswick (1970) found that males are less capable than females of expressing or receiving companionship support from their spouses. His research also supports the view than inadequacy of expressiveness is greatest for the less educated males. Although inexpressiveness may be found among males at all socioeconomic levels, it is especially among the lower class male that expressiveness is seen as being inconsistent with his defined masculine role.

There may be some signs that conditions which have contributed toward the creation of the inexpressive male are in the process of decline. The deemphasis in distinctiveness in dress and fashions between the sexes, as exemplified in the "hippy" movement can be seen as a reaction against the rigidly defined distinctions between the sexes which have characterized American society. The sexless look, as presently being advanced in high fashion, is the logical end reaction to a society which has superficially created strong distinctions between the sexes. Along with the blurring of sexual distinctions in fashion may very well be the shattering of the strong, silent male as a glorified type. There is already evidence of sharp criticisms of the inexpressive male and exposure of him as constituting a "hangup." Marriage counselors, sensitivity group leaders, "hippies," and certainly youth in general, are critical of inexpressiveness, and candid honesty in interpersonal relations. Should these views permeate American

society, the inexpressive male may well come to be regarded as a pathetic tragedy instead of the epitome of masculinity and fade from the American scene. Not all may applaud his departure, however. While those interested in more satisfactory male-female relationships, marital and otherwise, will probably gladly see him off, those concerned with more stable marital relationships may greet his departure less enthusiastically. Although it should remove an important barrier to satisfaction in all male-female relationships via an increase in the male's capacity for emotional response toward females, by the same token it also may remove a barrier against emotional entanglement in relations with females outside marital relationships and thus threaten the stability of marriages. If one finds the inexpressive male no longer present one of these days, then, it will be interesting to observe whether any gains in the stability of marriage due to increased male expressiveness *within* this relationship will be enough to offset losses in stability emanating from increasing displays of male expressiveness *outside* it.

## REFERENCES:

Auerback, Alfred. The Cowboy Syndrome. Summary of research contained in a personal letter from the author, 1970.

Balswick, Jack O. The Effect of Spouse Companionship Support on Employment Success. *Journal of Marriage and the Family*, 1970, **32**, 212-215.

Benedict, Ruth. Continuities and Discontinuities in Cultural Conditioning. *Psychiatry*, 1938, 1, 161-167.

Blood, Robert and Donald Wolfe. *Husbands and Wives: The Dynamic of Married Living*. Glencoe, Illinois: The Free Press, 1960.

Cox, Harvey. Playboy's Doctrine of Male. In Wayne H. Cowan (Ed.) *Witness to a Generation: Significant Writings from Christianity and Crisis (1941-1966)*. New York: Bobbs-Merrill Company, 1966.

Hurvitz, Nathan. Marital Strain in the Blue Collar Family. In Arthur Shostak and William Gomberg (Eds.) *Blue-Collar World*. Englewood Cliffs, New Jersey: Prentice Hall, 1964.

Komarovsky, M. *Blue-Collar Marriage*. New York: Random House, 1962.

Mead, Margaret. *Sex and Temperament in Three Primitive Societies*. New York: William Morrow and Company, 1935.

Manville, W. H. The Locker Room Boys. *Cosmopolitan*, 1969, **166** (11), 110-115.

Popplestone, John. The Horseless Cowboys. *Transaction*, 1966, 3, 25-27.

Rainwater, Lee. *Family Design: Marital Sexuality, Family Size, and Contraception*. Chicago: Aldine Publishing Company, 1965.

# IV. Social Institutions

An institution is an organized, patterned system of social relationships. Institutions play a vital part in the social structure: they lend shape and order to society and serve many important social functions. In simple societies, institutions are few; but as a society grows larger and more complex, a whole range of specialized institutions emerges to meet the varied requirements of social existence. Among the most important institutions in contemporary America are the familial, educational, economic, political, legal, religious, medical, and military systems.

Few if any of these institutions have escaped criticism in recent years. They are often experienced as entities separate from society and from everyday life—as distant, coercive, unresponsive, and even oppressive. The rate of institutional change in a rapidly changing society is necessarily uneven, and many critics have charged that our institutions are behind the times, ineffectual, or even the source of our most severe social problems.

The readings in this section focus on some of our most significant institutions. Topic 12 presents marriage and the family from three different viewpoints. David R. Mace sets forth a spirited defense of that much-maligned institution, the nuclear family. John Rothchild and Susan Berns Wolf, on the other hand, explore a major alternative to the nuclear family—communal living—and describe what it is like to live in a commune. Morton Hunt's article on "The Future of Marriage" takes a broad perspective, surveying the state of the institution in modern America and exploring some alternatives and their chances of success.

Topic 13 contains four articles on the institution of education. In her article, Lillian Zach looks at a major controversy in American education, one laden with racial overtones—the use and misuse of IQ tests. The role of the schools in society is a topic that sociologists have debated for decades: Can schools actually change society, or will they always tend to reflect it? Mary Jo Banc and Christopher Jencks offer the controversial view that our attempts to create equal educational opportunity as a route to greater social equality have in fact made very little difference—with the implication that efforts to engineer this kind of social change through the schools have been somewhat misdirected.

One attempt to use education as a means to promote greater social equality is the policy of "open admissions," which guarantees any high-school graduate admission to a college or university. The City University of New York (CUNY) was one of the first major institutions of higher education to adopt such a policy, permitting students with poor academic preparation to enter the university. At the same time, CUNY also created several ethnic studies departments in the early 1970s. The policies became a source of heated political conflict among the various ethnic groups in New York City—blacks, Jews, Italians, Puerto Ricans, and others. Theodore L. Gross, former dean of humanities at City College of New York, a branch of CUNY, has written a sensitive, introspective account of open admissions and its political and human consequences. Originally entitled "Open Admissions: A Confessional Meditation," the article was retitled "How To Kill A College: The Private Papers of a Campus Dean" when it appeared in *Saturday Review* in 1978. The title change, ironically, made Gross's article a focus for political debate over open admissions. CUNY President Robert E. Marshak, for example, issued a long "open letter" to Gross, characterizing the article as condescending, insulting, and slanted; several months thereafter, Gross was forced to resign as dean. Nonetheless, it is our view that the essay is a careful, thoughtful, and valuable discussion of an explosive topic and its attendant educational, social, and political issues.*

One nation that uses education consciously to *retard* social equality is the Republic of South Africa. In that country, a major function of the educational institution is to inculcate in the young a sense of the legitimacy—and even sanctity—of the policy of *apartheid*: racial separation and the rule by a white minority of a nonwhite majority. As are all other institutions in South Africa, education is based upon race. At the top of the heap are the whites, who attend free schools with modern facilities and equipment; at the bottom are the blacks, who must pay for the opportunity to attend overcrowded, ill-equipped, delapidated schools. Nevertheless, whether a child is designated "White," "Coloured," "Asian," or "Bantu," he or she is taught equally that the system of *apartheid* is best for all. In "Apartheid Education" Ian Robertson describes the shocking way in which the South African government uses education as a tool to support a system of racial domination.

The sociology of religion is one of the most interesting of sociological subdisciplines. Topic 14 examines two belief systems, religion and science. In the aftermath of the youth counterculture of the late 1960s, increasing numbers of young people in Western industrial societies began joining Eastern, or Eastern-derived religious movements; shortly thereafter Christian fundamentalist sects began gaining favor among many young people. The turn to the East was highly publicized by such "happenings" as the Beatles adopting

---

* For an account of the controversy surrounding the article, see Larry Van Dyne, "Dean Under Fire for Article," *Chronicle of Higher Education*, March 6, 1978, pp. 3 ff.

their own guru, the Maharishi Mahesh Yogi, founder of TM (Transcendental Meditation); the attempts by distraught parents to "kidnap" their own children from religious groups and "deprogram" them; the flashy life styles of a Korean religious leader with ties to the Korean CIA; and an Indian teen-age "perfect master." Such Eastern religious groups tend to be located in college areas; indeed, Harvey Cox refers to the area in Cambridge, Massachusetts, around Harvard Square as a veritable "Benares on the Charles." In his article, an excerpt from his book *Turning East*, Cox describes some of those who have turned to the East and their reasons for doing so. Science, too, is a belief system just as religion is, and it can lead to the creation of scientific myths. In "Science and Myth" a leading French scientist, Pierre Auger, discusses some scientific myths.

Topic 15 consists of three articles on economic systems. The first recounts an incident in the lives of a hunting and gathering group, the San (Bushmen) of the Kalahari desert. In "Eating Christmas in the Kalahari" Richard Borshay Lee describes the reaction of the San and his own lesson in humility when he decided to give an ox to the group of San with which he was living. In so doing he provides us with a fascinating glimpse into the economic system of a small-scale human society and into the value system that supports it.

The next two articles, by contrast, deal with modern capitalism in the United States. Ernest Fitzgerald takes a close look at the largest United States bureaucracy, the Pentagon, whose relationship with the rest of the military-industrial complex is regarded by many sociologists as one of the most severe and intractable problems in our society. Mark Dowie and Tracy Johnston describes in detail what can happen when a modern industrial firm places profits ahead of human safety. Their account of the development and marketing of the Dalkon Shield, an intrauterine device, though shocking, is not unique. Other companies in recent years—in the United States, Europe, and Japan—have failed to alert the public to the potential dangers of their products. In the case of the Dalkon Shield, seventeen women using the device died before any action was taken.

Topic 16 deals with the institution of politics. Ralph Nader's often single-handed David-and-Goliath battles with government bureaucracies and wayward corporations form the subject of Julius Duscha's article. In his essay, former Massachusetts Congressman Michael J. Harrington takes a critical look at the lobbying process and shows how powerful interest groups—in this case the National Rifle Association—are able to influence public policy. Finally, Andrew Kopkind takes a look at the growing strength of "America's New Right." Led by individuals such as Ronald Reagan and Anita Bryant, and utilizing direct mail techniques, the New Right is riding issues like abortion, ERA, the Panama Canal, gun control, and gay rights to become a powerful political force in the late 1970s and early 1980s.

# IN DEFENSE OF THE NUCLEAR FAMILY

## David R. Mace

*David R. Mace is professor of sociology at the Behavioral Sciences Center of the Bowman Gray School of Medicine in Winston-Salem, North Carolina. A founder of the American Association of Marriage and Family Counselors, Dr. Mace has written many books and articles about marriage and the family.*

A newspaper columnist, reviewing some notable features of the decade of the sixties, made special reference to the attack on the nuclear family. This represented, he said, a dramatic reversal in our value system, because it implied a rejection of the very foundation on which our traditional culture was built.

Surprisingly enough, the attack has not stimulated a very vigorous defense. Ill-founded accusations against the nuclear-family system have been received with indifference or even complacency. In this short essay I propose to examine the matter a little more closely.

### What Is the Nuclear Family?

Harold Christensen defined the nuclear family as "the least common denominator of family organization." It consists of one husband, one wife, and the children born to them. According to G. P. Murdock, it normally performs four basic functions: control of sexual access, control of procreation, education of children, and economic cooperation. It could still function if these roles were diminished in number or in degree—but not if all were eliminated.

Structurally the nuclear family is, as its name implies, a *nucleus*. It can be "extended" in three ways: first, by adding blood relatives and their dependents—grandparents, brothers and sisters, nieces and nephews, with their respective relatives by marriage; a second form of extension could be brought about by introducing multiple

marriage; a third could occur through the adoption or inclusion of unrelated persons.

Extended families do not, of course, stand in contrast to nuclear families, as is often implied. Most extended families use nuclear families as building blocks. In this sense, the nuclear family has been regarded as universal. Murdock, in his monumental and much-quoted study *Social Structure*, found it in every one of the two hundred fifty human societies he examined. M. J. Levy and L. A. Fallers have, however, pointed out that, although nuclear families are indeed components of most extended families, in some cases nuclear functions are so diluted that the extended families are not effective units.

In sharp contrast to these diluted nuclear families, Talcott Parsons has drawn attention to the "isolated nuclear family" in our contemporary society. Industrialization has brought high social mobility, which has weakened extended-family ties, while urbanization has broken down the close neighborhood communities in which families supported each other. The result is that many nuclear families have been forced to rely too exclusively on their own resources, and this has led in some instances to acute relational stress.

### Why Is the Nuclear Family Under Attack?

A sampling of the polemical literature soon reveals that the reasons for the attack on the nuclear family are seldom related to any serious attempt to understand its functioning. In nearly every instance, the attack is really against something else, and the nuclear family is used as a convenient scapegoat. Here are four examples of the oblique reasoning that occurs frequently:

1. Marriages today are breaking down at an increasing rate so there must be something unworkable about our contemporary family system, which is the nuclear family.

2. Many parents and children are alienated from each other. This "generation gap" must be the result of the nuclear family; so we must find a better family system where it won't occur.

3. Individual freedom is being stifled in the tight, close, author-

itarian atmosphere created by family life. The nuclear-family system must be to blame for this.

4. The sense of true community has been lost in our culture. The nuclear-family system must be the cause. We must therefore break it up in favor of more-open community groupings.

All the misfortunes listed here—the brittleness of our marriages, the alienation of the generations, the loss of the sense of person-hood, and the superficial competitive character of community life—are perfectly legitimate causes for complaint and cry out for remedial action. However, they are all incidental results of vast social changes, to which neither our society in general nor our family system in particular have yet been able to accommodate themselves. To accuse the nuclear family of being the *cause* of this situation, when it is in fact a *victim* of it, is poor reasoning and gross injustice. In fact, I believe that enabling nuclear families to function effectively could do more to mitigate these evils than almost any action we could take at the present time. In other words, the attack on the nuclear family is a classic example of the mistaken policy of throwing out the baby with the bath water.

## Families in Transition

Prophets of doom are today telling us repeatedly that marriage and the family are outworn and obsolete institutions in the final stages of decay and will soon be replaced by something better. This picture is irresponsible, dangerous, and grossly inaccurate.

The family is a most durable and, surprisingly, a most flexible institution. It has been with us for a very long time and has weathered many storms. As Panos Bardis has expressed it, "In view of man's nature, as well as of the conditions prevailing on our planet, the family is a virtually indestructible institution, which, throughout history, has been capable of resolving seemingly insoluble problems, and surviving cataclysmic catastrophes."

What Clark Vincent has called the "adaptive function" of the family has been grossly underrated, because for a long time in our Western culture it has not been brought into play. The chief role of the family is to provide a secure foundation upon which the culture may build, by feeding into our communities a steady stream of new citizens who understand, accept, and will uphold the values that make the culture distinctive. Consequently, the family responds very slowly and cautiously to cultural change. The result is that it appears to *resist* change; although what it is actually doing is de-manding time to make the necessary adaptation.

This is the situation with which we are presently confronted. Today's unprecedented range and rapidity of cultural change, well documented in Alvin Toffler's *Future Shock*, is exerting tremen-dous pressure on the family, as on all other social institutions. It is now quite clear that many of the characteristic features of our traditional marriage and family system cannot and should not sur-vive. A process of reconstruction is actively taking place, of which there is abundant evidence.

So the family *is* now in transition. But what is the *nature* of that transition? It is our failure to understand this clearly that has, I believe, caused most of our confusion.

It has been vigorously contended that the only way to deal with the traditional family, which admittedly is functioning poorly, is to change its *structure*. The blame for all our troubles has been placed on the pattern that the family has assumed in our Western society.

But what if it should happen that the real cause of the trouble lies not in the structure—the particular persons involved or the way in which they are grouped together—but in the manner in which they perceive each other and interact with each other?

Suppose that our real need is not change of structure, but change of function?

## The New Companionship Emphasis

The "companionship family" is not a new idea. Ernest W. Bur-gess, the "father" of American family sociology, saw it clearly a generation ago. In 1945 he published, with Harvey Locke as co-author, a large book entitled *The Family—From Institution to Companionship*.

This title exactly describes the nature of the change that is now actively taking place in our family system. The families of the past were rigidly structured, legally fenced in, hierarchical, and often tyrannical; their relationships were dominated by custom, ritual, and predetermined roles. Families took this form because the societies they served were so fashioned. The traditional family was, quite properly, the foundation stone of the traditional culture.

The new emerging family is quite different. Our contemporary open society requires, not citizens schooled to conform and to obey, but men and women with a strong sense of autonomy, fully aware of their identity, and able to assume responsibility for their actions and to make creative use of freedom. The traditional family was simply not "tooled up" to turn out such products, and it must therefore be reconstructed in order to do so. The "com-panionship family" is the form we now need. It is an entirely workable pattern. Millions of such families are already operating successfully in our culture, though they are receiving little or no attention.

These highly successful families retain the nuclear pattern. In-deed, they demonstrate that *the nuclear family works much better on a companionship basis*. The traditional nuclear family was essentially a power structure based on a system of authority and submission that was unable to foster creative relationships in an atmosphere of love and intimacy. The new companionship emphasis makes such creative relationships its central goal.

This new nuclear family is, therefore, ideally suited to the task of raising and training citizens for our new society. In "What I Have Learned About Family Life" (*The Family Coordinator*, April 1974), I said:

> The functioning nuclear family provides at once the model and the training school for the kind of human society we are trying to build. It is a microcosm of that larger world in containing both sexes and a variety of ages. In a manageable setting it enables its members to give and to get in just proportion. It trains them to be sensitive to the needs of others, to work together for common goals, to succor each other in times of crisis, and to find joy and gladness in shared delights. Its product is the kind of citizen who has learned to respect law and order; who is conscientious in his work, honest in his deal-ings, kind and charitable in his judgments, warm and affectionate in his friendships. We desperately need large numbers of just such people. And I frankly know of no way to get large numbers of them except to work for the increase of the kind of families that produce them.

## Facilitating Functional, Not Structural, Change

But why, if this new form of the family is emerging to replace the old, are marriages breaking down and parents and children alienated from each other on such a scale? Some degree of disinte-gration is of course inevitable in a culture passing through sweep-ing social change. But that does not fully explain our present pre-dicament. The real problem is that *we have made a tragic error in estimating what is wrong and what must be done to put it right*.

Motivated often by high idealism, we have been trying to improve human relationships by destroying the structure of the family, instead of helping to change its functioning. We have looked to "alternative life-styles" to bring about improved human relationships and embarked on a series of social experiments that while interesting and valuable in themselves could not possibly produce a viable and durable substitute for family life.

What we need to change is not the way in which people are grouped together in social systems, but *the manner in which they interact with each other as persons.* It is not the nuclear family that is at fault. It represents a magnificent natural grouping that provides the ideal setting for learning to relate to others. What is wrong is that the nuclear family has not yet been renovated to produce the new kind of people who are needed to live in our new kind of world. So our culture is full of malfunctioning nuclear families, many of which are breaking down. We need to enable them to function in the new mode.

How can this be done? Ernest Burgess made it clear that the transition in our family life would not go smoothly unless we provided the services that would be necessary. He tried to spell out what these services would be. But another decade was to pass before Nelson Foote and others began to see clearly that a new kind of training for relationships was going to be needed. He coined the term "interpersonal competence" in 1955, and it became increasingly clear that the old ways of training people to relate to each other needed to be supplemented, and even replaced, by new patterns. Learning to perform prescribed roles, like actors on a stage, was not enough. New and more flexible ways of interacting could alone make possible the kind of depth relationships we now saw to be essential for creativity and personality growth.

## Some Promising New Developments

We now stand on the threshold of exciting and promising new insights that can free nuclear families to function at very high levels of creativity. But this can only happen through intensive and extensive retraining in the skills needed for depth communication, for empathy, and for conflict resolution for the constructive management of anger in intimate relationships. Progress made in the past five years could be spectacular.

The new approach is gaining ground. We are at last beginning to see that true personality growth means learning to relate effectively to others, that *the unit of human society is not the individual but the dyadic relationship.* This new understanding will lead us to rediscover the power of the nuclear family as the natural unit of society, in which the ideal conditions exist for effective relational growth. A grass-roots movement is already taking place across North America that is leading to a proliferation of programs for marriage enrichment and parent effectiveness. An attempt is already being made to coordinate these new beginnings through the Association of Couples for Marriage Enrichment (ACME), which my wife and I helped to establish in 1973. Professional interest in this field is growing quickly—in the areas of research, preventive clinical services, and education and training.

Our attempts to jettison the nuclear family will not succeed. They have already cost a high price in terms of a disturbing increase in social pathology. We would be better employed in well-planned and sustained efforts to enable nuclear families in our midst to make the transition from the institutional to the companionship emphasis. This transition will not be easy, and it will take time. But I am personally convinced that helping to bring it about represents the best hope for the future of our society.  ●

# 35

# CHILDREN OF THE COMMUNE
## GROWING UP WITH FIVE KIDS AND SIX PARENTS

Illustrations by Lou Myers
by John Rothchild and Susan Berns Wolf

BERNSIE is about to draw with a green crayon on the living room wall of the Cosmic Circle commune where we are visiting. Susan (co-author) interrupts her conversation with one of the women here, rushes across the room yelling, "Berns, don't do that," and gives four-year-old Berns the usual two-minute lecture on how paper is for drawing and walls are not for drawing. "I don't have any paper," says Berns. Susan is on the way out the front door to get some paper, her journalistic duties forgotten in the call of motherhood, when Eloise stops her. Eloise is the freckly-faced 16-year-old who manages to look as fresh as an airline hostess even when she's wearing a Jimi Hendrix tee shirt. "It's OK," says Eloise. "Why waste your paper? Why waste your time? She can draw on the wall. Everybody else does." And Eloise points to a large expanse of wall on the far end of this massive room they call the Cavern, a wall covered with homemade paintings and penciled graffiti like you find in neglected

men's rooms. Berns directs herself to that wall, and her "Duck with Cigar in Mouth" becomes part of the permanent collection of the Cosmic Circle.

We could see immediately how this place had changed family living. It eliminated the need for about 90 per cent of the protective sorties we have come to call "parenthood." Children roamed this giant room—created by tearing the walls out of three brownstone houses and connecting them—without a worry of breaking, staining, or reducing the resale value of anything. Being in this room was like visiting a truck of refugees who had piled up their most useful possessions in a hurried flight from a homeland. Form gave way to function on every level. Bicycles hung on the wall instead of paintings. Shoes were thrown in a large cardboard box next to the front door. The dining-room table, a rectangular one that sat 20 people, was often covered with sawdust, carpentry tools, and boards glued together with vise grips. The piano over in the corner was missing

some keys, and its top was carved like a public picnic table. The floor was cluttered with used auto parts, darts, empty tobacco cans, discarded record jackets. The couches and pillows, strewn around the room in no particular order, were the kind that only a college freshman would buy from a college senior. It was the first living room we had seen where one worried more about what the things might do to the children than what the children might do to the things.

The people who occupied this room were urban professionals who had all emerged, three-and-a-half years ago, from regular houses with walls and Danish furniture and hardwood floors. Some of them still drove to work in the mornings, but you could see from the Cavern that there had been a change of mind. A woman named Mary, whom we first met while she was taking a bath in a porcelain tub that stuck out from under the staircase into the kitchen area, told us she had come here to "simplify her life." The house was bought with cash,

176

she said. The new inhabitants, 20 of them then, did all the wall-ripping themselves, and picked up old furniture from garage sales. "We didn't allow ourselves to keep anything we really cared about." she said. "Later, we discovered some people had stashed their good stuff secretly in bonded warehouses."

Five children lived here (six, if you count Eloise) without the props that we thought basic to an urban child's life—the props that still filled the entire back end of the car we were traveling around the country in. The five children occupied two of the upstairs bedrooms, bedrooms without any doors. They slept on floor mats, and what possessions we could see in those two bedrooms would not have filled a single large cardboard box. Amy, the 40-year-old matriarch of this place, who wore leftover cocktail dresses and gave the guided tours, was quite proud of the fact that the children had stripped down their "baggage" to a few items of clothing and a bicycle for each of them. Plus the Turtle, of course. The Turtle was collectively owned and managed by the children. It was a large ferroconcrete structure in the backyard, stocked with food, cots and a working gas stove, where grownups were forbidden to enter.

For some reason, Amy neglected to show us the garage room full of toys. Michael finally did. Michael was a seven-year-old who grabbed onto six-year-old Chauncey the moment we arrived, and the two were rarely heard from again. It was a case of two children desperate for playmates. Chauncey and Michael played mostly in a dirt pile next to the Turtle, making toys from sticks

and rocks and loose string, but once in a while Chauncey would take Michael into our portable suburb for some factory-made caps or balloons. It was during one of those visits to our car that Michael brought up the "toys in the back room." Michael took Chauncey to the white-shingled garage behind the house, opened the door, and revealed Christmas morning. Incredible piles of stuff gathering dust on the floor—Erector sets, Monopoly games, dolls, swim masks, Lionel trains in triplicate. Michael didn't pick anything up or even suggest playing with it; he just seemed to want to prove that it was there.

"Oh, *that* stuff," Amy later said. "I forget it's out there. When we came here, there were a lot of hassles about what belonged to whom, about broken things and who broke them. We had a meeting and decided to relegate the toys to the garage, where the grownups wouldn't be bothered. But, you know, the kids hardly ever go in there. Now it's just a toy drop, a forgotten place to throw the birthday presents that the grandmothers send."

AT THE CIRCLE commune, toys and boxes of books were not part of the landscape; after Michael showed Chauncey the garage, its door was never opened again during our visit. Possessions were relegated to an unimagined secondary status—it was a common cliché that commune children were more apt to share their things; but here, the entire question of things did not appear to be that important. Things were useful, but not worth fighting for, and we didn't see any fights over people's

possessions.

The lack of order in the physical surroundings heightened the impression that these children were being raised in a bus station. It was extraordinary being in a house for two days and still not being able to fix the relations between all the people. From the first morning, caught in the anarchy of 15 people trying to cook their own breakfasts, we were totally disoriented. Two men in business suits, Steve and Bill, went out the door like suburban husbands—but husbands to whom? Women and children mingling together, but which belonged to which? Amy introduced us around, but nobody drew dotted lines from one to the other with accustomed phrases like, "This is my mother," or "That is my son." John (co-author) had an intense conversation with a man named Boog, a fat man with a tattoo on his arm who gave John his theories on the benefits of beating children. Boog neglected to tell him that he had only been here for two months and had no children himself.

At the Cosmic Circle, different grownups were involved with the children, to the point that it was difficult to connect mother with child. Children were also given more room to work things out on their own—which augmented our difficulty. When little three-year-old Dixie fell down and bumped her head, everybody was in the house, and they all heard the thump that usually makes a real parent come running, but nobody came. Dixie sat there at the foot of the stairs, crying in the middle of a pile of shoes, for what seemed like five minutes.

Finally it was 16-year-old Eloise who got up off the floor, came over to Dixie,

Sometimes I think the children are being raised in a bus station.

we don't see any fights among the children.

we're self sufficient.

picked her up and patted her head. The crying stopped. "You couldn't be the mother," John said, knowing that she wasn't. "No," she said. "But we have a rule here. When a child has a problem, the nearest person is the parent."

Aside from the fact that the nearest person to Dixie was always Eloise, the system seemed to work out well. The other children spread out their physical needs among grownups and themselves to the point that they could hardly be called a bother. For people who despair at the number of glasses of water they pour for their children each day, the number of questions they must answer, the number of times they have to say "don't," this group arrangement had a lot of potential.

How can you accept sharing the basic responsibility for your children? It wasn't as simple as shared baby-sitting, which is how we had envisioned the advantages of communes. And it wasn't as simple as at another house we visited, where everybody could share in avoiding the children by repeating, "They're on their own trip, man." Here people dealt directly with other people's children, and to do that, they had to give up some of the pre-emptive parental rights that we still believed in.

Mary, a vivacious-looking woman who was one of the founders of this place, said that was one of the hardest things about living here, letting other people deal directly with your children. That and sexual jealousy. "One thing that happened when we first got here," she said, "was people would yell at my kids [Mark and Michael] or take a swat at them, and I got pissed off. It got so

that when somebody else would tell Michael to do something, he would turn around and say, 'You can't tell me, you're not my mommy.' We discussed how to get him beyond this notion, and Steve suggested that *I* was the problem. I denied it at first, but later I had to admit it. I liked Michael saying that, it gave me a certain sense of my power over him. I mean, I still had him in some special way. It's hard to give that up."

THERE WERE a lot of theories about how these children were different than they had been in the nuclear families into which they had been born. The most repeated was Amy's theory that the Circle children were "growing themselves up." That meant a lot of things—nine-year-old Judy's being able to stay in the Turtle and cook there, Eloise's responsibility for the little girl Dixie, all the children's freedom to decide when to go to bed, what to wear, with whom to sleep and even whether or not to go to school. But one choice, misbehavior, was no longer a sign of liberation at the Cosmic Circle. "We went through that bullshit in the beginning," Amy said, "letting them run all over us. But we couldn't keep a house together that way." Here there were penalties for fighting, stealing, breaking things, not working. Usually, Amy said, the penalty was isolation. And here the children had a lot of work to do.

They began their work after Bill, Steve and Joanie, a nurse, left for outside jobs, and Mary, Amy, Eloise and assorted adult floaters would sit in a corner and talk. The talk mostly centered around psychological interactions, so the

feeling we got from the children sweeping and dusting around the grownups was of janitors at Esalen. Michael, the seven-year-old, would carry plates in from the big table and try to impress Chauncey (Susan's six-year-old) with how many he could carry at once. Judy would scrape and start the dishwasher, and complain about the number of plates and why didn't they use paper ones. Ten-year-old Mark would sweep for a while always shooting an extra puff of dust in the grownups' direction, and then take down a big canful of grass and begin rolling joints. It took us a while to realize that this was a regular job and was listed on the sign-up sheet for daily chores.

There was nothing strenuous about the work here, but the way the children went about it, we could see a new attitude—the difference between helping and working. Helping is when the children's chores become more tedious for the grownups than if the grownups did them themselves. Helping out, in our experience, resulted in soap on the floor, broken Windex bottles, half-made beds, and a lot of nagging questions from Chauncey and Bernsie. Of course, they were younger than most of these children. But what impressed us here was that the Circle children did not help out. They worked. Their jobs were part of the regular "rotation sheet" for the day, not token chores to be later completed by parents.

But too much can be made of this working thing. The Circle children stretched out their jobs with a certain solemn flourish because they had little else to do. They weren't going to school, except for Karen, Steve and Amy's

Eloise is a constant temptation to the forty year old men.

Eloise is willing to come out and deal with strange grownups on a person to person level.

It's good to help out.

nine-year-old kid. The others had admittedly fallen behind. Mark had missed the entire fifth grade and was floundering with his reading. The only things we saw him try to read were comic books.

So the days at the Circle were imbued with listlessness for the children, a state of affairs which resembled that in many other urban communes we saw. The children were all occupied to a certain degree, but the alternative life was not a full life for most of them. Mark especially had never really adjusted from the days of baseball practice, plays and school activities. We became his action for the week, and he depended on us to take him to the store, the park and movies.

Other neighborhood children didn't come over to the Cosmic Circle. Amy said it was because the Circle people were so "far-out." She talked like they were in danger of being thrown out of town any minute. She made us promise we wouldn't identify the city where the commune was located. It's true, the house appeared a little odd, but the people looked and talked like other professionals in their middle 30s, and Steve and Bill and Joanie were close enough to the regular world to hold down good jobs. Amy exaggerated the daring of the living experiment, like people who hoped their phones were tapped. But her sense of paranoia and cynicism was shared by the children, who never ventured down the street and were not visited by neighbors from what even Mark called "the bullshit materialistic, ego-tripping asshole world."

What were the grownups doing while the children were bumbling around inchoately? They were talking. In fact, the main purpose of the Cosmic Circle seemed to be analyzing every nuance of every relationship. Maybe it was because the place was kept alive, economically, by Steve and Bill, the two urban psychologists. Bill said what they had hoped for, before a lot of the original people left the commune, was a giant "behavior laboratory." But that hadn't worked out, and now they settled on a lot of informal encounter groups, and on a weekly, more elaborate session, called Encounter Night. We visited Encounter Night to see how the children fit into the main business of the urban commune.

ENCOUNTER NIGHT was a version of the meetings that take place in every commune, when people get together to even scores and vent frustrations so they can stand each other for another week. It's amazing how many hours this activity took up, as many hours as most families spend in front of the television set. Here they had no television, and they didn't go to church, but Encounter was definitely a religious occasion, or as religious as you can get with urban psychologists who think of divine revelation as a psychomotor deception. Here they had elevated the simple complaint to the level of mystical experience.

Steve, who was the prime mover of the commune, presided over the meeting, attended by all the children except Dixie, and by all the grownups. For these meetings, he took off his business suit and put on white guru robes and held a glittery cheerleader's baton called the Magic Stick. For a man with a balding head and a big nose and a successful paunch that dominated his five-foot-five frame, Steve managed to look less convincing in these guru clothes. Actually, he looked like Friar Tuck going off to meet the Maharaj Ji. Steve was in his glory at these meetings, standing over the rest who had put pillows in a circle around him. He flailed his arms around so dramatically you could see his Accutron watch ticking high up on his forearm.

You had to wait for the Magic Stick to be able to speak. It started to make the rounds. The children sat very attentively, as if they understood the seriousness of this event. They did not hold the baton, but just passed it along to the nearest grownup. At first we could not tell if they were allowed to speak. The children held onto and smoked the joints, which were flowing in the other direction. The motto could have been: Children should be stoned and not heard.

The meeting progressed rather like a poker game. It started out with a few simple exchanges about the rules. Steve reminded everybody about the work board, said that nobody had signed up for weeding the garden, and that they might all have to do it over the weekend. Amy reminded everybody to pay his or her monthly food and rent bill. Joanie the nurse suggested that more people use the dental floss she copped from the hospital. Bill complained that the food buyer for the month (Mary) had been putting too much money into vegetables and not enough into desserts. He also accused unnamed people of having raided two chocolate cream pies in the middle of the night.

It was all impersonal, for a few rounds of the stick. But then people started the more direct attacks, and Amy, Boog,

Steve, Mary and Joanie began to eye each other with a gambler's suspicion. Personal weaknesses came into play. Amy mentioned that Boog the carpenter, who had been hanging out there for two months, hadn't been doing his work. "I see vise grips on the table," she said. "I see wood and glue. But I don't see any work. And that's why we are paying your room and board." Boog the bulldog didn't let that pass. When the stick got around to him, he said he resented being a "slave laborer" during the day. "If I didn't have to open every stuck bottle and do half the work the women are supposed to do around here," he said, "I'd get a lot more shelves done."

Mary said she resented that "stupid, chauvinistic remark" and then took the meeting into the thicket of high-stakes personal interplay. "While we're on the subject of Boog," she said, with off-handed amusement, "I don't like having a hard-hat around here during the day. But what I really don't like is that he thinks commune women are an easy lay." That brought some laughter. The psychologist, Bill, was the next to speak. In his driest clinical voice he suspected that Mary was *flirting* with Boog, that Boog's "come-ons weren't all that self-generated." That remark made Mary mad. She said it was ridiculous. She also didn't like the "off-the-cuff psychological bullshit from somebody who isn't here most of the time."

Several such interchanges took place, beginning with a complaint and ending with an intervention from one of the psychologists. Bill and Steve would lay in wait for a certain level of irrationality and then strike with clinical swiftness.

That way, they were never on the defensive and always had the last word. But whatever Bill and Steve and the rest were doing, the children seemed to lose interest. A lot of what was said was remarkably childish for grownups who supposedly had been refining the art of living together. (Mary called Joanie a "lousy cunt" for refusing to help her at the grocery store.) But neither Mary's children nor Joanie's took special notice. The children seemed to accept verbal hostility like children of drunk parents accept drunkenness.

Sometime around 9 p.m., when the comments were getting trivial, one of the children finally took the stick. It was Karen, the dumpy, black-haired girl with the American flag patch on her blue jeans. She opened up in an extremely loud and confident voice—there were no verbally timid children here. "I want to say something about Amy," she said. "I think other people have noticed it, too. She's been real bossy lately. She hassles me about school, and does stuff like accidentally drop pans outside my room to wake me up. What are pans doing on the second floor?

"She knows school is my business. But she can't handle it. Just 'cause she's the oldest woman in the house, she still thinks she can tell everybody what to do. It's a big ego trip."

Karen's delivery was a little shrill, but it was effective. It was unusual to see a nine-year-old take on a grownup in an open field like this, especially when the grownup was her mother. She was aware of her mother's effect on her, of her mother's designs on her, in a way that made her seem much older than her nine

years. It was somehow unsettling to witness that kind of awareness in a little kid.

It was also unsettling to Amy. She would deny it later, but you could see it in her face. She was trying to look impassive, in a Big Nurse sort of way, but she was failing. Her face was cocked. You could sense her mind behind it, all her years of wisdom, loading up with ammunition for a big volley back at Karen. She never got to retaliate, though, and the commune itself buffered what might have been the usual nuclear family reaction. Before Amy could get her hands on the stick, it went to Mary, who supported what Karen had said. That cooled Amy out considerably, and by the time she got to speak she managed to sound pleasant. "I know what the problem is," Amy said. "It's the big Jewish mother that captures me at night, when I'm in a weakened condition. When I get pushy, it's really her talking." It was the presence of the other people that gave Karen the impetus to criticize her mother in what seemed to be a constructive way.

The results of this meeting hinted at another possible advantage of communal life. It was a natural check on the invisible mother. Amy's meddling was not permitted by the group, or at least the group gave Karen a way to express her opposition to it. How many nine-year-old girls have that opportunity? Left alone in a house, Amy would not have let go of her anger long enough to hear what Karen had to say. And how did Karen even know what to say? It wasn't the freedom of speech that was impressive, it was a kind of emotional distance which allowed Karen to see her mother's faults clearly, see her mother as a person,

...that Helen's made it with Bill and with Karen's father, Harry and Joanie's taken up with Bill and Bill's wife has left with another man leaving Dixie behind...

They are potentially lasting relationships that didn't work out.

They're compensating.

unravel the mystery of her parents a little earlier than some of us who begin to do it when we go to college.

Karen was the most tied to her parents of any of the children here. Maybe because she was the daughter of the only original married couple that still remained. She spent quite a lot of time with her mother, she did her homework, she went to school, and she carried on in many ways like she was still a part of a nuclear family. She had already picked up the psychological jargon of her father, Steve. She even looked like her parents—dumpy and fluttery. And yet she already had a clearly defined notion of her emotional rights, not just property rights, but her rights to be spared from the effects of her mother's admittedly neurotic behavior.

SOMETIMES, EVEN with all the analyzing, there were total freakouts. One morning there was a major commotion down the hall, from one of the bedrooms that had no doors. It was a male voice saying, "Hey, kid, don't do that," with mild impatience at first, and then again, "Don't do that," now more threatening, and finally, "I'm going to kick that little bastard out in the hall." Then Mary said, "Don't be rough with him, he doesn't understand." Later we found out that Michael had gone in there to pull the covers off his mother's lover, a weekend visitor from somewhere. Mary tried to make light of it, but Michael appeared to be quite upset. He and Chauncey, who had played for several days without a problem, got into a fight and had to be separated. Michael, usually a cheery figure, sulked around and peri-

odically ran up to the male visitor and pretended to pinch him in the ass. The visitor, a man named Jeremy, pretended to swat Michael away like a mosquito, but you could see that Michael was perturbed. Mary said he had pulled the cover trick several times since she and her husband had broken up a year earlier.

Commune life had torn every one of these families apart. Maybe, as Mary suggested, they would have been torn up anyway, but in a place with no doors and walls and a belief in total openness, the children knew everything. No attempt was made to hide lovers or to soften the blows of divorce and attendant recriminations. Mark and Michael had arrived here with a mother and a stepfather, and they knew the ex-Hertz agent turned rock musician who had taken their mother away from their stepfather. They also knew each lover from the succession of men their mother had seen since. Mark was even able to say, with some accuracy, that his mother had "the hottest pants in the commune." Michael could not be so jocular about it.

The line on the children was that since they had spent more of their lives in a communal place, they could handle the floating relationships and the disruptions better than the parents. It was part of a new notion of progress that they had, that Circle children would overcome some of the pettiness, some of the possessiveness, some of the ugly competitiveness, that the grownups carried here.

It was hard to say for sure, but it didn't seem to us that the children were handling the parental disruptions any better than the parents.

HOW DIFFERENT were these Circle children who had emerged, three-and-a-half years beforehand, from nuclear families? The commune certainly had not had a homogenizing effect on them, like what reportedly happened when the family structure was broken in China. The commune had not cut them off from certain aspects of Americana—they knew all the television shows. Even though they had no television set, they knew the Waltons, "Sesame Street," quiz programs. We asked Mark where he got this TV knowledge. Was there a kind of kid osmosis at work here? And he said, "Grandmother." That was another thing, the "grandmother factor." They all visited their grandmothers during the summer or for a week here and there, a week, Amy said, "of getting presents and being spoiled." It was a deliberate part of the training. "I don't want them to grow up not knowing about the kind of world we left behind," Amy said. "If they get a little of it now, maybe they won't go back to it."

How far were these children from the world their parents left behind? They had the communal house; it was like a Depression house with the extra people and commotion and mealtimes and the entertaining disorder of *You Can't Take It with You*. The house without walls gave them all a lesson in demythologication—there was no way to live in that place and come out of it honoring parents as parents, or sanctifying the Office of Parenthood. The children were too adept at psychological probing, too aware of the revealed foibles of their own parents to believe that parents are

LOUMYER

more than people.

The children's independence had nothing to do with rules or the absence of them—if anything, they had more responsibility than regular urban children. The Circle children had a kind of independence of spirit that derived from the presence of the group. Eloise, who said she had never gotten along with her real family, had in effect invented a new family at the Circle. She said living at the Circle improved her relationship with her mother, with whom she visited from time to time. Judy, when she was having particular trouble with her mother Joanie, could find room to stay away from her. Mark and Michael could spread their need for adult contact among a lot of people. There were no apparent sibling rivalries, possibly because every child knew a grownup who thought he or she was special. It was reminiscent of Aldous Huxley's *Island*, where the children had the right to choose parents from the people they got along with best. "We scoff at arranged marriages," Amy said, "as being clumsy and cruel. But what about arranged childhoods? The way things are set up in most families, children never have the chance to know it can be any other way."

AT THE SAME time, there was a conspiratorial hush about the place which tended to isolate these children from the larger world around them. When Circle members did invite outsiders from the neighborhood, it was for symbolic exercises like the Race, which took place every couple of months. The Race was part of a day of games and activities in the backyard, when Steve was in his glory, walking around giving speeches on the virtues of group living.

The Race occurred when everybody lined up on a chalk marker, as if they were ready for the hundred-yard dash, and Steve shot off a blank starter pistol, and the entire community took off. They ran in circles, screaming wildly, over bushes and around trees, until they all fell down in mock exhaustion. Then they lined up and did it again, until nobody

had the energy to get up. "There is no finish line in life," Steve was happy to point out to the onlookers, "and there is no finish line here. Everybody wins his own race."

They talked about living without competition, about how incompatible it was with communal spirit, and yet many of them were holding down competitive jobs on the outside. Steve, especially, was conscious of the irony, enough so that every time he came home from his office, he would throw down his coat, and declare, "That's the end of the bullshit for today, man." We asked him why he always had to say that, why he couldn't just come in and sit down. "I still have to work," he said, "but I want the children to know that I am just putting up with it. It isn't that I like to do it."

It took awhile to see through that fantasy, and what finally did it was Steve's studies. Steve, apparently, had been testing the kids all along, giving them the same psychological and intelligence batteries that most kids get in schools. He said he did them to prove to his own colleagues that the children had not been damaged by communal life, to encourage other parents to live this way. But it seemed that Steve did the studies for his own benefit, to prove to himself that the kids were still bright. It was not achievement he cared about but raw intelligence; he talked about the children's uniformly high IQs.

And the children also talked about intelligence. Karen, especially, was always postulating that "that was an intelligent statement," or "that was a dumb statement." Mark, the least academic of all of them, introduced himself as the "smartest person in the commune." I think he might have doubted that; but one very conventional thing about all these children was that they were verbally aggressive and often snide. Snideness was not discouraged at the Circle; it was valued as proof of mental agility.

It was part of the confusion. Intellectual activity was valued here; it took up most of the adults' time, and talk put money on the table. Bill and Steve could

come home and throw down their coats in a flourish, but it didn't hide the excitement on their faces when they discussed their work. The children knew all this; they heard Mary talk about the garden and about "self-sufficiency" but they didn't quite believe it. Eloise was totally committed to the commune; she had no desire to return to school. But the others, I think, saw through Steve's noncompetitive posture—they would be back in school next year. It was part of an unresolved drama of all urban communes: how can you let your kids drop out and still let your colleagues know they have 140 IQs?

The other confusion had to do with the role of the separate families in this communal place. Behind all the apparently open exploration of sexual relationships was a conventional belief in monogamy. The grownups were honest about it, of course, and honesty was a first step away from suburban hypocrisy, but they exaggerated the importance of that honesty in changing their children's attitudes about marriage and sex. Judy's protest against her mother and Michael's pulling covers off the lovers are classic examples of kids freaking out about a divorce or a separation—the extra honesty did not seem to have helped in those two situations. The kids did carry their parents' belief in families—Mark talked a lot about who his girlfriends were; Karen accused Judy of being too sullen to have boyfriends. There was no resolution, in the Circle, of the jealousy and loyalty questions plaguing many families. In this area, as in so many others, we found people living in the urban communes we visited grappling with the same problems plaguing nuclear families today, exploring earnestly but with no complete resolution in sight.

*Excerpted from the book* The Children of the Counter-culture © *1976 by John Rothchild and Susan Berns Wolf, published by Doubleday & Co., Inc. Rothchild is an editor for the* Washington Monthly; *Wolf is a former film editor.*

# the future
# of marriage

## By MORTON HUNT

*under the pressure of subcultures and social move-
ments, matrimony is changing from the old patriarchal
pattern to a new form of partnership*

OVER A CENTURY AGO, the Swiss historian and
ethnologist J. J. Bachofen postulated that early man
lived in small packs, ignorant of marriage and indulging
in beastlike sexual promiscuity. He could hardly have
suggested anything more revolting, or more fascinating,
to the puritanical and prurient sensibility of his time, and
whole theories of the family and of society were based
on his notion by various anthropolgists, as well as by
German socialist Friedrich Engels and Russian revolu-
tionist Pëtr Kropotkin. As the Victorian fog dissipated,
however, it turned out that among the hundreds of primitive peoples still on earth — many of whom lived much
like early man — not a single one was without some
form of marriage and some limitations on the sexual
freedom of the married. Marriage, it appeared, was
a genuine human universal, like speech and social
organization.

Nonetheless, Bachofen's myth died hard, because it appealed to a longing, deep in all of us, for total freedom to
do whatever we want. And recently, it has sprung up from

its own ashes in the form of a startling new notion: Even
if there never was a time when marriage didn't exist, there
soon will be. Lately, the air has been filled with such
prophecies of the decline and impending fall of marriage.
Some of the prophets are grieved at this prospect — among
them, men of the cloth, such as the Pope and Dr. Peale,
who keep warning us that hedonism and easy divorce are
eroding the very foundations of family life. Others, who
rejoice at the thought, include an assortment of feminists,
hippies and anarchists, plus much-married theater people
such as Joan Fontaine, who, having been married more
times than the Pope and Dr. Peale put together, has authori-
tatively told the world that marriage is obsolete and that
any sensible person can live and love better without it.

Some of the fire-breathing dragon ladies who have given
women's lib an undeservedly bad name urge single women
not to marry and married ones to desert their husbands
forthwith. Kate Millet, the movement's leading theoretician,
expects marriage to wither away after women achieve full
equality. Dr. Roger Egeberg, an Assistant Secretary of
HEW, urged Americans in 1969 to reconsider their inherited
belief that everyone ought to marry, And last August, Mrs.
Rita Hauser, the U.S. representative to the UN Human

Rights Commission, said that the idea that marriage was primarily for procreation had become outmoded and that laws banning marriage between homosexuals should be erased from the books.

So much for the voices of prophecy. Are there, in fact, any real indications of a mass revolt against traditional marriage? There certainly seems to be. For one thing, in 1969 there were 660,000 divorces in America — an all-time record — and the divorce rate seems certain to achieve historic new highs in the next few years. For another thing, marital infidelity seems to have increased markedly since Kinsey's first surveys of a generation ago and now is tried, sooner or later, by some 60 percent of married men and 30 to 35 percent of married women in this country. But in what is much more of a departure from the past, infidelity is now tacitly accepted by a fair number of the spouses of the unfaithful. For some couples it has become a shared hobby; mate-swapping and group-sex parties now involve thousands of middle-class marriages. Yet another indication of change is a sharp increase not only in the number of young men and women who, dispensing with legalities, live together unwed but also in the *kind* of people who are doing so; although common-law marriage has long been popular among the poor, in the past few years it has become widespread — and often esteemed — within the middle class.

An even more radical attack on our marriage system is the effort of people in hundreds of communes around the country to construct "families," or group marriages, in which the adults own everything in common, and often consider that they all belong to one another and play mix and match sexually with total freedom. A more complete break with tradition is being made by a rapidly growing percentage of America's male and female homosexuals, who nowadays feel freer than ever to avoid "cover" marriages and to live openly as homosexuals. Their lead is almost certain to be followed by countless others within the next decade or so as our society grows ever more tolerant of personal choice in sexual matters.

Nevertheless, reports of the death of marriage are, to paraphrase Mark Twain, greatly exaggerated. Most human beings regard whatever they grew up with as right and good and see nearly every change in human behavior as a decline in standards and a fall from grace. But change often means adaptation and evolution. The many signs of contemporary revolt against marriage have been viewed as symptoms of a fatal disease, but they may, instead, be signs of a change from an obsolescent form of marriage — patriarchal monogamy — into new forms better suited to present-day human needs.

Marriage as a social structure is exceedingly plastic, being shaped by the interplay of culture and of human needs into hundreds of different forms. In societies where women could do valuable productive work, it often made sense for a man to acquire more than one wife; where women were idle or relatively unproductive — and, hence, a burden — monogamy was more likely to be the pattern. When women had means of their own or could fall back upon relatives, divorce was apt to be easy; where they were wholly dependent on their husbands, it was generally difficult. Under marginal and primitive living conditions, men kept their women in useful subjugation; in wealthier and more leisured societies, women often managed to acquire a degree of independence and power.

For a long while, the only acceptable form of marriage in America was a life-long one-to-one union, sexually faithful, all but indissoluble, productive of goods and children and strongly husband-dominated. It was a thoroughly func-

tional mechanism during the 18th and much of the 19th centuries, when men were struggling to secure the land and needed women who would clothe and feed them, produce and rear children to help them, and obey their orders without question for an entire lifetime. It was functional, too, for the women of that time, who, uneducated, unfit for other kinds of work and endowed by law with almost no legal or property rights, needed men who would support them, give them social status and be their guides and protectors for life.

But time passed, the Indians were conquered, the sod was busted, towns and cities grew up, railroads laced the land, factories and offices took the place of the frontier. Less and less did men need women to produce goods and children; more and more, women were educated, had time to spare, made their way into the job market — and realized that they no longer had to cling to their men for life. As patriarchalism lost its usefulness, women began to want and demand orgasms, contraceptives, the vote and respect; men, finding the world growing ever more impersonal and cold, began to want wives who were warm, understanding, companionable and sexy.

Yet, strangely enough, as all these things were happening, marriage not only did not lose ground but grew more popular, and today, when it is under full-scale attack on most fronts, it is more widespread than ever before. A considerably larger percentage of our adult population was married in 1970 than was the case in 1890; the marriage rate, though still below the level of the 1940s, has been climbing steadily since 1963.

The explanation of this paradox is that as marriage was losing its former uses, it was gaining new ones. The changes that were robbing marriage of practical and life-affirming values were turning America into a mechanized urban society in which we felt like numbers, not individuals, in which we had many neighbors but few lifelong friends and in which our lives were controlled by remote governments, huge companies and insensate computers. Alone and impotent, how can we find intimacy and warmth, understanding and loyalty, enduring friendship and a feeling of personal importance? Why, obviously, through *loving* and *marrying*. Marriage is a microcosm, a world within which we seek to correct the shortcomings of the macrocosm around us. Saint Paul said it is better to marry than to burn; today, feeling the glacial chill of the world we live in, we find it better to marry than to freeze.

The model of marriage that served the old purposes excellently serves the new ones poorly. But most of the contemporary assaults upon it are not efforts to destroy it, they are efforts to modify and remold it. Only traditional patriarchal marriage is dying, while all around us marriage is being reborn in new forms. The marriage of the future already exists; we have merely mistaken the signs of evolutionary change for the stigmata of necrosis.

Divorce is a case in point. Far from being a wasting illness, it is a healthful adaptation, enabling monogamy to survive in a time when patriarchal powers, privileges and marital systems have become unworkable; far from being a radical change in the institution of marriage, divorce is a relatively minor modification of it and thoroughly supportive of most of its conventions.

Not that it seemed so at first. When divorce was introduced to Christian Europe, it appeared an extreme and rather sinful measure to most people; even among the wealthy — the only people who could afford it — it remained for centuries quite rare and thoroughly scandalous. In 1816, when president Timothy Dwight of Yale thundered against the "alarming and terrible" divorce rate in Connecticut, about one of every 100 marriages was being legally dissolved. But as women began achieving a certain degree of emancipation during the 19th Century, and as the purposes of marriage changed, divorce laws were liberalized and the rate began climbing. Between 1870 and 1905, both the U.S. population and the divorce rate more than doubled; and between then and today, the divorce rate increased over four times.

And not only for the reasons we have already noted but for yet another: the increase in longevity. When people married in their late 20s and marriage was likely to end in death by the time the last child was leaving home, divorce seemed not only wrong but hardly worth the trouble; this was especially true where the only defect in a marriage was boredom. Today, however, when people marry earlier and have finished raising their children with half their adult lives still ahead of them, boredom seems a very good reason for getting divorced.

Half of all divorces occur after eight years of marriage and a quarter of them after 45 — most of these being not the results of bad initial choices but of disparity or dullness that has grown with time.

Divorcing people, however, are seeking not to escape from marriage for the rest of their lives but to exchange unhappy or boring marriages for satisfying ones. Whatever bitter things they say at the time of divorce, the vast majority do remarry, most of their second marriages lasting the rest of their lives, even those whose second marriages fail are very likely to divorce and remarry again and, that failing, yet again. Divorcing people are actually marrying people, and divorce is not a negation of marriage but a workable cross between traditional monogamy and multiple marriage; sociologists have even referred to it as "serial polygamy."

Despite its costs and its hardships, divorce is thus a compromise between the monogamous ideal and the realities of present-day life. To judge from the statistics, it is becoming more useful and more socially acceptable every year, Although the divorce rate leveled off for a dozen years or so after the postwar surge of 1946, it has been climbing steadily since 1962, continuing the long-range trend of 100 years, and the rate for the entire nation now stands at nearly one for every three marriages. In some areas, it is even higher. In California, where a new ultraliberal law went into effect in 1970, nearly two of every three marriages end in divorce — a fact that astonishes people in other areas of the country but that Californians themselves accept with equanimity. They still approve of, and very much enjoy, being married; they have simply gone further than the rest of us in using divorce to keep monogamy workable in today's world.

Seen in the same light, marital infidelity is also a frequently useful modification of the marriage contract rather than a repudiation of it. It violates the conventional moral code to a greater degree than does divorce but, as practiced in America, is only a limited departure from the monogamous pattern. Unfaithful Americans, by and large, neither have extramarital love affairs that last for many years nor do they engage in a continuous series of minor liaisons: rather, their infidelity consists of relatively brief and widely scattered episodes, so that in the course of a married lifetime, they spend many more years being faithful than being unfaithful. Furthermore, American infidelity, unlike its European counterparts, has no recognized status as part of the marital system; except in a few circles, it remains impermissible, hidden and isolated from the rest of one's life. This is not true at all levels of our society, however: Upper-class men — and, to some extent, women — have

long regarded the discreet love affair as an essential complement to marriage, and lower-class husbands have always considered an extracurricular roll in the hay important to a married man's peace of mind. Indeed, very few societies have ever tried to make both husband and wife sexually faithful over a lifetime; the totally monogamous ideal is statistically an abnormality. Professors Clellan Ford and Frank Beach state in *Patterns of Sexual Behavior* that less than 16 percent of 185 societies studied by anthropologists had formal restrictions to a single mate — and, of these, less than a third wholly disapproved of both premarital and extramarital relationships.

Our middle-class, puritanical society, however, has long held that infidelity of any sort is impossible if one truly loves one's mate and is happily married, that any deviation from fidelity stems from an evil or neurotic character and that it inevitably damages both the sinner and the sinned against. This credo drew support from earlier generations of psychotherapists, for almost all the adulterers they treated were neurotic, unhappily married or out of sorts with life in general. But it is just such people who seek psychotherapy; they are hardly a fair example. Recently, sex researchers have examined the unfaithful more representatively and have come up with quite different findings. Alfred Kinsey, sociologist Robert Whitehurst of Indiana University, sociologist John Cuber of Ohio State University, sexologist/therapist Dr. Albert Ellis and various others (including myself), all of whom have made surveys of unfaithful husbands and wives agree in general that:

• Many of the unfaithful — perhaps even a majority — are not seriously dissatisfied with their marriages nor their mates and a fair number are more or less happily married.

• Only about a third — perhaps even fewer — appear to seek extramarital sex for neurotic motives; the rest do so for nonpathological reasons.

• Many of the unfaithful — perhaps even a majority — do not feel that they, their mates nor their marriages have been harmed; in my own sample, a tenth said that their marriages had been helped or made more tolerable by their infidelity.

It is still true that many a "deceived" husband or wife, learning about his or her mate's infidelity, feels humiliated, betrayed and unloved, and is filled with rage and the desire for revenge; it is still true, too, that infidelity is a cause in perhaps a third of all divorces. But more often than not, deceived spouses never know of their mates' infidelity nor are their marriages perceptibly harmed by it.

The bulk of present-day infidelity remains hidden beneath the disguise of conventional marital behavior. But an unfettered minority of husbands and wives openly grant each other the right to outside relationships, limiting that right to certain occasions and certain kinds of involvement, in order to keep the marital relationship all-important and unimpaired. A few couples, for instance, take separate vacations or allow each other one night out alone per week, it being understood that their extramarital involvements are to be confined to those times. Similar freedoms have been urged by radical marriage reformers for decades but have never really caught on, and probably never will, for one simple reason: What's out of sight is not necessarily out of mind. What husband can feel sure, despite his wife's promises, that she might not find some other man who will make her dream come true? What wife can feel sure that her husband won't fall in love with some woman he is supposed to be having only a friendly tumble with?

But it's another matter when husband and wife go together in search of extramarital frolic and do their thing with other people, in full view of each other, where it is free of romantic feeling. This is the very essence of marital swinging, or, as it is sometimes called, comarital sex. Whether it consists of a quiet mate exchange between two couples, a small sociable group-sex party or a large orgiastic rumpus, the premise is the same: As long as the extra-marital sex is open, shared and purely recreational, it is not considered divisive of marriage.

So the husband and wife welcome the baby sitter, kiss the children good night and drive off together to someone's home, where they drink a little and make social talk with their hosts and any other guests present, and then pair off with a couple of the others and disappear into bedrooms for an hour or so or undress in the living room and have sex in front of their interested and approving mates.

No secrecy about that, certainly, and no hidden romance to fear: indeed, the very exhibitionism of marital swinging enforces its most important ground rule—the tacit understanding that participants will not indulge in emotional involvements with fellow swingers, no matter what physical acts they perform together. Though a man and a woman make it with each other at a group-sex party, they are not supposed to meet each other later on; two swinging couples who get together outside of parties are disapprovingly said to be going steady. According to several researchers, this proves that married swingers value their marriages: They want sexual fun and stimulation but nothing that would jeopardize their marital relationships. As sociologists Duane Denfeld and Michael Gordon of the University of Connecticut straight-facedly write, marital swingers "favor monogamy and want to maintain it" and do their swinging "in order to support and improve their marriages."

To the outsider, this must sound very odd, not to say outlandish. How could anyone hope to preserve the warmth and intimacy of marriage by performing the most private and personal sexual acts with other people in front of his mate or watching his mate do so with others?

Such a question implies that sex is integrally interwoven with the rest of one's feelings about the mate—which it is —but swingers maintain that it can be detached and enjoyed apart from those feelings, without changing them in any way. Marital swinging is supposed to involve only this one segment of the marital relationship and during only a few hours of any week or month; all else is meant to remain intact, monogamous and conventional.

Experts maintain that some people swing out of neurotic needs; some have sexual problems in their marriages that do not arise in casual sexual relationships; some are merely bored and in need of new stimuli; some need the ego lift of continual conquests. But the average swinger, whatever his (or her) motive, normal or pathological, is apt to believe that he loves his spouse, that he has a pretty good marriage and that detaching sex—and sex alone—from marital restrictions not only will do the marriage no harm but will rid it of any aura of confinement.

. . .

In contrast to this highly specialized and sharply limited attitude, there seems to be a far broader and more thorough rejection of marriage on the part of those men and women who choose to live together unwed. Informal, nonlegal unions have long been widespread among poor blacks, largely for economic reasons, but the present wave of such unions among middle-class whites has an ideological basis, for most of those who choose this arrangement consider themselves revolutionaries who have the guts to pioneer in a more honest and vital relationship than conventional marriage. A 44-year-old conference leader, Theodora Wells,

and a 51-year-old psychologist, Lee Christie, who live together in Beverly Hills, expounded their philosophy in the April 1970 issue of *The Futurist:* " 'Personhood' is central to the living-together relationship; sex roles are central to the marriage relationship. Our experience strongly suggests that personhood excites growth, stimulates openness, increases joyful satisfactions in achieving, encompasses rich, full sexuality peaking in romance. Marriage may have the appearance of this in its romantic phase, but it settles down to prosaic routine. . . .The wife role is diametrically opposed to the personhood I want. I [Theodora] therefore choose to live with the man who joins me in the priority of personhood."

What this means is that she hates homemaking, is career oriented and fears that if she became a legal wife, she would automatically be committed to traditional female roles, to dependency. Hence, she and Christie have rejected marriage and chosen an arrangement without legal obligations, without a head of the household and without a primary money earner or primary homemaker—though Christie, as it happens, does 90 percent of the cooking. Both believe that their freedom from legal ties and their constant need to rechoose each other make for a more exciting, real and growing relationship.

A fair number of the avant-garde and many of the young have begun to find this not only a fashionably rebellious but a thoroughly congenial attitude toward marriage; couples are living together, often openly, on many a college campus, risking punishment by college authorities (but finding the risks smaller every day) and bucking their parents' strenuous disapproval (but getting their glum acceptance more and more often).

When one examines the situation closely, however, it becomes clear that most of these marital Maoists live together in close, warm, committed and monogamous fashion, very much like married people: they keep house together (although often dividing their roles in untraditional ways) and neither is free to have sex with anyone else, date anyone else nor even find anyone else intriguing. Anthropologists Margaret Mead and Ashley Montagu, sociologist John Gagnon and other close observers of the youth scene feel that living together, whatever its defects, is actually an apprentice marriage and not a true rebellion against marriage at all.

Dr. Mead, incidentally, made a major public pitch in 1966 for a revision of our laws that would create two kinds of marital status: individual marriage, a legal but easily dissolved form for young people who were unready for parenthood or full commitment to each other but who wanted to live together with social acceptance, and parental marriage, a union involving all the legal commitments and responsibilities — and difficulties of dissolution — of marriage as we presently know of. Her suggestion aroused a great deal of public debate. The middle-aged for the most part condemned her proposal as being an attack upon and a debasement of marriage while the young replied that the whole idea was unnecessary. The young were right: They were already creating their own new marital folkway in the form of the close, serious but informal union that achieved all the goals of individual marriage except its legality and acceptance by the middle-aged. Thinking themselves rebels against marriage, they had only created a new form of marriage closely resembling the very thing Dr. Mead had suggested.

. . .

If these modifications of monogamy aren't quite as alarming or as revolutionary as they seem to be, one contemporary experiment in marriage *is* a genuine and total break with Western tradition. This is group marriage — a catchall term applied to a wide variety of polygamous experiments in which small groups of adult males and females, and their children, live together under one roof or in a close-knit settlement, calling themselves a family, tribe, commune or, more grandly, intentional community and considering themselves all married to one another.

As the term intentional community indicates, these are experiments not merely in marriage but in the building of a new type of society. They are utopian minisocieties existing within, but almost wholly opposed to, the mores and values of present-day American society.

Not that they are all of a piece. A few are located in cities and have members who look and act square and hold regular jobs; some, both urban and rural, consist largely of dropouts, acidheads, panhandlers and petty thieves, but most are rural communities, have hippie-looking members and aim at a self-sufficient farming-and-handicraft way of life. A very few communes are politically conservative, some are in the middle and most are pacifist, anarchistic and still or New Lefist. Nearly all, whatever their national political bent, are islands of primitive communism in which everything is collectively owned and all members work for the common good.

The communism extends to—or perhaps really begins with—sexual collectivism. Though some communes consist of married couples who are conventionally faithful, many are built around some kind of group sexual sharing. In some of these, couples are paired off but occasionally sleep with other members of the group; in others, pairings off is actively discouraged and the members drift around sexually from one partner to another— a night here, a night there, as they wish.

Group marriage has captured the imagination of many thousands of college students in the past few years through its idealistic and romantic portrayal in three novels widely read by the young—Robert Heinlein's *Stranger in a Strange Land* and Robert Rimmer's *The Harrad Experiment* and *Proposition 31*. The underground press, too, has paid a good deal of sympathetic attention—and the establishment press a good deal of hostile attention—to communes. There has even been, for several years, a West Coast publication titled *The Modern Utopian* that is devoted, in large part, to news and discussions of group marriage. The magazine, which publishes a directory of intentional communities, recently listed 125 communes and the editor said, "For every listing you find here, you can be certain there are 100 others." And an article in *The New York Times* last December stated that "nearly 2000 communes in 34 states have turned up" but gave this as a conservative figure, as "no accurate count exists."

All this sometimes gives one the feeling that group marriage is sweeping the country; but, based on the undoubtedly exaggerated figures of *The Modern Utopian* and counting a generous average of 20 people per commune, it would still mean that no more than 250,000 adults—approximately one tenth of one percent of the U.S. population—are presently involved in group marriages. These figures seem improbable.

Nevertheless, group marriage offers solutions to a number of the nagging problems and discontents of modern monogamy. Collective parenthood—every parent being partly responsible for every child in the group—not only provides a warm and enveloping atmosphere for children but removes some of the pressure from individual parents; moreover, it minimizes the disruptive effects of divorce on the child's world. Sexual sharing is an answer to boredom and solves the problem of infidelity, or seeks to, by declaring extramarital experiences acceptable and admirable. It avoids the success-status-possession syndrome of middle-class family life by turning toward simplicity, communal ownership and communal goals.

Finally, it avoids the loneliness and confinement of monogamy by creating something comparable to what anthropologists call the extended family, a larger grouping of related people living together. (There is a difference, of course: In group marriage, the extended family isn't composed of blood relatives.) Even when sexual switching isn't the focus, there is a warm feeling of being affectionally connected to everyone else. As one young woman in a Taos commune said ecstatically, "It's really groovy waking up and knowing that 48 people love you."

Other writers, including those who have sampled communal life, also talk about the problems of leadership (most communes have few rules to start with: those that survive for any time do so by becoming almost conventional and traditional) and the difficulties in communal work sharing (there are always some members who are slovenly and lazy and others who are neat and hardworking, the latter either having to expel the former or give up and let the commune slowly die).

A more serious defect is that most group marriages, being based upon a simple, semiprimitive agrarian life, reintroduce old-style patriarchalism, because such a life puts a premium on masculine muscle power and endurance and leaves the classic domestic and subservient roles to women. Even a most sympathetic observer, psychiatrist Joseph Downing, writes. "In the tribal families, while both sexes work, women are generally in a service role. . . . Male dominance is held desirable by both sexes."

Most serious of all are the emotional limitations of group marriage. Its ideal is sexual freedom and universal love, but the group marriages that most nearly achieve this have the least cohesiveness and the shallowest interpersonal involvements: people come and go, and there is really no marriage at all but only a continuously changing and highly unstable encounter group. The longer-lasting and more cohesive group marriages are, in fact, those in which, as Dr. Downing reports, the initial sexual spree "generally gives way to the quiet, semipermanent, monogamous relationship characteristic of many in our general society."

Not surprisingly, therefore, Dr. Ellis finds that most group marriages are unstable and last only several months to a few years; and sociologist Lewis Yablonsky of California State College at Hayward, who has visited and lived in a number of communes, says that they are often idealistic but rarely successful or enduring. Over and above their specific difficulties, they are utopian—they seek to construct a new society from whole cloth. But all utopias thus far have failed, human behavior is so incredibly complex that every totally new order, no matter how well planned, generates innumerable unforseen problems. It really is a pity, group living and group marriage look wonderful on paper.

. . .

All in all, then, the evidence is overwhelming that old-fashioned marriage is not dying and that nearly all of what passes for rebellion against it is a series of patchwork modifications enabling marriage to serve the needs of modern man without being unduly costly or painful.

While this is the present situation, can we extrapolate it into the future? Will marriage continue to exist in some form we can recognize?

It is clear that, in the future, we are going to have an even greater need than we now do for love relationships that offer intimacy, warmth, companionship and a reasonable degree of reliability. Such relationships need not, of course, be heterosexual. With our increasing tolerance of sexual diversity, it seems likely that many homosexual men and women will find it publicly acceptable to live together in quasi-marital alliances.

The great majority of men and women, however, will continue to find heterosexual love the preferred form, for biological and psychological reasons that hardly have to be spelled out here. But need heterosexual love be embodied within marriage? If the world is already badly overpopulated and daily getting worse, why add to its burden—and if one does not intend to have children, why seek to enclose love within a legal cage? Formal promises to love are promises no one can keep, for love is not an act of will; and legal bonds have no power to keep love alive when it is dying.

Such reasoning—more cogent today than ever, due to the climate of sexual permissiveness and to the twin technical advances of the pill and the loop—lies behind the growth of unwed unions. From all indications, however, such unions will not replace marriage as an institution but only precede it in the life of the individual.

It seems probable that more and more young people will live together unwed for a time and then marry each other or break up and make another similar alliance, and another, until one of them turns into a formal, legal marriage. In 50 years, perhaps less, we may come close to the Scandinavian pattern, in which a great many couples live together prior to marriage. It may be, moreover, that the spread of this practice will decrease the divorce rate among the young, for many of the mistakes that are recognized too late and are undone in divorce court will be recognized and undone outside the legal system, with less social and emotional damage than divorce involves.

If, therefore, marriage continues to be important, what form will it take? The one truly revolutionary innovation is group marriage—and, as we have seen, it poses innumerable and possibly insuperable practical and emotional difficulties. A marriage of one man and one women involves only one interrelationship, yet we all know how difficult it is to find that one right fit and to keep it in working order. But add one more person, making the smallest possible group marriage, and you have three relationships (A-B, B-C and A-C); add a fourth to make two couples and you have six relationships; add enough to make a typical group marriage of 15 persons and you have 105 relationships.

This is an abstract way of saying that human beings are all very different and that finding a satisfying and workable love relationship is not easy, even for a twosome, and is impossibly difficult for aggregations of a dozen or so. It might prove less difficult, a generation hence, for children brought up in group-marriage communes. Such children would not have known the close, intense, parent-child relationships of monogamous marriage and could more easily spread their affections thinly and undemandingly among many. But this is mere conjecture, for no communal-marriage experiment in America has lasted long enough for us to see the results, except the famous Oneida Community in Upstate New York; it endured from 1848 to 1879, and then its offspring vanished back into the surrounding ocean of monogamy.

Those group marriages that do endure in the future will probably be dedicated to a rural and semiprimitive agrarian life style. Urban communes may last for some years but with an ever-changing membership and a lack of inner familial identity; in the city, one's work life lies outside the group, and with only emotional ties to hold the group together any dissension or conflict will result in a turnover of membership. But while agrarian communes may have a sounder foundation, they can never become a mass movement, there is simply no way for the land to support well over 200,000,000 people with the low efficiency productive methods of a century or two ago.

Agrarian communes not only cannot become a mass movement in the future but they will not even have much chance of surviving as islands in a sea of modern industrialism. For semiprimitive agrarianism is so marginal, so back-breaking and so tedious a way of life that it is unlikely to hold most of its converts against the competing attractions of conventional civilization. Even Dr. Downing, for all his enthusiasm about the "Society of Awakening," as he calls tribal family living, predicts that for the foreseeable future, only a small minority will be attracted to it and that most of these will return to more normal surroundings and relationships after a matter of weeks or months.

Thus, monogamy will prevail; on this, nearly all experts agree. But it will almost certainly continue to change in the same general direction in which it has been changing for the past few generations; namely, toward a redefinition of the special roles played by husband and wife, so as to achieve a more equal distribution of the rights, privileges and life expectations of man and woman.

This, however, will represent no sharp break with contemporary marriage, for the marriage of 1971 has come a long way from patriarchy toward the goal of equality. Our prevalent marital style has been termed companionship marriage by a generation of sociologists; in contrast to 19th Century marriage, it is relatively egalitarian and intimate, husband and wife being intellectually and emotionally close, sexually compatible and nearly equal in personal power and in the quantity and quality of labor each contributes to the marriage.

From an absolute point of view, however, it still is contaminated by patriarchalism. Although each partner votes, most husbands (and wives) still think that men understand politics better; although each may have had similar schooling and believes both sexes to be intellectually equal, most husbands and wives still act as if men were innately better equipped to handle money, drive the car, fill out tax returns and replace fuses. There may be something close to equality in their homemaking, but nearly always it is his career that counts, not hers. If his company want to move him to another city, she quits her job and looks for another in their new location; and when they want to have children, it is seldom questioned that he will continue to work while she will stay home.

With this there is a considerable shift back toward traditional role assignments. He stops waxing the floors and washing dishes, begins to speak with greater authority about how their money is to be spent, tells her (rather than consults her) when he would like to work late or take a business trip, gives (or withholds) his approval of her suggestions for parties, vacations and child discipline. The more he takes on the airs of his father, the more she learns to connive and manipulate like her mother. Feeling trapped and discriminated against, resenting the men of the world, she thinks she makes an exception of her husband, but in the hidden recesses of her mind he is one with the others. Bearing the burden of being a man in the world, and resenting the easy life of women, he thinks he makes an exception of his wife but deep-down classifies her with the rest.

This is why a great many women yearn for change and what the majority of women's liberation members are actively hammering away at. A handful of radicals in the movement think that the answer is the total elimination of marriage, that real freedom for women will come about only through the abolition of legal bonds to men and the establishment of governmentally operated nurseries to rid women once and for all of domestic entrapment. But most women in the movement, and nearly all those outside it, have no sympathy with the anti-marriage extremists, they very much want to keep marriage alive but aim to push toward completion the evolutionary trends that have been under way so long.

Concretely, women want their husbands to treat them as equals; they want help and participation in domestic duties; they want help with child rearing; they want day-care centers and other agencies to free them to work at least part time, while their children are small, so that they won't have to give up their careers and slide into the imprisonment of domesticity. They want an equal voice in all the decisions made in the home — including job decisions that affect married life; they want their husbands to respect them, not indulge them; they want, in short, to be treated as if they were their husbands' best friends — which, in fact, they are, or should be.

All this is only a continuation of the developments in marriage over the past century and a quarter. The key question is: How far can marriage evolve in this direction without making excessive demands upon both partners? Can most husbands, and wives have full time uninterrupted careers, share all the chores and obligations of homemaking and parenthood and still find time for the essential business of love and companionship?

From the time of the early suffragettes there have been women with the drive and talent to be full time doctors, lawyers, retailers and the like, and at the same time to run a home and raise children with the help of housekeepers, nannies and selfless husbands. From these examples, we can judge how likely this is to become the dominant pattern of the future. Simply put, it isn't, for it would take more energy, money and good luck than the great majority of women possess and more skilled helpers than the country could possibly provide. But what if child care were more efficiently handled in state-run centers, which would make the totally egalitarian marriage much more feasible? The question then becomes: How many middle-class American women would really prefer full-time work to something less demanding that would give them more time with their children? The truth is that most of the world's work is dull and wearisome rather than exhilarating and inspiring. Women's lib leaders are largely middle-to-upper-echelon professionals, and no wonder they think every wife would be better off working full time — but we have yet to hear the same thing from saleswomen, secretaries and bookkeepers.

Married women *are* working more all the time — in 1970 over half of all mothers whose children were in school held jobs — but the middle-class women among them pick and choose things they like to do rather than *have* to do for a living; moreover, many work part time until their children have grown old enough to make mothering a minor assignment, Accordingly, they make much less money than their husbands, rarely ever rise to any high positions in their fields and, to some extent, play certain traditionally female roles within marriage. It is a compromise and, like all compromises, it delights no one — but serves nearly everyone better than more clear-cut and idealistic solutions.

Though the growth of egalitarianism will not solve all the problems of marriage, it may help solve the problems of a *bad* marriage. With their increasing independence, fewer and fewer wives will feel compelled to remain confined within unhappy or unrewarding marriages. Divorce therefore can be expected to continue to increase despite the offsetting effect of extramarital liaisons. Extrapolating the rising divorce rate, we can conservatively expect that within another generation, half or more of all persons who marry will be divorced at least one. But even if divorce were to become an almost universal experience, it would not be the *antithesis* of marriage but only a part of the marital experience; most people will, as always, spend their adult lives married — not continuously, in a single marriage, but segmentally, in two or more marriages. For all the dislocations and pain these divorces cause, the sum total of emotional satisfaction in the lives of the divorced and remarried may well be greater than their great-grandparents were able to achieve.

Marital infidelity, since it also relieves some of the pressures and discontents of unsuccessful or boring marriages — and does so in most cases without breaking up the existing home — will remain an alternative to divorce and will probably continue to increase, all the more so as women come to share more fully the traditional male privileges. Within another generation, based on present trends, four of five husbands and two of three wives whose marriages last more than several years will have at least a few extramarital involvements.

Overt permissiveness, particularly in the form of marital swinging, may be tried more often than it now is, but most of those who test it out will do so only briefly rather than adopt it as a way of life. Swinging has a number of built-in difficulties, the first and most important of which is that the avoidance of all emotional involvement — the very keystone of swinging — is exceedingly hard to achieve. Nearly all professional observers report that jealousy is a frequent and severely disruptive problem. And not only jealousy but sexual competitiveness: Men often have potency problems while being watched by other men or after seeing other men outperform them. Even a regular stud, moreover, may feel threatened when he observes his wife being more active at a swinging party than he himself could possibly be. Finally, the whole thing is truly workable only for the young and the attractive.

There will be wider and freer variations in marital styles — we are a pluralistic nation, growing more tolerant of diversity all the time — but throughout all the styles of marriage in the future will run a predominant motif that has been implicit in the evolution of marriage for a century and a quarter and that will finally come to full flowering in a generation or so. In short, the marriage of the future will be a heterosexual friendship, a free and unconstrained union of a man and a woman who are companions, partners, comrades and sexual lovers. There will still be a certain degree of specialization within marriage, but by and large, the daily business of living together — the talk, the meals, the going out to work and coming home again, the spending of money, the lovemaking, the caring for the children, even the indulgence or nonindulgence in outside affairs — will be governed by this fundamental relationship rather than by the lord-and-servant relationship of patriarchal marriage. Like all friendships, it will exist only as long as it is valid; it will rarely last a lifetime, yet each marriage, while it does last, will meet the needs of the men and women of the future as no earlier form of marriage could have. Yet we who know the marriage of today will find it relatively familiar, comprehensible — and very much alive.

# 37

# THE IQ

☐ **Intelligence testing, from basis to implications,** continues to be the center of heated debate. Despite a history which is almost three quarters of a century long and despite the fact that the IQ is by now a household term in America, mental tests are still reeling under the impact of criticisms which term them, among other things, invalid, misleading, and based upon false assumptions of human development.

In a highly controversial article published in December 1969, Arthur Jensen, a professor at the University of California at Berkeley, proposed that compensatory education failed to raise the IQ of black children because of a biological difference in the way these children learn. The topic became incendiary; psychological, educational, political, and racist groups began interpreting the data to suit their views. Arguments and criticisms continue. Yet, unquestionably, the Stanford-Binet, the Wechsler Scales, and certain group tests do provide useful information, and the tests remain the most relied-on source for sorting children according to their presumed learning ability. Is it any wonder that teachers are uncertain what to believe about intelligence testing?

Binet's original intent was to develop an instrument to determine which children in Paris were retarded and in need of special education. In 1905, he produced the first Binet scale, designed to measure a retarded child's intelligence and compare it to the intelligence of normal children the same age. There was no attempt to determine whether the child's retarded learning was genetic or curable.

In 1912, German psychologist Wilhelm Stern suggested that one could express the developmental level, or mental age, of a given child as the age at which the average child achieved equivalent ability. If mental age (MA) were used as a ratio to the child's chronological age (CA), one could arrive at a brightness index, now called the Intelligence Quotient (IQ).

Like Binet, Stern did not claim that the test measured inborn capacity. In 1914, he wrote, "No series of tests, however skillfully selected it may be, does reach the innate intellectual endowment, stripped of all complications, but rather this endowment, in conjunction with all influences to which the examinee has been subjected up to the moment of testing. And it is just these external influences that are different in the lower social classes. Children of higher social status are much more often in the company of adults, are stimulated in manifold ways, are busy in play and amusement with things that require thinking, acquire a totally different vocabulary, and receive better school instruction. All this must bring it about that they meet the demands of the test better than children of the uncultured classes."

But H. H. Goddard, who brought the test to America in 1910, had a very different viewpoint. Dr. Goddard translated the test into English for use at the Vineland Training School for the mentally defective. Perhaps it was an act of fate that the man who brought mental testing to this country was someone who emphasized the importance of heredity on human behavior.

Goddard was working with grossly defective children, and one can speculate that he was probably not convinced they could be educated. (Further, the chances are they were biologically defective as well as mentally retarded.) Goddard became intrigued with the notion that, being able to measure innate intelligence, we had the means for a sweeping program of social reform, with every man working on his own mental level. Soon, mental testing was adopted in every training school and teachers college in the country. Few stopped to consider that perhaps the innate intelligence which Goddard postulated and the intelligence measured by the test were not the same. Shortly thereafter, in 1916, L. M. Terman revised the Binet Scale at Stanford University to give birth to the Stanford-Binet, the standard of today's intelligence test. The test was revised and updated in 1937 and 1960. The rapid growth of compulsory education in the United States required some means to identify the intellectual capacities of pupils in the schools, and the Stanford-Binet seemed to fill the bill.

When the intelligence test is evaluated solely in terms of its value to meet specifically defined, immediate situations, its usefulness has proven itself. A good case in point can be seen in its use since the start of World War I to screen men for the armed forces. In these instances, the mental test has provided the means for appraising what an individual

# DEBATE

**LILLIAN ZACH,** *associate professor of psychology and education, Ferkauf Graduate School of Humanities and Social Sciences, Yeshiva University, New York.*

**Moratorium on Standardized Testing**

"This Representative Assembly directs the NEA to immediately call a national moratorium on standardized testing, and at the same time to set up a task force on standardized testing to research and make its findings available to the 1975 Representative Assembly for further action."

The above "Item of New Business" was passed by the NEA Representative Assembly in Atlantic City, New Jersey, in June 1972. In another action on this subject, the Representative Assembly passed Resolution 72-44, Standardized Tests, which says:

"The NEA strongly encourages the elimination of group standardized intelligence, aptitude, and achievement tests to assess student potential or achievement until completion of a critical appraisal, review, and revision of current testing programs."

could do, here and now, as the product of his biological inheritance and his training and background.

But as testing proliferated, some problems became apparent. Testing in America was growing along two separate paths. One was in the real world of the school, the armed forces, and the industrial plant. The other was in the halls of academe, where the basic theoretical issues of intelligence were not yet settled. This lack of a universally accepted theoretical framework led to the anomolous situation in which intelligence is defined as that which intelligence tests test.

Herein lies a dilemma: Intelligence was only vaguely defined by the test maker, but the tests were used to define intelligence. This is perhaps the greatest failure of the testing movement in the United States. The pragmatic value of the mental test is undiminished. Test scores are good indicators of functioning abilities as long as their limitations are clearly understood, but these scores should not be used outside of their immediate significance. The failure lies not in the mental tests themselves, but in the perversion of the test results by investigators and social philosophers who use numbers in support of particular far-reaching positions. It is unfair both to the person tested and to the test itself to say that the scores of any one individual represent support for broad statements concerning human development.

There is nothing inherently wrong with practical definitions as long as they are clearly understood. The tests, after all, were developed to measure those aspects of human behavior which correlate well with scholastic achievement. In order to succeed in school, an individual must demonstrate certain types of abilities. If we develop tests to measure these abilities and if they prove to be valid and reliable instruments, we are measuring some form of intellectual ability. But if we lose sight of what we are measuring and if we claim for the test qualities for which it was never intended, we can be led into invalid implications.

**The IQ, like the MA, is nothing but a score. The** IQ indicates a child's performance on a test in the same way that a score of 80 on an arithmetic test does, except that intelligence tests purport to measure more general learning skills. Further, the scores merely reflect the child's performance on a specific test at a given time. The difference between the IQ and other test scores is that intelligence tests are standardized. Standardization means that the same test items are developed and revised on a large group, representative of the population for whom the test is designed— U.S. elementary school students, for example. Standardization also requires that the same test be administered under the same carefully controlled conditions to all who take the test. This means that a given child's score can be compared with scores obtained by other children of the same age on whom the test was originally standardized. It also permits prediction of the chances that in later testing a given child will obtain a score which is close to the original score, and further, to what extent a given child's

performance is the result of the construction of the test rather than his own ability.

In order to interpret the results of standardized tests, certain fundamental assumptions are implicit. It is assumed, for example, that test norms are fair, since they are based on a representative national sampling of children. But this does not take into consideration the fact that the national sample is weighted heavily by average white children.

Since the mental test purports to measure basic learning capacities, it is also assumed that the items which make up the test are of two types—information which for the most part all children have been exposed to or situations to which no one has been exposed.

For items based upon supposedly equal opportunities of exposure, it is possible to reason that a child who has learned what he has been exposed to is bright; one who has not done so is not bright. Observation tells us that this does not have to be true.

In my own testing experiences, I found that many black children who had just come North gave as response to the question, "Who discovered America?" the answer, "Abraham Lincoln." The response is obviously wrong and adds no points to the IQ score. But does this response mean that this child has no ability to learn or does it merely reflect the child's background? In certain ways, the answer could be considered a meaningful and pertinent response.

For items to which no one has been exposed and which therefore demand "on the spot" learning, similar problems arise. Usually, tests try to utilize nonverbal materials like blocks and puzzles as a way of minimizing factors like education and experience. But these are not equally novel experiences for all children. Many youngsters are familiar with educational toys long before they enter school. (Even more important, and less easy to identify, are factors related to "learning to learn" and test-taking abilities.)

Another assumption is that the mental test is a sampling of behaviors which directly reflect the general capacity for learning. Actually, all available intelligence tests are direct measures only of achievement in learning. We wrongly equate the inferences from scores on IQ tests to some native inherent trait. Many persons think of intelligence as a discrete dimension existing within the individual and believe that different people have different amounts of it. In a certain sense this is true, but one's intelligence is not a characteristic of a person so much as it is a characteristic of the person's behavior. We can only hope to measure or observe manifestations of it.

It is also not possible to add up the elements of someone's intelligence in the same way that you can count the number of fingers on his hand. Although two people can have the same IQ score, they may demonstrate quite different abilities by virtue of the fact that they succeeded on different parts of the test. All too often, undue weight is given to an IQ score, although numerical assignment of a child to a man-made concept, untied to real characteristics of the child, tells us very little. Even more unfortunate, parents and some teachers are led to believe that the IQ concept has deeper significance than its meaning as a score.

Unquestioning faith in descriptive concepts reaches the height of absurdity in the notion of overachievers —a word used to describe children whose classroom performance is higher than their IQ scores would predict. The concept makes no sense at all because it says, in effect, that although these children are achieving, they do not have the ability to do so. Their success is laid to other factors, such as motivation. It's like telling the child who had the highest batting average in the Little League that, on the basis of batting practice, he's really a very poor hitter. He only did it because he wanted to.

The danger in a meaningless concept like over-achieving is that children so designated may not receive as positive a recommendation for college as other children with the same grades but higher IQ scores. Few stop to consider that the methods used to judge ability must have been inadequate and that terms like IQ, MA, and overachievement are man-made.

In view of all the drawbacks, one might reasonably ask, then, why do we continue using mental tests? Even though many have argued for abandoning them, most psychologists still feel that they have value. In most cases, we can describe, evaluate, and even predict certain kinds of behavior much better with tests than without them. The paradox exists that most psychologists, who were responsible for the tests, have never given them as much weight as those in schools and industries who use and misuse them.

While various practical problems were being con-fronted, the academic world of psychology was still trying to resolve many basic issues about intelligence testing. One of these, the focus of several decades of research, concerned the whole heredity-environment controversy—the battle over nature versus nurture.

Not all psychologists in America were convinced that the IQ was the highly predictive, hereditarily determined measure it was held to be by Goddard and his followers. It wasn't long before studies were reported which demonstrated that not only was the IQ not fixed but that it could be altered with training, experience, and changes in adjustment patterns.

Although research was reported from all over the nation to support one or the other position, two distinct battle camps could be located. One group, at the University of Iowa, came to be known as the environmentalists. The other, at Stanford University, supported the significance of heredity. After a while, it seemed as if the heredity-environment controversy had settled down into a comfortable compromise: Most people were content to accept the notion that the IQ is the result of the interaction between the gene structure and the environment.

Everyone knew that the argument was not settled, however, probably because people were asking the wrong kinds of questions. Instead of asking how *much* is contributed by heredity and environment respectively, they should have been asking *how* each makes its particular contributions.

For example, in our present state of knowledge, nothing will enable a child who is born deaf to hear. How differences in environment can affect his future development, however, is a terribly significant factor: With appropriate educational procedures he can develop into a literate, communicating adult; without them, he can remain illiterate and uncommunicative. Concentrating on heredity versus environment obscures the more important problem of determining how education can help each child best use what he has at his disposal.

In recent years, the black community has become more and more vociferous in its objections to the mental test as being biased against them. The outcry has been especially strong against group testing because these tests depend almost entirely on the child's ability to read. Since the child has to read the questions in order to answer them, blacks question whether the test measures capacity to learn or ability to read. They also argue that IQ tests are self-fulfilling predictions. A child with a low IQ score is placed in slow learning classes, where he learns less, thereby supporting the original score. Prompted by such arguments, many major school systems abandoned group intelligence testing. Individual tests like the Stanford-Binet and the Wechsler Scales are less subject to criticism, since, hopefully, the trained psychologist ensures that the test is administered properly under an optimum testing climate, and is able to evaluate better to what extent a given child's performance is influenced by emotional, motivational, educational, and socioeco-nomic factors.

**Some people have suggested that we discard the** IQ test entirely and substitute for it a battery of achievement tests. The problem is that since the achievement test is a sampling of what a child has learned, usually in specific academic subjects, the achievement battery does not provide much information about general learning skills. Others have looked to new methods of measurement which could meet the limitations and criticisms posed by our current models.

One such method has been developed by John Ertl at the University of Ottawa. Dr. Ertl records the brain response to a flashing light by placing electrodes on the motor cortex. By averaging the responses, which are recorded on a computer so as to eliminate noise, he arrives at a score, known as the *evoked potential*, which he claims is a culture-free index of intellectual functioning.

Several drawbacks can be cited to Ertl's approach. For one thing, he has no strong theoretical rationale to support his hypothesis that more intelligent people respond faster to stimulation than do less intelligent ones. The results he reports may be explained, not by the greater (or lesser) strength of the brain, but by the fact that some people are better able to pay attention and to fixate on the light source. In addition, correlations with IQ, although significant, are low—as are correlations on retesting with the same subject. In view of all this, in my opinion, it is doubtful that Ertl's method can be of real use to the teacher, at least at this time.

Previous attempts had been made at developing culture-free scales. For example, an effort was made to remove the middle-class bias of IQ tests by changing the wording of questions and by introducing content more relevant to the lower-class child's background and life experiences.

The results were unsuccessful, and since the task of developing culture-free tests poses difficult problems, it seemed to make better sense to concentrate on improving the environment of the culturally deprived rather than on changing our tests.

As a result, many special programs were started that were designed to educate children from the lower socioeconomic strata. In too many cases, these programs were established in an atmosphere of emergency, with little planning and with limited knowledge of what should constitute suitable curriculums for such classes. Professional educators were not too surprised, therefore, when these programs failed to raise the IQ of black children.

Using the failure of these programs and an impressive array of statistical data, Dr. Jensen shocked many educators when he proposed that the reason these programs failed can be traced to an hereditary inferiority in black children. The great fear this aroused in the minds of socially oriented psychologists and educators is that it might be possible, by misinterpretation, to obtain "proof" that no matter what compensatory education the black child receives, he remains inferior in intellect. Another possible interpretation is that the schools are not to blame if black children fail to achieve academically.

*The IQ Argument: Race, Intelligence, and Education* (Library Press. 1971), a recent publication by Hans J. Eysenck, a British psychologist, lends support to Jensen's position. Actually, there was nothing so new about Dr. Jensen's position; it's the old nature-nurture controversy in new clothes. It is a fact that blacks as a group score lower than whites as a group on intelligence tests. It is also a fact, however, as Jensen notes, that many blacks score higher than a very large number of whites. People concentrating on the main conclusions in the article tend to forget this.

I recently received a rather touching letter from a young black boy attending an Ivy League college. He wrote: "I was interested that the specific areas in which Jensen indicated blacks were inherently inferior are precisely those areas in which I scored highest in my class. Maybe it was luck." Even he had lost sight of the fact that the Jensen data refer to averages and not to individuals.

It is unfortunate that Jensen presented his material within the context of a racial issue, since the emotional impact of this tends to negate all of what he has to say. Despite its incendiary qualities, the Jensen paper has the major merit of reminding us that we are dealing with a biological organism and that the educational environment is only one of the many influences affecting the growth and development of a given individual.

Black people as a group in America are poor, and poor people are subject to all kinds of health risks deriving from prenatal conditions and malnutrition. The relationship between poverty, health, and learning failure is now receiving the attention it deserves. It is becoming clear that not only does malnutrition play a role in retarded intellectual development but that more than one generation may have to be well-fed before all the effects of dietary deficiency are overcome.

Jensen was premature in evaluating just what portion of the black child's biological structure actually resides in the genes. It is difficult to evaluate the amount of damage caused by health hazards resulting from poverty, or to say how even slight changes in environment can produce large changes in behaviors, even where those behaviors are linked to genetics and biology.

Another criticism of the Jensen material is that the public does not have a clear appreciation of just what kinds of information can be validly drawn from heritability data. The method used by Jensen and Eysenck can only tell what proportion heredity contributes to the variance of a specified trait in a given population under existing conditions. The data cannot tell us the reason for a given child's low intelligence, the origin of ethnic differences in test performance, or what educational intervention programs can accomplish.

Jensen's article should be credited with helping us recognize that compensatory programs of education in their beginning phases were inadequately structured. That he used these

poorly planned programs as a basis for postulating hereditary inferiority in blacks is a major weakness. His reasoning could have proceeded the other way. If the programs failed to raise IQ scores, why place the onus on the black child's shoulders? Why not look at what's wrong with the programs?

**A peculiar characteristic of Ameri**-can education is that, although we give lip service to meeting the needs of individual children, we seldom follow through with concrete actions. We meet the needs of individual children as long as they respond to the existing curriculum, but when a child fails to learn under the existing structure, we assume there is something wrong with him. If "meeting the needs of individual children" is to become meaningful, we should consider the possibility that perhaps a particular teaching method is all wrong for a particular child.

Certainly, we can't make wholesale prescriptions for black children as if they were all alike. A black child who is not doing well in school may be more like a white child who is similarly unsuccessful than he is like an achieving black child. The problem of understanding learning deficiencies and of locating appropriate pedagogy for overcoming them is not something we know too much about. The storm over the Jensen article may provide the impetus toward working for a true understanding of education and individual differences.

A first step might well be to define our aims and come to grips with why we test. Are we concerned with measuring the amount of cognitive ability an individual is born with, or do we wish to appraise, by sampling performance, the level of adaptive capacities at his disposal?

Do we seek to predict, by way of one or several tests, what an individual will do 20 years from now? Or do we seek to know how and at what stage educational circumstances might be arranged for the individual to achieve his highest level of intellectual functioning ability? Piaget, among others, has never been impressed with standard IQ tests because they do not lead to an understanding of how intelligence functions. His work is not based on predictions, but rather on assessments of the presence or absence of the essential abilities related to intellectual functioning.

Schools must decide what is the purpose of testing. If all we wish is to separate the bright child from the dull child, the brain-damaged from the neurologically intact, the retarded learner from the gifted, and to attach labels to the children in our schools, we can go on using tests the way we always have, and the argument over genes will continue. But if we mean what we say about meeting individual needs, we can put tests to better use.

The intelligence test, not the IQ score, can tell us the level of the child's functioning in a variety of tasks which measure general intelligence and which are intimately correlated with classroom learning. The goal of testing then becomes to describe the developmental level the

child has attained. The next step requires that educators and psychologists together formulate the educational environment necessary to raise the child to the next developmental level. □

# 38

# The Schools and Equal Opportunity

BY MARY JO BANE AND CHRISTOPHER JENCKS

## Quality education will reduce socioeconomic inequality, the reformers claim. This is a delusion. Schools have few long-term effects on the later "success" of those who attend them.

Americans have a recurrent fantasy that schools can solve their problems. Thus it was perhaps inevitable that, after we rediscovered poverty and inequality in the early 1960s, we turned to the schools for solutions. Yet the schools did not provide solutions, the high hopes of the early-and-middle 1960s faded, and the war on poverty ended in ignominious surrender to the *status quo*. In part, of course, this was because the war in Southeast Asia turned out to be incompatible with the war on poverty. In part, however, it was because we all had rather muddleheaded ideas about the various causes and cures of poverty and inequality.

Today there are signs that some people are beginning to look for new solutions to these perennial problems. There is a vast amount of sociological and economic data that can, we think, help in this effort, both by explaining the failures of the 1960s and by suggesting more realistic alternatives. For the past four years we have been working with this data. Our research has led us to three general conclusions.

First, poverty is a condition of relative rather than absolute deprivation. People

*Mary Jo Bane is a research associate at the Center for Educational Policy Research, Harvard University, and a contributing editor of SR/EDUCATION. Christopher Jencks is an associate professor of education at Harvard. He is the coauthor, with David Riesman, of* The Academic Revolution.

feel poor and are poor if they have a lot less money than their neighbors. This is true regardless of their absolute income. It follows that we cannot eliminate poverty unless we prevent people from falling too far below the national average. The problem is economic inequality rather than low incomes.

Second, the reforms of the 1960s were misdirected because they focused only on equalizing opportunity to "succeed" (or "fail") rather than on reducing the economic and social distance between those who succeeded and those who failed. The evidence we have reviewed suggests that equalizing opportunity will not do very much to equalize results, and hence that it will not do much to reduce poverty.

Third, even if we are interested solely in equalizing opportunities for economic success, making schools more equal will not help very much. Differences between schools have very little effect on what happens to students after they graduate.

The main policy implication of these findings is that although school reform is important for improving the lives of children, schools cannot contribute significantly to adult equality. If we want economic equality in our society, we will have to get it by changing our economic institutions, not by changing the schools.

### Poverty and Inequality

The rhetoric of the war on poverty described the persistence of poverty in

the midst of affluence as a "paradox," largely attributable to "neglect." Official publications all assumed that poverty was an absolute rather than a relative condition. Having assumed this, they all showed progress toward the elimination of poverty, since fewer and fewer people had incomes below the official "poverty line."

Yet, despite all the official announcements of progress, many Americans still seemed poor, by both their own standards and their neighbors'. The reason was that most Americans define poverty in relative rather than absolute terms. Public-opinion surveys show, for example, that when people are asked how much money an American family needs to "get by," they typically name a figure about half what the average American family actually receives. This has been true for the last three decades, despite the fact that real incomes (incomes adjusted for inflation) have doubled in the interval.

During the Depression the average American family was living on about $30 a week. A third of all families were living on less than half this amount, which made it natural for Franklin Roosevelt to speak of "one-third of a nation" as ill-housed, ill-clothed, and ill-fed. By 1964 mean family income was about $160 a week, and the Gallup poll found that the average American thought a family of four needed at least $80 a week to "get by." Even allowing for inflation, this was twice what people had thought necessary during the Depression. Playing it safe, the Johnson administration defined the poverty line at $60 a week for a family of four, but most people felt this was inadequate. By 1970 inflation had raised mean family income to about $200 a week, and the National Welfare Rights Organization was trying to rally liberal support for a guaranteed income of $100 a week.

These changes in the definition of poverty were not just a matter of "rising expectations" or of people's needing to "keep up with the Joneses." The goods and services that made it possible to live on $15 a week during the Depression were no longer available to a family with the same real income ($40 a week) in 1964. Eating habits had changed, and many cheap foods had disappeared from the stores. Housing arrangements had changed, too. During the Depression many people could not afford indoor plumbing and "got by" with a privy.

# The reforms of the Sixties failed because they focused only on equalizing opportunity rather than on reducing economic differences.

By the 1960s privies were illegal in most places. Those who still could not afford an indoor toilet ended up in buildings that had broken toilets. For these they paid more than their parents had paid for privies.

Examples of this kind suggest that the "cost of living" is not the cost of buying some fixed set of goods and services. It is the cost of participating in a social system. It therefore depends in large part on how much other people habitually spend to participate in the system. Those who fall far below the norm, whatever it may be, are excluded. Accordingly, raising the incomes of the poor will not eliminate poverty if the cost of participating in "mainstream" American life rises even faster. People with incomes less than half the national average will not be able to afford what "everyone" regards as "necessities." The only way to eliminate poverty is, therefore, to make sure everyone has an income at least half the average.

Arguments of this kind suggest not only that it makes more sense to think of "poverty" as a relative rather than an absolute condition but that eliminating poverty, at least as it is usually defined in America, depends on eliminating, or at least greatly reducing, inequality.

## Schooling and Opportunity

Almost none of the reform legislation of the 1960s involved direct efforts to equalize adult status, power, or income. Most Americans accepted the idea that these rewards should go to those who were most competent and diligent. Their objection to America's traditional economic system was not that it produced inequality but that the rules determining who succeeded and who failed were often unfair. The reformers wanted to create a world in which success would no longer be associated with skin color, economic background, or other "irrelevant" factors, but only with actual merit. What they wanted, in short, was what they called "equal opportunity."

Their strategy for achieving equal opportunity placed great emphasis on education. Many people imagined that if schools could equalize people's cognitive skills this would equalize their bargaining power as adults. Presumably, if everyone had equal bargaining power, few people would end up very poor.

This strategy for reducing poverty rested on a series of assumptions that went roughly as follows:
1) Eliminating poverty is largely a matter of helping children born into poverty to rise out of it. Once families escape from poverty, they do not fall back into it. Middle-class children rarely end up poor.
2) The primary reason poor children cannot escape from poverty is that they do not acquire basic cognitive skills. They cannot read, write, calculate, or articulate. Lacking these skills, they cannot get or keep a well-paid job.
3) The best mechanism for breaking this "vicious circle" is educational reform. Since children born into poor homes do not acquire the skills they need from their parents, they must be taught these skills in school. This can be done by making sure that they attend the same schools as middle-class children, by giving them extra compensatory programs in school, by giving their parents a voice in running their schools, or by some combination of all three approaches.

Our research over the last four years' suggests that each of these assumptions is erroneous:

1) Poverty is not primarily hereditary. While children born into poverty have a higher than average chance of ending up poor, there is still an enormous amount of economic mobility from one generation to the next. A father whose occupational status is high passes on less than half his advantage to his sons, and a father whose status is low passes along less than half his disadvantage. A family whose income is above the norm has an

even harder time passing along its privileges; its sons are typically only about a third as advantaged as the parents. Conversely, a family whose income is below average will typically have sons about a third as disadvantaged as the parents. The effects of parents' status on their daughters' economic positions appear to be even weaker. This means that many "advantaged" parents have some "disadvantaged" children and vice versa.
2) The primary reason some people end up richer than others is not that they have more adequate cognitive skills. While children who read well, get the right answers to arithmetic problems, and articulate their thoughts clearly are somewhat more likely than others to get ahead, there are many other equally important factors involved. The effects of I.Q. on economic success are about the same as the effects of family background. This means, for example, that if two men's I.Q. scores differ by 17 points—the typical difference between I.Q. scores of individuals chosen at random—their incomes will typically differ by less than $2,000. That amount is not completely trivial, of course. But the income difference between random individuals is three times as large and the difference between the best-paid fifth and the worst-paid fifth of all male workers

# "Inequality is not mostly inherited: It is re-created anew in each generation."

averages $14,000. There is almost as much economic inequality among those who score high on standardized tests as in the general population.
3) There is no evidence that school reform can substantially reduce the extent of cognitive inequality, as measured by tests of verbal fluency, reading comprehension, or mathematical skill. Eliminating qualitative differences between elementary schools would reduce the range of scores on standardized tests in sixth grade by less than 3 per cent. Eliminating qualitative differences between high schools would hardly reduce the range of twelfth-grade scores at all and would reduce by only 1 per cent the disparities in the amount of education people eventually get.

Our best guess, after reviewing all the evidence we could find, is that racial desegregation raises black elementary school students' test scores by a couple of points. But most of the test-score gap between blacks and whites persists, even when they are in the same schools. So also: Tracking has very little effect on test scores. And neither the overall level of resources available to a school nor any specific, easily identifiable school policy has a significant effect on students' cognitive skills or educational attainments. Thus, even if we went beyond "equal opportunity" and allocated resources disproportionately to schools whose students now do worst on tests and are least likely to acquire credentials, this would not improve these students' prospects very much.

The evidence does not tell us why school quality has so little effect on test scores. Three possible explanations come to mind. First, children seem to be more influenced by what happens at home than by what happens in school. They may also be more influenced by what happens on the streets and by what they see on television. Second, administrators have very little control over those aspects of school life that do affect children. Reallocating resources, reassigning pupils, and rewriting the curriculum seldom change the way teachers and students actually treat each other minute by minute. Third, even when the schools exert an unusual influence on children, the resulting changes are not likely to persist into adulthood. It takes a huge change in elementary school test scores, for example, to alter adult income by a significant amount.

*Equal Opportunity and Unequal Results*
The evidence we have reviewed, taken all together, suggests that equalizing opportunity cannot take us very far toward eliminating inequality. The simplest way of demonstrating this is to compare the economic prospects of brothers raised in the same home. Even the most egalitarian society could not hope to make opportunities for all children appreciably more equal than the opportunities now available to brothers from the same family. Looking at society at large, if we compare random pairs of individuals, the difference between their occupational statuses averages about 28 points on the Duncan "status scale" (the scale runs from 0 to 96 points). The difference between brothers' occupational statuses averages fully 23 points on this same scale. If we compare men's incomes, the difference between random pairs averaged about $6,200 in 1968. The difference between brothers' incomes, according to our best estimate, probably averaged about $5,700. These estimates mean that people who start off equal end up almost as unequal as everyone else. Inequality is not mostly inherited: It is re-created anew in each generation.

We can take this line of argument a step further by comparing people who not only start off in similar families but who also have the same I.Q. scores and get the same amount of schooling. Such people's occupational statuses differ by an average of 21 points, compared to 28 points for random individuals. If we compare their incomes, making the additional assumption that the men have the same occupational status, we find that they differ by an average of about $5,300, compared to $6,200 for men chosen at random.

These comparisons suggest that adult success must depend on a lot of things besides family background, schooling, and the cognitive skills measured by standardized tests. We have no idea what these factors are. To some extent, no doubt, specialized varieties of competence, such as the ability to hit a ball thrown at high speed or the ability to persuade a customer that he wants a larger car than he thought he wanted, play a major role. Income also depends on luck: the range of jobs available when you are job hunting, the amount of overtime work in your plant, good or bad weather for your strawberry crop, and a hundred other unpredictable accidents.

Equalizing opportunity will not, then, do much to reduce economic inequality in America. If poverty is relative rather than absolute, equalizing opportunity will not do much to reduce poverty, either.

*Implications for Educational Policy*
These findings imply that school reform is never likely to have any significant effect on the degree of inequality among adults. This suggests that the prevalent "factory" model, in which schools are seen as places that "produce" alumni, probably ought to be abandoned. It is true that schools have "inputs" and "outputs," and that one of their nominal purposes is to take human "raw material" (*i.e.*, children) and convert it into something more "useful" (*i.e.*, employable adults). Our research suggests, however, that the character of a school's output depends largely on a single input, the characteristics of the entering children. Everything else—the school budget, its policies, the characteristics of the teachers—is either secondary or completely irrelevant, at least so long as the range of variation among schools is as narrow as it seems to be in America.

These findings have convinced us that the long-term effects of schooling are relatively uniform. The day-to-day internal life of the schools, in contrast, is highly variable. It follows that *the primary basis for evaluating a school should be whether the students and*

*teachers find it a satisfying place to be.* This does not mean we think schools should be like mediocre summer camps, in which children are kept out of trouble but not taught anything. We doubt that a school can be enjoyable for either adults or children unless the children keep learning new things. We value ideas and the life of the mind, and we think that a school that does not value these things is a poor place for children. But a school that values ideas because they enrich the lives of children is quite different from a school that values high reading scores because reading scores are important for adult success.

Our concern with making schools satisfying places for teachers and children has led us to a concern for diversity and choice. People have widely different notions of what a "satisfying" place is, and we believe they ought to be able to put these values into practice. As we have noted, our research suggests that none of the programs or structural arrangements in common use today has consistently different long-term effects from any other. Since the character of a child's schooling has few long-term effects, and since these effects are quite unpredictable, society has little reason to constrain the choices available to parents and children. If a "good school" is one the students and staff find satisfying, no one school will be best for everyone. Since there is no evidence that professional

This article is based on research done by Christopher Jencks and his colleagues at the Center for Educational Policy Research, Harvard University, with the support of the Carnegie Corporation of New York. The research group started in 1968 by re-examining the data on the effects of schooling gathered by the Equality of Educational Opportunity Survey (EEOS), whose most famous product was the "Coleman Report." It also reanalyzed Project Talent's longitudinal study of students in 100 high schools plus many smaller studies. In addition, Jencks reviewed, and in some cases reanalyzed, data on adult occupational status and income gathered by the U.S. Bureau of Census and by the National Opinion Research Center, as well as many smaller studies. The complete results are presented in *Inequality: A Reassessment of the Effect of Family and Schooling in America* by Christopher Jencks and Marshall Smith, Henry Acland, Mary Jo Bane, David Cohen, Herbert Gintis, Barbara Heyns, and Stephan Michelson educators know appreciably more than parents about what is good for children, it seems reasonable to let parents decide what kind of education their children should have while they are young and to let the children decide as they get older.

Short-term considerations also seem decisive in determining whether to spend more money on schooling or to spend it on busing children to schools outside their neighborhoods. If extra resources make school life pleasanter and more interesting, they are worthwhile. But we should not try to justify school expenditures on the grounds that they boost adult earnings. Likewise, busing ought to be justified in political and moral terms rather than in terms of presumed long-term effects on the children who are bused. If we want an integrated society, we ought to have integrated schools, which make people feel they have a stake in the well-being of other races. If we want a society in which people are free to segregate themselves, then we should apply that principle to our schools. There is, however, no compelling reason to treat schools differently from other social arrangements, including neighborhoods. Personally, we believe in both open housing and open schools. If parents or students want to take buses to schools in other neighborhoods, school boards ought to provide the buses, expand the relevant schools, and ensure that the students are welcome in the schools they want to attend. This is the least we can do to offset the effects of residential segregation. But we do not believe that forced busing can be justified on the grounds of its long-term benefits for students.

This leads to our last conclusion about educational reform. Reformers are always getting trapped into claiming too much for what they propose. They may want a particular reform—like open classrooms, or desegregation, or vouchers—because they think these reforms will make schools more satisfying places to work. Yet they feel obliged to claim that these reforms will also reduce the number of nonreaders, increase racial understanding, or strengthen family life. A wise reformer ought to be more modest, claiming only that a particular reform will not harm adult society and that it will make life pleasanter for parents, teachers, and students in the short run.

This plea for modesty in school reform will, we fear, fall on deaf ears. Ivan Illich is right in seeing schools as secular churches, through which we seek to improve not ourselves but our descendants. That this process should be disagreeable seems inevitable; one cannot abolish original sin through self-indulgence.

That it should be immodest seems equally inevitable; a religion that promises anything less than salvation wins few converts. In school, as in church, we present the world as we wish it were. We try to inspire children with the ideals we ourselves have failed to live up to. We assume, for example, that we cannot make adults live in desegregated neighborhoods, so we devise schemes for busing children from one neighborhood to another in order to desegregate the schools. We all prefer conducting our moral experiments on other people. Nonetheless, so long as we confine our experiments to children, we will not have much effect on adult life.

*Implications for Social Reform*
Then how *are* we to affect adult life? Our findings tell us that different kinds of inequality are only loosely related to one another. This can be either encouraging or discouraging, depending on how you look at it. On the discouraging side, it means that eliminating inequality in one area will not eliminate it in other areas. On the encouraging side, it means that inequality in one area does not dictate inequality in other areas.

To begin with, genetic inequality is not a major obstacle to economic equality. It is true that genetic diversity almost inevitably means considerable variation in people's scores on standardized tests. But this kind of cognitive inequality need not imply anything like the present degree of economic inequality. We estimate, for example, that if the only sources of income inequality in America were differences in people's genes, the top fifth of the population would earn only about 1.4 times as much as the bottom fifth. In actuality, the top fifth earns seven times as much as the bottom fifth.

Second, our findings suggest that psychological and cultural differences between families are not an irrevocable barrier to adult equality. Family background has more influence than genes on an individual's educational attainment, occupational status, and income. Nonetheless, if family background were the only source of economic inequality in America, the top fifth would earn only about twice as much as the bottom fifth.

Our findings show, then, that inequality is not determined at birth. But they also suggest that economic equality cannot be achieved by indirect efforts to manipulate the environments in which people grow up. We have already discussed the minuscule effects of equalizing school quality. Equalizing the amount of schooling people get would not work much better. Income inequality among men with similar amounts of

**The primary basis for evaluating a school should be whether the students and teachers find it a satisfying place to be.**

schooling is only 5–10 per cent less than among men in general. The effect is even less if we include women.

If we want to eliminate economic inequality, we must make this an explicit objective of public policy rather than deluding ourselves into thinking that we can do it by giving everyone equal opportunity to succeed or fail. If we want an occupational structure which is less hierarchical and in which the social distance between the top and the bottom is reduced, we will have to make deliberate efforts to reorganize work and redistribute power within organizations. We will probably also have to rotate jobs, so that no individual held power very long.

If we want an income distribution that is more equal, we can constrain employers, either by tax incentives or direct legislation, to reduce wage disparities between their best- and worst-paid workers. We can make taxes more progressive, and we can provide income supplements to those who do not make an adequate living from wages alone. We can also provide free public services for those who cannot afford to buy adequate services in the private sector. Pursued with vigor, such a strategy can make "poverty" (*i.e.*, having a living standard less than half the national average) virtually impossible. Such a strategy would also make economic "success," in the sense of having, say, a living standard more than twice the national average, far less common than it now is. The net effect would be to make those with the most competence and luck subsidize those with the least competence and luck to a far greater extent than they do today. Unless we are prepared to do this, poverty and inequality will remain with us indefinitely.

This strategy was rejected during the 1960s for the simple reason that it commanded relatively little popular support. The required legislation could not have passed Congress, nor could it pass today. That does not mean that it is the wrong strategy. It simply means that, until we change the political and moral premises on which most Americans now operate, poverty and inequality will persist at pretty much their present level. Intervention in market processes, for example, means restricting the "right" of individuals to use their natural advantages for private gain. Economic equality requires social and legal sanctions—analogous to those that now exist against capricious firing of employees—against inequality within work settings. It also requires that wage rates, which Americans have traditionally viewed as a "private" question to be adjudicated by negotiation between (unequal) individuals or groups, must become a "public" question subject to political control and solution.

In America, as elsewhere, the long-term drift over the past 200 years has been toward equality. In America, however, the contribution of public policy to this drift has been slight. As long as egalitarians assume that public policy cannot contribute to equality directly but must proceed by ingenious manipulations of marginal institutions like the schools, this pattern will continue. If we want to move beyond this tradition, we must establish political control over the economic institutions that shape our society. What we will need, in short, is what other countries call socialism. Anything less will end in the same disappointment as the reforms of the 1960s. □

# 39

# HOW TO KILL A COLLEGE
## The Private Papers of a Campus Dean

WHO SHOULD BE ADMITTED to America's colleges and universities? For the past several years, that question, in one context or another, has underlain the hottest issues in higher education. The current Supreme Court case of Regents of the University of California v. Allan Bakke [SR, October 15, 1977] stems directly from it. But well before Bakke, in the wake of the student rebellions of the late Sixties, there was the inflammatory issue of "open admissions."

While it varied from school to school, open admissions meant a drastic, across-the-board lowering of admissions standards. The purpose was to reach the masses of blacks, Hispanics, and other young people traditionally excluded by all but the junior colleges. More than Bakke, open admissions challenged fundamental educational precepts, particularly the credo that standards always had to be maintained—else the university would suffer grievously.

Several institutions adopted a form of open admissions. Among them were such disparate schools as the University of Alaska, the University of Arkansas, and the Federal City College (now the University of the District of Columbia). None did so with the sweep—and the resulting controversy—of CUNY, the City University of New York. The burden of CUNY's decision fell on the City College of New York, an outstanding academic institution with a long, proud tradition of educating young—but usually white—people of poor economic circumstances.

In the article below, the City College's dean of humanities reflects on the gains, the losses, and the meaning of the entire experience for American education.

by Theodore L. Gross

MY OFFICE is in Lincoln Corridor, on the ground floor of an old Gothic building called Shepard Hall, at the City College of New York, 138th Street and Convent Avenue, Harlem. Outside this office, on makeshift benches, students congregate—black, Puerto Rican, Asian, and varieties of ethnic white—playing radios, simulating sex, languidly moving back and forth to classes, dancing and singing, eating and studying and sleeping and drinking from soda cans or from beer bottles wrapped in brown paper bags.

As the dean of humanities, I move among these students unnoticed and conduct my business in adjacent rooms that feature telephones and filing cabinets, typewriters, a copying machine, a Dictaphone, and a wall of books that from the Anglo-Saxon point of view represent the best that has been thought and said.

As an administrator, I am responsible for the teaching of foreign languages, English and speech, music, art, drama, and, because of circumstances peculiar to this urban college, Asian and Jewish studies. The two other ethnic studies departments—black and Puerto Rican studies—report to the dean of social science, who lives on the other side of Lincoln Corridor. Fifteen thousand students, day and evening, are enrolled in courses—to speak only of the humanities—ranging from Shakespeare to Eldridge Cleaver, from Beethoven to Ellington, from Confucius to Martin Buber, from Basic Writing I for the poorly prepared to creative writing taught by the most sophisticated American novelists. The student population is multiethnic: 33 percent black, 21 percent Spanish, 12 percent Jewish, 11 percent Asian, and diminishing percentages of Italians, Irish, Ukrainians, Serbo-Croatians, and Slavs—a microcosm, as we proudly say, of the world.

It was not always so. In the Sixties, the college was almost entirely white and predominantly Jewish. Enthroned on a hill overlooking Harlem, it was an urban institution with high academic standards, a citadel that for more than 50 years had existed undisturbed amid the surrounding black community. As educators, we at the City College were representative of the decade. We had abolished requirements and prerequisites and had arranged elective courses in a cafeteria curriculum that made basic skills and basic knowledge seem irrelevant, structure obsolete, and sequential study unimportant. The historical perspective was already so suspect that the liberal arts college functioned primarily on the pleasure principle. Students enrolled in the courses they wanted. Economic growth was everywhere, and we could afford small classes, independent study, and esoteric subjects.

During those years, an occasional summer riot created fear in the minds of those who were sending their children to the campus on St. Nicholas Heights. At other times, assassinations like those of Malcolm X and Martin Luther King, Jr., and local uprisings starring Stokeley Carmichael and H. Rap Brown stirred discomfort in white liberals like me. These events and other "minor incidents," as we called them, seemed like campfires that were easily extinguishable—until they flared more frequently and burned closer to the campus. By 1969 the flames were in our buildings. Decent human beings wrangled with one another: Blacks confronted Jews, liberals shouted at conservatives, the young grumbled at their seniors, the swingers taunted the sedate, women warned male administrators, Asians and blacks and Puerto Ricans cau-

cused against the so-called white imperialist educators of the City College.

Politics dictated educational policy. Arguments that had once been contained within classrooms and dining rooms raged through loudspeakers on the campus, while television and newspapers and radio recorded this page in the changing history of New York. White educators who had blessed student protégés in the names of Melville, Joyce, and Kafka were now being asked by minorities to say no in thunder to a form of education that had been exclusive, intellectually elitist, unresponsive to colored Americans, and unyielding in its demand for only—*only*—academic excellence.

The minorities' demand, in turn, seemed ideologically sound and in the best tradition of liberalism: A public institution of higher learning should educate all the citizenry. What group of self-pronounced liberals could refuse that opportunity? (We faculty members were whites whose parents had been Irish or Italian or Jewish immigrants out of one ghetto or another, supporters of Roosevelt, Truman, and Stevenson. After growing up in the streets of Brooklyn and the Bronx, we had struggled to disembarrass ourselves of every ethnic odor so we might reach that fine point of middle age when we could drive from surrounding white suburbs into the City College. We worked in Harlem. Some of us never wanted to admit that

---

**"In desperate measures redolent of Madison Avenue, the faculty created sexy courses to attract students: gay literature, Jewish fertility. Then they tried to sell the courses with gaudy posters."**

---

fact, but we walked or drove through Harlem to get to work; we moved on its edges between classes; we ate in a faculty cafeteria that overlooked the scarred landscape below. Metropolitan colonialists. Most of us were still liberal, however, and we felt a vague sympathy for open admissions, as though it symbolized a retribution for past social sins.)

But beyond the platitudes and the posturings, what exactly should the new education be? And were we who had degrees from Columbia and from New York University, who had been trained to preserve the best that has been thought and said— were we prepared to teach Shakespeare to a student who two years earlier had been struggling to compose coherent sentences? And could he learn to read Shakespeare, even if we learned how to teach him to do so? Should he be taught to read Shakespeare at all? Or should he, if he had to enter college, be given the liberation of literacy—itself enough to be learned in four brief years—and sent on his way to ply a trade, watch television in the evenings, and maybe read—if he should read at all—*Time* magazine? Did we have an obligation to educate everyone, even in a democracy, by means of college?

We had no choice. The city's Board of Higher Education told us to implement an open admissions policy that would assure every high school student, regardless of his record, acceptance at a college of the City University. For guaranteed entrance to the senior colleges, the high school graduate had to have a scholastic average of 80 percent or had to be ranked in the upper half of his class. But the allocation system depended upon the student's own selection of a college within the City University system, and when fewer well-prepared

high school graduates made the City College their first choice—fundamentally because of its Harlem location— those with lower scores were admitted. We had planned to initiate this dramatic change in our admissions policy by 1975, but pressures from minorities and from some students and faculty could not be resisted, and open admissions was begun five years earlier.

The impact was particularly severe at the City College of New York, where academic achievement had been like a code of honor that never included considerations of class, race, religion, or national origin. The City College had been the great tuition-free institution whose diploma had had so special a meaning for alumni—the hard-earned diploma of the poor. The alumni had been proud that they had been admitted to the proletarian Harvard, as the college was often called, and proud that they had been graduated; proud that they had studied with Jonas Salk and Alfred Kazin, Bernard Malamud, Arthur Kornberg, and A. M. Rosenthal; nostalgic about their youthful poverty and grateful to have escaped it through the college; strong-minded about their remembered hunger for learning and eager to preserve the meaning of their academic achievement.

Some of them were bitterly disaffected by open admissions and renounced their alma mater because they believed it had betrayed the standards they had struggled to achieve. But most were bewildered by this new generation of students for whom the college had to "soften" those standards. These alumni distrusted the arguments about deprivation—hadn't they themselves been deprived?—but they sensed that the quality of this current deprivation was different, linked to a racist society that they had disavowed; and even if it wasn't different, they could afford to be generous. Like many successful people, they wished to be tolerant and understanding, and they tried to fathom the meaning of open admissions as explained by the administrators of the City College, who had no choice but to be generous.

IN MAY 1970, I was elected chairman of an English department composed of 125 full-time people and a range of part-time professors: visiting poets, novelists, and journalists. By the end of August, as a consequence of the open admissions policy, I had hired 21 additional full-time faculty members to teach what we called basic writing. Within a year, open admissions greatly altered our educational mission. A department that had offered 70 percent of its courses in literature and the rest in some form of basic written composition now offered the reverse.

These basic writing courses were deeply remedial. The problem for one third of the open admissions students was literacy, for another third, competence, for the last third, college level English. In addition, the students themselves were altogether different. Suddenly, Asians and blacks and Hispanics crowded the classrooms, bringing with them language and dialect problems that prevented them from understanding the most elementary texts, face-to-face with a faculty that was intellectually unprepared and emotionally unwilling—liberals up against the wall. The faculty experienced a shock of cultural recognition, and I tried to build instant rhetorical bridges that seem even more rhetorical today than they did in 1970. In a newsletter distributed within the English department that year, I wrote:

Many of us have been trained for an elitist profession, but we are asked to perform democratic tasks; we have written dissertations on Spenser, but we are teaching remedial writing; we are committed to the book, but the students have been culturally shaped by television and film; we have studied a body of culture that is fundamentally Anglo-Saxon, but we teach many students who are black and Asian and Spanish; we pay homage to the history of English literature, but we are surrounded by the consequences of American history and the political presence of America; we are in an "English" department, but our work is involved with the literature and with the language that is spoken by Americans.

I list all of these paradoxes collectively because they form a background against which we seek to accomplish our central desire: the humanistic training of a new generation of students.

All true, I suppose, but the older professors who struggled to teach sentence fragments were scarcely appeased; they would not change. The younger faculty—those whom I had hired in late August—were indeed writing dissertations on Spenser, and their graduate studies pulled them away from the hard reality of their teaching; they were academic schizophrenics, holding what seemed to be two opposing ideas—literacy and literature—in their mind at the same time.

Everywhere one turned were crowds; confusion; the sweet smell of pot in the student lounge; students lined up to register in the hallways of huts; others waiting for conferences outside the little offices of English professors; still others crowded into the dining rooms and bookstore or packed into rented quarters on Broadway and 134th Street, overlooking the grim steel tracks of the IRT.

The excessive numbers of students, the inadequate physical conditions, and the poor preparation—if not outright resistance—of the faculty all strained the implementation of open admissions. For a college, after all, is like a home: Without a foundation, it crumbles. When open revolt by a faculty does not occur, as in the Sixties, then lethargy invades the teachers' spirits, as in the Seventies, and they come not to care. Everyone begins to complain about facilities, pension benefits, the quality of lunchroom food, and extraneous matters of the flesh; and the favorite subject seems to be early retirement.

Anyone who had ever passed through the City College knew that the physical conditions there were as bad as almost anywhere else in urban America. But once the student had entered the classroom, the peeling walls and encrusted windowpanes vanished—the electricity of mind compensated for everything. I remember having taught "Tintern Abbey" to the belching music of a city bus, and it worked. Now everything seemed plebeian—particularly the minds of the students.

Into the midst of the radical change at work in the university came the teachers' union and "affirmative action," which ultimately were additional contributions to mediocrity. So was the hoary practice of tenure. At one end of the age spectrum, a department chairman confronted senior professors who had the smug choice of whether or not they would cooperate in the implementation of open admissions—an academic noblesse oblige. At the other end, the union so protected nontenured faculty that it was virtually impossible to dismiss them.

Minorities, including now impatient women, used affirmative action to leap into positions of power or to retain their jobs. Minorities were underrepresented on the faculty, and one could scarcely contemplate dismissing a black, a Puerto

Rican, or a woman unless he or she was utterly incompetent. One knew that not only the union but also special interest groups, in and out of the university, would apply pressure: the Citizens' Commission on Human Rights, a campus women's caucus, B'nai B'rith, the Sons of Italy, the NAACP, community organizations—the list seemed endless. Such conditions were not conducive to courage on the part of the faculty or to educational leadership and academic freedom; and the history of open admissions—from this angle of vision—is a history of political, educational, and moral compromises.

THE BLACKS and Puerto Ricans and Asians arriving at the City College came from working-class families in which television and radio were the exclusive sources of information and in which there was no tradition of learning, no special association with books, no clear commitment to the purposes or possibilities of higher education. The problem that controlled all others was literacy.

Open admissions students needed a vast amount of attention in their attempt to master the writing of English. One could find some comprehension among them during the discussion of a reading assignment, and class sessions were animated with an intensity not experienced in the "relevant" Sixties; but the students' writing barely made sense. The greatest difficulty for blacks, for example, seemed to be to put an "s" on the third person singular. Puerto Ricans and Asians had bilingual problems that prevented them from reading conventional college texts and from writing college compositions; on occasion, a student would even arrive with an interpreter so that he could register for classes. Yet the Asians were remarkable students of engineering and mathematics; and the blacks and Puerto Ricans had a real feeling for literature, sociology, and political science.

The open admissions students brought to their work a motivation that was like a hunger. I remember a drug-dazed white girl in the Sixties who slumped in her seat, her guitar beside her, stoned out of her mind, turned off by "irrelevant" education, while I tried to persuade her that *King Lear* was worth reading. That scene was unimaginable in the Seventies. One was almost tempted to suggest that the criterion for entrance to college be motivation, not preparation or the ability to produce high scores. But motivation is not measurable, and the experience of open admissions argues, most dramatically, that adequate preparation is essential to success.

The need for students to master English was clear to everyone; and on a fundamental level, instruction in basic writing was carried on intensively. In 1970 almost 90 percent of City College students took some form of remedial instruction in writing—an incredible situation for any American college, let alone one that had had a great academic tradition. Seven hundred students were placed in Basic Writing 1, and 1,700, in Basic Writing 2. The other students were placed in Basic Writing 3, the equivalent of our former freshman English.

Few people wanted to confront the unappealing implications of language retardation; they blamed the high school teachers, who blamed the junior high school teachers, who blamed the elementary school teachers, who blamed the parents, who blamed the schools, whose chairmen and faculty and principals (many of them City College graduates) blamed us for having implemented open admissions and for not maintaining standards against which their students could measure themselves. When underemployed foreign language teachers were retrained for remedial work, most resisted it, and the students resisted them. When history teachers were used, they lectured on history to students in remedial classes who needed to know about subject and verb agreement. Faculty and administration were impatient with the work of teaching basic writing (it never seemed to produce "quantifiable" results) and acted as though it would eventually go away. But the subject proved to be the most difficult to teach—one that required a stretching of the imagination and a tolerance rarely asked of "intellectuals." It also required that the teachers grow, too, a simple charge that they stop judging and labeling their students and attempt to understand them.

Many educators across the country were defending the student's "right to his own language," so that he would be protected against what was called "the cultural imperialism" of standard English. One read in the journals that black and **Puerto Rican** students would lose their idiosyncratic ethnicity, the special coloration of their language, their creativity. One listened to arguments against computerized America with its computerized language, the horrors of sociological jargon, the doublespeak of politicians, the Watergate grammar, the linguistic freakiness of Madison Avenue. A student's voice is his character, so the argument went, and should not be lost in the supermarket language of bland and utilitarian America.

It was an interesting rhetorical argument but a deceptive one—especially in regard to minority students, whose proficiency at the standard language was tantamount to learning the art of breathing the special air of America. The kind of deep creativity that is manifested in a private language—the blues or *Huckleberry Finn* or some of the poetry of Langston Hughes—is all the more powerful precisely because its vernacular clashes with the standard public language. The two languages must be simultaneously held in the mind of the reader as well as of the writer, at whatever counterpoint can be productively sustained. Indeed, one reason why the language of creativity has lost its power is that the repressed emotions it once released are now on the newsstands, debased by their easy availability. In any event, for most students, writing is expository, and exposition is standardized and should be clear (like Auden's windowpane) and logical. It is the obligation of every English teacher to give students this primary skill.

At the City College we were too overwhelmed by the immensity of our problems to engage in theories about language acquisition. We never surrendered the conviction that our first obligation was to offer the conventional language conventionally, and we tried to teach those underprepared students in the way that we had taught thousands of other freshmen. At the same time, we struggled to invent new pedagogical devices that would make our teaching more effective. But despite all the goodwill that a lifetime of liberalism and academic training dictated, the nagging doubt grew that we might not be able to take an eighteen-year-old who suffered deep linguistic shortcomings and bring him to college level verbal competence.

Those of us who were asked to implement open admissions strained so hard to be successful that we didn't have the time to call into question the expectations imposed upon us by minorities and, more important, by ourselves. When our conservative colleagues screamed that the standards were falling, we answered by saying that the record wasn't in yet. When we

failed to bring students to the appropriate level of literacy, we blamed ourselves—we hadn't been adequately trained or we lacked patience or we'd set our standards too high.

But in fact we had false expectations. Open admissions students came with a sense of fear and self-doubt, confronting a standard language that was rendered even more complicated by their need to master, at the same time and in the same place, the separate language of biology or psychology. Their entire miseducation and bookless past rose to haunt them, and all the audiovisual aids and writing laboratories and simplified curricular materials we tried could not turn the trick.

The mistake was to think that this language training would be preparation for college education when what we were really instilling was a fundamental literacy that would allow social acculturation to occur. We were preparing our students to be the parents of college students, not to be students themselves. And the impossible burden that we assumed was one properly meant for the community colleges of the City University. In the strictest sense, the two-year college—the most powerful single phenomenon to appear in higher education during the past two decades—should be the bridge from the community to the senior college. The junior college is where the openness of open admissions should manifest itself.

If a senior college undertakes the policy, it either must alter most of its programs in the humanities and social sciences or face a student drift into "soft" subjects that do not require an exacting competence in language. The latter happened at the City College. The traditional disciplines of philosophy and history and literature and political science diminished in significance and popularity because students felt unprepared for them. We expected too much too fast from students, and we betrayed the notion of open admissions by holding students to standards they could never hope to meet. But articulating these conclusions at the time, even if they had been clear in one's mind, was impossible.

Clouding the issues of literacy and of open admissions, and every consequent question of how to give a liberal arts education in an urban setting, was the sudden primacy of ethnicity

---

**"What really gnawed away at our innards and left us hollow...what coursed in our bodies like an incurable illness was our growing realization and fear that in middle age we no longer had a profession."**

---

and race. It conditioned everyone's response because it was central to the purpose of open admissions. In a college that had originally been almost entirely white and that was now half composed of minority students, race touched every educational issue—from black art to black journalism, from black history to black music. No record of this fitful period can be intelligible unless one understands the implications of racial tensions, vibrating at every meeting, working across and into the mind of everyone who cared.

THE DRAMATIC MOMENT came in the fall of 1971, at a large and raucous meeting of the Faculty Council, when new departments of ethnic studies were being considered. The City College's minorities wanted the power that departments represent, and they brought to the meeting dozens of students and friends and political figures from the Harlem community who crowded the room, sitting on the floor and perching on window ledges. The intention was cultural intimidation of the white faculty, and the intention was fulfilled.

Like a thunder that speaks only to the emotions, the rhetoric rolled that October afternoon, and as the black and Puerto Rican and Asian spokesmen denounced our "racist" university in the midst of that "racist" society, the minority students (allowed to sit in the hall but not to participate) surrounded the white faculty members and cheered, clapped, and hissed until it became clear that reason would not prevail.

One white conservative rose to denounce the academic shallowness of ethnic departments. Another mocked the arbitrary definition of a department (an ethnic group had to be represented by at least 5 percent of the student body before applying for departmental status): Why only black, Puerto Rican, Asian, and Jewish departments? Why not Italian and Irish and Ukrainian? But the vocal white conservatives were small in number, even though their silent brothers and sisters were sizable. The conservatives were not the leaders of the campus. They had no students following them down the corridors and crowding their offices, and their loud protests fell on the embarrassed ears of the squirming white liberals in the middle of the room.

Then the parade began. With black and Hispanic students seated around the room, like the inner ring of the enclosing black community, with nontenured minority faculty confronting tenured white faculty, with the president of the college and the dean of liberal arts and science on the podium, the liberals rose vaguely and uncomfortably to express their sympathy for the creation of ethnic studies departments, regretting the haste with which they were developed, of course, but still in sympathy. It was clear to me that black and white were the colors of the day, that the unknown (the interdisciplinary ethnic departments) would ultimately have to coexist with the known (the clearly structured, power-based departments that represented the academic disciplines), and that gray was a color for the colorless. It was not the moment for subtlety or intellectual discrimination.

So, with the gravest misgivings about simpleminded ethnicity and politically oriented courses and mediocre faculty hired on the spot; with these private doubts aggravated by the thought that the creation of these departments *was* hasty, ill-conceived, an intellectual disgrace, and unfair to faculty and students—especially to future minority students for whom the college was being changed; but also with the unwillingness to be associated with academic reactionaries whose advocacy of "standards" and "excellence" seemed to be just another version of the *Übermensch* (superman) syndrome—with all of these contradictory emotions running through me, compounded by personal disgust at the thought that I might be doing the bidding of an administration that simply wanted to solve a nasty problem as quickly as possible and by memories of having written about ethnic literature but of never having felt free to teach a course in black culture and of having been criticized by blacks for even touching the materials—I remembered Norman Mailer's easy remark that "Every compromise makes you less of a man," and I walked to the podium and compromised:

"We are being asked for an expression of faith in this administration that has dealt fairly with us on so many other matters.... I, for one, am ready to express that faith."

The departments were created, and the following months brought courses that could only encourage militant separatism: "Organized and Disorganized Crime in the Black Community"; "The Contemporary Black Family" ("A normal Negro child, having grown within a normal family, will become abnormal on the slightest contact with the white world"); "The Prisoner as Political Hero"; "Protest and Rebellion Within Ante-Bellum America"; "Prisons and Concentration Camps" ("After Attica, the entire system of corrections and penology must be reexamined"); "Seminars in Revolutionary Decolonization" ("The tradition of revolution as presented in the classic portrayals of European and American experiences does not attempt to present the sociological basis of revolutions through a consistent theoretical analysis").

Each new course was a brick that heightened the wall of segregation between black studies and other programs of the college. With less intensity and self-conscious purpose and overt anger, many of the courses in the departments of Asian, Jewish, and Puerto Rican studies served to further the same insular tendency: Asians talking to Asians, Jews brooding with each other over the holocaust, Puerto Ricans structuring a culture. Each of these groups developed some courses that were valuable in themselves; but they also developed, despite their efforts, an effect of self-isolation, a defensiveness that too often took the form of petty academic politics.

Now a decade has passed, and the fire has not burned us after all—although some extraordinary leaders have been killed. But it has singed our sensibilities in ways not easily forgotten. The academic home we live in has been altered to accommodate other voices in other rooms and, with luck, in our own rooms. That passionate intensity experienced on so many college campuses had little to do with education and much to do with establishing racial bases of power. Now that the fire has subsided, it is possible to draw a few conclusions that may seem rational.

The creation of ethnic studies departments at the City College and throughout the nation represented an educational capitulation to extreme political pressure by minority groups. Once black studies was established, Puerto Rican, Asian, and Jewish studies had to follow; and before long, courses in ethnic history and sociology and literature were conflicting with those of the traditional departments. The result, with few exceptions, is a curriculum that has the faculty and students of ethnic studies departments ghettoized in separate corners of the colleges. Each ethnic group raises its own consciousness at the expense of general education. Attempts to develop courses and programs in comparative ethnicity have failed, and the minorities in these departments feel more alienated than before.

Creating ongoing departments was wrong, and those with empty hands are the minorities for whom they were created. Overt bigots from the traditional departments were not displeased at the isolation of the new departments, for they knew that open admissions pupils—the less well-prepared pupils—would segregate themselves in ethnic studies while the intellectually secure and confident students would work with more substantial subject matter in their own departments. The well-intentioned liberals agreed to the creation of these departments out of no deep ideological impulse, with no real purpose or passion. They accepted the change cynically and mocked its results privately. They accepted it because to do so was easy. And like the society, the college became fragmented and divided.

American education—American culture at large—is integrative, and the subject matter cannot be obfuscated in the name of ethnic heritage or women's studies or homosexual studies or experimental studies. The appropriation of knowledge for some personal need is one reality. That is the reason most of us have for learning anything. But to use knowledge solely to further a cause will ultimately debase the knowledge because it is being manipulated for a narrow purpose. The student is allowed to evade personal responsibility and unique humanity for an abstraction that has an absolute quality and a finality; the student's use of his knowledge is too predictable, too tendentious.

It is insufficient to claim—as defenders of these programs do—that a college teaches students, not subject matter, and that therefore students should explore what they wish, however they wish. This is a sentimental argument, so relativistic and shifting that it blurs an essential educational vision that judges priorities, that sets forth objectives and skills, that knows its own inherent meaning. It offers the students themselves—no more, no less. It offers no leadership. It points in no direction.

The full implications of open admissions had little meaning for people at either end of the educational spectrum: those who advocated a narrow ethnicity and those who for so long had considered themselves the custodians of an unvarying culture. Even those who supported professional education most vigorously failed to acknowledge the need for vast resources to improve the language skills of the new undergraduates. Scientists claimed that too many students were placed in basic writing courses and accused the English department of self-aggrandizement, of shoring up its British Empire; social scientists continued to give short-answer tests. The liberal arts faculty complained about expensive programs for bright students, whom they never saw in their classrooms, and about students in remedial classes, whom they did not want to teach.

Where were the old liberal arts students who simply wanted to study philosophy or literature or history? Where were those who could not be programmed, who weren't so absolutely certain of their careers, who weren't so utterly nervous about job security, and who came to us with a literacy we took for granted? Gone. Gone to colleges of the State University. Gone to Queens and to Hunter. Gone to the suburbs and the exurbs and the hinterlands. And with their flight something faded from our own lives—a passing purpose, a pointed passion.

What really gnawed away at our innards and left us hollow, what began to create a sad yet anxious look in our eyes and a dreadful listlessness in the way we moved through classes or sat at committee meetings, what dulled our lunchroom conversations and made us depend more on each other than on the students—who had always been the great reward for teaching at the City College—what coursed in our bodies like an incurable illness was our growing realization and fear that in middle age we no longer had a profession.

Elective courses in literature, languages, philosophy, and history attracted only a handful of students; and though we defended the study of the humanities in the most elegant rhetoric, fewer and fewer students were interested in our subjects. Those few who might have cared had no incentive to prepare

for graduate school since teaching jobs were unavailable. The number of majors plummeted so that the heart of the heart of our disciplines was gone. Worse still, most students were no longer motivated to read—assignments grew shorter and even those were rarely read. In desperate measures redolent of Madison Avenue, the faculty created sexy courses to attract students: gay literature, Jewish fertility. Then they tried to sell the courses with gaudy posters or notices in campus newspapers. In the sweaty gym during registration, too many of the faculty were no better than barkers at a circus sideshow touting the attractions awaiting behind the tent flap. Student enrollment determined departmental strength. College had become a kind of cheap academic stock market, and teachers were stockbrokers in an inflationary educational economy.

All of these forces developed, Pelion upon Ossa, a scramble for infinite options to satisfy every taste or lack of taste, until the college bulletin resembled the smashed windows of a very large house, a house that had once been considered home. An academic home. There was no vision, however singular it might have been, that offered a future to the educators and that would return the faculty members' professions to them. The numbers were appalling: professional education for 700 students in architecture, education, engineering, nursing, biomedicine, law, and the performing arts; 1,700 who needed remedial work; and a handful of students in liberal arts and sciences who were genuinely ready for a college education—they were now called "honors students."

The natural tendency was to expand the professional programs and to view liberal education deductively, to establish career goals and then to shape the education for them accordingly. The general economic condition of the city and of the nation encouraged parents, students, and educators to move in this direction—to clutch at what seemed to promise a chance of survival in a confusing age. The study of languages, literature, philosophy, history, physics, and mathematics on their own terms seemed impossible, given the desires and needs of the students, given the pressures of a decaying city, given the budget (which finally ran out on May 28, 1976, forcing the City University to close for two weeks while we listened to wrangling politicians and lined up, for the first time in our lives, for unemployment compensation). As each career program was established, the traditional disciplines in liberal arts and sciences were placed in a service relationship to vocationalism—as though the only way the disciplines could be made interesting or relevant was by attaching them to practical programs.

Today, open admissions has ended in New York City for lack of funds. But the urban conditions that prompted it will remain to haunt us as memories of what we failed to achieve. Inevitably, one returns in education to the basic questions of what the student *knows* upon graduation and especially of what skills of interpretation he possesses. If he does not know something of philosophy and history; if he has not developed the critical skills that enable him to distinguish the moral from the immoral, flatulent language from genuine, art from artifact—then he is not educated. Discrimination is essential: intellectual discrimination. That and lengthening the critical attention span, so atomized by television and radio and newspapers and a hundred forces colliding with the eye and the ear. And acquiring the understanding of a few great texts—a few will suffice—that have lived beyond their moment in time. And achieving the self-reliance that grows from the authority of knowing some things well.

Knowledge is certainly not enough. It should lead to wisdom, which carries vision in its meaning. But without knowledge, wisdom is hard bought. And knowledge cannot be only the sociology and economics and political science of the moment, ever shifting, stimulating an anxiety that stems from uncertainty, fogged by statistics that carry with them apparent truth. Without a past, what future can we have? ◉

*Theodore L. Gross is dean of humanities at the City College of New York. A scholar of American studies, he has recently served as general editor of* America in Literature *(John Wiley, 1978). This essay is part of the first chapter of a work in progress,* The Humanities in Higher Education.

# 40

# Apartheid Education

## Ian Robertson

The South African educational system has been relatively neglected by students of *apartheid*, largely because the attention of researchers and critics has been diverted by many of the more immediately arresting features of that society. But the regime itself regards education as one of the most important pillars of the entire South African social order, and it deliberately and explicitly uses the schools as a tool for indoctrination and social control. The form and content of South African education are dictated by the traditional ideology of Afrikaner nationalism and are directed toward a single goal: that of preparing each child to occupy a niche in a highly segregated and stratified society, with the relative position and appropriate attitudes of the individual being determined by the criterion of skin color.

An ideology is a belief system that derives from social structure and functions to legitimate the material interests of the group that creates and disseminates it. The dominant ideology in South Africa as in any other society is the ideology of the dominant group, in this case the Afrikaners. This ideology, usually termed "Christian Nationalism" by its adherents, is the product of the Afrikaners' historical experience. Their history, from the time of their arrival on the African subcontinent until the present, has been one of a struggle for survival—against the physical environment, against the indigenous peoples, against British imperialism, and now against all those inside and beyond South Africa's borders who wish to bring about the downfall of Afrikaner hegemony. As Calvinists believing in the doctrine of individual predestination, the early Dutch settlers and their descendants readily came to believe in the predestination of entire peoples as well; they saw the continued survival of their language, culture, and identity as the work of God, and their mission in Africa as that of exercising trusteeship over the heathen.

*A "Coloured" elementary school near Capetown, South Africa. In South Africa, every person is classified by race and entered into the population register accordingly. The racial categories are "White," "Coloured," "Asian," and "Bantu." The quality of education a child receives depends on his or her "race," with whites receiving by far the best education and blacks (Bantus) the worst. But the education of all children is permeated by the concepts of CNE, which seeks to justify white minority rule.*

In 1832, Dutch trekkers who had left the Cape Colony in disgust at the British insistence on racial equality before the law, faced their climactic battle with the Zulus at Blood River. On the night before the battle they made a solemn covenant with God, promising that if they were granted victory they and their descendants would remember the day forever. The biblical parallels—the flight from the land of oppression, the covenant with God, the battles with heathen peoples, the quest for the promised land—did not pass unnoticed by the trekkers. The day of the battle is now a national holiday in South Africa, on which a small segment of the population duly gives thanks to God for its victory over the major segment a century and a half ago. The text much quoted on these occasions in Genesis 17:7–8:

> And I will establish My covenant between Me and thee and thy seed after thee in their generations, for an everlasting covenant, to be a God unto thee and thy seed after thee. And I will give to thee and to thy seed after thee the land wherein thou art a stranger, all the land of Canaan for an everlasting possession; and I will be their God.

The result of the historical experiences of the Afrikaner has thus been the creation of a highly nationalist, strongly authoritarian, and extraordinarily cohesive group, clinging with a desparate tenacity to its control of a country in which it is a tiny minority, and believing that the slightest compromise may herald its utter destruction. This group has evolved an ideology grounded in the memory of conflict, oppression, and the danger of racial extinction—an ideology characterized by a wary, ethnocentric, defensive attitude to all who are excluded on the grounds of race, language, and religion from the *volk*.

In ideal type at least, the ideology of Christian Nationalism comprises the following related beliefs: (1) The Afrikaners are a chosen people, destined by God to work his will in southern Africa; this divinely determined task is, in the first instance, to Christianize the heathen. (2) Western civilization is an attribute inextricably linked to white skin color; it cannot be transmitted to other races except in distorted form. (3) The culture of the blacks, although it has some intrinsic merit, is inferior; this inferiority derives from the innate inferiority of the blacks themselves. (4) Racial purity is a moral imperative, to be maintained at any cost. (5) Fundamentalist Calvinism, as revealed by the Dutch Reformed churches of South Africa, is the only true religion. (6) As in the past, there are evil forces abroad in the world dedicated to the destruction of Afrikanerdom. (7) The preservation of the traditional norms of the *volk* is essential if these challenges are to be withstood in the future.

These are not the principles enunciated in South African Information Department publications intended for foreign consumption, but they are echoed again and

again in South Africa itself at the very highest levels of public debate. Let me give a few examples. At the Day of the Covenant ceremony in 1970, Prime Minister Vorster declared:

> It should be clear to everyone who has made a study of South African history that the people of South Africa have been placed here with a definite purpose.
>
> It is not impossible that the people of South Africa might be faced with a situation similar to that of the Battle of Blood River in the future. But no matter what happens, we know that our forefathers had two things on their side. They realized the power of positive prayer and they had the courage to stand alone against overwhelming odds.[1]

At a similar ceremony the following year, the prime minister developed his theme:

> Blood River stands as a symbol of hope for South Africa. . . . It is becoming clear that the enemies of a country do not any more depend on troops but on the aid they receive from inside the borders of the country they want to conquer. This is the softening-up process being used by the advance forces of the enemy and we in South Africa must counteract this. . . . The people of South Africa must know that it dare not lay down arms against the enemy forces that are confronting South Africa today. It would not be a laying down of arms, but the grave of civilization here.[2]

*Die Kerkblad*, the official organ of the Dutch Reformed church, has editorialized:

> In this dangerous world we are almost totally isolated. . . . Two million Afrikaners stand alone against the world population of about 3000 million. It is to be expected that as the threats approach us like savage monsters, more will have to be spent on police and defense. . . . There is not one of the people [in the world] which, if it suits it, will not simply sacrifice us.[3]

The Reverend D. J. Vorster, brother of the prime minister and at the time head of the Dutch Reformed church, has explained:

> We are a conservative church, and we have always been and will continue to be. Our only guide is the Bible. Our policy and our outlook on life are based on the Bible. We firmly believe that the way we interpret it is right. We will not budge one inch from our interpretation to satisfy anyone—in South Africa or abroad. The world may differ from our interpretation. This will not influence us. The world may be wrong. We know we are right, and will continue to follow the way the Bible teaches us. . . .
>
> It is true the Bible teaches that all men are equal. But the Bible also teaches that there are differences between men. We believe in the Bible, and thus we believe, accept, and teach both concepts equally. That, in brief, is the racial theology of the Dutch Reformed Church.[4]

And *Die Transvaler*, mouthpiece of the Nationalist party, commented in a typical editorial:

In Britain and America, the spiritual capitulation of the white man is the order of the day, to such an extent that the British people are apparently prepared to become a bastard race within a few generations.... The liberalistic sickness will not continue.... The liberalistic striving after equality will be rejected. When liberalism disappears and a normal situation rules again, common South Africa will be praised because it did not want to go with the stream.[5]

South Africa's policies do not always reflect this rhetoric consistently; the regime is often more flexible than some critics allow. But the ideology of Christian Nationalism sets the standard against which policies are judged and in terms of which modifications must be justified. Particularly in the field of education, public policies conform with startling fidelity to this ideology. The link between the ideology and actual educational practice is to be found in a document entitled *Manifesto for Christian National Education* (CNE), first published in 1948 after a nine-year process of consultation with "the whole of Afrikanerdom." A few quotations from the document give some idea of its flavor:

> Our Afrikaans schools must not be merely mother tongue schools.... they must be places where our children are soaked and nourished in the Christian-National spiritual and cultural stuff of the *volk*.... We will have nothing to do with a mixture of languages, of culture, of religion, or of race.

> By Christian instruction ... we mean instruction and education given in the light of God's revelation in the Bible expressed in the articles of faith of the three Afrikaans churches.... The Bible should shape the spirit and direction of all other subjects.

> By National instruction we mean instruction ... in which adequate expression is given ... to the National principle of love for one's own ... so that the child is introduced thoroughly and with pride to the spiritual-cultural inheritance of the *volk*.

> The trend of instruction in all subjects must correspond with the Christian and National attitude.... Every pupil must be moulded into a Christian and National citizen ... so that each one ... shall respect, preserve and perpetuate the Christian and National character of the family, the church, the community and the State.

> Every people is attached to its own native soil alloted to it by the Creator.... History must be taught in the light of God's decreed plan for the human race ... God ... willed separate nations and peoples.

> Higher education should have the same foundation.... Institutions must expound Christian science positively, contrast it with non-Christian science. The professors and lecturers must be convinced Christian and National scientists.

> The instruction of the Coloured people should be regarded as a sub-division of the vocation and task of the Afrikaner to Christianize the non-European races of our country.... This trusteeship imposes on the Afrikaner the solemn duty of seeing that the Coloured people are educated in accordance with Christian and National principles.... The Coloured man can and will only be truly happy when he has been Christianized, for then he will be proof against his own heathen ideology and all sorts of foreign ideologies that give him the illusion of happiness but leave him in the long run dissatisfied and unhappy. We believe he can be made race-conscious if the principle of *apartheid* is strictly applied in his teaching.... The financing of Coloured education must be placed on such a basis that it is not provided at the cost of European education.[6]

It is difficult to regard this program as being in any sense Christian, national, or even education, but it has become the basis for educational policy in South Africa. CNE has been endorsed by the Nationalist party congresses, by successive ministers of education, by the DRC, by the Afrikaans press, and by all Afrikaans teachers' organizations. The extreme distaste of English-speaking South Africans for CNE, and in particular the vigorous opposition of the predominantly English-speaking province of Natal, has delayed the full implementation of the program for many years. Ever since the Nationalist party assumed office in 1948, however, it has been slowly and systematically applying CNE principles, gradually centralizing control of education in order to do so. This process and its consequences can be seen in three major areas of the educational system: white schools, black schools, and the universities.

## WHITE SCHOOLS

The application of CNE principles to white elementary and secondary schools has focused on the segregation of English- and Afrikaans-speaking pupils, the centralization of control of education, and the introduction of new, uniform national syllabuses that present "separate development" in uncritical and glowing light.

Education at the elementary and secondary levels was already racially segregated when the Nationalist party took office in 1948, but control of education rested almost entirely in the hands of the four provincial authorities, three of which had previously been dominated by United party administrations. Soon after 1948 all the provinces but Natal fell under Nationalist party control, and the former three began, stealthily at first, to introduce CNE principles into white schools. Thus we find the administrator of the Transvaal writing in the journal of the Afrikaans teachers' association of the province:

> A white consciousness must be fostered in every pupil. ... The transmission of the policy of Separate Development of white and native is the task of the school. We must strive to win the battle against the non-white in the classroom rather than on the battlefield.[7]

And the general secretary of the same association declared:

> In no era of history did the future of white and Christian civilization look as dark as now. . . . Principals are urged to act as field generals in the campaign against liberalism. . . . No separate lesson is required; inculcate a little with each lesson.[8]

So strong was the opposition of Natal to CNE that the anomalous position of the province was tolerated for almost twenty years, until the passage of the National Education Policy Act in 1967. This act stripped the provinces of most of their control over white education, empowered the national minister of education to determine "general policy," and specified that "the education of schools shall have a Christian character" and that "education shall have a broad national character."

The passage of the act has been followed by the introduction of uniform syllabuses throughout the white schools system. One interesting innovation, introduced in 1972, is a compulsory high-school course entitled "Youth Preparedness." Among the items in the syllabus are these:

> Our national heroes and the message of their lives. School heroes. Our national monuments and our duties in respect of them.
>
> Rules and laws. Their function, origin, and values. Results of disobedience.
>
> South Africa's task in the world.
>
> The Bantu. Dangers of detribalization. Our missionary task.
>
> Modern tendencies and their causes. Conservative groups and decadent groups.
>
> Anchors for the ship of life: the Bible, religion, the family, the church, the nation.
>
> Youth and religion. The role of drink, drugs, and decadent music.
>
> Authority and freedom. All authority comes from the hand of God. The place and function of authority at every stage of man's life.
>
> The servitude of dissipation. Planned attempts to cut young people adrift from their anchors. Techniques used. Pseudo-anchors. The rehabilitation of those who have gone astray.
>
> The Christian philosophy of life. Communism and religion. Communism in practice. Ideologies that pave the way for communism. How communism can be combatted by (a) the application of Christian principles (b) education.[9]

The centralization of educational control also enabled the regime to eliminate dual-medium schools—schools attended by both Afrikaans and English pupils who were taught in both languages. Earlier United party administrations in the provinces, dedicated to the ideal of white national unity, had encouraged the development of these schools; the Nationalists, committed to mother tongue education by CNE dogma and generations of fears about the survival of Afrikaans, abolished them. All white children are now obliged to attend a single-medium school teaching in the language of the home, irrespective of parental wishes. The Afrikaans child is now educated in the pure, hothouse atmosphere of the CNE school; the English child, taught by English teachers who have little sympathy for the Christian National ideology however hard the regime tries to impose it, is marginally more fortunate. Both, however, grow up with minimal opportunity for social interaction and the development of mutual understanding.

School curricula have been substantially reformed, mainly by including instruction in *apartheid* in whatever syllabuses—history, geography, civics—can be made to accommodate it. In no textbook is there any indication whatever that there are any alternatives to or even reasoned criticisms of "separate development"; it is presented as an ineradicable, noncontroversial aspect of the social order.

School textbooks for white children make absorbing if disturbing reading. The fetish of race purity, for example, leads to some interesting distortions of history, for the authors have both to assert the purity of the white race and explain away the existence of more than two million Afrikaans-speaking half-castes, the coloureds. One method is to flatly deny the facts:

> In some non-white countries that the whites penetrated centuries ago, the whites began to marry with the non-whites almost immediately, and bastard populations arose. In South Africa this did not happen. . . . Our forefathers believed and we believe today that God himself made the distinctions between the peoples of the earth. For that reason it is not good if whites intermarry with non-whites.[10]

Another method, slightly more ingenious, is to befuddle the issue:

> The Coloureds are, in the same way as the Afrikaners, an indigenous ethnic group of this country. These two population groups came into being more or less at the same time in the same part of the country.[11]

Several texts emphasize the taboo attached to sexual and even social relations across the color line. One history text declares:

> The sin of blood mixture between a white man and a nonwhite woman—or the other way around—falls in great measure on their children and their children's children. Their children are unacceptable to self-respecting whites and are unacceptable to self-respecting bantu. Can anyone have it in his heart to commit a deed that will cast his children and his children's children into disgrace in the years that lie ahead?[12]

And another text states:

Yes, our forefathers believed that like must seek like. Also, the non-whites do not like the bastardizing of their people. During the years gone by the whites therefore remained white and the non-whites, non-white. It has become the traditional principle that . . . there is no blood mixing, and there is no eating, drinking, or visiting together. The principle is also entrenched in various laws. The living together of white and non-white is not only a great shame, but it is also forbidden by law.[13]

Perhaps a little inconsistently, the text also asserts:

Every white . . . surely does not need a law to pledge him to maintain his loyalty to his own traditions and pattern of culture. We whites' traditions must beat in our blood and in our being.[14]

The attitude of the texts to the black population is either hostile or patronizing. One text states flatly that "from the very beginning, the whites and blacks were sworn enemies,"[15] and texts typically treat other population groups as "problems"—one, for example, has chapters on "the Hottentot problem," "the Basuto problem," "the Zulu problem," and the "South African Indian problem."[16] Another text informs its readers:

It is actually not only the white South African's skin which is different from that of the non-white. The white stands at a higher level of civilization and is more developed. The whites must so live, so learn, and so work that we do not sink to the level of civilization of nonwhites. Only then will the control of our country be able to remain in the hands of the whites.[17]

The texts even treat the abolition of slavery in South Africa as a still-controversial issue, and deal almost exclusively with its personal and financial disadvantages to the slaveowners. One text describes the emancipation of the slaves in the Cape Colony as an "unsavory incident," and goes on to say, in outright contradiction of a mass of historical evidence:

Slavery in the Cape Colony differed radically from the slavery in other parts of the world. . . . In the Cape the slaves were handled by their masters in a respectable, civilized, and Christian manner. This must be attributed in the main to the deep-rooted religious sense of the Dutch-Afrikaans colonist. The great blunder that the British government made, was that it took no account of [this fact]. . . . The slave laws that were made for the colonists severely curtailed the powers and rights of the slave owners by degrees, and exposed them to all kinds of humiliations.[18]

Civics texts go to great lengths to justify the racial division of labor and the reservation of skilled jobs for whites:

Their simple and inexpensive manner of living makes the Bantu much cheaper workers than the Whites, Indians, or Coloureds, and for this reason extensive use is being made of Bantu labor. . . . The Bantu love repeti-

tion which is reflected in their songs and dances, and they are therefore preeminently suited to the performance of routine tasks and work of a repetitive nature in the factories.[19]

Another text takes up a similar theme:

Equal pay for equal work, which after all sounds very nice if a person does not think about it, brought it about that the whites had to make do in life with the same wages as those the non-whites are paid. Such a thing was impossible for most whites, seeing that the non-white's style of life requires less money than that of the white.[20]

The text then suggests the following as the basis for a class discussion:

Debating point: What characteristics will distinguish a genuinely South African labor union?
    There will be only white members.
    It will adopt a Christian standpoint.
    "White South Africa first" will be its motto.[21]

Several texts present religious dogma as historical fact. The following passage opens a school history text:

Adam and Eve, the first people, were fully developed and civilized. They had no clothes, cars, trains, streets, and houses like ours, but just as people in 6000 years will still have the same civilization as ours, so does our outward form of civilization differ little from that of Adam and Eve. They were innately good and civilized, but through their disobedience and the fall of man, they fell into a state of disgrace. From then on, they and their descendants would have an incessant struggle. Adam however obtained from God permission to work the earth. . . . It is the command of God that people carry out. The execution of this command, for better or worse, we trace in history.[22]

The divine mystique of the Afrikaner is treated in similar fashion:

Nations are creations of the Lord God. They did not simply arise at will. Further, we believe that the Almighty also determines nations' existence in life and plan of life. The Lord thus has a goal in the creation of a nation. This is also very decidedly the case with the South African nation.

Taking all the circumstances into account, the coming into existence and the continued existence of the white Christian civilization in spite of the mass of non-whites, can be seen as nothing less than a providence of the Almighty.

We believe that Providence planted us more than three centuries ago on the Southern corner of Africa because He had a definite purpose with us.[23]

The remarkable aspect of this sledgehammer approach to indoctrination is that it is probably quite superfluous. White children arrive at school thoroughly socialized into the norms governing race relations in South Africa, and the education system has at most a reinforcement rather than a conversion function: it provides for the continuing legitimation of the existing order and the blanket annihilation of potential alternatives. So many other agencies of control operate to serve the same ends, however, that the minute care with which CNE is applied in the schools must be seen more as a manifestation of pathological insecurity than as a political imperative. The very atmosphere of the schools, irrespective of the indoctrination that occurs within them, seems guaranteed to produce a conformist philistinism. The emphasis is on orthodoxy, regimentation, compulsory sports, and rigorous discipline, including public beatings as routine classroom procedure. There is a national system of twice-yearly examinations based on work prescribed down to the minutest detail, even to the particular stanzas that are to be studied in a certain poem in a specific anthology. In a high-school graduation examination, for example, one question asks the salary of a character in Dickens' *Great Expectations*.[24] Teacher experimentation or deviation from the predetermined syllabus is utterly precluded. Such an atmosphere offers little opportunity for personal development or critical thought.

Two other extracurricular influences deserve mention. One is the South African Broadcasting Corporation (SABC), a state monopoly that has recently been transferred to the control of the Education Department in recognition of its potential role in that field. The SABC radio services pour forth an incessant barrage of *apartheid* propaganda, and television, recently introduced into South Africa, is to have a "Christian and broad national character" and to be supervised by, to quote the charmless phrase of an SABC commission on the subject, "norm-conscious officials." A second influence is the South African Defense Force, into which all male whites are drafted after leaving school. Draftees are subjected to an intensive indoctrination program, described by the minister of defense in these terms:

It is not enough merely to take up an anti-communist stand. A positive message must be offered in its place. The best answer is probably the Nationalist Party, which is not simply an anti-party, but which has a positive message for South Africa, and, in fact, for the whole world. It is my intention to give trainees instruction in their spare time to equip them spiritually to meet the dangers of communism.[25]

This "instruction" has included the systematic presentation of literature from the American John Birch Society.

## BLACK SCHOOLS

The CNE manifesto stipulated three basic principles for the education of the indigenous African population: that it should be of a special kind, adapted for the supposed distinctive characteristics of the blacks; that

it should be in the vernacular; and that it should not be paid for at the expense of the whites. The regime has acted on all three principles.

When the Nationalist party took office in 1948, all black school education was under the control of the provinces and was operated primarily by religious missions. Within a year, the new government had established a commission to "formulate principles and aims of education for natives as an independent race, in which their . . . inherent racial qualities . . . are taken into consideration."[26] In its report, the commission recognized that blacks showed "an extreme aversion to any education especially adapted for the bantu," but recommended a new system of schooling that would provide for "the transmission and development of the bantu cultural heritage."[27]

What this would mean in practice was outlined in Parliament by Dr. H. F. Verwoerd, later to become prime minister but at the time minister of native affairs:

Education must train and teach people in accordance with their opportunities in life according to the sphere in which they live . . . Good racial relations cannot exist when the education is given under the control of people who create wrong expectations on the part of the native himself. . . . Native education should be controlled in such a way that it is in accordance with the policy of the state. . . . Racial relations cannot improve if the result is the creation of a frustrated people.[28]

A few months later he elaborated this position in one of the most remarkable utterances of his career:

The general aims . . . are to transform education *for* natives into Bantu Education. . . . A bantu pupil must obtain knowledge, skills, and attitudes which will be useful and advantageous to him and at the same time beneficial to the community. . . . The school must equip him to meet the demands which the economic life of South Africa will impose on him.

There is no place for him in the European community above the level of certain forms of labor. . . . For that reason it is of no avail for him to receive a training which has as its aim absorption into the European community. . . . Until now he has been subject to a school system which withdrew him away from his own community and misled him by showing him the green pastures of European society in which he was not allowed to graze. . . .

What is the use of teaching a bantu child mathematics when he cannot use it in practice? . . . That is absurd. Education is after all not something that hangs in the air.[29]

The Bantu Education Act of 1953 transferred control of black elementary and high schools from the provinces of the central government, and made it illegal for anyone to establish or conduct schools for blacks without government permission. Syllabuses were drawn up by the new Department of Bantu Education, and schools

*A class at St. Mark's Community School in Capetown, South Africa—a school for "Coloured" children. The facilities in all nonwhite schools are far inferior to those in white schools.*

were required to operate under government supervision. All the religious denominations except the Catholic church and the Seventh Day Adventists declined to maintain their schools under these conditions, and the schools were taken over by the government.

One of the regime's first steps after passage of the act was to introduce the vernacular as the medium of instruction in black schools, which had previously used English (or much more rarely, Afrikaans) after the first four years of elementary school. In part this policy stems from a projection of the Afrikaner's own insecurities about his language onto other groups, but the main reasons for the change lie deeper. The intention is twofold: to imprison blacks within their tribal culture by denying them the window on the world that easy acquaintance with the English language might provide and to emphasize ethnic divisions among the various black tribes by reinforcing their cultural differences and depriving them of a common *lingua franca*. In its effort to preserve the "traditional culture" of the blacks, the Department of Bantu Education has had to develop a brand-new technical jargon—even for the names of the days of the week—because the vernaculars lack the necessary specialized vocabulary. The language used in schools now diverges so markedly

from that used in homes that it is scornfully referred to in the black community as "school Xhosa," "school Zulu," and so on. The vernacular was introduced in the face of the strongest opposition from black teachers and parents, and it is noteworthy that as some control of education is being transferred to the new bantustans, the homelands authorities are reverting to English as the medium of instruction. In the black schools in the rest of South Africa, however, the vernacular is still used.

White teachers have been eased out of the system, although white administrators occupy the upper echelons of power. The supervision of black teachers is both rigorous and paternalistic. The departmental *Bantu Education Journal*, which contains various exhortations and policy pronouncements, is circulated in schools and must be signed by each teacher as an indication that he or she has read and absorbed the contents. The departmental magazine *Bantu* is also distributed free in the schools for the edification of both teachers and pupils; announcing this step in Parliament in June 1955, Dr. Verwoerd commented with pride that the black people were now nearing "the other side." An examination of the relevant issue of *Bantu* in June 1955 affords a most suggestive insight into Dr. Verwoerd's gratification over the matter. The magazine contains the following poem, eminently worthy of reproduction for its content if not for its style:

### Dr. Verwoerd: Minister of Native Affairs

Dr. Verwoerd, thou art the shepherd of the black races,
Thou art the defender of the Bantu, our rock, our mountain,
Thou art our refuge and our shield.
The mountain that saves us, our refuge.
The Saviour who rescued us in time of need.

We the Bantu boast and say, "Glory unto thee Dr. Verwoerd,"
And to all who are defenders of the Bantu;
We were amidst the seas of fear,
Fearing the government of malefactors, trapped in the nets of hypocrites. We were in fear.

Thou showed us compassion because we have no guilt,
Thou led us because there was no-one to lead us in our works,
We shall never forsake thy laws, for they bring
Plenty, wisdom, and knowledge.

Dr. Verwoerd, thou art with us! Glory unto thee our redeemer,
Praises be unto Dr. Verwoerd, the defender of the Bantu,
He that helped our chiefs by giving them good laws,
He that gave our schools proper education,
Because he knew what we needed and could not manage.[30]

Every effort has also been made to apply the parsimonious principle that education for blacks should not be conducted at the expense of the whites. Before the passage of the Bantu Education Act, black schools were funded from central government revenue. The new school system was financed by a fixed block grant from central revenue of R14 million per year (R1 equals $1.15), plus a proportion of the poll tax—a tax imposed on all blacks but not paid by any other population group. It became Nationalist party dogma that the block grant was not on any account to be increased, and the sum was pegged at this level for almost twenty years, during which its value was steadily eroded by inflation. Any increases had to come from the blacks themselves. The poll tax was therefore increased, and the entire sum eventually made over to the Bantu Education account. Black children were and still are charged school fees, unlike whites, whose education is free. Black communities are even expected to bear half of the cost of new school buildings; only when the structure stands virtually shoulder-high does the depart-

ment pay for the roof and fittings—and even so, many applications for equalization grants have been turned down because the department's funds for the purposes are exhausted. Black communities even raise money to pay for extra teachers to relieve the burden on the grossly understaffed schools. Thus the poorest section of the community is obliged to make the greatest sacrifices for what is the worst education system in the country.

Challenged to justify the refusal to increase the block grant from central revenue, the deputy minister of bantu education replied that he was not even prepared to discuss:

> the unhealthy aspect of continually stuffing the Bantu with more money and spending more on their education than they can absorb, of giving him more education than he can need in proportion to his economic position. . . . South Africa is doing as much, and more, for Bantu Education than the Bantu can absorb.[31]

Perhaps more to the point, the minister of bantu education admitted: "The money being spent on Bantu Education is not being spent out of love for the Bantu, but for the future of the whites.[32] Yet these fiscal arrangements finally broke down under the impact of inflation, the increase in the black school-age population, and, perhaps most importantly, the demands of an economy that cried out for more workers who were at least semiliterate and semiskilled. Throughout the sixties the department was obliged to engage in permanent deficit funding, and since 1972 the black schools have again been financed from general revenue, although still at an entirely inadequate level.

Every aspect of the system suffers from the continuing lack of funds. Black teachers earn on average less than a third of the salaries of white teachers with similar qualifications. Lack of teacher training facilities has meant that most black teachers are grossly underqualified: in the early seventies some 70 percent of them had not themselves completed high school, and more than 15 percent had not even completed elementary school.[33] Teacher-pupil ratios have increased from 1:41 in 1953 to over 1:60 today. More than half the schools operate a "double session" system, serving in effect as two schools—one occupying the buildings in the morning and one in the afternoon. Libraries, which may contain only books whose titles appear on lists published periodically by the *Bantu Education Journal*, are almost nonexistent: throughout the sixties the amount of money allocated to school library purchases for the entire system average R5000 per year. Spending on scientific equipment is at a more handsome but hardly generous level: R35,000 per year, spread over more than eight thousand schools.[34] School feeding programs have been cut: in 1953, R1.7 million was spent for this purpose; in 1961, R73,000; in 1966 and subsequently, nothing —although surveys at the time the program was being eliminated showed that 60 to 70 percent of black schoolchildren were recognizably malnourished, while 50 percent needed medical attention.[35] The per capita pupil expenditure dropped from R17 per pupil in 1954 to R11 per pupil in 1962; since then it has increased once more and now stands at around R25, about one-seventh of that spent on a white child.

Education for blacks remains voluntary, although there are plans to make attendance through the first four grades compulsory. In the early seventies over 90 percent of black schoolchildren were in elementary school, more than two-thirds of them in the first years, and about 10 percent of black children between the ages of seven and fourteen were not in school at all. The majority drop out after four or five years of school, after a curriculum consisting largely of religious instruction, singing, gardening, the vernacular, elementary arithmetic, and enough English or Afrikaans to follow simple commands. It is the government's policy to discourage permanent black settlements in the so-called white urban areas, and for this reason it is reluctant to establish secondary schools for blacks in these areas. In 1970 there were only twenty secondary schools catering for high-school pupils in the urban areas of the entire country, or one school for every eighty thousand youths living in these areas. In many places, notably Johannesburg and its environs, large numbers of black pupils have been turned away from secondary schools because there are no facilities for them. Less than four thousand blacks graduate from the Bantu Education schools each year, compared with more than thirty thousand whites who graduate from the white schools.

What have the few who graduate finally achieved? A report of the department records "aspects where the Department has achieved particular success".

Bantu pupils who have achieved matriculation [graduation] standard . . . show proof of the following:

1. They use clear, neat, uniform and easily legible handwriting.
2. They write their mother-tongue fluently and correctly, and speak it faultlessly.
3. They have no need to be ashamed of their knowledge of both official languages in written or in spoken form.
4. Most of them are also able to converse freely in at least one other Bantu language.
5. When they work with figures they are neat and accurate to such an extent that they have gained recognition for the outstanding quality of the work they perform in this sphere.[36]

These are curious claims. To boast neat handwriting as the prime product of thirteen years of school is, to say the least, suspect. To assert that the pupils write their language correctly and speak it faultlessly is simply untrue, since the median mark in the matriculation examination is 52 percent. To claim that they need not be ashamed of their command of English or Afrikaans is meaningless. To brag of the pupils' capacities to converse in other bantu languages is rather curious, since no bantu language other than the vernacular is taught in any Bantu Education school; such facility as the pupils may have has been acquired elsewhere. And the boast about the arithmetic capacity of the pupils is entirely unjustified: the median mark in arithmetic examinations is 35.5 percent.[37]

Education for Indians and coloureds follows a broadly similar pattern. The government took control of Indian education from the provinces in 1964. In the preceding decade, the average pass rate in the matriculation examinations was 75 percent; in 1964 it dropped to 48 percent, and in the following year to 34 percent. The director of Indian education explained that the problem was that Indian pupils were "taking courses not suited to their attributes and abilities and beyond their scope," a statement that heralded the introduction of a more "suitable" curriculum in 1972. When coloured education was similarly being taken over by the central government, the opposition in Parliament attempted to insert a clause in the legislation guaranteeing that coloured children would have an educational standard equal to that of whites. The minister of coloured affairs rejected the amendment: "Many coloured people cannot cope with the education whites receive." The minister declared:

> There are basic faults in Coloured education. We shall give no inferior education, but we shall most certainly give Coloured people differentiated education. It would not help to give them only academic education, and then throw them on the market as frustrated people.[38]

It has a depressingly familiar ring.

## THE UNIVERSITIES

The university is potentially a repository of critical thought in society. It is not surprising, therefore, that the CNE manifesto urged state intrusion into higher education, or that the English-language universities, one of the most nonconformist elements in South African society, have been continually assailed by the regime. Ever since it assumed office the government has perceived the exercise of academic freedom in South Africa as a threat to its totalitarian designs. Academic freedom involves the right of a university to engage in the free and unfettered pursuit of truth without being subject to the whims and dictates of transient political authority. The concept necessarily implies a high degree of university autonomy in decisions about who will teach, who will be taught, and what will be taught. Each of these pillars of academic freedom has been steadily eroded since 1948.

Two distinct traditions have existed in the universities of South Africa. One is the liberal tradition of the old Cape Colony under British rule—a tradition which, however attenuated it has become, stems directly from the intellectual mainstream of Western civilization and the values of humanism. This tradition is found in the English-language universities, however inconsistent they may have been in their adherence to it; above all, they have never deviated from their view that they should be entitled to admit students of every race. The second tradition is a particularist one, founded on the belief that race is a primary characteristic of the individual and that the appropriate relations between races are segregated and hierarchical. This tradition is deeply embedded in the Afrikaans-language universities, which see themselves as an organic part of the Afrikaans community, a place from which all "alien" influences and ideas are to be eliminated. As the principal (president) of the Afrikaans University of the Orange Free State expressed it:

> The university belongs to the *volk*, and therefore must be from the *volk*, of the *volk*, and for the *volk*, a *volk* university, anchored in the traditions of the *volk* in accordance with its conception of life and the world, and therefore on a Christian national basis.[39]

When the Nationalists took office there were eight universities in South Africa, four Afrikaans and four English; and there was one "university college"—an institution that could not award its own degrees—for blacks. The English universities admitted blacks under varying conditions: Cape Town and Witwatersrand universities did so freely, but imposed social segregation on students outside the classroom; Rhodes university admitted only a limited number of blacks; and Natal university imposed both social and academic segregation, admitting blacks freely but teaching them in segregated classrooms.

Throughout the fifties the government became progressively more agitated at the presence of the tiny black minorities in the English universities. In 1958 Dr. Verwoerd, then prime minister, declared:

> We do not want non-Europeans in the same university as the young European students of today, who are the leaders of tomorrow. We do not want Europeans to become so accustomed to the native that there is no difference between them and the natives.[40]

In 1959 the government secured passage of legislation euphemistically entitled the Extension of University Education Act. The act provided for the establishment of a series of ethnic universities for each of the major sections of the nonwhite population, with the new institutions being under the direct control of the central government. This legislation evoked some of the strongest opposition the government has ever faced in South Africa, both outside and within Parliament, where the opposition forced the longest debates and sittings in South African parliamentary history. Since the passage

of the bill, no black has been permitted to register at a white university without a permit, granted only if the student wishes to take a course unavailable elsewhere, and even then only in exceptional circumstances.

There are now five ethnic universities in South Africa: one each for the Indians, the coloureds, the Xhosa, the Sotho, and the Zulu; Africans who are not members of the Xhosa, Sotho, or Zulu attend the college of the most closely related group. Each college has a white principal and a predominantly white faculty, and is governed by a council whose members are approved by the regime. The councils, in fact, are packed with officials of government departments and with principals of Afrikaans universities, never previously noted for their concern with black higher education. There are separate dining room and faculty lounges for the white and black faculty, and faculty members are precluded by their conditions of contract from criticizing any aspect of government policy whatever. Control of students is equally strict; the ethnic colleges have almost identical regulations, which provide that no student society may be formed without permission, that a faculty supervisor must attend all meetings, that resolutions to be put to meetings must be approved beforehand by the principal, and that no student may leave the campus area or invite a visitor to it without permission. The particularist emphasis of the Afrikaans universities finds its counterpart in the new ethnic colleges. The principal of the Zulu college, for example, has described his institution in these terms:

> It is situated in purely Zulu territory. Its aims are the development of the Zulu community . . . the development of the Zulu language, the training of staff to be expert in the Zulu culture and the problems of education affecting the Zulu . . . and the encouragement of research into problems of importance to the Zulu.[41]

It is of these institutions that the minister of bantu administration and development has declared, "they are equal to all universities, not only in South Africa, but in the academic world as a whole."[42]

South African universities thus no longer have the right to determine whom they will teach. Their right to determine what they will teach and what research they will do is subject to a less formal control. The universities, operate, however, in an atmosphere that is both stifling and fearful. The presence of spies and informers on campus, documented in many instances and publicly complained of by the principals of the English universities, must have an effect in every classroom. The example of the fate of colleagues whose research has ventured into sensitive areas and elicited banning orders discourages critical social inquiry. The banning of books and periodical literature poses a continuing problem to the academic community; the Publications Control Board has banned over 40,000 books, films, magazines, papers, and records since 1965.[43] Even the possession of a Nobel Prize for literature seems to excite rather than allay the suspicions of the board; among the authors featured on its list of undesirable, obscene, blasphemous, or offensive literature are Jean Paul Sartre, Norman Mailer, John Steinbeck, Ernest Hemingway, Bertrand Russell, William Burroughs, Vladimir Nabokov, D. H. Lawrence, Philip Roth, Karl Marx, Robert Graves, Erskine Caldwell, Leon Uris, Bernard Malamud, William Faulkner, Edna O'Brien, John Updike, François Sagan, James Baldwin, Mario Puzo, and Brendan Behan. Political science students learn about communism or African nationalism from anticommunist or antinationalist tracts; faculty members may apply for a permit to keep banned books for scholarly study, but the books must be kept under lock and key and may not be seen by students. A large number of South African radicals, inside of the country and abroad, are banned or listed under the Suppression of Communism Act, and their words may not be quoted in print or verbally; their ideas thus remain largely unknown even in the universities.

Even academic associations are segregated. In 1962 the minister of education wrote in these terms to all learned societies that received government grants:

> It has been decided with reference to scientific and professional societies, no mixed membership is allowed and where this exists a separation must be effected immediately. . . . Non-white societies should be combined by way of affiliation into national societies, which can appoint one or two representatives to attend periodically certain executive meetings of the national societies for whites. In this way channels can be created not only for the interchange of ideas, but also to pass on to non-white scientists the knowledge which has crystallized out in congresses and conferences of white scientists.[44]

This document becomes even more fatuous in the light of the fact that of the twelve thousand members of the societies concerned, only *eight* were not white—and of these, four were Chinese.

One indication of the way the mores of the surrounding society can intrude on the university may be gleaned from the fate of the editor of the Cape Town student newspaper when he published a report about a campus debate on religion. One speaker was quoted as having declared that "God is dead." For publishing this quotation, the editor was charged and convicted of blasphemy. The charge sheet alleged that he:

> Did wrongfully and unlawfully blaspheme God, the Supreme Being . . . by spreading or circulating a disbelief in the Supreme Being, and in contemptuously ascribing to the Supreme Being acts inconsistent with His attributes.[45]

The right of the university to determine who shall teach and do research has also been undermined in many ways. The government screens intending faculty and research students from abroad, and has refused entry visas to those whose views might be offensive or whose research might be unwelcome. Faculty at the ethnic colleges may be arbitrarily dismissed for reasons unrelated to their academic competence; one was fired for having suggested that the pace of "separate development" was too slow. Several South African academics, including full professors of some eminence at the universities of Cape Town and the Witwatersrand, have been banned or listed under the Suppression of Communism Act and prevented from setting foot in a classroom, from teaching any person including their own children, and from publishing their research findings, even on such innocuous subjects as endocrinology. Mr. Vorster has explicitly stated that these steps were taken to prevent the "influence" of these scholars over their students. In the ethnic colleges, politically suspect black students are not permitted to do graduate research, and indeed on more than one occasion an ethnic college has expelled its entire student body after it had displayed symptoms of unrest. The English universities cannot admit black research students on the basis of merit, and even those few who receive government permits to study at white universities risk having the permits withdrawn at any time if their work or attitudes offend the regime. Since 1968, the government has prevented the English universities from appointing black faculty. In that year the University of Cape Town attempted to hire a black anthropologist, and was forced to withdraw the offer after the regime had threatened new legislation empowering the minister of education to reduce or cut off the government subsidy—representing the bulk of university revenue—of universities that flouted its wishes. The university complied, but the legislation was passed anyway: South African universities may now be in effect bankrupted if, "in the minister's opinion," they do not conform to "lawful requirements."

South African students are as divided as the universities they attend. Most Afrikaans students belong to the Afrikaans Student Bond (ASB), a fanatically reactionary body that is one of the most right-wing elements in the entire country. The ASB refuses to have anything to do with other student organizations except under the most peculiar conditions; in 1971 its president declared that "contact and dialogue between Afrikaners and Coloureds is not wrong, provided that the contact and discussion is aimed at greater separation between them."[46] Most English students belong to the National Union of South African Students (NUSAS), a liberal organization that attempted to retain a multiracial membership until the early seventies, although it has since recognized that it can no longer speak for black students. The organization has been a favorite target for Mr. Vorster's attacks; he has variously described it as a "breeding ground of adders," "offspring of vipers," "sons of serpents," and, in imagery less serpentine but equally clear in its general import, "a red cancer in our midst," "young pink liberals playing with fire," and "corrupters of our youth whom no decent person would touch with a bargepole." Leaders of the organization have been routinely banned since 1966. Many black students joined the South African Students Organization (SASO), which was formed in 1968 by blacks disillusioned at what they felt was the patronizing stance of the white liberals in NUSAS. Strongly influenced by the American black power movement, the organization emphasized black solidarity and discouraged contact with whites. The existence of SASO posed a dilemma to the regime. On the one hand the organization appeared to advocate black separatism and to reject any multiracial alternative, an approach that the government commends. On the other hand, SASO was militantly opposed to *apartheid*, rejected "separate development," and urged the unity of all the ethnic groups. For five years the government equivocated, but in 1973 it served the entire leadership of SASO with banning and house arrest orders, and has since harassed the organization to virtual extinction.

In the final stages of their education, then, Afrikaans students have generally turned out as the government wished them to be: nationalist, conservative, and conformist. Black students have developed the sense of racial exclusivity that was intended for them—but not through being led there by their "trustee" so much as through being pushed into this position by bitterness and resentment. English students, escaping some of the rigors of CNE in their elementary and secondary schools and then exposed to the more liberal climate of their universities, remain on the whole mildly critical of the regime, but their outlook is hardly radical.

Shaped by an ideology that is grounded in an anachronistic system of racial privilege, South African education contributes in countless ways to the inexpressible cruelty of *apartheid*. For the blacks, education offers little more than a training for menial roles in a white-dominated economy, and as such it is little more than a preparation for servitude. The black high-school children recognize this fact; at the time of writing they have been taking part for several months in a nationwide boycott of their classes, in the conviction that Bantu Education is worse than no education at all. It was the black high-school pupils, too, who played the leading part in the protests and rioting that shook urban centers throughout 1976, and who paid dearly in the loss of lives and liberty in the repression that followed. For the whites the educational system offers every material advantage, but at the cost of distorting their intellects and emotions through the organized encouragement of prejudice and bigotry.

The tenets of CNE have been successfully applied, but ultimately the South African educational system will fail in its objectives. Like so many other institutions in South Africa, the educational system prevents com-

munication and understanding among the various population groups; instead, it fosters resentment and hatred. The system recognizes no common nationhood, no shared human needs; it aims rather at the maintenance of white and particularly Afrikaner supremacy through the deliberate reinforcement of cleavages in the population. Yet, it is those very cleavages that may well, in the long run, precipitate an upheaval that will bring to an end Afrikanerdom's stubborn defiance of the twentieth century. If racial tensions in South Africa increase to an intolerable point, leading to a conflagration that tears apart that unhappy society and brings Afrikaner hegemony to a violent and wretched end, then "Christian National Education" will surely be accounted as one of the factors contributing to that conclusion.

## NOTES

1. *Natal Mercury*, 17 December 1970.
2. *Star*, weekly edition, 18 December 1971.
3. *Die Kerkblad*, November 1970.
4. Quoted in *Daily News* (Durban), 29 March 1965.
5. *Die Transvaler*, 29 March 1965.
6. Education League, *Manifesto for Christian National Education* (Johannesburg, 1948).
7. *Onderwysblad*, 1 July 1961.
8. Transvaal Onderwysersunie circular to school principals, quoted in National Union of South African Students, *The Citizen, Politics, and Education* (Cape Town, 1964).
9. Quoted in *Dome* (University of Natal), 23 June 1972.
10. L. C. Bekker and G. J. Potgieter, *Voortligting vir St VIII* (Johannesburg, 1961), p. 32.
11. F. A. Van Jaarsveld; *New Illustrated History for Senior Certificate, Vol II: General History* (Johannesburg, 1969), p. 296.
12. L. C. Bekker and G. J. Potgieter, *Voorligting vir St VIII*, Johannesburg 1960, p. 29.
13. Bekker and Potgieter, *Voorligting*, 1961, p. 32.
14. Ibid., p. 31.
15. B. G. Lindeque, *Geskiedenis: Algemene en Suid-Afrikaanse vir St VIII* (Cape Town, 1954), p. 81.
16. A. N. Boyce, *Europe and South Africa: A History of the Period 1815–1939* (Johannesburg, 1960).
17. Bekker and Potgieter, *Voorligting*, 1960, p. 33.
18. J. F. E. Havinga, G. F. Robbertse, and A. G. Roodt, *Geskiedenis vir St VII* (Johannesburg, 1960), p. 120.
19. J. J. Muller, G. H. P. de Bruin, and J. L. du Plooy, *New History for the National Junior Certificate, Part I—Std VI* (Cape Town, 1969), pp. 108–9.
20. Bekker and Potgieter, *Voorligting* 1961, p. 23.
21. Ibid., p. 24.
22. Havinga, Robbertse, and Roodt, *Geskiedenis*, 1960, p. 5.
23. Bekker and Potgieter, *Voorligting*, 1960, pp. 29–45.
24. *Sunday Times* (Johannesburg), 23 August 1970.
25. *Rand Daily Mail*, 3 November 1966.
26. Terms of reference to the commission on native educa-

tion, in *Report of the Commission on Native Education 1949–1951* (Pretoria, 1951).

27. Ibid., p. 164.
28. *House of Assembly Debates*, 15 June 1959, 8319 ff.
29. Quoted in Brian Bunting, *The Rise of the South African Reich* (London, 1964).
30. *Bantu*, June 1955.
31. Quoted in National Union of South African Students, *Fact Paper on Bantu Education* (Cape Town, 1968).
32. Quoted in National Union of South African Students, *Bantu Education: Education or Indoctrination?* (Cape Town, 1963).
33. South African Institute of Race Relations, *Survey of Race Relations in South Africa, 1971* (Johannesburg, 1972), p. 261.
34. Muriel Horrel, *Bantu Education to 1968* (Johannesburg, 1968), p. 73.
35. South African Institute of Race Relations, *Fact Paper 4 (Johannesburg, 1960)*.
36. Department of Bantu Education, *Annual Report, 1968* (Pretoria, 1969), p. 104.
37. See also W. G. McConkey, "Bantu Education: A Critical Survey, with Illustrations," *Theoria* 38 (May 1972): 1–45.
38. Quoted in Bunting, *Rise of the South African Reich*, p. 215.
39. Quoted in David Welsh, "Some Political and Social Determinants of the Academic Environment," in *Student Perspectives on South Africa*, ed. Hendrick van der Merwe and David Welsh (Cape Town, 1972), p. 21.
40. *Cape Argus*, 19 March 1958.
41. P. W. Cook, "Some Aims and Objectives of a Bantu University College," in *Education and Our Expanding Horizons*, ed. R. G. Macmillan, P. D. Hey, and J. MacQuarrie (Pietermaritzburg, 1962).
42. *Rand Daily Mail*, 24 August 1967.
43. *Rand Daily Mail*, 5 March 1971.
44. Quoted in UNESCO, *Apartheid and Its Effects on Education, Science, Culture, and Information* (Paris, 1967).
45. *Sunday Times* (Johannesburg), 3 September 1967.
46. *Sunday Tribune* (Durban), 4 July 1971.

# EASTERN CULTS AND WESTERN CULTURE: WHY YOUNG AMERICANS ARE BUYING ORIENTAL RELIGIONS

BY HARVEY COX

## What are they looking for, the millions who have been touched by this neo-Oriental religious revival? And are they really finding it?

*An old Zen story tells of a pilgrim who mounted his horse and crossed formidable mountains and swift rivers seeking a famous roshi, or wise man, in order to ask him how to find true enlightenment. After months of searching, the pilgrim located the teacher in a cave. The roshi listened to the question, and said nothing. The seeker waited. Finally, after hours of silence, the roshi looked at the steed on which the pilgrim had arrived, and asked the pilgrim why he was not looking for a horse instead of enlightenment. The pilgrim responded that obviously he already had a horse. The roshi smiled, and retreated to his cave.*

IN THE PAST DECADE, this country has seen dozens of Eastern religious cults and movements spring up and flourish, attracting thousands of American youths who are searching for truth, brotherhood, and authority. What has provoked this neo-Oriental religious revival? Who are the people caught up in it? Why have they left some more conventional religious life—or none at all—to become seekers or adherents in these new spiritual movements? What

does it all mean for American culture?

Large numbers of people are involved in this quest, not just a fringe group. And the extent of their interest has no precedent in American religious history. Although overall estimates vary widely—partly because the movements themselves tend to overstate their membership—I would guess that by now several million Americans have been touched one way or another by some form of neo-Oriental thought or devotional practice. I base this guess not only on the number of actual adherents, but also on those who practice—regularly or sporadically—various forms of meditation, or whose practice of karate or the martial arts goes beyond self-defense to their underlying Buddhist philosophy.

To learn why people join these movements and practice these disciplines, I and some of my students at Harvard Divinity School spent three years informally studying dozens of such groups currently operating in Cambridge, Massachusetts. Some of the students were already involved in the movements, while most of them were just curious about what meaning they had to their adherents, why people had joined, and what they were looking for.

To find out, we visited the centers to observe, participate in the meetings and the rituals, and talk with the devotees.

Cambridge is known throughout the country primarily as the home of Harvard University. But in recent years it has also become a thriving center of Eastern religious cults and movements, prompting one of my friends to call it "Benares-on-the-Charles."

Within walking distance of Harvard Square, one can find dozens of different neo-Oriental religious movements. A few blocks away stands the Zen center, furnished with black silk cushions, bells, an appropriately wizened and wise-looking resident master, and a visiting Zen swordplay instructor. In the basement of a nearby Episcopal church, the Sufi dancers meet twice a week to twist and turn like the legendary whirling dervishes in a ritual circle, chanting verses from the Koran. Down the street is the Ananda Marga center, specializing in a combination of meditation and community action.

A few blocks south sits the headquarters of the Hare Krishnas, officially known as the International Society for Krishna Consciousness. There, the devotees hold a weekly feast of savory Indian food and a somewhat less piquant

Paul Plumadore

# "I decided to concentrate not on what the movements and leaders claim to offer, but on what the individuals who turn to them actually find."

introductory lecture on the mysteries of the Krishna devotion. The clean-shaven followers of the chubby young guru, the Maharaj Ji, have a meeting place near Central Square. A group of self-styled Sikhs, immaculately clad in white robes, turbans, and daggers, have opened a vegetarian restaurant called the Golden Temple of Conscious Cookery. Nearby is the International Student Meditation Center, founded several years ago by the Maharishi Mahesh Yoga, the best known of the swamis of the late '60s, where one can learn the art of "transcendental meditation." Recent arrivals include the followers of guru Sri Chinmoy, a former postal clerk living in Queens; the Dharma House, founded by Chogyam Trungpa Rinpoche, the Tibetan Buddhist lama; and dozens of smaller, less stable groups devoted to yoga, Tai Chi, and other exotic pursuits.

I knew that no matter how hard I tried to maintain scholarly objectivity, my inner distrust for all "opiates of the people" might continue to influence me. But I decided to do the study anyway. Although my prejudice against some of the movements was undeniable, I was at least fully aware of it.

During the first several weeks of the study my students and I all had a marvelous time. Together and separately we attended dozens of meditation sessions, feasts, satsangs, introductory lectures, inquirers' meetings, worship services, and study circles. The groups we visited were invariably hospitable. We asked questions, read stacks of tracts and pamphlets, watched, listened, and filled up stacks of tape cartridges. For once we were getting something straight from the source instead of from textbooks.

With all our research, however, I felt something was lacking. As the notebooks piled up, I began to wonder what it would feel like to be on the inside of one of the movements. No one can hope to experience another person's faith as he does. And as a Christian and a professional theologian I realized I was neither a genuine Oriental pilgrim nor an authentic seeker. I was intrigued, curious, fascinated, but not a devotee. Still, I realized I would have to pursue some kind of "inside" knowing and feeling if I were going to understand the disciples I

was studying. So I tried to become as much of a participant as I could. I did not merely observe the Sufi dancers; I whirled too. I did not just read about Zen, or visit centers; I "sat." I chanted with the Hare Krishnas. I stood on my head, stretched my torso, and breathed deeply with the yoga practitioners. I spent hours softly intoning a mantra to myself in a favorite form of Hindu devotional practice.

I became a participant not because I thought there was actually something in it for me, but because I wanted to nourish my capacity for empathy. I wanted to find out what I could about the lure of the East on the visceral level. This participant-observer phase of my inquiry took me far away from Benares-on-the-Charles. It led me to spiritual centers in California, Colorado, Texas, and Vermont, and into conversations with Zen abbots, Sufi drummers, and Divine Light devotees.

Only after my search became personal did I finally hit on an approach which seemed both faithful to the movements, and helpful in interpreting them to other people. I had become interested in Eastern spirituality for personal reasons, with a host of internal reservations. My purposes were clearly different from those advanced by the teachers themselves. I was quite sure that mine was a most unusual case. I soon discovered, however, it was not. Once I got to know them, nearly all the people I met turned out to have personal reasons that often had little to do with the official teaching of the movement's leaders. This discovery provided me with the clue I needed. I decided to concentrate not on what the movements and their leaders claim to offer, but on what the individuals who turn to them actually find.

he "East turners" we found in these movements have not moved to India to live in an ashram. They have not left home for the Orient to dwell in a Tibetan temple or a Zen monastery. They still live in Texas or Ohio or New York or somewhere else in the United States. They have not

gone East, they have *turned* East. There are true seekers and frivolous dilettantes, converts and fellow travelers. Their interest comes in widely varying degrees of seriousness and persistence: some merely sneak a glance at a paperback edition of the *I Ching* or try some yoga postures; others find that one of the Eastern practices becomes important to them; others leave everything behind and sleep on mats in a Hare Krishna temple.

One way to find out what kind of people join these movements is to determine the standard sociological data of their social class, age, race, sex, education, and ethnic background. Such studies have been done, but they leave much unsaid. The participants tend to be young, in their late teens or early 20s. Although some early teen-agers learn how to do yoga, or read a little Eastern philosophy, few become seriously involved until late adolescence. The 20s are the prime turning time.

The Eastern religious movements are made up almost exclusively of white, educated, middle- and upper-middle-class young people. Most have at least begun college, although some have dropped out after a year or two. Men and women seem to participate in fairly equal numbers, but men control the leadership groups. There is no predominance of any particular regional background, although more of the devotees seem to come from urban than from rural areas, probably because the movements are generally based in cities.

These young people come from all religious denominations, with relatively more from liberal Protestant and reform Jewish backgrounds than the proportion of these groups in the general population would suggest. This is not surprising, considering the urban, middle-class, educated milieu in which these groups recruit most of their members. Few come from strongly atheistic or unusually pious homes. They seem to have received some religion from their parents, but not enough to satisfy them.

Despite all these statistics and data and categories, we still don't know much about the actual human beings who have made this decisive choice. So my students and I asked the people

"Most of the members of these communities seem to be looking for simple friendship...the search for a supportive community."

themselves to tell us in their own words what they found in the groups they belonged to. Their answers varied, but as we sorted through them, several definite patterns emerged.

1. Most of the members of these movements seem to be looking for simple human *friendship*. The reply we heard most often, especially from those actually living in religious communes or ashrams, told a story of loneliness, isolation, and the search for a supportive community. To paraphrase a large number of replies:

*They seem to care for me here. I was bummed out, confused, just wandering around. When I first came here I didn't know what they were talking about. They all seemed crazy, and I told them so. But that didn't seem to bother them. They took me in. They made me feel at home. Now I feel like I'm a part of it, an important part, too. I belong here. It's where I was meant to be.*

The newer the convert, the more likely this reply. After a few weeks, however, the novices begin to learn a more theologically proper answer, such as, *Krishna called me here*, or *It was my karma*. Many seekers who drift into such movements looking for intimacy quickly learn to express their reasons in the group argot. But the need for plain friendship is clearly their chief motivation. They are looking for warmth, affection, and close ties of feeling. They don't find it at work, at school, in churches they attend, or even at home. But they do seem to find it, at least for a while, in the community of devotees. The groups we visited provide an island of companionship in what the adherents feel is a world devoid of fraternity.

2. The East turners are also looking for a way to experience life directly, without the intervention of ideas and concepts. They seek a kind of *immediacy* they have not been able to find elsewhere. Even though some young people drift from movement to movement, they do not seem to be looking for just another kick or "trip" to add to their collection.

Most are serious, and want a real, personal encounter with God, or simply with life, nature, and other people: *All I got at any church I ever went to*

*were sermons or homilies about God, about "the peace that passes understanding." Words, words, words. It was all up in the head. I never really felt it. It was all abstract, never direct, always somebody else's account of it. It was dull and boring. I'd sit or kneel or stand. I'd listen to or read prayers. But it seemed lifeless. It was like reading the label instead of eating the contents.*

*But here it really happened to me. I experienced it myself. I don't have to take someone else's word for it.*

This testimony of direct experience became more understandable when we noticed that nearly all the neo-Oriental movements include instruction in some form of spiritual discipline. Initiates learn the primary techniques of prayer, chanting, contemplation, or meditation. Teachers rely not only on words, as in most Western religious training, but also on actual techniques—either quite simple, as in transcendental meditation, or complex, as in Zen—for inducing the desired forms of consciousness. At the local Zen center, for example, the teachers sit you down immediately to face a blank wall, and smilingly refuse to answer all but the most elementary questions until you have taken the practical step of trying to meditate. Even after that they keep the ideas to a minimum. Practice and direct exposure are the keys to the kingdom.

3. Some East turners are looking for *authority*. They have turned East to find truth, to lay hold on a message or teaching they can believe and trust. They join these groups as refugees from uncertainty and doubt. They often stress the role of the particular swami or guru whose wisdom or charismatic power has caused such a change in their lives: *I tried everything. I read all the books, went to lectures, listened to different teachers. But all that happened was that I got more confused. I couldn't think straight any more. I couldn't get myself together or make any decisions. Then I met him, and what he said finally made sense. Everything finally clicked. I knew he was for real. I could tell just from the way he spoke that he knew. Now my confusion is over.*

The quest for authority results from a wide range of factors documented by

dozens of sociologists: the dissolution of conventional moral codes; the erosion of traditional authorities; the emergence of what Alvin Toffler, the author of *Future Shock*, once called "overchoice." As a result, large numbers of people have begun to suffer a kind of choice-fatigue. They hunger for an authority that will simplify, straighten out, assure; something or somebody that will make their choices fewer and less arduous. For some, the search for authority ends at the swami's feet.

4. A smaller number of people told us in one way or another that they had turned to the East because somehow it seemed more *natural*. These people also seem to have changed their faith-orientation more self-consciously than others, and with deliberate rejection of what they consider the effete, corrupt, or outworn religious tradition of the West. They see in Eastern spirituality a kind of unspoiled purity. In contrast to Western faith, the East seems artless, simple, and fresh. They could often tell us why they had turned *from* some Western religion more clearly than they could say why they had turned *toward* the East.

*Western civilization is shot. It is nothing but technology and power and rationalization, corrupted to its core by power and money. It has no contact with nature, feeling, spontaneity. What we need to do now is learn from the Oriental peoples who have never been ruined by machines and science, who have kept close to their ancestors' simplicity. Western religion has invalidated itself. Now only the East is possible.*

The people who talked to us in this vein were often the most widely read and best educated of the East turners. They could often cite evidence more specifically and phrase their arguments more clearly than the others. Though they did not put it this way themselves, to me their decision to turn East often seemed to have some of the quality of a purification ritual. It was as though they were going through the Western equivalent of a bath in the Ganges, shedding the tainted and the impure.

These then are the reasons most East turners cite for their choice: they seek friendship; a direct experience of God

## "Religious teachings, Eastern or Western, can be transformed into commodities, priced, and made available to prospective buyers."

and the world; a way out of intellectual and moral confusion; and a kind of innocence, or a way of life unmarred by technological overkill. This list of goals shows that East turners are really not very different from anyone else. They are looking for what many other people in America are looking for today. They have merely chosen a more visible and dramatic way of looking. The real question, of course, is will they find it?

he ironic aspect of the Turn East is that it is occurring just as many millions of Asians are involved in an epochal "Turn West" toward Western science and technology, Western political systems, and Western cultural forms. Just as this great awakening to history has begun to occur in the real Asia, millions of Americans have fallen in love with an Asia that is disappearing, or maybe never existed: the "mysterious Orient" of the old Western myth. In fact, those who yearn for what they call an "Oriental" approach today are really opting for an archaic rather than a historical way of life. They may be turning back instead of turning East.

Two kinds of replies from East turners disturb me because they reveal a quest that will lead not just to disillusionment but to frustration and bitterness. One can sympathize with those who hope to regain a lost innocence—a world free of complications, a world of black and white choices. But eventually they will find out that no such world will ever be found. For maturity means learning to live in a complex, shades-of-gray world.

I feel similar qualms about those who long for an authority so unquestionable and total that they would not have to make hard decisions or chew through choices on their own.

At first, converts to these movements often do seem to find a kind of new innocence. They are "blissed out" with their hassle-free life. The emphasis many of these groups place on the inner life, plus their relegation of secular society to an inferior form of reality, means that adhering to their teachings

will remove the uncomfortable tensions of school, work, or home. Since money, power, and, in some cases, even the capacity to make choices are viewed as illusory or insignificant, the causes of most political tussles disappear. The problem is that the nasty issues of work, politics, and the rest do not really disappear, and even East turners must eventually grapple with them. But as devotees they must do so with a world view that gives them little help, because it refuses to recognize that the problems even exist.

I am also troubled by the pursuit of an absolute religious and moral authority that will relieve the discomfort of making decisions. People who hunger for this kind of authority over them suffer from the wounds dealt out by parents, schools, and jobs where they have never been encouraged to flex their decision-making capabilities. But in order to mature, the last thing they need is one more perfect master to solve their problems for them.

They need friends and families and larger settings in which their confidence in their own capacities will be strengthened.

What the East turners are doing is hardly a prescription for a general cure; rather, it is a symptom of a malaise with which we must all contend. Religious remedies to the ills of a culture take two basic forms: one tries to get at the underlying causes of the malady; the other provides a way for people to live in spite of the illness, usually by providing them with an alternative miniworld, sufficiently removed from the one outside so that its perils are kept away from the gate. The East turners have almost all chosen this second form. The only solution they offer to other people is to join them in their miniworld.

But if we all join them, it would soon be a maxiworld with all the problems back again. Part of the answer is that these movements cannot be the answer for everyone. Some East turners have found a haven from the impersonality and vacuousness of the larger society, and, some would say, of its churches. They have rightly located the most severe symptoms of our ailing era. But their solution, though it may work for them individually, at least for a while, is

ultimately no solution for the rest of us.

s for the movements themselves, I also worry about their future. For the business of America is business, and that includes the religion business. The greatest irony of the Eastern religious movements is that in their effort to present an alternative to the Western way of life, most have succeeded in adding only one more line of spiritual products to the American religious marketplace. They have become a part of the consumer culture they set out to call in question.

This consumerization of the new religious movements should not surprise us. After all, the genius of any consumer society is its capacity for changing anything, including its critics, into items for distribution and sale. Religious teachings and disciplines—Eastern or Western—can be transformed into commodities, assigned prices, packaged attractively, and made available to prospective buyers.

Conspicuous consumption is no longer a mark of distinction. What we have in its place is something I call the new gluttony, which transforms the entire range of human ideas and emotions into a well-stocked pantry. Today, only the old-fashioned glutton still stuffs his mouth with too many entrees. The new glutton craves experiences: in quantity and variety, more and better, increasingly exotic, and even spiritual. Today's money does not lust after houses, cars, and clothes, but travel, drugs, unusual sights and sounds, exotic tastes, therapies, and new emotional states. If disgrace haunts the affluent, it is not apt to be for failing to *have* something, but rather for failing to have *tried* something. The very thought that out there lurks an experience one has not had now sends the affluent into panic.

No doubt economists as well as theologians could advance explanations for why we are moving from a greed for things to a gluttony of experience. In a system based on encouraging greed, people eventually become sated. It is hard to sell still another television set to the family that already has one in every room. There is a limit somewhere

# "No deity, however terrible, no devotion, however deep, no ritual, however splendid, escapes the voracious process of trivialization."

to what most people can stack up.

With experiences, however, there seems to be no such limit, and the experience merchants do not need to plan obsolescence or invent style changes. Their product self-destructs immediately, except for one's memory. Last year's model is unusable not for any reason as trivial as changing hemlines but because it is gone.

Economists can explain the new gluttony in the classical terms of a movement from goods to services. It is the old story of expanding markets, finding new resources and developing novel products. But now the product is an experience that can be sold and delivered to a customer. The resources are virtually infinite for the imaginative entrepreneur, and the market is that growing group of people whose hunger for accumulating mere things has begun to decline.

I think there is an element of spiritual gluttony in the current fascination with Oriental spirituality. We should not blame this on the Oriental traditions themselves, most of which are highly sensitive to the pitfalls of spiritual pride. Nor can we blame the often anguished people who are driven by forces they can neither control nor understand toward searching out more and more exhilarating spiritual experiences.

If there is any fault to be allocated, it lies not with the victims but with the buyer-seller nexus within which the new religious wave is marketed. Despite what may be good intentions all around, the consumer mentality can rot the fragile fruits of Eastern spirituality as soon as they are unpacked. The process is both ironic and pathetic. What begins in Benares as a protest against possessiveness ends up in Boston as still another possession.

No deity, however terrible, no devotion, however deep, no ritual, however splendid, is exempt from the voracious process of trivialization. The smiling Buddha himself and the worldly wise Krishna can be transformed by the new gluttony into collectors' trinkets. It was bad enough for King Midas that everything he touched turned to gold. The acquisition-accumulation pattern of the new gluttony does even more. Reversing the alchemist's course, it transforms

rubies and emeralds into plastic, the sacred into the silly, the holy into the hokey.

The gods of the Orient mean one thing there, and something quite different here. This is not to be blamed either on the gods themselves, or on their original devotees, or on their new seekers. It happens because when the gods migrate, or are transported to a civilization where everything is to some extent a commodity, they become commodities too.

The culture barrier that a commodity culture erects against the possibility of genuine interreligious exchange is formidable. It raises the question of whether we in the West can ever hear the voice of the East, can ever learn about the Buddhist or Hindu paths without corrupting them in the process.

Although America today *seems* uncommonly receptive to spiritual ideas and practices from the East, the truth is that we are not really receptive to them at all. True, no stone walls have been erected to keep the pagans out. No orders of Knights Templar have ridden forth to hurl back the infidels. The gates are open, and the citizens seem ready to listen. No wonder many Eastern teachers view America as a fertile ground in which to sow their seeds.

But curiously it is precisely America's receptivity, its eagerness to hear, explore, and experience, that creates the most difficult barrier to our actually learning from Eastern spirituality. The very insatiable hunger for novelty, for intimacy, even for a kind of spirituality that motivates so many Americans to turn toward the East also virtually guarantees that the turn will ultimately fail.

The final paradox is that Easterners have never claimed to be able to save the West. Frequently they deny having any interest in doing so, even if they could. They rarely send missionaries here, and they accept Western novices with reluctance. Although the Westernized versions of Eastern faiths often claim to bring salvation to the West, at this point they betray the spirit of their sources, and actually worsen the Western dilemma by advertising more than they can deliver.

The spiritual crisis of the West will not be resolved by spiritual importa-

tions or individual salvation. It is the crisis of a whole civilization, and one of its major symptoms is the belief that the answer must come from Elsewhere. The crisis can be met only when the West sets aside myths of the Orient, and returns to its own primal roots.

Eventually the spiritual disciplines of the Orient will make a profound contribution to our consciousness and our way of life. Some day, somewhere, we will hear the message the East has for us. But we can only begin to know the real Orient when we are willing to let go of the mythical one. And we can only begin to hear the message of the Oriental religious traditions when we are willing to confront the inner dislocations in our own civilization that caused us to invent the myth of the East in the first place. And when we are willing to do that, we may realize, like the truth seeker in the Zen parable, that what we are seeking so frantically elsewhere may turn out to be the horse we have been riding all along.  ♫

---

Harvey Cox graduated from the University of Pennsylvania, and then attended Yale Divinity School, from which he received a bachelor of divinity degree in 1951. He served as Protestant chaplain at Temple University and director of religious activities at Oberlin College. He also worked for the American Baptist Home Mission Society, and taught at the Andover-Newton Theological Seminary.

In 1962, Cox received a Ph.D. in history of philosophy of religion from Harvard University. He has been a member of the faculty of Harvard Divinity School since 1966, and is now chairman of the Department of Applied Theology. He has taught courses there in contemporary theology, religion and society, and the Church and social change.

Professor Cox is the author of *The Secular City*, *The Seduction of the Spirit*, and *Turning East* from which this article has been adapted.

For more information, read:
Cox, Harvey. *The Seduction of the Spirit*, Simon and Schuster, 1973, $8.95; paper, 1974, $2.95.

Glock, Charles Y. and Robert N. Bellah, eds. *The New Religious Consciousness*, University of California, 1976, $14.95.

Graham, Aelred. *Contemplative Christianity*, Seabury, 1975, $6.95.

Needleman, Jacob. *The New Religions*, Doubleday, 1970, $6.95; paper, Pocket Books, $1.50.

Trungpa, Chogyam. *Cutting Through Spiritual Materialism*, Shambhala, 1973, paper, $4.25.

# 42
# SCIENCE AND MYTH

Talk of machines that "think", computers having "nervous breakdowns", "flying saucers" is creating a new kind of myth hiding behind the cloak of science.
Here a leading French scientist discusses modern myths in relation to a true understanding and popularization of science.

*by
Pierre Auger*

To the sensational progress of science—and of physics and biology in particular—what is generally called the general public reacts in three different ways.

Some admire and even wax enthusiastic about the daring exploits of astro-physics and molecular biology. Without being really able to add to their own knowledge, they sense the grandeur of this amazing adventure of the human mind.

Others are struck, above all, by the technical achievements which follow in the wake of scientific progress, such as communications satellites, supersonic flight, and exploration of the moon and of the ocean floor. The power of man equals, and in certain fields surpasses, that of the gods of antiquity.

There is a third attitude, however, which is wholly compounded of the anxiety and distrust inspired by scientific progress and at the same time—perhaps even primarily—by the attendant technical progress. Where are we heading with these machines and computers? Can we be sure that these atomic, space and genetic adventures are not going to end in disaster?

Thus, if the writer on scientific subjects is to cater for every category of

**PIERRE AUGER**, *is a leading French physicist and former Director-General of the European Space Research Organization (ESRO) which he helped to set up. He was head of Unesco's Department of Natural Sciences from 1948 to 1959 and is the author of "Current Trends in Scientific Research", a comprehensive survey of world scientific and technological research published by Unesco in 1961, 3rd edition 1963*

reader, he must not take the easy path and be content with tending and feeding the sacred fire of the first group we have described, and with providing fresh grounds for the enthusiasm of the second group. He must take care to reassure the third group, and this he must do by re-establishing the truth, not the truth pure and simple, for the truth is complex and often abstract, but the naked truth by which I mean stripped of the fantastic trappings with which it is all too often embellished by publicists—! dare not call them writers—who are either naive and ill-informed themselves or else unscrupulous popularity-hunters.

There is no denying that this is a very difficult task. It is even regarded as an impossible one by some people of sound judgement who see the attempts of science writers to acquaint the general public with certain fields of knowledge as leading simply to the creation of a new kind of mythology.

I can be quite frank here and admit that they are often right. This is certainly one of the main rocks on which the efforts of those known as popular science writers come to grief. It is a rock never struck by the writers of those works of fiction in scientific garb which fill library-shelves labelled "science-fiction". Here, the creation of myths is the avowed aim.

A word of warning however. It is essential that the mythical nature of such books be clearly indicated so that there is no mistake about what is being offered for public consumption. There has been too much talk of machines that think, computers that get nervous breakdowns and flying

saucers with little green men from outer space. From all this there seems to have been born a kind of myth which people are beginning to take as scientific fact.

But let us look at what the popular science writer can do to communicate knowledge instead of new myths. First of all, what distinguishes a scientific theory from a myth?

Here I am using the word myth to signify an explanation or theory of natural or human phenomena and events, like those handed down by tradition in ancient times and those still transmitted in this way by so-called uncivilized peoples following the thought processes of "the savage mind" described by Claude Lévi-Strauss.

These myths make use of figures with human characteristics and animals gifted with supernatural powers, but they also present abstract forces such as Fate or mana, particularly those secreted in certain objects.

The expression "scientific theory" is also used to signify explanations of natural—and, if need be, human—phenomena, and although these explanations do not make use of human figures or animals, they nevertheless attribute specific properties to certain objects which secrete forces and are capable of generating phenomena and bringing about events.

Examples of such objects are magnetized or electrically charged bodies, and radioactive or fissile substances. The analogy is so strong as to cause confusion in some cases and myths then grow up around machines,

## The legend of the magnetic mountain

Magnetism was such a mysterious phenomenon that it gave rise to a whole mythology among the Ancients. The geographer Ptolemy wrote that, near present-day Borneo, there existed mountains "of such great powers of attraction that ships are built with wooden pegs, lest the iron nails should be drawn from the timbers" with disastrous results (left). The legend of the magnetic mountain was repeated in "A Thousand and One Nights" and was accepted as true until early in the 17th century when men such as William Gilbert, "the Galileo of magnetism", laid the foundations of modern theories. Below, the lines of force in a magnetic field as drawn by James Clerk Maxwell in 1865.

Photo from "Hortus Sanitatis" Mainz 1491 Senckenbergische Library, Frankfurt-am-Main, Fed. Rep. of Germany

Photo Bibliothèque de Genève

magnets, high-tension cables and ships. A good example is the cargo-cult that grew up around the steamers bringing wealth to the islands of the Pacific.

I shall be told that the educated public of the developed countries will not fall a prey to such confusion. But it is precisely on this point that I would be tempted to share—if only very partially—the pessimistic opinion I mentioned earlier.

Are we quite sure, in fact, that the information given by the popular science writers is always properly understood in the scientific sense? Is there not a tendency among the general public, or a large section of it, simply to trust the presumably competent dispensers of information and to be content with metaphors and rather vague analogies.

To give an example, it is said quite commonly that space engineers have managed to put a satellite in orbit, or that it has gone off its trajectory and fallen into the sea. In this case, it seems clear that the orbit and the

trajectory are thought of as abstract objects which the satellite may follow or leave just as a train does the track, or a car the road. This is understandable since we model our conceptions on familiar facts and events.

Unfortunately, the model in this case is a bad one and leads to false ideas about space mechanics. It is perhaps appropriate to use the term myth, in this instance, by comparison with those myths about the planets or the sun in which the heavenly body followed real paths laid down by the gods.

We have another example in radioactivity and radium. A veritable myth had grown up around these glamorous words, and every mineral water and even some beauty creams used to boast of being radioactive, for this was a guarantee of efficacy. We have recently witnessed a spectacular reversal of the myth, since radioactivity is now considered dangerous—because of fallout—and the labels on the mineral water bottles and jars of beauty cream have been surreptitiously brought up to date.

What has to be done, people will say, is to give more detailed information, explain the laws of celestial mechanics, and throw light on the real nature of radioactivity, striking the balance between its benefits, as in the treatment of cancer, and its dangers. They are right of course, and this is what many serious popular science writers are doing, backing up the very effective—and, it must be said, even essential—efforts being made at all levels of the education system.

Only piecemeal improvements will be made in this way, however, when the subjects being dealt with are particularly in the news. A more general strategy must be adopted if we are not to rest content with small tactical victories.

In this connexion, I would like to make a suggestion based on the concept of a "model". A model, which is basically nothing more than the concrete representation of an abstract theory, is a tool for thought—and even for discovery—which is very useful both in making scientific progress and in giving an account of such progress, scientists being no different from other men in the way they think. To make myself clear, I shall draw a parallel between myths and models, and first of all, I shall recall a few facts from the history of science.

Scientists usually take pride in presenting their results in the most perfect and most elegant form, without giving any idea of the gropings, the false starts, and the hard intellectual and experimental work which led up to them.

It is understandable that they should wish not to overburden their writing with details which have ceased to be of current interest. On the other hand, how worthwhile it would be to follow step-by-step the thought and the labour of this or that great discoverer in his exploration of new scientific fields.

In the few cases where this has been possible thanks to an autobiography or a series of published papers, it has made an exciting and instructive study. We can see the part played by models and preliminary plans which are like scaffolding to be removed when the building has been completed.

These models are often concrete ones, sometimes visualized as improvised mechanisms. This was so in the case of James Clerk Maxwell, for example, who had experimented with models of rollers centred on the lines of magnetic force and representing the movements of electricity. Once his equations had been established, all the apparatus was discarded and the equations are now elegant, perfect and abstract. They are also completely incomprehensible to anyone who has not undergone a lengthy initiation.

Many models remain very useful, however, even when the knowledge they represent has been outdated by more general theories. Bohr's planetary model of the atom, for example, still serves quite adequately to interpret many properties of the atom and the molecule. It has the further advantage of being sufficiently visual to be easily accepted by non-specialists.

The even older model of the elastic atoms of the kinetic theory of gases continues to be employed. A great English scientist admitted that he still used it to help him think out his ideas. "When I think of the thermic agitation of the atoms of a gas", he said, "I cannot help seeing little red and white balls knocking against each other." Of course he knew very well that the model was inadequate.

This is the heart of the matter and one of the big differences between models and myths. The model is partial, incomplete and provisional, constructed to be useful for a time (sometimes a very long time!) and then superseded. The myth, on the other hand, is total and definitive from the outset and in this draws close to belief. We shall find other characteristics which carry it at the same time farther away from scientific theory.

But do not theories themselves run the risk of changing into myths if they are treated too much as if they were absolutes? We have the old example of phlogiston which gave metals their sheen and hardness and which resisted the theory of oxidation so stubbornly.

Are we not also justified in saying that absolute time has become a myth still perpetuated by many educated people although it is nothing more than a model which is very adequate on most occasions but must yield to the four-dimensional universe of Minkowski and Einstein.

There is an obvious defence against myths: it is built into the scientific method itself which considers theories good as long as they account for phenomena in the best possible way and especially when they represent a minimum number of arbitrary rules and parameters for a maximum number of facts explained. In the realm of myths, on the other hand, there is one myth for each fact or occurrence to be explained, just as the ancient Romans had a different god for each of life's events, no matter how insignificant.

Here we come to the most sensitive point—the one which is the chief worry, not to say nightmare, of the modern lovers of myth—the touchstone of experiment. A theory, however fine it may be, gives way when confronted with a contradictory fact established by experiment. A myth does not give way but argues, evades and finds often purely verbal loopholes.

This is true of the myth of the waves which are emitted by thinking minds—the thought waves in telepathy—the fluids or waves operative in water-divining, "second sight", extra-sensory perception, and so on. Experimental demonstrations to the contrary have no effect on myths and this is an excellent way of distinguishing them.

This is not to say that theories must be immediately confirmed by experiment if they are to be considered scientifically respectable. Experimental confirmation might not come for some time. Researchers will devote all the more effort to this task if the theory has internal logic, is linked with other scientific fields, and synthesizes numerous facts already known, all these being the characteristics of a good theory.

One example is Pauli's hypothesis of the existence of the neutrino, a particle having no mass, no magnetic field, no electric charge and hardly any effect in its passage through matter but which made it possible to restore to their place under the general laws of the conservation of energy and the quantity of movement, absolutely sure experiments lying apparently outside their scope.

"The neutrino is a myth", said some physicists. Experiments have nevertheless shown that it exists, and it plays a fundamental role in nuclear physics. Two or three other hypotheses of this kind are currently being tested, namely the quark, the parton and the intermediate boson. They are good hypotheses which are awaiting the verdict of experiments. They are not myths.

If we wish to explain this to a wide public which is so often impressed by the romantic aspect of the myths we spoke about earlier, and also of the myths concerned with vitalism, vital force and vital impulse, we must lay stress on the quantitative, measurable and calculable aspects of correct theories, as opposed to the resolutely and purely qualitative character of myths.

The rotational force of spiritualists' turning tables has never been measured nor the speed of propagation of telepathic waves and for very good reasons. Calculations of the neutrino's precise energy and velocity (that of light) were made even before it was found and they proved to be correct.

The case of the neutrino is obviously a perfect example. There is no reason, however, why the serious popular science writer should penalize himself by disregarding the fact that all classes of readers are attracted by accounts—sometimes full of the unexpected and even of a kind of romanticism—of the great scientific discoveries and movements, of the opening up of the great avenues of science.

Several books could be quoted which tell of adventures in connexion with the life of a scientist or the development of a school or laboratory, and which are full of memorable anecdotes, some of which have a genuine scientific interest since the real life situations they describe show how scientific thought develops.

What a lot there is to learn from books like these, either for young people attracted towards science or even for the general reader seeking a better understanding not only of the findings of research but also of "how it was done" and how such discoveries are made.

Books like these bring out the rôle of scientific information, in other words, of knowledge of what has already been done, the rôle of the imagination which makes it possible to get out of the rut and discover new paths, and the rôle of chance— or of luck, as some would say—a rôle which has often been grossly exaggerated by sensation-mongering commentators, and "forgotten" by those who have benefited from it.

They are wrong, anyway, for there is nothing more superbly human than the power of the mind to launch a new train of thought from facts or remarks which will be overlooked by people who are incapable of wonder. The classic examples are Henri Becquerel's discovery of radioactivity, the result of choosing a uranium oxide salt as a fluorescent substance, and Donald Glaser's bubble chamber inspired by a glass of beer.

The "personalized" history of science can also be a way of admitting the general public into the laboratory and showing the amount of work, thought, experimental skill and, finally, patience that underlies great discoveries and breakthroughs. Pasteur defined genius as endless patience and Newton said that he had discovered the law of gravity by thinking about it.

I believe that a great effort must be made to bring people who have never been inside a research institute to appreciate the true value of the work done by all those research workers whose names will never get into the headlines but who make a vitally important contribution to scientific progress.

The danger of presenting the daily life of research workers in this way— particularly on television—lies perhaps in the contrast with the descriptions given in science fiction, which, needless to say, depict only dramatic situations.

There is a risk of taking the poetry out of science—or at least out of research—thus serving the cause of those who place in opposition the famous "two cultures" of Lord Snow (1). To my mind, the remedy lies in the fullest possible integration of all the activities of the human mind and, I should like to add, good taste and sensitivity.

Who is going to write the "Works and Days" of the scientific research worker? Possibly this is asking too much, but it is certainly worthwhile to describe the aspects of science's current values which have a high intellectual and even artistic quality.

One of the characteristics of Science—with a capital S—which has become more and more obvious over

(1) In his book "The Two Cultures", Lord Snow compares humanistic and scientific cultures through interviews with engineers, scientists and men of letters which he uses to show the cleavage between them.

the last fifty years is its unity. The general public must realize that in science there no longer exists a juxtaposition of subjects classified according to the order introduced by Auguste Comte or following a less strictly linear order, but instead an immense network of facts and theories forming a pattern from which there emerges the outline of a veritable structure encompassing the whole of nature, from the universe to living beings.

This structure cannot be understood unless it is analysed down to the components of matter and energy, for it is at the level of atoms and molecules that physics, chemistry and biology meet. We must penetrate as far as the nucleus of the atom and its constituent elements in order to add astronomy and cosmology to the other sciences.

Mathematics, of course, are everywhere and our world is indeed the one which Pythagoras had imagined. "All things are numbers", he said, but what would he have thought of the vast field now covered by numbers?

Beginning with the simplest, there is the number 2, following unity and introducing diversity; it might be said to be the atom of diversity from which it is possible to build up the most extreme complexities, just as all the matter of the universe can be derived from the hydrogen atom and the neutron.

Then there are the quantum numbers which are small integral numbers—or half-integral or even third-integral numbers, at the extreme limit—while at the other end of the scale of complexities, the chains of macromolecules of chromosomes offer possibilities of combinations numbering thousands of millions. Here, too, the structure is simple, however, because we need only four symbols to write the great book of the anatomy and physiology of Man! Mathematicians will say that two would be enough, but the chains would then be much longer and perhaps too long to remain stable.

Here, then, are two of the great ideas which are shaping the future development of science: the quest for a structural unity which is no longer just an intellectual need but is gradually becoming discernible and definable and the quest for a complexity which underlies the extreme variety of beings (or objects) and phenomena in the universe.

The first trend has often been called reductionism, and it cannot be denied that it has been dazzlingly successful, although, it has not led to the discovery of unity in some areas of research, even when followed by geniuses like Einstein. There are still four forces which cannot be expressed in terms of each other and these are the Strong Nuclear force, the Weak Interaction, Electromagnetism and the Force of

Gravitation. Nevertheless fresh hopes are raised every day.

The second line of research has recently been extremely successful in the field of biology with genetics and molecular biology, and is gaining ground each day. It holds out the hope that we may come to understand the mechanisms of cellular differentiation, immunity, and perhaps cancer.

The small and, especially, the very big molecules forming the links of the chains of these systems of reaction, catalysis, energy exchange, electrons and protons, are more and more frequently the subject of scientific treatises and articles. They represent a world which is enclosed within the living world but is generally imperceptible.

In fact, until the end of the last century it was virtually only in handling plants that this arsenal of complex and active substances, which composed the pharmacopoeia of antiquity and were also the preserve of the cook, dyer and perfumer, had been recognized and used. Today, as well as these essences and alkaloids, there is a growing list of the proteins comprising the various enzymes and coenzymes found in this protoplasm which used to be compared to a drop of egg-white!

To bring the non-scientific public to appreciate the value of such research work, we must, of course, highlight the two characteristics of science: knowledge and utility. There must be a better understanding of the world around us, and thus a link-up with the intellectual mission of humanism. People must also learn how this knowledge is used in technical applications and inventions calculated to improve man's lot, so that science is seen in its social rôle. This rôle is not a straightforward one, as the current problems of industrialization show, but knowledge is a prerequisite.

This brings us back to the origin of the three attitudes which we mentioned at the beginning: the beauty, utility and dangers of science. We have to sail a stormy sea, guided by the stars, taking advantage of favourable currents and avoiding reefs.

This is possible only if the crews, ratings as well as captains, retain confidence in themselves, their reason and their vigilance and, like latter-day Ulysses, allow themselves to be led astray neither by the siren voices of all the mythologies nor by the risk of avoiding the Charybdis of Hermetism and the ivory tower only to founder on the Scylla of defoliations and nuclear explosions.

I am not a believer in the religious sense of the word, but I nevertheless think, like the Church, that the greatest sin is despair, and for Man to despair of science and knowledge would be to despair of himself. ∎

# 43

# *Eating Christmas in the Kalahari*

## *by Richard Borshay Lee*

The !Kung Bushmen's knowledge of Christmas is thirdhand. The London Missionary Society brought the holiday to the southern Tswana tribes in the early nineteenth century. Later, native catechists spread the idea far and wide among the Bantu-speaking pastoralists, even in the remotest corners of the Kalahari Desert. The Bushmen's idea of the Christmas story, stripped to its essentials, is "praise the birth of white man's god-chief"; what keeps their interest in the holiday high is the Tswana-Herero custom of slaughtering an ox for his Bushmen neighbors as an annual goodwill gesture. Since the 1930's, part of the Bushmen's annual round of activities has included a December congregation at the cattle posts for trading, marriage brokering, and several days of trance-dance feasting at which the local Tswana headman is host.

As a social anthropologist working with !Kung Bushmen, I found that the Christmas ox custom suited my purposes. I had come to the Kalahari to study the hunting and gathering subsistence economy of the !Kung, and to accomplish this it was essential not to provide them with food, share my own food, or interfere in any way with their food-gathering activities. While liberal handouts of tobacco and medical supplies were appreciated, they were scarcely adequate to erase the glaring disparity in wealth between the anthropologist, who maintained a

two-month inventory of canned goods, and the Bushmen, who rarely had a day's supply of food on hand. My approach, while paying off in terms of data, left me open to frequent accusations of stinginess and hard-heartedness. By their lights, I was a miser.

The Christmas ox was to be my way of saying thank you for the co-operation of the past year; and since it was to be our last Christmas in the field, I determined to slaughter the largest, meatiest ox that money could buy, insuring that the feast and trance dance would be a success.

Through December I kept my eyes open at the wells as the cattle were brought down for watering. Several animals were offered, but none had quite the grossness that I had in mind. Then, ten days before the holiday, a Herero friend led an ox of astonishing size and mass up to our camp. It was solid black, stood five feet high at the shoulder, had a five-foot span of horns, and must have weighed 1,200 pounds on the hoof. Food consumption calculations are my specialty, and I quickly figured that bones and viscera aside, there was enough meat—at least four pounds—for every man, woman, and child of the 150 Bushmen in the vicinity of /ai/ai who were expected at the feast.

Having found the right animal at last, I paid the Herero £20 ($56) and asked him to keep the beast with his herd until Christmas day. The

next morning word spread among the people that the big solid black one was the ox chosen by /ontah (my Bushman name; it means. roughly, "whitey") for the Christmas feast. That afternoon I received the first delegation. Ben!a, an outspoken sixty-year-old mother of five, came to the point slowly.

"Where were you planning to eat Christmas?"

"Right here at /ai/ai," I replied.

"Alone or with others?"

"I expect to invite all the people to eat Christmas with me."

"Eat what?"

"I have purchased Yehave's black ox, and I am going to slaughter and cook it."

"That's what we were told at the well but refused to believe it until we heard it from yourself."

"Well, it's the black one," I replied expansively, although wondering what she was driving at.

"Oh, no!" Ben!a groaned, turning to her group. "They were right." Turning back to me she asked, "Do you expect us to eat that bag of bones?"

"Bag of bones! It's the biggest ox at /ai/ai."

"Big, yes, but old. And thin. Everybody knows there's no meat on that old ox. What did you expect us to eat off it, the horns?"

Everybody chuckled at Ben!a's one-liner as they walked away, but all I could manage was a weak grin.

That evening it was the turn of the young men. They came to sit at our evening fire. /gaugo, about my age, spoke to me man-to-man.

"/ontah, you have always been square with us," he lied. "What has happened to change your heart? That sack of guts and bones of Yehave's will hardly feed one camp,

EDITOR'S NOTE: *The !Kung and other Bushmen speak click languages. In the story, three different clicks are used:*

*1. The dental click (/), as in /ai/ai, /ontah, and /gaugo. The click is sometimes written in English as tsk-tsk.*

*2. The alveopalatal click (!), as in Ben!a and !Kung.*

*3. The lateral click (//), as in //gom. Clicks function as consonants; a word may have more than one, as in /n!au.*

let alone all the Bushmen around /ai/ai." And he proceeded to enumerate the seven camps in the /ai/ai vicinity, family by family. "Perhaps you have forgotten that we are not few, but many. Or are you too blind to tell the difference between a proper cow and an old wreck? That ox is thin to the point of death."

"Look, you guys," I retorted, "that is a beautiful animal, and I'm sure you will eat it with pleasure at Christmas."

"Of course we will eat it; it's food. But it won't fill us up to the point where we will have enough strength to dance. We will eat and go home to bed with stomachs rumbling."

That night as we turned in, I asked my wife, Nancy: "What did you think of the black ox?"

"It looked enormous to me. Why?"

"Well, about eight different people have told me I got gypped; that the ox is nothing but bones."

"What's the angle?" Nancy asked. "Did they have a better one to sell?"

"No, they just said that it was going to be a grim Christmas because there won't be enough meat to go around. Maybe I'll get an independent judge to look at the beast in the morning."

Bright and early, Halingisi, a Tswana cattle owner, appeared at our camp. But before I could ask him to give me his opinion on Yehave's black ox, he gave me the eye signal that indicated a confidential chat. We left the camp and sat down.

"/ontah, I'm surprised at you: you've lived here for three years and still haven't learned anything about cattle."

"But what else can a person do but choose the biggest, strongest animal one can find?" I retorted.

"Look, just because an animal is big doesn't mean that it has plenty of meat on it. The black one was a beauty when it was younger, but now it is thin to the point of death."

"Well I've already bought it. What can I do at this stage?"

"Bought it already? I thought you were just considering it. Well, you'll have to kill it and serve it, I suppose. But don't expect much of a dance to follow."

My spirits dropped rapidly. I could believe that Ben!a and /gaugo just might be putting me on about the black ox, but Halingisi seemed to be an impartial critic. I went around that day feeling as though I had bought a lemon of a used car.

In the afternoon it was Tomazo's turn. Tomazo is a fine hunter, a top trance performer (*see* "The Trance Cure of the !Kung Bushmen," NATURAL HISTORY, November, 1967), and one of my most reliable informants. He approached the subject of the Christmas cow as part of my continuing Bushmen education.

"My friend, the way it is with us Bushmen," he began, "is that we love meat. And even more than that, we love fat. When we hunt we always search for the fat ones, the ones dripping with layers of white fat: fat that turns into a clear, thick oil in the cooking pot, fat that slides down your gullet, fills your stomach and gives you a roaring diarrhea," he rhapsodized.

"So, feeling as we do," he continued, "it gives us pain to be served such a scrawny thing as Yehave's black ox. It is big, yes, and no doubt its giant bones are good for soup, but fat is what we really crave and so we will eat Christmas this year with a heavy heart."

The prospect of a gloomy Christmas now had me worried, so I asked Tomazo what I could do about it.

"Look for a fat one, a young one . . . smaller, but fat. Fat enough to make us //gom ('evacuate the bowels'), then we will be happy."

My suspicions were aroused when Tomazo said that he happened to know of a young, fat, barren cow that the owner was willing to part with. Was Toma working on commission, I wondered? But I dispelled this unworthy thought when we approached the Herero owner of the cow in question and found that he

had decided not to sell.

The scrawny wreck of a Christmas ox now became the talk of the /ai/ai water hole and was the first news told to the outlying groups as they began to come in from the bush for the feast. What finally convinced me that real trouble might be brewing was the visit from u!au, an old conservative with a reputation for fierceness. His nickname meant spear and referred to an incident thirty years ago in which he had speared a man to death. He had an intense manner; fixing me with his eyes, he said in clipped tones:

"I have only just heard about the black ox today, or else I would have come here earlier. /ontah, do you honestly think you can serve meat like that to people and avoid a fight?" He paused, letting the implications sink in. "I don't mean fight you, /ontah; you are a white man. I mean a fight between Bushmen. There are many fierce ones here, and with such a small quantity of meat to distribute, how can you give everybody a fair share? Someone is sure to accuse another of taking too much or hogging all the choice pieces. Then you will see what happens when some go hungry while others eat."

The possibility of at least a serious argument struck me as all too real. I had witnessed the tension that surrounds the distribution of meat from a kudu or gemsbok kill, and had documented many arguments that sprang up from a real or imagined slight in meat distribution. The owners of a kill may spend up to two hours arranging and rearranging the piles of meat under the gaze of a circle of recipients before handing them out. And I also knew that the Christmas feast at /ai/ai would be bringing together groups that had feuded in the past.

Convinced now of the gravity of the situation, I went in earnest to search for a second cow; but all my inquiries failed to turn one up.

The Christmas feast was evidently going to be a disaster, and the incessant complaints about the meagerness of the ox had already taken the fun out of it for me. Moreover, I was getting bored with the wisecracks, and after losing my temper a few times, I resolved to serve the beast anyway. If the meat fell short, the hell with it. In the Bushmen idiom, I announced to all who would listen:

"I am a poor man and blind. If I have chosen one that is too old and too thin, we will eat it anyway and see if there is enough meat there to quiet the rumbling of our stomachs."

On hearing this speech, Ben!a offered me a rare word of comfort. "It's thin," she said philosophically, "but the bones will make a good soup."

At dawn Christmas morning, instinct told me to turn over the butchering and cooking to a friend and take off with Nancy to spend Christmas alone in the bush. But curiosity kept me from retreating. I wanted to see what such a scrawny ox looked like on butchering, and if there *was* going to be a fight, I wanted to catch every word of it. Anthropologists are incurable that way.

The great beast was driven up to our dancing ground, and a shot in the forehead dropped it in its tracks. Then, freshly cut branches were heaped around the fallen carcass to receive the meat. Ten men volunteered to help with the cutting. I asked /gaugo to make the breast bone cut. This cut, which begins the butchering process for most large game, offers easy access for removal of the viscera. But it also allows the hunter to spot-check the amount of fat on the animal. A fat game animal carries a white layer up to an inch thick on the chest, while in a thin one, the knife will quickly cut to bone. All eyes fixed on his hand as /gaugo, dwarfed by the great carcass, knelt to the breast. The first cut opened a pool of solid white in the black skin. The second and third cut widened and deepened the creamy white. Still no bone. It was pure fat; it must have been two inches thick.

"Hey /gau," I burst out, "that ox is loaded with fat. What's this about the ox being too thin to bother eating? Are you out of your mind?"

"Fat?" /gau shot back, "You call that fat? This wreck is thin, sick, dead!" And he broke out laughing. So did everyone else. They rolled on the ground, paralyzed with laughter. Everybody laughed except me; I was thinking.

I ran back to the tent and burst in just as Nancy was getting up. "Hey, the black ox. It's fat as hell! They were kidding about it being too thin to eat. It was a joke or something. A put-on. Everyone is really delighted with it!"

"Some joke," my wife replied. "It was so funny that you were ready to pack up and leave /ai/ai."

If it had indeed been a joke, it had been an extraordinarily convincing one, and tinged, I thought, with more than a touch of malice as many jokes are. Nevertheless, that it was a joke lifted my spirits considerably, and I returned to the butchering site where the shape of the ox was rapidly disappearing under the axes and knives of the butchers. The atmosphere had become festive. Grinning broadly, their arms covered with blood well past the elbow, men packed chunks of meat into the big cast-iron cooking pots, fifty pounds to the load, and muttered and chuckled all the while about the thinness and worthlessness of the animal and /ontah's poor judgment.

We danced and ate that ox two days and two nights; we cooked and distributed fourteen potfuls of meat and no one went home hungry and no fights broke out.

But the "joke" stayed in my mind. I had a growing feeling that something important had happened in my relationship with the Bushmen and that the clue lay in the meaning of the joke. Several days later, when most of the people had dispersed back to the bush camps, I raised the question with Hakekgose, a Tswana man who had grown up among the !Kung, married a !Kung girl, and

who probably knew their culture better than any other non-Bushman.

"With us whites," I began, "Christmas is supposed to be the day of friendship and brotherly love. What I can't figure out is why the Bushmen went to such lengths to criticize and belittle the ox I had bought for the feast. The animal was perfectly good and their jokes and wisecracks practically ruined the holiday for me."

"So it really did bother you," said Hakekgose. "Well, that's the way they always talk. When I take my rifle and go hunting with them, if I miss, they laugh at me for the rest of the day. But even if I hit and bring one down, it's no better. To them, the kill is always too small or too old or too thin; and as we sit down on the kill site to cook and eat the liver, they keep grumbling, even with their mouths full of meat. They say things like, 'Oh this is awful! What a worthless animal! Whatever made me think that this Tswana rascal could hunt!'"

"Is this the way outsiders are treated?" I asked.

"No, it is their custom; they talk that way to each other too. Go and ask them."

/gaugo had been one of the most enthusiastic in making me feel bad about the merit of the Christmas ox. I sought him out first.

"Why did you tell me the black ox was worthless, when you could see that it was loaded with fat and meat?"

"It is our way," he said smiling. "We always like to fool people about that. Say there is a Bushman who has been hunting. He must not come home and announce like a braggard, 'I have killed a big one in the bush!' He must first sit down in silence until I or someone else comes up to his fire and asks, 'What did you see today?' He replies quietly, 'Ah, I'm no good for hunting. I saw nothing at all [pause] just a little tiny one.' Then I smile to myself," /gaugo continued, "because I know he has killed something big.

"In the morning we make up a party of four or five people to cut up and carry the meat back to the camp. When we arrive at the kill we examine it and cry out, 'You mean to say you have dragged us all the way out here in order to make us cart home your pile of bones? Oh, if I had known it was this thin I wouldn't have come.' Another one pipes up, 'People, to think I gave up a nice day in the shade for this. At home we may be hungry but at least we have nice cool water to drink.' If the horns are big, someone says, 'Did you think that somehow you were going to boil down the horns for soup?'

"To all this you must respond in kind. 'I agree,' you say, 'this one is not worth the effort; let's just cook the liver for strength and leave the rest for the hyenas. It is not too late to hunt today and even a duiker or a steenbok would be better than this mess.'

"Then you set to work nevertheless; butcher the animal, carry the meat back to the camp and everyone eats," /gaugo concluded.

Things were beginning to make sense. Next, I went to Tomazo. He corroborated /gaugo's story of the obligatory insults over a kill and added a few details of his own.

"But," I asked, "why insult a man after he has gone to all that trouble to track and kill an animal and when he is going to share the meat with you so that your children will have something to eat?"

"Arrogance," was his cryptic answer.

"Arrogance?"

"Yes, when a young man kills much meat he comes to think of himself as a chief or a big man, and he thinks of the rest of us as his servants or inferiors. We can't accept this. We refuse one who boasts, for someday his pride will make him kill somebody. So we always speak of his meat as worthless. This way we cool his heart and make him gentle."

"But why didn't you tell me this before?" I asked Tomazo with some heat.

"Because you never asked me," said Tomazo, echoing the refrain that has come to haunt every field ethnographer.

The pieces now fell into place. I had known for a long time that in situations of social conflict with Bushmen I held all the cards. I was the only source of tobacco in a thousand square miles, and I was not incapable of cutting an individual off for noncooperation. Though my boycott never lasted longer than a few days, it was an indication of my strength. People resented my presence at the water hole, yet simultaneously dreaded my leaving. In short I was a perfect target for the charge of arrogance and for the Bushmen tactic of enforcing humility.

I had been taught an object lesson by the Bushmen; it had come from an unexpected corner and had hurt me in a vulnerable area. For the big black ox was to be the one totally generous, unstinting act of my year at /ai/ai, and I was quite unprepared for the reaction I received.

As I read it, their message was this: There are no totally generous acts. All "acts" have an element of calculation. One black ox slaughtered at Christmas does not wipe out a year of careful manipulation of gifts given to serve your own ends. After all, to kill an animal and share the meat with people is really no more than Bushmen do for each other every day and with far less fanfare.

In the end, I had to admire how the Bushmen had played out the farce—collectively straight-faced to the end. Curiously, the episode reminded me of the *Good Soldier Schweik* and his marvelous encounters with authority. Like Schweik, the Bushmen had retained a thoroughgoing skepticism of good intentions. Was it this independence of spirit, I wondered, that had kept them culturally viable in the face of generations of contact with more powerful societies, both black and white? The thought that the Bushmen were alive and well in the Kalahari was strangely comforting. Perhaps, armed with that independence and with their superb knowledge of their environment, they might yet survive the future. ∎

# 44

# THE PENTAGON AS THE ENEMY OF CAPITALISM

## by Ernest Fitzgerald

### The main threat to free enterprise comes not from anti-capitalist ideologists but from government support of inefficient, wasteful, and non-competitive practices.

"What do we care whether they perform?" asked the then-Secretary of the Treasury John Connally. "We are guaranteeing them basically a two hundred and fifty million dollar loan. Why for? Basically, so they can hopefully minimize their losses, so they can provide employment for thirty-one thousand people throughout the country at a time when we desperately need that type of employment. That is basically the rationale and justification."

Secretary Connally provided this bit of attitudinal insight in response to complaints by Sen. William Proxmire, who was questioning the absence of *quid pro quo* in guaranteeing the famous "bailout" loan for Lockheed Aircraft Corporation in June of 1971. Senator Proxmire had offered the old-fashioned notion that corporate beneficiaries of taxpayer largess promise something in return. As it is, they are insulated from the normal perils of the marketplace. Thanks to a system that often awards contracts to the neediest rather than the most efficient and that permits staggering "overruns"

*Ernest Fitzgerald is credited with first bringing the Lockheed C-5A scandal to public attention, and as a result he lost his job as deputy assistant secretary of the U. S. Air Force. Now a consultant to the congressional Joint Economic Committee, he is the author of* The High Priests of Waste, *a study of the policy of deliberate overspending in military procurement.*

of the agreed upon price, American military contractors have gained what seems to be a permanent lien on the federal treasury. In so doing, they have undermined not only their own ability to turn out quality products at a reasonable price but the skills and motivation that are basic to the nation's entire economic structure as well.

The principal threat to American capitalism as we have known it comes not from anti-capitalist ideologists but from government support of inefficient and incompetent practices that are the antithesis of a free economy. It is difficult, if not impossible, to maintain an open economic system in which efficiency and excellence are basic determinants when the largest single complex in it is arbitrary to the point of being quixotic, and wasteful to the point of being massively irrational. How ironic that the one institution most intimately identified with the preservation of the American business system—the Pentagon—should turn out to be its enemy.

C-5A Transport—*Since 1969 there have been "no airplanes at all, just overruns."*

The Proxmire-Connally exchange took place in connection with Lockheed's commercial air-bus program. Secretary Connally's philosophy was already widely accepted for government grants on military programs. The last congressional authorization for airplanes in Lockheed's C-5A transport plane contract for the air force occurred in 1969. Nevertheless, each year since then, Congress has approved hundreds of millions of dollars for overruns on the same project. No airplanes at all, just overruns. In 1970, the year before the Connally candor, the same pitch in almost the same words had been made by supporters of unlimited grants to Lockheed. Rising in support of the annual Lockheed overrun grant, Sen. Herman Talmadge of Georgia had intoned in his rich porkchop accent, "I make no apology for not wanting to throw forty thousand people out of work in one fell swoop." Sen. Alan Cranston of California, a noted liberal, voiced the same concern:

And, of course, it would be a disastrous result for the eighty-seven thousand workers who hope to continue their employment with Lockheed and with the benefits of seniority, retirement plans, and so forth.

Senators Talmadge and Cranston were roused to their oratorical (and arithmetically inconsistent) outpourings by the mere suggestion that the Senate should determine what would be done with the annual Lockheed grant before authorizing the money. Had some tightwad actually proposed withholding the taxpayers' hard-earned money, senatorial rhetoric in support of the corporate handouts would have soared to an even higher pitch.

Although Lockheed officials perfected the art of revealing their latest bone-headed flop in order to rationalize tapping the public till, they were by no means the first to practice it. Back when

Wide World

I was in the Pentagon, General Dynamics nearly doubled its profits by increasing the cost of the misbegotten F-111 fighter bomber by about 500 per cent and delivering a product markedly inferior to the one they had promised to build originally. When a few penny pinchers proposed saving a few hundred megabucks (Pentagonese for a million dollars) by squeezing some of the fat out of the contractor prices, the F-111 program chief, Maj. Gen. "Zeke" Zoeckler killed the attempt by proclaiming that "inefficiency is national policy." General Zoeckler went on to explain that big contractor boondoggling was necessary for attainment of "social goals."

In fairness to Lockheed and General Dynamics, I should point out that the pattern of rewarding failures on the part of big military contractors is the rule rather than the exception. On January 26, 1969, *The Washington Post* published a summary of a study by Richard Stubbing of the Bureau of the Budget (now the Office of Management and Budget) showing that big Pentagon contractors with the worst records of meeting their contractual commitments consistently showed above-average profits on their military business.

The operative phrase here is "big Pentagon contractors." The Pentagon usually takes a strict-constructionist view of contract enforcement with smaller firms, which are thereby often driven into insolvency. Unfortunately, despite all the public-relations baloney put out by then-Secretary of Defense Melvin Laird and his former deputy David Packard the practice of shoveling money to big contractors—regardless of their performance—continues today. Litton Industries and Grumman Aircraft Corporation are both threatening to die and foul the economic air if they are not given access to public money to pull themselves out of the hole.

Regardless of their performance, the bumbling giants demand that the taxpayers furnish whatever money they say they need. Worse, the national adminis-

tration seems always to end up supporting their demands. Sometimes, to anesthetize the public, there is a little carefully staged fighting—the Lockheed bail-out is one example—but in the end the Pentagon and its supporting cast of contractors unite to pick the public pocket.

MILITARY BOONDOGGLING by the giant contractors has many bad effects, including what Senator Proxmire wryly calls "unilateral gold-plated disarmament." The soaring costs of inefficiency and bungling usually necessitate cutbacks in planned quantities of military hardware, and the acceptance of substandard products further degrades true capability and military readiness. However, since the top generals and admirals are willing to accept overpriced junk, perhaps the ordinary people shouldn't worry about it.

The *economic* effect of the Great Military Boondoggle is a graver concern, and its true nature is little understood. This is so despite the billions of words that have been spouted about new economic priorities since the combination of the bungled Asian war and weapons-procurement scandals caused the American public to suspect for the first time that our military juggernaut was not functioning as advertised. It is true that the "new priorities" pleaders forced the dominant Keynesian school of economists to think seriously about end products of economic activity. Most of these economists, especially those in government, appeared to view "making jobs" as a laudable economic objective whether the end products were farm-to-market roads, shoes for the civilian market, bomb craters in the Asian bush, or amputations in military hospitals. Confronted with such realities, most academic economists now admit that certain end products may be more economically and socially desirable than others, and speak loftily about lost-opportunity costs. Unhappily, none of this new rhetoric has yet been translated into the mainstream of economic calculations. The costs of bombing, cutting off legs, boondoggling at General Dynamics, and —to add philosophical balance—hanging around the office at HEW all increase the gross national product, add to something called gross aggregate demand, and are presumed to have salutary economic effects.

While there are perhaps a dozen major economic effects of Pentagon spending, each worthy of separate essays or even books, the most fundamental and long term of them is the damage done to the competitive position of our producing industries in world markets. From 1892 through 1970, the United States consistently sold more merchandise abroad than foreigners sold in the United States. The big machine could really grind out the goods. It was so efficient that the United States could pay its industrial managers and workers far more than their foreign counterparts got and still compete with them in their own back yards.

Then, in the late 1950s and 1960s, things started slipping. The United States began to lose out in market after market. By mid-1971 it became clear that the nation was headed for its first full-year trading deficit of the century. The margin of superiority in overall industrial efficiency was no longer sufficient to offset wage and salary differentials. The country ended calendar year 1971 with a trade deficit of $2.01 billion.

Many economists belittled the problem, pointing out that the trade deficit was a minuscule part of our skyrocketing gross national product and arguing that concern over the problem was merely a hang-over from outmoded mercantilist policies. After all, the United States was the world's financier, and the proceeds from its foreign investments offset trading losses, so there was nothing to worry about. But as an international trading competitor, the nation was definitely sick, and despite the Nixon administration's harsh, dictatorial economic remedies, the patient's condition deteriorated. Through the third quarter of 1972, the trade deficit had deepened to an annual rate of $7.06 billion.

What went wrong? For one thing, the foreigners, especially America's World War II enemies, became more productive and efficient. The most popular explanation is that these countries replaced their bombed-out industrial plants with brand-new, efficient facilities while U. S. modernization lagged. One reason why it lagged, as Prof. Seymour Melman has pointed out, is that huge chunks of available investment funds have been sunk into military bases and equipment instead of new plants. Another reason is national overhead expenses. Among the overhead accounts, U. S. welfare costs went up rapidly, but so did competitors'. The non-productive area where the United States outspent

all of its competitors was in operating and maintaining its military machine. The situation is analogous to that in private industry, with military forces equivalent to guard forces of a private manufacturing firm. Enormous expenses have been added to the cost of American products, either in the form of direct taxes or inflationary deficit spending, which has increased the costs of everything the country makes. On top of that, the United States has generously footed the bill for a major portion of its competitors' guard forces, thereby compounding the inequity.

None of the damage discussed so far is irreparable. It could be cured in large part simply by national leaders shifting emphasis on placement of investment funds and control of national overhead expenses. Not so with direct productive activities. Here we are dealing with human problems, work habits, managerial skills, and motivation. This is the area where the United States has enjoyed its greatest competitive advantage in the past. This is also the area where it has been hurt the worst, perhaps permanently, by the Pentagon's excesses.

Starting with the earliest settlers, American workers performed prodigious feats. Driven by necessity, encouraged by the hope of ownership of productive property usually denied to their European counterparts, the American work force demonstrated its energy, skill, and intelligence in developing a new country in record time. The industrial revolution reached the United States in a uniquely American form; that is, it took full advantage of the existing superior work force. As the American economy grew, wage-incentive plans tied to systematically measured productivity became commonplace in most industries. Reduction of the labor required per unit of product became the major focus of industrial management. Output per worker soared, and the United States became the world's dominant industrial power. Industrial-management disciplines declined during World War II, but the country recovered somewhat after the war; and with former competitors either devastated or exhausted, it remained dominant. America's current and perhaps chronic sick spell began getting serious during the "missile gap" controversy of the 1950s and early 1960s. This gap later was revealed to be non-existent, but the taxpayers didn't know it at the time, and they were easily persuaded to cough up whatever amounts the Pentagon called for to close it. After all, closing the gap was supposed to deter the Russians, who, Americans were told, planned to roast the free world with nuclear warheads.

During this period the Pentagon literally had so much ballistic-missile money that spending it all was difficult. This problem was solved for them by giant contractors who quickly geared up to relieve them of the burdensome funds. The surfeit of money had striking effects on the operations of the Air Force's major ballistic-missile contractors. Labor efficiency, never very high in these plants, sank to unbelievably low levels. Labor outputs 40 per cent below competitive standards became the norm. During the period 1960–65, these same contractors' overhead expenses per direct labor hour almost doubled, and overall rates of pay increased 50 per cent. All this took place during a period of relative price stability, during which industrial pay generally was increasing by about 3 per cent per year.

The permissiveness spawned by the flood of money in the ballistic-missile business soon spread to all the big Pentagon contractors. Smaller contractors and commercial producers had to follow suit to stay competitive for employees, services, and goods. The upsurge of military orders aimed at intensifying the Asian war made the problem more virulent, and before long America's whole industrial body was exhibiting symptoms of the Pentagon boondoggle syndrome.

Where were the nation's leaders while all this was going on? Conditioned to expect rescue by business or military leaders in the finest traditions of the *Reader's Digest*, Americans might have expected some gruff free-enterprisers and generals with the look of eagles to demand a halt to the national binge. They didn't—because they were too busy corrupting themselves. Arm in arm, big business and the military brass systematically set out to rationalize their failures and, in the process, raid the Treasury. Admiral Hyman Rickover, the only high-ranking maverick on military procurement, described the situation in testimony before the Joint Economic Committee on April 28, 1971:

> . . . large defense contractors can let costs come out where they will, and count on getting relief from the Department of Defense through changes and claims, relaxations of procurement regulations and laws, government loans, follow-on sole-source contracts, or other escape mechanisms. Wasteful subcontracting practices, inadequate cost controls, shop loafing, and production errors mean little to these contractors, since they will make their money whether their product is good or bad; whether the price is fair or higher than it should be;

whether delivery is on time or late. Such matters are inconsequential to the management of most large defense contractors, since, as with other regulated industries, they are able to conceal the real facts concerning their management ineptitude from the public and from their stockholders, until they stumble finally into the arms of government for their salvation.

THE SPECTACLE of rich incompetents stumbling into the government's arms is distressing for a number of reasons. The boondoggling infection appears to be debilitating our entire producing body. Worse, there are indications that the infection has eaten into the collective corporate brain. If only factory workers and other people whose jobs are subject to easy definition, and perhaps mechanization, were affected, the economy could probably work its way out of the difficulty. Unfortunately, the business and government leaders, who should be steering the nation back onto the right track, seem to be the most affected.

"Conservatives" lament the debilitating effects of continued welfare payments to poor families. But if welfare families are not motivated to escape their non-productive, subsistence-level lives, why on earth should non-productive or even counterproductive corporate executives, already living off the fat of the land, be motivated to strenuous exertions? After all, running an efficient factory is grubby, demanding, confining work. Why bother, when it is

so much easier and more sociable to cozy up to the White House, the procurement generals, and the armed-services committees?

Given existing motivations, it is unrealistic to expect the leaders of the military spending complex—the Typhoid Marys of the boondoggle infection—to cure themselves. To be sure, the corporate members of the complex are in some trouble. Unfortunately, their outlook is that of the alcoholic who has the shakes on a fifth a day. They think another pint of their poison will set them right again. They do not seem to realize that the root of their problem is that they have been drunk on money since the beginning of World War II.

Instead of attempting to cure our national industrial sickness by purging the source of infection, national political leaders seem content to concentrate on cosmetic actions, which may temporarily conceal but will not cure the problems. Rather than requiring the bloated and indolent giant contractors to shape up, it appears that the Nixon administration is determined to pump increasing amounts of money into them. Current plans call for increasing Pentagon spending from the present level of about $80 billion per year to at least $112 billion in seven years. This presumes both an end to the Asian war and "austerity" for the military. The "realistic" projection, an alternative stoutly supported by Pentagon insiders, calls for an increase to $141 billion in the same period. Even under the austerity ground rules, the money for the big-weapons contractors is projected to increase by 81 per cent between fiscal years 1973 and 1980, by far the largest

percentage increase among the various budget slices.

Since the new order of things seems to follow the pattern of receiving from the giant firms in accordance with their abilities to produce, and giving money to them in accordance with their needs, it is tempting to call the evolving system corporate communism. Yet the distribution of benefits is far too narrow to satisfy the Marxist ideal of giving to each according to his needs. Only the politically favored giants and their hangers-on will benefit. Only big contractors appear to be regarded as politically reliable conduits for redistribution of resources taken from producers.

Meanwhile, the favorites who receive ever-increasing amounts of public money will become ever more lazy, non-productive, and infectious. The fatter the industrial giants become, the less they will be able to sustain themselves and the more public support they will need. The evolving political economic system seems more in accord with the outlook of Louis XVI—who took from the common folk and gave to the nobility—than with modern Communist despots. The taxpaying peasants will just have to adjust to supporting their betters while competitive advantages are dissipated.

So unless current trends are reversed, the system that gave the United States industrial dominance in the past may be finished. Some observers, thinking of sweated workers and wide class divisions, will see this as a good thing. Still, the old machine was vastly productive, even though its benefits were never widely shared. It might be repaired, brought up to date, and used again.  □

# 45

# A CASE OF CORPORATE MALPRACTICE

By Mark Dowie and Tracy Johnston

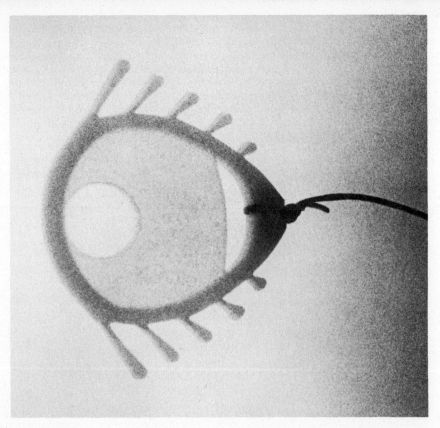

[ The Dalkon Shield was hailed as a promising new method of birth control—until 17 women using it died. Here for the first time is its full story. ]

I N 1971, Dr. Hugh J. Davis, associate professor of gynecology at Johns Hopkins, decided to write up his experiments with a new intrauterine device he had been using at the university's family planning clinic. He heads the clinic, which is part of one of the country's most prestigious medical schools. The clinic, like the John Hopkins Medical School, is in the middle of one of the worst ghettos in Baltimore, and Davis spends a lot of his time prescribing pills, inserting IUDs and advising poor black and Latin American women how to prevent unwanted children. One of the many lawyers who do the talking for him now says Davis thinks of pregnancy as "a social evil—contributing to poverty, unhappiness and unrest."

Although Davis's book, a slim volume sprinkled with charts and graphs and called *The Intrauterine Device for Contraception*, was not stacked up alongside the cash registers of bookstores across the country, many doctors read it eagerly. The results of research performed under the auspices of Johns Hopkins could certainly be trusted, and doctors everywhere were anxious for information about the various plastic loops and squiggles and paper-clip-like things they had inserted in over three million women in America. They still know almost nothing about intrauterine devices, except that somehow a foreign object in the uterus usually prevents pregnancy.

At that time, the entire subject of contraception was especially controversial. Pill men and IUD men were known to exchange bitter comments at conventions and engage in primitive avoidance rituals if they discovered each other at the same party. The Davis book, since it came from Hopkins, was discussed by most everyone in the field and widely reported on in women's magazines.

In his book, Davis gives evidence that the IUD is a better birth control device than the Pill—almost as efficient and much safer. More important, he indicates that a certain new IUD recently put on the market works better than any of the old ones.

To be sure, Davis doesn't directly recommend the Dalkon Shield over the Lippes Loop, the Saf-T-Coil, the Copper-7 or its other competitors; such recommendations in medical texts are considered highly unprofessional. The Shield's experimental results just look a lot better. The comparisons appear to be thorough, scientific and convincing. On every graph, on every chart and in every analysis, the Dalkon Shield is first.

The only thing the book does not say about the Dalkon Shield—and the full story has not been told before—is that Davis had not only tested it, he had invented it, along with his good friend Irwin Lerner, and he was making money on every new Shield sold. At the time the book was published, Davis had already made $250,000 on the sale of the Shield to the A. H. Robins Company, one of the largest pharmaceutical houses in the U.S. In five years' time, before the Shield would be removed from the market amid increasing publicity about deaths and injuries to women who used it, Davis would earn well over $300,000 more in royalties and consultants' fees.

N O ONE KNOWS exactly how many women have been killed by the Dalkon Shield. As of last January, 17 American women had died. There have been a number of deaths since, but the government totals and releases such figures only once a year. Statistics from the dozens of other countries where the Shield has been in use—mostly in the Third World—are fragmentary or nonexistent. In other ways, too, the full story of the device that has left untold hundreds of women sterile, and that is still in use by more than a million women around the world, has been hard to get. Doctors do not easily reveal secrets about each other. Also, all the principal characters in this story are under orders from their lawyers not to speak, for the Dalkon Shield has become one of the most litigated products in pharmaceutical history.

Since Davis would not talk to us, it was difficult to get a full picture of this paradoxical man, who teaches at a leading university and runs a clinic for the poor, yet who succumbed to the temptation of making big money by the most unethical means. We could assemble only a fragmentary picture of him from others' reports. Thomas Kemp, a lawyer handling many of the cases for Robins, describes Davis as "tall," "neat " and a man of "overwhelming heart." Davis's wife says she hopes the true story about her husband will get out, but she doesn't know what it is. "Work is work and home is home," she says on the phone over the sounds of children giggling, and Davis doesn't mix the two. Still another picture of him comes from a woman who once worked in his clinic, who described him as "the most efficient man I ever met." She said he once used a vacation to have

his appendix taken out, just so that he would lose no work time if he ever got appendicitis.

Luckily for our story, though, there are sworn depositions in the Dalkon case, and although Davis is cagey and doesn't reveal a thing when he talks to lawyers, Irwin Lerner is a garrulous guy and tells the story of the Dalkon Shield with relish.

"Win" Lerner is an inventor, really. He started off in 1948 as an electrical engineer in oil development. He went on to computers and then typewriters, where, he claims, he developed the Selectric. In 1960 he got interested in the medical supplies field and started working for a company making polyethylene tubing, blood test equipment, automatic pipettes and all sorts of things a burgeoning medical market could use. He met Hugh Davis in 1964, while trying to push one of his inventions, and the two men liked each other right away. Also, they realized, according to Lerner, how they "could use each other's expertise."

T HE DAVIS-LERNER association started out as business (they worked on several products together from 1964 to 1967) but it soon turned into friendship. In fact, it was on Christmas Day, 1967, while the two families were opening presents and sitting around Davis's home in Baltimore, that the idea for inventing a new IUD came to them.

Each man claims it was the other who first came up with the idea, but whatever the case, both were very excited about it. The two men would call each other up at midnight and three o'clock in the morning to discuss the project. Davis would tell Lerner the little that was known about IUDs and the failures of the ones already on the market: they caused pain, cramps and bleeding; they didn't work; they came out. And Lerner would discuss ways of solving each problem. For the expulsion problem, they had a unique solution: a disk-like IUD with stubby tentacles whose barb effect would hold the device in the uterus. Within a few months Lerner had his first model of the Dalkon Shield, and in August, Davis took a few of them fresh from the Pee Wee Plastic Company, where they had been manufactured, and inserted them into some patients at his clinic. Patients had heard about dangers from the Pill and were quite willing to try a different contraceptive. Initial results looked good, and one month later Lerner applied for

Dr. Hugh Davis testifies before the Senate subcommittee on birth control.

a patent.

Instead of donating the device to a medical institution for study, Lerner and Davis decided to market it themselves and to get private physicians across the country to test it for them. Lerner says Davis had some money from Hopkins, which he used to buy Dalkon Shields, and over a one-year period, Davis inserted 640 of them into women (558 clinic patients, 82 private patients) and carefully noted down the "results." He wrote them up and published them in February 1970 in the *American Journal of Obstetrics and Gynecology,* the leading journal in the field. They were remarkable to say the least, especially the pregnancy rate—the lowest among all IUDs (1.1 per cent). The article concluded, "Taken all together, the superior performance of the Shield intrauterine device makes the technique a first choice method of contraception control."

Meanwhile, other doctors across the nation were beginning to hear about the device that had impressive Johns Hopkins statistics behind it, and many were sending for it to try out on their own patients.

*One of the people who read of Dr. Davis's exciting discovery was Mary Bolint. She was a junior at the University of Arizona in Tucson at the time and was engaged to Ned Ripple. She planned to go to law school after college, so she wanted to wait to have children until after she finished four more years of school. Contraception was an important factor in her life, and so she informed herself about such things. "What makes me angriest*

*now," she says today, "is that I didn't just go to my doctor and let him put whatever he wanted in my body, I studied all the statistics carefully." She read glowing reports of the Dalkon Shield in a feminist health book and asked her doctor if she should have one. Since he too had heard favorable reports, and since a model had been specially designed for women who had never had children, he inserted a Dalkon Shield into Mary's uterus. Carefully following the instructions that accompanied the product, he warned her that she might experience some minor discomfort and slightly heavier bleeding with her period. The pain, however, was immediate and acute. Mary returned to her doctor, who told her it would subside. It did, but her first period was profuse and painful. Again, her doctor promised that once her system grew used to the device all would be well.*

*After a few months the pain during her period became tolerable. Mary and Ned were married, and she was accepted into law school during her senior year. She continued to study hard and became an avid modern dancer.*

[I: DAVIS'S "SCIENTIFIC" RESEARCH]

The rise of the Dalkon Shield really began with Davis's research at Hopkins, and the more closely you look back on it, the less scientific it appears. For one thing, the women tested didn't sign any consent forms, so no one knows what Davis told them about the fresh-off-the-drawing-board gadgets he was putting into their uteri. Also, many people claim that Davis regularly told his IUD patients to use spermicidal foam during the tenth to seventeenth days of their cycle, which would leave it unclear whether his study reported the contraceptive effects of the Dalkon Shield or of the foam. Davis said the people who came to his clinic wouldn't use foam even if they were told to, but that is questionable. In any case, Davis admits that at least some of the 82 private patients in his study might have taken his suggestion to use foam, and that makes his research findings dubious. It is as if, in studying a new headache remedy, he had told patients to take aspirin as well. Also, the study sounds less impressive when you realize there was an average of only 5.5 months testing per woman—not much time to get a reliable pregnancy figure.

Hindsight aside, however, after the *Journal of Obstetrics and Gynecology* article was published, the Dalkon Shield began to take off. Additional help had

come to Lerner and Davis on New Year's Eve, 1969, in the form of Dr. Thad Earl. He was a small-town practitioner from Defiance, Ohio, and had inserted the Shield into some of his own patients and thought it was a great idea. He offered Lerner, Davis and their lawyer, Robert Cohn, $50,000, and got a 7.5 per cent interest in what became "The Dalkon Corporation." (The name was probably an amalgam of Davis, Lerner, and Cohn.)

Lerner had been the inventor, Davis the scientist whose research at a famous institution had validated the invention, Cohn the lawyer who had put together a corporate framework that would allow everyone to get rich, and now, finally The Dalkon Corporation had what it needed to get off the ground: Thad Earl, the enthusiastic salesman willing to go on the road drumming up publicity. If you don't have a large marketing organi-

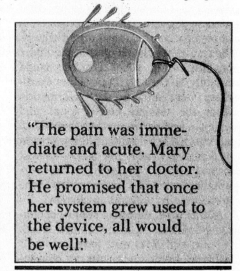

"The pain was immediate and acute. Mary returned to her doctor. He promised that once her system grew used to the device, all would be well."

zation or the capital to advertise, about the only effective way to sell a new medical product is to set up demonstration booths at medical conventions. Earl proved to be an energetic salesman. IUDs were not, at the time, classified as drugs, so Dalkon Shields could be hawked just like new office furniture to doctors browsing in convention hallways. Earl passed out the Shields from his booth and showed everyone the impressive testing results of Dr. Hugh Davis of Johns Hopkins.

*One warm spring day toward the end of her senior year in college, while Mary Bolint was shopping for dinner, she began to feel uneasy. Suddenly an enormous wave of nausea swept over her. She left her groceries and walked as fast as she could to her car, where she lay down in the back seat. She had been dancing all afternoon, preparing for a summer arts festival, and hoped that she was simply overtired. She remained dizzy and confused, however, and had to ask a friend to drive her home. Her main worry was appendicitis. That would have spoiled her summer of dancing and working. She worked as a nurses' aide in the local hospital and was saving her money for law school.*

*She made it home, cooked a small dinner and went to bed early—tired and sore. The pain grew worse through the night and at six a.m. she woke her husband Ned. She barely had enough strength left to ask him to take her to the hospital, and he rushed her to the emergency ward, where her condition was quickly diagnosed as appendicitis. When the doctors opened her up, however, they found a healthy appendix, but large abscesses on her ovaries. They drained the abscesses, took out her appendix and sewed her up. When she awoke she told her doctor she was using a Dalkon Shield and asked him if he thought it should be taken out. He said he didn't think it was necessary since he had never heard of IUDs causing infection, but that he would remove it if she wanted. She decided to leave it in and was released from the hospital in a few days. She returned home satisfied that she had made the right decision. The infection was gone and, even if the Dalkon Shield was uncomfortable, it couldn't be as dangerous as the Pill.*

[II: DALKON GOES NATIONAL]

It was 1970, and the scene was a medical convention in Ohio. Thad Earl was there selling Dalkon Shields and found himself set up in a booth next to one run by John McClure, a salesman for A. H. Robins Company. The two men began talking; their chit-chat quickly turned to business talk, and suddenly the promoters of the Dalkon Shield had a big break beyond their greatest dreams.

Robins is headquartered in Richmond, Virginia, and has assets of $186 million and subsidiaries in more than a dozen foreign countries. Tranquilizers and appetite suppressants are among the best-selling products of its large line of drugs; it also makes cosmetics, Robitussin cough syrup, Chapstick and Sergeant's Flea Collar, which *Forbes* business magazine accused of killing pets.

At the time Thad Earl and John McClure got to talking outside their convention booths, Robins was looking for an entry into the growing contraceptive market. Its rivals Schmidt and Ortho had captured the Pill business and were be-

ginning to reap enormous profits from their own IUDs. When McClure started chatting with Earl, he didn't waste time. Within a few days after their meeting, Robins' acquisition manager flew to Defiance, Ohio, to watch Earl make a few insertions of the Dalkon Shield and to talk medicine and markets. A week later the company's medical director, Dr. Fred Clark, flew to Baltimore to meet Hugh Davis.

Davis told him, by Clark's account, "that the company that takes the Dalkon Shield must move fast and distribute

Mary Bolint: "What makes me angriest is that I studied all the statistics carefully."

much merchandise and really make an inroad 'in the next eight months.' " Several other people Davis knew were working on similar devices. The courtship quickly intensified; both sides were eager to consummate.

Within a few days Lerner and Cohn, Dalkon's lawyer, flew to Richmond to work out a deal. After three days of negotiating, everyone returned home richer. Robins paid The Dalkon Corporation $750,000 for the patent, which was split among Lerner, Davis, Earl and Cohn according to their interests in the Corporation. Also, an agreement was made (and this is where the big money comes in) that the four men would split ten per cent royalties on all gross sales of the Shield by Robins in the U.S. and Canada. Finally, Earl was retained by Robins as a $30,000-a-year consultant for three years; Davis consulted at $20,000 a year for five years; and Lerner consulted for one year at $12,500 and two more at $2,500.

As the deal was being made, however, something was discovered that proved to be a portent of troubles ahead. Dr. Fred Clark, the Robins official who had flown up to Baltimore to meet Hugh Davis, dictated a three-page memorandum to the files on his return to Richmond. In it he said that of the 832 patients Davis had tested so far, 26 had become pregnant. This would raise the pregnancy rate from the previously published 1.1 per cent to close to three per cent. The dates on the Clark memo show that Hugh Davis was aware of this new, less impressive result back in February when his *Journal* article was published.

(Robins lawyers claim that Fred Clark's memo about a higher pregnancy rate is merely a typo. They say Clark never read the typed version of the notes he dictated and that he meant to say "an additional six" rather than "26." But their claim sounds weak, for there is other material in the subpoenaed files that indicates Clark did not believe Davis's figures were as impressive as he had first heard.)

Although not quite the corporate equivalent of a smoking gun, the memo has become an important document in the Dalkon affair. It indicates that both Davis and Robins are guilty of promoting the Dalkon Shield with false statistics. The crucial importance of the pregnancy rate becomes clear when you imagine a fetus having to share a uterus with a small crab-shaped piece of plastic. Most of those 17 deaths were due to blood poisoning caused by infection and spontaneous abortion among women who got pregnant while wearing the Dalkon Shield.

[III: THE "FLYING UTERUS"]

Readers of five national medical journals in December 1970 found themselves looking at a remarkable two-page advertisement. It became known in Robins' ad department as the "flying uterus" ad, and it was Robins' way of beginning the vigorous promotion of the Dalkon Shield it had bought only six months earlier. The ad's art page is a painting by a prominent medical artist, Arthur Lidov. It shows a cross-sectioned uterus floating through the sky towards the reader with a Dalkon Shield nestled in it. The Shield looks like some sort of space bug out of the pages of Ray Bradbury—it's about the size of a small fingernail, is made of white plastic and its most notable feature is the little spines or legs surrounding it to keep it from slipping out of the womb. It also has a "tail" or piece of string attached to facilitate medical removal.

It turns out that the string is more important than it would seem. In fact, technically speaking, it is the culprit of the Dalkon affair. According to most researchers (although not Robins) who have since studied it, its construction (which is multifilament, meaning several threads wound together) acts like the wick of a kerosene lamp and allows bacteria from the vagina to creep up and enter the uterus, where massive infections leading to blood poisoning, and eventually death, can result.

The copy on the companion page of the advertisement, with the "scientific" findings from Dr. Hugh Davis's earliest research, boasts of the 1.1 per cent pregnancy rate, and says nothing about the women in the study also using foam or being tested for an average of less than six months. Davis is impressively footnoted as a research physician with citations from the articles he published. He is not cited as a businessman who had just collected $250,000 from his share of the sale of the Shield to Robins.

[ONWARD AND UPWARD]

For the next few years, everything went wonderfully for Robins. The Dalkon Shield was inserted into 3.3 million women in the U.S. and overseas. Robins reaped huge profits from it (each device had only a few cents' worth of plastic in it, but sold for $4.35 retail). The Shield was hailed as the latest thing in IUDs, particularly good for women who had not yet had children. E. Claiborne Robins, Sr., chief executive officer of the company started by his grandfather in 1878, was proud of his officers and was looking forward to the day when the Dalkon Shield would be as familiar a product as Chapstick.

*Not long after her "appendectomy," when the abscesses on her ovaries had been discovered and drained, Mary Bolint again began feeling pain and nausea. She went directly to the gynecologist in the hospital where she was working for the summer. He tried in his office to remove her Dalkon Shield but was unable to do it, and so she was put in an operating room where it was removed surgically. For two days after the operation Mary remained in the hospital, running a temperature of 104 degrees and experiencing almost constant dream-like hallucinations. When her tem-*

*perature returned to normal several days later, she was sent home with antibiotics. She was still too weak to work or dance, so she stayed home to cook for Ned, who was working. She grew weaker day by day, and finally her parents convinced her to come home to Louisiana, where they could take care of her. Her mother flew to meet her and took Mary to the plane. When they arrived in New Orleans, a flight attendant had to carry Mary off. After she had been home for a few days the fever returned and again she was*

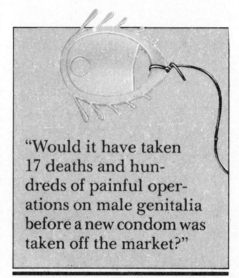

"Would it have taken 17 deaths and hundreds of painful operations on male genitalia before a new condom was taken off the market?"

*rushed to the hospital, where she was found to have septicemia, or blood poisoning. For ten days she was kept in intensive care, receiving intravenous antibiotics. During that time, her appendectomy scar burst open from new abscesses on her ovaries, which were again drained. When she finally regained her strength after a month, she flew to San Francisco to join Ned and begin law school. She hoped at last that she could put the painful memories behind her and look ahead to law school, a career, a good marriage and, someday, children.*

[ENTER A WOMAN]

Up to this time all the characters on the corporate side of the Dalkon history have been men. (One wonders how different this story might be had the subjects of their experiments and sales been men also: would it have taken 17 deaths and hundreds of painful operations on male genitalia before a new variety of condom, say, was taken off the market?) But one woman played a role in the discovery of the Dalkon Shield's dangers, although, unfortunately, her warnings

were ignored by higher-ups.

She is Dr. Ellen (Kitty) Preston, a Southern woman who got her M.D. in 1950. She had worked as a physician in private practice and for the State of Virginia Health Department before coming to Robins to be chief of the Antibacterial and Miscellaneous Division (the Shield came under Miscellaneous). In 1971, Preston wrote a memo to medical director Fred Clark (the same Robins official who had flown to Baltimore to meet Hugh Davis and had discovered Davis had been using inflated statistics). In her memo, Preston said that she and Daniel French, president of Robins' Chapstick Division, were concerned that the Dalkon's multifilament tail might display "wicking qualities." She was predicting the source of the very problem that was to lead to so many injuries and deaths among women who used the Shield. On August 20, 1971, Clark replied with a curt letter saying that it was not up to Drs. Preston and French to test the Shield. He indicated in the letter that he was passing the problem to Dr. Oscar Klioze, the company microbiologist. But did he ever do so? In a sworn deposition four years later, Dr. Klioze said he had never heard of the Preston and French memos, and when he was shown them he swore he had never seen them.

It was one of Dr. Ellen Preston's duties to answer medical inquiries from doctors regarding the Shield. After her rebuff by Clark, she responded to at least one doctor who wrote asking about the possibility of "wicking," saying that as far as Robins knew, such a problem did not exist.

Robins must have been having some second thoughts about the Shield's safety, for around this time it did its own testing, came up with a pregnancy rate of 2 per cent, somewhat higher than Davis's, and cited the new figure as well in its ads. However, some other studies done at the same time that showed vastly greater pregnancy rates—one by Dr. Johanna Perlmutter at Beth Israel Hospital in Boston (10.1 per cent) and one by the Kaiser Medical Center in Sacramento (5.6 per cent)—Robins simply chose to ignore.

*Two weeks after she had arrived in California to enter law school, Mary Bolint again began experiencing fever and nausea. She went to a doctor and told him her history. He examined her and said she had a new large abscess on her left ovary and that if it burst she might die. Very scared and sick, Mary decided to fly back to Lancaster, Pennsylvania, where her father-in-law, a doctor, could supervise her medical care. On the plane east she began to wonder if it would ever end. She was going in for her fourth operation in four months.*

*While she was under anesthesia, the surgeon made a six-inch incision from her navel down to the top of her pubic bone and two 1½-inch incisions on either side of her abdomen to drain the infection. The doctors were working to save her reproductive organs, but cautious not to give her too many pain-killing drugs because her nervous system was by now so weak. Mary lay in bed for two weeks with tubes and needles running in and out of her body and was in constant excruciating pain.*

*When she recovered and again flew home to Louisiana to recuperate, she was badly scarred all over her abdomen, emotionally drained but dimly grateful that she would still be able to have children.*

[AN INCRIMINATING SLIP]

Let us backtrack in time a little to take up another strand of the Dalkon story. It is an important one, for it involves a slip for which—in the unlikely event that the law is enforced justly— one of the principals could go to jail.

In January 1970 the controversy over the damaging side effects of oral contraceptives was at its height, and a Senate Subcommittee headed by Senator Gaylord Nelson was holding hearings on the subject. One of the experts on contraception they called in to testify was Dr.

Hugh Davis. Davis took a stand against birth control pills with high estrogen content and for IUDs, especially "the new ones" that have been developed. He disapproved of the collection of information regarding the side effects of the Pill, saying that they were vastly "underreported." He said information regarding contraception supplied to women is not adequate, and that gynecologists aren't all that informed about it either. "They are busy," he said. "They read the brochures and information that the drug houses tend to pump into them, I am sorry to say."

It is true that IUDs are generally safer than the Pill, but, sensing that Davis might have some special stake in his strong case for the IUDs, one of the committee members asked if he had a patent on any intrauterine device. Davis mentioned an IUD (not the Dalkon Shield) he had co-invented ten years earlier that was never marketed. The time to tell it straight came, however, when the question was put more bluntly.

"Then you have no particular commercial interest in any of the intrauterine devices?"

"That is correct," replied Dr. Davis.

For the first time in the whole murky history of the Dalkon Shield, someone had clearly and indisputably broken the law: Davis had committed perjury. In flatly lying under oath to the Senate Subcommittee, Davis had committed a felony—one that carries a prison sentence of up to five years and one for which a

whole host of people, from Alger Hiss to one or two of the lesser Watergate defendants, have done time in prison. To date, Davis has not been indicted or charged.

[IV: THE TROUBLE BEGINS]

The first hint of trouble for Robins in the Dalkon matter came in 1973, and it came, surprisingly, from a man in an Army uniform. He was a witness at a federal hearing called to discuss whether or not medical devices should be subject to the same kind of controls as regular drugs. The hearings dealt with every device imaginable, from pacemakers to artificial kidneys, but on May 30 Army Major Russel Thomsen stole the show by recounting his experiences with the Dalkon Shield. Like so many doctors, he said, he had trusted his medical journals and assumed their editors made sure their authors and advertisers were responsible. On the strength of Robins' advertisements and Davis's article, he had convinced his patients to switch to the Dalkon Shield, only to see them go through a great deal of suffering because of it. Thomsen described cases of septic abortion, pelvic inflammatory disease, massive bleeding, incessant cramps. Some of his patients had almost died. He said he was "revolted" by the gap between the glossy advertising claims and the occurrence of serious and even fatal complications. His testimony about the gruesome effects of the Dalkon Shield was in most major American newspapers the following morning.

After the Dalkon Shield became a public issue, a flood of reports like Thomsen's began coming in from throughout the country. After a year of such information-gathering, Robins got word, finally, of a death in Arizona due to the Shield. From this point on, Robins at last began to act responsibly. The company went to the Food and Drug Administration with the information, and when four more deaths were reported soon after, Robins decided to send out a strongly worded "Dear Doctor" letter to every physician in the country. The letter warned doctors about possible septic abortion and death from the Dalkon Shield and recommended that women who got pregnant with the Shield be given therapeutic abortions. Similar warnings were printed on the packages of new Shields being manufactured. All this seems reminiscent of the Surgeon General's warning on cigarette packs, with one difference: as with prescription

# Read The Label, But Not Too Closely

The A. H. Robins Company took a number of hasty actions in its eagerness to get the Dalkon Shield selling faster than its competitors; nowhere was their salesmanship more embarrassing than over the copper question. Back in 1970, Hugh Davis publicized the fact that copper sulphate (which makes up about five per cent of the Shield's composition) had contraceptive properties. The salespeople at Robins decided to publicize this, even though they had no evidence that the copper did anything other than make the Shield's plastic less brittle. Detail men in the field were instructed to add "copper content" to their sales pitch, and they did.

In April 1971, however, the FDA began inquiring about the copper in the Shield. If copper was actually released into the uterus, this would make the Shield not a "device" but a "drug," and it would have to be withdrawn from the market for a lengthy and expensive testing period to meet federal requirements. Robins quickly scrambled to rewrite its sales monograph, removing all references to copper being released, and explained that the copper was blended into the plastic only to enhance malleability and "radiopacity." It "has *no effect* in the contraceptive effectiveness of the Shield." (Robins' emphasis.)

drugs, the ultimate recipient never gets to see the label.

Things began looking bad for Dalkon sales. Within weeks of the Dear Doctor letter, the Planned Parenthood Federation sent a memorandum to its 700 membership clinics. It suggested that they immediately cease prescribing the Shield and recommended that they call in all patients then wearing it, advise them of the dangers and offer a substitute contraceptive. They also said the 26.4 per cent of the women in their clinics fitted with the Dalkon Shield experienced severe cramps and bleeding.

Davis was interviewed by the press around this time. He was known as the Shield's co-inventor, but not as someone who still owned a piece of the action. "The whole thing has been blown out of proportion by a certain amount of deliberate design," he reportedly said. "There are large commercial forces that are quite interested in selling new IUDs."

• • •

While all the fuss was going on, the Food and Drug Administration began hearings on the Dalkon Shield. Robins executives were frightened, and the highway from its headquarters near Richmond to Washington was soon filled with scouts and lobbyists it was sending to the hearing. According to Dr. Richard Dickey, a member of the FDA's Ob/Gyn Committee, which conducted the hearing, "throughout the entire proceedings the halls and offices of the FDA were crawling with the Robins men. It was disgusting."

Finally, though, before the FDA committee made its recommendations, Robins itself suspended sale of the Shield. It was a difficult decision for the company, as Dalkon had recently moved into the lead in national IUD sales. But in 30 short days, the deaths reported to the FDA had risen from four to seven and the septic abortions from 36 to 110. By this time, also, many people were pointing to the possibility of "wicking," which was the subject of the Preston/Clark memos written back in 1971. Now, in 1975, Robins knew its product was commercially dead, and wanted to forget it. Only, as things turned out, it couldn't.

*The day Mary Bolint was scheduled to leave Louisiana to fly back to California for another try at law school and a normal life with her husband, she came down with a high fever. Despairingly, she checked into the hospital again. When doctors opened up her abdomen this time, they found that the infection was everywhere. To save her life they performed a complete hysterectomy and rinsed her peritoneal cavity with antibiotic fluid. During recovery, the intern told Mary that for a while he couldn't get a blood pressure on her and her pulse measured 150.*

*"I knew from working as a nurses' aide," she says, "that it meant death, but you know, I didn't care. In fact I was relieved. My skin was gray, my hair was falling out and I weighed about 100 pounds."*

[BUSINESS AS USUAL]

Throughout the rise and fall of the Dalkon Shield, one irony is how seldom anyone actually broke the law. Hugh Davis did, when he perjured himself by telling senators he had no commercial interest in any IUD. But his having that interest in the first place in a harmful device he and the Robins Company were vigorously promoting by questionable means was not really illegal.

Most doctors we talked to either avoided comment on the Dalkon controversy or seemed to genuinely consider it business as usual. Even Dr. John Brewer, editor of the *American Journal of Obstetrics and Gynecology*, sidestepped the issue. We asked him if he considered it unethical for Davis to have published an article in his journal praising the IUD Davis co-owned, without revealing his financial stake.

"I don't know what you're talking about and I consider it no business of mine."

# How Much They Made

| | Sale of Patent | Estimated Royalties | Consulting | Estimated Gross Sales | Total |
|---|---|---|---|---|---|
| **Irwin Lerner** | $412,500 | $555,000 | $15,000 | | $982,500 |
| **Hugh Davis** | $262,500 | $350,000 | $100,000 | | $712,500 |
| **Thad Earl** | $56,000 | $75,000 | $90,000 | | $221,000 |
| **Robert Cohn** | $75,000 | $100,000 | | | $175,000 |
| **A. H. Robins Co.** | | | | $16,000,000 | $16,000,000 |

"But we know lawyers have been taking depositions from you," we persisted.

"I just answer their questions," Brewer replied. "Until you told me this minute, I had no idea of what it was all about, and I don't want to know."

Others in the medical profession say this kind of conflict of interest is fairly common. Many medical researchers are paid by drug companies to test new products and don't mention that fact in their statistical write-ups. Aside from his distortion of statistics, the main thing medical people consider unusual about what Davis did is that he developed the Dalkon Shield while using the clinic and the prestige of Johns Hopkins. Doctors who are out to make big money in the medical market are usually not at medical schools.

A 1976 law (passed largely because of the Dalkon controversy) will make it somewhat harder for anyone to profiteer from a new medical device in precisely the same manner Davis and the Robins Company did. Medical devices are now subject to many of the same kinds of government monitoring and approval as drugs have been.

Nonetheless, we can still expect drug companies to rush new drugs and devices onto the market as fast as whatever the current law allows. Not because the companies mean harm, but because they have no choice. If a drug or device is tested more cautiously or for a longer time than the law requires, or advertised with less distortion or oversell than the law permits, someone else will corner the market with a competing product. That's why Hugh Davis warned Robins the company had to "move fast and distribute much merchandise."

As long as there is a free market for medical products, that's the way business will be done. Indeed, though there have been civil lawsuits aplenty as a result of the Dalkon Shield, the whole affair has been considered so normal a way of conducting free-enterprise medicine that Johns Hopkins took no action against Davis, state medical authorities censured neither Davis nor Earl and the government left the A. H. Robins Company and The Dalkon Corporation alone.

[EXPORTING OUR TROUBLES]

A product that has been heavily promoted and advertised gathers a certain kind of momentum, a momentum that can carry it right over obstacles like bad publicity, studies of its dangers and the

like. In the case of the Dalkon Shield, this momentum brought a curious coda to its story: throughout the entire controversy over the Shield, long past the time Major Thomsen had testified before the Senate committee, past the time Robins sent out its "Dear Doctor" letter, past the time Planned Parenthood and HEW clinics stopped using them and right up to the moment Robins took the Shield

"That's the way business will be done. The whole affair has been considered a normal way of conducting free-enterprise medicine."

off the market, the U.S. foreign aid program was busily sending huge quantities of the device to more than 40 countries throughout the world.

The Agency for International Development's population control program is in the hands of Dr. R. D. Ravenholt, a man whose enthusiasm for birth control as a solution to the world's problems borders on the fanatical. When one of us visited his office several years ago she found it filled with charts of female reproductive organs, packages of condoms, and models of a small vacuum cleaner-like device Ravenholt was promoting at the time as the latest in birth control techniques. When she got up to leave, he said "Here, take these," reaching into a small box overflowing with little packets of Pills.

"But I don't use Pills," she replied.

"That's all right," he said. "Give them to your friends."

Only when the FDA ruled the Shield unsafe (which was some time *after* Robins had stopped selling it) did Ravenholt and AID try to recall any Shields. They managed to get back fewer than half of the 769,000 Shields they had given away.

[V: WHERE ARE THEY NOW?]

Today Mary Bolint has regained her

health, but her entire abdomen is a mass of scar tissue. She can never have children. For a long time, she says, she could not think about the Dalkon Shield. Now she is one of many women engaged in lawsuits against the A. H. Robins Company and Hugh Davis, Irwin Lerner, Thad Earl and Robert Cohn.

Robins spent $5 million in litigation costs over the Shield last year, and more suits are yet to come. The company is setting aside a reserve from its profits to cover future lawsuits, and its stock value has dropped sharply. All told, though, Robins' corporate health is not bad: profits were up 26 per cent in the first half of 1976.

Hugh Davis still teaches at Johns Hopkins and still heads the university's Family Planning Clinic. He does not return phone calls from the press. Thad Earl is still in private practice, although he has moved to Arizona. "Win" Lerner is still an engineer, working for himself at "Lerner Labs." Like the others, he has been told by his lawyers to say nothing, but he is the only one who sounds frustrated with this prohibition. Lerner would like to tell the whole story, he says, but he can't. The Dalkon Corporation still exists, he adds, and maybe someday it will come up with a new product.

Dr. Ellen Preston, the woman whose memo about "wicking" first pinpointed the danger of the Dalkon Shield, still works for A. H. Robins in Virginia. She has been forbidden by company lawyers to talk about the case with anyone.

Some 800,000 women in the United States and an estimated 500,000 in other countries are still wearing the Dalkon Shield as a birth control device. Planned Parenthood and several similar groups have considered recommending that all women wearing Shields have them removed immediately. But these organizations have decided not to do so, for recently it has been discovered that removal of the Shield frequently causes lesions of the cervix, followed by serious infection.

---

*Mark Dowie is general manager of Mother Jones. He is the author of* Transitions to Freedom, *a book on the problems of ex-prisoners. Tracy Johnston is a freelance writer whose work has appeared in* The New York Times Magazine, The Village Voice, Redbook *and elsewhere.*

# 46

*Nader's Raiders is their name, and whistle-blowing is their game . . .*

# Stop! In the Public Interest!

By JULIUS DUSCHA

WASHINGTON.

THEY said that he couldn't last, that he would spread himself too thin, that he would burn himself out, that the press and the public would tire of his moralistic, monastic, Martin Luther life style and that then he, too, would succumb to the pleasures of the flesh. That was what they were saying about Ralph Nader after he burst upon the public conscience five years ago at a supercharged Senate hearing, challenging the gumshoe tactics General Motors had used against him.

Well, they were all wrong. Some of the Chevrolets of 1966 are already on the junk heap, but not Ralph Nader. He has become an institution at least as formidable as General Motors. Some say Nader and his followers constitute a corporation, perhaps even a conglomerate. Wow! Ralph Nader, Chairman of the Board.

Nader, now 37 years old, is no longer a lonely figure bravely fighting off the excesses of governmental

JULIUS DUSCHA is the director of the Washington Journalism Center and author of "Arms, Money and Politics."

and corporate bureaucracy and standing up all by himself for consumers. With him now are Nader's Raiders—hundreds of students, housewives, lawyers, professors, engineers and scientists throughout the country who are working or have worked for him part-time and a handful of lawyers, a teacher or two and a few other professionals who have enlisted full-time and who operate from his several redoubts in Washington.

The result is an avalanche of reports, books, television programs, testimony at Congressional and administrative hearings, lawsuits, petitions, letters to government and corporate administrators and campaigns to organize college students in a nationwide consumers' crusade.

IT is not all just talk, either. Nader and his Raiders get things done. Last year they were moving forces in pushing a tough air-pollution bill through Congress; in getting workmen's safety legislation approved by Congress; in persuading the Senate to turn a mushy consumer bill into a meaningful Consumer Protection Agency; in winning a court case that

forced the Administration to review all the remaining uses of the herbicide 2,4,5-T, and in convincing the National Highway Safety Bureau that 200,000 G.M. trucks had potentially dangerous wheels.

And that's not all Nader's Raiders accomplished last year. Reacting to their first assault on a Government agency, the Federal Trade Commission continued to implement suggestions made by some of the early Raiders back in 1969. The Interstate Commerce Commission and the Food and Drug Administration instituted some long-overdue reforms pinpointed by Raider reports on those two agencies.

Two Raiders dispatched to West Virginia mounted an assault on Union Carbide's pollution smokestacks and low tax bill in the state. Partly as a result of the Raiders' activities, the company agreed to clean up its polluting plants and pay higher taxes.

Some Raiders have even joined the Establishment. William Howard Taft IV, one of the first Raiders, is a special assistant to Caspar W. Weinberger, Deputy Director of the Office of Management and Budget. Raider

Reuben B. Robertson III is Chairman of the Consumer Advisory Committee to the Civil Aeronautics Board. Nader himself is a member of the National Highway Safety Bureau's Advisory Council, but sends Lowell Dodge of his Center for Auto Safety to represent him at meetings because he doesn't think the council is important enough for his time. And Edward F. Cox, another of the original Raiders, appears to be about to marry Tricia Nixon.

There are only 20 or so full-time members of Nader's Raiders (the name was coined by a newspaperman), but their energy and effectiveness make it seem as if there were at least 2,000. A half-dozen senior Raiders, most of them around 30, work out of Nader's three-year-old Center for Study of Responsive Law. Each earns only $10,000 to $15,000 a year.

A few blocks away a dozen Raiders just out of law school (each paid about $4,500 a year) make up Nader's newly organized Public Interest Research Group. In adjoining closetlike offices in the National Press Building, Nader's Center for Auto Safety and Professionals for Auto Safety operate with a full-time staff of one and many volunteers.

Then there is the Center for Law and Social Policy, a five-man public-interest law firm with 12 law-student internes, which is not directly associated with Nader but represents him and his Raiders in some of their suits. Finally, the Project for Corporate Responsibility runs the Campaign to Make General Motors Responsible with the advice of Nader and the help of a Raider.

Ralph, as everyone in Washington calls Nader, continues to work out of his $80-a-month room near Dupont Circle and a $90-a-month unmarked office in the National Press Building, dropping in daily on his various enterprises and scoffing at the idea that he has become a corporation.

"This," he says, "is an experiment in *not* developing a bureaucracy. We bring people in who are interested in a particular subject and give them front-rank responsibility. They don't report to somebody who then reports to somebody else. I get together with them regularly. We have a constantly fluid, conversational system."

"It's orchestrated chaos," says 25-year-old Mark J. Green, a lawyer attached to the Center for Study of Responsive Law. "Have you been down to that office? It's impossible. I work at home because I can't get anything done when I go down there."

INSTITUTION, corporation, conglomerate, fluid conversation pit, orchestrated chaos—whatever it is that Nader has wrought, it works surprisingly well for him.

He has found a way to turn youthful energy into amazingly productive work. Beginning in the summer of 1967 with five law-school internes, he built up his corps of summer Raiders to 100 in 1969 and 200 last year. While they are in Washington, the young Raiders do a lot of spadework for the reports Nader and his senior Raiders publish later in the year. And once the Raiders are back at school they are eager to help with problems Nader would like checked out in New York, Boston, Chicago, San Francisco or wherever a Raider happens to be.

The concept is that reasonably bright young men and women with a background in the law, engineering or the sciences can easily grasp the deficiencies of governmental and corporate bureaucracies. Nader now seems to have institutionalized the program on a year-round basis, and the part-time Raiders continue to churn out more material than Nader and his handful of full-time Raiders know what to do with.

And Nader still inspires youth, though he is no gentle perpetrator of participatory democracy. He is an authoritarian with a mania for detail and perfection. He does not approve of cigarette-smoking, let alone marijuana, and at times last summer his dictatorial handling of the Raider program pushed many of its participants to the brink of revolt. But still young people are attracted to him because he accomplishes things.

"I had done all sorts of antiwar protesting," said 22-year-old Mrs. Collot Bruce, the blond daughter of novelist Albert Guerard. She is the part-time director of Professionals for Auto Safety and a full-time Georgetown University law student. "But I didn't think I could change anything that way. At first the idea of working on auto safety didn't appeal to me. I'm more concerned about corporate collusion, but now I'm convinced that I can help make corporations more responsive through auto safety."

Mrs. Bruce is typical of Nader's Raiders—white, upper-middle-class, from one of the best schools (in her case Radcliffe), modishly dressed but not determinedly sloppy. Blacks are not attracted, and many Negro activists regard Nader's attacks on the Establishment as middle-class protests and irrelevant to their causes. Nor are there any freaked-out long-long-hairs around.

Not only is Nader authoritarian with his own Raiders: he can also be ruthless in his legislative tactics and his bouts with bureaucrats. During the drafting of consumer legislation last year he frequently got his way by threatening to go over the heads of Congressional staff aides to their patron Senators or Representatives or to the press.

"If you don't do what he wants," one staff aide said, "he's prepared to go to his friends in the press and publicly denounce you."

And Nader has no qualms about denouncing his friends, either. A 1970 report by some of the Raiders scathingly criticized Senator Edmund Muskie's record on air pollution. Liberal Senators were appalled, but the report stiffened Muskie's backbone and helped push him into supporting a tough bill requiring a 90 per cent reduction in automobile pollution by 1975. Senator Abraham Ribicoff of Connecticut, the man who in 1966 provided Nader with the forum in which he exposed G.M.'s efforts to shadow him, also felt Nader's wrath last year. When, during debate on the Senate floor, Ribicoff accepted several compromising amendments to his consumer bill, which Nader had been so active in shaping, Nader emerged from the galleries where he had been watching the horse-trading and denounced Ribicoff to reporters.

In dealing with governmental bureaucracy, Nader has perfected a familiar Washington tactic which drives administrators up walls. Through a friend working in an agency, Nader will find out that a long-pending decision favorable to one of his causes is about to be made public. He then will write a letter to the administrator in charge demanding to know why this decision has not been made for lo! these many months. Copies of the letter go to Nader's many friends in the Washington press corps, and when, within a few days, the governmental decision is dutifully announced, Nader gets credit for once again cracking open the bureaucracy.

As Senators and Raiders alike have discovered, joining up with Nader is like enlisting in the Army. He demands total fealty to his concept of the public good.

Raider pay is low and the hours are long. "One hundred hours a week is ideal," Nader says, and he's not kidding. He still works those hours himself, and recently told a friend that he had spent only $5,000 on his personal needs last year. The friend believes him because Nader is as meticulous in keeping track of his own expenses as he is in following amendments on the Senate floor.

Nader frowns on Raiders' going off for summer weekends at the beach, and was unhappy with one aide who took a long Thanksgiving weekend last year without leaving behind a telephone number where he could be reached. Raiders quickly get used to midnight calls from the boss with his marching orders for the next day or two.

He hassles his Raiders over cigarettes (but half of them still smoke) and over the cars they drive (he still does not have one). A lot of Raiders own Volkswagens, which Nader considers to be particularly dangerous but which the Raiders like because they are economical. Despite the pressures, though, few Raiders resign.

"I'll still be a Raider when I'm 60," says Mark Green, who has 35 years to go and is finishing a mammoth study of Government antitrust activities. "Imagine sitting up in a Wall Street office being the 10th man on an antitrust suit, working on the 13th count of the suit. The responsibility I have here is the largest I could possibly think of having at my age."

Nader is a lawyer and has great faith in a lawyer's approach to problems and in legal solutions to them. Usually he finds out what a Raider is interested in and tries to give him a research assignment within that range. He tells the Raider to begin by reading everything he can find about the subject. The reading is followed by extensive interviewing. Finally Nader sits down with the Raider to decide whether the end product should be a report, a book, a letter to a Government administrator or a public denunciation of some person or agency.

But the styles of the Raiders vary enormously. Some, like 30-year-old John C. Esposito, can be abrasive and arrogant, spoiling for a public confrontation. A dark-haired, brooding man with penetrating eyes and a penchant for sports shirts and bell-bottom trousers, Esposito went to work for Nader in the summer of 1966 and is now a senior Raider.

Esposito wrote the report on "Vanishing Air" which Nader put out last spring and which sought to tear apart Senator Muskie's record on air-pollution legislation. But such is the power of Nader and his Raiders that Esposito was routinely admitted thereafter to meetings organized by Muskie aides to get industry and reformers together for discussions of the 1970 air-pollution legislation.

LIKE 36-year-old Gary Sellers, other Raiders become fascinated with the legislative process and its inevitable compromises, and learn how to use the system on Capitol Hill to their advantage. Now the senior Raider in charge of the neophytes at Nader's Public Interest Research Group, Sellers also works part-time for Democratic Representative Phillip Burton of San Francisco.

A short man with longish brown hair, a taste for long cigars and a generally conspiratorial view of the world, Sellers spent much of last year helping steer occupational-safety legislation through Congress. Burton is a member of the House Education and Labor Committee, which handled the legislation, and Sellers used his position on Burton's staff as a way to get into secret committee meetings where legislative tactics were discussed.

"I have no problem serving two masters," Sellers said. "Ralph's and Phil's passion and concern are coextensive. The arrangement turned out very well for both of them."

Like William Harrison Wellford, some Raiders look and talk as if they were displaced scholars. Nearly bald at 31, Harrison Wellford is a soft-spoken North Carolinian who was a valedictorian at Davidson College, has a master's degree from Cambridge University, is a doctoral candidate in government at Harvard and has won Marshall, Danforth and Woodrow Wilson Fellowships.

More than any other single person, Wellford is responsible for the recent decision by the Environmental Protection Agency to conduct a crash study to determine whether all uses of the herbicide 2,4,5-T should be ended.

During a lengthy study of the Agriculture Department which has resulted in a two-volume book, "Sowing the Wind," to be published this spring, Wellford became an expert on herbicides and pesticides. His knowledge was used by four environmental organizations which filed a

makes $30 a week, another $40 and the third $75) and several volunteers.

The aides range from a young man fulfilling his conscientious-objector's obligation, to a young woman who goes to law school at night and by day studies the use of air bags to prevent injuries in automobile crashes, and a physicist who works at the U.S. Patent Office.

It was Dodge who put together information about potentially dangerous wheels on

ical study of the F.D.A. Still another is James R. Michael, who is completing a massive citizens' handbook on access to the Federal agencies.

Other reports and studies are under way on supermarkets; property taxes; consumer credit; banks; the influence of large law firms like Washington's Covington & Burling, whose most celebrated partner is Dean Acheson; the domination of the state of Delaware by the du Pont Company; the power of the First National City Bank in New York; the pollution caused by pulp and paper mills in Maine; General Motors' commitment to safety work and the abatement of air pollution, and the relationship of Government agencies to think tanks.

**"To encourage more people to put public responsibilities above bureaucratic allegiances, Nader organized a 'Whistle-Blowers' Conference."**

suit that led to the decision by the new Environmental Protection Agency, which recently took over the Agriculture Department's authority to regulate herbicides and pesticides.

Raiders have shown again and again what one man can do in Washington if he spends full-time on a single issue or bird-dogging one agency, and no one has been more successful than 30-year-old Lowell Dodge, the director of Nader's Center for Auto Safety. Dodge's office in the National Press Building is hardly wider than the door leading into it and not much deeper than a walk-in closet.

Dodge's sole assignment is the National Highway Safety Bureau, which was created by the first piece of legislation resulting from Nader's crusade in Washington—the 1966 Highway Safety Act. A neat, black-haired man who rides a bicycle to work from his Capitol Hill apartment, Dodge supervises the activities of three paid assistants (one

200,000 G.M. trucks built between 1960 and 1965. By pressing their case, Dodge and some public-interest lawyers got the Highway Safety Bureau to reverse a previous decision and issue a warning about the truck wheels.

Dodge has also completed work with Nader and an engineer named Ralf Hotchkiss on a book entitled "What to Do With Your Bad Car: A Manual for Lemon Owners." Profits from the book will be used to help finance and expand the center.

"Sure, that little Center for Auto Safety is effective," said an official of the Highway Safety Bureau. "Many a night I've spent late at the office trying to 'Nader-proof' a regulation. The pipelines this guy has into the agency are unbelievable."

ANOTHER Raider, James S. Turner, is Nader's expert on the Food and Drug Administration and the author of "The Chemical Feast," a crit-

Helping Nader keep track of everything is 30-year-old Theodore Jacobs, a classmate at Princeton and Harvard Law School who gave up a Wall Street law practice three years ago to come to Washington, first as chief counsel to the National Commission on Product Safety and since last spring as Nader's chief of staff.

"When I was practicing law in New York," said Jacobs, an intense man with receding but bushy hair and rimless glasses, "Ralph would drop into my office when he was in town, pick up some will or trust I was working on, glance at it, put it down with disdain and ask: 'How can you spend the rest of your life on stuff like that?'"

Jacobs is bringing some order out of Nader's orchestrated chaos, but he is also seen by some Raiders as a divisive influence. Some consider Jacobs an opportunist who waited to sign on until Nader was firmly established. Others believe Jacobs shields Nader too much from his staff. And still others think Jacobs is not a true believer in the Nader muckraking style, but is more interested in steering old friend Ralph into politics.

Jacobs and Nader's senior Raiders work in an old three-story office building just below Dupont Circle. There is not even a sign on the door, and the offices are furnished with second-hand desks and hand-me-down chairs (one in a corner of Jacobs's office is propped up with a chunk of 2 by 4). Everywhere there are files—in old metal cabinets, in cardboard boxes, in wooden apple crates, on book shelves made from planks and bricks. The Public Interest Research Group is jammed into a warren of offices in an old apartment house five blocks away.

The Center for Study of Responsive Law is tax-exempt and meets its $250,000-a-year budget largely with money from foundations and profits from the sales of Raiders' books. Major contributions have come from the Philip M. Stern Family Fund, Carnegie Corporation, Norman Fund, Jerome Levy Foundation and from the automobile muffler king turned liberal philanthropist, Gordon Sherman of Midas International.

The Public Interest Research Group is not tax-exempt, and is thus free to lobby. Its annual budget of $170,000 comes from Nader's speaking fees, which range up to $2,000 an appearance, and from the $280,000 out-of-court settlement in his libel suit against G.M. The Center for Auto Safety is financed by Consumers' Union, and Professionals for Auto Safety stays in gear with money from speaking fees.

Finances are a constant problem, and Nader is frequently criticized, even by his friends, for failing to build a dues-paying constituency. He is thinking about trying to raise money through magazine and newspaper advertisements and direct-mail solicitations. Nader has put an experimental ad in The Progressive magazine, and it met with some success. But it costs money to raise funds

through ads and mailings, and Nader is reluctant to expend what little capital he has. He is also impatient with Raiders who keep after him to find a financial angel.

"People are always asking me why we can't get some Jean Paul Getty to finance us," Nader says, "but it doesn't work that way. You have to go at it 60 different ways. If someone will come in and work for room and board, fine, or if his family will support him, fine. That's

## 66Says one of Nader's Raiders: 'Ralph would have been a great camp counselor.'99

the same as a $4,000 or $5,000 contribution right there. It's always going to take bits and pieces like that."

DESPITE Nader's great impact in some areas, most of the governmental and corporate bureaucracy still sits there, impassive and largely unmoved by the Raiders.

"It troubles me," says Jacobs, "that we haven't got the formula to translate concern for public problems into effective means for change."

It troubles Nader, too. In a recent conversation in Jacobs's office at the Center for Study of Responsive Law, Nader munched on some cookies baked by a Raider's wife and talked about his and the Raiders' future. He hasn't changed much in five years—wavy black hair a little longer but by no means modish; the shadows under his eyes a little more pronounced; his dark features perhaps a little sharp-

er. But he looked as though he were wearing the same rumpled dark gray suit, narrow dark green tie, white shirt and scuffed black shoes he wore in 1966.

Offering the tin of cookies to the others in the room—"Have one; they're good. Homemade"—and then taking a couple himself, Nader began: "What we've been trying to do is all converging now. Wherever you look the consumer is defied, whether it be the goods and services he buys, the Government services with which he is supposed to be provided or governmental and corporate pollution of the environment.

"Take the Government first," he continued, reaching for another cooky. "There have been more studies than I care to count on the Civil Service which show men willfully changing regulatory law, willful lassitude, willful manipulation of legal processes.

"How can we develop rights for citizens to initiate censure actions for public officials? Now they get decorated instead of being fired. When a citizen is adversely affected by pesticides and the Agriculture Department knowingly suppresses information about violators of the laws regulating pesticides, as has happened, why shouldn't a citizen have the right to make the public officials involved responsible for their actions?

"We're interested in the democracy, and this is more fundamental than participatory or representative democracy. We need a fundamental change in our structure so that people can initiate actions to make sure public officials are acting responsibly. I'm talking about rights plus remedies plus legal responsibilities so it can be a citizen versus the I.C.C. or the F.D.A. A civil servant should be forced to make the law work, and if he won't do it he should be censured or expelled from the Government."

**T**URNING to corporations —and taking another cooky —Nader said: "The question of the constitutionality of the corporation will be one of the biggest struggles of the next decade. It will be a greater struggle than the New Deal. The corporations must assume more responsibility for what they do. We have a right to know how much pollution is being dumped where by what corporation. Corporations are now running the ball game, and we must look at them in terms of the scene today, not in terms of their origins in the 18th and 19th centuries."

One way Nader sees to attack the problem of individual responsibility in the bureaucracies of both the Government and corporations is to turn what he calls "whistle-blowing" into an honorable action. "A 'whistle-blower,'" says Nader, "is anyone in any organization who draws a line in his own mind where responsibility to society transcends responsibility to his organization."

An example of "whistle-blowing" that Nader often cites is the G.M. engineer who first came to him with details of the tendency of Corvairs to roll over. To encourage more people to put public responsibilities above bureaucratic allegiances, Nader had one of his Raiders organize a "Whistle-Blowers' Conference" in Washington recently. At the all-day meeting in the Mayflower Hotel, speakers included Ernest Fitzgerald, a former Defense Department employe who first blew the whistle on the excessive costs in the C-5A plane contracts.

Nader has also advocated legislation giving protection to persons working for the Government or for corporations so they may be free to speak out on public-interest problems within their bureaucracies. He also has urged professional societies to make

known their readiness to defend members who seek to put the public interest above their private interests as employes.

Ever the optimist, but still pragmatic, Nader likes to reply to questions about his successes and failures with: "We always fail. The whole thing is limiting the degree of failure."

But Nader is not a man to dwell on the past. He is always looking ahead, at the moment to his "whistle-blowing" concept, to the expansion of an Oregon project that encourages students to tax themselves to finance public-interest law and research groups, to the passage of consumer legislation this year—"It will be a vintage year for consumers"—and to the development of more public-interest law offices in Washington.

"Ideally," he says, "after a report comes out on an agency like the I.C.C., filled with facts and statistics, we ought to see to it that at least a four-man law firm is set up to specialize in the I.C.C., to begin filing suits, to be a full-fledged pressure group. We need to begin this institutional monitoring on a mass basis. We know exactly what has to be done, but it takes a lot of people and money to do it."

**A**LTHOUGH Nader is usually tagged simply as a "consumer advocate" by the newspapers, he is much more than that. He is an ombudsman; a symbol to all the little people of the world; a one-man court of last resort that receives an average of 1,500 letters a week from the helpless; an inspiration to college students; the man who turned the phrase "public-interest law" into a whole new concept of the legal profession. But is he a revolutionary?

"To what extent is he interested in basic reform?"

mused a Senate staff aide who has dealt extensively with Nader and is a personal friend. "I honestly don't know. He's not much of a philosopher, is he? A lot of guys up here think that he deliberately tailors his strategy so as not to frighten off too many people."

"Ralph wants change," says old friend Ted Jacobs, "but we're not revolutionaries. Basically, Ralph wants people to be accountable for their actions. Ralph believes that the system of injustice in this country was built up block by block, and that any effort to remedy it will have to be done block by block. The basic problem we're dealing with is law and order — the law and order of corporations."

A former Government official who has dealt extensively with him says: "Nader more than any other single individual has contributed to the denigrating attitude America's young people have toward government. He has deprecated government on every major campus in this country."

"For a fellow who is so critical of the law," noted a prominent Washington lawyer who has fought more than one battle with Nader, "he has an extravagant faith in the ability of the law to right wrongs, but all of us are doing things quite differently because he's around."

"He's changed the realities we all had to deal with," said Charles Halpern, who heads up the public-interest law firm that handles many of Nader's suits, "and he's made a new world for us."

"People working for Ralph," said Raider Mark Green, "are not imbued with a sense of politics and power but with a concern for issues. We're not on ego trips. Ralph has a very effective way of psyching up his staff. He has so much enthusiasm, and that gets a lot of work out of people. Ralph would have been a great camp counselor.

"Ralph's ideal is true competition, with vigorous Government regulation to keep people competing. Socialism doesn't interest Ralph. When Ralph thinks of socialism, he doesn't think of Lenin. He thinks of Paul Rand Dixon [the former F.T.C. chairman so mercilessly criticized in the first Raider report] because he knows there will always be guys like Dixon trying to run things." ∎

# 47

# THE POLITICS OF GUN CONTROL

## REP. MICHAEL J. HARRINGTON

In April 1971, a special assistant to the Secretary of the Treasury named G. Gordon Liddy represented the Administration in a panel at the annual meeting of the National Rifle Association. Liddy, described by the NRA's magazine the *American Rifleman* as an "attorney, conservationist, and pistol shooter," told his audience that the Administration opposed gun registration and had established an "open, clear dialogue" between the White House and the firearms field. "High ranking members of the White House staff," he pointed out, "have already held two mutually helpful conferences at the White House with representatives of firearms organizations, manufacturers, and gun publications."

The NRA and its allies are doing well in their battle to frustrate advocates of gun control in this country. Yet it seems to me that the so-called gun lobby remains an enigma to its opponents, who feel on much firmer ground in analyzing the oil lobby, the dairy lobby, the highway lobby and the AMA. Most lobbies represent readily definable business interests, and that makes them easy to understand and criticize. General knowledge of the gun lobby is more limited: its sources of funds, the nature of its political tactics, the base of its membership—even its motives—are difficult to pin down.

The lobby's shadowy image is perhaps one major reason that the issue of gun control itself is so perplexing. Environmentalists have won some modest victories over the oil companies in the 1970s, and consumer advocates have forced some setbacks on the car manufacturers, but citizen activists have made little headway on gun control. To understand why, it is necessary to consider not only the lobby but the qualities of pro-control advocates, the attitudes of the American public, and the nature of Congressional response to organized and disorganized group interests.

Founded in 1871 by some officers of the New York National Guard—who had been distressed by the ineptitude of Northern riflemen during the Civil War—

*Michael Harrington is a Democratic Congressman from the 6th District, Massachusetts. He was elected in 1969 and serves on the Foreign Affairs Committee.*

the National Rifle Association today numbers more than a million dues-paying members. That makes it larger than all but three of the country's labor unions (the Teamsters, the Steelworkers and the UAW) and more than three times as big as Common Cause. The association operates out of its own modern 8-story structure in Scott Circle in Washington, where it employs a full-time staff of 250, maintains communications with 11,500 affiliated clubs, works on programs in marksmanship and firearms safety, plans and sponsors thousands of annual shooting tournaments, and publishes the *American Rifleman*. As the governing body of competitive rifle and pistol shooting in the United States, the NRA sponsors the big annual tournament for gunmen, the National Matches. Because of its semi-official status, the association also selects the rifle and pistol teams who represent the United States in the World Olympics and the Pan-American games. Its impressive range of activities is backed by assets of $19 million and an annual budget of almost $8 million.

The association is not the sum of the gun lobby armada, however, but rather its highly visible and imposing flagship. Central to the lobby's unapparent economic power are the country's gun manufacturers (Remington Arms, Winchester, Browning Arms, Colt Industries, Smith and Wesson, Savage Arms, Sturn-Ruger, Daisy) and gun dealers (New York's dignified Abercrombie & Fitch, Interarmco in Virginia), which do an estimated annual business of $1.5 billion. The gun industry's financial support is essential to the NRA, since 22 per cent of the NRA's annual income flows from manufacturer and dealer advertising in *American Rifleman*.

The industry's money also goes directly into the treasuries of sympathetic politicians. When Common Cause successfully sued the Committee to Re-Elect the President last September to force identification of secret campaign donors, a total of $345,000 was recorded from dominant shareholders of a single gun manufacturing interest—the Olin Mathieson Corp., whose Winchester-Western Division is one of the country's two largest gun makers. This dollar figure made Olin the fourth largest known source of contributions to the committee during the period before April 7, 1972, at which time new disclosure requirements went into effect.

Also charter members of the gun lobby are an astonish-

255

ing number of national hunting and sporting publications (*Field & Stream,* with an annual circulation of 1.5 million; *Guns and Ammo,* with 200,000; *Shooting Times, Sports Afield, Trap and Field, Shooting Industry, Argosy, Guns and Hunting, Gunsport, Gun World, Guns*), all of them pipe lines to the 21 million Americans who participate in hunting, and all of them recipients of advertising revenue from the firearms industry.

Surprisingly, the lobby includes conservation and wildlife preservation groups like the National Wildlife Federation, the Wildlife Management Institute, the Isaac Walton League, and numerous state wildlife and conservation departments. The key to this improbable environmental link is also economic—firearms hunters spend about $72 million a year on hunting licenses and $27 million a year in federal excise taxes on guns and ammunition, most of which is committed by state laws to conservation and wildlife programs.

Finally, the membership of the NRA includes hundreds of state and local political leaders, more than twenty-five Congressmen, and the President of the United States, who became a "life member" in 1957 and who remains officially on the rolls, though the Administration claims he resigned after the 1968 election.

Despite these varied and impressive trappings of power, the most formidable source of the gun lobby's clout lies in its grass-roots following—those million NRA members, 21 million hunters and an estimated 60 million American households which have guns. For the most part, these people are decent and law-abiding, and the importance they attach to firearms defies the arguments of gun-control proponents in Congress and elsewhere.

The views of those who oppose gun control are easy to describe: people have the right to bear arms for pleasure and self-protection without interference from big government; criminals will get guns despite gun-control laws; all gun-control proposals—whether they advocate registration, licensing, record keeping, or anything else—are undesirable because they will lead inevitably to other more restrictive measures.

Gun-control opponents promote these beliefs through several methods.

*They make use of political contacts in the executive branch and Congress,* as the Gordon Liddy incident illustrates.

*They use campaign contributions* from sources like the Olin Corp.

*They put the pressure on opposing groups.* This past June, *American Rifleman,* in an editorial entitled, "Say Goodbye to the Y?," reported that the YWCA "had thrown its full feminine weight" behind gun control at its annual assembly. The group's decision "may turn out to be a self-inflicted financial problem," the *Rifleman* observed. "The Sportsmen's Alliance of Michigan, a highly active and vocal organization of gun owners, has already expressed the view that its members should refrain from contributing to community drives whose proceeds go in part to supporting the YWCA. Others may follow suit." They may indeed, but they probably wouldn't have if the magazine hadn't given the ploy national circulation.

*They use their extensive media connections to misstate the details of proposed bills, and to play to fears about race, government domination and subversion by radicals.* In July 1965, when the modest proposals to regulate mail-order sales were first proposed in the Senate, *Guns and Ammo* ran an article called "The Real Facts Behind S. 1592" which began, "If you, as a collector, hunter, target shooter, gun dealer, gunsmith, or small manufacturer, wish to lose your rights to own guns, to go hunting, target shooting, or deal in firearms, read no further. This bill will ultimately confiscate your guns, and make it impossible for you to hunt or stay in business."

In fact, the 1965 proposal, which was not enacted into law until three years later, was a thoroughly mild reform. All persons selling firearms are now required to obtain a federal license, the interstate sale of firearms through the mails is prohibited, and the possession of firearms by certain people—including convicted criminals, aliens residing illegally in the United States, and mental incompetents—is forbidden. The law poses no threat whatsover to respectable collectors, hunters, target shooters, gun dealers, gunsmiths or small manufacturers.

Later that year, after the Watts rioting, *Guns and Ammo* editorialized, "In the final analysis, rampaging hoodlumism such as experienced in Los Angeles, Chicago and other major cities may yet be a blessing in disguise which will do a great deal to preserve our precious right to keep and bear arms."

*But most of all, the lobby stirs an avalanche of grass-roots sentiment, usually in the form of letters.* Ultimately, as I suggested earlier, it is the lobby's outside following, rather than its inside connections, that most effectively discourages Congressional action. The lobby's ability to elicit letters from its constituency is phenomenal.

During the 1965 controversy, for example, the NRA sent a bulletin to all its members, urging them to write the President and Congress about the mail-order bill. "Write now," urged the NRA, "or it may be too late." Included with the letter was a list of instructions, entitled, "How to Write Your Letter." The bulletin featured exhortations like, "Do not doubt for one second the effectiveness of your one voice," and "If the battle is lost, it will be your loss and that of all who follow you."

*Guns and Ammo* chimed in, saying in its August issue, "Nothing impresses an elected lawmaker as much as a massive amount of mail from people who vote in his district. It is the one proven way to persuade a legislator to act."

Journalist Richard Harris describes in *The New Yorker* the results the association's bulletin produced:

> During the month preceding the campaign set off by the NRA, the White House received fifty letters on S. 1592 [the Senate bill], divided just about equally pro and con. During the following month, it received 12,000 letters, all but a few opposing the bill. Within two weeks after Orth [an official of the NRA] alerted his followers, the Subcommittee to Investigate Juvenile Delinquency [which was handling S. 1592] got 1,400 letters, forty-seven of them favoring the bill, and the Commerce Committee [also considering the legislation] got over 2,000, four of them favoring it.

The reaction was predictable. Sen. Jacob Javits was quoted as saying, "I have received an enormous amount of mail, really enormous, almost unbelievable, expressing opposition to this bill." Sen. Gale McGee of Wyoming said, "I can recall no issue, either international or domestic, in my tenure in the Senate that has aroused the people of Wyoming as this one."

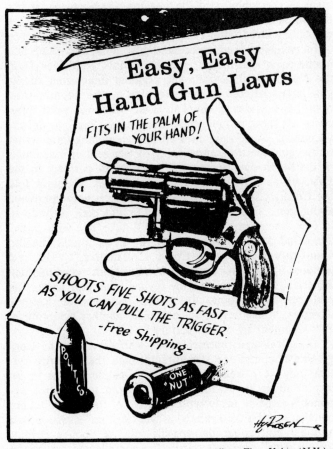

Albany Times-Union (N.Y.)
*Praise the Law and Pass the Ammunition!*

Three years later, the deaths of Robert Kennedy and Martin Luther King triggered a temporary counter reaction in favor of gun control, but even then the lobby was so strong that the bill which finally passed was a much amended ghost of its former self. The lobby, however, still declared war on supporters of the 1968 measure, and chose its targets for political retribution accordingly. "Every Congressman who lost his seat in 1970 is convinced he lost because he voted for the gun-control bill," said Rep. Abner Mikva, a leading control advocate, who lost his own seat two years later. *American Rifleman*, in an article reviewing plusses and minuses of the 1970 elections, began the column by quoting Maryland's Joseph Tydings, another spokesman for control who had just lost his re-election fight in the Senate, as saying, "I suppose this will discourage others from taking on the gun lobby."

At this point in a discussion of gun control and Congress' failure to support it, control advocates can be expected to point out that, as early as April 1938, the Gallup poll showed 84 per cent of the American public in favor of requiring firearms registration. In eight polls conducted by the Gallup organization between 1959 and 1972, posing the question, "Do you favor or oppose a law requiring a police permit to buy guns?," those in favor have never dropped below 68 per cent.

Given these polls, supporters of control say, the politician should realize that he has little to fear from the gun lobby, that the lobby simply looks bigger than it is by generating an intense reaction from its hard-core membership, and that, in fact, the case for gun control is almost universally conceded.

However, a special interest does not necessarily have to convince a politician that its positions reflect the feelings of the majority of voters in his district or state. In elections, politicians worry not only about the views of the majority but about the possible sources of the *margin* of victory or defeat. They believe that most of their constituents make up their minds according to their general perceptions of a variety of issues, and that supporting a concept like gun control is not likely, by itself, to win many additional votes. On the other hand, elected officials may sense that the anti-control voters mobilized by the gun lobby are apt to engage in a kind of bullet voting, and decide their voting preferences on the basis of the gun question alone. This view of gun-control opponents and other special interest voters, which is not calculated but intuitive, leads the politician to treat particular groupings in his area—union people, peace activists, members of particular professions—with great care, especially if they have a high degree of internal organization. Politicians want very much to avoid controversy, and will go a long way to placate people who harass them.

In that case, it may be asked, why haven't gun-control supporters organized to provide the margin of victory or defeat in the other direction? The answer, I think, is the same that explains why there is no well-organized group to oppose the oil interests on the depletion allowance or the medical-health establishment on national health insurance: "special interests" can focus resources and efforts, while the "general interest" is by definition broad, unfocused and difficult to defend.

The pro-gun control forces in this country tend to be governmental agencies and officials concerned with the entire area of crime prevention, religious and civic organizations whose primary activities lie elsewhere, "public interest" and "citizen action" groups designed to represent the public against the special interests but spread thin across the entire spectrum of political issues, and public figures who lend their names and time to the cause. Thus, in 1972 the Americans for Democratic Action assembled a coalition which included Detroit Mayor Roman Gribbs, the American Baptist Convention, Common Cause, the ACLU, the AFL-CIO, the UAW and the American Jewish Committee. In 1968, after the shock of the assassinations, former astronaut John Glenn chaired an "Emergency Committee for Gun Control" composed of people like Warren Beatty, Truman Capote, Joe DiMaggio, Vince Lombardi and Archibald Cox.

Both coalitions were modestly funded, loosely organized, and designed to self-destruct at the conclusion of the particular legislative fight then being waged. The National Rifle Association, meanwhile, was going full steam before they started and after they disbanded.

Currently, consumer groups, tax reform groups, political reform groups and women's groups all see gun control as a desirable goal, but the issue falls in the chinks between each organization's specific program planks. "We're an organization of somewhat limited resources," an official of the National Women's Political Caucus said recently, "and we've had to devote those resources to matters directly affecting women's ability to participate in the political process. As far as gun control is concerned, I can't think of a time when the issue has even come up."

The only group which now exists solely to promote gun control and organize for its adoption is the National Council for a Responsible Firearms Policy, headed by David Steinberg. Steinberg is the most informed and thoughtful proponent of gun control in the country, but because the council is small and unable to attract substantial funds, he must serve as its only staff member in a part-time capacity. He circulates on Capitol Hill, consulting with committees and interested Congressmen, providing solitary counterbalance to the NRA's 250 employees on the other side of the issue.

Thus, members of Congress confront a situation in which a special interest is organized to threaten them with the margin of defeat, while the "public interest" is represented with tenacity and dedication, but without adequate backing. Under such circumstances, it might still be reasonable to expect our elected political leaders to *lead,* to take the dangerous but responsible policy position, and to find ways to educate and mobilize those substantial majorities who, according to the Gallup poll, agree with gun control.

In fact, quite often a politician may feel that he could defeat the economic, political and media strength of a given special interest—if he devoted a major part of his political capital to the effort. But very likely he will have a variety of such interests to cope with, and rather than take on all of them, he is apt to fall back to one of the first precepts of play-it-safe politics: people often don't give you credit for agreeing with them, but they never forget when you disagree. The politician, particularly the incumbent, is likely to settle for the *status quo* and keep his boats from rocking.

In my opinion, this outlook characterizes much of the behavior of Congress, which ordinarily takes so much time to see which way the wind is blowing that the storm is over before it ever acts—whether in response to the war in Vietnam, Presidential vetoes of social programs, or the gun situation.

Moreover, the Congressional inclination toward caution becomes more pronounced in the absence of Presidential pressure to act. The 1968 laws regulating mail-order sales passed only after President Johnson, acting through people like Atty. Gen. Ramsey Clark, made the matter a legislative priority. Attitudes changed greatly in the White House after 1968, as I attempted to illustrate at the beginning of this article.

These points about interest group tactics and the re-actions they draw from politicians are probably true for many controversies. But it seems to me that there are attributes of the gun question which make it distinct from, say, the oil lobby problem and the pharmaceutical lobby problem. While the gun lobby has many of the marks of a conventional special interest which sets out to frustrate a widely acknowledged "public interest," quite a few members of Congress are disturbed by the grass-roots element of the lobby, and the nagging apprehension, if not the outright conviction, that the voters in their areas are not telling Dr. Gallup everything he ought to know.

In weighing these apprehensions, it is important that intellectuals, journalists, reformers and politicians from the Northeast understand the regional dimensions of the gun issue. Almost everywhere else in the country—the South, the Midwest, the Far West, wherever rural influences are more pronounced—firearms are basic to the environment. According to Carl Bakal, a long-time writer on the gun question, an amazing 59 per cent of individuals in the South own a gun, compared to 34 per cent in the East. An aide to South Dakota Sen. James Abourezk told the *Chicago Tribune,* "Our constituency is very emotional about guns. Guns are a way of life and their attitude is, if you take away my guns, you'll take my wife next." *The Wall Street Journal* wrote, in an editorial, "Behind Gun-Control Furor: A Clash of Cultures," "The real pressure for gun control comes from cosmopolitan America, which sees it as the plainest common sense. The real resistance comes from the redoubts of bedrock America, which sees gun control as another symptom of encroachment by a new culture."

The rural area representatives who dominate the Congressional committee structure through the seniority system may very well feel they have ample reason to interpret those thousands of letters from gun-control opponents as being fairly representative of their constituents' convictions. To their minds, a "yes" or "no" question in a national poll about the specific idea of "police permits to buy guns" does not mirror the complicated feelings of the voters back home.

Similar conclusions have apparently been reached in the White House, where the Administration's ardent courtship of the National Rifle Association fits nicely into its "Southern strategy" and its appeals to "Middle America." To many politicians, as well as to many other observers, there appear to be a number of social and cultural factors in American life today which make broad, unambivalent public support of gun control unlikely.

One can begin by reciting the historical factors, unique to the United States—our nostalgia for the American frontier, reverence for self-reliance and individual strength, and insistence on a tough kind of masculinity in our country's males. In a quite pessimistic essay, *America as a Gun Culture,* historian Richard Hofstadter writes that "for millions of American boys, learning to shoot and above all graduating from toy guns and receiving the first real rifle of their own were milestones of life, veritable rites of passage that certified arrival at manhood."

These traditional inclinations have assumed a fresh tone of immediacy with the stunning growth of the nation's crime rate. Millions of citizens genuinely fear their neighborhood streets after dark, and the notion of defending oneself and one's family, of "fighting back," rather than relying solely on the police, has apparently gained great appeal, despite the proven impracticality and ineffectuality of such efforts. Women enroll in self-defense courses, *New York* magazine chronicles the growth of citizen vigilante groups, Sen. William Proxmire evokes a national reaction when he stands up to two muggers who accost him during his jogging. "I wouldn't want to see a lot of gun-control laws," a young volunteer for a major women's rights organization remarks, "if it would deprive women of a means of defending themselves."

An additional current of feeling reinforces public reservations about gun control, a current which, if anything, is apt to grow stronger in light of Richard Nixon's disturbing use of Presidential power. "Another belief of American gun enthusiasts enjoys a wide currency in the United States, extending to a good many liberals, civil libertarians, and even radicals," historian Hofstadter remarks. "It is the idea that popular access to arms is an important counterpoise to tyranny."

A dozen years ago, invocation of this fear of centralized government as a reason for resisting gun control would have been dismissed as near paranoia. Now, while Professor Hofstadter rightly describes belief in the value of "popular access to arms" as both naive and dangerous, the suspicions behind the belief perhaps cannot be so easily argued away. Recent evidence has emerged of the government's illegally wiretapping newspapermen and its own officials, misusing data-bank information, burglarizing private offices, and spying on dissident groups. It isn't altogether surprising that many people might hesitate to accept assurances that the federal government would never abuse its regulatory powers over firearms.

*The Christian Science Monitor,* a consistent advocate of gun control, recently featured an article with the headline, "Many Gun Owners Distrust Government." When considerable numbers of citizens come to distrust the individuals they have democratically elected to office, that seems to me one of the greatest tragedies which can befall a democracy.

I have been most concerned with describing the nature of the gun lobby. Though I have not discussed them here, the arguments for gun control—the statistics on the number of firearms homicides, the correlation in particular states between strict control laws and low firearms murder rates, and the history of effective gun control in England and other countries—are quite well known. A question remains: what can be done to advance the cause of gun control in the face of the forces I have been discussing?

A wholly satisfactory answer would require an additional article, but I can suggest some ways to begin. First, gun-control supporters should proceed with an awareness of the issue's complexities, and especially with respect and empathy for the concerns which motivate the grass-roots opposition.

Second, gun control should be made part of a tough, effective anti-crime program for the nation. Conventional liberal analyses of national issues have not been cohesive and convincing in the area of crime prevention; yet many Americans will hesitate at the most modest regulation of their firearms as long as they feel threatened by criminals.

Third, gun-control advocates should work to elect a President who will curb the federal government's increasing incursions into individual civil rights and liberties, as well as institute an anti-crime program which includes gun control. Given the imperfections of Congress and the regional strength of the gun lobby, strong national leadership on the issue must come from the Chief Executive.

The activist core of the gun lobby—the NRA, the manufacturers and dealers and the hunting and gun publications—will persist in fighting effective gun control. But the grass-roots element, essential to the lobby's continued strength, could, in my opinion, be persuaded of the merits of the pro-control position. These people have been grief-stricken by the assassinations of the last decade, believe in the responsible use of firearms, wish to be free of the fear of crime, and want to trust their government. In the past, liberal reformers have had trouble talking persuasively to "bedrock America" about gun control—or, for that matter, about the welfare problem, civil rights, dissent, the cities, the 1972 Presidential election and change in general. However, these are the people who have to be convinced; then progress in gun control could very likely follow.   □

# 48

# AMERICA'S NEW RIGHT

## By Andrew Kopkind

**A decade after the antiwar movement, the left is in eclipse. But another activist campaign is gaining momentum. The issue this time: save the nuclear family**

The talk of Bensenville, Illinois, is all about women's liberation, homosexual rights and abortion. Like thousands of communities around the country, this placid, featureless town in the far western reaches of suburban Chicago has suddenly been ignited by the burning social issues of the decade. The *Bensenville Chronicle* is heavy with hortatory letters and earnest editorials. The auditorium at Blackhawk Junior High School rings with righteous rhetoric. Groups of militant women have left their noodle rings and needlepoint and meet into the night to draft pamphlets, plan demonstrations and raise their consciousness. As this short summer wanes, the grassroots movements in Bensenville show all the familiar road signs of popular political struggle that Americans have been reading about since the sixties: that is, every sign but one. In Bensenville, the arrows all point right.

Dorothy Waldvogel, a 46-year-old mother, Mormon and militant in the Bensenville backlash, sells sweet corn by the streetside on the outskirts of town. In the lush, late harvest season, her farm wagon is laden with the ripe vegetables she and her husband grow on 53 acres of leased land. Behind the stand, her 1968 Buick LeSabre is filled with propaganda produce no less ripe than the corn: copies of "The Phyllis Schlafly Report" ("International Women's Year: A Front for Radicals and Lesbians"), a wallet-size comic book denouncing the Equal Rights Amendment ("Do you want the SEXES fully integrated like the RACES?"), and Xeroxes of a letter of commendation and support Waldvogel received from North Carolina's Senator Jesse Helms, a Washington anchor for the anti-ERA, anti-homosexual and anti-abortion axis.

"You sort of hear things that you don't really feel good about," Waldvogel said, recalling the first phases of her radicalization in right-wing politics last winter. "There was abortion, and then the homosexual movement was getting *so* big. And then Illinois was the key state for the ERA. You know something is wrong, but you need someone to tell you how to get involved.

"So some of the girls down at the church made up a list of state legislators—I don't know how they got the names, but they did. I sat down and wrote 65 letters, all about the importance of the family and how male and female are different. I mean, how can a law make males and females the same? To me, the ERA is an attack on our system of life—call it tradition—the way that God intended it to be."

Waldvogel's convenient theology may be widely disputed; the unisex Hell prophesized by ERA opponents could exist nowhere on this earth. But she can find convincing confirmation of her belief system in the mundane success of her comrades' campaigns to make God's Word into common law. Beyond Bensenville blow winds of change that have dramatically shifted direction since the late storms of liberal and Left protest subsided.

The ERA was defeated in Illinois and every other state (save Indiana) where it's been at issue in the last two years; chances for its ratification by at least four more states in time for the

261

# Anti-abortion action

On August 16, the National Conference of Catholic Bishops announced a drive to stamp out abortion in every aspect of public policy and private practice in America. Even before the current outbreak of anti-abortion fervor, nine states had voted to call a Constitutional Convention to write an abortion prohibition; anti-abortionists vow that the question will be put to every state legislature come January, and if 25 more ratify the call, the first such convention since 1789 will be assembled. "And that would be the most dangerous political game in American history," ACLU Director Aryeh Neier has warned.

Illinois has led the way in the holy war against abortion. It was, after all, in Chicago that anti-abortion pickets heckled Jimmy Carter just as his campaign for the presidency was picking up steam, and Auxiliary Bishop Alfred Abramowicz made "right-to-life" an issue by bringing up the delicate subject at a Carter rally. And Congressman Henry Hyde, author of the federal anti-abortion laws, is an Illinois native son.

Milking the sacred cow for all it's worth is Joseph Scheidler, chief organizer for a coalition of anti-abortion forces in Illinois, loosely grouped under the title "Illinois Pro-Life Coalition, Inc." Scheidler holes up in a murky office behind the Chicago Board of Trade at the edge of the Loop. A single secretary juggles the phones, makes excuses for missed appointments, and passes out literature showing mutilated fetuses; meanwhile, Scheidler commands the troops in the nation's most successful campaign against abortion.

Scheidler was reportedly a week away from ordination as a priest when he slid back into secular life and opted for a career as a lay crusader. "And it *is* a crusade," he told me amiably. "We are righteous as hell. We consider ourselves the good guys, the white hats."

Two years ago, Scheidler's crew succeeded in getting the state legislature to pass the most restrictive anti-abortion law in the country–making it illegal even to *advocate* "prohibited" acts of abortion. That law was stopped by a court injunction, but this year the legislature passed four more anti-abortion laws in its place.

"It was an orgy of repression," Lois Kraft, a Chicago attorney who works with right-to-abortion groups, said with a shudder. The laws banned Medicaid abortions, again prohibited advocacy of certain abortion rights, and protected doctors who refused to perform or assist in abortions, even in cases where a mother's life is in danger.

Scheidler tries to be careful to keep the abortion issue separate from other causes, but his enthusiasm sometimes will not allow sharp distinctions. One August day, for instance, his anti-abortion telephone "action line" was running on about "welfare fraud" and its connecton, somehow, to "abortion mills." He claims to get 250 or 300 calls a day on his hot-line, and the subliminal messages are not lost on the callers. They will respond, sooner or later, with reflex reaction on the range of New Right issues.
—**A.K.**

1979 deadline new seem bleak. Ordinances guaranteeing protection against discrimination to homosexuals lost decisively in the South Florida referendum as well as in city councils and state capitols across the nation; previously progressive Austin, Texas, for example, voted down a gay rights bill that the local Civil Liberties Union director said "would have passed with all flags flying" two years ago. Congress, the Supreme Court and several state legislatures have grievously wounded the new body of laws giving women the right to choose abortion, and the nation Catholic hierarchy is steamrolling the drive for an anti-abortion amendment to the U. S. Constitution.

Behind the New Right vanguard on the "pro-family," anti-liberation front are troops fighting scores of battles that may seem separate, but appeal to the same backlash sensibilities. Sooner or later, pro-family activists find themselves *pro*: death penalty, Laetrile, nuclear power, local police, Panama Canal, saccharin, FBI, CIA, defense budget, public prayer and real estate growth. More likely than not, they are *anti*: busing, welfare, public employee unions, affirmative action, amnesty, marijuana, communes, gun control, pornography, the 55-m.p.h. speed limit, day-care centers, religious ecumenism, sex education, car pools and the Environmental Protection Agency. Of course there are exceptions everywhere; Boston's leading conservative theorist, David Brudnoy, is as passionately for gay rights as he is against abortion rights. Former

John Birch Society director John Rousselot, now a California congressman, says privately that he is for freedom of choice with marijuana as well as Laetrile. But the overwhelming political significance lies in the new conjunction of all those issues, not in the exceptions.

Liberals, radicals, reformists and progressives who have done battle these many years on the opposite side of those questions would like to believe that the ideology and the logistics of the new right wing movements are devised and controlled by a few conspirators at the top—Phyllis Schlafly, Jesse Helms, a Catholic cardinal here or a John Birch birdwatcher there: a handful of Reaganites, racists and young Republicans. But the Left's devil theory is no more plausible than the Right's. There is a great social upheaval at the heart of America that now finds an expression in the new constellation of traditionalist, individualist and fundamentalist movements. It feeds the established politicians and practitioners of the Right, and it is well fed by them. But to disregard its authentic roots in home-town America is to misread the new national mood, and to become its more vulnerable victim.

Nobody's perfect, but Dorothy Waldvogel is as nearly perfect a product of the new social backlash as may be found in its Midwest heartland. "I'd rather be home cooking and caring for my family, doing embroidery, than what I'm doing," she told me earnestly. "But a force greater than myself is magnetically drawing me to pursue it. I guess I feel a responsibility to inform other

women what's going on. We've just got to protect the family.

"The family!" she repeated excitedly. "Where else can you go at Christmas but back to your family?"

If a lonely Whopper in a deserted Burger King is the pervasive fear-fantasy of the American seventies, turkey and the trimmings *en famille* is surely an alternative of choice. There may be other credible options, but none is immediately apparent in Bensenville. For Dorothy Waldvogel, as for many other women of her social location, "the family" is the best available rock in a storm-tossed sea of contradictions.

Out there on Thorndale Road where she sells her produce and peddles her pamphlets, the contradictions tumble down at every turn. The pastoral peace is shattered by the artillery thunder of jets streaking across the cornfields from O'Hare Airport, just a few miles to the east. Suburbia is approaching almost as fast: a "Locate Your Business Here" sign has gone up a few hundred yards down the road from the Waldvogel farm stand, and a fast-food franchise occupies a nearby intersection. Soon enough, there will be no land left for planting.

Bensenville's biggest billboard advertises the Unisex Hair Styling shop, and despite Waldvogel's nostalgia for strict sex roles, she shows up each morning at the old stand in men's shoes, white socks, blue jeans, a plain shirt—and hair as long and loose as Peter Frampton's unisex hair stylist ever created. Only a thin veneer of pale lipstick prevents her full participation in the integrated sex model.

"I understand what women go through," Waldvogel confided. "I've been divorced. I know about unequal credit laws. I couldn't get the water company to put the bill in my name. I needed that law against sex discrimination. But I don't know what these women libbers are trying to do with this country except get us stirred up. I think to myself, what are they doing to me out there? *What are they doing?*" Her voice rose in passion and evident fear, just as a customer pulled up to the stand for two dozen ears.

Married and a mother before she was 17, Waldvogel held her first family nucleus together for a quarter of a century. She and her husband built a successful janitorial service in an Indiana town, then sold it to a partner whose business behavior was a bit too sharp for the Waldvogels' liking. They had moved to Arizona and begun a similar business when she decided her husband was no better than their previous partner. "We just didn't hold to the same values," she said flatly.

One day during the worst years of her domestic turmoil, Mormon missionaries came to the door on a proselytizing tour, and in a flash Dorothy Waldvogel saw the light. "I had been hooked on cigarettes and I hated myself for it, but when I started going to church I was able to stop smoking," she confessed. "That's what churches are supposed to do — to teach us to understand ourselves and to do what's good for us."

What was good for her was to leave her husband, pack up the kids, and return to her roots in the Midwest — where she promptly met a Mormon widower; she was remarried in a year. Life was complete with the new family, the farm stand, embroidery and church socials — until the ERA vote came up in Illinois. In the supporting warmth of Mormon conservatism, Waldvogel began her activist career by lobbying legislators against ratification. Then she "and a bunch of the girls" made a bigger plunge into politics. One night last June, they piled into a car and headed for their state's preparatory meeting for the International Women's Year National Conference scheduled for November in Houston.

The 50 state IWY meetings have provided the battlegrounds this year in the eruptive war of women against women. The purpose is to set agendas and choose delegates for Houston; but the real prize of battle is the definition of feminism: whether Americans will accept the new terms of liberation, or restore an earlier concept of womanhood based on separation and inequality. Sizable stores of political power reside in each camp.

Despite furious fights, feminists of the left — led by the National Organization of Women in a coalition of liberationist groups — have been able to withstand the fire from anti-ERA, anti-lesbian, anti-abortion forces of the Right. There have been some disasters for the NOW side: Mormons in Utah, fundamentalists in Mississippi and Catholics in several midwestern states have routed the Left with religious fervor. But at the June meeting in Normal, Illinois, 500 women bearing backlash banners were beaten by the NOW liberationists after bitter political confrontations.

Whatever else that event was, it became a major milestone in the political odyssey of Dorothy Waldvogel.

"I have never been the same since," she said with a shake of her long hair. She and "the girls" walked out in protest against the Left's "manipulation" of the meeting, and caucused later with the assistance of organizers from Phyllis Schlafly's ferocious Eagle Forum, the nationwide anti-ERA commissariat, based in a suburb of St. Louis, Missouri. What they all decided was to make a permanent counter-revolution against women's liberation in Illinois.

Waldvogel hurried back to Bensenville and began writing letters and pamphleteering. She broke into print on the "Opinion" page of the *Bensenville Chronicle*, decrying the resolutions of the Normal IWY meeting, which advocated "rights for homosexuals, gays and lesbians to marry and adopt children. We need to unite," she argued, "if we are to stop the destruction of our families and the decline of moral values being thrust upon us."

So enthusiastic was the response to that letter that Waldvogel was propelled to the leadership of the backlash movement in Bensenville. She easily got the use of a hall at Blackhawk Junior High for a rally of her partisans. By the merest coincidence, Phyllis Schlafly was due to pass through Bensenville that night on her way to the airport (by a circuitous but opportune route) and agreed to address the throng. Almost 300 people packed the room, donated $105 in small change (reimbursing Waldvogel for the cost of printing flyers) and convinced Waldvogel that her immediate future, at least, lay in political organizing.

"I've gone all around town," she reported proudly. "I went over to the Catholic church and talked to the priest. I told him that we as Christians have to unite against the evil that's taking over this country. It's evil to allow murder of little babies under our Constitution. It's evil to allow homosexuals to marry and be adoptive parents. It's evil to have federally funded day-care centers, although it's not evil to have babysitters of your

own—as long as you don't encourage it in the whole country. It's evil to bus your children across the city when you live across the street from a perfectly good school."

She gave me a perfectly good, ripe red tomato and a tiny cardboard amulet of Morton's salt. It was perfectly delicious. I jumped down from my perch on her wagon and prepared to leave Bensenville when she indicated she had one last thought to convey.

"You see," she began, "there are evil things and there are good things and we are put on this earth to choose. That's our whole purpose. My own belief is that Lucifer is trying to make it hard for people to have children, to have families. So I *have* to get involved. I can't just stay home and do nothing. After what I've learned, I can't think of anything any more. I put down an afghan I was making for my daughter's graduation that day I went to the meeting at Normal, and I can't even finish it."

Far from Thorndale Road, the "magnetic force" compelling Dorothy Waldvogel to action may be less mysterious than she imagines. The contradictions of her life and hard times and her own social predicament seem genuinely perplexing; but its political display in particular issues is arranged by cynical and often sinister figures in the institutions and offices of the organized Right.

For although Lucifer and the Lord may be contending for Waldvogel's soul, it is more immediately Phyllis Schlafly, Jesse Helms and other earthlings who are fighting for her body—for the phalanxes of their movements, their organizations, and their election campaigns. The New Right of small-town women, urban Catholics and working-class whites starts only with unformed fears and perplexities. Someone else, with different interests, other agendas and wider connections will translate them into a coherent political force.

"The New Right is led by the old fascists," argues NOW president Ellie Smeal. "It's the same old people who have been around since Joe McCarthy's time and the beginning of the John Birch Society. But now they're wrapping themselves in the cloth of 'the family,' instead of racism and super patriotism. The old right of the fifties never died; it's just been reborn."

What is *new* about the New Right is its generation in the "pro-family" issues and its creation of a logical place for women leaders in those concerns. The "traditional" family is indeed being transformed; no right-wing fanatic has to convince Americans that the old styles of long, stable marriages, lots of loving children, extended family structures, and firm sex-role stereotypes are out of fashion—if not yet out of existence.

But while the hidden economic and political pressures that distort the old forms are extremely complicated, symbolic enemies are easier to conjure out front. Homosexuals, abortionists and liberated women make perfect targets of convenience for baffled and misled traditionalists. The "government"—in disrepute on several scores—can be blamed for every imagined affront to family stability and piety, from busing and day-care centers to prayer prohibitions and *Hustler* on the newsstands.

"In a peculiar way, the predominance of women in all these new right-wing groups seems to be another version of women's liberation," national ACLU Director Aryeh Neier observed recently. "Women are asserting themselves and taking on serious political responsibilities."

Similar binds do not entail like solutions. Dorothy Waldvogel in Bensenville and her New Left counterparts in Berkeley or the Bronx may have similar problems with their marriages, their work and their utility companies. They may feel attracted and repelled by strict sex roles, consumerist capitalism, and government interventions in their everyday affairs. They may both yearn for a peaceable kingdom, a happy home and a turkey dinner. But one chooses the women's movement and the other the backlash.

The busing battles in Boston, Louisville and Los Angeles have all been led by newly politicized women. In Boston, for example, Elvira "Pixie" Palladino rode her notoriety as a busing protester on the streets of one Italian working-class neighborhood into an at-large elected seat on the city's School Committee. In Los Angeles, Bobbi Fiedler parlayed her anti-busing activism into an election victory over an entrenched liberal member of that city's Board of Education.

Women were in the vanguard of the furious campaign in Wheeling, West Virginia, to rid school libraries of "progressive" and "permissive" textbooks. Women helped organize the successful recall election this summer in LaCrosse, Wisconsin, which removed five members of the local school district who had voted to fire a brutally authoritarian school principal; the principal is now back on the job. Ellen McCormack made startlingly strong showings in many states last year with her anti-abortion presidential candidacy. Governor Ella Grasso of Connecticut, elected as a conventional liberal, has made most of her political hay on backlash issues, such as her opposition to gay rights, marijuana-law liberalization and abortions for the poor. Anita Bryant and Phyllis Schlafly are perhaps the two most powerful "populist" political figures of the year: they have slowed, though not stopped, the forward march of the two great movements for human liberation of the seventies.

None of that comes as a surprise to Ellie Smeal. "In fact, we *are* a threat," she says confidently of women in the liberationist movement. "So the right-wing men are organizing their women in self-defense. I don't feel that the real opposition to us is 'frightened women'; women are no more scared of this world than are men. The real power is held by the men who gain from our inequality. Women make 57 percent of the income that men make, so someone out there is getting two workers for the price of one."

It is true that behind the women of the New Right lurk men in a political role—whether the women recognize it or not. Women have the time—and a taste for moral issues taught early in life by custom and society—to do the low-level organizing, while men make the profits.

"Look at religion," Smeal advised me. "The churches are made up of women, but policy is made by the men." The education system operates on the same principle. And, increasingly, district-level political campaigns are staffed by women workers—while men pull the last levers.

What is *old* about the New Right, then, is its manipulation—however late or limp—by the old men in the old institutions. Politicians such as Georgia Congressman Larry McDonald, Illinois Congressman Henry Hyde, Utah Senator Orrin Hatch and North Carolina Senator Jesse Helms have seized upon "pro-family" sentiment in the way they and their fellows once used "pro-American" patriotism to rally reaction and build a right-wing movement in America.

Suddenly this summer, it is growling again. Not many weeks ago, informal meetings of right-wing organizers began in Washington to swap strategies and make plans for the coming campaigns. "The first meeting consisted of about a dozen people from conservative organizations who committed themselves to the opposition on a number of specific issues, like the Panama Canal treaties," a veteran Washington lobbyist (who is cautious enough to insist on anonymity) reported. One key strategist was Paul Russo, once a Reagan campaign field worker, who now acts as a liaison between the Republican National Committee and the far-right movements.

Russo represents his boss, Charles Black, campaign director of the GOP committee, who until recently headed up a militant new right-wing outfit called the

# Backlash culture

Manifestations of the New Right are not always immediately discernible. Future-shocked housewives may provide the political impetus, but the "New Right style" is swathed in sophistication and is embraced most heartily by old lefties, gays and kids. Thus:

• When Barry Manilow thrills his teeny-bopper fans with a medley of commercial jingles, it's more than Corporate Art. "You deserve a break today" and "Have it your way" provide a subliminal message for the otherwise impotent citizen. New Populist anthems?

• Punk rock assumes a family against which to rebel and seeks to reaffirm a sense of gender-imperative. Butch is back—even for girls.

• Imamu A. Baraka, nee LeRoi Jones, a reborn Communist, denounced homosexuality as a "class" disease.

• New York liberal intellectuals, chafed by semantics and despairing of public taste, finally drew the line at *Hustler* and engaged in a bitter dispute over Larry Flynt's Constitutional rights.

• Left-wing pragmatists view the ERA and Gay Rights as political kamikaze runs.

• The new "decadence," once part of a gay subculture, has been mass-marketed and homogenized. Computerized disco franchises—identical as Burger Kings—now provide the youth of America with a no-fault exhaust system.

• The Unique Clothing Warehouse, a hip purveyor of recycled uniforms and other military gear, has opened an annex at Macy's.

• Cocaine, the preferred drug of the Third Reich, is now the preferred drug of the Bloomingdale's circuit.

• The last scene from *Star Wars* is a direct, shot-by-shot steal from *Triumph of the Will*, a documentary by Hitler's propagandist, Leni Riefenstahl.

• Erstwhile Yippie Jerry Rubin is attending a seminar in Money Consciousness.

• Self-help books proselytize power as its own justification; mediocrity as its own reward.

• New women's sex novels of the confessional genre contain the same moral as gothics and *Cosmo* . . . and echo the sentiments of this summer's hottest single: "I need a man!"

• Mental health, once a national concern, has been regurgitated as the Me Decade. *I* deserve a break today.

—Tracy Young

**Dorothy Waldvogel at her vegetable stand: "How can a law make males and females the same?"**

National Conservative Political Action Committee (NCPAC). The NCPAC's fund-raiser is Richard A. Viguerie, the mercurial reader and adviser for extremist campaigns and causes—from George Wallace ($6 million) to Senator Strom Thurmond to former California Education Superintendent Max Rafferty, and indirectly to Anita Bryant and Phyllis Schlafly. Viguerie is also one of the dozen key strategists in the Washington area meetings.

Viguerie's publication, *Conservative Digest*, lays out the lines of the new political strategy in an interview with Mike Thompson, the publicist for Anita Bryant's successful campaign to defeat the gay anti-discrimination ordinance in Dade County, Florida.

"We will bring together people who have never been politically involved before," Thompson enthused, "or people who have been involved but not on the same side. We will probably be a catalyst, and these people will go on to work together for other issues and candidates."

Thompson is a PR man and perennial rightist candidate (he has run for Congress and state offices) who struck gold—or at least orange—with the Bryant crusade. Now he has left the O.J. Queen and is striking out on his own: on the trail of what he sees as the "new majority" of Democrats, blue-collar workers and Jewish voters who are liberal on other issues, but conservative on "the family." Already, Thompson said, the force of the New Right has been felt in Florida. "A kind of cooperation" developed between the Bryantites and the Schlaflyites that helped defeat the ERA in the sunshine state; Florida senators who were inclined to favor equal rights for women voted against the amendment, he thought, because of the ERA's "homosexual implications." Thompson now chairs the Florida Conservative Union—the local arm of the American Conservative Union—and is preparing the massive advertising campaign to defeat the Panama accords.

Thompson's opposing general in the Dade County wars was Ethan Geto, a savvy political consultant for New York liberal candidates, who flew into Florida to do battle with Bryant in the last several weeks of the referendum campaign. Geto arrived at the front unaware of the larger implications of the "life styles" issue he was supporting.

"It started becoming clear down there that this was part of a national right-wing political thrust," Geto reflected recently. "There's been a major shift from the old issues of economics, foreign policy and big government to such things as abortion, women's rights, gay rights and marijuana. The political rip-off artists see that as the wedge to broaden their base and their strength."

Geto got the first clue to the new plan when the same names and the old familiar faces from anti-abortion, anti-feminist and anti-Castro movements began turning up in the anti-gay campaign. By referendum time, the local county Democratic party committee made the same connections—and endorsed the pro-gay side as much in self-defense as in sympathy. "They realized gay rights wasn't an abstract issue anymore," Geto concluded, "but an organizing vehicle for their old opponents from the Republican right-wing."

The relationship between the militant mass movements and the manipulative elite organizations is extremely complex.

Beside the NCPAC and the Republican campaign committee, some of the groups and personalities involved are:

• The American Legislative Exchange Council, a new network of conservative state legislators and national congressmen, which is now drafting backlash bills for introduction at all levels of government.

• The Heritage Foundation, a tax-exempt, right-wing think tank, funded last year by Joseph Coors of Colorado beer fame, which gives "intellectual content" to right-wing projects. One early idea was Coors' plan to create a "Fourth Network" for conservative television programming and production.

• The Committee for the Survival of a Free Congress, now headed by Paul Weyrich, formerly of The Heritage Foundation. Weyrich says, "My bag is organizing"—specifically, the defeat of liberal congressmen and their replacement by reactionaries. Richard Viguerie has raised substantial funds for the Committee in direct-mail campaigns.

• The Conservative Caucus, thought to be the "key connection" of New Right grass-roots organizing efforts for candidates and causes. TCC is run by Howard Phillips, a former Young American for Freedom, who was Nixon's last director of the Office of Economic Opportunity. Phillips' job at OEO was to scuttle the anti-poverty program—as scuttle he did. His dream for the caucus is to place hundreds—thousands, even—of activists in every congressional district in the country: something like a network of Committees for the Defense of the Counterrevolution.

• Citizens for the Republic, the personal political vehicle for the future travels of Ronald Reagan, wherever they may lead. Reagan's recent presidential aspirations have been heavily subsidized by Coors.

Beneath the bland names of those general groupings, the issues of the New Right connect in byzantine ways:

• The campaign to legalize Laetrile is organized by an ad hoc "Committee for Freedom of Choice in Cancer Therapy, Inc.," a virtual subsidiary of the John Birch Society. The "legislative representative" of the group is the ubiquitous Larry McDonald of Georgia, author of the anti-gay legislation. McDonald received the fifth biggest bundle of campaign donations among all the 435 congresspeople elected in 1974; among his contributors were the Coors brewery, H.L. Hunt family and the Birch Society's National Council.

• The American Enterprise Institute, a long-time conservative center for right-wing policy studies, recently sponsored a classy "Round Table" on the saccharin controversy. Speaking for saccharin was Congressman James G. Martin of North Carolina, whose major political cause this year is repeal of the "Delaney Amendment," requiring proof of the safety of foods and drugs *before* they are allowed on the market. Food and drug companies despise the Delaney rule. Martin's 1976 election victory was funded in large part by the National Conservative Political Action Committee.

• The National Drive to Defeat Liberal Democrats is a special project of the National Republican Congressional Committee, which promotes the policies of the G.O.P.'s far-right flank. The National Drive is gearing up to defeat 45

---

## On Capitol Hill, "The mail is running ten-to-one, a *hundred*-to-one against busing, abortion, gay rights," moans a liberal lobbyist

---

"ultra liberals" in the 1978 congressional elections. A crucial complaint against all of them is their support for laws which "redistribute your income to people who can, but won't work." At the right end of the spectrum, "welfare recipient" is invariably defined as "welfare cheater."

• Jesse Helms is holding hearings this month on the "Leftist" manipulation of the various state preparatory meetings for the International Women's Year Conference. Stop-ERA activists hoped he could turn the hearings into a latter-day Un-American Activities Committee production, with lesbians and women's libbers in the old roles of comsymps and fellow travelers. Dorothy Waldvogel has been invited to testify. Helms is also a leading opponent of ratification of the Panama Canal treaty, as is the anti-gay, anti-ERA, anti-abortion Senator Orrin Hatch of Utah. Helms and Hatch are instrumental supporters of Howard Phillips' Conservative Caucus. TCC's major campaigns have been against gay rights and the ERA. Chairman of the TCC is Governor Meldrim Thomson of New Hampshire, a troglodyte among Republican neanderthals.

• The *South Boston News Digest*, once the house organ of anti-busing ROAR, soon became the voice of the grass-roots New Right in Massachusetts. Its columns lay out the range of issues of concern to the new movements. Favorite causes last spring were the expansion of nuclear power facilities and the abolition of car pools. Editor Paul Walkowski believes that car pools undermine the individualist traditions of American life. *SBND* writer John Ciccone sees the nuclear protest as a pinko plot. ROAR people periodically make Man-Man raids on feminist meetings; South Boston whites attack gays of all races, as well as blacks and Hispanics of all sexual persuasions. Congressman Larry McDonald—a former member of the National Council of the John Birch Society — is a hero of the paper, as he is a forthright comrade of Meldrim Thomson in the governor's attacks on the anti-nuke Clamshell Alliance. Two members of McDonald's office staff, John and Louise Rees, are known to have infiltrated liberal organizations and have supplied McDonald with confidential documents from those groups' files. McDonald later inserted them in the litigation-proof Congressional Record. McDonald's office was the source of false reports, trumpeted by Thomson, that the Clamshell Alliance would engage in "terrorism" at the Seabrook nuclear plant during the demonstrations last May. Thomson's major political projects as governor have been the construction of nukes and the demolition of a gay students organization at the University of New Hampshire. The U.S. Labor Party, the quack political cult embracing the worst of left and right paranoia, is closely allied with Thomson, as well as with Boston City Councilor Albert "Daper" O'Neil, a veteran anti-busing campaigner.

Like anti-war and civil rights workers of yore, the New Right takes its campaigns from the streets into the election booths, concentrating huge amounts of energy and time in targeted districts.

"I see some issues as taking such a priority in terms of what we as a society are all about, where we are going in the future, that I have to say that it is perhaps the priority of our century," a Cook County anti-abortion militant named Marie Prime said in a television documentary on the issue. "I will always support the candidate who has the pro-life position." With spirit like that, no candidate in the state can afford to dismiss the issue next time at the polls.

"There's no question that the right is getting increasingly successful on Capitol Hill," Vicki Otten of the Americans for Democratic Action said nervously. The *anti* people are winning bigger and bigger majorities. In 1976 a partial anti-abortion bill was defeated two-to-one; this year the House accepted a *total* prohibition by almost the same margin, the other way. In the Senate, it's been the Democratic liberals who have gone over to the Right on the issue—Ted Kennedy, Humphrey, Leahy —all of a sudden they're scared. In the House, the new freshmen of '76 were supposed to make up the most liberal Congress in history. But they've made it one of the most conservative. Their mail is running ten-to-one, a *hundred*-to-one against busing, abortion, gay rights. It's phenomenal! They believe that 'life-style' issues will reelect them or defeat them, and so they're voting with the 'anti's.'"

The growing strength of the New Right showed itself in Congressman Larry McDonald's success in passing an amendment to a legal services bill which forbids government-funded legal aid in cases of discrimination against homosexuals. McDonald was practically laughed off the floor of Congress when he first proposed his amendment. Then he called for a vote on the record, and the frightened representatives passed it 230 to 133.

The function of the life-style, pro-family, moral issues in the Right's political scheme is to make the moderates and the liberals near the center run scared. It is already a cliché of columnar journalism in Washington that the political vectors of the country all run right. But, in their divinations of a "national mood," the columnists ignore the essential importance of right-wing organization and its purposes. Real power and commanding interests rest on the nexus of "moral" and "emotional" issues. Dorothy Waldvogel and the girls in Bensenville may not realize it, but their outrage in Illinois can be redeemed for cash benefits and political privileges in Washington. In the not-so-old days, politicians on the Left understood that functional importance of grass-roots activism and used it for their own schemes, wise or foolish. White civil-rights sympathies and middle-class anti-war sentiments were converted into progressive policies that began to redistribute power and wealth: from the well-off to the poor, from whites to blacks, from the countryside to the cites, from South to North, from old to young. Suburban liberals who joined one candlelight vigil were enrolled as troops in the war on poverty, as supporters of Chicano unions, as voters for liberal candidates, as participants in a "culture of the left." In time, everyone of that tendency felt part of a movement, many movements, or "the Movement."

Suburban conservatives and small-town moralists are now drafted as soldiers for the armies of the Right and consumers of its culture. "The Movement" now is located 180 degrees around from the 1967 position. What counts now, as then, are the deeper connections of power and politics beneath the pious rhetoric, the strong currents beneath the surface froth.

Phyllis Schlafly may support and finance anti-ERA organizing around the country, but as the ACLU's Neier noted, "She hasn't made the movement, it made her." In the same way, the Catholic hierarchy is giving anti-abortion activists a big boost now, but a year ago one leading layman in Chicago was heard to wonder "when Cardinal Cody would get off his fat ass" and catch up with the movement.

The Reborn Right began organizing at the bottom of the political pyramid, much as the New Left did in the sixties. In fact, the parallels between the two native American movements, one progressive and the other reactionary, are striking.

"We learned a lot from the Left organizations," Bircher Congressman John Rousselot told me one afternoon as we chatted over bean soup in the House dining room. "Sometimes it's been conscious, sometimes not. But a lot of conservatives have learned from groups like Common Cause, the unions, and the ACLU.

"One thing we learned," Rousselot continued, excitedly pounding the table with his forefinger, "is that organizations like Right To Life have paid off in votes right here."

Rousselot knows how the grass-roots Right has turned Congress around, how it has profoundly shaped the Carter Administration, and how it is succeeding in every state legislature in the country. The governors who still have the temerity to veto anti-abortion and pro-death penalty laws are often over-ridden. Gay rights hasn't a chance in any major constituency in the country (with the possible exception of San Francisco's gay ghetto) in the foreseeable future.

Former liberals are hiding their progressive pasts in the nearest available closets. For example, the latest anti-homosexual crusader is Adam Walinsky, a campaign advisor to New York mayoral candidate Mario Cuomo, and a former legislative assistant and speechwriter for Bobby Kennedy. I can remember the day in early 1968—in my Washington apartment—when Walinsky made plans to leave congressional politics and join Tom Hayden's movement in the streets to end the war and bring socialism to America. At the last minute, Kennedy's decision to run for president kept Walinsky out of the Chicago Conspiracy. Now, not even 10 years after, he has joined the anti-liberation lobby.

There is no single, simple way to explain the success of the New Right, much less to predict its future trajectory. The victories of the Right this year have been permitted, to some extent, by the failure of a liberal opposition—the consequence of the Left's own cynicism, disillusionment and isolation.

The New Left and its descendants have been notoriously maladroit in reaching people whose background and behavior diverge from its young, white, cool cosmopolitan styles and middle-class status. Serious and progressive urban feminist organizers are impatient with Middle American housewives who are not quickly captivated by the blinding truths of Women's Liberation. A depressing case in point concerned a clutch of pro-feminist Catholic women from a working-class district in Chicago who attended the Illinois International Women's Year planning session as partisans of the NOW liberationists. They were soon dismayed, however, at the way their own "leaders" demanded strict adherence to the ideologically pure position on abortion. The Catholic women personally favored the right of women to choose abortion, but they knew they could not go back to their neighborhoods and organize other women on the basis of the purist platform that the middle-class, largely Protestant and Jewish feminists pushed through in Normal.

Nothing is gained by the Left in dismissing their antagonists as "right-wing nuts," as one bitter Chicago feminist called them. There is too much nuttiness around these days and a fair portion of it can be found in the precincts of the New Right. It's hard to discern much logic or reason, for example, in any of the stated arguments that Larry McDonald or Phyllis Schlafly make against the ERA. But the women who oppose the amendment are as diverse a lot as those in favor. There are the jeans-clad young mothers of the suburban New Right and the blue-haired Republican ladies of the Old; there are those who believe every farfetched fantasy of the Schlaflyites—that the ERA will foist coed toilets, battlefield breastfeeding and compulsory female ditchdigging on helpless American

# Satan's plan for Arizona

The resurgent right has already won important electoral victories in Arizona, which showed a surprising flurry of New Left activity in the early years of the decade. Ron Asta, a young maverick champion of environmental and consumer causes, was elected to the Pima County (Tucson) Board of Supervisors on a "progressive" platform in 1972. Within four years, he had gathered a new coalition of like-minded folks who succeeded in winning offices in 24 consecutive elections. And then the backlash hit.

"They beat me last year on the 'no-growth' issue." Asta told me. "They used our campaign tactics—door-to-door canvassing and mass mailers. But behind these 'good government coalitions' were the old Reagan campaigners, and behind them were the Chamber of Commerce, the banks, the utilities, the builders, the new car dealers, the realtors and the old-line regular Democrats." Within a few months, the New Right coalition had defeated most of Asta's comrades in the state legislature and had recalled all four of the progressives on the Tucson City Council.

"They used a whispering campaign against us," Asta said.

PHOTOGRAPH BY TERRY MOORE

"They said, 'Asta lives in a singles apartment and wears beads and he's probably a homosexual.' They said Jo Cauthorn, a state representative, doesn't wear a bra and she probably doesn't raise her kids properly. There was a bunch of ugly stuff about a gay man who was murdered in a bar; they let the two people convicted of the murder off with incredibly light sentences. They still haven't passed the ERA in Arizona. One Phoenix legislator calls ERA 'Satan's plan for Hell on Earth.' That's what's happening down here." —A.K.

womanhood; and there are others who treat the anti-ERA campaign as a symbolic confrontation with modernist doctrine.

"I feel sorry for people who are trying to hold on to yesterday," NOW's Ellie Smeal said sorrowfully; but she has no good way to help them loose the grip.

For no one has yet devised a believable alternative to the old family forms and social values, the decay of which has thrown so many Americans into a reactionary snit. The Left experiments with communes, collectives, open marriages, living together, same-sex couples and the like. The Right clings to the old formulas for marriage, religion and sex roles—long after their content has been compromised and only the skeletal structures remain. Accidents of class, ethnicity and geographic context—as well as quirks of character—can determine which side a person will choose.

For in the end, we are all

squeezed in the same inexorable vise. Dorothy Waldvogel and her unknown feminist counterparts are natural allies, not enemies. As Congressman John Rousselot told me, the pro-pot and pro-Laetrile issues are virtually identical—except that one has been captured by the left, the other by the right.

What is breaking up the family are the demands of the system—call it what you will—for women workers at low pay, for routinized work schedules, for education tracked to job slots, for high rates of consumption, for waste and for profit. Scraps of the proceeds of that system have for years been thrown to the most underprivileged members of society in hopes that they will not upset the social applecart; the rest stays in the board rooms at the top. Inevitably, the Waldvogels of this world get the short change, and it is they who are crying in pain. It is a pity that they yet mistake their fellow sufferers for their true tormentors. ●

# V. Social Change

Social change is an inevitable and continuing process in all societies. Some societies, of course, change much more slowly than others. In simple, traditional societies, change may scarcely be noticeable, and grandparents may expect their grandchildren to live much the same lives as they have done. In comparatively recent times, however, the modernization process, based on a shift from agricultural to industrial production, has made headlong social change a dominant feature of most contemporary societies. Change in the United States is now so rapid, and the pace of accumulation of new knowledge so great, that for perhaps the first time in history the young may have more relevant technical knowledge about the world than their parents. Today we can hardly conceive the kind of life our grandchildren might lead.

Social change comes from many sources, notably discovery, invention, and diffusion of cultural elements from one society to another. And change always brings problems with it, largely because it tends to be uneven, with change in one area of society lagging behind change in another. For example, medical science has slashed the death rate, but religious and other attitudes favoring a high birth rate have been slow to respond to this change. The result is a global population explosion of potentially frightening consequences.

Paul R. Ehrlich is probably the foremost spokesman for the view that population is the world's most pressing problem. Not everyone agrees, how-

ever, with the views he expresses in the first article in Topic 17. In the following selection, John Maddox argues forcefully that those who foresee an ecological doomsday are exaggerating the perils. In his essay, Peter F. Drucker takes a sober and realistic look at the costs of protecting the American environment and saving the ecology movement from becoming merely an impractical and short-lived fad.

Topic 18 considers six diverse issues in modern industrial society. The first article, by Robert J. Trotter, examines some recent research on a suspected (but still unproven) connection between urban crowding and crime. Next, Herb Denenberg, formerly the commissioner of insurance in Pennsylvania, argues that the American health-care system is rigged to produce a self-perpetuating inflation of medical costs, insurance costs, and hospital facilities and services.

The third article considers the power of the press. It is an old adage that the pen is mightier than the sword; on occasion, however, it may also be mightier than the state. The power of the press has been demonstrated in the past: Through his articles, a British journalist helped bring about the liberation of Bulgaria more than a century ago; at about the same time, Austrian journalist Theodore Herzl began writing about an independent Jewish state in what was then a corner of the Ottoman empire, an effort that eventually resulted in the creation of modern Israel more than three decades ago. Modern media—especially television—helped end the war in Indochina in the 1970s. And, of course, the media (notably newspapers such as *The Washington Post* and *The New York Times*) helped expose the excesses of the Nixon administration, writing an end to the era of the "Imperial Presidency." Nevertheless, while the media can act as an important constraint on the excesses of government and business in a democratic society, what forces can counterbalance the power of the press? Tom Bethell and Charles Peters argue that an ironic outcome of the Nixon era is that we are now entering an era of the "Imperial Press."

The compilation of data about the private lives of individuals by private and government organizations is an important issue in Western society, especially when the data are shared with other organizations and when the individual is not given access to his files and cannot rebut the charges contained in them. In the United States, the Freedom of Information Act was passed to correct such abuses. Unfortunately, the act permits the agencies controlling the files to decide arbitrarily what records will and will not be made public. John Seigenthaler describes his experiences with charges made against him in FBI files; the story is particularly chilling as Seigenthaler is a respected member of the establishment.

Since the early 1970s, terrorists of almost every conceivable ideology have captured the attention of the world: Palestinian terrorists murdered eleven Israeli athletes at the Munich Olympics, American diplomats in the Sudan, and dozens of people in airline terminals in various European cities; Japanese terrorists killed Christian pilgrims in Israel; West German terrorists carried out a series of bloody murders and kidnappings; South Moluccans committed several hijackings; right-wing terrorists in Argentina, Chile, and Uruguay, among other countries, systematically assassinated political opponents while the police turned a blind eye. These events and countless others committed by terrorists are generally considered separately from cases of the use of force by established governments—some of which, no doubt, are equally brutal and senseless. Walter Laqueur, a distinguished political analyst, argues, however, that contrary to conventional wisdom, terrorism is no more than a nuisance at present. He considers and demolishes several of the myths about terrorism.

Finally, in an adaptation from their book, Jeremy Rifkin and Ted Howard discuss some of the implications of the discovery of recombinant DNA—genetic engineering—and ask, "Who Should Play God?"

An important vehicle for social change and for confronting the problems that change brings is the social movement, the subject of Topic 19. In the past two decades we have witnessed a number of influential social movements: civil rights, peace, women's, gay rights, and so on. Social movements tend to have their own life cycles, starting with a shared belief that something should be changed, proceeding to the establishment of informal groups dedicated to change, then moving to the institutionalization of the movement if it begins to achieve success, and finally leading to the disappearance of the movement when its goals have either been met or frustrated decisively. James S. Kunen, a student rebel of the late 1960s, discusses some of the respects in which he, his former comrades, and the United States have changed since that time and some of the ways in which they have remained the same. In the final article, Jeff Greenfield examines those unlikely revolutionaries, the Beatles, and their influence on contemporary culture, which has changed in significant ways as a direct and indirect result of the music and life styles they pioneered and popularized.

## ADVENTURES OF THE MIND

# POPULATION CONTROL

## By PAUL R. EHRLICH

Population control is a loaded concept. It seems to conjure up different images in the minds of different people. To some the images are of horrors: fetuses killed by abortionists, sterilants put in water supplies by mad scientists, poor families taxed into oblivion for having too many children, minorities threatened with genocide. To others, the images are of salvation. The world in which we live is vastly overpopulated and we are faced by a wide array of hideous problems—war, racism, food shortage, pollution, and so on. People are destructive in many ways, and the more people there are the worse things get. Therefore, the solution is to limit the size of the population. If only there were fewer people, our problems would be solved.

Obviously, neither of these sets of images is realistic. While it is quite true that there is a major population component in many human problems, and that rapid population growth can prevent us from solving any of them, it is not true that controlling the size of the population will automatically bring on a golden era. For instance, if the population of the United States were stabilized at its present size while current trends in American behavior continued, a little over 200 million Americans would soon exhaust most of Earth's rich deposits of resources and in the process greatly degrade the life-support capacity of our planet's ecosystems. In addition, such problems as racism, poverty, and international aggressiveness would persist, al-

though they would be somewhat more amenable to solution. On the other hand, the picture of population control as some sort of fiendish plot is hardly accurate either. Draconian measures are not really called for. In theory one might "control" population growth by killing people, just as one might "control" crime by shooting everybody suspected of being a criminal. But there are more humane and socially desirable ways of controlling population growth, just as there are other ways of controlling criminal behavior.

Before discussing the intricacies of population control further, it is wise to ask whether or not it is necessary. If there were no crime, there would be no reason to devise programs to control criminal behavior. If there are no problems associated with population growth, there is no reason to discuss possible programs of population control. Today, however, no informed person considers population growth innocuous. It is true that some people and even some "scientists" can be found who will derogate the population problem. But one can still find people and even "scientists" who think the world is flat or who attempt to guide their lives by astrology. In the last several years, science has moved from the stage of generalized concern over population growth to efforts to influence public policy on the matter. Individual spokesmen have been joined recently by various groups. In 1970, the Governing Board of the American Institute of Biological Sciences released the following statement:

WHEREAS, scientific studies have clearly identified as a threat to human life and to its quality the current high rate of population increase and consequent overpopulation both in the United States and elsewhere, and

WHEREAS, immediate measures must be taken to correct the population growth in the United States; therefore be it

RESOLVED, that it is essential that the Government accelerate its efforts toward implementing all methods of humane birth control at the earliest feasible time.

In 1970 also, the report of the Study of Critical Environmental Problems (SCEP), sponsored by the Massachusetts Institute of Technology, was published and it called attention to the global nature of various ecological problems and to the population component in them. In 1972, a group of scientists under the leadership of Dennis and Donella Meadows at MIT published a popular report of their work entitled *The Limits of Growth*—a document clearly designed to influence public policy—which emphasized the ways in which population growth is mortgaging the human future. Almost simultaneously, the British journal

*The Ecologist* produced a "Blueprint for Survival," endorsed by a very distinguished group of thirty-five English scientists. A major thrust of the blueprint was toward population control. Perhaps most important, in the spring of 1972 the *Report of the President's Commission on Population Growth and the American Future* was published. A diverse group of distinguished Americans, including many laymen, had examined the impact of population growth on our lives and its potential impact on the lives of our children and had come to the conclusion that there were no benefits to be gained, and many costs to be incurred, from further increasing the number of Americans.

Why is there such unanimity about the need for limiting the numbers of people in the United States and in the world? The reasons are many and complex, but can be briefly summarized:

1. The rapid growth of the world population threatens to worsen an already marginal food situation. Although we are not certain what factors will limit the amount of food that can be produced, we know that at any given time the supply is finite. At the moment if all the food in the world were distributed equitably among the 3.8 billion people living on the planet Earth, everyone would have just enough calories and not quite enough high-quality protein. Since food *is not* equitably distributed, many people are overfed while large numbers go hungry. It is estimated that ten to twenty million people die prematurely every year because their diets are inadequate in some respect. For the past twenty years or so, food production has barely kept pace with population growth. This means that the proportion of hungry people has remained more or less constant, but their *number* has steadily increased. Specialists in food production have expressed grave doubts that even the most strenuous efforts can keep per capita food production at the present inadequate level for more than another twenty to thirty years. Moreover, these estimates take no account of the possibility of a collapse of world fisheries or large-scale crop failures, events which would result in massive famines.

2. The most serious environmental problem facing humanity is the simplification of ecological systems. Complex natural ecological systems supply many indispensable services: they dispose of wastes, they help to maintain the quality of the atmosphere, they provide control of most pests, and they constitute a "library" of genetic information which people can draw on to develop new kinds of crops, antibiotics, vaccines, and so on. The stability of these all-important ecological systems is related to their complexity. Unfortunately, many human activities, particularly agriculture, constitute a serious assault on that complexity and thus on the life-support systems. Thus one result of attempts to produce more food for a rapidly growing population could be an inadvertent, large reduction in the carrying capacity of the planet for human life. By attempting to feed five billion people in 1984, we may make it impossible to feed even two billion in the year 2000! Many other activities that support human populations also reduce ecological complexity: the clearing of land for dwellings, highways, and factories; the building of dams; overfishing; strip mining; and the release of persistent poisons. Most of these assaults on ecosystems tend to increase as population grows, and some increase disproportionately; two million people may do much more than twice as much damage as one million.

It must be emphasized that, as long as human activities are seriously damaging the ecological systems of the Earth, the planet is *by definition* overpopulated. There is some confusion about this among some non-ecologists, who are prone to deny that we are overpopulated on the grounds that damage could be avoided if there were "less affluence" or "better technology." Unfortunately for their argument, overpopulation must be *measured in terms of the animals (or people) as they exist*, not of hypothetical animals behaving differently. If a population of rat-eating cats begins to exhaust the supply of rats so that the cats start dying of hunger, then there is an overpopulation of cats. The possibility that the cats might all be able to survive if some learned to eat squirrels does not alter the fact of overpopulation. Neither would the information, supplied by a cat historian, that cats had once actually fed on squirrels. Overpopulation exists when the numbers of an animal increase until its population begins to deplete its resources, degrade its environment, or (in the case of humans) press on its values. Thus overpopulation can, in theory, be caused or cured without changes in population size.

Of course, people are not cats; presumably they can much more readily change their behavior. And it is quite true that appropriate changes in behavior could dramatically reduce the impact of today's 3.8 billion people on the environment and thus reduce the degree of overpopulation. Indeed it might be possible—with redistribution of wealth and food, less meat-eating, intensive recycling of resources, replacement of automobiles with mass transit, less manufacturing of all kinds, less frivolous use of power and resources—to design a world in which 3.8 billion people can live without overpopulation. But we do not at present know enough about the system to be sure.

The situation is, however, rendered much more serious because the population, great as it already is, is growing so rapidly that it will double in about thirty-five years, unless some extraordinary event intervenes. Moreover, stopping population growth cannot be accomplished overnight. As Bernard Berelson, President of the Population Council, wrote in 1970, ". . . if the replacement-sized family is realized for the world as a whole by the end of this century—itself an unlikely event—the world's population will then be 60 percent larger or about 5.8 billion, and due to the results of age structure [the proportion of people of different ages] it will not stop growing until near the end of the next century, at which time it will be about 8.2 billion, or about 225 percent the present size. If replacement is achieved in the developed world by 2040, then the world's population will stabilize at near 15.5 billion about a century hence, or well over four times the present size."

In other words, there is a long "braking time" if we attempt to halt population growth by slowing the flow of people into the population—that is, by limiting the number of births. Of course there is always that grim alternative, the end of population growth through an acceleration in removal of people from the population—an increase in the death rate. Population growth could be stopped in its tracks by worldwide famine, or plague, or thermonuclear war. Worldwide today there are, annually, about thirty-four births per thousand people in the population and only some fourteen deaths. The balance can be restored by lowering the former or by raising the latter (or some combination of the two). Then the size of the population would be stable—we would have achieved zero population growth (ZPG).

Since no population can grow forever, it is inevitable that the balance *will* be restored. We will have ZPG. The only questions are when and how. For reasons already indicated, I think the time is soon. The question of how remains to be resolved. In any animal but man, there would be no choice—overpopulation ordinarily results in increased death rates, sometimes accompanied by "compulsory" reductions in birthrates. *Homo sapiens* alone has the option of choosing to limit its population size by voluntarily controlling the birthrate. If it is not exercised soon, however, the option may expire.

Assuming this peculiarly human option is to be exercised, how can the population be controlled? For a long time, the answer of establishment sociologists and demographers was: through family planning. The basic idea here was that if people were given the chance to plan their families, to have only the number of children they *want*, then population growth would be slowed or halted. Family planning has received wide support among intelligent and humane people simply because it involves an obvious social good—preventing the births of unwanted children. It is mainly the question of the efficacy of family planning as a route to population control that has led to controversy. As Justin Blackwelder succinctly put it, "... 'family planning' means, among other things, that if we are going to multiply like rabbits, we should do it on purpose. One couple may plan to have three children; another couple may plan seven. In both cases they are a cause of the population problem—not a solution to it."

What are the sources of faith in family planning as an effective device for limiting population growth? One is the relatively low birthrates in the developed countries (DCs) in contrast to those in underdeveloped countries (UDCs). It was in the DCs that the family planning movement originated; it is in those countries that people today have the widest access to the means of birth control; ergo, family planning leads to low birthrates and, eventually, ZPG. Another source of faith is the belief that people, given the opportunity to choose the size of their families, will make socially responsible decisions, considering not just their own needs, but those of their children and of society as well.

There are a number of serious problems with the first view. The fundamental "cause" of the population explosion is a decline in death rates in the human population, a decline which began at the time that agriculture was invented some 10,000 years ago. As living conditions improved with advances in agriculture, industrialization, and the conquest of epidemic disease, the decline in death rates accelerated dramatically. But there were no significant changes in birthrates, which remained close to their primitively high levels. Then, around 1850, birthrates in Europe and North America began to drop, and continued to drop until the second quarter of the twentieth century, when they levelled off. The family planning movement was in part a result of the changing attitudes toward family size that caused the decline in birthrates. The organizations that grew from it probably directly affected only a minority of people, but their influence in changing restrictive laws and public attitudes toward the practice of birth control certainly accelerated the birthrate decline.

However, the decrease in birthrates has not, in general, been sufficient to halt population growth in the DCs. Indeed, demographic data seem to indicate that DC populations will continue to grow at rates which will double them about once per century, on the average, if no steps beyond family planning are initiated. There are those, however, who are not worried by this. Some demographers seem to have a mystical belief that birthrates and death rates automatically move from a primitive state of balance where both rates are high to a new state of balance where both are low. This change is called the demographic transition. These individuals believe that birthrates in DCs must fall further—that

the demographic transition will be "completed." Still other demographers and many family planners see no need for ZPG in the near future, and approve of slow growth.

On a much more sophisticated level, demographer Charles Westoff has recently contended that simply eliminating unwanted births might substantially reduce the population growth rate in the United States. This conclusion has been challenged by another respected demographer, Judith Blake. Recent data support her position that the proportion of unwanted births has been greatly reduced since 1965, allowing little room for further decrease in the number of unwanted births. Changes in the average age of mothers, widespread use of oral contraceptives, and loosening of abortion laws in some states are some of the factors that have operated to reduce unwanted births.

The entire matter is further confused by the recent decline in United States birth-

rates at a time when more and more women are entering what are normally their "peak" reproductive years. No one can say with certainty why this is occurring. It might be because of improvements in the availability of contraceptives and easier access to abortion. It could be a result of the intensive propaganda efforts of organizations like ZPG and "population nuts" like me—indeed some recent data indicate this could be one factor. But much as I would like to give the credit to the family planners (or take it myself!) I suspect other factors to be more important. One is suggested by population biologist K.E.F. Watt of the University of California at Davis. Dr. Watt believes that this dramatic drop is due to the economic difficulties recently encountered by young people attempting to enter the job market. There is intense competition for positions in the labor force among those just joining it at the ages just prior to normal peak reproduction. Another possible factor is the rising tide of

women's liberation with its emphasis on nonchildbearing routes to fulfillment. But, in fact, it is not now possible to assign cause to this birthrate drop with certainty—all we can do is be pleased and hope it continues.

The second assumption of the family planning promoters, that individuals given the opportunity to choose the size of their families will automatically respond to the needs of society, has also been strongly attacked. Recent surveys done in connection with the work of the President's Commission indicate an increase in social responsibility as a factor in childbearing in the United States, but this has only occurred after an intensive propaganda program. In contrast, in other DCs and in UDCs there are few data indeed to indicate that considerations of the problems of overpopulation have any influence on the childbearing decisions of couples. The factors which enter into decisions on the number of children a couple "wants" are at best only partially understood. It is clear, for instance, that desired family size dropped in Western nations following industrialization. A major cause of this trend seems to have been a change in the perceived role of children. In an agricultural society, children tend to be greatly valued for their potential as farm labor—they can become economically active at a very early age. They also serve as a form of old-age insurance in societies which lack social security. Large families provide the best insurance for a surviving son to inherit the farm and support the parents in their old age.

In urban industrial societies the pattern tends to be changed. The traditional association of generations tends to break down, as does the unchanging pattern of existence generation after generation. People see both opportunities to better themselves and opportunities for the betterment of their children. Increasing restrictions on child labor make children less and less of an economic asset, while decreased mortality rates reduce the need for large numbers of children to insure a surviving son. Moreover, savings, pension plans, and governmental social security programs have reduced the need for sons to support elderly parents.

Under such circumstances, people in the late nineteenth and early twentieth centuries wanted to have fewer children, and indeed had fewer children. They managed to have fewer children long before organized family planning became a reality. This, in fact, is not very surprising, since virtually all people have exercised some control over their reproductive activities. In many "primitive" societies, various combinations of contraception, abortion, infanticide, and taboos affecting sexual relations normally regulate the size of families. In eighteenth-century England infanticide was institutionalized as "baby farming."

It is fair to say, then, that the major element in the world population problem today is *not* the birth of too many unwanted children, but the birth of too many *wanted* children. People are choosing to have more children than is good for the health of human society — more children than is good even for the health of those children. Therefore one could hardly expect a program emphasizing "freedom of choice" in childbearing to achieve population control. To reach that end society must find ways to influence the family size chosen.

Many family planning groups now do just that. Within the United States, Planned Parenthood chapters often go far beyond simply making contraceptives available to those who desire them; they actively try to influence desired family size. Especially in the western United States, Planned Parenthood groups colaborate with more radical organizations such as Zero Population Growth (ZPG) in attempting to persuade couples to limit their reproduction. Outside the United States, some governmental family planning programs have begun to extend into the area of population control. For instance, the family planning program in India now emphasizes the desirability of the two-child family.

The idea of population control is thus acceptable to some individuals, organizations, and governments. They accept the necessity for society to influence the reproductive activities of its members in order to produce a population size which will permit the continuing health of society. That is the essence of population control. Two major problems remain. The first is to convince more individuals, organizations, and governments that action is required. The second is to determine the most humane and least socially disruptive means of achieving population control, so that convictions can be converted to actions.
control. Two major problems remain. The first is to convince more individuals, organizations, and governments that action is required. The

second is to determine the most humane and least socially disruptive means of achieving population control, so that convictions can be converted to actions.

In the United States both tasks appear relatively easy. Concern over the population explosion is continually growing, and the report of the President's Commission almost certainly foreshadows governmental action within the next few years. Some people will undoubtedly remain adamantly opposed to population control for philosophical, religious, or pecuniary reasons, but broad acceptance seems assured. We are fortunate in the United States that only rather minor measures seem required to depress average family size well below the replacement rate. It is possible that we will be able to halt our growth before the end of the century and perhaps initiate a gradual decline which, over a period of perhaps a century or two, could greatly alleviate our population-related problems.

What sorts of measures would be effective? It is only guesswork, but I suspect that giving all citizens access to contraceptives and abortions on request, coupled with strong governmental support of equal rights for women and a small-family ideal will be effective. Accessibility to the means of birth control has been increasing steadily for nearly a century, so all that is required is the culmination of a long trend. The trend to liberalize abortion laws has also been in the right direction, although recently powerful conservative forces have attempted to force a return to the situation where only rich women can have safe abortions. Women's liberation should, of course, be supported for its own sake; but as more and more women find fulfillment outside of childbearing, there probably will be a "bonus" in the form of lower birthrates. The biggest job will be persuading the government to revise its present pro-population growth stance and to initiate a campaign to convince American couples that it is selfish, irresponsible, and unpatriotic to have more than two children. The

government should already be doing that, because overbreeding *is* selfish, irresponsible, and unpatriotic.

Suppose for a moment that Americans take the appropriate steps to bring our population size under the rational control of society. What can be done about population growth in the other rich nations? And what about the catastrophically rapid growth now occurring in the UDCs? All too often population control is viewed as a plot by rich white people to suppress the poverty-stricken and colored people of the world. And unhappily, in the minds of some members of our society, that is precisely what population control means. It is, therefore, critical that population control be achieved in the United States with great care to avoid *any* overtones of racism or bias against the poor.

If the United States can set an example for the world by controlling her population with equity and humanity, then a major barrier to world population control will be overcome.

Once we have started in that direction the stage will be set for an all-out effort to control the population of the Earth before it is too late. The most satisfactory and effective ways of achieving this goal (beyond ensuring that knowledge and the means of birth control are everywhere available) will undoubtedly be different from country to country. But several themes should be virtually universal: provision of social security for old people, finding creative roles for women other than childbearing, placing the emphasis on the *quality* of one's children rather than their *quantity,* and directing societal effort toward improving the chances for all our children to grow up in a world relatively free of fear and want.

What is required is no less than a transformation of the social, political and economic systems of the world, for population control alone will not solve our problems. But it *is* necessary. Whatever your cause, it is lost without population control. ⬛

# 50

# THE DOOMSDAY SYNDROME

The environmentalists, a leading British scientist charges, may be the most insidious of all plunderers of our planet. Using "a technique of calculated overdramatization," they have deflected attention from the genuine ecological issues we face and blinded us to solutions that exist now. BY JOHN MADDOX

Prophets of doom have multiplied remarkably in the past few years. It used to be commonplace for men to parade on city streets with sandwich boards proclaiming, "The End of the World is at Hand!" They have been replaced by a throng of sober people—scientists, philosophers, and politicians—proclaiming that there are more subtle calamities just around the corner. The human race, they say, is in danger of suffocating itself by overbreeding, of poisoning itself with pollution, of undermining its essential character by tampering with heredity, and of weakening the basic structure of society through too much prosperity.

The questions that these latter-day doomsayers have raised are complex and interesting; the spirit in which they are asked is usually too jaundiced for intellectual comfort. Too often, reality is oversimplified or even ignored, so that there is a danger that much of this gloomy foreboding about the immediate future will accomplish the opposite of its intention. Instead of alerting people to important problems, the "doomsday syndrome" may be as much a hazard to human survival as any of the environmental conundrums society has created for itself.

Nobody doubts the sincerity of the contemporary prophets of calamity, and nobody would disagree that modern society is confronted with impor-

*John Maddox is a theoretical physicist and the editor of the prestigious British scientific journal,* Nature.

tant tasks that must be tackled with a sense of urgency. In advanced societies machinery must be devised for the more equitable treatment of the poor and the disadvantaged. Urban life, although better than it used to be, surely leaves much room for improvement. Even where medical care is excellent, ways of preventing untimely death and unnecessary disease remain to be discovered. And in less-developed societies there are the more basic tasks of providing people with adequate food, housing, and schooling. These are difficult problems, but they are capable of solution in the foreseeable future if enough time and money are spent on them. By contrast, the questions the doomsayers generally raise are rhetorical ones, either because they are based on incorrect premises or because they are unanswerable with the knowledge we possess at the present moment. The risk is that too much preoccupation with the threat of distant calamity will lead to a kind of quietism by diverting our attention from good works that might be accomplished now.

The doomsday cause would be more telling if it were more securely grounded in facts, as well as better informed by a sense of history and an awareness of economics. The major defect in the argument that calamity is just around the corner is its imprecision. Some doomsayers fear that the burning of fuel on the scale to which modern industry is accustomed will wreck the earth's climate, but few meteorologists

are able unambiguously to endorse such prophecies. Others fear that the use of pesticides will irrevocably damage the human race, but that is an overdramatic statement of the need to carefully regulate the way in which such chemicals are sprayed on crops. Still others fear that modern biology, with its artificially fertilized eggs and its detailed understanding of genetic processes, will create a race of robots, but such a concern flies in the face of the past five centuries of medical history, for the most part a consistent record of humane endeavor. In short, the weakness of the doomsday prophecies is that they are exaggerations. Many of them are frighteningly irresponsible.

The flavor of these prophecies of disaster is well illustrated by the work of Dr. Paul Ehrlich, whose book *The Population Bomb* startled a good many people when it was published four years ago. "The battle to feed all of humanity is over," Ehrlich wrote. "In the 1970s the world will undergo famines, hundreds of millions of people are going to starve to death in spite of any crash program embarked on now." Ehrlich went on to describe in a somber way the rate at which the population of the world is increasing, the inconveniences that are likely to result therefrom, and some ways of striking a better balance between the population growth and available resources, especially in developing parts of the world.

Nobody will deny that it is important to control, if not the size of a population, then its rate of growth. In advanced societies population control is increasingly becoming an accepted function of good government. In developing countries it is generally recognized as a prerequisite to economic progress. Ehrlich's warning of imminent famines on a massive scale is unrealistic. The truth is that the total production of food on the earth is now increasing much faster than the population. For most of the Sixties, the population of the world grew at about 2 per cent a year, while agricultural production in the same period increased by 2.7 per cent annually. And in the past few years there has been especially encouraging progress in the hard-pressed countries of Southeast Asia and India, where food production has increased nearly twice as fast as population, due largely to the introduction of new strains of wheat and rice. Nor is there any reason to believe that the "green revolution" will slow down in the coming years. Population control is therefore desirable, not as a means of avoiding calamity, but because it can accelerate the steady improvement of the human condition.

Famine is only one of several hypothetical catastrophes that are said to flow from population growth. Ehrlich and other doomsayers argue that high population density produces individual disorientation and increased social tension. One common argument for supposing that crowding as such is bad for people starts from experiments that have been carried out with laboratory animals, principally rats. The best-known experiments, performed by Dr. John B. Calhoun, showed that rats kept in unusually crowded conditions developed all kinds of psychological disturbances—mother rats took to infanticide, males became unnaturally aggressive, and the mortality rate rose. So is it not reasonable to suppose that people living in metropolitan areas will be more disturbed than those who live in rural areas? With growing population densities, will not violence within and between countries become that much more prevalent? These are common suspicions. Dr. Ehrlich and his wife, Anne, in their book *Population, Resources, Environment*, write that there are "very high correlations among rates of population growth . . . and involvement in wars."

The trouble is that the analogy between rats and people is at best tenuous—gregariousness of the kind that led to the development of cities thousands of years ago distinguishes the human race from rodents. And the belief that violence and war accompany crowding rests on the most shaky statistical basis. Who, after all, would claim that the Netherlands, the most crowded of

all Western European countries, is more given to violence than, say, the United States?

Implicit in these dire warnings of the consequences of population growth is a misleading method of prediction that gives more credit to simple arithmetic than it deserves. If the population of the world is at present doubling every thirty-five years, does it necessarily follow that the population will multiply by a fourfold factor in the next seventy years, so as to reach 14,000 million by the year 2040? In *The Population Bomb* Ehrlich is scornful of those whom he calls "professional optimists . . . who like to greet every sign of

"Alarm does not provide the best atmosphere for finding rational solutions to worrisome problems. Aesop knew what happened to shepherd boys who cried wolf too often."

dropping birth rate with wild pronouncements about the end of the population explosion." And even in the more soberly written *Population, Resources, Environment*, he chooses to base predictions of the future population of the earth on the most pessimistic calculations appearing in studies funded by the United Nations, which assume that there will be no change in the fertility of women of childbearing age between now and the end of the century. In reality, however, there are already signs that fertility is declining in developing countries in exactly the same way as, but possibly more rapidly than, it declined in Western Europe between fifty and a hundred years ago. One of the strangest features of Ehrlich's description of the population explosion is the bland assumption that the social forces that have brought about stability in the developed countries—the improvement of the quality of education and medical care, for example—are inapplicable elsewhere. Is it any wonder that the predominantly Western preoccupation with the population explosion seems like patronizing neocolonialism to people elsewhere?

In much the same way that environmentalists worry about the effects of population growth on our physical and psychological well-being, so, too, they decry its effect on natural resources. In the United States, at least, this is an honorable tradition going back to the

end of the nineteenth century, when Gifford Pinchot, head of the U.S. Forest Service, wrung his hands over the prospect that timber in this country would be used up in roughly thirty years, that anthracite coal would last for only fifty years, and that other raw materials such as iron ore and natural gas were being rapidly depleted. Seventy years later the same complaints are heard. The environmentalists have coined the phrase "our plundered planet" to express their anxiety about the probability that petroleum will be much less plentiful a century from now and that the time will soon come when high-grade copper ores are worked out. The fallacy in this reasoning is that society has never been uniquely dependent on the balance of raw materials in common use at a particular time. If copper becomes scarce or merely expensive, more aluminum will have to be used in its place. If natural diamonds are expensive, then we will make them synthetically. In any case, although supplies of such raw materials are known to be limited, the point at which they seem likely to be exhausted tends to recede with the passage of time so as to be always just over the horizon. Indeed, despite what the environmentalists say, the present time appears to be one in which forecasts of scarcity are less valid than ever. Petroleum may be much harder to obtain a century from now, but in the past few years scientists have laid the foundations for wresting energy from hydrogen and minerals such as uranium in large quantities, so that future decades will be much better off than anybody could have expected even a decade ago. And, however strange it may seem, the real economic cost of extracting such metals as lead and copper from the ground is still decreasing as exploration and the techniques of mining and metallurgy become more efficient. In terms of their availability at least, the earth's resources are becoming more and more plentiful.

Ecological catastrophe is also high on the list of public fears for the future. As another leading doomsayer, Dr. Barry Commoner, puts it in *The Closing Circle*, ". . . in our unwitting march toward ecological suicide, we have run out of options." What he and the other environmentalists who echo his opinions wish to imply is that the relation between people and the environment is so delicate, and the dependence of the human race on its surroundings so complete, that many of the effects of our activity on the natural world may destroy the capacity of the earth to support life.

One recipe for ecological disaster, for example, holds that pollution of the surface layers of the oceans by insecticides or chemicals may destroy the microscopic plants that turn the energy of sunlight into chemical form, help to support marine life of all kinds, and replenish the oxygen in the atmosphere. Another theorizes that the accumulation of carbon dioxide produced by the burning of fossil fuels may so increase the temperature on the surface of the earth as to transform the present pattern of weather and perhaps even melt the Antarctic ice. Fortunately, these chains of events are by no means inescapable. For one thing, the processes that are supposed to lead to disaster are only imperfectly understood. Moreover, their scale is still puny in relation to the size of the earth's envelope—the ecosphere, as it is called.

Tiny though the earth may appear from the moon, it is in reality an enormous object. The earth's atmosphere alone weighs more than 5,000 million million tons, more than a million tons of air for each human being now alive. The water on the surface of the earth weighs more than 300 times as much—in other words, each living person's share of the water would just about fill a cube half a mile square. So while it is not entirely out of the question that human intervention could at some stage bring about changes in the ecosphere, for the time being the vast scale on which the earth is built should be a great comfort to us all.

But even if the human race is unable to harm the ecosphere significantly, is there not a danger that it may destroy itself more directly? In the past few years the nature of biological research has been repeatedly held up as a potential threat to man's survival. Genetic engineering is a somber phrase, no doubt, conjuring up visions of long rows of test-tube babies bred to governmental specifications. But the concept is less frightening when one recalls that horse breeders and plant growers have been practicing it for centuries. And why should communities that have rejected the eugenic devices already available—forced choice of marriage partners, for example, or selective infanticide—throw their principles to the winds now that molecular biology has come along?

Even the quite real prospect of artificially fertilizing human eggs does not contain the seeds of unwelcome social upheaval that many people suppose. The truth is that the most obvious uses of these new techniques are therapeutic, not subversive. To be sure, biological research has raised novel ethical problems. How, for example, does a doctor decide which of several equally needy patients should have access to an artificial kidney machine or receive a kidney that becomes available for transplant? But the fact that these problems are novel is neither an argument against the new techniques nor a justification for the belief that biological research is full of unmanageable social dangers. What justification can there be for the supposition that the same medical men who have developed antibiotics for the treatment of infectious disease and vaccines for its prevention will seize on the new developments to pursue malevolent objectives?

But what of the possibility that science and technology may undermine the integrity of society in much more subtle ways? This is an old fear, of course, which in its crudest form amounts to unregenerate obscurantism. In the past few years the theme has appeared again in a revised and updated form. In his book *Reason Awake*, Dr. René Dubos writes: "Man has always lived in a precarious state, worried about his place in the order of things. In the past he was threatened chiefly by natural forces that he could not control, and he experienced fear because of ignorance of the cosmos and of his own nature. Now threats and fears derive in large measure from science and its technologies, paradoxically the most characteristic products of human reason." And elsewhere he adds, "Most would agree that science and technology are responsible for some of our worst nightmares and have made our societies so complex as to be almost unmanageable."

The flaw in these protestations is that they label technology, and the science from which it springs, as a subversive force in society. It is true, of course, that technical innovations frequently have unexpected consequences. This has always been the case. Who would have guessed fifty years ago that the motor car would create the suburbs of North America? The fact that ocean beaches are so much more crowded now than half a century ago is also a consequence of the tremendous expansion of the automobile industry. But is it sensible to wish that internal combustion engines had not been invented for the sake of avoiding overcrowding at the beaches? Is it not preferable to enjoy the other benefits of the invention and to regulate the crowding of beaches by other means? And in any case, where such developments are in question, is it not entirely misleading to suggest that the automobile industry has grown to its present size for reasons connected with the character of technology and not because a need for its product became apparent? On issues like this, the doomsday literature is dishonest.

The introduction of the wheel into primitive societies must similarly have been attended by unforeseen developments. Then, as now, the immediate benefits of innovation may be predictable, but the more distant consequences, beneficial or harmful, are harder to foresee. The moral, of course, is that governments have a responsibility to ensure that most of the social consequences of technological progress are positive ones. To pretend with Dr. Dubos that such discrimination is impossible and that all technology is therefore suspect is to suggest that society is powerless to regulate its own affairs. The argument that technology is an all-powerful juggernaut pressing the humanity out of society usually cloaks a pessimistic belief in the impotence of social institutions. The challenge is not to keep science and technology at bay but to control them and, in particular, to make sure that they do not become dehumanizing influences on our lives.

One of the most common misconceptions about technology is that it consists entirely of gigantic, tax-supported programs for sending rockets to the moon. In reality, most technologists work toward much less spectacular objectives—building safer and cheaper bridges, for example, or devising ways of drying coffee without loss of flavor. Those who complain about technology and its effects would be on stronger ground if they concerned themselves with devising ways for society to exploit science and technology. The key question is, *Who* says *which* innovations are worthwhile? Some decisions have to be made by individuals in their role as consumers. Others are left to manufacturers. Still others, which have a political flavor in the most general sense, must be taken by governments acting on behalf of the communities they represent. Governments have all too often been unwilling to shoulder their responsibilities. They have, for example, accepted the introduction of jet planes without taking into proper consideration the extra noise such aircraft cause. They have encouraged industrial development without thinking sufficiently about the unavoidable side effects of industry, pollution being chief among them. They have encouraged urbanization without paying enough attention to city planning.

Were these the complaints of the environmentalists, their cause would be entirely laudable. But by slipping into the pretense that science and technology have between them established such a powerful hold on society's development that the survival of the human race may be undermined, they have side-stepped the real issue, which is to guide, not eliminate, technological progress. There is no reason to think that technology will be less valuable in the future than it has been in the

## Many environmentalists talk about the misuses of pesticides in the same apocalyptic terms they once used to describe the horrors of nuclear weapons.

past in liberating men and women from drudgery and so improving the quality of their lives. Paradoxically, the environmental message, at least in its crudest form, is self-defeating.

The main reason the message is so often presented so crudely goes back to the origins of the modern environmental movement. The first environmentalists were probably the scientists who, toward the end of World War II, sensed that the development of nuclear weapons posed a grave threat to the human race. In 1945 Dr. J. Robert Oppenheimer, the scientific director of the Los Alamos program that produced the first atomic bomb, made the point with characteristic eloquence: "In some crude sense which no vulgarity, no overstatement can quite extinguish, the physicists have known sin, and this is a knowledge which they cannot lose."

Throughout the Fifties the campaign to ban the testing of nuclear weapons picked up momentum. In the early years of the decade the first test explosions of hydrogen bombs carried the scientists' initial sense of alarm to a far wider spectrum of the population. In 1954, when four Japanese fishermen were killed by radioactive dust from a thermonuclear explosion, the entire world was given a vivid demonstration of the potential destructiveness of nuclear energy. By the late Fifties nuclear weapons tests had become commonplace, and the amount of radioactive fallout was reaching intolerable levels. The discovery of strontium 90 in the skeletons of young children was a powerful assault on the public conscience. With military strategy still dominated by plans for thermonuclear retaliation, it is no wonder that the decade ended with the sense that Doomsday was just around the corner.

At about the same time, ironically, the concern of the early environmentalists with the perils of nuclear explosions to human health began to win wide acceptance, and in 1963 the major powers signed a treaty prohibiting above-ground testing of nuclear weapons. Suddenly, the environmentalists constituted an army that had tasted blood but seemingly had no further battles to fight. The year before, Rachel Carson had published her now-famous study of the misuses of pesticides, *Silent Spring*, thereby launching an entirely new phase of the environ-

mental movement. **The problem was** that many environmentalists continued to use the same apocalyptic rhetoric they had employed so effectively to express their indignation over the unregulated dissemination of nuclear weaponry —a truly apocalyptic danger—to describe a much more subtle and complex phenomenon.

Miss Carson herself was concerned almost entirely with the way in which insecticides were being used in the United States. Many of her complaints were well founded—it is absurd that insecticides should have been employed to clear insects from inland lakes with such abandon as to kill the fish as well as the insects. Another of her many cautionary tales described how the use of an insecticide similar to DDT against the Japanese beetle in the cornfields of the Middle West made life easier for a still more dangerous pest, the corn borer, which normally was preyed upon by the Japanese beetle. In this and other ways she marshaled enough evidence to demonstrate that pesticides should be more carefully regulated. The most seriously misleading part of her narrative involves the relating of horror stories about the misuse of DDT to create the impression that there are no safe uses for pesticides at all.

Rachel Carson thus set the tone of much subsequent environmental literature by employing a technique of calculated overdramatization. The silent spring itself was an apocryphal season in "a town in the heart of America" created by Miss Carson's fertile imagination. Her book begins with what she calls "a fable for tomorrow." Once,

all life seemed to live in harmony with its surroundings. . . . But then a strange blight crept over the area and everything began to change. Some evil spell had settled on the community: mysterious maladies swept the flocks of chickens; the cattle and sheep sickened and died. Everywhere was a shadow of death. The farmers spoke of much illness among their families. In the town the doctors had become more puzzled by new kinds of sickness appearing among their patients. There had been several sudden and unexplained deaths, not only among adults but even among children, who would be stricken suddenly while at play and die within a few hours.

The calamity, of course, was caused by the use of pesticides. Miss Carson goes

on innocently to reveal that "this town does not actually exist, but it might easily have a thousand counterparts in America or elsewhere in the world." By playing this literary trick on her readers, she provided not merely graphic illustration of the fact that excessive amounts of pesticide could kill animals as well as insects but also a sense that excessive use was almost unavoidable.

Paul Ehrlich's *The Population Bomb* is a splendid illustration of how the technique of calculated exaggeration has flourished. After a tautly written account of how "the battle to feed all of humanity" has been lost, sufficiently vivid to have most readers on the edges of their seats, Ehrlich concludes with the smug apology that he, like any scientist, "lives constantly with the possibility that he may be wrong." However, no harm will be done if *his* argument proves false, Ehrlich continues, for "if I am wrong, people will still be better fed, better housed and happier . . . ." The difficulty, of course, is that alarm does not provide the best atmosphere for finding rational solutions to those problems that are truly worrisome. Aesop knew what happened to shepherd boys who cried wolf too often.

Barry Commoner also uses Miss Carson's technique. In his book *Science and Survival*, for example, he writes that "as large a body of water as Lake Erie has already been overwhelmed by pollutants and has in effect died." The truth is now what it was when the book appeared in 1963, namely, that Lake Erie has indeed been seriously afflicted by pollution, for such a shallow body of water could not be expected to remain unchanged under the assault of the vast amount of sewage and industrial effluent that surrounding cities discharge into it. But throughout the 1960s the lake somehow managed to support a thriving fishing industry. In 1970 it yielded 25,000 tons of fish. Nobody can know for certain why the trout have been replaced by other species of fish—is it in fact the sewage or perhaps the influence of the Welland Canal, which, bypassing Niagara, connects Lake Erie to Lake Ontario? By now it seems to have been generally agreed that something must be done to limit the discharge of effluents into Lake Erie, but the proclamation that the lake is already "dead," whatever such a phrase may mean, has probably given Lake Erie more prominence than it deserves. To be fair, in his more recent book, *The Closing Circle*, Commoner does not say the lake is dead but merely that "we have grossly, irreversibly changed the biological character of the lake and have greatly re-

## Because the use of aluminum cans indicates a highly developed economy, the extremists have created the false impression that prosperity is the enemy.

duced, now and for the foreseeable future, its value to man." But even this more moderate statement of his position is dubious if the assertion of the irreversibility of the damage is taken at face value.

Implicit in the pessimistic outlook of many ecologists is a common stand on the nature of living things and their relationship with the environment. In *Science and Survival* Commoner has a chapter entitled "Greater Than the Sum of its Parts," which attempts to demonstrate that the properties of living things cannot be explained solely in terms of the properties of the molecules that make them up.

There is, I believe, a crisis in biology today. The root of the crisis is the conflict between the two approaches to the theory of life. One approach seeks for the unique capabilities of living things in separable chemical reactions; the other holds that this uniqueness is a property of the whole cell and arises out of the complex interactions of the separable events of cellular chemistry. Neither view has, as yet, been supported by decisive experimental proof. The molecular approach has not succeeded in showing by experiment that the subtly integrated complexity and beautiful precision of the cell's chemistry can be created by adding together its separate components. Nor has the opposite approach, as yet, discovered an integrating mechanism in the living cell which achieves the essential coordination of its numerous separate reactions.

In its essence this argument echoes the old nineteenth-century belief in what was then called "life force"—a special quality of living things—whose credibility has steadily diminished ever since the first laboratory synthesis a century and a half ago of substances usually considered by-products of life. The modern equivalent of this neovitalism holds that the "web of life"—as Darwin termed the way in which different species are linked together by their mutual dependence—is so complicated that it cannot be submitted to the methods of mathematical analysis. This is one of Commoner's arguments. In the trivial sense, of course, the point is incontrovertible—who would seriously set out to calculate the weight of a full-grown locust when it would be much simpler, and probably safer as well, simply to put it on a scale? But

this does not imply that the weight of a locust is in principle incalculable, that there are features of the ecosphere that lie beyond the scope of conventional science. Among the environmentalists there is a temptation to emphasize the unity of the living world in circumstances when it would be more appropriate to consider different parts of it separately. After all, the special character of science is its ability to understand complicated problems by breaking them into their constituent parts.

What happens when scientists attempt to examine the world in its entirety is beautifully illustrated by the controversial Club of Rome study published last spring, entitled *The Limits to Growth*. The study, carried out at MIT under the leadership of Dr. Dennis L. Meadows, is based on a computer simulation of the world and purports to show that many of the more gloomy prophecies of the environmentalists can be upheld by mathematical calculations. The computer is programed with information about the population of the world (for this purpose broken down into three numbers representing the population of children between zero and fifteen, the population of adults of reproductive age, and the population of those whose reproductive life is over), as well as a number indicating the amount of money invested in industrial capital, another indicating the amount of arable land, one that is supposed to stand for the stock of unrenewable resources, and one that is meant to be a measure of pollution. The object of the exercise is to calculate how these and several other interrelated variables will change in the course of time. In my opinion the results fully justify Gunnar Myrdal's description of the study as "pretentious nonsense."

To cite one example, the stock of nonrenewable resources such as minerals will obviously decrease over time at a rate determined in part by the size of the world's population and by the quantity of material consumed each year by a single individual, which is in turn dependent on the amount of industrial output per person and ultimately on the investment in new factories of various kinds. Dr. Meadows and his colleagues calculate that if there is "no major change in the physi-

cal, economic, or social relationships that have historically governed the development of the world system," there will come a point in the next century when the diminishing stock of natural resources brings about a decrease of industrial growth, a consequent decrease in the amount of food available per person, and then, in due course, a return to the bad old days of the eighteenth and nineteenth centuries, when the death rate rose rapidly because of starvation and even an increasing birth rate was unable to prevent a population decline.

The first thing to be said about such a prediction is that even the best possible computer model is no better than the assumptions about the real world with which it is programed. And even very large computer models, such as Dr. Meadows's, are never large enough to take into account all the possible relationships between one thing and another. So it is no wonder that the Club of Rome study has been forced to make drastic simplifications that even the extremists in the environmental movement usually manage to avoid.

The most serious error in the study involves something economists call aggregation—the combining of things that ought not to be considered as one. For example, the authors have been compelled by the limitations of their equipment to represent the totality of pollution on the earth by a single number, based on world industrial production. Having lumped pollution and industrial production together, the authors cannot take into consideration the obvious fact that modern technology can control the first without affecting the second at all.

These simplifications, apparently built into the Club of Rome's computer model, make nonsense of the study. To add another example, *The Limits to Growth* represents the world's stock of nonrenewable resources with a single number. In one particular calculation it was assumed that the amounts of nonrenewable resources in the earth's crust in 1970 were the equivalent of 250 years' supply at the then rate of consumption. On the face of things this was a generous assumption, for the known reserves of a great many common materials such as lead and mercury are unlikely to last nearly so long. But the history of the past few decades has shown clearly enough that relatively scarce materials are constantly being replaced by more common ones —copper, for instance, has been superseded by aluminum in many branches of the electronics industry. Moreover, by representing the present stock of raw materials with a single number, the study has overlooked a cardinal law of economics, which holds that increasing scarcity and, consequently, higher prices would stimulate exploration for new materials and also make it more practical to mine ores of lower quality.

In general, economics is not the strong suit of the environmentalists. And, unfortunately for their case, most of the issues they tend to present as questions of life or death for the human race are essentially questions of economics. Consider urban air pollution. The overriding issue is not whether cleaner air can be provided (we know it can) but how much taxpayers, and in particular the owners of cars and factories, are prepared to pay for that amenity. Exactly the same is true of the noise produced by jets, the overcrowding of beaches, and even the extent to which farmers are allowed to use pesticides. On such issues there is a need for a better understanding of the economics of the communal good.

Because the relationship between communities and their surroundings is often determined by economic considerations, it is not surprising that different communities should have different objectives and that each should strike its own balance between exploitation and conservation. This is another way of saying that only prosperous communities will pay much attention to environmental amenities. One of the more serious dangers of the extremist wing of the environmental movement is that by insisting on the catastrophic implications of present tendencies, it may alienate the countries of the developing world, not yet rich enough to aspire to the kind of pollution-free future on which the more prosperous nations have set their sights. This was plain enough at the United Nations Conference on the Human Environment held in Stockholm last June, where it proved to be extremely difficult to hammer out a common platform, partly because of the inevitable conflict of interest between rich and poor nations.

The extremists have created the false impression that prosperity itself is the enemy. After all, cars are so numerous on the roads of a wealthy nation because its citizens are able to pay for them. And the heaps of aluminum cans that deface a countryside indicate that consumers can afford the added expense of disposable items. But insisting on the relationship between prosperity and pollution obscures the incontrovertible truth that the level of prosperity now common in developed nations has also purchased better health services, educational systems, and a host of other social benefits to which less fortunate nations still aspire. To people in the developing world environmental concerns are simply not of the highest priority.

The political consequences of this tactlessness by people from industrialized societies are serious. The intellectual sins committed by the environmentalists are more serious still. The common justification of their technique of deliberate exaggeration is the claim that it is necessary to stir people up, to get things done. But people are easily anesthetized by overstatement, and there is a danger that the environmental movement will fall flat on its face when it is most needed, simply because it has pitched its tale too strongly. □

# 51

The high cost of protecting our future

# SAVING THE CRUSADE

by Peter F. Drucker

E VERYBODY TODAY IS "for the environment." Laws and agencies designed to protect it multiply at all levels of government. Big corporations take full-color ads to explain how they're cleaning up, or at least trying to. Even you as a private citizen probably make some conscientious effort to curb pollution. At the same time, we have learned enough about the problem to make some progress toward restoring a balance between man and nature. The environmental crusade may well become the great cause of the Seventies—and not one moment too soon.

Yet the crusade is in real danger of running off the tracks, much like its immediate predecessor, the so-called war on poverty. Paradoxically, the most fervent environmentalists may be among the chief wreckers. Many are confused about the cause of our crisis and the ways in which we might resolve it. They ignore the difficult decisions that must be made; they splinter the resources available for attacking environmental problems. Indeed, some of our leading crusaders seem almost perversely determined to sabotage their cause—and our future.

Consider, for example, the widespread illusion that a clean environment can be obtained by reducing or even abolishing our dependence on "technology." The growing pollution crisis does indeed raise fundamental questions about technology—its direction, uses, and future. But the relationship between technology and the environment is hardly as simple as much anti-technological rhetoric would have us believe. The invention that has probably had the greatest environmental impact in the past twenty-five years, for instance, is that seemingly insignificant gadget, the wire-screen window. The wire screen, rather than DDT or antibiotics, detonated the "population explosion" in underdeveloped countries, where only a few decades ago as many as four out of five children died of such insect-borne diseases as "summer diarrhea" or malaria before their fifth birthday. Would even the most ardent environmentalist outlaw the screen window and expose those babies again to the flies?

The truth is that most environmental problems require technological solutions—and dozens of them. To control our biggest water pollutant, human wastes, we will have to draw on all sciences and technologies from biochemistry to thermodynamics. Similarly, we need the most advanced technology for adequate treatment of the effluents that mining and manufacturing spew into the world's waters. It will take even more new technology to repair the damage caused by the third major source of water pollution in this country—the activities of farmers and loggers.

Even the hope of genuine disarmament—and the arms race may be our worst and most dangerous pollutant—rests largely on complex technologies of remote inspection and surveillance. Environmental control, in other words, requires technology at a level at least as high as the technology whose misuse it is designed to correct. The sewage-treatment plants that are urgently needed all over the world will be designed, built, and kept running not by purity of heart, ballads, or Earth Days but by crew-cut engineers working in very large organizations, whether businesses, research labs, or government agencies.

## Who will pay?

T HE SECOND AND EQUALLY DANGEROUS delusion abroad today is the common belief that the cost of cleaning the environment can be paid for out of "business profits." After taxes, the profits of all American businesses in a good year come to sixty or seventy billion dollars. And mining and manufacturing—the most polluting industries—account for less than half of this. But at the lowest estimate, the cleanup bill, even for just the most urgent jobs, will be three or four times as large as all business profits.

Consider the most efficient and most profitable electric-power company in the country (and probably in the world): the American Power Company, which operates a number of large power systems in the Midwest and upper South. It has always been far more ecology-minded than most other power companies, including the government's own TVA. Yet cleaning up American Power's plants to the point where they no longer befoul air and water will require, for many years to come, an annual outlay close to, if not exceeding, the company's present annual profit of $100 million. The added expense caused by giving up strip mining of coal or by reclaiming strip-mined land might double the company's fuel bill, its single largest operating cost. No one can even guess what it would cost—if and when it can be done technologically—to put power transmission lines underground. It might well be a good deal more than power companies have ever earned.

WE FACE AN ENVIRONMENTAL CRISIS because for too long we have disregarded genuine costs. Now we must raise the costs, in a hurry, to where they should have been all along. The expense must be borne, eventually, by the great mass of the people as consumers and producers. The only choice we have is which of the costs will be borne by the consumer in the form of higher prices, and which by the taxpayer in the form of higher taxes.

It may be possible to convert part of this economic burden into economic opportunity, though not without hard work and, again, new technology. Many industrial or human wastes might be transformed into valuable products. The heat produced in generating electricity might be used in greenhouses and fish farming, or to punch "heat holes" into the layer of cold air over such places as Los Angeles, creating an updraft to draw off the smog. But these are long-range projects. The increased costs are here and now.

Closely related to the fallacy that "profit" can pay the environmental bill is the belief that we can solve the environmental crisis by reducing industrial output. In the highly developed affluent countries of the world, it is true that we may be about to de-emphasize the "production-orientation" of the past few hundred years. Indeed, the "growth sectors" of the developed economies are increasingly education, leisure activities, or health care rather than goods. But paradoxical as it may sound, the environmental crisis will force us to return to an emphasis on both growth and industrial output—at least for the next decade.

## Overlooked facts of life

THERE ARE THREE REASONS FOR THIS, each adequate in itself.

1) Practically every environmental task demands huge amounts of electrical energy, way beyond anything now available. Sewage treatment is just one example; the difference between the traditional and wholly inadequate methods and a modern treatment plant that gets rid of human and industrial wastes and produces rea-

sonably clear water is primarily electric power, and vast supplies of it. This poses a difficult dilemma. Power plants are themselves polluters. And one of their major pollution hazards, thermal pollution, is something we do not yet know how to handle.

Had we better postpone any serious attack on other environmental tasks until we have solved the pollution problems of electric-power generation? It would be a quixotic decision, but at least it would be a deliberate one. What is simply dishonest is the present hypocrisy that maintains we are serious about these other problems—industrial wastes, for instance, or sewage or pesticides—while we refuse to build the power plants we need to resolve them. I happen to be a member in good standing of the Sierra Club, and I share its concern for the environment. But the Sierra Club's opposition to any new power plant today—and the opposition of other groups to new power plants in other parts of the country (e.g., New York City)—has, in the first place, ensured that other ecological tasks cannot be done effectively for the next five or ten years. Secondly, it has made certain that the internal-combustion engine is going to remain our mainstay in transportation for a long time to come. An electrical automobile or electrified mass transportation—the only feasible alternatives—would require an even more rapid increase in electrical power than

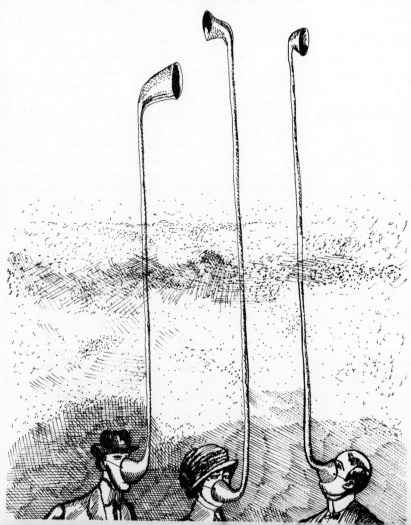

any now projected. And thirdly it may well, a few years hence, cause power shortages along the Atlantic Coast, which would mean unheated homes in winter, as well as widespread industrial shutdowns and unemployment. This would almost certainly start a "backlash" against the whole environmental crusade.

2) No matter how desirable a de-emphasis on production might be, the next decade is the wrong time for it in all the developed countries and especially in the U.S. The next decade will bring a surge in employment-seekers and in the formation of young families—both the inevitable result of the baby boom of the late Forties and early Fifties. Young adults need jobs; and unless there is a rapid expansion of jobs in production there will be massive unemployment, especially of low-skilled blacks and other minority group members. In addition to jobs, young families need goods—from housing and furniture to shoes for the baby. Even if the individual family's standard of consumption goes down quite a bit, total demand—barring only a severe depression—will go up sharply. If this is resisted in the name of ecology, environment will become a dirty word in the political vocabulary.

3) If there is no expansion of output equal to the additional cost of cleaning up the environment, the cost burden will—indeed, must—be met by cutting the funds available for education, health care, or the inner city, thus depriving the poor. It would be nice if the resources we need could come out of defense spending. But of the 6 or 7 per cent of our national income that now goes for defense, a large part is cost of past wars, that is, veterans' pensions and disability benefits (which, incidentally, most other countries do not include in their defense budgets—a fact critics of "American militarism" often ignore). Even if we could—or should—cut defense spending, the "peace dividend" is going to be 1 or 2 per cent of national income, at best.

But the total national outlay for education (7 to 8 per cent), health care (another 7 to 8 per cent), and the inner city and other poverty areas (almost 5 per cent) comes to a fifth of total national income today. Unless we raise output and productivity fast enough to offset the added environmental cost, the voters will look to this sector for money. Indeed, in their rejection of school budgets across the nation and in their desperate attempts to cut welfare costs, voters have already begun to do so. That the shift of resources is likely to be accomplished in large part through inflation—essentially at the expense of the lower-income groups—will hardly make the environmental cause more popular with the poor.

The only way to avoid these evils is to expand the economy, probably at a rate of growth on the order of 4 per cent a year for the next decade, a higher rate than we have been able to sustain in this country in the postwar years. This undoubt-edly entails very great environmental risks. But the alternative is likely to mean no environmental action at all, and a rapid public turn—by no means confined to the "hard hats"—against all environmental concern whatever.

## Making virtue pay

THE FINAL DELUSION is that the proper way to bring about a clean environment is through punitive legislation. We do need prohibitions and laws forbidding actions that endanger and degrade the environment. But more than that, we need incentives to preserve and improve it.

Punitive laws succeed only if the malefactors are few and the unlawful act is comparatively rare. Whenever the law attempts to prevent or control something everybody is doing, it degenerates into a huge but futile machine of informers, spies, bribe givers, and bribe takers. Today every one of us—in the underdeveloped countries almost as much as in the developed ones—is a polluter. Punitive laws and regulations can force automobile manufacturers to put emission controls into new cars, but they will never be able to force 100 million motorists to maintain this equipment. Yet this is going to be the central task if we are to stop automotive pollution.

What we should do is make it to everyone's advantage to reach environmental goals. And since the roots of the environmental crisis are so largely in economic activity, the incentives will have to be largely economic ones as well. Automobile owners who voluntarily maintain in working order the emission controls of their cars might, for instance, pay a much lower automobile registration fee, while those whose cars fall below accepted standards might pay a much higher fee. And if they were offered a sizable tax incentive, the automobile companies would put all their best energies to work to produce safer and emission-free cars, rather than fight delaying actions against punitive legislation.

Despite all the rhetoric on the campuses, we know by now that "capitalism" has nothing to do with the ecological crisis, which is fully as severe in the Communist countries. The bathing beaches for fifty miles around Stockholm have become completely unusable, not because of the wicked Swedish capitalists but because of the raw, untreated sewage from Communist Leningrad that drifts across the narrow Baltic. Moscow, even though it still has few automobiles, has as bad an air-pollution problem as Los Angeles—and has done less about it so far.

We should also know that "greed" has little to do with the environmental crisis. The two main causes are population pressures, especially the pressures of large metropolitan populations, and the desire—a highly commendable one—to bring a decent living at the lowest possible cost to the largest possible number of people.

The environmental crisis is the result of success—success in cutting down the mortality of infants (which has given us the population explosion), success in raising farm output sufficiently to prevent mass famine (which has given us contamination by insecticides, pesticides, and chemical fertilizers), success in getting people out of the noisome tenements of the nineteenth-century city and into the greenery and privacy of the single-family home in the suburbs (which has given us urban sprawl and traffic jams). The environmental crisis, in other words, is very largely the result of doing too much of the right sort of thing.

To overcome the problems success always creates, one has to build on it. The first step entails a willingness to take the risks involved in making decisions about complicated and perilous dilemmas:

• What is the best "trade-off" between a cleaner environment and unemployment?

• How can we prevent the environmental crusade from becoming a war of the rich against the poor, a new and particularly vicious "white racist imperialism"?

• What can we do to harmonize the worldwide needs of the environment with the political and economic needs of other countries, and to keep American leadership from becoming American aggression?

• How can we strike the least agonizing balance of risks between environmental damage and mass starvation of poor children, or between environmental damage and large-scale epidemics?

## An environmental crime?

**M**ORE THAN TWENTY YEARS AGO, three young chemical engineers came to seek my advice. They were working for one of the big chemical companies, and its managers had told them to figure out what kind of new plants to put into West Virginia, where poverty was rampant. The three young men had drawn up a long-range plan for systematic job creation, but it included one project about which their top management was very dubious—a ferroalloy plant to be located in the very poorest area where almost everybody was unemployed. It would create 1,500 jobs in a dying small town of 12,000 people and another 800 jobs for unemployed coal miners—clean, healthy, safe jobs, since the new diggings would be strip mines.

But the plant would have to use an already obsolete high-cost process, the only one for which raw materials were locally available. It would therefore be marginal in both costs and product quality. Also the process was a singularly dirty one, and putting in the best available pollution

controls would make it even less economical. Yet it was the only plant that could possibly be put in the neediest area. What did I think?

I said, "forget it"—which was, of course, not what the three young men wanted to hear and not the advice they followed.

This, as some readers have undoubtedly recognized, is the prehistory of what has become a notorious "environmental crime," the Union Carbide plant in Marietta, Ohio. When first opened in 1951 the plant was an "environmental pioneer." Its scrubbers captured three-quarters of the particles spewed out by the smelting furnaces; the standard at the time was half of that or less. Its smokestacks suppressed more fly ash than those of any other power plant then built, and so on.

But within ten years the plant had become an unbearable polluter to Vienna, West Virginia, the small town across the river whose unemployment it was built to relieve. And for the last five years the town and Union Carbide fought like wildcats. In the end Union Carbide lost. But while finally accepting federal and state orders to clean up an extremely dirty process, it also announced that it would have to lay off half the 1,500 men now working in the plant—and that's half the people employed in Vienna. The switch to cleaner coal (not to mention the abandonment of strip mining) would also put an end to the

"Practically every environmental task demands huge amounts of electrical energy, way beyond anything now available. . . .This poses a difficult dilemma. Power plants are themselves polluters."

Eugene Mihaesco

800 or so coal-mining jobs in the poverty hollows of the back country.

There are scores of Viennas around the nation, where marginal plants are kept running precisely because they are the main or only employer in a depressed or decaying area. Should an uneconomical plant shut down, dumping its workers on the welfare rolls? Should the plant be subsidized (which would clearly open the way for everybody to put his hand in the public till)? Should environmental standards be disregarded or their application postponed in "hardship" cases?

If concern for the environment comes to be seen as an attack on the livelihood of workers, public sympathy and political support for it is likely to vanish. It is not too fanciful to anticipate, only a few years hence, the New (if aging) Left, the concerned kids on the campus, and the ministers in a protest march against "ecology" and in support of "the victims of bourgeois environmentalism."

## Third World ecology

IN THE POOR, DEVELOPING COUNTRIES where men must struggle to make even a little progress in their fight against misery, any industry bears a heavy burden of high costs and low productivity. Burdening it further with the cost of environmental control might destroy it. Moreover, development in these countries—regardless of their political creed or social organization, in Mao's as well as in Chiang Kai-shek's China and in North as well as in South Vietnam—cannot occur without the four biggest ecological villains: a rapid increase in electric power, chemical fertilizers and pesticides, the automobile, and the large steel mill.

That poor countries regard those villains as economic saviors confronts us with hard political choices. Should we help such countries get what they want (industrialization), or what we think the world needs (less pollution)? How do we avoid the charge, in either case, that our help is "imperialistic"? To complicate matters, there is a looming conflict between environmental concern and national sovereignty. The environment knows no national boundaries. Just as the smog of England befouls the air of Norway, so the chemical wastes of the French potash mines in Alsace destroy the fish of the lower Rhine in Belgium and Holland.

No matter what the statistics bandied about today, the U.S. is not the world's foremost polluter. Japan holds this dubious honor by a good margin. No American city can truly compete in air pollution with Tokyo, Milan, Budapest, Moscow, or Düsseldorf. No American river is as much of an open sewer as the lower Rhine, the Seine, or the rivers of the industrial Ukraine such as the lower Dnieper. And we are sheer amateurs in littering highways compared to the Italians, Danes, Germans, French, Swedes, Swiss, and Austrians—although the Japanese, especially in littering mountainsides and camp grounds, are clearly even more "advanced."

If not the worst polluter, however, the U.S. is clearly the largest one. More important, as the most affluent, most advanced, and biggest of the industrial countries, it is expected to set an example. If we do not launch the environmental crusade, no one else will.

We shall have to make sure, however, that other nations join with us. In the absence of international treaties and regulations, some countries—especially those with protectionist traditions, such as Japan, France, and even the United States—may be tempted to impose ecological standards on imports more severe than those they demand of their own producers. On the other hand, countries heavily dependent on exports, especially in Africa and Latin America, may try to gain a competitive advantage by lax enforcement of environmental standards.

One solution might be action by the United Nations to fix uniform rules obliging all its members to protect the environment; and such action is, in fact, now under official study. The United States might help by changing its import regulations to keep out goods produced by flagrant polluters—allowing ample time for countries with severe poverty and unemployment problems to get the cleanup under way. We have good precedent for such an approach in our own history. Forty years ago we halted the evils of child labor by forbidding the transportation in interstate commerce of goods produced by children.

Such a course, however, will demand extraordinary judgment. Unless we persuade other nations to join with us—and set an example ourselves—we may well be accused of trying again to "police the world."

## Choosing the lesser evils

THE HARDEST DECISIONS AHEAD are even more unprecedented than those we have been discussing. What risks can we afford to take with the environment, and what risks can we *not* afford to take? What are the feasible trade-offs between man's various needs for survival?

Today, for example, no safe pesticides exist, nor are any in sight. We may ban DDT, but all the substitutes so far developed have highly undesirable properties. Yet if we try to do without pesticides altogether, we shall invite massive hazards of disease and starvation the world over. In Ceylon, where malaria was once endemic, it was almost wiped out by large-scale use of DDT; but in only a few years since spraying was halted, the country has suffered an almost explosive resurgence of the disease. In other tropical countries, warns the UN Food and Agricultural Organization, children are threatened with famine, because of insect and blight damage to crops resulting from restrictions on spraying. Similarly, anyone who has lately traveled the New England turnpike will have noticed whole forests defoliated by the gypsy moth, now that we have stopped aerial spraying.

What is the right trade-off between the health hazard to some women taking the pill and the risk of death to others from abortions? How do we balance the thermal and radiation dangers of nuclear power plants against the need for more electricity to fight other kinds of pollution? How should we choose between growing more food for the world's fast-multiplying millions and the banning of fertilizers that pollute streams, lakes, and oceans?

Such decisions should not be demanded of human beings. None of the great religions offers guidance. Neither do the modern "isms," from Maoism to the anarchism popular with the young. The ecological crisis forces man to play God. Despite the fact that we are unequal to the task, we can't avoid it: the risks inherent in refusing to tackle these problems are the greatest of all. We have to try, somehow, to choose some combination of lesser evils; doing nothing invites even greater catastrophe.

## Where to start

CLEANING UP THE ENVIRONMENT requires determined, sustained effort with clear targets and deadlines. It requires, above all, concentration of effort. Up to now we have had almost complete diffusion. We have tried to do a little bit of everything—and tried to do it in the headlines—when what we ought to do first is draw up a list of priorities in their proper order.

First on such a list belong a few small but clearly definable and highly visible tasks that can be done fairly fast without tying up important resources. Removing the hazard of lead poisoning in old slum tenements might be such an action priority. What to do is well known: burn off the old paint. A substantial number of underemployed black adolescents could be easily recruited to do it.

Once visible successes have been achieved, the real task of priority-setting begins. Then one asks: 1) what are the biggest problems that we know how to solve, and (2) what are the really big ones that we don't know how to solve yet? Clean air should probably head the first list. It's a worldwide problem, and getting worse. We don't know all the answers, but we do have the technological competence to handle most of the problems of foul air today. Within ten years we should have real results to show for our efforts.

Within ten years, too, we should get major results in cleaning up the water around big industrial cities and we should have slowed (if not stopped) the massive pollution of the oceans, especially in the waters near our coastal cities.

As for research priorities, I suggest that the first is to develop birth-control methods that are cheaper, more effective, and more acceptable to people of all cultures than anything we now have. Secondly, we need to learn how to produce electric energy without thermal pollution. A third priority is to devise ways of raising crops for a rapidly growing world population without at the same time doing irreversible ecological damage through pesticides, herbicides, and chemical fertilizers.

Until we get the answers, I think we had better keep on building power plants and growing food with the help of fertilizers and such insect-controlling chemicals as we now have. The risks are now well known, thanks to the environmentalists. If they had not created a widespread public awareness of the ecological crisis, we wouldn't stand a chance. But such awareness by itself is not enough. Flaming manifestos and prophecies of doom are no longer much help, and a search for scapegoats can only make matters worse.

What we now need is a coherent, long-range program of action, and education of the public and our lawmakers about the steps necessary to carry it out. We must recognize—and we need the help of environmentalists in this task—that we can't do everything at once; that painful choices have to be made, as soon as possible, about what we should tackle first; and that every decision is going to involve high risks and costs, in money and in human lives. Often these will have to be decisions of conscience as well as economics. Is it better, for example, to risk famine or to risk global pollution of earth and water? Any course we adopt will involve a good deal of experimentation—and that means there will be some failures. Any course also will demand sacrifices, often from those least able to bear them: the poor, the unskilled, and the underdeveloped countries. To succeed, the environmental crusade needs support from all major groups in our society, and the mobilization of all our resources, material and intellectual, for years of hard, slow, and often discouraging effort. Otherwise it will not only fail; it will, in the process, splinter domestic and international societies into warring factions.

Now that they have succeeded in awakening us to our ecological peril, I hope the environmentalists will turn their energies to the second and harder task: educating the public to accept the choices we must face, and to sustain a worldwide effort to carry through on the resulting decisions. The time for sensations and manifestos is about over; now we need rigorous analysis, united effort, and very hard work.  □

"Despite all the rhetoric on the campuses, we know by now that 'capitalism' has nothing to do with the ecological crisis, which is fully as severe in the Communist countries."

# CITIES, CROWDING & CRIME

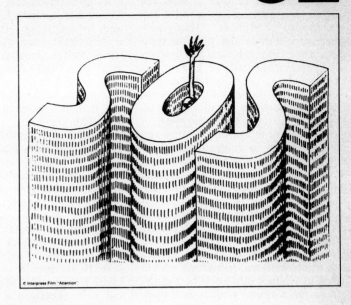

© Interpress Film "Attention"

## Recent studies strengthen the evidence that crowding contributes to social problems and crime

by Robert J. Trotter

Sexual perversion, irrational and excessive aggression, increased mortality rates, lowered fertility rates, maternal neglect of young, withdrawal and other psychotic behavior—these are among the reactions of rats, monkeys, hares, shrews and fish that have been experimentally forced to live in overcrowded conditions. Are overcrowded human populations subject to this type of psychological and physiological disintegration? Can such reactions, for instance, explain or in part account for crime in the crowded cities?

At the recent meeting of the American Psychological Association, psychologists reported results of new studies on the effects of crowding on humans. One study was conducted in the Netherlands, one of the most densely populated countries in the world (323 persons per square kilometer). Leo Levy and Allen N. Herzog of the University of Illinois Medical Center in Chicago compared high-density areas to low-density areas and found that higher density appeared to be positively related to such things as deaths due to heart disease, admissions to hospitals and mental hospitals, juvenile delinquency, illegitimacy, divorce and infant mortality. In Honolulu density was related to adult and infant death rates, TB, VD and prison rates. In Chicago one measure of density, the number of people per room, was correlated

with various types of social disintegration (SN: 4/15/72, p. 247). All of these findings tend to support some of the results of animal studies and suggest that human crowding is related to social disintegration and crime.

Arousal, stress, anxiety and frustration seem to be among the important results of crowding that can lead to personal and social degeneration. One thing that can sometimes lead to stress or anxiety, for instance, is infringement on personal space. Personal space or interpersonal physical distance (IPD) is defined as the area surrounding a person's body into which intruders may not come. Gay H. Price and James M. Dabbs Jr. of Georgia State University investigated the effects of age and sex on IPD. They found that personal space requirements become larger as children grow older. First grade boys and girls allowed another child to approach until a comfortable conversational distance was reported. Both boys and girls showed an IPD of 0.30 meters—about 12 inches. As children grow older, however, they need more personal space. Females in the 12th grade needed 0.45 meters and males the same age needed 0.60 meters. Other studies have shown cultural and racial differences in desired interaction distances. British and Germanic people prefer to interact at a greater distance than do Middle Eastern or Latin American people.

Blacks tend to interact at greater distances than do whites. Maintaining this personal space is not always easy in a crowded city, and overly close contact with strangers can sometimes lead to psychological discomfort and may even be perceived as threatening. This, in turn, can lead to arousal, anxiety and stress that can be physically harmful and that can sometimes lead to antisocial activity.

Yokov M. Epstein and John R. Aiello of Rutgers University have made physiological measures of arousal caused by crowding. Skin conductance levels were used as a measure of arousal. The subjects were monitored as they sat quietly in either a crowded or noncrowded room. Arousal increased over time in both conditions, but arousal increased significantly under the crowded conditions. And arousal was higher under all conditions for men.

In another set of experiments Epstein and Robert A. Karlin examined some of the social and behavioral effects of crowding. According to their definition, social crowding exists when the distance between individuals is less than the expected appropriate distance for a particular setting. What is appropriate in the bedroom, for instance, is not appropriate in the subway. Whenever the appropriate distance is not maintained, say Epstein and Karlin, stress reaction can result. Such things as heat, odors, noise and bodily contact add to the perception of crowding.

What happens socially when crowding is perceived? Groups of men and women were subjected to crowded and noncrowded conditions. They were given various tests and tasks to complete while their reactions and interactions were monitored. In general, report Epstein and Karlin, crowded men concealed their distress from each other, became competitive and developed attitudes of distrust and hostility—all of which can lead to aggression, stress and crime. Women, in contrast, have usually been subjected to social norms and training that allow them to react quite differently. They tend to share their distress. In a number of crowding experiments women reacted as if they were in the same boat rather than becoming competitive. They formed cooperative groups. There were usually positive sentiments between individuals. When asked to evaluate other members of the group, the crowded women gave more positive evaluations than did the noncrowded women or any of the men's groups.

One reason for criminal activity and social breakdown, therefore, may be that when crowded, men feel more negatively about each other, become more competitive, fight with each other and even become more disposed to engage in criminal activity to achieve their own ends at each other's expense.

A slightly different explanation is the "overload theory." Stanley Milgram of the City University of New York has explained how the overload theory works. People in overcrowded cities, he suggests, are constantly bombarded by sensory stimuli (horns honking, phones ringing, lights flashing, people talking, etc., etc.) at such a rate that not all stimuli can be processed. To adapt to this sensory overload, city people tend to allocate less time to each input, disregard certain low priority inputs and decrease involvement with other people. These factors lead to a lower level of social responsibility and hence a lower rate of intervention in criminal activity. Where intervention is not expected, crime rates tend to increase.

Experiments conducted by Donna Gelfand of the University of Utah tend to confirm Milgram's theory. People raised in small towns reported shoplifting (done by an experimenter) at about twice the rate of people raised in large cities. Gelfand suggests that people raised in rural areas learn that they must rely on their neighbors while city dwellers learn to rely on municipal services. Therefore, an urbanite who sees a crime being committed is likely to let the police handle it rather than

get personally involved.

Frustration also affects criminal activity, and frustration has become almost an accepted fact of city life. Annoying interruptions, for example, often lead to frustration. Ineffective phone service, traffic and parking problems, transit strikes, construction noises and many other daily happenings interrupt life and lead to frustrations. And frustrations can lead to criminal behavior, says R. Lance Shotland of Pennsylvania State University.

Milgram and Shotland demonstrated experimentally how frustration can play a part in property crimes. They sent letters inviting people to come to a Manhattan theater to rate a television program. As a reward the subjects were to receive transistor radios. The subjects rated the program and were told where they could pick up their radios. They were sent to different offices that were fronts for the experiment. The offices looked real. They were furnished and each contained a charity display with about $14 in bills and change in it. There were no people in the offices and the subjects were monitored by closed circuit television.

In the high-frustration condition a rude message in the office said that no more free radios would be distributed until further notice. No reason was given for the empty office. In the low-frustration condition the message was apologetic. It explained that the workers were ill and that the radios could be picked up in another office. In the high-frustration condition 18.7 percent of the subjects stole something from the office including charity money, ash trays, plants, tools, etc. In the low-frustration condition only 2.9 percent of the subjects took anything.

The frustrations of life are increased for the lower class members of society. The Report of the National Advisory Commission on Civil Disorder stated that "middle-class citizens, although subject to many of the same frustrations and resentments in dealing with the public bureaucracy as ghetto residents, find it relatively easier to locate the proper agency for help and redress." Therefore, says Shotland, "One might expect and obtain more criminal activity from the lower class as they are more frustrated. They cannot use communication with a representative of government or a real or theoretical law suit as a substitute for aggression. They do not feel that they have any control over the annoyance."

With good evidence that crowding does contribute to social problems and increased criminal activity, is there any hope that crime rates can be lowered in the already overcrowded cities? Hong Kong is the most densely populated

area in the world (3,912 persons per square kilometer) yet its crime rate is only half that of the United States (22 persons per square kilometer). So crowding need not always be a great contributing factor to criminal activity. Cultural attitudes are involved. The people of Hong Kong react differently to crowding than do the people of the United States. Similarly, women react differently to crowding than do men. But changing the cultural patterns, even if possible, would be only a long-range solution to the problems caused by crowding. It will be as difficult to achieve as eliminating poverty.

Architectural design, some have suggested, is a possible and more immediate solution to some of the problems caused by crowding. "Architecture will not eliminate poverty or other conditions surrounding it," says Shotland. But there are certain conditions that architecture can effect. Movable walls and ceilings can lend flexibility to a setting and allow people to increase personal space when necessary. Other architectural strategies can help make crime and criminals more visible and easier to report. But in areas where there is a high turnover of residents, says Shotland, intruders cannot be easily identified. All neighbors begin to look like strangers, and architectural design is not much help.

New York's Chinatown has traditionally had a low crime rate. But in recent years street crime has increased in Chinatown. Indications are that this may be due to an increase in population and immigration from the Orient. Little Italy, adjacent to Chinatown, has comparatively little crime. Architecturally, both neighborhoods are the same, a grid pattern of tenements. Little Italy, however, has a stable population and has not had a great influx of strangers. The residents know each other, says Shotland, and can and do recognize and challenge strangers. Correct architecture cannot guarantee a knowledge of one's neighbors but it can, he says, foster this knowledge by designing so there are only a small number of neighbors to be recognized. Increased contact between neighbors leads to friendships and raises the rate of bystander intervention. In conclusion, Shotland says, architectural design can only contribute toward the lowering of crime rates. It is not a panacea and is no guarantee of reduced crime rates.

A total solution to the many problems caused by crowding is not in sight. Ongoing and future research on human crowding should, however, continue to offer additional clues to the solution of crime in the crowded cities. ◻

# THE GREAT AMERICAN MEDICAL RIP-OFF: WHY PATIENTS ARE RUNNING OUT

## By Herb Denenberg

The modern miracle of medicine is not hooking someone up to a heart-lung machine and letting the blood flow in and out. It's hooking most of us up to health insurance policies and letting the money flow from patients to health care providers in a never-ending stream, with little or no regard for the value or quality of the health care being provided in return.

We spend more and more, financing ever-expanding hospitals, other capital plants, and medical technologies. This produces a self-perpetuating inflation of medical care costs, health insurance costs, and expansion of hospital facilities and services.

The medical care providers have outdone Midas. He had to touch things to turn them into gold. The medical care system no longer has to touch one item and then the next. It has the system rigged to run on automatic cycles, changing all the disease and death that comes within its purview into a steady river of gold.

### Rip-Off One:
### Automatic Inflation

Blue Cross and Blue Shield are the classic prototypes. There are 70 different Blue Cross and Blue Shield organizations, which operate in every state. Many of these plans are still dominated by doctors and hospitals, which control or strongly influence their boards.

In 18 states, Blue Cross still pays hospitals the cost of providing services, plus a bonus of about 2-to-5 percent. That cost-plus factor is rationalized as payment for contingencies, for free care provided by the hospital, for growth and development, or for some other purpose. What it assures is continued head-long expansion and frequent premium increases. Cost-plus contracts, as the

Defense Department discovered, are formulas for bankruptcy of the payer and exorbitant expenditures for the payee.

Blue Cross plans often work on the assumption of continuous and fantastic inflation. Blue Cross of Philadelphia is now writing group policies on the automatic assumption that there will be an 18 percent annual increase in hospital costs. It writes contracts on that assumption, with the proviso that the premium will be adjusted later. But the system is fine-tuned to assure that the greediest projections are realized.

These inflationary cycles can be largely explained by this hookup between health insurance and health delivery, but they are also facilitated by the assumption that the more you spend, the more likely the cure. In many cases, the reverse is true. The system is notorious for grinding people up by unnecessary surgery, excessive and unsafe hospitalization, and untested and dangerous technologies and therapies.

The classic example is the open-heart surgery unit. In Philadelphia alone, in recent years, there have been about a dozen units not operating at sufficient capacity, according to standards promulgated by medical experts. That means excessive costs and excessive mortality. Practice makes perfect; lack of practice makes cadavers.

Automatic inflation is encouraged by a system which puts new technology and procedures in place without testing their cost-effectiveness or even their medical effectiveness. And it's facilitated by the public's willingness to spend anything to cure illness, such free spending being further inspired at decision-making time if the bill is picked up by an insurance company rather than the patient.

And this is all established by a medical environment in which the patient's decisions are often made by the doctors, who seem to be captivated more by expensive technologies and intensive methods of treatment than by the patient's desires or welfare.

This trend is likely to get worse, not better. By the celebration of our tercentenary, we can look forward to one day in the hospital costing over $200 million. By then, undoubtedly, all of our resources will be devoted to health care, and everyone will have their own hospital bed. These numbers are based on straightforward projections which are no more farfetched than what we have now, with hospital costs inflating at the rate of $24 million a day (or $1 million an hour) across the country.

Blue Cross talks incessantly about cost and quality control, but is too timid and unimaginative to do anything substantial. Its recent New Year's resolution to control hospital costs and insurance premiums will require investigations of possible fraud and abuse, and internal screening to evaluate the necessity of hospitalization. This is generally a recital of basic and obvious steps that they should have taken years ago, and only proves Blue Cross is negligent and incompetent at protecting its subscribers.

But that is only rip-off number one. Health insurance is a never-ending telescopic array of rip-offs—or perhaps it can be more neatly compared to the sets of Russian dolls which fit one into another.

## Rip-Off Two: By and For Doctors

Both the health insurance and health delivery system are controlled by the providers of care rather than the recipients of care and the financers of care. This decision-making power is built into the very system, from top to bottom.

The Secretary of Health in many states must be a doctor. Most licensing and disciplining boards are dominated entirely by doctors or controlled by them. The hospital boards and other institutions within the system are responsive to doctors. Even the health insurers may be controlled directly and indirectly by providers. Blue Shield, which pays doctor bills, is often controlled by a doctor-dominated board of directors.

The results are outrageous. While Insurance Commissioner, I asked Pennsylvania Blue Shield what it did with a doctor it discovered perpetrating gross, fraudulent overcharges on that insurance plan. The answer: The doctor was asked to return the overcharges, without interest.

The fundamental malaise of the system, however, is not based on structure alone but on general attitudes. The public walks away from any decision that seems in any way to have a medically related component. The medical doctors, who often seem less than competent at resolving their own medical questions, are given *carte blanche* to decide broader economic and social questions,

such as which of their competitors in health care will be authorized to practice, to be licensed, and to be compensated under the health insurance system.

For example, the American Medical Association has often successfully opposed the development of nurse-midwives who are willing to work when women need them. Doctors have often frozen chiropractors out of the reimbursement schedules in Blue Shield policies, and it is the medical profession which has led the way in establishing unreasonable restrictions on lab technicians and paraprofessionals.

This unearned, undeserved, and unhealthy medical omnipotence can be neatly illustrated by one small provision found in many health insurance contracts. It provides that there will be payment for a medical consultant if he is requested by another doctor. If requested only by the patient, whose head and pocketbook are on the line, no provision is made for reimbursement.

The doctors can even put deadly pressure on alternative forms of health delivery which they do not like. For decades, segments of medicine have tried to thwart the growth of Health Maintenance Organizations (HMO's) such as Health Insurance Plan of New York and Kaiser-Permanente. These HMO's provide complete medical services for a fixed fee and often have doctors on a salaried basis. In this way, they cut incentives for excessive treatment and emphasize preventive medicine. The Federal Trade Commission has now launched one of its endless investigations into the anti-HMO conduct of certain groups of doctors.

## Rip-Off Three: Orthodoxy and Incest

By controlling the flow and direction of money, this insurance and delivery system stunts the growth of promising, economical innovations.

The system has always favored surgery, for example, rather than less expensive alternatives. Surgeons are the movers and shakers of medicine, the politicians of medicine, and their power is reflected in the handsome schedules of surgical payments commonly found in health insurance policies.

A surgeon who advises against surgery may not even be paid under an insurance contract. Surgeons counseling caution have little financial incentive to do so; surgeons who are cheerleaders for incisions prosper.

The predominance of much that is overdone in medicine is encouraged by the present health insurance system. Other notable examples are hospitalization rather than out-patient or home care; the ministrations of a medical doctor rather than some other health care provider such as a nutritionist, psychologist, chiropractor, or pharmacist; and the use of radical medical therapies such as surgery or drugs rather than diet, exercise, or some cheaper and safer alternative.

There are almost no dollars from the insurance system for prevention or education. The alcoholic or other drug addict, who might be best treated in a specialized facility, may not be insured at all for such care, because it is not in the confines of a traditional hospital. Hospitals are primarily the doctor's workshop and business, not the place to meet the needs of the patient.

Medical research, for example, means M.D. research, and other health care providers—such as osteopaths, chiropractors, pharmacists, podiatrists, optometrists, and others—are likely to be on the outside looking in. Groups of health care providers not viewed with favor by the M.D.'s get

virtually no Government research funding. Out of $1.2 billion in research grants offered to universities by the National Institute of Health in 1976, osteopaths received just $733,000, and chiropractors, nothing.

## Rip-Off Four:
## Self-perpetuation

The bulk of health insurance is written by the Blues (Blue Cross and Blue Shield), non-profit insurance companies often dominated by doctors and hospitals, and by mutual life insurance companies, which are supposedly controlled by policyholders, but which in fact are run by a small group of management.

This sets up unrestrained economic and political power which can lobby to perpetuate the present system. For example, public owners of Prudential, the largest insurance corporation in the world, received a little folder with their last premium notice. Labeled "A Message of Concern to Every American," it advocated a national health insurance system run "by the insurance industry in cooperation with the Federal government." Management can freely use policyholders' money to lobby to achieve their objectives.

Is there any control over all of this? In the case of most corporations, such lobbying expenses are not deductible, but IRS does not really enforce that provision, I've been told by Congressional staff researchers. But the question may be academic in case of a mutual life insurance company. When I asked Prudential about the deductibility of such lobbying expenses, it said its tax is based only on investment income. So it is apparently not penalized in any way by the IRS for free-spending lobbying.

This process of self-perpetuation is made easier by a regulatory system subject to the influence of insurers, and remote from anything vaguely suggestive of consumer influence. For example, 40 percent of the nation's insurance commissioners come right out of the insurance industry and go right back in when their government tenure is over. Even Governor Jerry Brown of California, who talks so much of consumer control, appointed a lifelong insurance executive as his insurance commissioner.

### Rip-off Five:
### The Unsold Majority

Despite the unique influence and power of the insurance industry, it leaves many Americans uninsured and underinsured. The costs of health care are one of the leading causes of bankruptcy, but the insurance industry hardly seems to be ready to respond at all to public needs, even when it might profit the insurers themselves.

The Congressional Budget Office has concluded that 114 million Americans have inadequate health insurance protection against the catastrophic cost of health care. Some of this vacuum is based on economic deprivation. But much of it is based on an inadequate sales effort by the health insurance industry and by Blue Cross and Blue Shield.

The main sales effort has been focused on group health insurance sales. Those not eligible for group coverage find themselves in an insurance no man's land. The health insurance industry and its salesmen view individual health insurance as involving too many claims, too much administrative work, and too much effort to justify it.

The life insurance salesman knows you'll only die once. The health insurance salesman knows he can expect multiple claims over the years.

This leaves room for marginal companies, which often shortchange and defraud the public. The worst of this was evidenced by health insurers selling by mail in the early 1970's. The widespread abuses of that era are gone, but similar abuse exists, and much of the industry still does not compete for individual health insurance. This problem is further complicated by limitations in the insurance law which restrict the types of groups eligible for group marketing.

If the insurance industry does not do a more effective job of selling individual coverage, alternative techniques should be considered, or new incentives introduced. Some of the deficiencies in the market could be eliminated by state insurance departments if they published usable and up to date "Shopper's Guides."

The "Shopper's Guide" which I authored as insurance commissioner not only described the kind of policies and provisions to look for, but also rated companies by financial strength and percentage of premium dollars returned to its policyholders. The Guide recommended against 16 of the 25 largest commercial health insurance companies. This tradition has been widely copied by other insurance commissioners but their guides have typically omitted the names and ratings of specific companies.

### Rip-off Six, Seven, Etc.

We still have Mickey Mouse policies, with tricky exclusions and laughable benefits, with unfair cancellation and non-renewal provisions, with unreadable language. We still have claims settlement policies that jerk the public around, with no-pay and slow-pay policies. We still have competition by variation and confusion, rather than that based on price and service.

A while back I checked out some cancer policies for sale and found they promised payment for treatment of cancer—but *not* the complications of cancer or adverse effects of its treatment. So if chemotherapy or radiation cause side effects requiring hospitalization, that hospital bill would not be covered.

We still have much of the traditional discrimination of health insurance against such groups as women and even newborn children. Many policies single out maternity benefits for sharp limitation. Some policies do not provide coverage for newborn infants for the first 14 days of their life. That's when they need hospital care the most, and needless to say, they are hardly in a position to assert their rights.

And we still have a predominance of financially questionable companies. Those with access to advice are usually told to stick to insurance companies that get at least an A rating from Best's

Insurance Reports, the leading publishing authority on insurance company strength. That excludes about 80 percent of licensed companies.

## Rights and Remedies

The health insurance rip-off is by no means unique. It's the classic model of what happens when the public sleeps on its rights and responsibilities, and lets some special interest group walk off with the store.

We have a health insurance and health delivery system subject to government of the providers, by the providers, and for the providers. We have to make the system subject to governance of the people, by the people, and for the people.

That is a task easy to formulate and difficult to execute. The public must understand the issues of health insurance and health care. The public must organize so it can exert its will on private institutions and government which influence health insurance and health care. And the public must start working its will on the personnel and politicians who run these systems at variance with the public's best interests.

First, the public has the right to know, but it also has the responsibility to find out. If the typical consumer would spend as much time finding out the answers *before* his decision as he spends crying after the results are in, all of our problems would be solved. He has to start eliminating companies of questionable financial strength and policies of questionable economic value. This process could be facilitated by consumer groups, by government, and by the media if they would provide meaningful and specific consumer information.

The same kind of know-how has to be exercised by consumers in making decisions about health care. A typical patient will plop onto an operating table at the faintest call for surgery, without a question and without exercising his or her own judgment, and often without a second medical opinion. He or she is now anesthetized into abdicating responsibility to a doctor who often has the willingness but not the competence to play God and to make decisions on matters peculiarly within the knowledge and competence of the patient. Only the patient has the information to de-

cide, for example, if he or she wants to run the risks of proposed surgery, drug therapy, or other medical treatment.

And that same patient and policyholder has a right and responsibility to have meaningful input, participation, and control in formulating the basic decisions incident to health insurance and health care. That means, for example, as a policyholder of Blue Cross and Blue Shield, he has some obligation to shift their focus from protecting and enriching doctors and hospitals, to saving the lives and bank accounts of patients and policyholders. That means that knowledgeable consumers should be sitting on Blue Cross boards.

Health insurers should be the countervailing force representing the consumer in the health delivery marketplace. In other words, the public has to make its health insurers perform like consumer cooperatives rather than provider puppets. The same might be said for hospital boards and health service agencies, the public bodies now operating in all communities, to police the authorization of hospitals and other new medical facilities.

In the final analysis, health insurance and medical problems have been and will continue to be political problems. We may change the technology, inflate the bills, expand the empires, but we will continue to have precisely the same kind of problems until we have a more responsive political system, propelled by the public.

What we have now in medicine and health insurance is simply the standard model of how our system lets those who control the system profit by it. Any change will require the most simple and yet most radical reform—participation and control by the public. We cannot make a system respond to the public interest if the public is not mobilized to formulate and insist on that interest.

The health insurance-health delivery system is a noble and enduring monument to our own failure to apply those pressures and to perform our responsibilities as citizens.  □

---

*Herb Denenberg served as Pennsylvania Insurance Commissioner from 1971 to 1974 and is a member of the Institute of Medicine of the National Academy of Sciences. He is currently a consumer reporter in Philadelphia.*

# 54

# The Imperial Press

## by Tom Bethell and Charles Peters

The day before Daniel Schorr was to testify before the House Ethics Committee, the Newspaper Guild held a press conference to drum up support for him. It was a solemn and awe-inspiring affair. The Guild, the labor union for journalists, had rounded up Seymour Hersh, Carl Bernstein, Mary McGrory, and various other big guns of the media, and it was clear that it considered the whole Schorr affair Serious Business. The press conference itself was held in one of the House's own office buildings. In front of the room was a row of media celebrities, and facing them was a row of less celebrated journalists who were reporting on the affair.

Anyone who looked at the Schorr case could see that Congress' vote to make the Pike Report secret was perfectly ridiculous. It was good that the report was published because there was no reason for the informa-

tion it contained to be kept out of the public's reach. Still, watching the press conference, one got the sense that perhaps things were going too far. Under the hot flame of self-righteousness, all sorts of principles were coalescing, so that it was becoming impossible to tell them apart. Protection of sources, First Amendment, people's right to know, freedom of the press, freedom of speech—these were the kind of weighty phrases being bandied about, and they all seemed to be very close—nearly identical—in meaning.

The procession of important journalists at the press conference began with Dan Rather of CBS, whose comments were representative of both the tone and content of the afternoon. "I am uncomfortable as a participant in events," he said, "preferring to cover events. If you believe nothing else believe this, that I decided to come here because I believe this matter is of such overriding importance, and

*Tom Bethell is a contributing editor and Charles Peters editor-in-chief of* The Washington Monthly.

because my conscience would not allow me to do otherwise. These words are said humbly, even prayerfully. . . ." On it went. Finally Rather got to the point, which was that "the issue is whether we are going to preserve something essential in a democracy: freedom of the press, including the freedom to protect sources of information. This is not for the benefit of reporters. It is for the benefit of listeners and viewers and readers. . . . The cause is America."

Such is the mood of the press these days: earnest, weary from the long battle. Mulling it all over somehow conjures up in the mind images of a long series of newsroom civics seminars: The managing editor is toiling over the next day's front-page dummy, deciding which arrangement of stories will most strengthen the spirit of freedom in his community, when his star reporter bursts in with leaked documents. They hold a fevered conference, wrestling with their consciences to determine whether publication of the documents will be in the public interest. Maybe they consult the Constitution, or the Jefferson-Adams letters. If they decide to go ahead, well, damn the consequences. . . .

The civics class may not precisely exist, but it's certainly the prevailing image these days. Amid all the press' self-promotion there's been a disruption of balance, by which a set of indisputably good causes begin to expand and envelop some other, not so indisputably good ones. It's understandable that nobody seems to be noticing this—the press usually notices people's little pomposities and obscurings of issues. If it's the press that's now the culprit, it's not likely to start chastising itself.

It's not likely, for instance, that the press will mention this, but if sources weren't protected, the reporters who so courageously protect them would be far less important themselves. The importance of reporters and the protection of sources seem, in fact, inextricably linked. Where would Woodward and Bernstein be today if Deep Throat had called a press conference?

The fact is that reporters have a direct stake in the encouragement of a timid government service. If sources weren't shadowy figures—if they were forced to speak up publicly and take their chances if they wanted to leak in the service of justice—the journalist wouldn't be the glamor-boy he is today; he wouldn't be holding press conferences. In adding up the pluses and minuses of total protection of sources, it ought to be remembered that the press' interest is not in having the noblest possible government. Federal employees with damaging information about the government are most useful to reporters when they are most afraid of losing their jobs. On the whole, they're most useful to the rest of us when they're not afraid, or cautious, or prone to hiding their true opinions and not telling the boss when he's doing something wrong. Precisely the opposite, in fact, is where the public interest lies.

## From Tradesmen to Professionals

It's not hard to see why the issue of reporters' importance should be such a key one today. Journalists in this century, to put it simply, have undergone a phenomenal rise in status, a rise similar to the one doctors and lawyers went through in the last century. They've gone from being tradesmen to being professionals. In the old days "the media" referred to a motley collection of $50-a-week newspapermen, not journalists (a journalist was some kind of a remote fop with a cane whom one never saw)— newspapermen with green eyeshades and half empty liquor bottles next to the typewriter. In 1922 the literary editor of the *Boston Herald* wrote that "as a citizen, a workman, a human being, the journalist is. . . nothing but a wage-earning servant, as impotent and unimportant, considered as an individual, as a mill hand." Only in the 1950s, in most instances, did general reporters begin to be paid more than the printers who worked downstairs in the pressroom.

Much of the change is due to the applaudable efforts of the Newspaper Guild, and most of its net effects are indisputably good. But the professionalization process is a tricky one; it carries with it a lot of excess baggage and mumbo-jumbo. It's not, that is, without elements of priestification as well. Professionals, once firmly established, tend to claim adherence to some noble higher principle that, by the way, allows them to greatly increase their own income and power while no one is looking, in a way that is often inimicable to the public interest. Everybody now recognizes that this has to some extent been the case with doctors and lawyers, so it was distressing, back at the press conference, to hear the comparisons that were being bandied about.

At one point in the press conference Larry Larson of the *Fresno Bee* read a statement written especially by the Fresno Four "for this news conference." The Four, who were briefly in jail for disobeying a judge's orders by printing secret grand jury testimony, had gotten to the heart of the matter:

"Sooner or later, we must make judges, congressmen, and others in official positions aware that newsmen, like lawyers, doctors and clergymen, adhere to professional ethics, which we cannot ignore. The public's right to know what their government is doing is a paramount concern in a free democracy. And the need for confidential sources is an important test of our profession."

In a similar vein, in another hearing room the next day at the actual House Committee hearing, Schorr had this to say in his defense: "For some of us—doctors, lawyers, clergymen, *and* journalists—it is an article of faith that we must keep confidential those matters entrusted to us only because of the assurance that they would remain confidential."

The Fresno Four and Schorr were right about the privileges that accrue to doctors, lawyers, and clergy. The effect of those privileges is only to help the person who has confidential information; it makes it easier for him to receive professional services. In the case of doctors' privilege, for instance, the patient will become more frank, in order that he may receive better health care and be spared embarrassment about his ailments; but since privilege or no privilege, a sick person will see his doctor, the doctor himself is hardly affected at all by the arrangement.

## Secrets That Have To Be Kept

In the case of reporters' privilege the equation is somewhat different. It is designed to encourage the passage of information from government officials to reporters, on the grounds that

such passage, absolutely unhampered, will always work to the public's benefit. While other professionals' privilege tends to keep more information secret, the press' tends to make more public, and it therefore has a greater impact on the world at large. In some cases, like Schorr's and the Pentagon Papers, that impact is good; but in others, it's not.

The Fresno case seems to be a good example, because it's hard to conceive, except in the most exceptional cases, of the publication of grand jury testimony as being in the public interest. As Nicholas Von Hoffman pointed out not long ago, grand juries are secret for a good reason: they are preliminary legal probes, in which "any accusation, any gossip, any surmise about anyone is admissible. There is no cross examination, no adversary questioning, no testing of evidence, no defense counsel." The whole system is undermined when its secrecy goes.

There are far more obvious cases, too, where secrets have to be kept. Anybody can see that it's a bad idea to protect leakers of the location of Polaris submarines, or missile silos, or troop movement orders—that, in fact, there should be some way that those leakers can be found and punished. The events of the last ten years have given leakers a pretty good name, but it's worth remembering that the precursors of Daniel Ellsberg were unsavory figures who, depending on their ideological leanings, gave defense secrets to the Soviet Union or the names of former Communists to Congressional committees.

The reporters at the Schorr press conference might have said to that, 'Sure, we recognize that there are leaks and leaks, but let *us* decide which ones are in the public interest and which ones aren't. We'll do it in the newsroom civics class. Just leave it to us.'

Here again, though, self-interest plays a part, because the press is, quite commendably, trying to sell papers, which sometimes precludes consideration of the public interest. Amid all the high-flown talk at the House Committee hearings, Clay Felker, owner of the *Village Voice*, admitted that he decided to publish the Pike Report without really reading it beforehand. He had just sort of leafed through it, he said. He knew it would make a nice, flashy cover headline, and that it would help the *Voice*, and on that basis he decided to publish it. The public interest seems to have been a minor character in the drama, at least until well afterward when Congress came around with questions.

The pursuit of the flashy headline can lead down some pretty dark alleys, ones only tangentially related to the public interest. The facts of the Fresno Four case are unclear (perhaps one of the Four will leak them in the public interest, but it's doubtful) but it is known that a *Fresno Bee* reporter had a skeleton key to the courthouse where the grand jury transcripts were kept. What if, in fact, he simply let himself into the courthouse, stole the transcripts, and walked out? Was that in the public interest? Or should he be punished like anyone else? Earlier this year this magazine got a manuscript in the mail suggesting that if privilege laws were enacted the Mafia might invest in newspapers in order to avoid testimony about their criminal activities. That seems a little farfetched, but you get the idea—it's unwise to sanction anything reporters might do on the grounds that it's part of their freedom of press.

## Custodians of Morality

If you assume that it's right that the government keeps some things secret, then the public's interest is this: that what really needs to be kept secret be kept secret, but that everything else be made public. It's clear that lately the government has gone much, much too far in the direction of secrecy, but the ideal alternative to that is not establishing the press as a unilateral, protected conduit of any secret government information it can get, with no restrictions. To expect the press, as custodian of morality in government, to police itself ideally here, with selling papers, reporters' status, and other self-interested issues so heavily at play, is asking too much. The idea behind government is that it ought to be a disinterested party, counterbalanced against itself; therein lies its great strength.

Under absolute reporters' privilege, the press has what amounts to veto power over all three branches of government, and therefore, since by its own account it's carrying out a quasi-governmental, Constitution-ordained function, it becomes a sort of fourth branch with more power than the other three. If Congress, or the President, or the courts, decide to keep something secret, and the press disagrees (which, given its interests, is extremely likely), then it simply publishes. It overrides.

So, to cut through all the talk about Freedom and Amendments and The People's Right we have this: there is a problem with the government's keeping too much information secret, and the press proposes to solve that problem by putting itself in a position where a great deal of secret information comes its way, and it, instead of the government, decides what the public should or shouldn't know. This notion has Present-Day Mistrust of Government stamped all over it; it reflects liberals' assumption that the government can't do anything involving civil liberties right, so we might as well give up on it.

The point, however, is that the government got to be that way through the commission of the very sins that are starting to appear in the press. It wasn't always that great masses of information were being held back from the American people; the chain of events is fairly recent, and can be easily traced. The power of the executive branch of government was, necessarily, greatly increased to cope with the Depression and World War II; and once that power existed in its amplified form, it began to be abused. The government-secrets problem is just one product of the imperial presidency; the mentality that put guards around the White House and filled its offices with yes-men also decided that vast amounts of information about the government should be kept from Americans.

Now, in response to all those horrors, we seem to be moving in the direction of an imperial press, produced by the Nixon era in the same way that the imperial presidency was produced by the Depression and World War II. But it ought to be clear by now that *anything* imperial is dangerous. Difficult choices in reporting the news are inescapable. The press should meet them courageously, but with some humility, too. The more self-righteous, pontificating press conferences it holds, the more fawning attention it gets, the more likely it is to slip into the same kinds of excesses it is trying to wipe out. ∎

# 55

# What the FBI Tells You about Your Own Files

## John Seigenthaler

allegations of Seigenthaler having illicit relations with young girls . . .
*—Report of Memphis FBI to FBI Director
Clarence Kelley, May 6, 1976*

I have been reporting and writing for this newspaper, The Tennessean, for most of the last 28 years—and this is the most difficult assignment I have undertaken.

This is a story about myself. It is personal. It is painful.

The allegations cited in the FBI communication printed above, dated May 6, 1976, are not true. But they were repeated, in substance, in another communication to FBI Director Kelley four days later, on May 10, 1976.

I found out about it in late June 1977—when, after more than a year of denial and delay, Director Kelley finally complied with provisions of Federal laws and sent me my FBI files. At least he sent me some of my files.

I have now been assured by ranking members of the Justice Department that the records cited in the May 6 and May 10 "telexes" will be purged from my records.

But as of this moment they are part of the "official" FBI files. I have been given access, under law, to some FBI reports mentioning my name. But nothing I have received from the Federal Bureau explains how such information could get into my files, why it was sent on May 6 to Director Kelley, or why it was repeated in another message to him a few days later.

The law which allows citizens the right to examine their files also allows the FBI to decide arbitrarily what records will not be shown. I am appealing Kelley's decision in my own case to try to get more information.

Like most Americans, I grew up believing completely in the integrity of the FBI. I know many agents I like and admire. The hard work of agents like them gave the Bureau a reputation which was unblemished for decades. I am aware that disclosing the mere fact that this material is in my files will raise doubts about me in the minds of some people. It will raise the inevitable questions: "If there is smoke isn't there fire? If the FBI had it in the files isn't it true?" That realization is why I would prefer not to write this.

But I appeared before a Congressional Committee May 20, 1976, and stated under oath that if I could get access to my FBI files I would publish what was there, no matter how scurrilous or scandalous or false.

I then wrote a letter to FBI Director Kelley, I told him I was convinced that his agency had collected defamatory gossip about me. I demanded access to my FBI records. I told Kelley that I was going to publish that material if I could get it.

Then, recently, I was honored in New York by the Sidney Hillman Foundation and given an award for "courage in publishing."

Having accepted that award, and having told Kelley I would publish what was in my files, and having sworn before a committee of Congress to do so, I can hardly lock it up in a filing cabinet now and forget it.

For years the FBI has engaged in a "vacuum cleaner" approach to intelligence gathering. That means that some FBI agents will solicit or accept any information, even hearsay, rumor or gossip, and put it into the Bureau's "raw files."

At the time I testified before Congress I had an idea that if I would voluntarily expose the "vacuum cleaner" method of information gathering that it might help stop that corrupt practice.

For some time it has been clear that J. Edgar Hoover, when he was FBI director, collected titillating tid-bits of gossip about high-ranking officials in Washington—members of Congress, Senators, Cabinet officers, even Presidents.

But nobody ever thinks the FBI is collecting common

300

gossip about them; nobody realizes that the "vacuum cleaner" is always turned on, possibly sucking up information about them. Before May, 1976, I did not suspect that the FBI had collected damaging or discrediting information about me. I didn't want to think that about myself; I didn't want to think it about the FBI.

Then on May 13 last year an FBI official named Homer Boynton, while visiting the Washington offices of the New York Times, made disparaging comments to members of the Times' staff about me and the Tennessean.

Boynton said, "Seigenthaler . . . is not entirely pure."

I don't know why he said it. I can't prove what he meant.

But for more than a year I have suspected the worst; now, having received my FBI records—or some of them—I know the worst. I know that in the week before Deputy FBI Director Boynton made those comments about my "purity" the FBI in Memphis sent two messages to Director Kelley which included false allegations that "Seigenthaler involved in having illicit relations" with young girls.

□

If this is a difficult story for me to relate, it also may be difficult for the reader to follow. It involves complex events and confusing relationships with the Federal Bureau of Investigation.

The job of a journalist is to make complexities simple and confusion easy to understand. Because of my personal stake in this story, I may fall short of doing the reporter's job.

My conflict with the FBI dates back more than a year—to May 5, 1976, the day before the first Memphis FBI telex was sent off to Kelley.

It was on that day that Mrs. Jacque Srouji, then a part-time copy editor for The Tennessean, was separated from the newspaper.

On May 3, 4 and 5 I had talked at length with her about what the FBI has since described as her "special relationship" with the Bureau. I was concerned about how that special relationship affected our newspaper's staff. On May 5 I made the difficult decision to dismiss Mrs. Srouji.

There is public controversy about why Mrs. Srouji was fired. Ultimately, I am confident, that controversy will be resolved. That will be another story for another day.

What is pertinent to this story is the date of her firing: May 5, 1976. It was the day before the first FBI telex went from Memphis to Director Kelley in Washington. Her dismissal became public knowledge in news accounts published in The Tennessean and other news-

papers on May 8. Two days later the second FBI telex was shot off from Memphis to Kelley in Washington.

Three days later I appeared at the Department of Justice in Washington to file a formal complaint with Justice officials about the FBI developing a "special relationship" with a member of the staff of The Tennessean. It was on that day—in fact at the very hour while I was filing the complaint—that Deputy Director Boynton showed up at the office of the New York Times and made his "not entirely pure" crack about me and The Tennessean.

The files I now have received from the FBI are maddeningly incomplete. For example, the May 5 and May 10 telexes have been heavily censored and excised by either Kelley or agents who make the decision as to what in my records I may not read.

Consider the May 6 "document." It appears to be a two-page telex. It has been so heavily censored that nothing appears on the first page but the notation that a "coded" "nitel" was sent to the "Director" from "Memphis" at 7:15 p.m.

Everything else on that first page has been deleted by the FBI. Kelley, in a letter that came with these documents, said this was to protect the privacy of others, including the source of the information.

On the second page of this "nitel" every word has been deleted by the FBI except what appears to be the last two and a half lines. Starting in what surely is the middle of a sentence, those lines read as follows:

"allegations of Seigenthaler having illicit relations with young girls, which information source obtained from an unnamed source."

When I first read that, I wondered how I would write this story, I was tempted to try to soften the blow by beginning: "The Federal Bureau of Investigation says I'm a dirty old man."

But it isn't a laughing matter to me, although I am sure that some of my friends—and some who are not my friends—are going to chuckle and chortle about my discomfiture at having to publish such a thing about myself.

I concluded there was no way to begin this account other than to repeat the worst of the damaging lines as the first words of this article.

What is there to conclude from the May 6 "nitel" to Kelley? It shows that sometime prior to May 6 the FBI "vacuum cleaner" turned in my direction and ingested this derogatory information. Some "source"— unnamed in the FBI documents I have received—had sucked up this gossip from some other source. The second source is "unnamed" according to that telex.

That means not even the FBI knows the original source who started the rumor about me.

I had waited for more than a year for a look at my FBI records. It was a year of frustrating exchanges of letters with Kelley and Justice Department officials in which I would regularly demand immediate access to my files, Kelley would deny those demands, I would appeal to other Justice Department officials, and then there would be interminable delays.

When I finally read the few words included in the May 6 telex I was reminded of a letter I had written to the FBI director on July 9, 1976. In that letter I stated that I was convinced "your agency solicits and files common gossip and rank character defamation, under the guise of 'investigating' . . ."

On July 21, Kelley wrote me: "I can assure you that the FBI does not solicit common gossip and rank character defamation."

When he wrote me those words he had in his possession the message sent him from Memphis May 6 quoting a "source" who quoted an "unnamed source."

He also had in his possession the telex sent him from Memphis on May 10. This one is three pages in length. Once again, as I read it I feel that I have been ripped off because either the FBI director or some of his agents have censored most of what it contained.

In addition, the copying machine used by the FBI in reproducing the document is a sad commentary on the technical equipment of the world's greatest investigative agency. Some of what I received is barely legible.

In the May 10 telex the FBI, once again, has blanked out everything that was on page one—except the fact that it was addressed to the "Director" from "Memphis" and that the teletype was "immediate," rather than a "nitel" as the May 6 communication had been. The rest of what was contained on that first page is blank— censored by the FBI. Most of the second page is blank. It is reproduced elsewhere as part of this story. On what appears to be the third line from the bottom one word appears: "volunteered."

The next line is mostly blank but it does contain three words, "heard rumors that."

What seems to be the last line on that page is mostly blank but near the end of the line is my name, "Seigenthaler"—followed by a comma.

Now, it is impossible to tell what those three lines really say. But the FBI official who censored those lines obviously wants me to know—or perhaps believe—that somebody "volunteered" that there were "rumors" around about "Seigenthaler."

Whether that came from "source" or "unnamed source" isn't spelled out quite as clearly in this message.

And what were the rumors heard about Seigenthaler? The first line (on page 3) is complete: "involved in having illicit relations with young females."

I am at a loss to explain the difference between "young girls" as set out in the May 6 communication and "young females" as included in the May 10 telex. It hardly sounds like a correction. Perhaps the agent in Memphis who sent the news to Kelley on May 10 thought it sounded less as if I had violated the age of consent if "young females" rather than "young girls" were involved in the "rumor." I hope that anonymous agent will understand if I fail to send him an anonymous note of appreciation.

The next sentence in the telex says: "Inasmuch as the information by the source concerning Seigenthaler was unfounded rumor, since it could not be corroborated (and then there is a blank space), no record of this information was made in Memphis files."

But somebody kept it in Washington FBI files. And from there, after more than a year of denial and delay, I finally got access to it. The language of the FBI message on May 10 leaves no doubt that it was "unfounded rumor" which could not be corroborated. As I read the telex it is obvious to me that the FBI actually tried to corroborate it, and failed.

And after more than a year that unfounded uncorroborated rumor has remained in my FBI files in Washington—where it rests today. And there it would remain forever were it not for current officials of the Justice Department who agree with me that it should be purged.

Still, Kelley wrote to me that he could assure me "the FBI does not solicit common gossip and rank character defamation."

In that same letter, Kelley said, "I am confident the records will speak for themselves."

Well, the documents are so heavily censored that they hardly speak at all. But insofar as they speak they leave no doubt in my mind that the FBI, even today, solicits—and keeps in its records—"common gossip and rank character defamation."

Last November, after I had protested the actions of the FBI and the statements by Boynton I received a letter of apology from the Department of Justice. In December, a second letter came from Justice Kelley and Boynton joined in this apology, this letter said.

Having now read my files I have a better idea of why that apology was forthcoming. I have difficulty understanding why it took from May until December.

But still the information I received is inadequate and incomplete. I suspect that means months of more appeals to get more information.

As I re-read the May 6 and May 10 telexes I have several reactions:

• The Federal privacy act bars the FBI from providing me any information about any other person whose name is in my files. That, I think, is a sensible provision designed to let me know what the FBI says about me, but protects others from my finding out what the FBI says about them. At the same time, as long as the Bureau continues to use a "vacuum cleaner" process of information gathering and allows unnamed sources to feed in false rumors, this provision will encourage bureaucratic abuse. It also will prevent those who are victims of that abuse from their accusers.

VOLUNTEERED
HEARD RUMORS THAT
SEIGENTHALER.

INVOLVED IN HAVING ILLICIT RELATIONS WITH YOUNG FEMALES.

INASMUCH AS THE INFORMATION FURNISHED BY THE SOURCE
CONCERNING SEIGENTHALER WAS UNFOUNDED RUMOR, SINCE IT COULD NOT
BE CORROBORATED, NO RECORD OF THIS INFORMATION WAS MADE IN MEMPHIS
FILES.

ALLEGATIONS OF SEIGENTHALER HAVING
ILLICIT RELATIONS WITH YOUNG GIRLS, WHICH INFORMATION SOURCE
OBTAINED FROM AN UNNAMED SOURCE.

*These are copies of censored pages of nearly illegible FBI telexes sent by the Tennessee FBI headquarters to Director Clarence Kelley on May 6 and 10, 1976. Sheet A (top left), the second page of a two-page telex sent May 6, reads, "allegations of Seigenthaler having illicit relations with young girls, which information source obtained from an unnamed source." Sheet B (top right), the second page of the three-page telex sent May 10, reads: "volunteered heard rumors that Seigenthaler." Sheet C (left), the third page of the same telex, reads: "involved in having illicit relations with young females. Inasmuch as the information furnished by the source concerning Seigenthaler was unfounded rumor, since it could not be corroborated, no record of this information was made in Memphis files." © The Tennessean.*

304

• This same provision that permits the FBI to determine what it will excise from documents will lead, inevitably, to the suspicion that the Bureau is covering up its own misdeeds in the process of censoring documents.

• There are many Americans who, I now am sure, have similar stuff in their files. There is no way for them to know how or when this may adversely affect their interests, or the interests of persons close to them.

• My hope that publishing the derogatory information about me might help cure the FBI practice of picking up such gossip and rumor has been dimmed by the tedious, tiring effort required to get even part of the records.

Kelley sent a letter accompanying the documents he provided me, listing the provisions of the law which permit him to withhold information in my records in order to protect others. His letter never even acknowledges that it was improper for the FBI to gather such material.

• My wife is outraged by what was in my FBI files. Outraged at the FBI and not at me, I am happy to report.

□

While the two telexes in May 1976 are the items in my FBI files which I found of the greatest interest, there were other documents which were intriguing.

Kelley actually forwarded me 78 pages of documents —the vast majority of them relating to the routine employment investigation done on my background when I went to work as an official of the Justice Department.

I had read that material when I became the Administrative Assistant to the Attorney General. It is made up of page after page of statements from people I knew who invariably said nice things about me.

In files I received from Kelley their names have been deleted to "protect" them. I remember most of them very well. They need no protection from me. I had known them in my neighborhood, at school, at work or at church. Some exaggerated my virtues beyond belief.

Then, in April 1975, there is another communication sent to the White House about my wife and me in response to another "name check" investigation. It mentions that there was a similar check made on both of us in 1972. It doesn't say why, and there is nothing in the documents reflecting anything more on the 1972 inquiry. Again, I am appealing for more details.

There is a highly interesting document showing the Bureau was interested in what was going on in our newspaper office in November 1967. At the top my name is listed, followed by a semi-colon. About half the one-page memo has been excised. The bottom half reads as follows:

"Toward the end of the conversation (here there is a blank where the name of the source has been blanked out) remarked that he had seen a memorandum from John Seigenthaler, Editor of The Tennessean, addressed to the staff of The Tennessean, regarding the feasibility of attempting to have some individual penetrate the security of government bases."

I remember the matter well. I had made a speech at Huntsville's Redstone Arsenal and thought the security there was lax. I suggested to our city editors that we try to get a reporter to slip through security, live for awhile on the base, then write a news story about it. The story never developed. But somebody told the FBI about it.

I suggested that we also should check other military bases to see whether security was lax. I mentioned AEDC at Tullahoma and Fort Campbell. These are also mentioned in the FBI document. The unnamed spy accurately told the Bureau that the purpose of it all was to "write an article" about security on these bases.

I don't remember writing any such memo to members of the staff. There is no such memo written by me in our files.

There was also in the FBI records sent to me a derogatory note: As a young serviceman I once turned up at home in Nashville when I should have been at MacDill Air Force Base in Tampa, Fla. The FBI reports that for this indiscretion I was consigned to "hard labor." Actually, I was restricted to barracks and given three weeks of "K.P." duty. Once again, this report is accurate. Kitchen Police duty is hard labor.

□

Director Kelley has denied my request to meet with him face to face and discuss the details of my files. I regret that. He did mention to me that I owe the FBI $7.80—or ten cents a page—as a copying fee for sending me the 78 pages of my FBI records.

The check will be in the mail shortly—but I don't like to pay. The quality of the "copying" was just too bad.

*John Seigenthaler is publisher of The Tennessean.*

# THE CONTINUING FAILURE OF TERRORISM

# 56

I T IS PART OF THE conventional wisdom of our time that terrorism is one of the crucial problems facing mankind. If repetition made an argument correct, this one surely would be. I have dealt with some of the myths about terrorism in a previous article; the present essay tackles a few more without, unfortunately, great hope of exhausting the topic. How much terrorism is there, and is it really increasing? Around the globe over the past decade perhaps some 10,000 people have been killed by terrorist actions; this includes both domestic and international terrorism, Latin America, Ulster, and the Middle East as well as Colonel Qaddafi's multinational flying circus. Such a figure obscures an immeasurable amount of tragedy and pain, but it is also true that as many people were killed in the Lebanese civil war in three months or perished in a few weeks in the Cambodian purge or in the Colombian *violencia*. More important, for the past three or four years the number of terrorist operations has shown a marked decline, most dramatically perhaps in the case of hijacking. There were more than fifty cases in 1970, whereas during the past year there have been only four or five.

Terrorism occurs in cycles; the most recent one reached its apex in the early 1970s and has been on the decline. The major terrorist groups of the late 1960s and early 1970s, such as the Tupamaros in Uruguay, the Brazilian ALN, the Canadian FLQ, the Weathermen, and the various European, North American,

and Japanese groups have been defeated. The Argentinian ERP and the Montoneros, who seemed so near to success only a few months ago, have suffered a setback from which they will probably not recover. The number of terrorist operations carried out by the Palestinian organizations had substantially decreased even before the Lebanese civil war. Dozens of books and thousands of articles have been written about the subject of Palestinian terrorism, but the number of Israelis killed in 1975 was about fifty—less than the number of victims in one night in Beirut.

There has been a minor resurgence of terrorism in Spain and in Mexico, but, seen on a global scale, the downward trend is quite unmistakable. American commentators have referred to the "stupendous cost" of such countermeasures as guarding American embassies abroad. Yet a little probing shows that the sum involved amounts to a mere $40 million, less than the projected cost of one B-1 plane. And as it has long been customary to guard embassies in any case—against thieves, for instance, or stray dogs—even if there is no terrorist danger, the real cost is probably much lower yet.

All this is not to say that terrorism will soon disappear. It has powerful international patrons and in the more distant future there is of course the danger of the use of unconventional weapons by terrorists. Even at the present stage, international (as distinct from domestic) terrorism could lead to limited war, but

Terrorists win the battle for publicity, but lose the war against repression

by
Walter Laqueur

*Walter Laqueur is the chairman of the Research Council of the Center for Strategic and International Studies in Washington.*

this has not happened. At present, terrorism is on the decline. The question remaining to be asked is, Why has this fact not yet registered?

## The publicity campaign

THE MEDIA ACT AS A selective magnifying glass: terrorism always exerts a strange fascination, especially from a safe distance. It has all the ingredients of a good story—mystery, quick action, tension, drama. It seems natural, therefore, that the media should give terrorism inordinate publicity. The vital importance of publicity has been realized by generations of terrorists all over the world: the terrorist act alone is nothing; publicity is all. The Algerian rebels of the 1950s quite deliberately transferred their struggle from the countryside to the capital, even though they suspected that they could not possibly win the battle for the capital. As one of them wrote, if ten enemies are killed in the *djebel*, no one will take notice, but even a small incident in Algiers will be picked up by the American press and prominently featured the next day in New York. He was quite right—the Algerians were beaten in the struggle for the capital, but they won the fight for publicity, which, in the long run,

was the decisive battle. What is news, certainly in the Western world, depends upon the presence of newspapermen and TV cameras. The case of Israel is most instructive in this respect. A massacre or a mass execution in a Third World country will rate at most a few paragraphs. However, if ten schoolgirls burn a tire in Bethlehem, all hell will break loose, for in Israel there is one of the heaviest concentrations of newspapermen on earth. This is partly because their editors believe that everything happening in Israel is most important and that world peace depends on it, and partly because Israel is one of only three or four countries left outside Europe, Japan, and North America in which journalists can move about freely. Let them try to cover terrorists training in Libya or an execution in Sudan, let them try to probe deeply into the struggle between terrorists and the army in Argentina, and they will soon find themselves in very serious trouble indeed. There is no such danger in Israel, and for this and other reasons the Israelis, however much they protest, will be overexposed for years to come.

Selective publicity, then, is one of the sources of misconception about terrorism: another is the vagueness—indeed, the utter carelessness—with which the term is used, not only in the media but also in government announcements and by academic students of the subject. Terrorism is used as a synonym for rebellion, street battles, civil strife, insurrection, rural guerrilla war, coups d'etat, and a dozen other things. The indiscriminate use of the term not only inflates the statistics, it makes understanding the specific character of terrorism and how to cope with it more difficult.

TERRORISM GREW OUT OF the time-honored tradition of tyrannicide; Brutus was a sort of terrorist; so were Wilhelm Tell and Charlotte Corday. The question of whether tyrannicide is permitted in certain circumstances has preoccupied generations of philosophers and theologians, and the general consensus is now that one cannot unconditionally condemn it except perhaps on the basis of a total, Gandhian commitment to nonviolence. For there are obviously cases in which there is no redress against tyranny, in which murder is no crime but a liberating act. Every terrorist would claim to be Wilhelm Tell fighting unspeakable despotism and cruelty, but, as a rule of thumb, one learns more about a terrorist group by looking at its victims than at its manifestos.

Contemporary terrorism has definitely changed its character: before the first world war systematic terrorism was on the whole limited to the Tsarist and Ottoman empires, which, by the exacting standards of that period, were about the most despotic regimes in the world. Today terrorism occurs only in democratic societies and in halfhearted authoritarian regimes; it no longer dares to challenge an effective dictatorship. As the character of terrorism has changed, so has the character of those practicing it. Even the bitterest foes of the Russian revolutionaries of the 1880s recognized their integrity, courage, and selfless devotion. Even to compare a Sofia Perovska (or an Emma Goldman) with the heroines of the 1970s—Patty Hearst, Bernardine Dohrn, or the late Ulrike Meinhof— is to invite ridicule.

Terrorism's strange fascination preoccupies many people, metaphysicians as well as popular novelists. Yet there is no more clarity about the phenomenon than there was eighty years ago, when a wave of assassinations, mainly involving freewheeling anarchists, shocked Europe and America. In the 1890s the behavioral sciences were in their infancy; all kinds of strange theories were bandied about: cranial measures of captured terrorists were taken, and a connection between terrorism and lunar phases was detected. Cesare Lombroso, the most distinguished criminologist of his day, found both a medical and a climatological explanation: terrorism, like pellagra and some other diseases, was caused by certain vitamin deficiencies, hence its prevalence among the maize-eating people of Southern Europe. He also found that the further north one went the less terrorism there was; Lombroso did not quite reach the North Pole in his investigations.

It is easy to poke fun at Lombroso's theory of vitamin deficiency, but the basic idea underlying it was not all that outlandish. For terrorists are usually angry and aggressive people, and it has long been known that there are some internal violence-generating factors and that some people have a lower violence threshold than others. Neurophysiologists have studied the correlation between aggressive behavior on one hand, and abnormal showings in electroencephalography, the function of adrenaline and thyroid secretion, the role of endocrinological disorders, and enzyme deficiencies causing hypoglycemia on the other. Their research has been inconclusive so far.

Political science has not made that much progress either since the early days. Large-scale cross-national investigations into the incidence of political violence have been undertaken in American universities for fifteen years; the correlations between terrorism and caloric intake, newspaper circulation, and the number of physicians have also been studied. A frustration and relative deprivation index has been established, using factor analysis, multiple regression, and other sophisticated statistical methods. Employment has been found for many doctoral students feeding facts and figures into computers. Only a few years ago hints were dropped about striking findings, and the general feeling in the profession was that a major breakthrough was just around the corner. Such optimism is no longer widespread, even though the computers are kept going. Suddenly people realized that the scales and models were not applicable to Communist countries, and perhaps not to Third World military dictatorships either. Doubt began to spread about whether it is always frustration that causes terrorism, and whether, even if it does, it can be measured. Statistical methods, in short, are of little help if underlying them there is confusion. Sweeping theories of the "terrorist personality" developed in the past have only contributed to this confusion.

Connections between terrorism and economic trends are at best tenuous. Terrorism in Uruguay and Argentina reached its peak

"One learns more about a terrorist group by looking at its victims than at its manifestos."

at a time of stagnation and economic crisis, but in Brazil it came at a time of rapid economic development. In Latin America it has occurred in the countries with the highest living standards, such as Cuba, Uruguay, and Venezuela, but also in those with the lowest. Nationalist terrorism has been rampant in Ulster, which is one of the poorest regions of the United Kingdom, and in relatively deprived Quebec. But it has also occurred in Euzkadi (the country of the Basques) and Croatia, which are among the most developed and prosperous parts of Spain and Yugoslavia. In short, the search for a magic formula and a comprehensive theory of terrorism is illusory. Terrorism can be understood only by studying historical and political experience and by taking into account the specifics of each situation, not by feeding into computers ten years of news items from the files of the *New York Times*.

## More repression, less terrorism

**W**E MAY BE ABLE TO do without a general theory of terrorism but greater clarity is needed to cope with concrete situations such as hijacking, the taking of hostages, et cetera. In this respect a great deal of emotion

has been engendered, and there is no denying that dealing with terrorists does indeed involve real dilemmas. This takes us back to the question of the origins of terrorism which occurs, some argue, wherever people have legitimate grievances. Remove the grievances, remove poverty, inequality, injustice, and lack of political participation, and terrorism will cease. These sentiments are shared by all men and women of goodwill but as a cure for terrorism they are of little value. Given the complexity of the world, concessions to one national group will almost invariably result in injustice to another. Latin-American terrorists maintain that they fight for greater political freedom and social justice; there is no reason to disbelieve their claims. Yet what little one knows about the personalities leading these groups does not inspire confidence, for these would-be *caudillos* are elitists, not radical democrats.

If any lesson can be drawn from the experience of several decades of terrorism, it is the uncomfortable and indeed shocking conclusion that the more the injustice and repression, the less terrorism there is. In other words, terrorism succeeds only against nonterrorists, namely groups or governments which refrain from responding to indiscriminate murder with equally indiscriminate repression. Terrorism continues in Ulster not because the terrorists are invincible but because the British government treats the violent men of both sides decently, unlike the Brazilians or Iranians, Russians or Yugoslavs. A professor of law in testimony to a Congressional committee said recently that he was not sure whether deterrence against terrorism worked. He could not have been more mistaken: the problem, alas, is not whether terrorism can be stamped out; even fifth-rate dictatorships have managed to achieve this. The real issue is, of course, the price that has to be paid to eradicate terrorism.

The nonconcession policy of the present administration, as stated both publicly and informally, has been bitterly attacked by critics in the Foreign Service, among whom demoralization is said to have spread. They understandably fear their fate if they should have the misfortune of becoming hostages one day. Their criticism is based on arguments which are by now familiar: they do not know if deterrence really works; being beastly to the terrorists will not solve the problem.

One can certainly sympathize with the concern shown by members of the Foreign Service and their spokesmen. When around the turn of the century an anarchist took a few shots at Umberto I, the king of Italy said that this was an inevitable professional hazard. It would be unrealistic to expect such philosophical resignation (or sense of duty) in our day and age, and a first secretary at an embassy will rightly argue that he is not a king. Nevertheless, an individual's concern for his own survival does not necessarily add conviction to his arguments.

Each terrorist action is different, and there may indeed be cases in which concessions may be advisable—not because the victim is very prominent but because there is no reason to assume that appeasement will encourage further terrorist attacks. This means in practical terms greater leniency in dealing with groups that are not particularly dangerous, such as the South Moluccans, but firmness toward those that are. This applies in particular to the new brand of international terrorism; it is quite unrealistic to suggest "drastic action" against terrorists after they have retired to the coffeehouses of Tripoli or Benghazi. It is equally unrealistic to call for action from the United Nations, such as the establishment of an international court dealing with terrorist activities. Various international conventions exist with the purpose of combating terrorism; they may be of interest to lawyers and insurance companies, but they have not the slightest practical importance. Bilateral pacts (such as the agreement between the United States and Cuba) may be of some help, but hoping for cooperation on a global scale is quite unprofitable. The Sixth Committee of the General Assembly of the United Nations has been debating the subject for several years, and it has been even less successful **than the old and** much ridiculed League of Nations. These discussions will no doubt go on for many years to reach an utterly predictable result.

APPEASING TERRORISM does not offer a solution, and as the danger of the use of nonconventional weapons moves nearer it is no longer even a short-term palliative. Prof. Bernard Feld, the distinguished physicist, once discussed the nightmarish consequences of the disappearance of twenty pounds of plutonium from government stocks. What if the mayor of Boston received a note to the effect that a terrorist group had placed a nuclear bomb somewhere in central Boston, accompanied by a crude diagram which showed that the bomb would work? Would the scientist not have to advise the mayor to surrender to blackmail rather than risk the destruction of his hometown? But one successful case of blackmail leads to another, and what would our scientist's advice be if faced with contradictory threats by extreme left-wing and right-wing, or nationalist-separatist groups? A policy of surrender would lead to constant tyranny by small groups of people or, more likely, to anarchy and destruction, unless of course society learns to live with blackmail.

There is the danger of overreacting to terrorism, of focusing one's attention and marshaling one's efforts against a minor irritation which, for all one knows, may never outgrow the nuisance stage. Paradoxically, while terrorism is on a small scale, it is not really that important what kind of approach is taken. Once a society faces a determined terrorist onslaught it will choose a hard-line policy anyway, as shown, for instance, by Turkey and Iran, by Israel and Egypt—not to mention Latin America. For terrorism is blackmail, and the victim of blackmail is less likely to forget and to forgive than the victim of almost any other crime: he feels a special sense of outrage because it is not just his life or property that has been affected. He has been humiliated; his elementary human rights, his dignity and self-respect have been violated. To argue that this counts for little, to maintain that one should always be guided by expediency, is asking too much of human nature, especially if the expediency is really no more than the rationalization of surrender.

Terrorism, to summarize, is no more than a nuisance at present. One day mankind may be threatened by the weapons of superviolence, but, if these should ever be used, it is of course at least as likely that this will be done by governments or, in the case of chemical or biological agents, perhaps by individuals. There is the certainty that society will not be able to satisfy the demands, justified or unjustified, of all its members. There is equally the certainty that some individuals will at some future date have the skill and the determination to dictate their wishes to society. Such action would, of course, be irrational, leading sooner or later to destruction without precedent. It is not certain, unfortunately, whether this perspective will deter individuals or small groups of people convinced that society or the whole world ought to be punished if their demands are not met. These are the disquieting prospects for the more distant future. For all one knows, they may never materialize, but, if they do, the peril will have to be faced without panic and hysteria. It is for this reason more than any other that the muddled thinking on terrorism, the myths and the humbug, could be one day a source of great danger. □

# 57

# Who Should Play God?

The Sociological Implications of Genetic Engineering

## JEREMY RIFKIN and TED HOWARD

On a few momentous occasions in mankind's history, the body of accumulated human knowledge has spawned dramatic new inventions and discoveries which people, in turn, have used to regulate, control, and moderate the external world — the discovery of fire, the invention of the wheel, the formulation of written language, the discovery of the principles of gravity, and the development of the internal combustion engine. The splitting of the atom and the dawn of the nuclear age is the latest development in this long pursuit of means by which to harness nature.

Now a dramatic new scientific discovery has given some of us the power, for the first time, to shift attention from shaping and controlling the external world of matter and energy to shaping and controlling the internal world of life itself. With the discovery of DNA and its workings, scientists have unlocked the very secrets of life. It is only a matter of a handful of years before biologists will be able to change the evolutionary wisdom of billions of years by creating new plants, new animals, and new forms of human and post-human beings.

Today, only a tiny handful of people are privy to the secrets of life and how to manipulate and change it. Most of us are totally unaware of this new-found power. The concept of designing and engineering life, especially human life, is so utterly fantastic that it is difficult even to

*Jeremy Rifkin and Ted Howard are national co-directors of the People's Business Commission, a public interest group in Washington, D.C. This article is adapted from their new book, "Who Should Play God?" Copyright© 1977, 1978 by Center for Urban Education. Published by arrangement with Delacorte Press/Dell Publishing Co., Inc.*

comprehend its meaning and implications. Yet, even as the public is kept virtually ignorant of this unparalleled new scientific discovery, microbiologists are busy in hundreds of laboratories across the country spending tens of millions of dollars in pursuit of the "mastery of life."

Breakthroughs in genetics research are making genetic engineering feasible for the first time, an in-house memorandum prepared by Cetus, a West Coast corporation, proudly announced in 1975. "This concept is so truly revolutionary," the memo asserted, "that by the year 2000 virtually all the major human diseases will regularly succumb to treatment" by genetic procedures.

The most significant genetic breakthrough of recent years has been recombinant DNA — a laboratory technique for splicing together genetic material from unrelated organisms to manufacture novel forms of life. While the scientific community has become deeply divided over the health and safety problems presented by recombinant DNA (see "Life from the Labs," by Judith Randal, in the March 1977 issue), lay observers are increasingly questioning how this new technology will be used to modify human life as we know it.

The goals of today's genetic engineers range from the sublime to the ridiculous. The most modest among them advocate using genetic engineering to cure some 2,000 "monogenic" diseases — disorders caused by the malfunctioning of a single gene. Others are turning their attention to the artificial production of new strains of plants and "super" grains, while still others focus on redesigning various animal species to equip them to do society's unpopular jobs.

More ominous, however, are the well-credentialed and well-financed researchers who propose the complete restructuring of human life. Name your wildest fantasy (or nightmare) and some authority somewhere is seriously proposing it — from redesigning the human stomach so that people, like cows, will be able to consume cheap hay and grass to hybridizing a cross between man and lower primates. There are even genetic engineers who eagerly await the day when their work will produce the "final solution": the construction of a genetic superrace that will move far beyond *home sapiens* on the evolutionary ladder.

There was a time when all of this could be dismissed as science fiction. No more. No matter how wild or fantastic the scenarios today's prestigious scientists envision, it is clear that they themselves are in earnest. As a tool of human genetic engineering, recombinant DNA literally offers us the opportunity to move beyond ourselves on the evolutionary scale. Man, the engineer, may soon become man, the engineered.

Until recently, population control programs focused on decreasing the numbers of births. Now, with geneticists and social planners worrying aloud about the deterioration of the human gene pool, there is interest in limiting the types and quality of births as well. Bentley Glass, former president of the American Academy for the Advancement of Science, warns, "In an overpopulated world, it can no longer be affirmed that the right of the woman and man to reproduce as they see fit is inviolate. . . ." Glass contends that the right of parents to procreate must become a secondary consideration to the "right of every child to be born with a sound physical and mental constitution, based on a sound genotype."

Thanks to new processes for manufacturing life, scientists can offer at least eight possible ways of controlling reproduction: artificial insemination of a woman with sperm from her mate; artificial insemination of a woman with sperm from an anonymous donor; transplantation of an ovum (egg) from one woman to another and subsequent artificial insemination with sperm from either a mate or a donor; fertilization of an egg in vitro (glass) followed by implantation into a woman; extra-corporeal gestation ("test-tube" life); parthenogenesis (the development of an unfertilized egg); nuclear transplantation or cloning (the reproduction of a cell which has been given a "foreign" nucleus), and embryo fusion (the joining of two individual embryos to form a human with four biological parents instead of two).

The combination of microbiological manipulation with the new reproductive techniques opens the way to full-scale genetic engineering. Bio-engineering is on the verge of moving from promise to performance. Artificial insemination is already marketable, and its popularity is growing. One million living Americans have been born by this process, and the number is increasing by more than 20,000 each year. The ability to deep-freeze human sperm for virtually any length of time has fueled a budding national industry — the commercial sperm bank. Banks are located in twelve cities, and business has never been better. John Olsen, president of Cryogenic Laboratories in St. Paul, notes, "In the last two years, the number of physicians requesting and using frozen donor sperm has

doubled. We're having a difficult time keeping up with the requests coming in." Cryogenic supplies doctors in forty-five cities around the country.

Other methods of controlling reproduction represent a greater degree of sophistication. They are not yet perfected, but extensive experimentation has proceeded on each. The process of removing impregnated eggs from one herd animal and implanting them in the uterus of another animal of the same species is a widely used practice among animal breeders who combine artificial insemination with this embryo "flushing" and implantation to create super-herds of prize cattle.

At the next level of sophistication is the use of deep-

---

## High on XYY

At the turn of the century, anthropologists measured head sizes to find out who the criminal types were. Today, some scientists are looking at chromosome combinations. One recent controversy over chromosomes and criminal behavior is illustrative of the trend and the unwarranted assumptions that underlie it.

Over the last several years, lurid stories have appeared in the daily press about a rare breed of "super males" who have been programmed for murder and other violent crimes because of an extra chromosome in their genotypes. The normal male is born with an XY pair of sex chromosomes. In rare cases, a male is born with an extra Y chromosome from his male parent.

Several years back, some scientists began arguing that these special XYY individuals were prone to aggressive, antisocial, and crminal behavior because of their super maleness. Public interest is this theory was sparked when the press reported that mass murderer Richard Speck was an XYY type. (The rumor turned out to be false.)

Scientists have published more than 200 reports in specialized scientific journals on possible genetic causes of crime. Bentley Glass, former president of the American Association for the Advancement of Science, wrote in *Science* magazine that he looks forward to the day when "a combination of amniocentesis [intrauterine chromosome identification] and abortion will rid us of . . . sex deviates such as the XYY type." Two states, Massachusetts and Maryland, began screening male adolescents in juvenile homes for the extra Y chromosome, and genetic counseling services in Denver, New Haven, and Boston offered screening programs to pregnant women for a time.

The "chromosome connection" has become a fashionable theory. Yet the only comprehensive research done on the subject to date found that the chances of abnormal behavior manifesting itself in an XYY male is no greater than in an XY male. It appears that the only significant problem the XYY male faces over his XY counterpart is a tendency to be taller.

J.R. and T.H.

frozen embryo banks that permit long-term storage of "superembryos." The first success in this area occurred in 1972, when scientists at the Atomic Energy Commission's Oak Ridge Laboratory thawed and implanted frozen mouse embryos. At about the same time, scientists in England announced the birth of Frosty, a bull calf born from a deep-frozen embryo.

Researchers point out that there are considerable similarities in embryo implantation and development between such lower mammals as mice and rabbits, and humans. So far, a human egg transplant has not been attempted, but several egg depositories exist at universities across the country. Commercial human ova banks are right around the corner.

A related area of experimentation is the fertilization of an egg in the laboratory and its subsequent implantation into a woman, a technique which some scientists feel is likely to be general medical practice within ten to twenty years. This research is making significant contributions in the quest to produce test-tube life.

The ability to keep tissue alive in glass has been recognized since 1907, when frog cells were first grown in petri dishes. A few years later, a scientist removed a piece of tissue from a chicken heart and placed it in a glass container filled with fluid, where it lived for thirty-three years (outliving the scientist by two years). As far back as the 1940s, a scientist succeeded in fertilizing a human egg with sperm in a test tube.

Joseph Fletcher, professor of medical ethics at the University of Virginia School of Medicine, regards test-tube life as finishing the work begun by the contraceptive pill. Because laboratory-created life is "willed, chosen, purposed, and controlled," rather than emotionally or accidentally produced, Fletcher believes "laboratory reproduction is radically human compared to conception by ordinary heterosexual intercourse."

Researchers have succeeded in growing a mouse embryo in vitro through approximately half of its gestation period, and E.S.E. Hafez, chairman of the department of animal sciences at Washington State University, is certain that the day of complete test-tube life is nearer than most of us suspect. To drive home his point, Hafez once posed for a photo which appeared in a national news magazine. There, in full color, was the scientist, a set of test tubes labeled "man," "sheep," and "swine" held in his outstretched hands; the caption read, "the barnyard of the future — complete with farmer."

With our present technology, incubators can keep alive a baby born as many as three months prematurely. The key now is to gain control of the first twenty-four weeks of life. Robert Goodlin of Stanford has been a leader in the search for an artificial womb for more than a decade, and has developed a pressurized steel-and-glass world in which an oxygen-rich saline solution constantly bathes a fetus. Intense pressure — roughly the equivalent of pressure felt under water at a depth of 450 feet — drives oxygen through the skin so that the baby's lungs do not have to work. No fetus has survived in the chamber for more than forty-eight hours, but Goodlin is working on a

system to draw off carbon dioxide and waste materials that become deadly unless removed.

No genetic engineering possibility provokes more "sci fi" thinking than cloning. But cloning, the production of genetically duplicate individuals from the biological information contained in a single body cell, is clearly not science fiction. Within our lifetimes, carbon-copy human beings will walk among us.

Recombinant DNA has become an especially useful tool in cloning experiments. A scientist at Oxford has taken an unfertilized egg cell from an African clawed frog, destroyed the egg nucleus with ultraviolet radiation, and then successfully implanted cells taken from the frog's intestinal wall into the empty egg. The egg cell, equipped with the full chromosomal make-up necessary to become an African clawed frog, was then tricked into "thinking" it had been fertilized. The cell began to divide. A clone was born.

Researchers have yet to clone a mammal in this way, but experts agree that human cloning is on the horizon. The switch to control the reproductive power of the human cell is almost known.

Joshua Lederberg, a Nobel Prize winning biologist, is a leading proponent of human cloning. "If a superior individual — and presumably, genotype — is identified," he argues, "why not copy it directly, rather than suffer all the risks, including those of sex determination, involved in the disruptions of recombination [sexual procreation]? Leave sexual reproduction for experimental purposes."

Most scientists agree that, given enough research money, all these reproduction technologies can be operational within the next ten to thirty years. And many argue that selective breeding, using these technologies, is our only option if we are to survive as a society. Joseph Fletcher maintains that not to initiate such policies would be immoral and irresponsible, since we have a sacred duty to control our heredity, just as we accept the responsibility of controlling our social life and behavior. James Bonner of the California Institute of Technology assures us that selective breeding of children is really just an extension of our age-old practice of domesticating animals and plants, and should, therefore, not be viewed with alarm.

Proponents of genetic engineering assert that decisions to procreate cannot be trusted to the individual. Nobel Prize winner Linus Pauling proposes that a symbol showing one's genotype be tattooed on the forehead of every young person. "If this were done," says Pauling, "two young people carrying the same seriously defective gene ... would recognize the situation at first sight and would refrain from falling in love with one another." Pauling favors legislation along these lines.

In an article published by the National Aeronautics and Space Administration, James Bonner discussed a plan in which genetic material from each individual would be removed immediately after birth, and the individual would promptly be sterilized: "During the individual's lifetime, record will be kept of accomplishments and characteristics. After the individual's death, a committee decides if the accomplishments are worthy of procreation into other individuals. If so, genetic material would be removed from the depository and stimulated to clone a new individual. If the committee decides the genetic material is unworthy of procreation it is destroyed." Bonner contends, "The question is indeed not a moral one but a temporal one — when do we start?"

As selective breeding begins to eliminate certain genotypes that are deemed undesirable, gene surgery will soon be used to "upgrade" existing individuals. This year scientists in California were successful in turning bacteria into a cellular "factory" that manufactures the genes necessary to produce insulin, a substance required by diabetics. The next step is to "switch on" these genes to begin insulin production. Researchers hope there will soon be cures, not only for diabetes, but also for hemophilia, PKU, and Tay-Sachs disease.

Genetic engineers also talk of using genetic surgery to "adapt" people to existing environments. If certain workers are more susceptible than others to the harmful effects of particular pollutants and carcinogens, for example, adapting workers will be less expensive than eliminating dangerous chemicals.

Gene surgery could not only provide a hedge against disease, proponents of genetic engineering believe, but also improve worker satisfaction by adapting brain functions. As justification for extending genetic surgery to the redirection of human emotion and intellect, many molecular biologists maintain that schizophrenia and other "abnormal" psychological states result from genetic disorders. "There can be no twisted thought without a twisted molecule," a prominent neurophysiologist has stated. Reports supposedly demonstrating that crime, social protest, poverty, and intelligence are also the result of people's genetic make-up — not of institutional injustice — are being published in large numbers.

Gene surgery has a high priority within Government-funded medical research. The National Institute of General Medical Sciences yearly awards more than $117 million for its development. With advances in recombinant DNA, the possibilities of gene surgery are almost limitless, suggests one scientist: "If one considers the purpose of a drug to be to restore the normal function of some particular process in the body, then DNA should be considered to be the ultimate drug."

The goal of perfecting the human race (or portions of it) through biological redesign is, of course, not new. It has spawned some of the most brutal social and political movements of the Twentieth Century. Whenever dramatic new discoveries in genetics have been made, they have soon been translated into political and social programs. And whenever societies have wanted to alter the social, economic, or political life of specific classes, they have encouraged geneticists to experiment with new ways to accomplish such ends.

This symbiotic relationship between genetic engineering and social policy reached its most conspicuously abhorrent level in the genetic policies of Hitler's Third Reich. Long before Hitler's rise to power, however, American geneticists and social ideologues had begun working together to fashion similar policies designed both to eliminate the so-called inferior stock from the human species and, at the same time, to create a master race.

The early genetic engineering movement in this country was called "eugenics." It arose in the wake of the first massive immigration wave, militant union organizing drives, and the mushrooming growth of city slums in the late 1890s. It promised an easy cure for economic inequalities and social ills at a time when social reformers were increasingly disheartened and when science was being heralded as the linchpin of American greatness. Eugenics offered both a scientific explanation for social problems and a scientific approach to their solution.

Eugenics appealed to the country's "best people" — powerful old-line ruling families, and upper-middle-class academics and professionals who turned the ideology into a form of secular evangelism. They preached eugenics in university lecture halls, before professional conventions, and on political platforms from one end of the country to the other. The message was always the same: America's salvation hinged on its resolve to eliminate the biologically inferior types and breed the perfect human race.

The acceptance of eugenics by much of the general public was due, in large part, to the early and enthusiastic support of some of the most prominent scientists of the time. Almost half of the nation's geneticists became involved in the movement, believing they could help reverse what they saw as a decline in society's hereditary quality.

Eugenicists looked to sterilization as a major tool in their campaign to weed out biologically inferior stock from the American population. As a result of their relentless drive, tens of thousands of American citizens were involuntarily sterilized under various laws enacted by thirty states to cure everything from crime to feeble-mindedness. The extent to which sterilization mania was carried is perhaps best reflected in a bill introduced in the Missouri legislature calling for sterilization of those "convicted of murder, rape, highway robbery, chicken stealing, bombing, or theft of automobiles."

One of the most bizarre twists in the eugenics movement was the Fitter Family Contests run by the American Eugenics Society. Blue ribbons were presented at county and state fairs throughout the Midwest to those families who could produce the best family pedigrees. Families were judged on their physical and mental qualities right alongside the breeding contests for pigs and cows.

From its peak in 1924, the eugenics movement steadily declined, eventually collapsing with the stock market crash in 1929. With America's financial elite jumping out of windows and middle-class professionals and academics standing in unemployment lines alongside Italian, Polish, and Jewish immigrants, and blacks, and with responsible scientists exposing the racism of their colleagues, the myth that certain groups were biologically superior was no longer tenable.

The American eugenics movement lay dormant through World War II. But the bomb on Hiroshima

# Science and 'Progress'

For proponents and critics alike, the debate over genetic engineering has also become a debate over the fundamental assumptions concerning the role of science and the meaning of progress.

Chief among the scientific prerogatives now being contested is the right of total freedom of scientific inquiry — uninhibited by any outside controls. Such scientists as Edward Teller, father of the H-bomb, believe that a researcher should not deny himself a discovery by worrying about the social consequences. "I believed in the possibility of developing a thermonuclear bomb," Teller said. "My scientific duty demanded exploration of that possibility."

Behind such statements is the assumption that scientific inquiry, if left alone, will inevitably lead to important new insights and discoveries that will ultimately benefit mankind. To attempt to restrict the free flow of scientific inquiry, the purists maintain, is self-defeating, since it is the only method that has proven itself capable of advancing the interests of civilization.

Some scientists even suggest that all of the complex problems facing our industrialized system be handed over to their profession for resolution. John Platt, research biologist at the University of Michigan, for instance, believes that where problems exist, only "more scientific understanding and better technology can carry us past them." Platt argues that the escalating crisis of population expansion, hunger, nuclear proliferation, and urban decay can best be solved by a mobilization of the talent and resources of the nation's scientists, who are the only ones with the knowledge necessary to address such monumental problems.

When critics point out that science and technology are responsible for some of the critical problems facing society, the stalwarts argue that the problems are merely temporary nuisances which will, in fact, automatically correct themselves with the passage of time and the development of new scientific technologies superimposed on the old. There is really no alternative to the scientific and technological approach to problem solving, argues Dr. Bernard Davis of Harvard University. "We cannot unlearn the scientific method, which is available for all who wish to wrest secrets from nature."

But for the first time in recent memory scientists themselves are beginning to question these arguments. James Watson, who with Francis Crick discovered the double-helix structure of DNA, argues that the notion that science, if left alone to do "its own thing," will solve everybody's problems, is "a form of laissez-faire nonsense dismally reminiscent of the credo that American business, if left to itself, will solve everybody's problems. Just as the success of a corporate body in making money need not set the human condition ahead," says Watson, "neither does every scientific advance automatically make our lives more meaningful."

At the opening session of the National Academy of Sciences Forum on Recombinant DNA Research, Erwin Chargaff, professor emeritus of biology at Columbia University, remarked that in his long career as a teacher one of his favorite sayings to his students was, "Never say 'no' to an experiment." However, in the case of recombinant DNA, Chargaff told the audience of scientists, "I relinquish my old maxim." Chargaff attacked the long-held supposition that scientists should follow their research wherever it leads and should not be overly concerned about the effect it might have on the larger community. "I may damage myself as much as I want," stated Chargaff, "but not one iota of danger to others is permissible."

What Chargaff and other scientists are saying is that not all scientific advances are progressive, and that there are other ways of looking at progress than just through the scientific perspective. The problem, says biologist Ruth Hubbard, is "that in the last 300 to 400 years the scientific method has completely overshadowed all other ways of looking at truth and reality." Hubbard claims that the scientific approach is a narrow and limited way to look at reality, since it only acknowledges things as being true that can be measured and that are repetitive. "Other kinds of things are necessary in order to really understand what is going on," she argues, "and by downgrading these other non-scientific approaches to the world, we've gotten into a pretty bad shape."

J.R. and T.H.

---

sparked a new interest in genetics, as scientist and government officials began to worry about the effects of radiation on the gene pool. And the bomb also triggered a renewed interest in eugenics. Prominent scientists claimed that increased radiation was causing massive mutations in the human gene pool, and that these were spreading with each generation. In addition, they argued, breakthroughs in medical treatment of "genetically defective" individuals were keeping alive biologically unfit people who, in turn, were passing on their "defects" to their offspring.

The new eugenics — today called "sociobiology" — has caught on. And as the tools of genetic modification have acquired new sophistication, so has the genetic engineering rhetoric. Today's arguments are couched in less openly racist terms: Many modern-day eugenicists agree with Bernard Davis, professor of bacterial physiology at Harvard, that we need a eugenics program "aimed primarily at reducing the production of individuals whose genetic endowment would limit their ability to cope with a technologically complex environment."

Such pronouncements become of even greater concern when prominent scientists attempt to convince the public that institutional environmental reforms are useless.

The genetic engineers argue that man, the machine, is

not keeping pace with the advances that have been made in a larger environment that is becoming increasingly technologized. "Human culture has grown so rapidly," says Joshua Lederberg, "that the biological evolution of the species during the last hundred generations has only begun to adjust to it." Man is still imperfect, often unpredictable, and prone to subjective miscalculations. These imperfections have a dysfunctional effect on the rest of the techno-system. If we are to prevent the entire system that we have synthesized from collapsing on itself, as it is showing signs of doing, then the only hope, says the biological engineer, is to bring the last major component of the system into line with technical design. That means humanity itself.

Our schools are preparing us for the age of genetic engineering. More than one million school children are being given special drugs to control behavior attributed to "minimal brain dysfunction." Genetic injections are being discussed by scientists and educators alike as a means of improving the general intelligence of the population. Proponents of gene therapy contend that it is merely an internal aid to education — designed to achieve the same ends as calculators, computers, and videotapes.

The consumer market for mood altering genetic surgery is already so firmly established that even critics doubt it will be possible to forestall its widespread use as soon as it becomes available. Their pessimism is based on the fact that psycho-active drugs have, in just a few years, become the most heavily prescribed medications in the country, and are now used by more than 40 per cent of all women and 22 per cent of all men.

Ciba Geigy advertises that its anti-depressant, Tofranil, will help the individual readjust when "losing a job to the computer may mean frustration, guilt, and loss of esteem." Merck Company's Triavil is for people who are "sad or unhappy about the future. . .easily tired and who have difficulty in making decisions." The Sandoz Company claims its product Serentil is "for the anxiety that comes from not fitting in. The newcomer in town who can't make friends. The organization man who can't adjust to altered status within his company. The woman who can't get along with her daughter-in-law. The executive who can't accept retirement."

In a society in which millions of people feel increasingly alienated at the hands of the giant bureaucracies that regulate their lives, and powerless to cope with pollution, urban decay, unemployment, inflation, and a host of other problems, psycho-drugs offer the ideal solution. And any consumer who has become habitually addicted to the purchase of psycho-drugs is a ready market for a "genetic fix."

The Cetus Corporation knows this and is prepared. The significance of the power of genetic engineering cannot be exaggerated, Cetus contends in its in-house memo: "A new industry with untold potential is about to appear."

Recognizing this untold potential, Standard Oil of Indiana is spending $5 million to capture controlling interest in Cetus. Cetus shareholders with convertible preferred stock are being offered $330 a share for stock that cost only $100 a share less than five years ago. The giant corporation sees Cetus as a hedge against the world's dwindling oil reserves.

Cetus is only the tip of the iceberg of corporate involvement in genetic engineering. Seven major pharmaceutical companies are also engaged in the race to exploit this new industry, and a dozen more drug, chemical, and agricultural companies are poised to enter the field, which *Fortune* magazine predicts will soon become a "multibillion dollar industry."

Many scientists advocating genetic engineering have a financial stake in these corporations. On the board of directors and advisers at Cetus are such world renowned scientists as Joshua Lederberg, Stanley Cohen, associate professor of medicine at Stanford University Medical School and the acknowledged leader in the new technology of gene manipulation; Arnold Demain, professor of applied microbiology at MIT; and Donald Glaser, Nobel laureate and professor of physics and molecular biology at the University of California.

Broad-scale genetic engineering will probably be introduced to Americans gradually, almost imperceptibly. As each new genetic advance becomes commercially practical, corporations, aided by scientific expertise and Government approval, will attempt to exploit a new consumer need, either real or manufactured. Whether the genetic revolution or the social revolution prevails depends, ultimately, on how we respond. Restructuring the institutions of society means rejecting the technological imperative and making an active commitment. Genetic engineering, to succeed, will require only our passive acceptance. ☐

# 58

## Confessions of a middle-class drifter

# The rebels of '70

### By James S. Kunen

Times change.

My first car was a political decision. In 1969, a tiny Austin America sedan seemed to conform to the radical line. It was a *rational* vehicle, one designed to meet the needs of The People.

Its little engine could move four people without consuming much gas, therefore without greatly polluting the air, nor greatly depleting the earth's resources, nor requiring me to gather to myself an unseemly amount of wealth to support its appetites. And if hills slowed it up, that gave me the opportunity to relate to my environment. And if after a long journey I felt as though I had walked, it was good to feel something, it added *validity* to my experience.

*James S. Kunen is the author of "The Strawberry Statement" and "Standard Operating Procedure."*

Now here I am, a one-man energy crisis, behind the wheel of The Dream, a metallic blue '69 Chevy Malibu convertible (white top), 307 cubes to blast me wherever I want to be. Thanks to my installation of a cassette player The Dream has the capacity to shut down radio communication with the outside world while maintaining its internal entertainment function. It is in short, a mobile self-contained modular life support system, and a sleek one.

I'm steaming through the badlands of Montana, near the edge of the white world, so far from anywhere I practically don't exist. The road ahead shimmers into the July sky. I ram in a tape, the captured music recalling events, and places, and people that are not with me now. In this euphoric state there is one cause for which I can conceive of risking my life—The Passing of Trucks. I do it constantly.

Still, one thing bothers me, especially when I pass hitchhikers without picking them up: Have I become one of the people I used to be against?

I'm on my way to California. After 18 months as a conscientious objector, working with juvenile delinquents in the Massachusetts Department of Youth Services, I'm going to "drift around" the country. "You realize, of course, this all comes from the movies," said my friend Phil of the idea. He's right. I'm trying to be a drifter, but by virtue of trying I cannot succeed. I'm a middle-class drifter—a bogus drifter—far too purposeful ever really to cut loose.

In this case my purpose is to gather material for an essay on what my friends are doing these days, to see if it's true that, after shutting down campuses five years ago, they're entering establishment careers—what we used to call "selling out."

I'm not writing about blacks, because I don't know anything about blacks. I'm not writing about women, because when a woman fights her way to status and power, that's a radical act. I'm writing about white prep- and Ivy-educated males, class of '70, who were born to power but looked prime to reject it. I'm writing about the Middle Class Vanguard.

Just before I left on the trip a friend asked me how my new Joe Reporter Tape Recorder was working. I said it seemed to pick up voices very clearly from close up, but I wasn't sure it could pick up a speech at a rally.

"Jim," she said gently, touching my wrist, "they don't have rallies anymore."

"**S**CAB grapes! Scab store! Please don't shop here anymore!"
My prep-school friend Dick Casey and I were picketing, for the United Farmworkers, San Francisco groceries which carried nonunion grapes. It felt good to be good again, out in the streets, shouting for justice, but it also felt a little awkward. Our half-dozen co-picketers seemed strangely young, and the words of their chants sounded almost foreign. Occasionally, Casey and I would quietly slip in a "Ho Ho Ho Chi Minh . . ." or "Hey Hey L. B. J. . . . "—our language.

In the old days Casey used to battle police around the University of Buffalo. The students would march through the streets chanting, and then the police would shoot tear gas at them and charge them with clubs, and the students would run away, then reassemble and start marching again, until the police would charge them again.

One day in the spring of '70 Casey had been doing this for several hours, until it was time to go home for supper. There, it struck him. "I was just fighting the police, and now I'm eating supper. If I was really serious, why did I go home for supper, and why did the police let me?" He decided he wasn't really "fighting" police, who, after all, had guns. Whatever he did was at their indulgence. So he stopped. As did many others.

Since then, having graduated with a degree in English and a prize for writing, Casey's been a liquor-store clerk, a cabdriver, a house painter, a shingler of roofs and a cook. The last job avowedly was his idea of a meaningful career. "People gotta eat," he used to say, and he still talks fondly of opening a restaurant called "Working Class Heroes." But he moves around a lot—as does everybody; a six-month-old address book is a keepsake—and is often out of work.

In San Francisco he was getting incremental haircuts and going down every day to the "deployment office," as he calls it, looking for a menial job. He and executive positions are not attracted to one another. "What am I supposed to say, 'O.K., I'll be vice-president of Coca-Cola'?" More and more he'd like to be something: perhaps a film maker. His latest home effort was a two-minute animated Hamlet.

I told him that our mutual friend John Short had decided to leave his small-town newspaper job and go to law school.

"Dropping out, huh," Casey observed.

*"Growers get rich! Farmworkers starve!"*

**I**HAD been surprised when Short called me last May to break the news that he was going to law school. Why, I wanted to know. He sounded apologetic: "Getting licensed to drive your car, that's the whole structure of life," he explained. "Besides, I want to be powerful. I've found that whatever you do, you're going to take crap, and I'd rather take crap from people below me than from people above me."

John Short, Andover '66, Harvard '70, springs from an upper-class background. His family is wealthy and well-connected, and among his forebears was one desperate soul who risked everything on the Mayflower. Short used to be known at Andover for being "in a fog," but he had the moral acuity to help barricade a Dow recruiter in an office at Harvard way back in 1967.

Upon graduation he duly set about not making his fortune and not climbing to power, quietly working on a small-town newspaper, The Provincetown (Mass.) Advocate. He remembers that he "scoffed at the idea" of taking law-school entrance exams as a senior, and was "shocked" at the number of his friends who paused to do so before embarking on their pastoral pursuits. "They were hedging," he says, "and that's what we were against."

I followed Short during his first day of law school this September. Registration at Northeastern University's Gryzmish Law Center was held in a lecture room full of legless black plastic seats attached to long white linoleum-topped tables. The air was conditioned, the windows blinded, the walls cinder-blocked—a law-and-order building. Members of the entering class of '76 looked as though they were there to be booked. Short, an organic if very slightly paunchy 25-year-old in sneakers and permanently unpressed white dungarees, was typical of those shuffling from table to table getting things stamped, except that half of them were women.

"Hello, John!" called a Harvard classmate, Bart Gordon, from a few places back in line.

"Oh God," Short groaned.

"I didn't know *you* were going to be here. It kind of cheapens the whole experience."

Gordon was fresh from a commune in Vermont, where he'd lived "till I couldn't handle it anymore—living in a house for four with nine people, seeing people at breakfast every morning that I maybe could have gotten along with if I saw them every three weeks."

I asked Gordon if it were money that had brought him down to school. "No, I don't need money. My wife and the baby and I could live on $3,000 a year, with some help from our parents. But I want a skill. All my jobs in Vermont were unskilled labor. I was an unskilled carpenter, an unskilled farmer, an unskilled teacher. I want a skill —it's the ideal of meaningful labor." He added that it may be "a fantasy" that the law will be "meaningful labor."

When Gordon asked Short his excuse for being there, Short said he wanted to be a D.A., to go after "the real criminals." "The real criminals are sitting in offices, like some people's fathers."

"You're going to be going after people's fathers?" I asked.

"I don't know," Short answered. "What do I know about being a D.A.?"

What does one know about anything after 16 years of school? One knows how to go to school. Short and his classmates completed their computer cards with dispatch, consumed coffee, doughnuts, speeches. The registrar in-

formed them that 2,500 had applied to be in their class of 125.

"Few people here would admit this," Short whispered, "but it feels good in spite of yourself to hear that you're still 'prime material.'"

Afterwards, the freshmen recessed to a nearby room for sherry. Nothing could be more established than sherry. It prompted me to ask John —who, as a Democratic party official helped deliver Provincetown to McGovern—if his commitment to social change was void.

"I'm not committed in the same way I was in college," Short said. "It's such a youthful thing. I thought things then were—not so much *worse*, but—more *disgusting*. Now I just think things *exist*."

A few of Short's classmates brought a bottle of Taylor Cream over and sat down. The revelation that I was writing an article only confirmed their sense that they—going to law school at 25—represented a trend, a trend that might be called Bourgeois Chic.

Short figures he'll be in a position to do more good as a lawyer than as a demonstrator or anything that he was before. 'In college the standard thing to believe was that our parents and even people a few years older than ourselves were incomprehensibly shackled by their occupations. Today I'd say the most important thing in my life is my work."

"And how much would you look to get paid for it?"

"It's hard to say. I've said to friends that my goal is to

have a Pontiac with a telephone in it, and that bespeaks a certain amount of income. Pontiacs are basically for *arrives*, self-made men. That's probably what I want more than the Pontiac—to be known as someone who's really earned his money, because that obviously hasn't been true up to now, being a rich kid, a prepster."

"With a career and a Pontiac you can't help but get married, can you?" I asked.

Short sipped his *n*th sherry. "Fortunately, I retain a power not to look into the future. The civilizing process of going to law school does make the idea more palatable. The thing is, I just don't know any marriages that are successful among people within shouting distance of our age. Everyone fails. It's just horrible. The time to go into it would seem to be after you've settled on what you're going to be doing for the rest of your life."

Or it's settled on you.

"You don't make long-range plans," Dave Warren (Midwood High School '66, Columbia '70) told me. "You find yourself at a point and you take the next step that seems appropriate, which usually turns out to be the path of least resistance."

Proceeding in this fashion, Warren weaved his way into N. Y. U. Law School last year, after two years of "keeping his options open" with the deftness of a juggler. He supported himself as a public school teacher days while taking a full architecture course at night, until he decided he wanted to be better at something than he was going to be at architecture. When I called him recently,

he was too harried with studying to see me. I commiserated. "The essence of happiness," I said, recalling my experience as a happy 40-hour-a-week state employe, "is not having to take home any work."

"That's the essence of law — taking home work," he replied.

"You can do it," I said.

He said he knew he could. It was just a question of organization. "It's organization, man." And inspiration, he might have added. He psychs himself up for studying each night by first sitting down at his upright piano and banging out the theme from "The Defenders" TV show of our youth.

We soon managed to get together, rendezvousing at the sundial at Columbia, the erstwhile podium for innumerable speeches by Mark Rudd (now silent, hiding from the F. B. I.) and the loading platform for the police vans that hauled 400 of us away one night five years ago.

Warren sat down beside me on the stone pedestal. He looked around the broad plaza at the foot of Low Library and observed, "You know, I really think half the reason for everything that went on here was the way this place is laid out. It's a giant theater." On stage that fall day were large numbers of students who managed to walk to and fro without ever congregating. They looked like location footage for a documentary on libraries.

Warren shared my contempt for our successors in college. What do they *do?* It's not that they should be demonstrating, necessarily, though with over 100,000 political prisoners in United States-financed South Vietnam there's plenty to

demonstrate about. Maybe that's not their thing, and it has been done. But why don't they do *something?* Swallow goldfish, for instance. Swallowing goldfish is an existential statement, an assertion of the validity of the absurd in an absurd world, an outcry for something meaningful to do. But *these* kids. Waterbed heads.

My Andover friend Stan Olson, who's a teaching assistant at Clark University, tells me that his undergraduates say they're right to be preoccupied with grades and success, that *we* were the aberration. "I think it has something to do with whether Nixon's in high office during your adolescence," Stan explains.

It's a nice feeling, contempt. This way we don't feel that we're over the hill; there has been no succession. We are still what is happening, whatever has happened.

"I knew the times they were a-changin'," Dave said, "when Dylan bought a split-level house." But Warren distinguishes between buying in and selling out. "Back in '68, people were setting up a false dichotomy. Either you joined the establishment and sold out, or you set about fulfilling yourself. But you can work in the establishment and still work for your own ends. Working with the establishment is confronting the world.

What it comes down to is that Warren sees the establishment as the only game in town. "As established institutions have been losing their meaning, counterinstitutions lose their meaning. Like the Church used to be something to be against. Marriage. But as they lose their vitality, the meaningfulness of opposing them diminishes."

It's true. It used to seem that growing your hair long, setting yourself against the establishment, was a meaningful act. You knew it, because they'd come down on you. You'd be castigated, maybe assaulted. But today, for a middle-class white guy, oppression is very hard to come by.

With meaning in decay on all sides, Warren sees the world in "universal entropy." His reaction is to aim for self-sufficiency and . . . Stability.

"I'd like to set up something that's independent, whether a law firm or a bookstore, just some enterprise I could set up with people I like." As far as money goes, "doing something I like is more important that money," but in 10 years he'd like to be earning $30,000 to $40,000 — in 1973 dollars.

And ultimately, he would like a Relationship, "and you want it to be permanent, and you want it to be exclusive. You want somebody to grow old with."

One stark winter Monday in 1972 I was working the 7 to 3 shift at the Massachusetts Department of Youth Services' Campbell House in Lancaster. I was holding a counseling session, in which I shared my accumulated wisdom in weekly installments with one of the kids. She was telling me that she just could not get along with her father, who would throw her out of the house in the intervals between her running away. I was trying to show her that this did not necessarily mean that she was as worthless a person as she supposed, that such strained familial relationships were not

all that uncommon. "People don't really live like the 'Donna Reed Show', you know," I said.

**"They *don't!*" she replied.** In her 17 years that actually had never occurred to her.

**It had just then occurred to me.**

**So much of our life is spent perceiving illusions that we tend to measure reality against them instead of the reverse. Instead of dismissing Coke ads as unreal, I'm inclined to feel my life is inadequate in the fun department because it isn't like the Coke ads—"the Real Thing." It doesn't matter that I interpret and resist the ads, that I know what they're up to. Those images are in my mind.**

**At Columbia we used to joke about the need for a course:**

### Life 1001x - 1002y FUNDAMENTALS OF REALITY 6 pts.

**Fall term:** *The Meaning of Life.* Sex, love, work, wealth, leisure and ideology are examined as possible sources of meaning, with attention to the question, What do 70-year-olds know that 19-year-olds don't?

**Spring term:** *Selected Problems in Living.* Emphasized are taxes, insurance, automotive legal problems, subleases, contracts, credit, birth control, venereal disease, zoning, local government, divorce, social behavior, job-seeking and unemployment.

**We felt the need for some such instruction because we**

felt we had been shielded from experience by our affluent backgrounds. Having lived in the shadow of destitution, our parents had naturally sought not just to survive but to survive with room to spare. They strove to isolate themselves from suffering by interposing layer on layer of things between themselves and want — pushing suffering ever farther away.

But we grew to feel that perhaps suffering was not all that we were removed from. Reading an account of a childhood of poverty, I would get the feeling that *there* was *authentic* experience, more meaningful and more *real* than my own affluent existence. (As though there were a principle of conservation of value: the greater the monetary value of your milieu, the less the value of your experience). We felt that as characters in novels, we would not be very interesting.

THE goal of middle-class life — from the air inside a Cadillac to the curriculum of a prep school — is insulation and control. Even our "own" youth culture came to us packaged. We had a communal experience, of a sort — though it was not experienced communally — an atomized communal experience. Millions of times in thousands of dorm rooms, the class of '70 heard revolution on the stereo. But however savage the rhythm or radical the words, anything we heard we heard because The Corporation had decided we'd hear it — though its motive be that most innocent of all: making money.

The youth culture was so pervasive because it filled a vacuum. Affluence had given us, luxury of luxuries, four years with nothing to do: college. Unheard of numbers of "kids" were in college; we were unbelievably well set up, regaled with music "systems," diverted by studies, and yet feeling a vague malaise, beginning to suspect that we were not in touch with reality and did not know very much about it, that we ourselves were not *relevant*.

The most important activity among this crowd was drug-taking, the principal purpose of which was, as always, escape. But in this case the students were trying to escape a reality they suspected was unreal, and to probe the depths and heights for a more basic or transcendent Reality, which would inform their actions and allow them to begin to live, at last, after having been suspended in a perpetual state of "preparation."

Browsing through the cosmos we found that there were worlds other than the one our parents perceived, a discovery which eroded our received beliefs and certainties; and one side effect of the drugs was to put us all outside the law.

Meanwhile, our parents' world came up with its war, misrepresented as this and that but obviously — to any-one with the time to look into it, and we, protected by deferments, had time — a cynical imperialist operation. That we were lied to about the war intensified our scrutiny of how much of our given reality was illusion. It set us looking for other lies, which weren't hard to find. Universities not being very portable, many had remained behind after the core cities had turned black and poor. A Columbia student, for instance, didn't have to look very far to see the effects of racism in the land of equal opportunity.

We had concluded, correctly, that we were living in a rotten, corrupt, morally bankrupt, brutally exploitative system, failing to apprehend only that this meant the world was clicking along as usual.

We were outraged. To us the war was a moral offense, not a question of politics, and we reacted to it in moral, rather than political terms. We didn't try to mobilize interest groups, or manipulate one power concentration against another, or do any of those things that politicians know about. And, of course, we didn't have "a program." Insofar as our rhetoric was political, that was a response to the needs of the conceptual framework of older people.

When people used to demand of us, "But what's your program?" we'd dutifully come up with something that could pass for one, talking about taxes and things. We should have said, "Why should we have a program? We're the Scourge of the Earth, we're the Wrath of God, and you're asking us about programs?"

I never knew anyone who, at 19, was seriously interested in running the country. We were trying to *stop* something. We felt ourselves to be a purifying force, the force of life. Somehow by the strength of our youth the nation would be wrenched from the grip of death, cleansed, made new.

"The Movement," we were aptly named. Not the party or the revolution. The Movement — an undirected upheaval of the earth, an inarticulate force of nature. We weren't trying to convince the nation of anything. We were just trying to wake it up. Our "tactic" was an appeal to the nation's conscience, the existence of which we posited, apparently in error.

To our great surprise, we failed — never ending the war. (We had no way of knowing at the time that we had catalyzed Nixon's paranoia, driving him to acts which would bring about his downfall.) Failure was something we had never contemplated. The only question was when we would end the war, not whether we would end it. It didn't occur to us that the war might end because the Indochinese *won* it, nor that it might go on forever (beyond our lifetimes).

Our confidence and resolve had grown from our middle-class backgrounds just as surely as our naiveté. We were raised to believe that we could do anything if we worked hard enough at it, and, conversely, that if we failed to achieve something it could only be because we had not worked hard enough. There was never any mention in our households of the breaks, or fate, or the authorities, or the Will of God. Achievement flowed from effort like interest from principal.

If we wanted bombs to stop falling on Indochina, then bombs would stop falling on Indochina. But they did not. Unable to sustain ourselves in the face of failure, we withdrew. Three years after graduation I could find no one who could say for sure whether any aboveground remnant of S.D.S. exists.

**N**ONE of my friends went to Vietnam. Those of us who were called got out by getting 4-F's or by doing alternative service as conscientious objectors. All you need is to know the rules.

Some of us got involved in counterinstitutions — free schools, communes, co-ops — but, typically, we remained aloof, rejecting all organization and politics, rejecting *abstraction*. After years of dealing in policies and issues, we wanted jobs where you could see what you were doing. We were trying, after graduating from college, to begin to learn what life was like.

We avoided long-term commitments, and spent a lot of time not working at all. We were afraid of losing ourselves before finding them. Embarking on a career meant accepting definition, that is, finitude, stasis, the closing of options and narrowing of potential — and it was the same

with getting married. Once you decided with whom and where you'd live and what you'd do, it would be a matter of 15 new cars and a hearse.

Since we didn't need to "provide for" a woman in order to enjoy a relationship with her, career and marriage were two things we could do without. To no one did this become more apparent than to those who got married.

Not working toward a career, let alone not working at all, was also a rejection of the System within which success and exploitation, work and war, were of a piece in our minds. ("Work! Study! Get ahead! Kill!" we used to chant at Columbia.) It seemed the country was full of people who subsumed themselves in their work roles, deriving their identities from their functions, abdicating human will and responsibility, leaving the country to be run not by people but by a System, capable of anything.

Of course it was the System that enabled us to reject the System. It gave us time. There was no need — or opportunity — for everyone to be producing all the time. You can bet there aren't a lot of sensitive young intellectuals trying to find themselves in The People's Republic: "You can find yourself right out there in the rice paddies with everybody else, buddy."

We were terrified of working as hard as did our fathers, charter subscribers to the Protestant Ethic: Pay now, fly later. Olson up at Clark University, told me, "When I look at how incredibly difficult it is for me to do very little, then I can't even imagine what it must be like for

people to do a lot." He likes to think about the easy fortune he could make marketing draft-evader bracelets, each engraved with the name of an exile, to be worn until amnesty.

By not having any hopes now of finding meaning in a career, he's saving himself from any crushing disillusion later. "The people who freak out at 45 are those who *thought* they were getting somewhere." But not being career-oriented — not building anything to lean on — needs peer-group support. "Me and my friends," says Olson, a grad student in English, "we don't work at careers." But even among Olson's friends the attrition rate is climbing.

Strange to say, we—whose whole sense of "we" was built around being "kids" — are getting older. The other day I looked in the mirror and saw a single gray hair — which I decided not to pull, because it made me look very slightly distinguished — but more alarming is the thinning, no longer deniable. A lot of longhairs have thinning hair.

At 25, you find your own stories boring you. Half the Red Sox are younger than you are. It's easy to get fat. Country and Western lyrics suddenly make sense. And your father faces his mortality, which prompts you to think about your own.

The pressure mounts to make your deal, some sort of compromise between the quest for authentic experience and the need for identity, between adventure and security.

As I heard one character say to another in a late-night TV movie, "Doing nothing is a very difficult job. It requires a lot of concentration." And an older friend of mine confirms that when you turn 30, "You can relax in ways you couldn't before, because you're no longer plagued by all those options. That's what makes life so difficult in your 20's, all that glorious potential to grapple with."

"It's not easy living the way I do," says my Columbia classmate Larry Lane, now a graduate student of uncertain prospects. "I'm looking for something I can do — it doesn't have to be fun — just something I can *do*, as opposed to *be*. I'd love to *be* a doctor [his father's a dentist] and have everybody respect me, but there's no way I want to put on rubber gloves and *do* doctor things."

Right now he's thinking of writing poetry to be illustrated by his girl friend, but a lot of people wouldn't consider that doing anything, and in occasional chilling moments it appears to him they may be right. "Don't you think I'd like to come home to a big house and bounce a kid on my knee?"

IT'S been three years now that we've been on the outs. The world of the small job, the personal project, inevitably begins to seem constricting. Our middle-class *instinct* (subliminal, unshakable) to "make something of yourself," abetted by our social commitment — also rather hard to shake — drives us back toward the larger arena. We can't leave the running of the world entirely in the hands of the exec types, can we?

And as we find idealistic

gratification hard to come by, materialistic gratification becomes more attractive. I, for instance, used to think I could stop the war; then I thought I'd get realistic and instead save delinquents from lives of crime; finding that beyond my power, I resolved to show them a good time. My success in pursuit of even that modest goal was equivocal. After several months as a supervisor and associate of juvenile delinquents it came to me that I'd feel somehow more *confident* if I had a big car. On May Day of '72, I bought The Dream.

As Dave Warren says, "Whatever else you say about those bourgeois comforts, they sure are comfortable."

I agree with a friend who said, "You don't want to be in the position of not knowing where your next car is coming from." And money can be habit-forming. After the hook, the line and sinker are easy.

Summing up the last three years, John Short said, "People led whatever kind of life they had to in order to convince themselves that they were exercising free will." That done, having gained control of their lives, having insulated themselves from outside pressures, more and more holdouts are becoming late-signers.

The question is: will we, despite the hallucinations and barricades in our backgrounds, become indistinguishable from our parents?

We still take drugs, but mostly just grass, and that without any imputation of mystic import. In this period of Post-Mumbo-Jumbo Materialism the popularity of psychedelics has fallen along with that of transcendence.

Our attitude toward authority is still shaped by the clashes in college. To quote Olson, "Whenever I see a cop on my block I feel like I better flush all my books down the toilet."

Our political views would still look appropriate on leaflets. I spoke with 11 classmates across the country, and most would agree with Casey that "the United States is the world's leading reactionary force." Though everyone enjoys Watergate, no one buys it as the redemption of the System. It's so American — instead of purging a corrupt government we do a TV show on it. And we can't help recalling that there was no uproar when "radicals" were bugged. No one I know has the slightest doubt that the C.I.A. was behind the coup in Chile, but no one has any plans for doing anything about it either, since there are no bumper-stickers out and no organization to send five dollars to. The activists among us are those who volunteered a few hours for McGovern.

In our rowdy days we were told we couldn't change the world. I think we can't help but change the world, one way or another.

I was just talking to a friend of mine, who said, "I'm much happier now that I'm not 'a radical.' I stopped feeling guilty over just being alive in America."

And I said, "My father always held to the belief that young people would eventually abandon their idealistic visions and come around to appreciating the verities — like the overwhelming importance of money."

"Your father sounds like a very wise man," she said. ∎

# 59

# They changed rock, which changed the culture, which changed us

## By Jeff Greenfield

They have not performed together on stage for more than eight years. They have not made a record together in five years. The formal dissolution of their partnership in a London courtroom last month was an echo of an ending that came long ago. Now each of them is seeking to overcome the shadow of a past in which they were bound together by wealth, fame and adulation of an intensity unequaled in our culture. George Harrison scorns talk of reunion, telling us to stop living in the past. John Lennon told us years ago that "the dream is over."

He was right: When the Beatles broke up in 1970 in a welter of lawsuits and recriminations, the sixties were ending as well—in spirit as well as by the calendar. Bloodshed and bombings on campus, the harsh realities beneath the facile hopes for a "Woodstock nation," the shabby refuse of counterculture communities, all helped kill the dream.

What remains remarkable now, almost 20 years after John Lennon started playing rock 'n' roll music, more than a decade after their first worldwide conquest, is how appealing this dream was; how its vision of the world gripped so much of a generation; how that dream reshaped our recent past and affects us still. What remains remarkable is how strongly this dream was triggered, nurtured and broadened by one rock 'n' roll band of four Englishmen whose entire history as a group occurred before any of them reached the age of 30.

Their very power guarantees that an excursion into analysis cannot fully succeed. Their songs, their films, their lives formed so great a part of what we listened to and watched and talked about that everyone affected by them still sees the Beatles and hears their songs through a personal prism. And the Beatles themselves never abandoned a sense of self-parody and put-on. They were, in Richard Goldstein's phrase, "the clown-gurus of the sixties." Lennon said more than once that the Beatles sometimes put elusive references into their songs just to confuse their more solemn interpreters. "I am the egg man," they sang, not "egghead."

Still, the impact of the Beatles cannot be waved away. If the Marx they emulated was Groucho, not Karl, if their world was a playground instead of a battleground, they still changed what we listened to and how we listened

*Jeff Greenfield is a writer whose most recent book, "No Peace, No Place," deals with the rise of rock 'n' roll.*

to it; they helped make rock music a battering ram for the youth culture's assault on the mainstream, and that assault in turn changed our culture permanently. And if the "dream" the Beatles helped create could not sustain itself in the real world, that speaks more to our false hopes than to their promises. They wrote and sang songs. We turned it into politics and philosophy and a road map to another way of life.

The Beatles grew up as children of the first generation of rock 'n' roll, listening to and imitating the music of Little Richard, Larry Williams, Chuck Berry, Elvis Presley, and the later, more sophisticated sounds of the Shirelles and the Miracles. It was the special genius of their first mentor, Brian Epstein, to package four Liverpool working-class "rockers" as 'mods,' replacing their greasy hair, leather jackets, and on-stage vulgarity with jackets, ties, smiles and carefully groomed, distinctive haircuts. Just as white artists filtered and softened the raw energy of black artists in the nineteen-fifties, the Beatles at first were softer, safer versions of energetic rock 'n' roll musicians. The words promised they only wanted to hold hands; the rhythm was more insistent.

By coming into prominence early in 1964, the Beatles probably saved rock 'n' roll from extinction. Rock in the early nineteen-sixties existed in name only; apart from the soul artists, it was a time of "shlock rock," with talentless media hypes like Fabian and Frankie Avalon riding the crest of the American Bandstand wave. By contrast, the Beatles provided a sense of musical energy that made successful a brilliant public-relations effort. Of course, the $50,000 used to promote the Beatles' first American appearance in February, 1964, fueled some of the early hysteria; so did the timing of their arrival.

Coming as it did less than a hundred days after the murder of John Kennedy, the advent of the Beatles caught America aching for any diversion to replace the images of a flag-draped casket and a riderless horse in the streets of Washington.

I remember a Sunday evening in early February, standing with hundreds of curious collegians in a University of Wisconsin dormitory, watching these four longhaired (!) Englishmen trying to be heard over the screams of Ed Sullivan's audience. Their music seemed to me then derivative, pleasant and bland, a mixture of hard rock and the sounds of the black groups then popular. I was convinced it would last six months, no more.

The Beatles, however, had more than hype; they had talent. Even their first hits, "I Want to Hold Your Hand," "She Loves You," "Please Please Me," "I Saw Her Standing There," had a hint of harmonies and melodies more inventive than standard rock tunes. More important, it became immediately clear that the Beatles were hipper, more complicated, than the bovine rock stars who could not seem to put four coherent words together.

In the spring of 1964, John Lennon published a book, "In His Own Write," which, instead of a ghost-written string of "groovy guides for keen teens," offered word plays, puns and black-humor satirical sketches. A few months later came the film "A Hard Day's Night," and in place of the classic let's-put-on-a-prom-and-invite-the-TeenChords plot of rock movies, the Beatles and director Richard Lester created a funny movie parodying the Beatles's own image.

I vividly recall going to that film in the midst of a National Student Association congress; at that time, rock 'n' roll was regarded as high-school nonsense by this solemn band of student-body presidents and future C.I.A. operatives. But after the film, I sensed a feeling of goodwill and camaraderie among that handful of rock fans who had watched this movie: The Beatles were media heroes without illusion, young men glorying in their sense of play and fun, laughing at the conventions of the world. They were worth listening to and admiring.

The real surprise came at the end of 1965, with the release of the "Rubber Soul" album. Starting with that album, and continuing through "Revolver" and "Sgt. Pepper's Lonely Hearts Club Band," the Beatles began to throw away the rigid conventions of rock 'n' roll music and lyrics. The banal abstract, second-hand emotions were replaced with sharp, sometimes mordant portraits of first-hand people and experiences, linked to music that was more complicated and more compelling

*Beatles rising—Paul McCartney, Ringo Starr, John Lennon, George Harrison in 1963.*

than rock had ever dared attempt. The Beatles were drawing on their memories and feelings, not those cut from Tin Pan Alley cloth.

"Norwegian Wood" was about an unhappy, inconclusive affair ("I once had a girl/or should I say/she once had me"). "Michelle" and "Yesterday" were haunting, sentimental ballads, and Paul McCartney dared sing part of "Michelle" in French—most rock singers regarded English as a foreign language. "Penny Lane" used cornets to evoke the suggestion of a faintly heard band concert on a long-ago summer day. Staccato strings lent urgency to the story of "Eleanor Rigby."

These songs were different from the rock music that our elders had scorned with impunity. Traditionally, rock 'n' roll was rigidly structured: 4/4 tempo, 32 bars, with a limited range of instruments. Before the Beatles, rock producer Phil Spector had revolutionized records by adding strings to the drums, bass, sax and guitar, but the chord structure was usually limited to a basic blues or ballad pattern. Now the Beatles, with the kind of visibility that made them impossible to ignore, were expanding the range of rock, musically and lyrically. A sitar—a harpsichord effect—a ragtime piano —everything was possible.

With the release of "Sgt. Pepper" in the spring of 1967, the era of rock as a strictly adolescent phenomenon was gone. One song, "A Day in the Life," with its recital of an ordinary day combined with a dreamlike sense of dread and anxiety, made it impossible to ignore the skills of Lennon and McCartney. A decade earlier, Steve Allen mocked the inanity of rock by reading "Hound Dog" or "Tutti-Frutti" as if they were serious attempts at poetry. Once "Sgt. Pepper" was recorded, Partisan Review was lauding the Beatles, Ned Rorem proclaimed that "She's Leaving Home" was "equal to any song Schubert ever wrote," and a Newsweek critic meant it when he wrote: "'Strawberry Fields Forever' [is] a superb Beatleizing of hope and despair in which the four minstrels regretfully recommend a Keatsian lotus-land of withdrawal from the centrifugal stresses of the age."

"We're so well established," McCartney had said in 1966, "that we can bring fans along with us and stretch the limits of pop." By using their fame to help break through the boundaries of rock, the Beatles proved that they were not the puppets of backstage manipulation or payola or hysterical 14-year-olds. Instead, they helped make rock music *the* music of an entire international generation. Perhaps for the first time in history, it was possible to say that tens of millions of people, defined simply by age, were all doing the same thing: they were listening to rock 'n' roll. That fact changed the popular culture of the world.

■

Rock 'n' roll's popularity had never been accompanied by respectability, even among the young. For those of us with intellectual pretenses, rock 'n' roll was like masturbation: exciting, but shameful. The culturally alienated went in for cool jazz, and folk music was the vehicle for the politically active minority. (The growth of political interest at the start of the sixties sparked something of a folk revival).

Along with the leap of Bob Dylan into rock music, the Beatles destroyed this division. Rock 'n' roll was now broad enough, free enough, to encompass every kind of feeling. Its strength had always been rooted in the sexual energy of its rhythms; in that sense, the outraged parents who had seen rock as a threat to their children's virtue were right. Rock 'n' roll made you want to move and shake and get physically excited. The Beatles proved that this energy could be fused with a sensibility more subtle than the "let's-go-down -to - the - gym - and - beat - up - the - Coke - machine" quality of rock music.

In 1965, Barry McGuire recorded the first "rock protest" song (excluding the teen complaints of the Coasters and Chuck Berry). In his "Eve of Destruction," we heard references to Red China, Selma, Alabama, nuclear war and middle-class hypocrisy pounded out to heavy rock rhythms. That same year came a flood of "good time" rock music, with sweet, haunting melodies by groups like the Lovin' Spoonful and the Mamas and the Papas. There *were* no limits to what could be done; and the market was continually expanding.

The teen-agers of the nineteen-fifties had become the young adults of the nineteen-sixties, entering the professions, bringing with them a cultural frame of reference shaped in good measure by rock 'n' roll. The "youth" market was enormous—the flood of babies born during and just after World War II made the under-25 population group abnormally large; their tastes were more influential than ever before. And because the music had won acceptability, rock 'n' roll was not judged indulgently as a "boys will be boys" fad. Rock music was expressing a sensibility about the tangible world — about sensuality, about colors and sensations, about the need to change consciousness. And this sensibility soon spilled over into other arenas.

Looking back on the last half of the last decade, it is hard to think of a cultural innovation that did not carry with it the influence of rock music, and of the Beatles in particular: the miniskirt, discotheques, the graphics of Peter Max, the birth of publications like Rolling Stone, the "mind-bending" effects of TV commercials, the success of "Laugh-In" on television and "Easy Rider" in the movies—all of these cultural milestones owe something to the emergence of rock music as the most compelling and pervasive force in our culture.

This is especially true of the incredible spread of drugs —marijuana and the hallucinogens most particularly— among the youth culture. From "Rubber Soul" through "Sgt. Pepper," Beatle music was suffused with a sense of mystery and mysticism: odd choral progressions, mysterious instruments, dreamlike effects, and images that did not seem to yield to "straight" interpretation. Whether specific songs ("Lucy in the Sky with Diamonds," "A Little Help From My Friends") were deliberately referring to drugs is beside the point. The Beatles were publicly recounting their LSD experiences, and their music was replete with antirational sensibility. Indeed, it was a commonplace among my contemporaries that Beatle albums could not be understood fully without the use of drugs. For "Rubber Soul," marijuana; for "Sgt. Pepper," acid. When the Beatles told us to turn off our minds and float downstream, uncounted youngsters assumed that the key to this kind of mind-expansion could be found in a plant or a pill. Together with "head" groups like Jefferson Airplane and the Grateful Dead, the Beatles were, consciously or not, a major influence behind the spread of drugs.

In this sense, the Beatles are part of a chain: (1) the Beatles opened up rock; (2) rock changed the culture; (3) the culture changed us. Even limited to their impact as musicians, however, the Beatles were as powerful an influence as any group or individual; only Bob Dylan stands as their equal. They never stayed with a successful formula; they were always moving. By virtue of their fame, the Beatles were a giant amplifier, spreading "the word" on virtually every trend and mood of the last decade.

They were never pure forerunners. The Yardbirds used the sitar before the Beatles; the Beach Boys were experimenting with studio enhancement first; the Four Seasons were using elaborate harmonies before the Beatles. They were never as contemptuously antimiddle-class or decadent as the Kinks or the Rolling Stones; never as lyri-cally compelling as Dylan; never as musically brilliant as the Band; never as hallucinogenic as the San Francisco groups. John Gabree, one of the most perceptive of the early rock writers, said that "their job, and they have done it well, has been to travel a few miles behind the avant-garde, consolidating gains and popularizing new ideas."

Yet this very willingness meant that new ideas did not struggle and die in obscurity; instead, they touched a hundred million minds. Their songs reflected the widest range of mood of any group of their time. Their openness created a kind of salon for a whole generation of people, an idea exchange into which the youth of the world was wired. It was almost inevitable that, even against their will, their listeners shaped a dream of politics and lifestyle from the substance of popular music. It is testament both to the power of rock music, and to the illusions which can be spun out of impulses.

■

The Beatles were not political animals. Whatever they have done since going their separate ways, their behavior as a group reflected cheerful anarchy more than political rebellion. Indeed, as editorialists, they were closer to The Wall Street Journal than to Ramparts. "Taxman" assaults the heavy progressive income tax ("one for you, 19 for me"), and "Revolution" warned that "if you go carrying pictures of Chairman Mao/you ain't gonna make it with anyone anyhow."

The real political impact of the Beatles was not in any four-point program or in an attack on injustice or the war in Vietnam. It was instead in the counterculture they had helped to create. Somewhere in the nineteen-sixties, millions of people began to regard themselves as a class separate from mainstream society *by virtue of their youth and the sensibility that youth produced.*

The nineteen-fifties had produced the faintest hint of such an attitude in the defensive love of rock 'n' roll; if our parents hated it, it had to be good. The sixties had expanded this vague idea into a battle cry. "Don't trust anyone over 30!"—shouted from a police car in the first massive student protest of the decade at Berkeley—suggested an outlook in which the mere aging process was an act of betrayal, in which youth itself was a moral value. Time magazine made the "under-25 generation" its Man of the Year in 1967, and politicians saw in the steadily escalating rebellion among the middle-class young a constituency and a scapegoat.

The core value of this "class" was not peace or social justice; it was instead a more elusive value, reflected by much of the music and by the Beatles own portrait of themselves. It is expressed best by a scene from their movie "Help!" in which John, Paul, George and Ringo enter four adjoining row houses. The doors open—and suddenly the scene shifts inside, and we see that these "houses" are in fact one huge house; the four Beatles instantly reunite.

It is this sense of communality that was at the heart of the youth culture. It is what we wished to believe about the Beatles, and about the possibilities in our own lives. If there is one sweeping statement that makes sense about the children of the last decade, it is that the generation born of World War II was saying "no" to the atomized lives their parents had so feverishly sought. The most cherished value of the counterculture—preached if not always practiced—was its insistence on sharing, communality, a rejection of the retreat into private satisfaction. Rock 'n' roll was the magnet, the driving force, of a shared celebration, from Alan Freed's first mammoth dance parties in Cleveland in 1951, to the Avalon Ballroom in San Francisco, to the be-ins in our big cities, to Woodstock itself. Spontaneous gathering was the ethic: Don't plan it, don't think about it, *do* it—you'll get by with a little help from your friends.

In their music, their films, their sense of play, the Beatles reflected this dream of a ceaseless celebration. If there *was* any real "message" in their songs, it was the message of Charles Reich: that the world would be changed by changing the consciousness of the new generation. "All you need is love," they sang. "Say the word [love] and you'll be free." "Let it be." "Everything's gonna be all right."

As a state of mind, it was a pleasant fantasy. As a way of life, it was doomed to disaster. The thousands of young people who flocked to California or to New York's Lower East Side to join the love generation found the world filled with people who did not share the ethic of mutual trust. The politicization of youth as a class helped to divide natural political allies and make politics more vulnerable to demagogues. As the Beatles found in their own personal and professional lives, the practical outside world has a merciless habit of intruding into fantasies; somebody has to pay the bills and somebody has to do the dishes in the commune and somebody has to protect us from the worst instincts of other human beings. John Lennon was expressing some very painful lessons when he told Rolling Stone shortly after the group's breakup that "nothing happened except we all dressed up . . . the same bastards are in control, the same people are runnin' everything."

He was also being unfair. If the counterculture was too shallow to understand how the world does get changed, the forces that were set loose in the nineteen-sixties have had a permanent effect. The sensuality that rock 'n' roll tapped will never again be bottled up. The vestiges of the communal dream have changed the nature of friendships and life-styles and marriages, in large measure for the better. And with the coming of harder economic times, the idea of abandoning private retreat for shared pleasures and burdens has a direct contemporary practicality.

For me, the final irony is that the Beatles themselves have unconsciously proven the value of communality. As a group, they seemed to hold each other back from excess: McCartney was lyrical, but not saccharine; Lennon was rebellious but not offensive; Harrison's mysticism was disciplined (Ringo was always Ringo, drummer and friend). Now, the sense of control seems to have loosened. Paul and Linda McCartney seem tempted by the chance to become the Steve and Eydie of rock; Lennon is still struggling to free himself from a Fad of the Month mentality; George Harrison's Gospel According to Krishna succeeded in boring much of his audience on his recent concert tour. Perhaps the idea they did so much to spread several years ago is not as dead as all that; perhaps we all need a little help from our friends. The enduring power of that idea is as permanent as any impact their music had on us, even if they no longer believe it. ■

# We need your advice

Because this book will be revised regularly, we would like to know what you think of it.

Please fill in the brief questionnaire on the reverse of this card and mail it to us.

# Business Reply Mail

No postage stamp necessary if mailed in the United States

First Class
Permit No. 247
New York, N.Y.

Postage will be paid by

**Dale Tharp**
**Sociology Editor**
**Harper & Row Publishers Inc.**
**College Dept.**
**10 East 53rd St.**
**New York, NY 10022**

Sociology
2nd Edition

# SOCIOLOGY: CONTEMPORARY PERSPECTIVES 2nd Edition

I am a ___ student ___ instructor

Term used _____ 19 ____

Name _____

School _____

Address _____

City _____ State _____ Zip _____

# How do you rate this book?

**1.** Please list (by number) the articles you liked best.

_____   _____   _____   _____   _____

Why? _____
_____

**2.** Please list (by number) the articles you liked least.

_____   _____   _____   _____   _____

Why? _____
_____

**3.** Please evaluate the following:

|  | Excell. | Good | Fair | Poor | Comments |
|---|---|---|---|---|---|
| Organization of the book | ____ | ____ | ____ | ____ | _____ |
| Section introductions | ____ | ____ | ____ | ____ | _____ |
| **Overall Evaluation** | ____ | ____ | ____ | ____ | _____ |

**4.** Do you have any suggestions for improving the next edition?

_____
_____
_____

**5.** Can you suggest any new articles to include in the next edition?

_____
_____
_____
_____
_____
_____
_____
_____

**Thank you very much**

# Business Reply Mail

No postage stamp necessary if mailed in the United States

First Class
Permit No. 247
New York, N.Y.

Postage will be paid by

**Harper & Row Publishers Inc.**
**Attention: William Grillo**
**10 East 53rd St.**
**New York, NY 10022**

Now you may order individual c[...] PERSPECTIVES READER
SERIES directly from the publish[...]

The following titles are now available:

BEING HUMAN TODAY, Edited by Phillip [...] [...]nis T. Jaffe
Readings in ABNORMAL PSYCHOLOGY, [...]
(ISBN 0-06-043259-4) ($7.50)

Readings in ADOLESCENT PSYCHOLOGY, [...] [...]06-047057-7) ($7.95)

Readings in ADULT PSYCHOLOGY, Edited by L[...] [...] Jaffe
(ISBN 0-06-047054-2) ($7.95)

Readings in AGING AND DEATH, Edited by Steven [...] ($7.50)

Readings in ECOLOGY, ENERGY AND HUMAN SOC[...] [...]urch, Jr.
(ISBN 0-06-047058-5) ($7.50)

Readings in EDUCATIONAL PSYCHOLOGY, Edited by F[...] [...]nard J. Shapiro
(ISBN 0-06-047083-6) ($7.50)

Readings in HUMAN DEVELOPMENT, Edited by David Elki[...] [...]el
(ISBN 0-06-047055-0) ($7.50)

Readings in HUMAN SEXUALITY, Edited by Chad Gordon an[...] [...]BN 0-06-042399-4) ($6.95)

Readings in PERSONALITY AND ADJUSTMENT, Edited by Thon[...] [...]d Phillip Whitten
(ISBN 0-06-382534-1) ($5.95)

Readings in PHYSICAL ANTHROPOLOGY AND ARCHAEOLOGY, E[...] [...]vid E. Hunter and Phillip Whitten
(ISBN 0-06-043023-0) ($4.95)

Readings in SOCIAL PROBLEMS, Edited by Peter M. Wickman (ISBN 0[...] [...]053-4) ($7.50)

Readings in SOCIAL PSYCHOLOGY, Edited by Dennis Krebs (ISBN 0-06-043772-3) ($6.95)

Readings in SOCIOLOGY, Edited by Ian Robertson and Phillip Whitten (ISBN 0-06-045502-0) ($7.50)

---------------------------------------------------------------------------------------------

Please send me:

_____copies of_____ (ISBN)

_____copies of_____ (ISBN)

_____copies of_____ (ISBN)

_____copies of_____ (ISBN)

My check or money order in the amount of $_____ is
enclosed. (Harper & Row will pay the postage and handling.)

_____
Name

_____
[...]s

_____

_____
                          Zip